Police & Society

Second Edition

Roy Roberg
San Jose State University

John Crank
Boise State University

Jack Kuykendall
San Jose State University

Foreword by Lawrence W. Sherman

Roxbury Publishing Company
Los Angeles, California

Library of Congress Cataloging-in-Publication Data

Roberg, Roy
Police & Society, 2nd Edition / Roy Roberg, John Crank, and Jack Kuykendall.
  p. cm.
  Includes bibliographical references and index.
  ISBN 1-891487-17-5
1. Police—United States. 2. Police administration—United States. 3. Community policing—United States. I. Crank, John p., 1947– . II. Kuykendall, Jack L. III. Title.
HV8141.R6 1999
363.2363.2'3'0973—dc21   99-35450
                                                                                                CIP

POLICE & SOCIETY, 2ND EDITION

Publisher and Editor: Claude Teweles
Developmental Editor: Susan Converse Winslow
Production Editors: Cathy Yoo and Jim Ballinger
Production Coordinator: Dawn VanDercreek
Production Assistants: Raoul Limeres, Mike Sametz, and Josh Levine
Typography: Synergistic Data Systems
Cover Design: Marnie Kenney

Printed on acid-free paper in the United States of America. This paper meets the standards for
recycling of the Environmental Protection Agency.

ISBN: 1-891487-17-5

ROXBURY PUBLISHING COMPANY
P.O. Box 491044
Los Angeles, California 90049-9044
Tel.: (310) 473-3312 • Fax: (310) 473-4490
Email: roxbury@roxbury.net
Website: www.roxbury.net

Dedicated to those ethical, hard-working police executives and officers who do their best to improve our society through their efforts. And to those students in higher education who endeavor to contribute to society through a career in policing.

Further dedicated to those who put up with us through the rigors of writing this textbook: Arlene, Patty, Mary, and Alyssa and Casey.

Contents

Part I
The Police Role

Part II
Police Administration

Part III

Police Behavior

Part IV
Contemporary Issues

Suggested Websites
for Further Study

Chapter 1: Police in a Democracy

The Official Website of the White House
http://www.whitehouse.gov/

United States Supreme Court Collection
http://supct.law.cornell.edu/supct/

Uniform Crime Reports
http://www.fbi.gov/ucr.htm

The Oyez Project: U.S. Supreme Court Multimedia Database
http://www.oyez.org/

Chapter 2: Police History

Biosketch of Sir Robert Peel
http://members.tripod.com/kiffg/peel.htm

Herbert Hoover on the World Wide Web
http://www.cs.umb.edu/~rwhealan/jfk/hoover_links.html

National Sheriffs' Association (NSA)
http://www.sheriffs.org/

The Official Website of the Texas Rangers' Law Enforcement Agency
http://www.texasranger.org/

Links to Municipal, County, and State Law Enforcement Agencies Across
   the United States
http://www.officer.com
http://www.leolinks.com

United States Marshals Service
http://www.usdoj.gov/marshals/

United States Postal Inspection Services
http://www.usps.gov/websites/depart/inspect/

United States Secret Service
http://www.treas.gov/usss/

Chapter 8: Police Behavior

Chapter 9: Force and Coercion

Chapter 12: Cultural Diversity

Equal Employment Opportunity Act of 1972
http://www4.law.cornell.edu/uscode/42/2000e.html

Dallas Police Department
http://www.ci.dallas.tx.us/dpd/

The International Association of Chiefs of Police
http://www.theiacp.org/

Albuquerque Police Department
http://www.cabq.gov/police/

National Center for Women and Policing
http://www.feminist.org/police/ncwp.html

Law Enforcement Gays and Lesbians International
http://members.aol.com/legalint/index.html

Latino Peace Officers' Association
http://claraweb.co.santa-clara.ca.us/sheriff/lpoa.htm

National Organization of Black Law Enforcement Executives (NOBLE)
http://www.noblenatl.org/

Family and Medical Leave Act of 1993—U.S. Department of Labor
http://www.dol.gov/dol/esa/fmla.htm

Chapter 13: Stress and Officer Safety

Cincinnati Police Division
http://www.cincinnatipolice.org/

San Francisco Police Department
http://www.ci.sf.ca.us/police/

Police Stress
http://www.theroad.com.hk/policestress.html

Texas Commission on Law Enforcement Officers' Standards and
Training
http://link.tsl.state.tx.us/tx/TCLEOSE/

Chapter 14: Policing Futures

Mothers Against Drunk Driving (MADD)
http://www.madd.org/

Delaware State Police
http://www.state.de.us/dsp/index.htm

Gangs in Los Angeles, Including Links to Other Gang Websites
http://www.streetgangs.com/

Cybercrime
http://www.digitalcentury.com/encyclo/update/crime.html

Florida Association of Computer Crime Investigators
http://www.facci.org/

Acknowledgments

We extend our sincere appreciation to Claude Teweles, the publisher of Roxbury Publishing Company, whose strong support and nonbureaucratic style have made this process less onerous and certainly more enjoyable. As usual, his wit, humor, and insights have been valuable assets and have helped to establish an enjoyable working relationship. Susan Converse Winslow did an exemplary job of editing the text, and it is much improved as a result. We would also like to send our appreciation to the staff at Roxbury, including Jim Ballinger, Marnie Kenney, Dawn VanDercreek, and Cathy Yoo. Several reviewers made constructive and helpful comments with respect to the final manuscript, including: James Golden, University of Arkansas-Little Rock; Larry Gould, Northern Arizona University; Cary Heck, Arizona State University; Dennis Kenney, Police Executive Research Forum; Peter Kraska, Eastern Kentucky University; and Ken Mullen, Appalachian State University.

Thanks are offered to Andrew Giacomazzi, Boise State University, for creating the dedicated website for this text and the section entitled "Suggested Websites for Further Study," beginning on page xv.

We are also indebted to Cary Heck, Arizona State University, for writing the *Instructor's Manual/Testing Program* and *Student Study Guide* that accompany the book.

Finally, special thanks goes to Marie Simonetti Rosen, publisher of *Law Enforcement News,* for her kind assistance and for permitting us to reprint numerous articles that enhance the realistic view of policing presented throughout the text.

Foreword

Lawrence W. Sherman

Policing in America has always reflected the society that created it. In the mere century and a half since the New York City Police Department was founded in 1844, we have witnessed enormous changes in the ethnicity, education, technology, and values of the American police. But of all the changes, perhaps the most important has been the revolution in police research of the past three decades—a revolution on which this text, *Police & Society*, is based.

As recently as 1970, it was impossible to base police practices on the best evidence from research. Policing was a field built on theory rather than facts. Untested ideas from ancient philosophers had more effect on what police did than any hard-nosed analysis of the results of various police practices. Policing "by the seat of your pants" was not only the prevailing custom—it was the only option.

All this began to change rapidly with the creation of two new institutions: the Police Foundation of Washington, D.C., and the National Institute of Justice. The Police Foundation is an independent, charitable organization established by the Ford Foundation to foster innovation and improvement in American policing. The National Institute of Justice is the research arm of the U.S. Department of Justice. Both these organizations, separately and in collaboration, cast the mold for basing police work on research and facts rather than speculation and theory. Proof of this claim is abundant in the following pages of this text, which does an admirable job of communicating a vast array of research results in a coherent, comprehensible manner.

The collection and evaluation of research is not just an academic exercise. Research has literally saved lives and prevented injury. It has guided a generation of police executives to find new and better ways of protecting life, liberty, and property. It has changed the ways in which millions of police officers do their jobs all around the globe. And it has made policing a far "smarter" institution in the cybernetic sense: an institution more capable of learning from what it is doing so that it can alter its practices for better results.

The basic premise of this research is simple: assume nothing, take nothing for granted, accept no claim without some evidence based on observation. This is no different from the premise of the scientific method, which itself has transformed the society creating the police. Thus, the fact that policing is now based on research is proof of the title of this book: the police and society must be studied as a whole, because they cannot be separated.

Two major societal trends affect policing at the beginning of the 21st century. One is the demand for a more accountable government. Ever since the taxpayer revolts of the late 1970s, all government has been under pressure to show results. No longer are taxpayers satisfied to hear that x billion dollars were spent providing specific services. Now they want to know what the services accomplished. This difference between outputs (services) and outcomes (results) cannot be established without research. In the case of policing, the number of arrests police make or calls they answer may not mean anything to the taxpayer—unless it is linked to evidence that these outputs reduced crime.

The second major trend is the revolution in information technology. Now that police can track crime and their own activity in real time with great precision, they are increasingly doing so. This text shows what they can do what that information to produce a society that is freer and safer.

For any new police manager or police officer, this book is an excellent place to begin digesting the vast research done on policing in recent years. For citizens or taxpayers who wants to know whether their own police department is using the best practices available based on research, this book is also an indispensable tool. From patrol to investigations to personnel and politics, *Police & Society* provides a wide-ranging review.

For the student of criminal justice and criminology, this book will help you reflect on the implications of research for a free society. Just because we know things that "work" to reduce crime does not automatically mean we should necessarily *do* those things. The self-imposed limit to research is values—moral judgments that we as citizens must make about the kind of society we want. Here again, *Police & Society* does an admirable job of laying out the key issues. Any student interested in criminal justice will find much to ponder here about the relationship between research-based policing and democratic policing.

Many who read this book will pursue careers in policing. Others may follow careers in law or politics, in which they may come to make policies affecting policing. A very few may even go on to conduct research on policing. No matter where this book may lead you, you may trust it to get you off to an excellent start. ✦

> —Lawrence W. Sherman
> Greenfield Professor of Human Relations
> Director, Fels Center of Government
> University of Pennsylvania

Preface

Police & Society offers a comprehensive introduction to policing in the United States. It is both descriptive and analytical in nature, discussing historical perspectives and current knowledge regarding the process of policing, police behavior, and organization and operations. Contemporary issues and future prospects are also addressed. Throughout the text, an emphasis is placed on describing the relationship between the police and the community and how this relationship has changed through the years. The impact of this change on current police practices, especially with respect to community policing, is explored. To adequately explain the complex nature of police operations in a democracy, we have attempted to integrate the most important theoretical foundations, research findings, and contemporary practices in a comprehensible yet analytic manner.

The Second Edition has been substantially updated to incorporate the latest research, concepts, and practices in policing. All chapters have been significantly revised, and four new chapters have been added:

- Community Policing

- Police Management

- Change and Innovation

- The Future of Policing

The first three of these new chapters provide an important update and critical assessment of the police field's movement toward community policing, including definitions and concepts, management practices and policies, and processes of change and innovation. Examples of police departments on the cutting edge of community policing are profiled. The fourth new chapter, on the future of policing, takes a fresh look at the challenges facing police in the 21st century, the broad changes in ethnicity occurring in the United States, and the development and use of modem technology. In addition, the text has been reorganized into four essential parts, each building on the other: *The Police Role*, *Police Administration*, *Police Behavior*, and *Contemporary Issues*.

Important new topics covered include: crime prevention through environmental design; police subcultures and employee organizations; Police Paramilitary units (PPUs), compstat and zero-tolerance policing; computerized crime mapping; hot spots and crackdowns; domestic violence; guns, violence, and gangs; police corps and federal funding for higher education; changing diversity; pregnancy and maternity issues for women; sexual harassment; new forms of police stressors, including community policing, violent crimes, and litigation; and officer safety and fatality reduction.

In addition, several topics have been expanded from the First Edition. These include: the police role and history; police ethics and deviant behavior;

the use of force, brutality, and oversight mechanisms; women in policing; police suicide; and police pursuits.

In order to provide the most realistic and up-to-date view of the police, two types of offsets are provided. *Case Studies* boxes present important research findings and exemplary police programs. *Inside Policing* boxes provide brief descriptions of real-world police issues and operations as well as biographical sketches that highlight the contributions of important police leaders.

The Second Edition features an expanded glossary of key terms, and each chapter begins with a listing of key terms.

The following ancillaries are available to enhance instruction:

- A free *Student Study Guide* is included with every copy sold to students.

- A dedicated website, accessible through the main Roxbury website www.roxbury.net, supports the text.

- A revised and expanded *Instructor's Manual/Testing Program* is available in electronic or printed format.

- All figures and tables in the text are available in Powerpoint on CD.

Part I

The Police Role

Chapter One

Police in a Democracy

❖ ❖ ❖ ❖

Chapter Outline

❏ The Police Concept in a Democracy

❏ The Democracy-Police Conflict

❏ Democracy and the Rule of Law

❏ The Policing System

❏ Organizational Structure

     Other Types of Law Enforcement Organizations
     Municipal, County, and Regional Police

❏ The Role of Police in a Democracy

❏ The Expectation-Integration Model

     Environmental Expectations
     Organizational Expectations
     Legal Expectations

❏ Debates About the Role of the Police

     Legalistic or Political?
     Crime Fighter or Social-Service Worker?
     Proactive or Reactive?

❏ Police Values, Goals, and Strategies

❏ Summary

❏ Discussion Questions

❏ References

KEY TERMS	
case law	expectation-integration model
civil laws	goals
community	jurisdiction
community policing model	law enforcement strategy
community-building strategy	legal expectations
consolidation	legalistic model
contract law enforcement	organizational culture
crime fighters	organizational expectations
criminal laws	police
democracy-police conflict	police power
discretion	political model
education strategy	presence strategy
environmental expectations	private police

KEY TERMS (continued)	
proactive	special-jurisdiction police
procedural laws	strategies
public police	substantive laws
public safety	tribal police
reactive	task-force approach
rule of law	values
social-service providers	

The United States is a work in progress as our experiment in democracy continues to unfold. We are all participants in this experiment and by virtue of our studies or experience are well aware that representatives of government, like the police, should never be trusted completely. Before you begin this study of police in society, the authors ask you to answer one question: "If you were a suspect in a criminal case, would you trust the police to report accurately and completely what happened and what you and others involved did and said?" If the answer to that question is no, and from our students it almost always is, then you will begin to understand why the role of the police in a democracy is both complex and controversial.

Why do the police exist? What do they do? What are their problems? How have the police changed? How can the police be made compatible with democratic society? The central theme of this book is to attempt to answer these and related questions about police in the United States. Throughout this book the words *police* and *law enforcement* will be used interchangeably. Although police do more than enforce the law, that is their primary responsibility.

The book is organized into four sections:

1. The police role, which includes a discussion of the democratic context of policing and the police role, the history of police, and the transition toward community policing.

2. Police administration, which includes a discussion of management and organizational behavior, change and innovation, selection and development, and police field operations and selected problems.

3. Police behavior, which includes a discussion of behavior and discretion, police authority and the use of coercion, and police professionalism and accountability.

4. Selected present-day issues, including a discussion of higher education, cultural diversity, stress and officer safety, and the future of policing.

Most chapters contain two special sections called Case Study and Inside Policing. A Case Study box describes a specific activity or program of a police department. An Inside Policing section provides a brief description of "real world" police issues, excerpts from important research studies, and brief descriptions of the contributions of important historical and contemporary figures in law enforcement.

The Police Concept in a Democracy

The word **police** is related to the Greek words *politeuein*, which means to be a citizen or to engage in political activity, and *polis*, which means a city or state. These definitions emphasize the importance of the individual, the political process, and the state or government. How are individuals to be governed? All governments are vested with **police power** to regulate matters of health, welfare, safety, and morality because a society requires both structure and order if it is to be effective in meeting the safety, economic, and social needs of its members. One important expression of the police power in a society is a police, or law enforcement, organization.

The activities and behavior of the police are determined, in part, by the type of government of which they are a part. In more totalitarian governments, power is exercised by only one person (e.g., a dictator), a small number of individuals, or one political party. Generally, the established laws and policies that control all aspects of life are intended to maintain the interests of those in power; the social order is preserved at the expense of individual freedom. More democratic governments are based on the idea of the "participation of the governed." The members of a democratic society either directly participate in deciding the laws or they elect representatives who make such decisions for them.

Democracies are concerned about the rights and freedoms to be given to individuals and about the limits to be placed on government's use of the police power. This concern is usually addressed by creating a constitution. Constitutions may be either written or unwritten, but they serve the same basic purpose: to establish the nature and character of government by identifying the basic principles underlying that government. The Constitution of the United States identifies the functions of government and specifies in the Bill of Rights the rights of individuals relative to the government.

The United States has a constitutional democracy in which the exercise of power is based on the premise of the **rule of law**; that is, government by laws and not by individuals or organizations, such as the police. Ideally, laws that are created through a democratic process are more reasonable and more likely to be accepted by citizens than laws created by only a few individuals or by the most influential persons in society. And although democratic government does not always work in this fashion, ours has evolved so that the rule of law in practice has gradually become less tyrannical and more representative of the concerns of all citizens. One of the reasons that the rule of law is considered to be necessary is that proponents of democracy assume that individuals in power will be inclined to abuse their power (i.e., act in an arbitrary manner) unless they are controlled by a constitution, democratically developed laws, and the structure or organization of government.

The United States has a republican form of government that is decentralized (e.g., federal, state, and local units of government) to allow more people to participate in the political system and to limit the political power of those individuals elected to political office. Another important organizational feature of the U.S. government involves a "separation of powers," which results in three "branches": executive, judicial, and legislative. This separation exists to provide a system of "checks and balances" so that one branch of government will not become too powerful. Law enforcement is a responsibility of the executive branch.

Government and laws are created through a political process, or system. Being political means becoming involved in attempting to influence the way government resources (i.e., money, technology, and government employees and their knowledge, skills, and decisions) are used and what laws and policies are to be developed to guide governmental decision making, such as a police use-of-force policy. Voters, special-interest groups (e.g., the National Rifle Association or the National Association for the Advancement of Colored People), and elected officials are active participants in the political process. Theories of political decision making in a democracy include both pluralistic and elitist, or class, perspectives. The pluralistic perspective argues that debates, bargains, and compromises determine use of resources, laws, and policies. Further, although there are many different interests and groups in a society, no one group dominates. The elitist, or class, perspective argues that only a limited number of persons (e.g., the rich or special-interest groups) have real influence in the political process. This type of politics results in preferential treatment for the most influential and discrimination against those with little or no influence or power. A recurring problem in law enforcement is the frequency with which the police treat some persons preferentially while discriminating against others. This behavior is one reason why attempts to define the role of police in a democratic society are ongoing, with differing points of view about appropriate police activities and behavior.

The Democracy-Police Conflict

"Democracy is always hard on the police " (Berkeley 1969, p. 1). The police, in both concept and practice, conflict with some of the important characteristics of a democratic society. The police represent the legitimate force of government to compel citizens, if necessary, to obey laws that the majority of citizens, at least theoretically, have participated in creating. H. Goldstein describes the **democracy-police conflict** as follows: "The police . . . . are an anomaly in a free society. They are invested with a great deal of authority under a system of government in which authority is reluctantly granted and, when granted, sharply curtailed" (1977, p. 1).

To be successful, a democratic government must be based on a consensus, but when that consensus fails, the police are often the initial representatives of government that respond. For example, one of the common values of U.S. society is the importance of private ownership of property. Yet when one person steals another's property, this action reflects a failure of a consensus on this value. The creation of a police force is based, at least in part, on the idea that consensus cannot be completely achieved.

Another potential democracy-police conflict is related to the role of government. Government exists to represent and serve its citizens. Yet the police provide services that many in the society do not want (e.g., a traffic ticket or an arrest) but cannot avoid. Although citizens, in the abstract, may agree to be governed, in practice they often resist governmental (including police) intervention.

Democracy is also associated with some degree of freedom. While complete freedom is not allowed in any society, at least a democracy permits citizen participation in deciding how and when individual freedom will be restricted. However, the policies and procedures of the police and the decisions of individual police officers do not always include citizen participation. Consequently, the exercise of police authority tends to reflect an authoritarian orientation in an otherwise "free" society. Police are a constant reminder that freedom is limited.

Another important consideration in democracy is equality. The social-contract theory of government rests on the belief that democratic governments are founded on a contract to which all parties agree and in which all parties are equal. Nevertheless, the citizen and the police officer are not equals. Once the contract is established, represented by a constitution and laws, it must be observed. If it is not, the police exist to ensure compliance even if coercion is required (Berkeley 1969, pp. 1–5).

All these factors indicate why the opposite of a democratic state is often called a police state. Democracy represents consensus, freedom, participation, and equality; the police represent restriction and the imposition of the authority of government on the individual. That is why the police in a democracy are often confronted with hostility, opposition, and criticism no matter how effective or fair they may be. The democracy-police conflict must be addressed in some manner. As previously noted, democracies have attempted to cope with the exercise of government authority by emphasizing the importance of the rule of law.

Democracy and the Rule of Law

Police accountability to the rule of law is an important tradition in democratic societies. Reith (1938, p. 188) states that the basis for democratic policing "is to be found in rational and humane laws." The significance of the rule of law to democracy and the police is described in the Royal Commission Report on the British police:

> Liberty does not depend, and never has depended, upon any particular form of police organization. It depends upon the supremacy of . . . the rule of law. The proper criterion [to determine if a police state exists] is whether the police are answerable to the law and ultimately, to a democratically elected [government]. In the countries to which the term police state is applied . . . , police power is controlled by a [totalitarian] government [that] acknowledges no accountability to democratically elected (representatives), and the citizens cannot rely on the [law] to protect them. (1962, p. 45)

There are a number of ways to categorize laws; for example, laws may be civil or criminal and substantive or procedural. **Civil laws** are concerned with relationships between individuals (e.g., contracts, many business transactions, family relations); **criminal laws** are concerned with the relationship between the individual and government. Those behaviors that pose a threat to public safety and order (e.g., failure to get a driver's license, theft, rape, murder) are considered crimes. The prosecution of a crime is brought in the name of the people as represented by government officials (e.g., a prosecuting attorney). While police need to be familiar with both civil and criminal law, their primary concern is with criminal law.

In the criminal area, **substantive laws** are those that identify behavior, either required or prohibited, and the punishments for failure to observe these laws. For example, driving under the influence of alcohol is prohibited, and such behavior may be punished by a fine or imprisonment or both, and possibly by suspension of the privilege to drive a motor vehicle. **Procedural laws** govern how the police go about enforcing substantive laws, that is, the democratically determined process for exercising legal authority.

Important frames of reference for procedural criminal laws are the Bill of Rights (first ten amendments), the Fourteenth Amendment (see Table 1.1), and the **case law** (the written rulings of state and federal appellate courts) that more specifically defines when, and how, each procedure is to be used. When the police enforce substantive laws, their actions represent a restriction on individual behavior. When enforcing substantive laws, officers are supposed to follow procedural laws, which exist to restrict the police power of government and to reduce the possibility that police officers will abuse the power they have been given. The law not only provides the framework for police activity and behavior but is also intended to ensure that the police have a good reason (e.g., "reasonable suspicion" or "probable cause") to intrude into the lives of citizens. The enforcement of laws is considered less important than individual rights and the concern that government may abuse those rights. Procedural laws also balance what would otherwise be an unequal relationship between government and the individual because the government usually has more resources, and often has more public support, than has a suspect.

Even when the police have legal authority, however, they do not always enforce the law because of limited resources, public expectations, organizational priorities, and officer preferences. Rather, both the organization and the officer exercise **discretion**; that is, they make a choice concerning both what laws will be enforced and how that enforcement will take place. A number of factors influence police discretion; they will be discussed in chapter 9.

The Policing System

There are four basic types of policing in the United States: citizen-police officers, private police, public police, and public police who work in a private capacity. While all types of policing are discussed, this book is primarily about public police officers.

It is not uncommon for people in a democracy to participate in the policing process. As citizen-police officers we may make arrests when a felony, or in some states a breach of the peace, is committed in our presence. When we report a crime and cooperate in the subsequent investigation, we are participating in the policing process. Another type of citizen involvement is related to the legal doctrine of *posse comitatus*, in which individuals can be required to assist police officers. This involvement conjures up the image of the posse in Western movies, but it also includes the possibility that any of us, if requested, would be required to aid a police officer.

Vigilantism is another example of citizen participation in law enforcement. Historically, vigilantes were often community members (e.g., civic, business, or religious leaders) or mobs who took the law into their own hands. These groups developed as the result of a public perception that the

Table 1.1   The Bill of Rights and the Fourteenth Amendment

First Amendment

Congress shall make no law respecting an establishment of religion, or prohibiting the free exercise thereof; or abridging the freedom of speech or of the press; or the right of the people peaceably to assemble, and to petition the government for a redress of grievances. Criminal justice issues: public speeches, gatherings, and demonstrations.

Second Amendment

A well-regulated militia being necessary to the security of a free State, the right of the people to keep and bear arms shall not be infringed. Criminal justice issue: gun control.

Third Amendment

No soldier shall, in time of peace, be quartered in any house without the consent of the owner, nor in time of war, but in a manner to be prescribed by law. Criminal justice issue: none

Fourth Amendment

The right of the people to be secure in their persons, houses, papers, and effects, against unreasonable searches and seizures, shall not be violated, and no warrants shall be issued but upon probable cause, supported by oath or affirmation, and particularly describing the place to be searched and the persons or things to be seized. Criminal justice issues: search and seizure, search warrants, use of deadly force.

Fifth Amendment

No person shall be held to answer for a capital, or otherwise infamous crime, unless on a presentment or indictment of a grand jury, except in cases arising in the land or naval forces, or in the militia, when in actual service in time of war or public danger; nor shall any person be subject for the same offense to be twice put in jeopardy of life or limb; nor shall be compelled in any criminal case to be a witness against himself, nor be deprived of life, liberty, or property, without due process of law; nor shall private property be taken for public use without just compensation. Criminal justice issues: charging criminals, double jeopardy, due process or fair treatment if charged with a crime, self-incrimination or confessions.

Sixth Amendment

In all criminal prosecutions, the accused shall enjoy the right to a speedy and public trial, by an impartial jury of the State and district wherein the crime shall have been committed, which district shall have been previously ascertained by law, and to be informed of the nature and cause of the accusation; to be confronted with the witnesses against him; to have compulsory process for obtaining witnesses in his favor, and to have the assistance of counsel for his defense. Criminal justice issues: speedy and public trial, impartial jury from the area in which the crime is committed, being told of the charges, being able to ask questions of witnesses.

Seventh Amendment

In suits at common law, where the value in controversy shall exceed twenty dollars, the right of trial by jury shall be preserved, and no fact tried by jury shall be otherwise re-examined in any court of the United States, than according to the rules of the common law. Criminal justice issue: appeals in criminal trials.

Eighth Amendment

Excessive bail shall not be required, nor excessive fines imposed, nor cruel and unusual punishments inflicted. Criminal justice issues: staying in or getting out of jail while awaiting a trial, seriousness of the punishment.

Ninth Amendment

The enumeration in the Constitution of certain rights shall not be construed to deny or disparage others retained by the people. Criminal justice issues: none.

Tenth Amendment

The powers not delegated to the United States by the Constitution, nor prohibited by it to the States, are reserved to the States respectively, or to the people. Criminal justice issues: none.

Fourteenth Amendment

All persons born or naturalized in the United States, and subject to the jurisdiction thereof, are citizens of the United States and of the State wherein they reside. No State shall make or enforce any law which shall abridge the privileges or immunities of citizens of the United States; nor shall any State deprive any person of life, liberty, or property, without due process of law; nor deny to any person within its jurisdiction the equal protection of the laws. Criminal justice issues: What is due process and equal protection of the law?

existing law enforcement system was inadequate and corrupt or that it did not serve the interests of the vigilantes (Walker 1977, pp. 30–31). Although more common in the nineteenth century, this type of citizen involvement in law enforcement still occurs.

There are also both public and private police. **Public police** are employed, trained, and paid by a government agency; their purpose is to serve the general interest of all citizens. **Private police** are those police employed and paid to serve the specific purposes, within the law, of an individual or organization. A municipal police officer is a public police officer; a guard at a bank or department store is a private police officer. Public police may also serve in a private capacity. It is common for public police officers to work part-time in a private capacity, such as at a nightclub or shopping center.

Public police are part of the executive branch of government. As noted earlier, the government of the United States is divided into three branches to check and balance the use of government power. The *legislative branch* is elected representatives who make laws and ordinances; the *executive branch*, which has both elected (e.g., the president or governor or mayor) and appointed officials (e.g., a city manager), enforces those laws. The *judicial branch*, which has both elected and appointed judges, interprets the law and applies it to problems in a changing society. Police forces were established primarily to enforce, and follow, laws enacted by the legislative branch as interpreted by the judicial branch.

Public police organizations are also part of the *criminal justice system*, which includes the courts and correctional institutions. The police function as the "gatekeepers" of the criminal justice system because they determine who will be cited or arrested. The judicial branch and its representatives, including prosecuting and defense attorneys, process the accused. The correctional part of the system (e.g., probation, community treatment programs, jails, prisons, parole) rehabilitates or punishes convicted criminals.

Organizational Structure

The organization of the U.S. police tends to follow the geographical and political structure of the U.S. government. Each of the four levels of government—federal, state, county (or parish or borough), and municipal (city or town)—has police powers and may have its own police forces. The federal and state levels of government have many different police forces that tend to specialize in different types of law enforcement.

Although law enforcement organizations at each level of government are similar in some ways, they may also differ in the types of activities in which they engage. These activities are determined, in part, by their **jurisdiction,** the criminal matters over which they have authority. For example, the Internal Revenue Service's (IRS) jurisdiction is limited to internal revenue violations, which involve federal tax laws. The Federal Bureau of Investigation (FBI) is the generalist law enforcement agency of the federal government. It is charged with the investigation of all federal laws not assigned to some other agency (e.g., the Postal Service or the IRS). Local police enforce all laws that are applicable, including state laws and local ordinances, within the legally incorporated limits of a city or county.

The federal government has more than 60 agencies with law enforcement and investigative powers. State governments, in addition to bodies such as the state police or highway patrol (e.g., the Alaska Department of Public Safety or the New York State Police), may also include other governmental agencies (dealing with such matters as revenue collection, parks and recreation, and alcoholic beverage control) that have police powers. The most common type of county law enforcement agency is the county sheriff, but some counties also have investigators who work for prosecuting attorneys and public defenders. In addition, some counties have separate police and sheriff's departments (e.g., city and county of San Francisco). In such situations, the sheriff's department is usually responsible for operating the county jail and for assisting the courts but does not engage in policing activities. Finally, most municipal governments also have their own police force (e.g., Los Angeles Police Department). For the most part, both county sheriffs and local police are involved in patrolling, responding to calls for service, and conducting investigations; however, sheriffs' departments also invest substantial resources in managing jails and providing court services.

Figures 1.1 and 1.2 indicate the different activities of sheriff's departments and local police agencies. Table 1.2 identifies federal law enforcement agencies that employ more than 100 officers. The largest federal agency is the Immigration and Naturalization Service (INS), which has more than 12,000 officers. Table 1.3 identifies the number of sworn officers and nonsworn employees for local police, sheriff's departments, and state police. Municipal police departments have more sworn officers than the county sheriffs, state police, and federal agencies combined. Table 1.4 groups state and local departments by number of sworn officers. Approximately 57 percent of all local departments have less than 10 officers and about 78 percent have 24 or less. As used in Table 1.4, "local law enforcement" refers to municipal forces (13,353), county sheriffs (3,088), county police (55), tribal police (135), regional police (35), special police (1,366), and Texas constables (738). These are discussed later in the chapter.

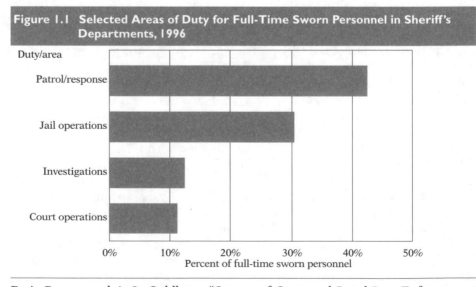

Figure 1.1   Selected Areas of Duty for Full-Time Sworn Personnel in Sheriff's Departments, 1996

B. A. Reaves and A. L. Goldberg, "Census of State and Local Law Enforcement Agencies, 1996." (Washington, D.C.: Bureau of Justice Statistics, 1998), p. 9.

Figure 1.2 Selected Areas of Duty for Full-Time Sworn Personnel in Local Police Departments, 1996

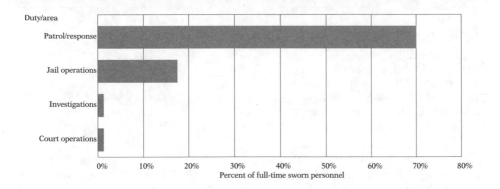

Percent of full-time sworn personnel

B. A. Reaves and A. L. Goldberg, "Census of State and Local Law Enforcement Agencies, 1996." Washington, D.C.: Bureau of Justice Statistics, 1998, p. 6.

Table 1.5 lists the municipal forces (32), the county sheriff's departments (11), county police (7), and regional, or consolidated, police forces with 1,000 or more sworn officers (3). The largest in each category are the New York City Police Department (36,813), Los Angeles County Sheriff's Department (8,014), Nassau County Police (3,099), and Las Vegas-Clark County Police Department (1,696). The New York City Police Department has almost three times the number of sworn officers as any other local, state, or federal agency.

Table 1.2 Federal Agencies Employing 100 or More Full-time Officers Authorized to Carry Firearms and Make Arrests, June 1996

Agency	Number of full-time federal officers
Immigration and Naturalization Service	12,403
Federal Bureau of Prisons	11,329
Federal Bureau of Investigation	10,389
U.S. Customs Service	9,749
Internal Revenue Service	3,784
U.S. Postal Inspection Service	3,576
U.S. Secret Service	3,185
Drug Enforcement Administration	2,946
Administrative Office in the U.S. Courts	2,777
U.S. Marshals Service	2,650
National Park Service	2,148
Bureau of Alcohol, Tobacco and Firearms	1,869
U.S. Capitol Police	1,031
U.S. Fish and Wildlife Service	869
GSA-Federal Protective Service	643
U.S. Forest Service	619
Bureau of Diplomatic Service	367
Amtrak	342
Bureau of Indian Affairs	339

Table 1.2	Federal Agencies Employing 100 or More Full-time Officers Authorized to Carry Firearms and Make Arrests, June 1996 (continued)	
Agency	Number of full-time federal officers	
U.S. Mint	224	
Bureau of Land Management	208	
Tennessee Valley Authority	194	
Bureau of Engraving and Printing	165	
Environmental Protection Agency	151	
Food and Drug Administration	128	
National Marine Fisheries Service*	117	
Library of Congress	108	

* A component of the National Oceanic and Atmospheric Administration.
B. A. Reaves, "Federal Law Enforcement Officers, 1996." Washington, D.C.: Bureau of Justice Statistics, 1997, pp. 2, 4.

Table 1.3	Employment by State and Local Law Enforcement Agencies, by Type of Agency and Employee, June 1996					
	State and local law enforcement employees					
Type of agency	Full-time			Part-time		
	Total	Sworn	Nonsworn	Total	Sworn	Nonsworn
Number of employees						
Total	921,978	663,535	258,443	97,770	47,712	50,058
Local police	521,985	410,956	111,029	61,453	30,970	30,477
Sheriff	257,712	152,922	104,790	22,412	10,845	11,567
Primary State police	83,742	54,587	29,155	1,303	132	1,171

B. A. Reaves and A. L. Goldberg, "Census of State and Local Law Enforcement Agencies, 1996." Washington, D.C.: Bureau of Justice Statistics, 1998, p. 2.

Table 1.4	State and Local Law Enforcement Agencies by Size of Agency, June 1996	
Number of full-time sworn personnel	Agencies	
	Number	Percent
All sizes	18,769	100%
1,000 or more officers	70	0.4%
500–999	80	0.4
250–499	188	1.0
100–249	604	3.2
50–99	1,085	5.8
25–49	2,028	10.8
10–24	4,018	21.4
5–9	3,624	19.3
2–4	3,663	19.5
1	2,245	12.0
0	1,164	6.2

B. A. Reaves and A. L. Goldberg, "Census of State and Local Law Enforcement Agencies, 1996." Washington, D.C.: Bureau of Justice Statistics, 1998, p. 5.

Table 1.5 Local Police Departments With 1,000 or More Sworn Officers, 1996			
Agency	Number of officers	Agency	Number of officers
New York	36,813	Palm Beach Co. Sheriff	1,620
Chicago	13,237	Baltimore Co. Police	1,535
Los Angeles	8,988	Atlanta	1,474
Los Angeles Co. Sheriff	8,014	Denver	1,427
Philadelphia	6,398	Memphis	1,420
Cook Co. Sheriff	5,309	Jacksonville-Duval Co. Police*	1,394
Houston	5,298	Riverside Co. Sheriff	1,357
Detroit	3,904	New Orleans	1,342
Washington	3,587	Charlotte-Mecklenberg*	1,286
Nassau Co. Police	3,009	San Jose	1,281
Baltimore	2,933	Seattle	1,237
Dallas	2,864	Prince George's Co. Police	1,230
Dade Co. Police	2,824	Newark	1,222
Suffolk Co. Police	2,744	Orange Co. Sheriff	1,221
Harris Co. Sheriff	2,484	Kansas City	1,173
Phoenix	2,433	Fort Worth	1,172
Milwaukee	2,105	Bexar Co. Sheriff	1,169
Boston	2,100	Sacramento Co. Sheriff	1,156
San Francisco	2,000	Pittsburgh	1,154
San Diego	1,986	San Bernardino Co. Sheriff	1,149
Honolulu	1,981	Nashville	1,129
San Antonio	1,872	Fairfax Co. Police	1,067
Columbus	1,730	Broward Co. Sheriff	1,029
Cleveland	1,729	Miami	1,012
San Diego Co. Sheriff	1,700	Oklahoma City	1,009
Las Vegas-Clark Co. Police*	1,696	Nassau Co. Sheriff	1,004
St. Louis	1,631		

* Regional or Consolidated Police Departments.

B. A. Reaves and A. L. Goldberg, "Census of State and Local Law Enforcement Agencies, 1996," (Washington, D.C.: Bureau of Justice Statistics, 1998), p. 6.

One of the more important sources for data about the number of police is *Crime in the United States* (or *Uniform Crime Reports*), which is an annual publication of the FBI and the Department of Justice. It also includes crime statistics and other police-related information, including the number of officers injured and killed and the number of women and minority officers. Another important data source is the *Municipal Yearbook*, published by the International City Manager's Association, which includes police employee and cost data as well as related management information (e.g., affirmative action programs and collective bargaining issues).

Some of the most comprehensive data can be found in the publications of the Bureau of Justice Statistics (BJS), which is part of the U.S. Department of Justice. Of particular interest are the Law Enforcement Management and Administrative Statistics (LEMAS) reports published by the BJS. Many states also have agencies that collect and disseminate data about police employment and expenditures, and many law enforcement agencies publish annual reports and have websites on the Internet.

Other Types of Law Enforcement Organizations

In addition to the basic structure of policing described above, there are other forms of public policing, including tribal police, public safety, consolidation, special-jurisdiction police, contract law enforcement, and task-force arrangements.

Tribal police are law enforcement agencies created and operated by Native Americans. Their jurisdiction is usually, but not always, limited to reservation land. These types of police agencies are separate from those law enforcement organizations operated by the Bureau of Indian Affairs, which is a federal agency.

The **public safety** concept involves the integration of police and fire-fighting services (and possibly other services like disaster preparedness, hazardous waste disposal, and emergency medical services). This integration can be limited to administrative matters, or it may also include the joint performance of both fire-fighting and police duties. When the duties or work is integrated, employees are trained to perform both police and fire-fighting activities.

Consolidation involves the integration of two or more police departments. This integration can be either by function or by organization. Functional, or partial, integration involves the combining of the same activity, perhaps communications or training. For example, two or more police departments may decide to share the same communication system or develop a common training program. Organizational integration involves two or more departments becoming one. This is usually a county and a city department, as in Clark County-Las Vegas, Nevada, or Duval County-Jacksonville, Florida, but it could also involve two or more cities.

Historically, it has been quite common for communities to consider the consolidation of police departments, particularly in urban areas. Supporters of consolidation argue that a larger police force can provide better service at lower cost. Although this argument is not always accurate, it does tend to generate some support for consolidation. Opponents of consolidation argue that if the community maintains control of its own police force, it will be more responsive to the needs of that community. Citizens often want to maintain direct control over the use of the police power in their community. Although functional consolidation of police departments is commonplace in urban areas, the complete consolidation of two or more police departments is rare.

Special-jurisdiction police usually have the same police powers as those officers employed in other police departments, but they tend to have jurisdiction in a specified area believed to require more specialized or separate law enforcement services. Colleges and universities often have their own police force (e.g., San Jose State University Police Department). Other examples include transit police (e.g., Bay Area Rapid Transit in California), park or recreation area police, and public school police. Table 1.6 provides data on the number and types of special-jurisdiction police.

Table 1.6 Special Police Agencies and Full-time Sworn Personnel, by Type of Jurisdiction, June 1996		
Type of special jurisdiction	Agencies	Full-time sworn personnel
Total	1,316	43,082
College/university campus	699	10,495
Natural resources/conservation laws	79	8,395
Public school district	117	5,247
Transportation system/facilities	28	4,274
Parks/recreation facilities	68	2,595
Criminal investigations	72	2,515
Airport	84	2,407
Waterways/harbors/ports	38	1,291
Public housing	13	1,245
Alcoholic beverage control	17	1,199
State capitol/government buildings	24	988
Medical school/facilities	42	894
Fire investigations	14	448
Agricultural/livestock laws	6	300
Commercial vehicle laws	1	197
Public sanitation district	3	193
Gaming/racing laws	5	190
Court services	1	140
Other	5	68

B. A. Reaves and A. L. Goldberg, "Census of State and Local Law Enforcement Agencies, 1996." Washington, D.C.: Bureau of Justice Statistics, 1998, p. 12.

Contract law enforcement, or policing, involves a contractual arrangement between two units of government in which one agrees to provide law enforcement services for the other. For example, a county sheriff's department might enter into a contract with a municipality to provide a given level of police service for a certain amount of money. The municipality might not wish to pay to establish its own police department or it might believe it would receive better services from the larger organization. Although it is possible to have a contractual relationship between any two governmental units, the most common one is between a county and a city. Contract law enforcement is quite common in many urban areas.

The **task-force approach** to policing is a form of functional consolidation but tends to be temporary (i.e., from a few weeks to years) rather than permanent. Some task forces, however, have lasted more than 20 years. Two or more departments may decide to create a task force to respond to crimes such as auto theft, drugs and related problems, a serial rapist, or a serial killer. Cooperative arrangements can exist at the local level (e.g., several municipal police departments and the county sheriff) or between local and state, or local and federal, law enforcement agencies (e.g., a drug or a gun and gang violence task force). A task force may also include representatives from other criminal justice agencies (e.g., probation and parole), or other governmental and community organizations (e.g., social services). What is unique abut this arrangement is that it involves the joint efforts of two or more police departments directed toward common problems.

Municipal, County, and Regional Police

Municipal, county, and regional police, when compared with state and federal law enforcement, have the most employees, cost the most money, respond to a majority of police-related problems, and tend to have a closer relationship with citizens. In addition, a substantial majority of social science research about the police concerns municipal and county agencies.

Although there are similarities, there are also considerable differences among law enforcement agencies. Police departments range in size from more than 30,000 officers to hundreds that have only one full-time or part-time officer. Some small communities are adjacent to urban areas; others are more isolated. Counties can be densely or sparsely populated. Although it is theoretically possible to create a number of categories or types of local departments using demographic, economic, social, and cultural variables, research has been primarily limited to the study of differences between rural and urban police.

Rural and urban police do not represent discrete categories; rather, both unincorporated areas (in counties) and incorporated areas (cities or smaller communities) vary in population numbers, population density, values, lifestyles, and problems. Consequently, it is often difficult to identify what is a rural or urban area or community. Nevertheless, differences have been noted between larger, more densely populated urban areas and those outside urban areas in which there are fewer people, usually 2,500 or less.

Although the urban crime rate tends to be higher than the rural crime rate, crime associated with urban areas is often exported to rural areas; for example, urban drug trafficking is a driving force behind the spread of drug use and the development of gangs in rural areas. Some of the crimes associated with rural areas include growing marijuana; thefts of crops, timber, and animals; and poaching. Some of the crimes in rural areas are more easily solved (i.e., an arrest is made) because homicide, rape, and assault are more likely to occur among acquaintances than in urban areas.

Sims describes other differences that exist between urban and rural police:

> Urban police tend not to live where they work, while rural officers do. . . . [R]ural law enforcement is personalistic and non bureaucratic, in contrast to the formality, impersonality and bureaucratization of urban police. Rural law enforcement involves . . . more face-to-face interaction and communication. [It also] . . . includes a greater . . . percentage of police-acquaintance contacts and . . . [fewer] police-stranger contacts. (1996, p. 45)

In addition, rural law enforcement officers, more than their urban counterparts, often work with lower budgets, less staff, less equipment, and fewer written policies. But they also appear to be more efficient than urban police and more respected by the public. The context in which rural police work takes place also affects their activities. Rural citizens may be more likely to rely on informal social controls (i.e., take care of the problem themselves) rather than report a "private" matter to the police. In addition, rural residents may be more likely to mistrust government and, therefore, may be more reluctant to share information (Weisheit, Falcone, and Wells 1994, 1996; McDonald, Wood, and Pflug 1996). Inside Policing 1.1 presents several comments by rural police officers concerning differences between rural and urban police.

Inside Policing I.I
Rural Police Work

Former Rural Police Officer

"The small town police officers are more in tune with the fact that if I'm a member of the Kiwanis, Lions Club or the Jaycees, these people can help me.... [In] New York [if]... you get into a bind they aren't going to help you as much. [Rural] ... police are very active ... in these types of organizations." (p. 81)

Rural Police Officer

"[When arresting someone] ... you can't act overly high and mighty with them, you won't get any cooperation. In big cities, that's what you do, you come on strong, 'I'm the boss.' That's often a very effective method there but not out here in the rural areas." (p. 82)

Rural Police Officer

"[M]ost ... training academies are geared for large, urban departments. I used to send somebody to the academy and when they came back I would have to ride herd on them for two months to get the academy out of them. At the academy, everything is treated very, very serious. All traffic stops are felonies un-

less proven otherwise. . . . In a small town, [citizens] are people first and suspects second. In a large town. . . [it is the reverse]." (p. 84)

Rural Police Officer

"Their [police and citizen's] kids go to the same school. You see [people] ... on the street, . . . in the grocery store. (Big-city cops) the officers are cold. They treat . . . [the good and the bad people] ... the same way." (p.86)

Small-Town Chief of Police

"I've had people in here to counsel ... [them] on their sex life because they think I'm the almighty, and can do that. I've had people come in here who are having trouble making ends meet, and we [help them] ... get welfare. Somebody needs a ride, like an elderly lady needs a ride to the doctor. We'll take her to the doctor and go get her groceries for her." (p.87)

Source: R. A. Weisheit, D. N. Falcone, and L. E. Wells. 1996. *Crime and Policing in Rural and Small-Town America*. Prospect Heights, Ill.: Waveland Press.

The next section begins the discussion of the role of police in a democratic society. First, it provides a conceptual framework that is useful in understanding the police role. Then follows a discussion of recurring debates about role and several methods used to identify the role of the police.

The Role of Police in a Democracy

The police are the major representatives of the legal system in their transactions with citizens. The police "adapt the universal standards of the law to the requirements of the citizen and the public . . . through their right to exercise discretion." They are also the "major emergency arm of the community in times of personal and public crisis." In carrying out their mandate, the police "possess a virtual monopoly on the legitimate use of force" (Reiss 1971; pp. 1–2).

The police also provide needed governmental and social services. In doing their job, the police often develop an intimate relationship with some citizens in a community:

> Police officers deal with people when they are both most threatening and most vulnerable, when they are angry, when they are frightened, when they are desperate, when they are drunk, when they are violent, or when they are ashamed. Every police action can affect in some way someone's

dignity, or self-respect, or sense of privacy, or constitutional rights. (President's Commission 1967, pp. 91–92)

C. B. Klockars suggests that there is a tendency to define the police in terms of goals (e.g., reduce crime) rather that the means or methods to achieve those goals (1985, pp. 8–13). Bittner (1970) believes that it is the means used by the police that tends to separate them from citizens and other government agencies. The police are authorized by government to use force (coercion) to compel individuals to comply with the requirements of criminal laws or force them to face the consequences.

The police can be defined as those nonmilitary individuals or organizations that are given the general right by government to use coercion to enforce the law and to respond to individual and group conflict involving illegal behavior. Although the military can be given police powers, this is not the group with which this book is concerned. Of course, the police use methods other than coercion, but this is what distinguishes them from other government agencies and employees. In the remainder of the chapter several aspects of the police role are discussed: compatible and conflicting expectations, recurring debates over roles, and values, goals, and strategies.

The Expectation-Integration Model

The police role is the part they are expected to play in a democratic society. There are three major sources of expectations concerning what the police should do and how they should do it: the environment, the police department, and the law. Figure 1.3 presents a depiction of an **expectation-integration model**. Each box indicates the different possible degrees of integration: substantial, partial, or minimal. As the degree to which expectations are shared and changes are integrated, the extent of role-related conflict either increases or decreases. When expectations from the three sources are compatible, there is minimal difficulty in deciding what the police should do and how they should do it.

Environmental Expectations

Societal trends and problems—in general and in each community—create an environment. Changing social and economic trends and problems in a society or a particular community often affect the police. For instance, there may be a rapid growth in population, an economic recession, a drug problem, or a gang problem. Although trends and problems in themselves do not create environmental expectations, police or citizen awareness of these issues may raise expectations concerning how the police should respond.

The community environment includes problems unique to a particular community, other private and public organizations, other criminal justice agencies, elected and appointed leaders, special-interest groups, identifiable neighborhoods, and the individual citizen. **Community** has different possible meanings—not only the legally incorporated area of a city or county but also individuals who live in the same area or neighborhood, work for the same organization, or share common concerns (e.g., members of an ethnic or religious group, teenagers, and senior citizens).

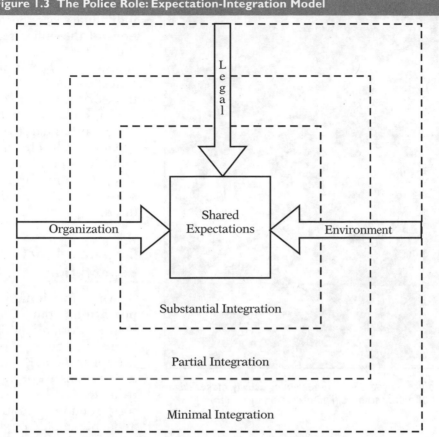

Figure 1.3 The Police Role: Expectation-Integration Model

Adapted from R. R. Roberg and J. Kuykendall, 1990. *Police Organization and Management: Behavior, Theory, and Processes.* Pacific Grove, CA: Brooks/Cole.

As the United States has become increasingly diverse in recent decades, the police relationship with multicultural communities has presented some unique problems. Different languages and cultural perspectives about the police have resulted in substantial changes in some police departments. Not only must the police interact effectively with diverse groups and individuals, they must also attempt to manage the conflicts between different cultural groups.

One of the most important, and recurring, police problems is the relationship between the police and a community that has, from the police point of view, a large number of suspects or individuals who are hostile to and critical of the police. This type of conflict between police and community has often been most pronounced in some areas inhabited by ethnic and racial minorities.

Each community is also made up of individual citizens, whose expectations of the police are determined by the citizens' educational background, personal experiences, and experiences of family, friends, and the media. Each person can interact with a police officer in at least six ways: as a suspect (including the recipient of a traffic ticket), a victim, a witness, an informer, a bystander, or a citizen interested in influencing police policies and practices. In

An officer, engaged in a crime fighting activity, makes an arrest of a drug suspect. (Photo: corbisimages.com)

each of the six roles, the individual's expectations of the police may differ; for example, a victim's expectations differ somewhat from those of a suspect. In addition, citizen expectations may be held by reasonable, well-informed individuals or by people who are uninformed, self-serving, or prejudiced.

Organizational Expectations

Organizational expectations come from both the formal and informal aspects of a police department. Formal expectations are derived from leaders; supervisors; training programs; and the goals, objectives, policies, procedures, and regulations of the police department. Informal expectations are derived from officers' peers and work group. Officers are strongly influenced by their work experiences and the way they adjust to the emotional, psychological, intellectual, and physical demands of police work. They must attempt to do their job in a manner that is acceptable to both the police department and their peers; they must try not to be injured or killed or allow other officers or citizens to be injured or killed; and their conduct must not provoke citizen complaints.

Together, formal and informal organizational (departmental) expectations create an **organizational culture** that can be defined as "the pattern of basic assumptions that a given group [the police] has invented, discovered, or developed in learning to cope with its problems of external adaptation and internal integration, [and] that have worked well enough to be considered valid" (Schien 1985, p. 9). The values and beliefs are concerned with what the police officer considers to be important and with his or her attitudes toward police work and the organization. An officer's norms become his or her basis for discretionary decision making. Not all formal organizational expectations concerning appropriate police work are incorporated into the values, beliefs, and norms of the officers. The validity of the formal expectations of police officers must first be "tested" in the "reality of the street." And formal expectations do not always pass this reality test. As a result, police behavior is influenced not only by what the department expects but also by the expectations of the organizational culture.

Legal Expectations

Legal expectations of the police are derived from substantive and procedural criminal laws and legal requirements that have resulted from civil suits. These laws provide the basic framework in which the police are supposed to function. Although the police do not always follow the law, legal expectations have a substantial influence on what they do and how they behave. In addition, as noted, the police do not enforce all laws; rather, they exercise discretion in deciding what laws to enforce and how to enforce them. These discretionary decisions may not always be compatible with what either the formal organization or the community expects.

Attempts to integrate environmental, organizational, and legal expectations have resulted in several recurring debates about the police role in society. Three of the most important of these debates are discussed below.

Debates About the Role of the Police

Historically, there have been recurring debates about the role of the police in democratic society. Although both sides of each debate have been influential in determining the police role, the extent of the influence of any particular perspective varies by community and time period. This aspect is discussed in more detail in chapter 2.

Legalistic or Political?

What is the most effective way to integrate the role of police into democratic society? At the extremes there are two alternatives: a rule-oriented way or one that is responsive and individualized. The former is a legalistic (or bureaucratic or quasi-military or professional or reform) approach, the latter is a political approach. The concept of a legalistic approach assumes that justice is a product of consistent application of laws and departmental policies and procedures. Ideally, these laws, policies, and procedures are rationally developed and free of any bias that would be inconsistent with the fundamental principles of the society.

The political view of the police role rests on one of two assumptions. One is that laws and the police primarily serve the interest of the most influential persons in a community. Such individuals are considered to be above the law, whereas others are treated more harshly. This view leads to politics of preference and discrimination. The second assumption focuses on responsiveness and individualization. Its advocates argue that strict enforcement of the rules does not take into account the uniqueness of the problems and needs of individuals and neighborhood groups in the community. Consistency is not required and preferential treatment and discrimination are unnecessary if police officers are professional. The police response should be lawful and a function of the situational context and community values as these relate to community problems.

This debate between the legalistic and the political approach emphasizes a long-standing tension in democratic societies—the rule of law versus community expectations. At the one extreme is the uncaring bureaucrat who never deviates from the rules and does not seek opinions about which rules

An officer engaged in a social service activity. (Photo: Mark C. Ide)

are important and when and how they should be applied. At the other extreme is mob rule. Ideally, public dissatisfaction would result in changes, but in a pluralistic society, with competing interests and demands on government services, changes can take considerable time and may indeed fail to occur at all. Consequently, those that provide the service are often called upon to tailor that service to the needs of a particular community. But how can they do this without providing preferential treatment for some (individuals, groups, neighborhoods) while discriminating against others? The answer to this question remains elusive and varies concerning how, or even if, it can be done.

The legalistic approach and the two assumptions of the political approach to the role of the police identify three possible types of police-community relationships. The next two chapters discuss three models in the evolution of policing: the political, the legalistic, and community. The **political model** refers to a police-community relationship that is plagued by problems of preferential treatment, discrimination, and corruption. The **legalistic model** is based on the assumption that political influence has a corrupting influence on policing; therefore, the police-community relationship must be more structured or bureaucratic. The **community policing model** is based on the desirability of the police being responsive to individuals and groups without engaging in preferential treatment or discrimination.

Crime Fighter or Social-Service Worker?

The debate whether the police should only fight crime or also provide social services influences the priority given to police activities, the type of personnel selected, the way officers are trained, and the styles of officers. Officers who consider themselves to be **crime fighters** believe that crime is a function of a rational choice made by criminals and that the primary police purpose is to patrol and conduct investigations to deter crime and apprehend offenders. Officers who consider themselves **social-service providers** believe that crime results from a variety of causes and there are other police activities like crime prevention education and community-building that may also reduce the crime rate. The social service orientation tends to result in more police-community involvement and a less aggressive and authoritarian approach to policing.

There are, of course, no "pure" crime fighters or social-service providers; however, the belief that police are, or should be, one or the other influences how the police role in a community will be constructed. Often the role expectations vary by source. Some communities or neighborhoods or groups may expect police to be crime fighters, whereas others may want a social-service orientation. Often, police officers themselves prefer to think of themselves as crime fighters. Attempts to resolve this debate have resulted in considerable research about the tasks and activities of the police. Beginning in the 1960s, critics of the emphasis on the crime-fighting role began to argue that police spent little time in actually responding to crime. This assertion was based on research studies that attempted to group police activities into such categories as law enforcement or crime fighting, service or social work, and administration (e.g., report writing). These studies were controversial because they did not produce the same results. In addition, there was, and is, a controversy concerning how certain police activities should be categorized. Some, such as patrolling and responding to crimes without making arrests (e.g., many disturbance calls), can be placed in either crime-fighting or noncrime-fighting categories. While task and activity studies are useful in identifying the amount of time police spend in different activities, they are not particularly useful in resolving this debate.

Proactive or Reactive?

Proactive police work emphasizes police-initiated activities of the individual officer and the department. **Reactive** police work is more a response to a problem by police when assistance is specifically requested by citizens. Giving a traffic ticket or other citation or conducting a field interrogation is a proactive act. Developing a response to a crime or other problem that is designed to keep a crime from occurring is proactive. For example, undercover decoy programs are proactive, as are "stakeouts" (following suspected career criminals) and picking up truants (who may be committing burglaries when absent from school). Responding to specific problems based on citizen requests and following up on those problems are reactive responses.

What is problematic about proactive responses is that they make the police more intrusive in the community; that is, they are more likely to initiate contacts or programs without being asked, and some proactive programs are potentially dangerous (e.g., stakeout and decoy programs). Being proactive can be associated with good management, but it may also be excessively intrusive and risky.

Which is more compatible with democracy—a police force that is primarily reactive or one that is substantially proactive? Although eliminating all proactive activity (e.g., giving traffic tickets) is probably not possible, it is possible to limit the number of police-initiated contacts and departmental programs. It is also important to distinguish the degree to which proactive police work is in response to community expectations or is entirely the result of the concerns of the police department. In some instances, professional police work has been associated with being proactive. What is clear, however, is that the more proactive, the more intrusive the police, and the more intrusive, the greater the risk to police officers, citizens, and democracy.

In order to define the police role and to attempt to resolve role debates, the police must first integrate diverse expectations by identifying their own values, goals, and strategies. Goals and values are also discussed in chapter 4.

Police Values, Goals, and Strategies

Values are fundamental assumptions that guide the department and the individual officer in the exercise of discretion. The values of the department determine police goals, how resources are used, strategies, and the style of officers. To illustrate the possible influence of values on the police role, two sets of values are listed in Table 1.7. The first listing tends to describe police work as primarily a law enforcement activity in which an officer should be primarily a crime fighter and a legalistic police-community relationship should exist. The second set of values suggests that the police officer is as much, or more, a social-service worker as a crime fighter and supports a politically responsive police-community relationship.

Table 1.7   Police Values

Law Enforcement-Oriented Values

1. Police authority is based on the law, and law enforcement is the primary police objective.

2. Communities can provide police with assistance and information in enforcing the law.

3. Responding to calls for service is the highest priority, and calls must receive the fastest response possible.

Law Enforcement-Oriented Values

4. Social and neighborhood problems are not the responsibility of the police unless they threaten the breakdown of public order.

5. Police, as experts, are best suited to determine crime-control priorities and strategies.

Community-Oriented Values

1. The police will involve the community in all activities, including the development of policies, that affect the quality of community life.

2. The police believe that strategies must preserve and advance democratic values.

Table 1.7 Police Values (continued)

3. The police must structure the delivery of service so that it will reinforce the strengths of the neighborhoods.
4. Employees should have input into matters that influence job satisfaction and effectiveness.

Adapted from R. Wasserman and M. H. Moore. 1988. *Perspectives on Policing: Values in Policing*. Washington D.C.: National Institute of Justice.

Goals are sometimes called purposes or objectives or aims. When the goals approach is used to define the police role, several goals are usually listed for the police. Table 1.8 provides, in no particular order, several possible police goals.

Table 1.8   Possible Goals of the Police

Prevention of crime
Reduction of the fear of crime
Maintenance of the peace
Protection of persons and property
Enforcement of laws
Detection of crime
Apprehension of offenders
Traffic control
Responsiveness to community needs
Management of intergroup conflict
Protection of individual rights
Provision of additional public services

Once the goals of a police department are identified, the next step is to determine how to achieve those goals most effectively. **Strategies** are those broadly conceptualized police activities that are assumed to have an impact on the attitudes and behavior of individuals. The four basic police strategies are law enforcement, presence, education, and community building.

Law enforcement strategies of the police invoke the formal sanctions of government (e.g., stopping suspicious persons, enforcing truancy and curfew laws, issuing citations, conducting investigations, and making arrests). The police **presence strategy** is that the police are visible, or identifiable, in the community; that is, wearing uniforms, patrolling in marked vehicles, and so on. Both strategies are based on the belief that a concern about the consequences of being caught by the police will deter criminal conduct.

For citizens, the **education strategy** involves providing knowledge and skills that will reduce the likelihood they will become victimized. The motivation for victims to use such knowledge and skills is based on their concern about, or fear of, the consequences of being the victim of crime. For potential and convicted criminals, education involves both appeals for moral behavior and clarifying the possible consequences of criminal conduct not only for themselves but also for the individuals they victimize; an example might be a program in which criminals and their victims discuss the harm done to the victims.

When the police use a **community-building strategy**, they are attempting, along with members of the community, to enhance the informal social controls of that community. The police do this by attempting to involve residents in various organizational (e.g., community association, neighborhood cleanup projects) and recreational activities (e.g., block parties, sporting activities). As community members become more active, they may become both more concerned about area problems and more likely to be helpful in attempting to solve those problems. If a sense of community develops, it may have a significant influence on the socialization process and the behavior of residents, who may become more watchful and more concerned about their neighbors, whom they are less likely to betray or victimize.

The law enforcement and presence strategies are more intrusive and punitive; consequently, when emphasized they are more likely to create citizen resentment and anger. The education and community-building strategies are not as likely to result in a negative community reaction.

An important related issue is how to combine strategies to achieve maximum police effectiveness in reducing crime while maintaining widespread community trust, support, and cooperation. When this is done successfully, and police officers follow the law and do not provide preferential treatment or discriminate, the democracy-police conflict is minimized.

The remaining chapters discuss police programs and methods that represent one or more of these strategies in action. The next chapter provides a brief history of the evolution of policing in the United States.

Summary

The word police is derived from the Greek words *politeuin* and *polis*. The type of police a society has is determined by its type of government—either totalitarian or democratic. In democratic governments there are a number of democracy-police conflicts. The rule of law is the most important means for dealing with this conflict. Laws represent rules that citizens are supposed to follow and that the police are supposed to follow in their relationship with citizens.

Police are defined as those nonmilitary individuals or organizations that are given the general right by government to use force to maintain the law, and their primary purpose is to respond to problems of individual and group conflict that involve illegal behavior. The police role, and what is considered to be appropriate activity and behavior, is determined by legal requirements, the police department, and the community. The greater the degree to which legal, organizational, and community expectations are compatible, the less the extent of role conflict for the police in a democratic society.

Conflicting expectations about the police have resulted in three recurring debates over their role: crime fighter or social-service provider, legalistic or political, and proactive or reactive. Three methods that are used to define the police role include the identification of values, the setting of goals, and the development of strategies used to accomplish goals.

Discussion Questions

1. Explain the difference between a police force in a totalitarian society and one in a democratic society.

2. Discuss the statement "Democracy is always hard on the police."

3. Why is the rule of law important to the democracy-police relationship?

4. Explain the difference between criminal and civil laws and between substantive and procedural laws.

5. Discuss the difference between law enforcement and community-oriented values as it relates to the police role.

6. What is the basic structure of law enforcement in the United States? Give examples of each type of police.

7. Explain the following organizational forms of policing: tribal, public-safety, consolidation, contract, and special-jurisdiction.

8. List and define the four police strategies.

9. What would a police department be like that was proactive and emphasized crime fighting?

10. Describe the expectation-integration model. How is this model related to the police role?

References

Berkeley, G. E. 1969. *The Democratic Policeman*. Boston: Beacon Press.

Bittner, E. 1970. *The Functions of Police in Modern Society*. Washington, D.C.: U.S. Government Printing Office.

Goldstein, H. 1977. *Policing a Free Society*. Cambridge, MA: Ballinger Publishing Company.

Klockars, C. B. 1985. *The Idea of Police*. Newbury Park, CA: Sage Publications.

Kuykendall, J. and Unsinger, P. 1979. *Community Police Administration*. Chicago: Nelson-Hall.

McDonald, T. D., Wood, R. A., and Pflug, M. A. (eds.). 1996. *Rural Criminal Justice*. Salem, WI: Sheffield Publishing.

President's Commission on Law Enforcement and Administration of Justice. 1967. *The Challenge of Crime in a Free Society*. Washington, D.C.: U.S. Government Printing Office.

Reiss, A. J., Jr. 1971. *The Police and the Public*. New Haven: Yale University Press.

Reith, C. 1938. *The Police Idea*. London: Oxford University Press.

Roberg, R. R., and J. Kuykendall. 1990. *Police Organization and Management: Behavior, Theory, and Processes*. Pacific Grove, CA: Brooks/Cole Publishing Company.

Royal Commission on the Police. 1962. *Report*. London: Her Majesty's Stationery Store.

Schien, E. H. 1985. *Organization Culture and Leadership*. San Francisco: Jossey-Bass.

Sims, V. H. 1996. "The Structural Components of Rural Law Enforcement: Roles and Organizations." In T. D. McDonald, R. A. Wood, and M. A. Pflug (eds.), *Rural Criminal Justice*, pp. 41–54. Salem, WI: Sheffield Publishing.

Torres, D. A. 1987. *Handbook of State Police, Highway Patrol and Investigative*. New York: Greenwood Press.

Walker, S. 1977. *History of Police Reform.* Lexington, MA: Lexington Books.

Wasserman, R., and Moore, M. H. 1988. *Perspective on Policing: Values in Policing.* Pamphlet. Washington, D.C.: National Institute of Justice.

Weisheit, R. A. 1996. *Crime and Policing in Rural and Small-Town America.* Prospect Heights, IL: Waveland Press.

Weisheit, R. A., Falcone, D. N., and Wells, L. E. 1994. "Rural Crime and Rural Policing." *National Institute of Justice: Research in Action.* Washington, D.C.: U.S. Government Printing Office.

For a listing of websites appropriate to the content of this chapter, see "Suggested Websites for Further Study" (p. xv). ✦

CHAPTER TWO

Police History

Chapter Outline

- ❏ Foundations of Policing
  - Early Policing
  - Policing in Nineteenth-Century England
- ❏ The Emergence of Modern Policing in the Unites States
  - The First City Police Forces
  - The County Sheriff
  - Vigilance Committees
- ❏ Modern Policing: The Political Model
  - Police Development
  - Criticism in the Progressive Era
- ❏ Modern Policing: The Legalistic Model
  - European Developments
  - Changes in the United States
  - Police Reform Movement
- ❏ State Police
  - Texas and Massachusetts
  - Pennsylvania
  - Highway Patrol
- ❏ Federal Law Enforcement
  - The Revenue Cutter Service and the U.S. Marshal Service
  - Postal Inspectors
  - The Secret Service
  - The Federal Bureau of Investigation
  - Additional Federal Law Enforcement Agencies
- ❏ Summary
- ❏ Discussion Questions
- ❏ References

Key Terms	
apprehension	marshal
Bertillon system	nightwatch
class-control theory	patronage system
commission approach	political model
constable	posse comitatus
constable-nightwatch system	prevention
crime-control theory	professionalization
disorder-control theory	sheriff
frankpledge system	state police
highway patrol	thief catcher
kin policing	urban-dispersion theory
legalistic model	vigilantes

Despite extensive research into policing since the 1960s, there are still no ❖ ❖ ❖ ❖
definitive answers as to what the police role should be or what particular activities are consistently more effective in reducing crime while maintaining
widespread community support, particularly among the poor and minority
members of society. Is it even possible for the police to be effective in reducing crime without providing preferential treatment for some while discriminating against others? This question identifies the fundamental police
problem in a democracy. The modern approach in responding to this problem is community policing, which is discussed in Chapter 3. Prior to community policing there were other approaches to making police compatible with
democracy. These approaches, called models of policing, are briefly discussed in this chapter.

Foundations of Policing

The history of policing begins with a consideration of kin police, Greek
and Roman police, and the development of policing in Europe, particularly
in England, because of that country's influence on the formation of modern
police departments in the United States.

Early Policing

One of the earliest methods of policing is known as **kin policing**, in
which the family, clan, or tribe enforced informal and customary rules, or
norms, of conduct. Often the response to a deviation from group norms was
brutal (e.g., a hand cut off for stealing or a brand on the forehead for being a
criminal). In effect, each member of the group had at least some authority to
enforce the informal rules (Berg 1992; 15–16).

The kin policing of clans and tribes began to change during the rise of the
Greek city-states and Rome. Until about 594 B.C. in Greece and the third century B.C. in Rome, public order was the responsibility of appointed magistrates, who were unpaid, private individuals. The first paid, public police officer was the *praefectus urbi,* a position created in Rome about 27 B.C. By 6 A.D.,
Rome had a large public police force that patrolled the streets night and day.
After the fall of the Roman Empire, anarchy tended to prevail on the European continent until the twelfth and thirteenth centuries when kings began to
assume the responsibility for legal administration.

Their approach included strengthening the **nightwatch**, a group of citizens who patrolled at night looking for fires and other problems, and ap-
pointing individuals to conduct investigations, make arrests, and collect
taxes. In some countries, such as France, mounted military patrols were also
employed.

In the twelfth century in England, **sheriffs** were appointed by the king to
levy fines and make sure that the **frankpledge system** worked. This system
for keeping order had existed for centuries and was based on an organization
of tithings (ten families) and hundreds (ten tithings). Eventually these hundreds became known as parishes, and several hundreds became known as a
shire. The area made up of several hundreds was similar to a contemporary
county.

❖ ❖ ❖ ❖   In this system, men over the age of 15 formed a **posse comitatus**, a group called out to pursue fleeing felons. In 1285 the Statute of Westminster mandated that every hundred appoint two constables to assist the sheriff. Like the sheriff, the **constable** inquired into offenses (conducted investigations), served summonses and warrants, took charge of prisoners, and supervised the night watch. By the thirteenth century, law was administered by magistrates, who were appointed by the king, and by sheriffs and constables. In the late 1200s, the office of justice of the peace was established in England. The county sheriff was responsible for policing a county and was assisted by the justice of the peace, who in turn was assisted by constables.

This arrangement was the foundation for a system of law enforcement that was to stay in place until the 1800s. Much of the work of these individuals, however, except the sheriff, was voluntary and not popular, so the practice of paying for substitutes became commonplace. In many instances, the same person was paid year after year to do the work of those who were appointed to the position but did not wish to serve. Often the substitutes were inadequately paid, elderly, poorly educated, and inefficient. These deficiencies did not help the image or effectiveness of policing in the eyes of the community.

At the end of the 1700s, families by the thousands began to move to newly established factory towns to find work. Patterns of lives were disrupted and unprecedented social disorder resulted. Existing systems of law enforcement, primarily the justice of the peace and the constable, were inadequate to respond to the problems associated with these changes.

In the **constable-nightwatch system** of policing, the constables, who were appointed by the local justices, patrolled their parishes during the day. The constables had limited power, and when they tried to obtain citizen assistance by raising the "hue and cry" to capture a fleeing criminal, they were more likely to be ridiculed than helped. At night, men of the watch were charged with patrolling deserted streets and maintaining street lamps. These individuals, however, were more likely to be found sleeping or in a pub than performing their duties.

In London, criminals had little to fear from this system of law enforcement, and they moved freely about the city streets. Victims of crime, if well-to-do, were protected by their servants and retainers (who formed a bodyguard or type of private police). Poorer citizens had no such protection. When property crimes were committed, the usual procedure was for the victim to employ a **thief catcher**. This person, usually an experienced constable familiar with the criminal underworld, would attempt, for a fee, to secure a return of all, or part, of the stolen property. Often the thief catcher would supplement his fee by keeping part of the stolen property for himself. Thief catchers were not interested in apprehending and prosecuting criminals but only in getting paid and returning all or part of the stolen property.

Critics of this approach to law enforcement began to suggest alternatives as early as the 1730s. In 1748 Henry Fielding wrote *An Enquiry Into the Cause of the Late Increase of Robbers*. Patrick Colquhoun published *A Treatise on the Police of the Metropolis* in 1795. Both books argued for a more effective approach to law enforcement (Johnson 1988, pp. 173–175).

Policing in Nineteenth-Century England

In response to the recommendations made in such books, several civic associations, such as the Bow Street Horse and Foot Patrol, were created to enforce the law in specific areas. By the early 1800s, at least nine such organizations existed in London. Their purpose was to detect and apprehend offenders. These civic associations were often, however, in competition to catch criminals, and their efforts were uncoordinated.

In 1822, Sir Robert Peel, the British home secretary, criticized the poor quality of police in London. In 1829 he was able to have passed the Act for Improving the Police In and Near the Metropolis, also known as the Metropolitan Police Act. This measure resulted in the creation of the first organized British metropolitan police force.

Initially, Charles Rowan and Richard Mayne were appointed to develop the force. They adopted a military structure and sought to employ the most competent personnel possible. There was considerable resistance, however, to this new police among the British populace. They feared the abuse of governmental authority, the kind of secret police that existed in other countries such as France, and limitations on individual freedom. Historically, Britain, like other countries, had many problems in this regard. Inside Policing 2.1 provides brief descriptions of the contributions of Peel, Rowan, and Mayne to the development of the English police.

Eventually the police became accepted, largely because their leaders— Rowan and Mayne—were strict about who they employed and how officers were to behave. By the 1850s, every borough and county in England was required to develop its own police force. The London system became a model for policing in England and to some degree for the United States (President's Commission 1967, pp. 3–5).

One of the most important principles of the Peelian approach was to emphasize the preventive aspects of law enforcement. This attitude resulted in police officers being distributed throughout the city in order to prevent crimes or to be close by when crimes occurred so that officers could make arrests and help victims. This idea was to become an important part of the development of police in the United States. Other principles were also implemented to guide the development of the new police force. Originally there were 12 principles; however, some of them dealt with the same issues. These principles are consolidated, rearranged, and presented in Inside Policing 2.2. As will be discovered later in the text, some of these principles have been called into question in recent decades in the United States, particularly numbers 2 and 4.

The remainder of this chapter is divided into three sections: the development of modern policing at (1) the local (county and municipal) level of government, (2) the state level, and (3) the federal level. The historical discussion of modern policing in this chapter ends in the 1960s but continues in Chapter 3 with a discussion of the development of community policing between the 1970s and 1990s.

Inside Policing 2.1 Founders of the British Police

Sir Robert Peel

In 1822 Robert Peel was appointed home secretary, the person responsible for internal security in England. One of his most important objectives was to establish an effective police force to respond to riots and crime problems. It took him seven years—until 1829—before he was successful. Because the idea for a new approach to policing was so controversial, Peel initially asked that the new police be established only in metropolitan London. He intended, however, that eventually a similar type of police organization would be established for all of Great Britain. Peel was a strong advocate of the concept of a civilian(rather than a military) police force that did not carry guns and that was put out in the community to patrol to prevent crime. The new police became known as Bobbies, after the founder of the department.

Colonel Charles Rowan

Charles Rowan was one of the first commissioners of the new police in London. He served in that capacity until 1850, when he retired. Rowan had a military background that prepared him for such service. Early in the nineteenth century he served under Major-General Sir John Moore, whose approach to dealing with his soldiers probably had a strong influence on how Rowan thought the police should relate to the public. Moore believed that officers should show respect for soldiers and treat them firmly and justly. Rowan wanted the same type of relationship to exist between police officers and citizens. Both he and Mayne encouraged officers to listen to citizen complaints and to be tolerant of verbal abuse by citizens.

Richard Mayne

Richard Mayne, an Irish barrister, served as a police commissioner until 1868. His extended service enabled the London police to develop a force that was well respected by citizens. Together with Rowan, he organized the force into numerous divisions that varied in size depending on the amount of crime in a division's area. Each division had a superintendent in charge, with inspectors, sergeants, and constables, in descending order of rank. Constables were placed in a blue uniform and armed with a short baton and a rattle (for raising an alarm). The uniform was designed so that it would not be similar to military dress. Mayne and Rowan were both concerned that a military-style police would have more difficulty in being accepted by the public.

Sources: Adapted from H. A. Johnson. 1988. *History of Criminal Justice*. Cincinnati: Anderson Publishing Company, pp. 173–175; D. R. Johnson. 1981. *American Law Enforcement: A History*. St. Louis: Forum Press, pp. 20–21.

The Emergence of Modern Policing in the United States

In the 1600 and 1700s the English colonists in America brought with them the system of policing that existed in England. This system included the

---

Inside Policing 2.2

Revised Peelian Principles of Policing

1. The police must be under the control of government.
2. The police must be organized along military lines to ensure stability and efficiency.
3. Police buildings should be located so they are easily accessible to citizens.
4. The public should be informed about the extent and nature of crime. The most appropriate method of evaluating the police is the amount of crime in a community.
5. Police officers should be distributed by time and area. To do this, it is important to keep records of police activities.
6. If a police organization is to be effective, its selection process and training program must be of high quality. New officers should be employed in a probationary status.
7. Police officers who have a good appearance will be more respected by the public.
8. Police officers should be able to control their temper and should emphasize a quiet, determined manner, rather than violent action, in dealing with citizens.
9. To ensure public confidence in the police, all officers must be easily identified; therefore, all officers should be given a number.

Source: Adapted from G. L. Kirkham and L. A. Wollan. 1980. *Introduction to Law Enforcement*. New York: Harper and Row, p. 29.

---

offices of justice of the peace, sheriff, constable, and night watch. Over time, the basic responsibility for law enforcement gradually shifted from volunteer citizens to paid specialists. This process of role specialization was the result of a growing and increasingly complex society attempting to master the physical environment and cope with human problems. One consequence of these economic, social, and technological changes was an increasing public concern about deviant and disruptive behavior.

Initially, the constable-nightwatch system of policing evolved as a response to the problems of maintaining order and enforcing the law. The system included a limited number of constables who had civil and criminal responsibilities and a patrolling nightwatch staffed with persons who were required to serve as a community obligation. As in England, this obligation was unpopular, and paid substitutes, who were often incompetent, were used until finally the nightwatch became a full-time, paid occupation.

This is the system that developed in the northern colonies, but in other areas there were different approaches to law enforcement. In the southern colonies, slave patrols, arguably the first form of modern policing, existed as early as the mid-1700s. In some colonies and later states, slave-patrol duty was a citizen obligation, much like duty in the nightwatch. Slave patrols were created to apprehend runaway slaves and to ensure that slaves did not revolt against their masters. In the parts of the West and Southwest that were influenced by Spain, the *alcalde*—a combination of sheriff and justice of the peace—was the most important law enforcement position. Nevertheless, the law enforcement system that was developed in the northern colonies gradually became the basis for local law enforcement throughout the country.

The First City Police Forces

Between the 1830s and the 1850s, a growing number of cities decided that the constable-nightwatch system of law enforcement was inadequate. As a result, paid daytime police forces were created. Eventually the daytime force joined with the nightwatch to create integrated day-night, modern-type police departments. In 1833 an ordinance was passed in Philadelphia that created a 24-person day force and a 120-person nightwatch, all of whom were to be paid. In 1838 Boston created a daytime force to supplement the nightwatch, and soon other cities followed. This arrangement provided the foundation for the emergence of modern policing: a force of officers in one department available 24 hours a day to respond, often through patrolling, to problems of crime and disorder (Bridenbaugh 1964; Lane 1967; Miller 1977; D. R. Johnson 1981).

Four theories have been suggested to explain the development of police departments. The **disorder-control theory** explains development in terms of the need to suppress mob violence. For example, Boston had three major riots in the years preceding the establishment of its police department (Lane 1967). Mob violence also occurred in other cities in the 1830s and 1840s. The **crime-control theory** suggests that increases in criminal activity resulted in a perceived need for a new type of police. Threats to social order, such as highway robbers and violent pickpockets (today called muggers), created a climate of fear. Concern about daring thieves and property offenses was also widespread in cities during this time (Johnson 1981).

The **class-control theory** regards the development of the police as a result of class-based economic exploitation. Its advocates note that urban and industrial growth coincided with the development of the new police. During this period, many persons of different social and ethnic backgrounds competed for opportunities that would improve their economic status. The resulting disruption prompted the middle and upper classes, usually white Anglo-Saxon Protestants, to develop a means to control the people involved, usually poor immigrants, sometimes not Anglo and often not Protestant. This theory holds that modern police forces were merely tools created by the industrial elite to suppress exploited laborers who were being used as fuel for the engine of capitalism (Cooper 1975; Johnson 1981). The last view, **urban-dispersion theory**, holds that many municipal police departments were created because other cities had them, not because there was a real need. Police forces were considered an integral part of the governmental structure needed to provide a stabilizing influence in communities (Mokkonen 1981).

There is some evidence to support all four theories; however, no single theory provides an adequate explanation. Although some cities had major urban disturbances before they established new police departments, others did not. Although there was also a public concern about crime, the degree of concern varied among communities. Some cities established after the 1830s and 1840s did not have mob violence or serious crime. Yet police departments were created because a governmental structure was assumed to include a police component similar to the ones that existed in older, larger cities. Police were also used to control class-based, economic unrest, but since many police officers often came from the dissident groups or had friends or family members who were participants, some police officers and departments resisted brutal or excessive responses.

The police departments established from the 1830s to 1850s—Boston in 1837, New York in 1844, Philadelphia in 1854—were loosely based on the Peelian model of the London police. As noted above, this model, designed by Peel, Rowan, and Mayne, emphasized prevention more than apprehension. **Prevention** was to be accomplished by dispersing police throughout the community to keep crime from occurring and to intervene when it did. **Apprehension,** or arrest, was not stressed because it was associated with secrecy, deceit, incitement, and corruption. Chapter 7 discusses the historical development of both the patrol and investigations functions in law enforcement.

The London model also included an elaborate structure based on military principles, strict rules of conduct, and well-defined management practices. Great care was taken in the selection and retention of police officers. Since the creation of a new police in England was controversial, the most important consideration was control of officer behavior. Community expectations and acceptance were the overriding concerns in the development and management of police.

In the United States, however, the establishment of the new police was not as controversial. Departments were generally based on the Peelian prevention concept, but there were minimal similarities beyond that point. Differences were essentially the result of three factors: social context, political environment, and law enforcement policies. The United States was more violent than Britain, politicians were more meddlesome, and the police were more decentralized and were expected to be locally responsive (Johnson 1981).

The County Sheriff

By the 1870s, most cities had a police department even if it consisted of only one person. In more rural areas the county sheriff was the dominant law enforcement officer. Inside Policing 2.3 describes the development and role of the sheriff.

Vigilance Committees

Another form of policing that was important during the nineteenth century was private, organized groups known as vigilance or vigilante committees. The word *vigilante* is of Spanish origin and means "watchman" or "guard." Whereas the term **vigilante** has several possible meanings, one definition of a vigilante group is a voluntary association of men (they rarely included women) who organized to respond to real or imagined threats to their safety, or to protect their property or power, or to seek revenge.

The behavior associated with vigilante movements ranges from attempts to provide reasonable due process to individuals suspected of criminal acts, to arbitrary, discriminatory, and brutal acts of revenge. The term *lynching* was originally used to describe public whippings carried out by a Colonel Lynch, head of a vigilante movement in the late 1700s in Virginia. Later this term was used to mean hanging. In southern states between 1882 and 1951, approximately 4,700 persons were lynched by unorganized mobs, a form of vigilantism. Most of the victims were black (Karmen 1983, pp. 1616–1618).

❖ ❖ ❖ ❖

Inside Policing 2.3 The County Sheriff

The office of sheriff was first established in the eighth century in England. Individuals who occupied this position were both powerful and influential. They served as the chief magistrates of the courts under their jurisdiction, collected taxes, and attempted to apprehend criminals. American colonists adopted the idea of the county sheriff, but by the time all the colonies were settled the duties of the office had been limited primarily to civil matters in the county and criminal law enforcement in areas where municipal police had no jurisdiction.

The sheriff became an elected official in the United States and, for many years, was paid based on fees received for serving summonses, subpoenas, and warrants and for looking after prisoners at the county jail. The sheriff became an important figure in Western states where local law enforcement was the responsibility of the sheriff and of town or city police officers, called marshals. Sheriffs usually were elected to office as representatives of the most influential groups in the county. Only a small portion of the sheriff's time was spent pursuing criminals. Other duties, such as tax collecting, inspecting cattle brands, punishing convicted felons, and serving court orders, proved to be more time consuming.

Because the sheriff occupied such a powerful position, many well-known individuals sought the office; such as "Wild" Bill Hickock and Willam B. "Bat" Masterson. Some gunfighters also served as a town marshal. Although stories of spectacular gunfights were associated with some sheriffs and marshals, they were actually rather rare events, much as the use of deadly force is rare in present-day law enforcement. Hickock killed only two men while he was a law enforcement officer in Abilene, Kansas, and one of them was a police officer who was coming to assist him. In fact, from 1870 to 1885, when Western cattle towns were the most active, only an estimated 45 persons died a violent death, and not all of these deaths involved a law enforcement officer.

Individuals who had "deadly" reputations as gunfighters were not necessarily the most deadly sheriffs. One such was John Slaughter, sheriff of Cochise County, Arizona, from 1886–1895. Slaughter was a prominent cattleman in the county. He used undercover police officers to obtain information and was very aggressive in pursuing criminals. He apparently had little confidence in the court system because he killed 12 "outlaws" that he arrested. His explanation was always the same—he had been forced to kill them.

In 1996 there were 3,088 sheriff's departments in the United States, with 257,712 employees, of which 152,922 were sworn officers. There are also some city sheriffs; for example, in the state of Virginia and in the cities of Baltimore and St. Louis. Three states—Alaska, Hawaii, and New Jersey—do not have the position of sheriff. And in some counties, for example, Dade County, Florida, and Denver County, Colorado, the sheriff is appointed. Many sheriffs' departments are small; almost two-thirds of them employ fewer than 25 deputies. There are 12 sheriff's departments, however, that have more than 1,000 personnel and 25 that have more than 600.

Although the primary responsibilities of the modern sheriff vary somewhat by department, the most typical include the following: (1) collect some types of taxes (in some but not all counties) and serve civil processes; (2) provide personnel (bailiffs) and security for the court system; (3) operate jails and other correctional facilities (such as prison farms); (4) maintain peace and order; (5) provide general law enforcement service in unincorporated areas (that is, those areas not in legally incorporated cities and towns); and (6) in some counties, provide contract law enforcement services. Of the total personnel, almost one-half work in either the jails or courts, and only about one-third engage in such activities as patrol and criminal investigation. Not all sheriff's departments provide law enforcement services and some do not operate jails.

Sources: B. A. Reaves and A. L. Goldberg. 1998. "Census of State and Local Law Enforcement Agencies, 1996." Washington, D.C.: Bureau of Justice Statistics; R. D. Pursley. 1991. *Introduction to Criminal Justice*. 5th ed. New York: Macmillan, pp. 132–135; D. R. Johnson. 1981. *American Law Enforcement: A History*. St. Louis: Forum Press, pp. 100–101; H. Abadinsky. 1987. *An Introduction to Criminal Justice*. Chicago: Nelson-Hall, pp. 155–159.

Vigilante movements were most common in the American West during the nineteenth century. Some of these movements have become the basis of movies, for example, *Heaven's Gate*, which is about the Johnson County War in Wyoming. Inside Policing 2.4 describes this war and several other vigilante movements of this period.

Interestingly, vigilante movements continue to exist to this day. The Guardian Angels are an example of a vigilante movement that started in New York City in the 1970s and subsequently spread to more than 60 cities. This is a group of teenagers and young males, including college students in some cities, who provide citizen patrols in high-crime areas (Berg 1992, p. 225). Initially, the police in many cities did not welcome the assistance of the Guardian Angels, but eventually a more cooperative relationship developed.

Any individual action or organized citizen effort that is designed to do something about crime, if not sanctioned by official law enforcement agencies, can be considered a form of vigilantism. Such movements are much less violent today, however, than in the nineteenth century because both law enforcement officers and members of the public are less tolerant of such behavior. And, as is true of the Guardian Angels, the police often cooperate with citizen law enforcement movements. Nevertheless, in some people's opinion, the word vigilante continues to be associated with mob violence and the inappropriate punishment of innocent victims.

The next two sections identify and describe two models of policing: the political and the legalistic (also called the reform, bureaucratic, and quasimilitary model). As discussed in chapter 1, these models indicate different approaches to managing the police-community relationship. Community policing, a third model, is discussed in chapter 3.

Modern Policing: The Political Model

From about the middle of the eighteenth century to the 1920s, local policing was dominated by politics; consequently, this era saw the development of what was essentially a **political model** of policing oriented to special interests. Politics influenced every aspect of law enforcement during this period: who was employed, who was promoted, and who was the chief of police or appointed to the police commission, a group of citizens appointed to "run" the police department in a manner approved by elected officials. To some degree even police arrest practices and services were determined by political considerations.

Police Development

Political and economic corruption was commonplace in police departments during this period. Although some officers were honest and responsible, a large number were neither. Police work during this period became decentralized and neighborhood oriented. Individual officers had a great deal of discretion and tended to handle minor violations of the law on a personal basis. The nature of the offense, whether or not the suspect treated the officer with "respect," what was known about the person's family, and prior activities, were all taken into consideration. Standards of enforcement often varied

❖ ❖ ❖ ❖   within cities, and local politicians played a more important role in determining enforcement priorities than did the chief of police.

Inside Policing 2.4
Vigilantism

Between 1767 and 1909 there were at least 326 organized vigilante movements in the United States. The 141 deadliest movements were responsible for 729 executions. Between 1849 and 1902 there were an estimated 210 vigilante movements in Western states and territories. Most of the vigilante violence took place in the states of Texas, Montana, and California. Although these movements were often controversial, in some areas they provided a type of law enforcement service. This service, however, tended to reflect the views of the members of the vigilance committees and their supporters. Consequently, some people were killed or run out of town because they opposed the vigilantes, not because they were criminals.

In San Francisco in the 1850s two vigilance committees were formed, one in 1851 and another in 1856. In each case, local businessmen became fed up with crime problems and the corruption among elected and appointed officials of government, including the police. Because of its proximity to the gold fields, San Francisco grew rapidly in the late 1840s. The city had become a haven for criminals, gamblers and prostitutes. In 1851, concerned about crime and its negative impact on business, 700 vigilantes sought criminals in the city. Of the criminals arrested, vigilante courts banished 14, had one whipped, and hanged four others.

Although the vigilance movement had widespread public support and some impact on the crime problem, its impact was short-lived. In 1856, businessmen again banded together, partly to deal with crime but also to attempt to discredit the political machine that ran the city. Nearly 8,000 citizens joined the movement and openly defied local government officials. They removed prisoners from the jails, conducted illegal searches, arrested a large number of individuals, and conducted "rigged" trials. Twenty-five men were deported and four were hanged. About 800 others left town because they were afraid of the vigilance

committee. The committee established its own political party, and one committee member was elected mayor.

Another example of a vigilance movement was the Johnson County War, which took place in Wyoming in 1892. The war developed as a result of a conflict between large cattle companies and small ranchers over the use of public lands for grazing. The large cattle companies resented the fact that small ranchers used this land and even considered some of the small ranchers to be cattle rustlers and thieves. At first, the large companies tried to have the small ranchers prosecuted as rustlers, but local juries would not convict them. And the small ranchers started to develop their own organization to offset the power and influence of the Wyoming Stock Growers' Association, which represented the large companies. Members of the association lynched two small ranchers, suspected of being thieves, and two others were murdered from ambush. Finally, the association organized a quasi-military group of gunmen to raid Johnson County to deal with the small ranchers.

This group of gunmen, or vigilantes, had a list of persons they were supposed to eliminate. They found two of the listed men at a ranch house and killed them. But this attack was observed and the other citizens of the county were alerted. The Johnson County sheriff organized a posse of more than 300 men, and they went looking for the vigilantes. Before a major battle could develop, the United States Cavalry intervened, but the vigilantes were allowed to go free because the governor of the state did not want them punished.

Sources: D. R. Johnson. 1981. *American Law Enforcement: A History*. St. Louis: Forum Press, pp. 92–96; A. A. Karmen. 1983. "Vigilantism." In S. H. Kadish, (ed.) *Encyclopedia of Crime and Justice*, Vol. 4. New York: Free Press, pp. 1616–1618.

Several trends converged in the mid-1800s that resulted in the creation of political machines that controlled cities, including the police department. As cities grew, there was an increasing need for municipal services, such as police, fire protection, and collection of garbage. Upper-class and middle-class citizens had the political influence to ensure that their needs were met, but many newly arriving immigrants, both native (from rural areas) and foreign born, did not. As the numbers of new arrivals increased, those with political ambition began to try to gain the political support of other newcomers. Often the leaders of these groups were successful and they took political control of many cities. Of course, upper-class and middle-class citizens in these cities did not give up their attempts to influence the political process or get elected to office. Even after they lost power, they played the role of critic of the political machines that emerged (D. R. Johnson 1981, pp. 17–55).

In order to be elected to public office, a candidate had to make promises to citizens. One of the most important promises was related to employment. Public jobs served as rewards for some individuals who supported the political party in power. Police jobs became an important part of this political **patronage system**. These types of jobs were popular because they required little or no skill and were paid well when compared to other jobs that also required minimal ability. Moreover, many officers often did little but frequent bars and pool halls when they were supposed to be working. These officers considered a police job a reward for supporting the political machine more than a real job.

Police departments were also of vital importance to the political machine's boss in his ability to maintain political control. The police were particularly useful during elections because they maintained order at polling booths and were able to determine who voted and who did not. Individuals who became police officers were often avid supporters of the political machine and would do anything to help keep it in power. After all, their jobs depended upon it. But they also supported it because the machine often represented a point of view that was consistent with their own.

The upper class and middle class often criticized the morality of ethnic immigrants and the poor, and they periodically tried to get the police to enforce a white, middle-class standard of morality by supporting legislation that attempted to control drinking, gambling, and prostitution. Nevertheless, even when criminal laws and ordinances were enacted in an attempt to regulate these activities, they were not always enforced because by the late nineteenth century many immigrants, particularly the Irish, were working as police officers, and many police officers were tolerant of such "vices" and even participated in them, on and off duty (D. R. Johnson 1981, pp. 17–55). Inside Policing 2.5 provides a brief description of what police work was like in the nineteenth century.

Criticism in the Progressive Era

By the 1890s, as cities began to grow larger and become more difficult to manage, the politically dominated, often corrupt, police departments came under increasing criticism. The criticism applied not only to the police but to all city services. All the problems attendant to large cities appeared to become important during this period: an increase in crime, population congestion,

Inside Policing 2.5
Policing in the Nineteenth Century

When the new police forces were established, applicants for positions essentially viewed the work as temporary because it was political. For example, in 1880 in Cincinnati 219 of 295 members of the police force were dismissed as the result of a change in elected officials. Police work did, however, have some positive features. When compared with other jobs that applicants might get (i.e., as a common laborer or a craftsman), salaries were attractive, and although temporary, the job still offered some security because once appointed, police officers could usually keep their jobs as long as the politicians they supported stayed in power.

The new police of the nineteenth century were intended to be distributed throughout the community in order to prevent crime. Many police departments, however, simply did not have enough personnel to patrol their communities. Patrol officers, who almost always walked, could cover only a small area. For a time, Chicago was able to patrol only 600 of 651 street miles, Cincinnati was able to patrol only 300 of 402 street miles, and Minneapolis could only patrol 25 of 200 street miles. In fact, in some cities, police did not patrol at all but stayed at the police station waiting to be called.

When on patrol, officers were faced with a potentially difficult task. They were expected to patrol in all types of weather, and they worked extremely long hours. Through most of the nineteeth-century officers were divided into two 12-hour shifts. Officers spent part of this time on patrol and part "on reserve" at the police station. In some cities, the weekly work period involved about 65 hours patrolling and 42 hours in a "reserve" capacity. While the length of time officers were required to work appears onerous, it is important to understand that even while on duty, patrol officers did not always engage in police work. Since many officers were essentially unsupervised while on patrol, they often frequented saloons, especially during inclement weather. One study of the Chicago police reported that patrol officers spent the majority of their time in saloons.

Patrol officers often encountered resistance to their authority even when making minor arrests. Most arrests (60 to 80 percent) were for drunkenness and disorderly conduct; the person arrested usually did not cooperate and had to be physically subdued. Sometimes bystanders would become involved, particularly when they disagreed with the police officer and tried to free the person being arrested. Once an arrest was made, the patrol officer had to transport the person arrested to the police station. Sometimes the prisoners walked, but some officers used a wheelbarrow to transport "tipsy prisoners." By the 1880s, the call box and horse-drawn patrol wagon were introduced. The patrol officer could "call" the station and a patrol wagon would be sent to transport the prisoner. Interestingly, the patrol wagon was hailed as an important innovation in police work.

The excessive use of force, or police brutality, was rather common during this period. Police work tended to be more personalized, and in some areas of a city police authority was accepted only if they could "back it up" with physical force. One of the most famous of all New York police officers was Alexander S. "Clubber" Williams. Evidently, his nickname was justly deserved. Lincoln Steffens, a prominent social critic of this period, commented about police brutality as follows: "Many a morning when I had nothing else to do I stood and saw the police bring in and kick out their bandaged, bloody prisoners, not only strikers and foreigners, but thieves, too, and others of the miserable, friendless, troublesome poor." It should be pointed out, however, that while there were complaints made about this type of behavior, it was also more accepted by citizens during this period.

Despite the widespread problems with citizen resistance and police brutality, police officers were not overly concerned with guns. As late as the 1880s there was no common practice regarding the carrying of weapons. In some cities they were authorized for all officers,

☞ whereas in other communities only certain officers carried them or they were carried only at night. By the latter part of the century, however, all police began to carry weapons because of the increasing violence in cities, violence that was often directed at the police officer.

One of the more controversial aspects of the police role was their involvement in labor disputes. While there is some evidence to support the idea that police (particularly state police) were used to suppress labor movements, other evidence suggests that many local police forces were sympathetic to the problems of the working class. Employers often complained that they could not depend on the police to break strikes. Many police officers were reluctant to do this because they were former "blue-collar workers" who would probably be returning to that type of work. Moreover, they often had friends and relatives who were involved in the labor dispute.

While nineteenth-century police officers may have been more brutal than their modern counterparts, they were also more likely to be involved in what can be called social-welfare activities. In fact, the police were one of the most important social-welfare institutions in cities. For example, the police were very active in assisting the homeless. Indigents were often given overnight lodging in police stations. In Philadelphia in the 1880s an estimated 127,000 persons per year slept at police stations. And usually these lodgers received some type of food. However, police officers did not allow anyone to make a practice of this, and people who tried were threatened with arrest and told to leave the city.

Source: S. Walker. 1977. *A Critical History of Police Reform*. Lexington, MA: D. C. Heath, pp. 1–25.

inadequate housing, health problems, waste disposal, and so on. The period from the mid-1890s to the mid-1920s became known as the Progressive Era in the United States because many of these types of problems, including poor working conditions and child labor, began to be addressed, not only in the public sector but in private enterprise as well.

Social critics began to argue that political power should change hands. These reformers were made up of religious leaders and civic-minded upper-class and middle-class business and professional people. They argued that government should be managed efficiently, public officials should be honest, and there should be one standard of conduct for everyone. The recommended reform model was based on the principles of industrial management because these principles were given credit for making the United States an economic success. Efficiency meant providing the highest-quality service at the least cost. To become efficient, organizations had to have centralized control under a well-qualified leader, develop a rational set of rules and regulations, and become highly specialized with duties and performance requirements specified for each specialized position.

The Progressive Era movement touched all aspects of American life. As it applied to government, it was based on three basic ideas: (1) honesty and efficiency in government, (2) more authority for public officials (and less for politicians), and (3) the use of experts to respond to specific problems. This movement and these ideas gained more and more credence as the country moved into the twentieth century. These changes also applied to police departments; gradually they began to shift away from a political orientation to more of a bureaucratic and legalistic approach to law enforcement (D. R. Johnson 1981, pp. 17–55).

Modern Policing: The Legalistic Model

By the 1920s, attempts to reform local policing, and to some degree state and federal law enforcement, were beginning to have an impact. From then to the 1960s was probably the most significant period in the development of policing in the United States because it established the foundations for the professionalization of law enforcement. **Professionalization** has a number of possible definitions. As used here it means an attempt to improve police behavior and performance by adopting a code of ethics and improving selection, training, and management of the police departments. Professionalism is discussed in more detail in chapter 10.

During this period a **legalistic model** (also called the professional or bureaucratic or reform or quasi- or semi-military model) of policing began to dominate thinking about police work. Essentially, it means that the police-community relationship should be based on law and departmental policy, because police (both as organizations and as individuals) should not be unduly influenced by politics or personal considerations when making decisions. One of the most important aspects of the legalistic model is related to the mission of the police. Advocates of this model thought that crime fighting should be the primary purpose of the police. They used this idea to mobilize support for their reforms and to improve the public image of the police. The police, in effect, began to emphasize the most dramatic aspects of their work (Johnson 1981, pp. 105–189).

Between about 1920 and the mid-1960s many police departments changed dramatically in the United States. Political meddling was substantially, but not entirely, replaced by efficient and centralized management and a commitment to professionalism. This change was the result of (1) European developments in criminalistics, (2) changes in American society and politics, and (3) the growth of the police reform movement.

European Developments

The first real attempt to apply the scientific method to police work took place in Europe. In many European police systems, officials were often university graduates, some of whom had been trained in the sciences. One of the most important scientific advances for police work was the **Bertillon system**, created by Alphonse Bertillon for identifying suspects. This system had four components: precise physical measurements, a detailed description of distinguishing features such as scars, a photograph, and later, fingerprints. Such information provided a scientific basis for identifying suspects and for developing a record-keeping system about criminals.

The Bertillon system provided the basis for scientific criminal investigation, which became a cornerstone for the emergence of professionalism in the United States. It was a rational and detached approach to law enforcement that contrasted with the political approach. Moreover, it provided a body of knowledge that could be transmitted to the police in training programs. Such a body of knowledge is crucial to the development of professionalism.

Changes in the United States

❖ ❖ ❖ ❖

American society and politics also began to change in ways that affected the development of policing. As the economy put more emphasis on industrial and consumer goods and rail and automobile transportation improved, more and more people moved to the suburbs. Many of them were white and middle-class. The population of cities began to change as increasing numbers of Spanish-speaking immigrants and blacks from the rural South arrived. Many of these newcomers were unskilled, poor, powerless, and in great need of city services. (Johnson 1981, pp. 105–189).

The Spanish-speaking and black neighborhoods were often plagued by extensive crime problems. Many police officers began to think of these neighborhoods as dangerous and troublesome areas in which to work. Given the fact that police forces, beginning with the slave patrols, had a long history of racist behavior, the tension between minority groups and the police increased and became an important factor in the numerous urban riots of the twentieth century. These riots began in East St. Louis in 1917 and were followed by several in 1919, at least seven during World War II, and numerous riots in the 1960s. There were 42 major-to-serious disorders in 1967 alone (National Advisory Commission 1968, pp. 35–206). Although there were many reasons for these riots, a significant factor was the behavior of police officers in minority neighborhoods.

Police Reform Movement

In the newly established suburban communities, the mostly white, middle-class inhabitants expected that government services would be based on the principles of efficiency and quality. The police were expected to be well-trained, courteous, use the best equipment, and employ the latest management techniques. Many of the reform ideas of the Progressive Era and the legalistic model of policing had a positive impact in these communities before they gained influence in larger, older cities, where a tradition of political interference was very difficult to change.

Among the more important developments during this period was the emergence of the **commission approach** to reform. When there was sufficient concern about police behavior in a community, prominent citizens and experts were appointed to commissions to conduct investigations and to make recommendations for change. Commissions were formed at both the local and national level.

In 1919 the Chicago Crime Commission was established to watch over the criminal justice system in Chicago. Unlike most other commissions that were created during the following decade, the one in Chicago became permanent. By 1931, 7 local, 16 state, and 2 national crime commissions had been established to investigate the police. Perhaps the best known of these was the National Commission on Law Observance, established by President Herbert Hoover in 1929. It was also known as the Wickersham Commission, for the man who headed the investigation. In 1931 the commission published 14 volumes, two of which were about the police. The other 12 were concerned with other aspects of crime and the criminal justice system. August Vollmer was the principal police consultant to the Wickersham Commission and was the author of the major report on the police (Walker 1977, pp. 125–134).

Vollmer's report identified what he thought were the most important problems in law enforcement: excessive political influence, inadequate leadership and management, ineffective recruitment and training, and insufficient use of the latest advances in science and technology. By 1931, it was widely accepted that these were the problems that needed to be addressed in police work. However, another report by the commission, on police lawlessness, overshadowed Vollmer's recommendations. It identified widespread police abuses, including the use of brutality, to secure confessions (Walker 1977, pp. 128–134). This problem is discussed in more detail in chapter 9.

After the Wickersham Commission published its reports, there was at least the beginning of a national consensus on the direction for the professionalization of the police. It was essentially toward a legalistic model in which laws and rules were enforced without regard to politics by well-trained and scientifically proficient, dedicated, honest employees who worked in a centralized department that was primarily concerned with crime fighting. Many police departments, however, remained substantially political well into the 1960s.

One of the most significant events of the twentieth century—the Great Depression of the 1930s—actually made police reform easier. With reduced funds available, there was less opposition to centralizing the police, and in many cities some local precinct stations were closed to save money. Centralization made it easier for chiefs of police to control their officers and also resulted in less meddling by politicians. In addition, for the first time, well-educated, middle-class Americans became interested in police work as a career because it offered job security (Johnson 1981, pp. 105–189).

By the 1930s, the reform themes—centralization, standardization of behavior through the development of policies and procedures, more education and training, selection and promotion based on merit, commitment to the goal of fighting crime, and use of the latest advances in science and technology—were well established.

By the 1960s, these reform ideas began to be questioned as a result of three important developments: urban riots, the civil rights movement, and the perception of an increasing crime rate. As minorities, and later women, became increasingly active in trying to change their status in society, and as people began to be more concerned about crime, the police became one focal point for criticism. By the mid-1960s, this concern was so great that two other national commissions were established, in part to address problems concerning the police. These were the President's Commission on Law Enforcement and Administration of Justice (hereinafter called the Crime Commission), established by President Lyndon Johnson in 1965, and the National Advisory Commission on Civil Disorders (hereinafter called the Riot Commission), established by President Johnson in 1967.

Like its predecessor, the Wickersham Commission, the Crime Commission focused on crime and the entire criminal justice system. The Riot Commission not only examined the criminal justice system but many aspects of civil disorders such as poor housing and unemployment. The recommendations of these two commissions concerning the police were a blend of previous reform suggestions plus new ones intended to make the police more responsive to the community. In effect, the legalistic model of policing that had been the basis of reform for several decades began to be challenged. However, this does not mean that its tenets were abandoned, only that some were debated and gradually began to be replaced with new ideas about the role of police.

❖ ❖ ❖ ❖

Four of the most prominent spokesmen for police reform in the legalistic era were August Vollmer, O. W. Wilson, William Parker (all discussed in the next three Inside Policing sections), and J. Edgar Hoover (discussed later in the chapter). They were controversial during their careers and have remained so as historians have provided examples of their abuses of authority

---

Inside Policing 2.6
August Vollmer

August Vollmer served first as town marshal and then as chief of police in Berkeley, California, from 1905 until 1932. He became one of the leading spokesmen for police professionalism in the first few decades of the twentieth century. He  advocated the principles of merit associated with the Progressive Era, as well as more education and training, adoption of the latest management techniques, and the use of science and technology. Vollmer was an advocate of the police officer as social worker, in the sense that he believed police should act to prevent crime by intervening in the lives of potential criminals, particularly juveniles.

Vollmer is often called the father, or dean, of modern police administration. Some of his important contributions include the early use of motorized patrol and the latest advancements in criminalistics. He suggested the development of a centralized fingerprint system that was established by the F.B.I.; he established the first juvenile unit, was the first to use psychological screening for police applicants, and the first to emphasize the importance of college-educated police officers.

Vollmer was also active in police professional organizations and on national commissions. He wrote several books and journal articles and conducted numerous studies of other police departments. He served as interim chief of police in Los Angeles in 1923–1924 and suggested many reforms for what was essentially a corrupt and inefficient police department. His critics tried to discredit him by attacking his morality. They induced a young woman to file a false paternity suit against him. This incident illustrates the difficulty of reforming some police departments during this period, not only in Los Angeles but in other cities as well.

Perhaps Vollmer's most important contributions were the promotion of people who worked for him in Berkeley and his emphasis on higher education for police officers. Many officers in Berkeley went on to successful administrative and academic careers. O. W. Wilson was perhaps Vollmer's most famous disciple. Another disciple who played a crucial role in academia was V. A. Leonard, who established the police science and administration program at Washington State University just after World War II and wrote many widely used textbooks in the field.

In the area of education Vollmer was instrumental in the establishment of police-training classes and later a criminology degree program at the University of California at Berkeley. He became a professor of police administration at Berkeley in 1929. He helped develop the first degree-granting program in law enforcement at San Jose State College (now University) in 1930. As a result of his efforts, higher education programs became increasingly acceptable.

After he retired as chief of the Berkeley Police Department he continued to serve as a consultant and to write about the police. He also kept in touch with many former employees. He died in 1955.

Sources: S. Walker. 1977. *A Critical History of Police Reform.* Lexington, MA: D. C. Heath, pp. 21–165; G. E. Caiden. 1977. *Police Revitalization.* Lexington, MA: D. C. Heath, pp. 210–217; G. F. Cole. 1989. *The American System of Criminal Justice.* 5th ed. Pacific Grove, CA: Brooks/Cole Publishing Company, p. 178.

Inside Policing 2.7
Orlando Winfield Wilson

O. W. Wilson worked in Berkeley, California, for August Vollmer from 1921 to 1925. At the same time, he completed his degree at the University of California. With Vollmer's recommendation he became chief of police in Fullerton, California, in 1925 but lasted only until 1926 because his ideas about modern law enforcement were not acceptable to many citizens in the community.

Wilson was considering another career when Vollmer recommended him as a possible chief for the Wichita, Kansas, police department in 1928. Wilson was selected for that position and over the next 11 years turned what was considered an inefficient and corrupt department into what some called the West Point of law enforcement. He left Wichita in 1937 because his strict enforcement of vice laws had alienated too many powerful citizens. He resigned under pressure, but not before creating what became a model for other police departments. Visiting dignitaries from other countries, who expressed a desire to visit a police department, were taken to Wichita by the U.S. State Department.

After Wilson left Wichita, he became a professor in the School of Criminology at the University of California at Berkeley from 1939 to 1960. His service was interrupted during World War II when he became a colonel in the U. S. Army. His job was to develop plans to rebuild police departments in countries that had been occupied by Axis Powers. After he left the army he returned to his teaching position.

In 1950 Wilson published the first edition of *Police Administration*, arguably one of the most influential books ever written about police in the United States. It describes in detail how police departments should be organized and managed. It was widely used in training programs, colleges, and universities, and as a basis for organizing and managing police departments in the United States and other countries until the 1970s, when Wilson's ideas began to be criticized. Nevertheless, the basic structure of many present-day police departments is the result of Wilson's ideas.

In 1960, while still teaching at Berkeley, Wilson agreed to serve on the committee to select a new police commissioner in Chicago. When the committee could not find an acceptable candidate, they offered the job to Wilson. He agreed and served until 1967; during that time he made many important changes which received widespread publicity and made Chicago a model of modern policing. One year after he retired, however, the Chicago police performed poorly in their attempts to manage the demonstrations at the 1968 Democratic Convention. This failure raised important questions about Wilson's effectiveness and the difficulty of changing police organizations. After his retirement Wilson moved to California and occupied his time writing and traveling until his death in 1972.

Wilson typified police leadership and management during the legalistic era. He believed politics had no place in policing, he was a strong advocate of centralized police management and strict discipline. He was also an articulate spokesman for police professionalism as it related to more training, and education, better salaries and benefits, and his definition of police management.

Source: Adapted from W. Bopp, 1977. *O. W. Wilson and the Search for a Police Profession.* Port Washington, NY: Kennikat Press.

and their racist and sexist behaviors. Despite this criticism their ideas about the police role and police management remain influential and have resulted in improved police performance in many areas.

The political era of often corrupt and inefficient policing was somewhat changed by the reforms of the legalistic era which, in turn, met criticism. The civic problems of the 1960s brought a new set of critics who wanted to over-

Inside Policing 2.8
William Parker

William Parker began his career as a patrol officer in Los Angeles in 1927. He then obtained a law degree and by 1934 was an assistant to the chief of police. He served in the Army during World War II, and worked closely with O. W. Wilson to rebuild the police departments in some European countries.

Parker was appointed police chief in 1950 after a scandal forced changes in the department. He was considered to be a very professional officer and the ideal candidate to reform the Los Angeles police. Over the next several years he reorganized the department in keeping with the legalistic model of policing espoused by Wilson and others. He centralized the department, improved recruitment and training, and worked hard to increase efficiency and reduce costs. He tended to emphasize the crime-fighting aspects of the police role. He wanted his department to become an effective crime-fighting machine, a "thin blue line" that separated the honest citizen from the criminal. Like both Wilson and Vollmer, he worked hard to eliminate excessive political influence in police activities.

Parker's idea of a good police officer was an individual who was scrupulously honest, tough-minded, competent, businesslike, and dedicated to the job. By the late 1950s, Los Angeles had become a model of a modern, professional, legalistic police department. The image of the department was enhanced by the television program *Dragnet* starring Jack Webb. This program was produced under the auspices of the Los Angeles Police Department and presented the image that Parker wanted to project.

Los Angeles continued to be the prototype for modern policing into the 1960s, but events of the mid-60s raised questions about the style of policing that Parker, and others like him, advocated. With the emergence of the civil rights movement the police became the focal point for black grievances. The discrimination that blacks had endured in the past became increasingly intolerable and riots occurred in many cities. The Watts riot in Los Angeles and a shootout with the Black Muslims that preceded it in 1962 resulted in increasing criticism of Parker and his concept of a professional police force. He died in 1966 amid this criticism.

Sources: Adapted from G. E. Caiden, 1977. *Police Revitalization.* Lexington, MA.: D.C. Heath, pp. 267–272; D. R. Johnson. 1981. *American Law Enforcement: A History.* St. Louis: Forum Press, pp. 119–121.

come the isolation of a professionalized police from citizen concerns and to develop new strategies and methods to respond to crime and order-maintenance problems. These subsequent changes, along with others, resulted in the emergence of what is now called community policing. About the same time (the mid-1970s) that the reforms began to be implemented, the crime rate began a decline that, so far, has lasted about 25 years. In chapter 3, the development of and controversies about community policing and the extent to which it contributed to a decline in crime are discussed. The next two sections of this chapter briefly trace the development of law enforcement at the state and federal levels.

State Police

Prior to 1900 only two states had a form of state police force—Texas and Massachusetts. The idea was slow to catch on. Not until the 1960s did all states have some form of state police.

Texas and Massachusetts

In Texas many inhabitants lived in rural isolation and faced dangerous problems such as widespread Indian raids. Consequently, the citizens decided to create a quasi-military force, called the Texas Rangers, to protect themselves. After Texas declared its independence from Mexico in 1836, the Rangers were well established. Originally designed for community defense, by the 1850s they were doing general police work. They pursued robbers, runaway slaves, and illegal immigrants from Mexico. Rangers tended to take the law into their own hands and to be very brutal in their treatment of prisoners, particularly minorities. Such behavior was commonplace well into the twentieth century. In 1935 Texas created a larger state police, the Department of Public Safety, which was given the responsibility of supervising Ranger activity, and their behavioral excesses were gradually reduced (Johnson 1981, pp. 161–162).

Massachusetts' experiment with a state police force was controversial. Rural residents and prohibitionists were disenchanted with the failure of city police to enforce laws against drinking, so the state legislature created a state police force and gave it general law enforcement responsibilities. Its primary task, however, was to enforce laws against vice. That was what it did in large cities, but in other areas it gradually won a reputation for effective detective work in robbery and murder cases. Nevertheless, controversy about its activities in cities continued, and the state police force was disbanded in 1875. A few state investigators were retained to work in rural areas.

Pennsylvania

The next appearance of a state police force was in 1905, with the establishment of the Pennsylvania State Police. In the Midwest and Northeast, as early as the 1860s, certain problems arose that proved difficult for local police to resolve. These problems were related to economic development, par-

A company of Texas Rangers, circa 1904. (Courtesy of State of Texas Department of Public Safety)

ticularly in the areas of mining and industrialization. A combination of an increasing crime problem in affluent rural areas coupled with the exploitation of workers and the workers' demands that such treatment stop resulted in levels of conflict and violence that were difficult to control.

Western Pennsylvania had more than its fair share of such problems. As a major mining region that attracted immigrant labor, it suffered ethnic and labor violence in the latter part of the nineteenth century. The violence became so extensive that President Theodore Roosevelt appointed a commission to look into a major coal strike in 1902. The result was the creation of the Pennsylvania State Police in 1905. This police force was unlike any other in the United States because it emphasized a military approach. All the officers had either national guard or army experience. The state police proved to be evenhanded in handling labor conflict, and the levels of violence began to decline. Like the Texas Rangers, however, state police officers tended to discriminate against "foreigners." In fact, officers were chosen, in part, because they had contempt for "foreigners."

Gradually, the Pennsylvania State Police began to expand its duties, and it began to do routine police work in rural areas throughout the state. Between 1908 and 1923, 14 states, mostly in the North, created state police forces based on the Pennsylvania model. Not all state police, however, were as evenhanded as Pennsylvania when it came to labor strife. In Nevada, Colorado, and Oregon the state police tended to side with organized business interests (e.g., mining). This bias became such a problem in Colorado that in 1923 the state police were disbanded (Johnson 1981, pp. 161–164).

Highway Patrol

Between the 1920s and the 1960s, state police forces began to take on new responsibilities. One of the most important was enforcement of traffic laws. With the increasing use of automobiles, the number of related problems—the

Pennsylvania State Police Officers, circa 1900. (Courtesy of Pennsylvania State Police)

violation of traffic laws, accidents, and the regulatory requirements associated with the registration of vehicles and the licensing of drivers—also increased. As the highway system grew, there was need for a statewide authority because many of the roads were outside the jurisdiction of cities. The automobile also gave criminals more flexibility: they could come and go more easily and avoid capture more readily.

This situation resulted in two approaches to the development of state law enforcement, a **state police** and a **highway patrol**. The former had broad law enforcement powers whereas the latter was generally limited to traffic enforcement. The highway patrol approach became more common. For example, in the 1920s, eight state police departments and six highway patrol units were established. In the 1930s, 18 units were created to deal with traffic and only eight to deal with general law enforcement (Johnson 1981, pp. 161–164). The differences between state police forces and state highway patrols are important. State police have their own criminal investigators, may have their own patrol force, gather criminal intelligence, and usually have a forensic science laboratory. State highway patrols concentrate on traffic and accidents on the state's roads and highways (Borkenstein 1977, pp. 1131–1134).

By the 1960s, all states had some type of state police or highway patrol or a combination of the two. They are usually responsible for traffic regulation on state roads and highways, and about two-thirds also have general police powers. State police often fill a void in rural law enforcement because they provide services where there are none or their assistance is requested by other law enforcement units (Cole 1989, p. 120). Inside Policing 2.9 briefly describes the development of the state police in Oregon, which was typical of other states during the 1920s and 1930s. Inside Policing 2.10 describes the Texas Department of Public Safety.

Inside Policing 2.9
The Oregon State Police

Discussions about the possibility of creating a state police force in Oregon began in 1918. During World War I the state had created an Oregon Military Police to protect shipbuilding plants, but it was disbanded after the war ended. Concern about problems associated with state policing continued because responsibilities were fragmented among several state departments. The State Traffic Department had already been established, but it was having a difficult time coping with the increasing number of automobiles on state highways. In 1929 it had only 50 officers to patrol the entire state. Prohibition was also proving to be a difficult problem. Increasingly, criminals were using cars and were able to avoid local police, who had jurisdiction only within city limits.

In response to these concerns, the state senate established the state police force on March 1, 1931. The force was designed by a committee that examined the Royal Canadian Mounted Police, the Texas Rangers, and the state police of New Jersey, Pennsylvania, and Michigan. The new force began operations on August 1. It was given the law enforcement responsibilities of several older state agencies, including the State Highway Commission (which governed the State Traffic Department), the Secretary of State, the Fish and Game Commission, the State Fire Marshals, and the Prohibition Commissioner. The responsibilities of this new police force included the enforcement of traffic laws, game and fish codes, all laws relating to arson and fire prevention, and laws against illegal liquor and drugs. In addition, the department was given law enforcement responsibilities throughout the state so the department could serve

☞ as a rural patrol force and assist local police.

The state police department was divided into four districts and 31 patrol stations. The first report of its activities was published in early 1933. Since 1931, the state police had made 415 arrests, written 181 traffic citations, reported on 200 liquor violations, and collected fines totaling about $17,000.

The state police were given additional responsibilities in 1939 and 1941. In 1939 a Crime Detection Laboratory was established at the University of Oregon Medical School; it was subsequently relocated in Portland. By 1989 there were six regional crime detection laboratories, which provided assistance to local police. In 1941 all fingerprint records and criminal photographs were transferred from the state penitentiary to the state police.

In the late 1970s the state police force was reorganized into the present five districts. By 1989 the number of patrol stations had increased from 31 to 45. By 1996, the number of personnel had increased from the original 95 to over 1,200.

Source: Oregon Department of State Police. *Memorandum.* March 15, 1989.

Inside Policing 2.10
The Texas Department of Public Safety

The Texas Department of Public Safety is the second (to the California Highway Patrol) largest state law enforcement agency in the United States. In 1996 there were 6,745 employees, of whom 2,873 were sworn officers. The goal of the department is to maintain public safety in Texas by preserving order and protecting the lives, rights, property, and privileges of state residents.

The administration division of DPS is responsible for the training academy, collecting and maintaining fingerprint files and crime records, managing the state's emergency operations and communications, and managing the concealed handgun licensing program. The traffic division issues driver licenses and identification cards, enforces traffic laws on rural highways, enforces commercial vehicle laws, supervises the motor vehicle inspection program, and provides security at the state capitol in Austin.

The criminal law enforcement division provides assistance to department officers and other law enforcement organizations. Its primary focus is on narcotics trafficking, organized crime and motor vehicle theft. This division also engages in crime analysis, maintains a crime lab and provides polygraph services. The Texas Rangers are also part of the DPS. They are one of the oldest law enforcement organizations in the United States. Rangers investigate major felonies such as murder, rape, robbery, white collar crime and government corruption. Rangers also provide assistance to other law enforcement organizations when requested.

Source: http://www.txdps.state.tx.us.

Some states also have other types of law enforcement agencies. Just as with the federal government, any state agency that regulates behavior that is punishable by fine or imprisonment may have a law enforcement component. States that have a park system or environmental laws, any form of legalized gambling, or state income taxes will usually have law enforcement officers associated with that activity. Many states also have an agency whose responsibility is to regulate the selling and distribution of liquor. A few states even have agencies that respond primarily to drug-related problems.

In addition to state police, state highway patrols, and the other types of agencies noted above, many states also provide law enforcement services to local jurisdictions; for example, special investigation assistance and crime labs for the analysis of physical evidence. There may also be a statewide computer system or systems to provide information about wanted persons and stolen property. Many states also gather and analyze crime-related information and provide the results to local police. All states now have some type of organization to set standards for the selection and training of police; for example, the California Commission on Peace Officers Standards and Training (POST).

Federal Law Enforcement

The development of federal agencies tended to lag behind those at the local level because the constitutional mandate for federal law enforcement is not clear. Prior to the Civil War there were three types of federal law enforcement activities.

The Revenue Cutter Service and the U.S. Marshal Service

In 1789 the Revenue Cutter Service was created to respond to problems of smuggling. In that same year the U.S. Marshal Service was established so that the federal courts would have officers to perform police duties. **Marshals** investigated cases of mail theft and crimes against the railroad. They also investigated murders on federal lands, but the majority of their responsibilities were civil. One of the more interesting aspects of the marshal's role was his law enforcement in the West, described in Inside Policing 2.11.

Inside Policing 2.11
Federal Marshals in the American West

U.S. Marshals were among the first law enforcement officials in the West. In federal territories they were often the only officials available to deal with criminals. Once a territory became a state, other law enforcement officials such as the sheriff, town marshal, or city police assumed responsibility for most law enforcement problems. However, because these local police officers had authority only in one jurisdiction, the U.S. marshal appointed some of them to be deputy marshals, which allowed them to pursue criminals outside the town or county.

Marshals usually had no law enforcement experience but were appointed because of their political connections. Often they were criticized for being inefficient and corrupt, much like city police of the nineteenth century. Their payment—rewards and fees—strongly influenced their priorities. Because rewards for catching criminals were rare,

most of a marshal's salary was determined by fees collected from serving civil processes. This system of payment lasted until 1896.

Marshals usually dealt with liquor smugglers, gun runners, and individuals who committed crimes involving the mail. The most infamous criminals were the train robbers. The railroads may well have been the most disliked industry in the nineteenth century. Although railroads played an important role in the development of the United States, the owners treated many citizens in a callous and indifferent manner. Consequently, train robbers were considered to be "heroes" by some people. This status contributed to the rise of romantic legends about such outlaws as the James, Younger, and Dalton brothers and Bill Doolin. But train robbers were hardly heroes. Jesse James initiated the idea of wrecking a train in order to rob it. Or they might ambush a train at a wa-

☞ ter stop and use dynamite or gunfire to steal the money or gold it carried.

After a robbery the outlaws would escape to some hideaway and then disperse. U.S. marshals might pursue them with a posse, but full-scale battles between a posse and gang were rare. More often, the outlaws were tracked down individually. Paid informants were very useful in this regard. They resulted in the demise of Bill Doolin and the Wild Bunch, who committed train robberies and bank holdups in the Oklahoma Territory in the early 1890s. Using informants, the local U.S. marshal was able to acquire enough information to track down each member of the gang. Most of the Wild Bunch died in shoot-outs with marshals, their deputies, and members of a posse. These shoot-outs were not in the open but usually during an ambush in which the outlaw was outnumbered and outgunned. Marshals were more inclined to use a shotgun than a "six shooter." When Doolin was finally located, he was killed by a shotgun blast fired by a deputy marshal, one of six hidden posse members who waited for Doolin to walk down the street.

Marshals played an important role in the American West. They were effective in developing informants and isolating outlaws. Perhaps their most important contribution was developing a basis for cooperation between different law enforcement bodies (i.e., town marshal and police, county sheriff) as federal territories became states.

Source: D. R. Johnson. 1981. *American Law Enforcement: A History*. St. Louis: Forum Press, pp. 96–100.

Postal Inspectors

Crimes involving the mail were a significant problem in the nineteenth century. Often these crimes were committed by postal employees, because many people sent money through the mail. Swindlers and confidence men also used the mail. Lotteries were a popular "scam"; people were asked to send a small amount of money to be eligible for an expensive prize. Of course, those who sent in money never heard from the lottery sponsors again. In the states, the Post Office assumed responsibility for all mail-related crimes. At first the postmaster used assistants to investigate crimes, but in 1836 the position of postal inspector was established. By the Civil War, postal inspectors were investigating robberies, embezzlements, and the counterfeiting of stamps, as well as post office employees involved in criminal activities.

The Secret Service

Although counterfeiting money had always been a problem at local and state levels of government, it became a very serious problem nationally when the federal government decided to issue a standard paper currency in 1861, at the time of the Civil War. The first attempts to suppress counterfeiting of national currency occurred in 1864, when the secretary of the treasury employed a few private detectives. In June 1865 the Secret Service was established. The first director, William Wood, distributed his agents among 11 cities and instructed them to work undercover to penetrate counterfeiting rings.

By the late nineteenth century, the Secret Service provided investigative services to other agencies of government that needed them, including the Postal Service, Customs Service, and Bureau of Immigration. In 1901 the task of protecting the President was added to the Secret Service's responsibility. In 1908 its role was limited to two major activities: protective services and counterfeiting (Johnson 1981, pp. 73–88).

The Federal Bureau of Investigation

In order to take over some of the duties the Secret Service had been performing for other agencies, the Bureau of Investigation was created within the Justice Department in 1908. This office began its work when the Secret Service transferred eight agents to the new bureau. It later became the Federal Bureau of Investigation, the general investigative law enforcement agency of the federal government.

The primary reason the FBI eventually became so highly regarded was the publicity surrounding its crime-fighting role in the 1930s. The two most important crimes involving the FBI were the kidnapping of the baby of ace flier Charles Lindbergh and the ambush murders of five people, including one FBI agent, in Kansas City. The Lindbergh incident was only one of several such cases in the late 1920s and 1930s. During this period criminals abducted several wealthy individuals or members of their families and held them for ransom. However, the Lindbergh case received the most publicity and the FBI was successful in identifying a suspect who was convicted and executed. In Kansas City, Pretty Boy Floyd and two companions tried to rescue a friend being taken to prison. Four police officers and one federal agent were killed. One of the criminals was captured, convicted, and executed. Floyd was killed by the FBI in a shoot-out, and the third was killed by other criminals.

Another event that added to the prestige and power of the FBI was the election of Franklin Roosevelt as president. He became a strong supporter of J. Edgar Hoover and the FBI and assisted in expanding the bureau's powers. The most important expansion was its responsibility to investigate cases of domestic espionage, counterespionage, and sabotage (Johnson 1981, pp. 172–181). The federal responsibility for enforcement of laws against drugs began in 1914 when the Harrison Narcotic Act was signed into law. The Bureau of Internal Revenue was given the responsibility for enforcing this act. It created a Narcotics Section, which within a few years became a major division. In 1930 the Federal Bureau of Narcotics was created, which became the Drug Enforcement Administration in 1973. In 1982 the DEA became part of the FBI.

By the 1920s, the U. S. Marshals Service, the Federal Bureau of Investigation, Postal Inspectors, the Secret Service, and the Narcotics Division of the Internal Revenue Service were the established federal law enforcement agencies. The one that received the most attention was the Federal Bureau of Investigation. Between the 1930s and the 1960s the FBI became the premier law enforcement body in the United States. J. Edgar Hoover was appointed to serve as Director in 1924. He became a national law enforcement leader and advocate of police reform in the 1930s and maintained this role into the 1960s. He is profiled in Inside Policing 2.12. Information about the current role and selected activities of the FBI is presented in Inside Policing 2.13.

Additional Federal Law Enforcement Agencies

By the 1990s there were many different types of federal law enforcement agencies and agencies that have a law enforcement component, that is, having some employees responsible for law enforcement activities. A listing of federal agencies with at least some law enforcement responsibilities was pro-

Inside Policing 2.12
John Edgar Hoover

J. Edgar Hoover was director of the Federal Bureau of Investigation from 1924 until his death in 1972. He first entered the Department of Justice in 1917, while attending law school. When he took over the bureau in 1924, it had just experienced a scandal and Hoover set out to reform the organization. Like O. W. Wilson and William Parker, he believed in a centralized command structure and improved recruitment and training. Interestingly, Wilson and Parker did not have a high regard for Hoover, and vice versa. This mutual disdain was the result of competition over leadership in the police reform movement and the fact that the FBI under Hoover looked down on local law enforcement.

The FBI began to receive national attention during the 1930s in its well-publicized campaign to catch infamous criminals such as John Dillinger. After some successes, the FBI became a national symbol of effective crime fighting. Hoover enhanced the bureau's reputation by establishing a national fingerprint file, providing assistance to local departments in training their personnel, and providing criminalistics services in some important criminal cases. In the 1960s the bureau also established a national computer system that included important crime-related information.

Perhaps the most important contribution to local law enforcement was the development of the FBI National Academy, which trained police managers from all over the United States. For many years this program was considered, and is still considered by some, to be the most prestigious in law enforcement. For the rank-and-file officers, the FBI provided what might be called traveling trainers, special agents who went from one police department to another to provide training in such things as criminal investigation and firearms, as well as management.

Hoover enhanced his reputation during World War II as the bureau pursued and arrested several spies. A fervent anticommunist, Hoover was criticized after the war for his involvement with Senator Joseph McCarthy, and in the 1950s and 1960s for his failure to respond effectively to the problems of organized crime. He was also criticized for his tactics in responding to civil rights issues. After Hoover's death it was discovered that the FBI often used illegal methods (e.g., wiretaps) to secure information about such civil rights leaders as Martin Luther King and to gather intelligence on activist groups. Hoover believed that communists had infiltrated the civil rights movement with the intent of using the race issue to destabilize the country.

Hoover is a good example of how a person in law enforcement can become very powerful. As a result of the investigations of his agents, he had access to a large amount of information about many important people in Washington and throughout the United States. Some critics have suggested that such knowledge was a significant factor in his being able to stay in office until his death at the age of 77. Some critics have even suggested that some presidents were fearful of Hoover's power. Nevertheless, despite these criticisms, Hoover did make important contributions to law enforcement in developing the FBI.

Sources: D. R. Johnson. 1981. *American Law Enforcement: A History*. St. Louis: Forum Press, pp. 171–180; G. E. Caiden. 1977. *Police Revitalization*. Lexington, MA: D.C. Heath, pp. 242, 286, 333.

Inside Policing 2.13
The Federal Bureau of Investigation

Founded in 1908, the Federal Bureau of Investigation is part of the United States Department of Justice. In 1997, it employed more than 11,000 special agents and 16,000 support personnel. The mission of the FBI is to uphold the ☞

law through the investigation of violations of federal criminal law; protect the United States from foreign intelligence and terrorist activities; provide leadership and law enforcement assistance to federal, state, local, and international agencies; and perform these tasks in a manner that is responsive to the needs of the public and is faithful to the Constitution of the United States.

The bureau's investigative activities are divided into seven programs: applicant background checks, civil rights issues, counterterrorism, financial crime, foreign counterintelligence, organized crime and drugs, and violent crimes and major offenders. Examples of investigations involving violent crimes and major offenders include searching for fugitives and escaped prisoners involved in FBI investigations; crime on Indian Reservations; assaulting, kidnapping or killing the president, vice-president, and members of Congress; kidnapping and extortion; sexual exploitation of children; and tampering with consumer products.

The headquarters of the FBI is in Washington, D.C. In addition, there are field offices in 56 major cities, including one in Puerto Rico. There are also 400 satellite offices, known as resident agencies, which house from one to 12 special agents. Both field offices and resident agencies are located according to crime trends and available resources. The FBI's role in international investigations (e.g., drugs, terrorism, financial crimes) has resulted in the establishment of 23 legal attaché offices in embassies around the world.

The FBI is also involved in numerous other activities, including managing several computer crime-related data bases, providing crime laboratory services to agents and other law enforcement organizations, and training programs for FBI agents and employees and officers from state and local police.

Source: http:www.fbi.gov.

vided in chapter 1. Table 2.1 identifies nine federal law enforcement agencies and briefly describes some of their activities.

Table 2.1   Selected Federal Law Enforcement Agencies

Bureau of Alcohol, Tobacco, and Firearms (ATF)

The ATF is part of the Department of the Treasury and is responsible for the investigation of laws covering the manufacture and sale of alcohol, tobacco, and firearms.

Drug Enforcement Administration (DEA)

The DEA is part of the Department of Justice, reports to the director of the FBI, and is responsible for the enforcement of laws related to the use of narcotics and dangerous drugs. It is primarily concerned with organized groups involved in producing and distributing illegal drugs.

Internal Revenue Service (IRS)

The IRS is a division in the Department of the Treasury. It collects taxes and investigates violations of federal tax laws. The IRS also supervises the legal alcohol industry and enforces certain explosives and firearms laws.

Immigration and Naturalization Service (INS)

The INS is part of the Department of Justice and is responsible for administering immigration and naturalization laws, which include determining who is to be admitted into or deported from the United States.

U.S. Customs

The Customs Service is part of the Treasury Department and is responsible for determining and collecting duties and taxes on goods imported into the United States. Agents work to control smuggling and revenue fraud, among other things. Agents also help to enforce environmental protection laws in coastal waters.

U.S. Marshals Service

The Marshals Service is part of the Department of Justice. Its legal authority is broad and includes such activities as serving federal warrants, locating federal parole and probation violators, investigating fugitives from other countries, providing security for federal courts, and protecting witnesses in federal criminal trials.

| Table 2.1   Selected Federal Law Enforcement Agencies (continued) |

U.S. Park Police

The Park Police is part of the Department of the Interior. Most officers are assigned to the Washington, D.C., area, where they are responsible for hosting and providing police services to visitors at the city's parks.

U.S. Park Rangers

The Park Rangers are part of the Department of the Interior and are responsible for law enforcement, among other things, in the national parks.

U.S. Secret Service

The Secret Service is part of the Treasury Department and is responsible for criminal activities involving counterfeiting and forgery and for protecting the president of the United States, the president's family, and other government officials.

Sources: R. D. Pursley. 1991. *Introduction to Criminal Justice*. 5th ed. New York: Macmillan; G. E. Rush, ed. 1986. *The Dictionary of Criminal Justice*. Guilford, CT: Dushkin.

Summary

The police heritage in the United States can be traced to classical Greece and Rome, and to developments in Europe, particularly England. The first form of policing in U.S. cities was the constable-nightwatch system, which existed from the 1600s to the 1930s. When this system proved to be inadequate, it was replaced by modern, integrated day-night police departments. Modern police departments at the local level have moved through three distinct periods of development, each dominated by a different model of policing. These models are the political, the legalistic, and community policing. Each model has a different conception of the police role and how police officers should interact with members of the community. Two of the models—the political and the legalistic—are discussed in this chapter.

State and federal police forces also have an interesting history. State police forces were created to respond to both law enforcement and traffic problems and to provide related services to local police. Federal law enforcement agencies have existed since the eighteenth century but were not well established until the middle of the nineteenth century. There are numerous federal law enforcement agencies and agencies with investigators working in a law enforcement capacity.

Discussion Questions

1. In what way did Sir Robert Peel and his ideas about policing influence the development of policing in the United States?

2. Describe the constable-nightwatch system of policing.

3. Identify and explain the characteristics of political policing. Why did political policing develop in the United States?

4. Identify and explain the characteristics of legalistic policing. Why did legalistic policing develop in the United States?

5. Discuss the contributions of August Vollmer and O. W. Wilson to the development of law enforcement.

6. Explain the difference between a state police force and a highway patrol. Give examples of the duties of each.

7. Briefly trace the development of federal law enforcement in the United States.

8. Discuss the role of the federal marshal in the American West.

9. Discuss the law enforcement career of William Parker.

10. Discuss the law enforcement career of J. Edgar Hoover.

References

Abadinsky, H. 1987. *An Introduction to Criminal Justice.* Chicago: Nelson-Hall.

Berg, B. L. 1992. *Law Enforcement: An Introduction to Police in Society.* Boston: Allyn and Bacon.

Bopp, W. J. 1977. *O. W. Wilson and the Search for a Police Profession.* Port Washington, NY: Kennikat Press.

Borkenstein, R. 1977. "State Police." In S. H. Kadish, ed. *Encyclopedia of Crime and Justice,* pp. 1131–1135. New York: The Free Press.

Bridenbaugh, C. 1964. *Cities In The Wilderness.* 2 vols. New York: Knopf.

Caiden, G. E. 1977. *Police Revitalization* Lexington, MA: D.C. Heath.

Cole, G. F. 1989. *The American System of Criminal Justice,* 5th ed. Pacific Grove, CA: Brooks/Cole Publishing Co.

Cooper, L. 1975. *The Iron Fist and the Velvet Glove.* Berkeley: Center for Research on Criminal Justice.

Johnson, D. R. 1981. *American Law Enforcement: A History.* St. Louis: Forum Press.

Johnson, H. 1988. *History of Criminal Justice.* Cincinnati: Anderson Publishing Co.

Karmen, A. A. 1983. "Vigilantism." In S. H. Kadish, (ed.), *Encyclopedia of Crime and Justice.* Vol. 4, pp. 1616–1618. New York: Free Press.

Kirkham, G. L., and Wollan, L. A. 1980. *Introduction to Law Enforcement.* New York: Harper and Row.

Lane, R. 1967. *Policing the City: Boston 1822–1882.* Cambridge, MA: Harvard University Press.

Miller, W. 1977. *Cops and Bobbies.* Chicago: University of Chicago Press.

Mokkonen, E. 1981. *Police in Urban America.* Cambridge: Cambridge University Press.

National Advisory Commission on Civil Disorders. 1968. *Report.* New York: New York Times Company.

Oregon Department of State Police. *Memorandum.* March 15, 1989.

President's Commission on Law Enforcement and Administration of Justice. 1967. *Task Force Report: The Police.* Washington, D.C.: U.S. Government Printing Office.

Pursley, R. D. 1991. *Introduction to Criminal Justice.* 5th ed. New York: Macmillan.

Reaves, B. A. 1992. *Sheriff's Departments, 1990.* Washington D.C.: Bureau of Justice Statistics.

Reaves, B. A., and Goldberg, A. L. 1998. *Census of State and Local Law Enforcement Agencies, 1996.* Washington, D.C. : Bureau of Justice Statistics.

Roberg, R. R., and Kuykendall, J. 1990. *Police Organization and Management: Behavior, Theory and Processes.* Pacific Grove, CA: Brooks/Cole Publishing Company.

Walker, S. 1977. *A Critical History of Police Reform.* Lexington, MA: D.C. Heath.

For a listing of websites appropriate to the content of this chapter, see "Suggested Websites for Further Study" (p. xv). ✦

Community Policing

Chapter Outline

Key Terms

aggressive law enforcement	co-production of public safety
broken-windows theory	CPTED
community-accountability	police legitimacy
conferences	problem-oriented policing (POP)
community-building strategy	SARA
community crime prevention	strategic management
community-oriented policing	team policing
community policing model (COP)	

The previous chapter described two modern police models and factors that led to the development of a third model, community policing. This chapter will provide a general framework for community policing and describe the transition that is taking place toward this model. Part of the discussion revolves around the precursor to community policing, known as team policing. Definitions and philosophy of community policing will be described, along with a discussion of where the concept is today in terms of evolution and practice. The final section of the chapter will discuss community policing and crime prevention—that is, the development of partnerships between the police and the community in the co-production of public safety.

Transition Toward Community Policing

The problems of the 1960s and the influence of the legalistic model of policing, as discussed in chapter 2, continued to be of concern to some police, political leaders, and academics in the 1970s and 1980s. These concerns tended to focus on (1) how the police should be evaluated, (2) the impact of increased research on the police, (3) how to manage police resources more strategically, (4) how to improve relations with minority groups, and (5) the role of the community in responding to crime. Each of these will be briefly described below.

How to Evaluate the Police

In the early 1980s, J. Q. Wilson and G. L. Kelling (1982) argued that the quality of community life should be an important consideration for the police. Their **broken-windows theory** suggests that once a neighborhood is allowed to run down, it can in a short period of time become an "inhospitable and frightening jungle." At the same time, research on the fear of crime suggested that citizen fear is more closely associated with neighborhood disorder (e.g., vandalism, graffiti, juvenile gangs, run-down and abandoned buildings, abandoned cars, and so on) than with the crime rate (Kelling and Moore 1988).

One obvious implication of this research was that the police should begin considering not only the crime rate as a measure of their effectiveness but also citizen fear of crime. To do this, however, the police would have to broaden their role to focus on "quality-of-life" issues, as defined by citizens. According to critics, the police would have to change their crime-fighting orientation, which usually meant emphasizing serious crimes, by putting more emphasis on minor violations (e.g., panhandling, loud juveniles, jaywalking, traffic violations), keeping order, community organizing, and community satisfaction. To that end, they would have to expand both the community relations and crime prevention activities associated with the service model and, in some instances, continue or increase strict law enforcement practices (e.g., saturate certain areas or "hot spots" of crime with officers, give numerous citations, conduct field interrogations, and make as many arrests as possible).

These **aggressive law enforcement** practices have long been part of the proactive police response to crime, dating back to the political model. At present, they are variously referred to as zero tolerance policing, saturation or aggressive patrol, and crackdowns. Some critics of the police believe that when the police advocate closer ties with the community, while continuing to engage in aggressive enforcement activities, they become the "iron fist in the velvet glove." This characterization is intended to describe what these critics consider to be the implicit deception of strict enforcement cloaked in community concern (Center for Research on Criminal Justice 1975).

Increased Police Research

Many of the recommendations for changing the police that have been made since the 1970s were the result of the increasing amount of research into policing practices. During the 1960s, the federal government took several steps that created an innovative climate in law enforcement. In addition to the Crime Commission in 1965 and the Riot Commission in 1967, the federal government created the Office of Law Enforcement Assistance (OLEA) in 1965 and passed the Omnibus Crime Control and Safe Streets Act in 1968. This act increased funding for OLEA, which became known as the Law Enforcement Assistance Administration (LEAA). From the late 1960s through the 1970s, hundreds of millions of dollars were invested to improve the criminal justice system (Caiden 1977, pp. 56–59).

The most important impact on the police was the large number of research studies that produced new knowledge about police methods and effectiveness. In addition, the LEAA (now called the National Institute of Justice, or NIJ) made grants and loans available to encourage individuals—both preservice and in-service—to pursue higher education. With this increase in students came an increase in faculty members, who also contributed to the growing body of knowledge about the criminal justice system.

Information about the police during the legalistic era was based largely on the experience and publications of classical writers (see chapter 4), who promoted a paramilitary approach to policing. By the 1970s, such information was being challenged by data derived from systematic research. Many of the challenges were in the areas emphasized by the legalistic model, such as patrol and investigation. Studies cast doubts on the effectiveness of reactive and random (or discretionary) patrol in controlling crime, the need for a rapid response to most citizens' requests for services, and the effectiveness of criminal investigators (detectives) in many cases. Although many of these studies had flaws, the research raised questions concerning the manner in which police invested their energies and the activities in which they engaged.

The police were also encouraged to broaden their use of research and the analytical process to solve problems. H. Goldstein (1979, 1987, see also 1990, p. 97), for example, recommended that the police begin to think in terms of problems rather than incidents; that is, they should change from an incident-based response strategy to a problem-oriented strategy (e.g., viewing a group of incidents as a potential problem). Goldstein argued that officers should not only try to determine the relationship between incidents that might be occurring in the same family, building, or area, but also consider alternatives other than law enforcement to try to solve problems. Goldstein's problem-oriented policing is now more commonly referred to as problem-solving policing.

Strategic Management

In the 1970s and 1980s the demand for police services increased. Although the police had modified their responses somewhat as part of the legalistic model, they still emphasized visible police patrol, investigation and apprehension, and rapid response to calls, particularly if a serious crime was involved. As demand increased, however, the police could not keep pace, so they had to search for alternative methods to respond to crime problems and citizen concerns. Not only were the traditional methods being overburdened, but their very effectiveness was being questioned. Concern about the effective and efficient use of police resources, the new research that questioned traditional police methods, and suggestions that police consider methods other than law enforcement to solve problems resulted in attempts to apply strategic management concepts to the police.

Strategic management involves the identification of organizational goals along with the most effective and efficient manner to achieve them. Police departments are not necessarily required to utilize patrol and investigations as their primary methods; rather, they should be free to experiment with alternative approaches. Departments that adopt this philosophy have the responsibility to determine the nature of policing in a democracy, alter or modify goals as the environment of policing changes, and determine (through systematic research and analysis) how best to achieve those goals.

As applied to the police, strategic management asks such questions as the following:

1. What are the fundamental purposes of the police?

2. What is the scope of their responsibility?

3. What is the range of possible contributions they can make to society?

4. What are the distinctive competencies of the police?

5. What are the most effective programmatic and technical means for achieving their purposes? (Moore and Trojanowicz 1988)

Instead of assuming that the police role is essentially predetermined, strategic management is based on a broader view. It adopts the perspective that the police have a distinctive part to play in society, but that this part, and the manner in which police play it, are variable over time and in different communities. As a community resource, the police can do many things in many different ways. Strategic management is simply a flexible approach to determining what those things should be and what ways are most effective and efficient. Inside Policing 3.1 provides more information about strategic management.

Minority-Group Relations

Historically, one of the most persistent and compelling problems confronting the police is their relationship with minority groups. Depending on the time period, a minority group could be Irish Americans, Italian Americans, Hispanics or Latinos, African Americans, Asian Americans, Native Americans, gays (and lesbians), or other groups. The police have had a long history of discriminating against members of minority groups, whose com-

---

Inside Policing 3.1
Strategic Management of the Police

The development of a "corporate strategy" involves making a purposeful choice, shaping the organization's identity and character, defining and redefining what needs to be accomplished, and using the organization's resources to attain goals in difficult, and possibly adverse, circumstances. Said another way, a corporate strategy involves determining a direction for the organization that is based on the organization's capabilities as related to opportunities and problems. In public organizations, managers often believe that they cannot make choices about purpose because that is the responsibility of policy makers (e.g., elected and appointed officials) outside the department. It is possible, however, and often desirable, for police managers, within the broad parameters of the role of police in democratic society, to consider a number of possible purposes for the department. This consideration involves identifying opportunities and problems in the department's environment to which the police have the capability to respond.

That is, police leaders do not necessarily have to assume that their mission is limited to controlling crime by enforcing laws. Rather, strategic management involves consideration of how a police department can make the most significant contribution to the communities in which it functions. When a manager assumes that the police have a "fixed" mission or predetermined ways to accomplish a mission, a police problem might be defined as: "how the police force might best be deployed to deal with predatory crime." From a strategic-management perspective, a manager would consider how to "use a large disciplined force . . . , that has access to transportation, and is available . . . around the clock, [and can] . . . make . . . [a] contribution to the quality of life within the community." In public organizations, like the police, an organization's strategy must identify goals that are legally permissible, have political support, and that the public believes are worthwhile. These goals must be achievable given the competency of the work force and the adequacy of knowledge about what is, and is not, effective.

One way of describing a strategy for police is to use the phrases "professional law enforcement" and "professional crime fighting" as statements of purpose, or in describing a mission. These phrases are based on the belief that the most important activities of the police involve enforcing laws that protect life and property. When the emphasis is on more serious legal violations, such as murder, rape, and robbery, it indicates a mission of "professional crime fighting." When broadened to include enforcement of traffic laws, health and safety laws, curfew ordinances, and other laws, the police mission is more appropriately characterized as "professional law enforcement." Another possible strategy is "crime prevention," which would include not only "professional law enforcement" and "professional crime fighting" but also the use of resources to educate the public as to how to protect themselves and their property. And it might also include the use of resources to respond to "correlates" of crime by developing programs to supervise children and teenagers, providing assistance to dysfunctional families, cleaning up neighborhoods, and so forth.

Source: Adapted from M. H. Moore and D. W. Stephens. 1991. *The Strategic Management of Police Departments: Beyond Command and Control*. Washington, D.C.: Police Executive Research Forum, pp. 14–27.

---

munities have often been plagued by serious crime and disorder. Numerous civil disturbances in the United States have been precipitated by police behavior considered to be inappropriate by minority groups.

The legalistic model of policing essentially saw the relationship with the community as bureaucratic and consequently was not considered to be sufficiently responsive to minority concerns. In its later stages, this model at-

Police and minority relationships have often been confrontational regarding police behaviors, even to the point of precipitating civil disturbances. (Photo: Mark C. Ide)

tempted to be more responsive by diversifying the police force, experimenting with team policing, and establishing community-relations programs. Although this approach improved police relationships with minorities, minority concerns about police behavior remained high.

In the 1980s, the public became increasingly fearful of crime, especially violence, gang activity, and drug use which were alarmingly portrayed by the media. Many police departments became more legalistic, proactive, and assertive. They tended to rely on aggressive patrol, field interrogations, citations, arrests, and increased undercover activities. These approaches, applauded by many minority leaders, also increased the tension between police and minority citizens, particularly African Americans and Hispanics. The perception that some police officers were brutal racists became widespread. In fact, this perception was often accurate, particularly as it applied to police use of excessive force. However, the degree to which such behavior was racially motivated or willful was much more difficult to determine. The movement toward community policing is viewed by many law enforcement leaders and academics as a way to attempt to reduce tension between minority citizens and the police.

The Community and Crime

Community theories concerning crime suggest that social order is more the result of informal social processes in the community than anything the police might do. This idea underscores the importance of involving citizens as "partners" in determining the police role and identifying solutions to quality-of-life problems. This goal has become known as the **co-production of public safety**, where the public shares some responsibility with the police in responding to crime, community disorder, and related problems. It also emphasizes the greater use of informal or neighborhood solutions and other community agencies, such as those for health, recreation, and counseling, to address problems. Because the police have considerable resources and expertise, they should assume a leadership role in motivating citizens to become involved and in coordinating the responses of other agencies. J. E. Eck and D. P. Rosenbaum describe this perspective as one of "community engagement," in which the police "help to create self-regulating, self-sufficient communities where levels of crime and disorder are contained by the efforts of local residents and local institutions" (1994, p. 8).

Team Policing

The decade of the1960s was a tumultuous era in the United States, as riots broke out in many cities. As noted above, in some instances the police actually provided the spark that precipitated these riots. Out of this crisis came the growing recognition that the police lacked responsiveness to, and understanding of, community expectations. Following the urban unrest, it became clear that a different style of police force would be necessary—one that could be more responsive to community needs. Thus, a major reorganization effort toward decentralization and increased community participation, known as **team policing**, was attempted in the early 1970s.

Team policing in the United States was based primarily on British precedents, especially the Aberdeen system, which originated in Scotland immediately following World War II, and unit beat policing, which was developed in the County of Coventry, England, in 1966 (Sherman, Milton, and Kelley 1973). The Aberdeen system was first established to counteract the low morale and boredom of single officers patrolling quiet streets; it allocated teams of five to 10 men on foot and in cars to move to different parts of the city that had the highest crime rates and numbers of calls for service. The increased workload eliminated boredom and loneliness. Unit beat policing was developed to utilize limited manpower more effectively; constables were organized into teams that remained in one specific area. Although the constables did not work as a team, they all fed information about their area to a central person, or collator, who was responsible for distributing information about the area to the other constables. Thus, by effectively using the collator to coordinate and exchange information, fewer constables could cover a wider geographic area.

Efforts in the United States often had elements similar to both the Aberdeen and unit beat policing systems. Team policing was first used by the Syracuse Police Department in 1968, and by 1974 as many as 60 departments across the country had attempted some form of team policing (Schwartz and Clarren 1977). According to L. W. Sherman, C. H. Milton, and T. V. Kelley (1973), in theory, team policing was based on reorganizing the patrol force to include one or more quasi-autonomous teams, with a joint purpose of improving police services to the community and increasing job satisfaction of the officers. The team is normally stationed in a particular neighborhood and is responsible for all police services in that neighborhood. It is expected to work as a unit and maintain a close relationship with the community to prevent crime and maintain order.

Sherman and his associates conducted a thorough evaluation of team policing in seven cities. Included in the study were two small cities—Holyoke, Mass. and Richmond, Calif.; two middle-size cities—Dayton, Ohio and Syracuse, N.Y.; two large cities—Detroit and Los Angeles; and one super-city—New York City. Although team policing had different meanings in each city, six of the seven programs attempted to implement three common operational elements: (1) geographic stability of patrol, that is, permanent assignment of teams of police to small neighborhoods; (2) maximum interaction among team members, including close internal communication among all officers assigned to an area during a 24-hour period, seven days a week; and (3) maximum communication among team members and the community.

The departments that were the most successful in implementing these three operational elements also had certain organizational supports in common, including: (1) unity of supervision (i.e., one supervisor responsible for a given area at all times), (2) lower-level flexibility in policy making, (3) unified delivery of services, and (4) combined investigative and patrol functions. Table 3.1 summarizes the operational and organizational elements of team policing in each city.

Table 3.1   Summary of Team-Policing Elements by City

Operational Elements	Dayton	Detroit	New York	Syracuse	Holyoke	Los Angeles (Venice)	Rich-mond
Stable geographic assignment	+	+	—	+	+	+	•
Intra-team interaction	—	+	—	—	+	+	+
Formal team conferences	—	+	—	—	+	+	+
Police-community communication	+	+	—	—	+	+	•
Formal community conferences	+	•	•	—	+	+	•
Community participation in police work	+	+	—	•	+	+	•
Referrals to social agencies	+		—	•	•	•	+
Organizational Supports							
Unity of supervision	+	+	—	+	+	+	+
Lower-level flexibility	—	—	—	+	+	+	+
Unified delivery of services	+	—	—	+	+	+	•
Combined patrol and investigative functions	+	+	•	+	+	+	+

Key:
+ the element was planned and realized
— the element was planned but not realized
• the element was not planned

L. W. Sherman, C. H. Milton, and T. V. Kelly, *Team Policing: Seven Case Studies, 1973.* Reprinted by permission of Police Foundation, Washington, D.C.

As can be seen from Table 3.1, there was wide variation by city in planning and implementing the various elements. Some programs achieved overwhelming success in certain areas. For example, the Venice (Los Angeles) team developed hundreds of block captains, who exchanged crime information with police on a regular basis; one team in Holyoke virtually abandoned preventive patrol since the citizenry informed them almost immediately of many crimes in progress. In both Dayton and Holyoke, community boards composed of representatives chosen by local groups (e.g., Parent-Teacher Associations, civic associations, tenant organizations) participated in police policy making; the Dayton team also used medical and welfare agencies for referrals the most frequently, instead of making arrests (Sherman, Milton, and Kelley 1973).

On the whole, however, most programs differed little from the traditional policing of the past. For instance, in none of the cities studied was a decentralized patrol style realized (i.e., authority and decision making were not delegated down to street officers). There appeared to be three major reasons why team policing either failed or reached only partial success:

1. Mid-management of the departments, seeing team policing as a threat to their power, subverted and, in some cases, actively sabotaged the plans.

2. The dispatching technology did not permit the patrols to remain in their neighborhoods, despite the stated intentions of adjusting that technology to the projects.

3. The patrols never received a sufficiently clear definition of how their behavior and role should differ from those of a regular patrol; at the same time, they were considered an elite group by their peers, who often resented not having been chosen for the project. (Sherman, Milton, and Kelley 1973, pp. 107–108)

Although it is apparent that team-policing experiments, to a large extent, failed owing to a lack of proper planning and training, it is also true that the amount of change required in switching from a highly bureaucratic, authoritarian structure to a decentralized, democratic one was simply too great—especially in a relatively short period of time. Another hurdle facing those departments attempting such a significant change was that no attempt had been made to establish a departmental climate of innovation. As will be noted in chapter 5, all these hurdles also confront police departments attempting to move to community policing.

Furthermore, because team policing is based on decentralized decision making for patrol officers, some police managers became concerned with the problem of accountability. For example, in another well-documented study in Cincinnati, Ohio, known as COMSEC (Community Sector Team Policing Experiment), top administrators had second thoughts about the program as it progressed. Although they wanted the teams to be responsive to the community, they "feared that with the promised autonomy and reduction in central control, their officers might become less productive or even corrupt" (Schwartz and Clarren 1977, p. 7). Of course, that is precisely why strong, bureaucratic, central control has been a mainstay in police administration over the past several decades (see chapter 4). The dilemma with such centralized control, however, is not only the lack of community responsiveness but also the reduction of morale among officers (who have less decision-making responsibilities).

Despite its drawbacks, team policing became the fad of the 1970s. But it soon became apparent that a "new" approach to policing was needed, one that was attuned to both community needs and officer satisfaction. In theory, team policing attempted to do both, but, for various reasons, in virtually every city in which it was attempted, the promises could not be fulfilled. Starting in the mid-1980s, new models of policing began to be developed.

Community and Problem-Oriented Policing

The legalistic model had provided the framework for police professionalism. Team-policing experiments had emphasized improved police services and relationships with the community, attempted new approaches in the organization and management of police departments, and stressed a broader role for the police (which, in turn, was expected to increase officer satisfaction). Taken together, these changes had resulted in the police gradually being directed away from strictly law enforcement toward social service and community problem solving.

The emphasis on a broader role for the police emerged as a new philosophy called **community-oriented policing (COP)**, and the emphasis on research contributed to the development of **problem-oriented policing (POP)**. In general, the initial development of community policing had a primary emphasis on establishing a working partnership with the community, whereas problem-oriented policing was concerned primarily with identifying and solving community problems , often, but not necessarily, with input from the community. The general evolution of the **community policing model** includes aspects of *both* community-oriented and problem-solving policing. Although it is possible to have one without the other, and some departments do, they are closely related and compatible. For one department's view on COP and POP, see Inside Policing 3.2. Community policing can be more effective if it uses problem-solving methods, and conversely, problem solving is more effective if there is widespread community input and support.

Inside Policing 3.2
COP and POP in Savannah

Problem-oriented policing, or problem solving, is a cornerstone of community policing in the Savannah, Georgia, police department. The department's view of the relationship between POP and COP was defined in an annual report as follows:

Problem-oriented policing is so closely related to community-oriented policing that, in order for either to be successful, the two must be considered effectively inseparable. POP strategies employ law enforcement as well as community resources to attack the problems [that] not only breed crime, but [also] contribute to other common annoyances [that] generate dissatisfaction in the community. This police [approach] eliminates, or at least mitigates, these conditions before they develop into incidents requiring police response.

Community-oriented policing removes the barriers that have traditionally existed between law enforcement and the public. By acquainting the police with the people they serve and, as a result, acquainting the public with individual officers, citizens no longer view police as nameless blue uniforms.

These different views, and how they apply to the department, were summarized by the patrol bureau commander as: "COP is the philosophy; POP is a strategy. This strategy is used throughout the department and starts with the initiation of a POP project."

Source: Adapted from Police Executive Research Forum. 1996. *Themes and Variations in Community Policing: Case Studies in Community Policing.* Washington, D.C.: Police Executive Research Forum, p. 74.

❖ ❖ ❖ ❖   It is also important to remember that problem solving is not associated with any particular solution to a problem; rather, the solution is contingent upon the analysis of the problem. Responses are situational rather than fixed. To provide a better understanding of the development of this process, problem-oriented policing is described below.

As noted earlier, Goldstein offers a pioneering approach to improving the police through a concept he terms problem-oriented policing. In formulating this new concept, he emphasizes that police departments (but not necessarily individual officers) had a history of being susceptible to the "means over ends" syndrome, that is, a tendency to place greater emphasis on improving traditional organization and operating methods than on the substantive outcome of their work. He believes that if the police are to improve operations and to mature as a profession, they need to concern themselves more directly with the end product of their efforts. Thus, the police should become problem oriented rather than incident oriented. Goldstein argues that they are too narrowly focused on specific incidents (i.e., they handle the same incidents time after time) and should instead become more involved with solving the problems that lead to these repeated incidents. As D. W. Stevens points out, "The police respond to and deal with the single incident, as if it had no history or future" (1990, p. 155). With this in mind, he further notes that

> About 60 percent of crime calls to which police respond originate from about 10 percent of the addresses in a city. Ten percent of the victims account for 40 percent of the reported crimes, and 10 percent of the criminals are responsible for about 55 percent of the offenses. The traditional incident-driven policing would normally not make the connections between these repeat calls, victims and offenders. (1990, p. 155)

A problem-oriented approach suggests that the police develop "a more systematic process for examining and addressing the problems that the pub-

Community policing involves community input and support to help police to identify and solve problems. (Photo: Mark C. Ide)

lic expects them to handle" (Goldstein 1979, p. 236). There are three key elements in this approach.

First, define problems more specifically. Broad categorical headings such as crime, disorder, or theft need to be more precisely defined in order to be dealt with more effectively. Definitions include such characteristics as time, location, participants' behavior and motivation, and other details of importance.

Second, research the problem—that is, gather and analyze basic data about the specific problem. It is important to obtain information from outside the department as well as within; citizens, businesses, and governmental agencies can provide additional insights and solutions regarding problems with which they are familiar.

Third, search for alternatives to present responses. A broad search for innovative solutions, extending beyond the police or criminal justice system, should be undertaken. Such alternatives might include various crime-prevention strategies, using civil law to require property owners to improve living conditions, organizing citizens to clean up an area, obtaining services from other governmental agencies (e.g., the street-cleaning department), or referring of individuals to public and private agencies for assistance (e.g., counseling or mediation).

Goldstein believes that the problem-oriented approach is an attractive approach to police change because it is an attempt to deal with problems rather than simply living with them. It not only taps police expertise but also calls for the police to become partners with other public agencies as well. He further argues that because such an approach is less likely to be seen as a direct challenge to the prevailing police value system (i.e., they are still dealing with the same types of incidents, but the process is changed), organizational reform efforts should be less difficult. This is an important point, since one of the primary problems with implementing team policing was the subversion of the programs by middle management.

In addition, such an approach should improve the working environment for officers, who would have much greater flexibility to take the initiative and be creative in solving problems. This improved work environment should lead to increased job satisfaction for the police and improved quality of police service provided to the community. Such a change would also utilize more effectively the potential of college-educated officers, "who have been smothered in the atmosphere of traditional policing"(Goldstein 1987, p. 28).

Two early programs that were based on principles similar to Goldstein's problem-oriented approach provide interesting examples of this process. The first is Baltimore County, Maryland, which implemented a more extensive foot-patrol program in which officers are responsible for gathering information pertinent to identifying community problems. One of the instruments designed to help them collect such data is the problem identification interview, shown in Figure 3.1, which is used to record citizen perceptions regarding "the existence of neighborhood disorder, contributing crimes, fear, satisfaction with the police response currently provided, and possible solutions (police service or otherwise)" (Scannell 1988, p. 35).

The second example is Newport News, Virginia, presented as Case Study 3.1, which involves a study by the National Institute of Justice on problem-oriented policing.The Newport News Police Department was the first to adopt problem solving through the **SARA** process (scanning, analysis, response, and assessment) as a department-wide standard method of operation.

Figure 3.1 Problem-Identification Interview

| Community Foot Patrol Program | PROBLEM IDENTIFICATION INTERVIEW | | DATE / / |

RESPONDENT'S PROFILE

☐ Business   ☐ Residence   Community Name _____

Address: _____   No. of Persons Interviewed _____

Years in Neighborhood: ☐ Less Than 1   ☐ 1 to 2   ☐ 3 to 5   ☐ Over 5

Age Group: ☐ Less Than 18   ☐ 18 – 29   ☐ 30 – 39   ☐ 40 – 49
            ☐ 50 – 59   ☐ Over 60

Sex: ☐ Male   ☐ Female

Race: ☐ White   ☐ Black   ☐ Oriental   ☐ Hispanic   ☐ Other

INTERVIEW QUESTIONS

1. When you think of neighborhood problems or crime, what are your concerns? _____

2. How often does this problem occur?
☐ Periodically   ☐ Isolated Incident   ☐ Constantly   ☐ Frequently

3. How has this problem inconvenienced you or changed your daily life? _____

4. What do you feel is the cause of the problem? _____

5. What do you feel could be done to correct the problem? _____

6. Do you feel the police department is responsive to the needs of your neighborhood. (i.e. have the police services been adequate in your neighborhood ?) If not, explain. _____

7. Do you feel the county government has been responsive to your neighborhood's needs? (Do not restrict to crime.) If not, explain. _____

8. _____
9. _____
10. _____

Source: From "Community Foot Patrol Officer (CFPO) Guidelines and Procedures," by J. Scannell, 1988, pp. 36–37. Reprinted by permission of Baltimore County Police Department, Towson, MD.

Community Policing Today

There has been considerable research and discussion concerning community policing. Many police departments have long had what they considered to be community-policing philosophy or programs, but they did not necessarily see this approach as an integral part of the police role, nor did they use it as a basis to reform individual departments. There remain a number of

Problem-Oriented Policing in Newport News

The theory behind problem-oriented policing is simple. Underlying conditions create problems. These conditions might include the characteristics of the people involved (offenders, potential victims, and others), the social setting in which these people interact, the physical environment, and the way the public deals with these conditions.

Designing Problem-Oriented Policing

Some departments had implemented problem-solving approaches as part of special units or projects; no department, however, had implemented a problem-oriented approach throughout the department. So an operational system had to be designed and tested. Newport News was chosen to undertake this task. It is a moderate-sized department, with 280 employees serving a population of 155,000. So it was small enough that changes could be made in a reasonably short time, but it served an urban population with many of the crime problems of big cities.

The Newport News Police Department assembled a task force of 12 members, representing all ranks and units. As this group had no experience at solving problems, they decided to test the system they were designing on two persistent problems: burglaries in an apartment complex and thefts from vehicles. It was understood, however, that all subsequent problems would be handled by officers in their normal assignments. As shown in Figure 3.2, the task force designed a four-stage problem-solving process, known as SARA. During the *scanning* stage, an officer identifies an issue and determines whether it is really a problem. In the *analysis* stage, officers collect information from sources inside and outside their agency. The goal is to understand the scope, nature, and causes of the problem. In the *response stage*, this information is used to develop and implement solutions. Officers seek the assistance of other police units, other public and private organizations, and anyone else who can help. Finally, in the *assessment* stage, officers evaluate the effectiveness of the response. They may use the results to revise the response, collect more data, or even to redefine the problem.

Figure 3.2 SARA: A Problem-Solving Process

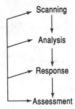

The heart of this process is the analysis stage. To help officers analyze problems, the task force designed a problem analysis guide. This guide separates the events that comprise a problem into three components:

1. Actors—victims, offenders, and others involved in the events.

2. Incidents—the social context, physical setting, and actions taken before, during, and after the events.

3. Responses—the perceptions of and responses to the problem by citizens and private and public institutions.

All officers of the rank of sergeant and above were trained in the use of the process and the guide, as well as on the research background of problem-oriented policing. The training also emphasized the need to encourage officer initiative in finding problems, collecting information, and developing responses. Officers throughout the department then began to apply the process and the guide. ☞

New Information and New Responses

Police managers have used the SARA process and the analysis guide to encourage officers to gather more information from a wider variety of sources than before. While studying problems, officers have reviewed literature, interviewed prostitutes and thieves, surveyed businesses, held conferences with local public and private officials, photographed problem sites, and searched title and tax records. As a result, the responses are more comprehensive than standard incident-driven reactions. This, too, is strongly encouraged by the department's managers. Some of the responses are improvements on standard tactics. For example, the department responded to the problems of downtown robberies and parking lot thefts by identifying, arresting, and incarcerating the most frequent offenders. But even in these examples, the involvement of people outside the criminal justice system was important. Other responses hardly involve the criminal justice process at all. While responding to other problems, officers have worked with businesses, the military, citizens' groups, state and federal agencies, and nonprofit organizations. So the resources used are as diverse as the problems themselves.

Implementing Problem-Oriented Policing

Problem-oriented policing involves a substantial change from current practice. The fully problem-oriented police department will be different from present departments in several ways:

- Problem solving will be the standard method of policing, not just an occasionally useful tactic.
- Problem-solving efforts will focus on problems of the public, not on police administration.
- When problems are taken on, police will establish precise, measurable objectives.
- Police managers will constantly look for ways to involve all members of the department in solving problems.
- These characteristics will be true of all departments that have committed themselves to problem-oriented policing. As these departments gain experience, they should develop three additional characteristics:
- Officers will consistently undertake thorough analyses, using data from many sources.
- Officers will engage in an uninhibited search for solutions to all problems they take on.
- All members of the department will be involved in problem solving.

Developing these characteristics will take time; police executives should plan to implement problem-oriented policing over a period of many years, rather than weeks or months.

Source: Adapted from J. E. Eck and W. Spelman. 1987. "Problem-Solving: Problem-Oriented Policing in Newport News." *Research in Brief*, Washington, D.C.: National Institute of Justice, January, 1987.

---

complex issues associated with community policing. This section will discuss some of these issues; the following section will provide examples of community policing programs.

Definitions and Philosophy

Perhaps the most fundamental question is, What is community policing? Is it a strategy of policing? Is it a vision of the future for the police? Is it a department-wide orientation or only a specialized appendage? According to R. Trojanowicz and B. Bucqueroux (1992, pp. 4–6), community policing (1) is a philosophy, not just an isolated program; (2) involves a permanent commitment to the community, including "average" citizens; (3) broadens the mission of the police beyond crime control; (4) provides full-service, personalized, and decentralized (i.e., localized) policing; (5) focuses on problem solving; (6) enhances accountability; (7) uses both reactive and proactive policing; and (8) must operate within existing resources.

The most frequently cited elements of community policing include the following:

- Defining police work more broadly.

- Reordering police priorities.

- Paying greater attention to neighborhood disorder and quality-of-life issues.

- Shifting to shared decision making with citizens.

- De-emphasizing bureaucratic processes in favor of results.

- Focusing on problem solving and prevention rather than on incident-driven policing (see Inside Policing 3.3 for an update on a computer program that helps police to focus on problem solving).

- Recognizing that the community plays a critical role in solving neighborhood problems.

- Restructuring and reorganizing police departments to encourage and reward a fresh set of police behaviors (Rosenbaum, Lurigio, and Davis 1998, p. 176).

According to W. A. Geller and G. Swanger, community policing involves a "strategic shift . . . toward the view that police can better help redress and prevent crime, disorder, and fear problems through active, multifaceted, consultative, and collaborate relationships with diverse community groups and public and private-sector institutions" (1995, p. 3). This strategic shift is based on the idea that "public safety [is] a community responsibility, rather than simply the responsibility of . . . the police." This change "transforms the police officer from an investigator and enforcer into a catalyst in a process of community self-help. Rather than standardized services, police services become customized" to individual communities (Osborne and Gaebler 1993, pp. 50, 174).

L. P. Brown (1989) has attempted to define community policing by identifying important characteristics of its philosophy and the benefits, that, in his opinion, are likely to result for both the community and the police (see Inside Policing 3.4).

As a department-wide philosophy that provides the foundation for the strategic use of police resources, community policing must take into account the three most fundamental questions asked about the police: (1) Who decides what the police role in a community will be? (2) What is that role? (3) What competencies are required in order to fulfill that role?

Who decides this police role is essentially a political question; community policing is based on the assumption that citizens will have substantial input in deciding such a role. Going further, it suggests that the police must act

---

Inside Policing 3.3
Computer Program Helps Put
Focus on Problem Solving

Police officers at a number of New England police departments have one less excuse for not pursuing a problem-solving approach to policing, thanks to an information module linked to their departments' records-management software. Microsystems Integrated Public Safety Systems, Inc., a computer software company, developed the Problem-Solver information module to be linked with its Crimetract records-management system. The idea for Problem-Solver came out of the frustrating difficulty in isolating data in police records-management systems that could be applied to problem solving. Although police departments typically collect a lot of information, it generally is not the type that an officer would need to perform the type of problem solving required in community policing.

Problem-Solver uses the SARA approach to problem solving, in which the user proceeds through the steps of scanning, analysis, response, and assessment. It draws on several sources of data in the records-management system—information on warrants, arrests, calls for service, crime hot spots, top offenders, including juveniles, orders of protection, citations, traffic summonses, and victims of repeat offenses—to help officers remedy problems on their beats. The data are used by the Problem-Solver module to ask officers specific questions about the problems they encounter. The answers are linked to a library of possible responses that the officer may use in attempting to solve the problem.

Currently, the module's library contains nearly 1,000 responses that were selected from existing literature on problem-solving efforts nationwide. About 300 questions have been developed that focus on three common crime problems related to domestic violence, gangs, and narcotics. The problem categories can be expanded to focus on other areas as well. Activities that have proven successful in solving a particular problem are recorded and stored in the module for future reference. In this way, virtually every officer has access to problem-solving capabilities.

The module also includes an assessment component to gauge the effectiveness of the response, as well as the time spent solving the problem and a before-and-after analysis of the situation. The system is flexible and does not require a successful resolution to utilize its other capabilities. Officers can go back to any of the SARA phases prior to implementing all of their responses. In this way, they can flip through all of the different components and map out all elements of the problem. This program empowers officers on the street to spend more time on patrol and problem-solving activities and less time wading through paperwork.

Source: Adapted from "One Less Problem When It Comes to Problem-Solving." 1998. *Law Enforcement News*, April 30: 1, 9. Reprinted with permission from *Law Enforcement News*, John Jay College of Criminal Justice, New York City.

Inside Policing 3.4
Characteristics and Possible Benefits of
Community Policing

Characteristics

1. The results of policing are as important as the process. Police obtain results by emphasizing the identification, analysis, and resolution of problems.

2. Police values that emphasize citizen involvement in matters that directly affect the safety and quality of neighborhood life are stressed.

3. The police must be accountable to each neighborhood in a community. Often, neighborhoods have different concerns, desires, and priorities. Of-

ficers must routinely interact with residents and keep them informed of police efforts to fight and prevent neighborhood crime.

4. Police departments, in both structure and authority, must be decentralized. Police officers must be allowed to participate in important decisions. A police department will establish a "mini-police station" in certain areas of the city.

5. Police departments share power with the community in a partnership to identify and solve problems. Power sharing requires that citizens take an active rather than a passive role because citizens have a great deal of information that is useful to the police.

6. Beat (area, sector, or district) boundaries are redesigned to coincide with natural neighborhood boundaries rather than being based on the needs of the police department.

7. Officers are given permanent assignments in terms of both the area in which they work and the shifts they work. This means that an officer should be assigned for at least six months, and possibly several years, to the same neighborhood.

8. Beat officers are empowered (i.e., given the responsibility and authority) to initiate creative solutions to neighborhood problems.

9. The role of supervision and management changes. For example, patrol officers become "managers" of their beats, while the supervisor becomes responsible for helping the patrol officer to identify and solve problems. Managers are responsible for obtaining the resources and support necessary to solve problems.

10. Police training programs change. At the recruit level, officers are provided information about the complexities and dynamics of the community and how the police fit into the larger picture. New officers are taught community organizing skills and leadership skills, as well as how to identify and diagnose problems.

11. Performance evaluation is based on the officer's ability to solve problems and to involve the community in crime fighting and neighborhood safety.

12. The management of requests for police service changes from responding only to each separate incident to trying to determine the reasons why such incidents occur and if they are related to a broader problem that can be addressed. Police responses to less serious incidents may be altered (e.g., telephone reports instead of sending a police officer) in order for officers to spend more time solving problems.

Benefits of Community Policing to the Community

1. The police make a commitment to prevent crime rather than just react to it.

2. Public scrutiny of the police is improved because more citizens know what police do and why.

3. Police officers are accountable for their behavior not only to the department but also to citizens.

4. Police services will be "customized" in that specific responses will be developed based on the needs of each neighborhood.

5. As citizens become more involved in police activities, the community will become more organized and therefore more effective in responding to problems.

Benefits of Community Policing to the Police

1. Police will receive greater community support.

2. The police will be able to share the responsibility for crime and disorder control with citizens.

3. Police officers will have greater job satisfaction because they will be able to see the results of their efforts at problem solving.

4. The communication and cooperation among units (e.g., patrol and investigations) in the police department will be improved.

5. Police departments will need to reexamine their organizational structure and managerial practices.

Source: Adapted from L. P. Brown. "Community Policing: A Practical Guide for Police Officials." *Perspective on Policing.* Pamphlet No. 12. Washington, D.C.: National Institute of Justice.

as community leaders in each neighborhood to ensure that a discussion about the police role takes place.

The role the police are to play depends on what the community wants, as long as it is not illegal, based on the citizens' ideas along with the expertise provided by the police. As a practical matter, the police often have more input than do citizens, but at least citizens are given the opportunity to participate. In some situations, citizens may have more information about community crime and disorder than do the police. Although the police may be reluctant to listen, that is precisely what they must do. Flexibility in using resources and solving problems is an important part of community policing.

What competencies are required in policing is a difficult question because, as noted in chapter 1, there is limited knowledge about the relationship between any particular police practice and the end result. Community policing addresses this problem by emphasizing the importance of research and evaluation. Police departments can become learning organizations (see chapter 5) as they experiment to improve police systems, the behavior of officers, and the results thereof.

Case Studies

There are many examples of community-policing programs. The following two examples—Knoxville, Tennessee, and Tucson, Arizona—were selected because their development was relatively well planned, documented, and implemented. These studies are primarily concerned with crime prevention and drug-related problems, although community policing is not limited to these areas. The studies do not describe the problems associated with implementation, which will be addressed in subsequent chapters.

Knoxville and Tucson began to experiment with community policing in the 1980s. After some initial success, they received a federal grant from the Bureau of Justice Assistance to demonstrate the importance of crime prevention as a major activity of equal status to patrol and investigative activities. The programs they developed had three phases: (1) the integration of crime-prevention and drug-prevention activities into all law enforcement operations; (2) the development of working relationships with other governmental agencies and community groups to assess the resources available and to develop action plans for specific neighborhoods; and (3) the implementation of the programs. See Case Studies 3.2 and 3.3.

New Duties and Community Feedback

These case studies provide an overview of the types of activities in which the police can become involved, but they do not describe how the individual police officer may be affected. Not only does community policing require significant departmental changes, it also requires that police officers perform new duties and learn new skills. Trojanowicz and Bucqueroux have identified possible "duties and activities" of a community officer (CO):

1. Performs law enforcement duties common to police patrol assignments.

2. Attempts to build an "atmosphere of mutual respect and trust" in order to develop a partnership with and between citizens to iden-

---

Case Study 3.2

Community Policing in Knoxville

After two successful programs dealing with drugs and prostitution, the Bureau of Justice Assistance gave Knoxville a grant to develop a crime-prevention program. In phase one, the Knoxville police addressed the meaning of such a program for the department. They also instituted training programs, not only for the police but also for leaders of other governmental and community agencies and several neighborhoods. To be successful, the police decided that they should take the following steps:

1. Emphasize a proactive response toward residents' fear of crime and victimization.
2. Enrich the line officer's job with greater community involvement.
3. Emphasize the police officer's role as part of a general human-service network rather than as someone who appears only when there is a problem.
4. Share the burden of solving neighborhood problems with other community agencies and groups.
5. Improve citizen-police interaction.
6. Expand the scope of traditional crime-prevention activities.
7. Elevate the professional stature of crime-prevention activities, that is, make it as important as patrol and investigations.
8. Provide a simple, straightforward process to effect systematic improvements in the delivery of services.
9. Develop police strategies based on interagency information-sharing and on research findings, rather than on belief or myth, to verify the effects of community involvement on levels of fear and victimization.

In phase two, Knoxville created a citywide task force including governmental agencies (e.g., fire departments, schools, utilities, courts, traffic engineering, and so on), political leaders, nonprofit organizations, citizen organizations, and business leaders. It involved as many persons as possible, particularly from those groups that might feel disenfranchised. This effort led to greater information sharing, and individual neighborhoods began to be profiled in order to improve understanding of their problems. The police department improved its crime-analysis capabilities and began to engage in neighborhood analysis by dividing the city into 33 small areas. Each neighborhood was described in terms of the following:

1. Crime rates and information about offenders.
2. Physical features, including street conditions, lighting, recreational areas, and building conditions.
3. School statistics, including truancy, dropout rate, vandalism, and violence.
4. Social information, including children and families at risk, poverty, and welfare.
5. Community conditions, including underreporting of crime, neighborhood concerns, social service needs, and juvenile problems.
6. Demographic information, including age, sex, and ethnicity.
7. How the land was being used at present and in the future.

After this analysis, one area was identified in which efforts to control drug activity did not seem to be working. When the drug sellers noted increased police activity, they would just move to a nearby street corner. Under community policing, the following steps were taken in addition to a law enforcement response:

1. Garbage and other debris were picked up and burnt-out and shot-out street lamps were replaced.
2. Traffic patterns were changed by adding speed bumps and barriers and by either closing certain areas to traffic or making them cul-de-sacs.
3. Business and building code violations were enforced.
4. The police consulted with the fire department to make sure they could still respond effectively even with the changes in the neighborhood.
5. Parks were changed to encourage citizens to use them in order to deter their use by drug pushers and users.

Source: Adapted from Bureau of Justice Assistance. 1993. "The Systems Approach to Crime and Drug Prevention: A Path to Community Policing." *Bulletin* 1, September.

Community Policing in Tucson

In phase one of Tucson's program, crime prevention was declared an emphasis of the entire police department. It was to be a part of, rather than apart from, patrol and investigations. No longer would crime prevention be the responsibility of just a small, specialized unit. Crime prevention was to become a goal for all officers, and all were to receive specialized training in this area. The police department even adopted a new mission statement: "The mission of the Tucson Police Department is to serve the public by furthering a partnership with the community to protect life and property, prevent crime, and resolve problems."

In addition to these changes, the department also developed training programs and created a crime-analysis unit. The officers assigned to this activity received special training and began to develop data that could be subjected to computer analysis. In addition, a process was developed to document the positive contacts officers had with citizens. Such contacts resulted in more citizen input into police activities, and, interestingly, citizens tended to desire both more police patrols and a faster response.

In phase two, neighborhood task forces, called community-action teams, were created. In addition, education in crime prevention was emphasized. Police officers were sent to crime prevention programs and to meet with representatives of other cities. This practice resulted in an emphasis on environmental design as a major part of the crime-prevention activities of not only the police department but also other organizations. The department also continued its crime-analysis activities. Twenty-eight neighborhoods were identified, and one was selected for a comprehensive response. A 12-part plan focused on general neighborhood cleanup, street lighting, street signs and traffic control, street names and numbers, speeding vehicles, pedestrian crosswalks, a lack of sidewalks, an underutilized park, an increased police presence, and a response to specific crime problems, such as burglary, gangs, and drugs.

In phase three, the police department began to expand the crime-prevention orientation throughout the organization and the community. A massive community-education program was undertaken to encourage citizens to volunteer and become involved in neighborhood improvement. A second neighborhood was selected for targeting. The community-action team, along with members of the local school district and leaders of city agencies, joined together to identify problems and develop strategies. A community survey was conducted to determine the concerns of residents. In order to give the neighborhood a sense of identity and to foster pride among its residents, a contest was held at a middle school to develop a neighborhood logo, which was placed on signs around the area. Schools in the area were declared drug-free zones, neighborhood cleanup was undertaken, traffic patterns were changed, and anti-graffiti programs were instituted.

Source: Adapted from Bureau of Justice Assistance. 1993. "The Systems Approach to Crime and Drug Prevention: A Path to Community Policing," *Bulletin* 1, September.

tify and prioritize problems related to crime, drugs, disorder, and fear.

3. Shares information with other officers in the department.

4. Identifies and analyzes problems using problem-solving techniques.

5. Educates community members about crime-prevention methods and engages in community building by organizing citizens and recruiting volunteers to assist the police in responding to, and solving, problems.

6. Mediates, negotiates, and resolves conflict among citizens and between police and citizens.

7. Visits homes, businesses, and schools to provide information about community policing.

8. Provides assistance to groups with special needs, such as the homeless, women, juveniles, the elderly, and the disabled.

9. Is concerned not only about crime and fear of crime but also about neighborhood decay and the residents' quality of life.

10. Networks with both public-sector and private-sector organizations to obtain support and cooperation in neighborhood projects. (1992, pp. 21–23)

One observational study in Cincinnati reflects the new content of the role of community policing (Frank, Brandl, and Watkins 1997). By comparing beat (traditional) officers' duties with the duties of specialized neighborhood (community) officers, it was found that neighborhood officers engage in a much broader range of nontraditional police activities than do regular beat or patrol officers. For instance, neighborhood officers spent a substantial amount of time engaged in community-based service activities, especially those related to community meeting activities, which consumes more time (11 percent) than any other activity except routine patrol. Furthermore, the service and problem-solving activities were performed to a much greater extent by neighborhood officers than by beat officers; not a single activity in the nontraditional community-based service category was found to be performed by beat officers. Interestingly, traditional crime-related activities (e.g., making arrests, issuing citations, making crime reports, serving war-

An important duty of community policing officers includes the education of community members. (Photo: Mark C. Ide)

rants) accounted for only about 5 percent of neighborhood officer time and about 18 percent of beat officer time. This research clearly establishes that the content of community policing can be substantially different from the content of traditional policing. Whether or not, and to what extent, such specialization is healthy (e.g., officer morale) and productive (e.g., should more or less of these tasks be performed throughout a community) remains for further investigation.

Evaluating officers on these new duties and activities requires an increased emphasis on the qualitative (versus quantitative) aspects of police work. Inside Policing 3.5 provides examples of an initial attempt by the National Center for Community Policing to build a foundation for performance evaluation of community police officers by establishing quantitative measurements of quality performance.

Inside Policing 3.5
Performance Evaluations of Community Officers

Building an Evaluation

In order to produce a performance evaluation for the community officer (CO), the kinds of measures used to assess the performance of the traditional patrol officer should be examined. Most patrol officers are evaluated on countable items such as the following:

- Radio calls: number and types of calls, alarm responses; reports written, time spent; follow-up required.

- Arrests: number and types of felony and misdemeanor arrests; warrants served; apprehensions of juveniles.

- Traffic: number and types of traffic stops; accidents and injuries; citations issued; time spent; motorist assists; parking tickets issued.

- Suspicious persons or situations checked or investigated: number and type; number of persons contacted; disposition; time spent.

- Property recovered: type and value of property; time spent.

- Administrative activities: roll call, court appearances, prisoner transport assignments, subpoenas served, reports written or taken, bar checks, and so on.

Statistics for crimes in the CO's beat area are a part of any performance evaluation; it is important to recognize, however, that these may be only indirectly related to the specific officer's per-

formance. Listed below are some outcomes that can be directly related to CO performance:

- Rates of targeted crimes: number and type; monthly and annual trends. (With input from the community, the CO may have prioritized specific crimes—for example, drug dealing or burglary.)

- Neighborhood disorder: social disorder—open use or sales of drugs, panhandlers, runaways, addicts, "winos," truants, curfew violations, prostitution, homeless, mainstreamed mental patients, unlicensed peddlers, gambling, loitering, unsupervised youngsters, youth gangs, and so on.

- Physical disorder: graffiti, abandoned cars, abandoned buildings, potholes, trash in yards, litter on streets, building code violations (residences and businesses), and so on.

The first-line supervisor and the CO can work together to decide which items apply, then develop ways to measure progress. Some items will be countable (see below) but the overall perception of improvement in neighborhood decay will require an on-site assessment from the first-line supervisor. The department can also survey residents periodically to assess their perceptions of progress toward improving the safety and quality of life in the area.   ☞

☞

- Calls for service: number and type; monthly and annual trends. New community policing efforts typically result in an increase in the number of calls for service from that area. Most effective CO's discover, however, that in time the number of such calls declines because some people tell the CO about problems in person or because residents begin handling more conflicts informally. Monitoring calls for service will help to verify that the CO is doing a good job in the area.

Examples of Quantifiable Problem-Solving Activities for COs:

- Social disorder: number and types of individual and group efforts undertaken by the CO; number of people involved; demographics of participants (e.g., race and income); participation of youth, area businesses, public agencies (e.g., social services), and nonprofit groups (e.g., Salvation Army).

- Physical disorder (beautification): Number and types of individual and group efforts undertaken by the CO; number of people involved; demo- graphics of participants (e.g., race and income); participation of youth, area businesses, public agencies (e.g., code enforcement), and nonprofit groups (e.g., Boy Scouts and Girl Scouts).

- Innovation: documentable incidents where the CO has demonstrated an imaginative approach toward problem solving; specific initiatives, for example, educational, athletic, and social activities for youth and families.

- Teamwork: if the CO works as part of a team with other officers (e.g., motor patrol or narcotics squad), the number of contacts or joint activities; outcomes; time spent; occasions when the CO's role was specifically to protect the other social-service agents or when the CO was a participant in group problem solving.

Source: Adapted from R. Trojanowicz and B. Bucqueroux. 1992. *Toward Development of Meaningful and Effective Performance Evaluations.* East Lansing: National Center for Community Policing, Michigan State University, pp. 23–27.

An integral aspect of community policing is feedback from the community with respect to the perceived needs of citizens and their level of satisfaction with the police. Thus, in community policing, the community also evaluates officers and the department. A number of departments have used community meetings for obtaining such feedback; others have employed door-to-door surveys conducted by officers; and a few with substantial resources (usually provided by grants) have conducted scientific community surveys (Wycoff and Oettmeier 1994). In Madison, Wisconsin, for example, surveys are routinely mailed to a sample of all citizens who have received service from the department in an effort to measure satisfaction and to improve service. Officers may receive evaluations directly from citizens; although the identity of the citizen is not known, the officer receives general information about the type of situation on which the evaluation is based. After reading the evaluation, the officer removes his or her identification from it and gives it to the supervisor. The individual responses are then pooled to examine whether the district as a whole is meeting citizen expectations (Wycoff and Oettmeier 1994).

Rhetoric or Reality: How Much Community Policing Is There?

In practice, there have been at least three community policing approaches used by police departments (Mastrofski, Worden, and Snipes 1995). The first approach, the **broken-windows theory**, stresses police attention to minor crimes and disorder (what has become known as quality-of-life concerns). The second approach, the **community-building strategy**, focuses on crime prevention, victim assistance, and building rapport with racial minorities. The third approach, **problem-oriented policing**, focuses on the underlying causes of crime and disorder and their prevention.

With this apparent shift toward community policing, however, the question remains how much actual community policing is there? This is an important, yet virtually unanswerable question at the moment because so many different definitions and approaches are being used by police departments. As D. H. Bayley has observed:

> Despite the benefits claimed for community policing, programmatic implementation of it has been very uneven. Although widely, almost universally, said to be important, it means different things to different people—public relations campaigns, shop fronts and mini-stations, re-scaled patrol beats, liaison with ethnic groups. . . Neighborhood Watch, foot patrols, patrol-detective teams, and door-to-door visits by police officers. Community policing on the ground often seems less a program than a set of aspirations wrapped in a slogan. . . . It is a trendy phrase spread thinly over customary reality. (1988, p. 225)

In an extensive national survey of 1,606 police executives' perceptions of community policing development in municipal, county police, and sheriff's departments (Wycoff 1995), almost half of the respondents reported that they had either implemented community policing (19 percent) or were in the process of doing so (28 percent). Implementation was most likely to be reported by medium (50 or more personnel) and large (100 or more personnel) departments. Community policing was most prevalent in the West, followed by the South, Midwest, and Northeast. Among departments that had implemented community policing for at least one year, 99 percent reported improved cooperation between citizens and police, 80 percent reported a reduction in citizens' fear of crime, and 62 percent reported fewer crimes against persons. Regarding potential negative consequences, 81 percent of the executives thought that crime might be displaced to an area that was not using community policing, 43 percent believed that responsiveness to calls for service would decline, and 15 percent anticipated an increase in officer or deputy corruption.

The survey further indicated that community policing departments were more likely than other police departments to report the following:

- Permanent neighborhood-based officers or stations.

- Designation of "community" or "neighborhood" officers.

- Foot patrol as a specific assignment of periodic expectation.

- Regularly scheduled meetings with community groups.

- Specific training and interagency involvement in problem identification and resolution.

- Use of regulatory codes to combat drugs and crime.

- Decision-making responsibility tied to geographically defined beat areas.

- Physical decentralization of field services and special units for problem solving and crime prevention.

- Increased citizen participation, including serving as volunteers and on citizen patrols, neighborhood watch programs, and attending a citizen police academy.

It was further discovered that despite support for community policing, no single approach emerged as a model. It was found that the two core components of community policing—community partnerships and problem solving—can be accomplished in a variety of ways. The means selected should fit the community's needs and the department's resources. It should also be recognized that the findings represent the perceptions of police executives and may not reflect actual levels or stages of community policing operations.

The 1997 Bureau of Justice Statistics national survey (Reaves and Goldberg 1999) of 700 large police agencies (over 100 officers) reported that 63 percent of county and 61 percent of municipal agencies had a formally written community policing plan, compared to only 38 percent of sheriff's departments and 33 percent of state police agencies. Approximately 80 percent of county and 79 percent of municipal departments had full-time community policing officers, with an average of 20 such officers. About 66 percent of sheriff's departments had full-time community policing officers, with an average of 11 each. This data suggests that most of these police departments are not in transition toward a "full-fledged" community policing mode, but rather, assign a certain number of specialists to a community policing position.

The BJS survey further indicated that in a large majority of municipal (80 percent) and county (73 percent) departments with 100 or more officers, all new recruits received training in community policing. Less than half of the sheriff's departments (49 percent) and state agencies (41 percent) required all recruits to undergo such training. With respect to in-service training, 91 percent of municipal, 83 percent of county, 79 percent of sheriff's departments, and 57 percent of state agencies, trained at least some of their in-service officers in community policing (with the emphasis most likely on the full-time community policing officers). Finally, nearly two-thirds of larger local police departments (65 percent) formed problem-solving partnerships with community groups, local agencies, or others through written agreements. A small majority (55 percent) also actively encouraged patrol officers to engage in problem-solving projects that utilized community policing concepts.

In another national study of 236 large metropolitan police departments by E. R. Maguire (1997), 44 percent reported that they had adopted community policing, 47 percent were currently in the planning or implementation process, and only 9 percent had no plans to adopt community policing. As Maguire noted, because of federal initiatives promoting community policing, it is likely that many of these "holdouts" will move toward community polic-ing in the near future. How far police departments are actually moving to-ward community policing, however, is another question in search of an an-swer, since there were no significant organizational differences reported among any of the departments in Maguire's study.

Another study of 228 municipal departments in 47 states by J. Zhao and Q. C. Thurman (1997) appeared to have similar results, in that although com-munity policing is primarily service oriented, crime control remained the pri-mary mission of most departments. It was inferred that the transition of po-lice departments from a paramilitary model to community policing is devel-oping at an evolutionary rather than a revolutionary pace in most communi-ties.

In a national study of community policing in nearly 6,000 non-urban po-lice departments serving populations of less than 50,000 (Maguire, Kuhns, Uchida, and Cox 1997), there were significant variations in levels of commu-nity-policing practices with respect to departmental size and geographic re-gion. Larger departments and those in the West practiced a wider range of community-policing activities. Although 80 percent of the departments de-veloped partnerships with other government agencies and 78 percent with schools, 68 percent also participated in antidrug programs; however, only 12 percent had a strategic plan for community policing, only 31 percent pro-vided community-policing training for officers, and only 51 percent met with the community to explain crime prevention techniques.

The federal initiatives noted above refer to the federal funding provided for community-policing officers and programs. For instance, between 1994 and early 1999, the Justice Department's Office of Community Oriented Po-licing Services (COPS) had funded nearly 90,000 new police officer positions throughout the nation (toward a total of 100,000) under the 1994 crime-con-trol act (i.e., the Violent Crime Control and Law Enforcement Act). In addi-tion, the 21st Century Policing Initiative, which builds on COPS, is expected to fund an additional 50,000 new police officers and provide funds for depart-ments to purchase the latest crime-fighting technology ("Clinton . . . for COPS Programs" 1999). Many state governments are also pushing community po-licing through the provision of grants, leadership, training, or some combi-nation thereof. For example, Washington became the first state to establish a mandated program promoting the development of a community policing philosophy by the state's police agencies through training seminars con-ducted by the state Criminal Justice Training Commission ("Washington in COP Push" 1990).

What does all this mean for the development of community policing? Simply that the scope and nature of the community-policing movement is still evolving, sometimes in a haphazard and disjointed manner, often as a specialized or independent part of the department. Although it is not possible to get a valid account of the number of police organizations *actually using* community policing, in general it appears that the field is unmistakably *evolving* in this direction—although "full-fledged" community policing is not being implemented as quickly as some in policing would suggest. We should recognize, however, that community policing *is* a *revolutionary* concept; con-sequently, any change process must be studied and interpreted from this per-spective—that is, it will not be a quick process. Imagine for a moment what the response of social workers might be if we asked them to become, in large part, crime fighters. In a similar vein, community models of policing—the role, the skills required, and the culture— are quite different from traditional models of policing.

It is too early to tell whether community policing in the long run will prove to be more desirable than other models of policing. For example, the so-called failure of the legalistic model was more the result of political assessments than of objective analysis. Likewise, support for community policing is based more on politics than on systematically acquired data; although it should be recognized that a good amount of evaluation research on community-policing programs is currently ongoing, much of it supported by federal funding. It is likely, as more is learned, that community policing will be modified in some manner. On the one hand, some cities that have experimented with it have already de-emphasized it in favor of methods associated with the legalistic model and a zero-tolerance policy (i.e., more citations, arrests, field interrogations, rapid response, and use of specialized aggressive enforcement teams). On the other hand, because of the ambiguous nature of community policing, some police managers prefer a more concrete, yet contemporary, label for police activity and are adopting the phrase *problem-solving* policing.

Whatever changes occur in community policing, they are more likely to be related to activities or programs (e.g., reduced social service, foot patrol, and problem solving) than to the overall philosophy. Although not all citizens want to discuss, and have an impact on, the police role, it is clear that some do. To the extent that the police have increasingly accepted the right of the public to have a meaningful participative role in police work, community policing is most likely here to stay.

Community Policing and Crime Prevention

The expansion of the police role in community policing to include partnerships with the community, through governmental, social, and educational agencies, significantly expands the benefits in protecting neighborhoods from crime and fear of crime. In other words, through the co-production of public safety with the community, crime prevention is no longer perceived solely as the responsibility of the police. Described below are several approaches to crime prevention that are closely aligned with a community policing model; each of these approaches may overlap to some degree and benefit from the others.

Crime Prevention and Police Legitimacy

One of the promising approaches to crime prevention is based on the study of procedural justice and suggests that police legitimacy may help prevent crime (Sherman 1997). **Police legitimacy** is the public confidence in the police as fair and equitable (Eck and Rosenbaum 1994). For instance, T. Tyler (1990) found a correlation across a large sample of Chicago citizens between perceived legitimacy of police and willingness to obey the law. The legitimacy of the police was measured by citizen evaluations of how they were treated in previous encounters. Perhaps the strongest support for this concept can be found in the reanalysis of the Milwaukee Domestic Violence Experiment (Paternoster, Brame, Bachman, and Sherman 1997) in which it was found that if police acted in a procedurally fair and respectful manner when arresting assault suspects, the rate of subsequent domestic violence was significantly lower than when they did not. It appears that police legitimacy through community policing can have an impact on crime and should be given increased consideration. For example, in a review of six community-policing evaluations (Skogan 1994), all showed positive or improved perception of police in the experimental areas, and in a review of Chicago's community policing program (see chapter 5) there was at least one positive impact on crime in every district (Skogan and Hartnett 1997).

Crime Prevention and Community ·

Community crime prevention is based on the assumption that if a community can be changed, so can the behavior of those who live there. Attempts to change communities include the following: (1) organizing the community to improve and strengthen relationships among residents to encourage them to take preventive precautions, and to obtain more political and financial resources; (2) changing building and neighborhood design to improve both public and police surveillance, which improves guardianship; (3) improving the appearance of an area to decrease the perception that it is a receptive target for crime; and (4) developing activities and programs that provide a more structured and supervised environment (e.g., recreation programs).

Although community crime prevention is closely associated with the community policing movement, the evidence of its effectiveness is limited, in part, because of the lack of understanding of social relationships within neighborhoods and how crime is influenced by both the broader community and societal trends. Perhaps the most promising approach to responding to high-crime areas is to focus on the relationship between the poverty of youth and crime. High-crime areas have a large number of criminals and victims in comparison to other areas; consequently, while developing programs to support, socialize, and supervise youth, it is also important to protect the "fearful, vulnerable, and victimized" (Hope 1995).

One interesting program currently being developed by the Australian Federal Police is an alternative procedure to prosecuting juveniles known as **community-accountability conferences** (Sherman 1997). The program is used only in cases in which the offender admits guilt and the victim is willing to attend a mixed conference, made up of offenders, victims, families, and friends. The conference is led by a trained police officer who focuses the discussion on what happened, the amount of harm caused, and how the harm may be repaired. The officer tries to ensure that all involved, but especially victims, have a say. An agreement for repaying the cost of the crime to the victim is reached; in cases where there is no settlement, prosecution results. Some research on interviews with victims and offenders indicates that the procedure greatly increases respect for police and a perception of justice, regardless of the outcomes. "This method may turn out to have long-term effects on police legitimacy in the eyes of both juvenile offenders and their families, which could in turn reduce crime" (Sherman 1997, 8–30).

Crime Prevention Through Environmental Design

❖ ❖ ❖ ❖

The basic principles of **crime prevention through environmental design (CPTED)** include target hardening, where access to neighborhoods and buildings is controlled and where specific areas are surveilled to reduce opportunities for crime to occur, and territorial reinforcement, where a sense of security is increased in settings where people live and work through activities that encourage informal control of the environment. CPTED overlaps with community policing by localizing police services, collaborating with other city agencies (e.g., parks or utility departments) to resolve problems, and maintaining regular police-citizen communication about neighborhood problems. Frequently, both community policing and CPTED use the SARA problem-solving model (described earlier) as a key ingredient of their approach (Fleissner and Heinzlemann 1996). Inside Policing 3.6 describes some of the strategies that may be applied through CPTED.

Inside Policing 3.6
Crime Prevention Through Environmental Design: Strategies and Trends

What Police and Residents Can Do

Police departments, community residents, and local officials all have roles to play in implementing a comprehensive CPTED and community policing strategy to promote public safety in private neighborhoods, business areas, and public housing.

Police can do the following:

- Conduct security surveys for residents and provide security improvements such as adequate lighting and locks.

- Conduct patrols of parks and other public spaces to eliminate crime and drug use.

- Use their substations to inform residents of high-risk locations in the neighborhood.

- Work with urban planners and architects to review the designs and plans in order to enhance community security.

- Prepare educational materials for building owners and managers to deal with problem tenants and improve the livability and security of rental units. These materials are useful because they address not only the design of the physical environment but how the environment can be more effectively managed to improve safety.

- Control traffic flow to reduce the use of streets by criminals and increase neighborhood cohesion and resident interaction. Streets can be closed or traffic diverted to create residential enclaves that give residents greater control of their environment.

Residents can do the following:

- Engage in cleanup programs to remove trash or graffiti.

- Carry out programs to improve the appearance, safety, and use of public spaces.

- Conduct their own patrols to identify neighborhood problems.

- Join an organized block watch program.

Specific crime prevention activities include:

- Security in parks. Parks can be refurbished, lighting can be installed, and opening and closing times can be scheduled to improve security. Adopt-a-park programs can be used to involve residents in cleaning up trash and litter and providing information to police about illegal activities being carried out in recreational areas. Recreational events ☞

can be scheduled to increase the community's informal social control of these places.

- Building regulations. Local government can be encouraged to use building codes as well as inspection and enforcement powers to increase environmental security. The owners of deteriorated or abandoned buildings can be required to repair, secure, or demolish them. Provisions related to security can also be incorporated into the city building code. These provisions include target-hardening tactics (e.g., better locks, strengthening of doors, and better lighting) as well as security standards for the design of the structure and site.

Civil Remedies

Civil actions can be used against building owners or tenants to control criminal activity or the inappropriate use of property. These actions may include the following:

- Obtaining title to abandoned property by community-improvement associations.

- Using nuisance abatement along with inspections by public works, building, fire, housing, or utility authorities to control criminal behavior or drug use in specific buildings or settings.

- Encouraging leases that contain language that controls illegal activities of tenants.

- Enforcing liquor laws to control violence and disorderly behavior around bars or liquor stores (especially at closing times).

- Using anti-trespassing laws to control unwanted loitering.

Trends

One general trend has been for CPTED and community-policing strategies to reinforce each other as they focus on comprehensive problem solving, the promotion of working relationships with the community, and the development of education and orientation programs that can assist residential and business groups as they address specific neighborhood problems—especially those dealing with crime and the environment.

The development of these initiatives affects various factors, such as the level of communication and cooperation among police, city, staff, and residents; the type, amount, and use of community education and orientation programs; and the methods by which crime-prevention programs are described, measured, and evaluated. Currently, these factors apply more to law enforcement agencies because modifying a community-policing model may require changes of significant magnitude. As CPTED evolves, however, its extension from just looking at the manmade environment to looking at how the natural setting is used and managed will also entail significant change for other public agencies involved in promoting safer and more livable communities.

Source: Adapted from D. Fleissner and F. Heinzlemann. 1996. "Crime Prevention Through Environmental Design and Community Policing." *Research in Action*. Washington, D.C.: National Institute of Justice, pp. 3–4.

In trying to build a more crime-free environment, some cities are requiring police input on building designs. In Tempe, Arizona, for example, an ordinance was passed that requires police approval of any commercial building, park, or residential housing development built in the city. Tempe police officers review construction blueprints and visit building sites to ensure that crime-prevention features are built into the designs; officers address issues such as parking lot locations, lighting, and the placement of plants and counters in stores. The goal is to provide employees and residents with a better view of their surroundings and to reduce places where criminals may hide. Getting police involved in building designs for crime prevention is similar to the long-established practice of the city's relying on fire department officials to help determine building codes for fire prevention purposes ("Building a More Crime-Free Environment" 1998).

CPTED is becoming a well-used practice as communities try to determine innovative ways to reduce crime. Police departments in eight of the nation's 10 largest cities have followed Tempe's lead to some degree, including those in New York, Los Angeles, Houston, Detroit, Dallas, Phoenix, San Antonio, and San Diego. For instance, in Los Angeles, police officers have input into any development going up in the city, but their suggestions, unlike those in Tempe, are not binding. Suggestions made by LAPD officers include landscaping with smaller bushes to improve visibility; using curved walls as opposed to sharp edges, which create hiding places; and locating parking lots within plain sight of building occupants. In San Diego, which is moving toward establishing an ordinance similar to Tempe's, officers have been working with city planners regarding building design, but, as in Los Angeles, their suggestions are not yet binding ("Building a More Crime-Free Environment" 1998).

Public Health and Crime Prevention

Where the criminal justice system tends to view violent crime as a problem of public order, public health officials consider violent crime to be intentional injuries that are part of the health problems in a community. Such officials are less concerned about the intentions (the moral culpability) of the offender than they are about identifying risk factors indicative of violence, including "persons at greater risk of disease or injury and the places, times, and other circumstances that are associated with increased risk" (Moore 1995, p.224). In general, risk factors can be grouped into three categories: structural or cultural, criminogenic commodities, and situational. Structural or cultural risk factors include poverty and violence on television. Criminogenic commodities include when and under what circumstances guns, alcohol, and drugs are available. Situational risk factors include "festering, unresolved disputes" between couples, spouses, tenants and landlords, and gangs (Moore 1995).

Gradually, the police are learning more about the strategies or combination of strategies that are the most effective in responding to crime, citizen fear of crime, and citizen attitudes. As this body of knowledge grows, and as more police executives become aware of and apply this knowledge, the authors believe that the police, in cooperation with the public, will be able to substantially improve their impact on crime.

Summary

The community policing model, based on the belief that citizens and police should work together to identify and solve community problems, is transforming the field. Community policing is a philosophy that includes a number of different types of programs and methods. Although it has been adopted in some form by many departments, in practice there is still uncertainty over what it actually is and how effective it may ultimately be.

Team policing, the precursor to community policing, was developed largely as a response to urban unrest in the 1960s. From this crisis, it became clear that the police lacked a responsiveness to, and understanding of, community needs and expectations. In the late 1960s, the police began to reorganize the patrol force into specific neighborhood teams with the dual purpose of improving police services to the community and increasing job satisfaction of the officers. For the most part, team-policing efforts were unsuccessful; attempting to switch from a highly centralized, authoritarian structure to a decentralized, democratic approach, in a relatively short period of time, proved to be too difficult an undertaking. Nevertheless, team policing provided the catalyst for community policing, which accepted the right of the community to have a participative role in police work. This role has led to the concept of the co-production of public safety, where the public shares some responsibility with the police in responding to crime, disorder, and related problems. It is believed that this closer working relationship with the public will not only help to improve police-community relations but also help control local crime and disorder.

Discussion Questions

1. Define the broken-windows theory of crime; how does this theory relate to aggressive law enforcement?

2. What is strategic management and how can it be applied to the police?

3. Discuss the meaning and practice of the co-production of public safety.

4. Describe the purpose of team policing and common operational elements. What are the major reasons team policing had only limited success?

5. Initially, community and problem-oriented policing were viewed as two distinct approaches; describe the emphasis that was placed on each approach.

6. Describe Goldstein's three key elements to problem solving and the problem-solving process known as SARA.

7. Describe the characteristics of community policing and give examples of programs.

8. Based on the answer to the above question, make up your own definition of community policing.

9. Discuss the status of community policing today and what you believe its future will be.

10. Briefly define CPTED and provide several examples of how it can be used in the community.

References

Bayley, D. H. 1988. "Community Policing: A Report from the Devil's Advocate." In J. R. Greene and S. D. Mastrofski (eds.), *Community Policing: Rhetoric or Reality*, pp. 225–237. New York: Praeger.

Brown, L. P. 1989. "Community Policing: A Practical Guide for Police Officials," *Perspectives on Policing*. Pamphlet No. 12. Washington, D.C.: National Institute of Justice.

"Building a More Crime-Free Environment." 1998. *Law Enforcement News*. November 15: 5.

Bureau of Justice Assistance. 1993. "The System Approach to Crime and Drug Prevention: A Path to Community Policing," *Bulletin 1*, September.

Caiden, G. E. 1977. *Police Revitalization*. Lexington, MA: D.C. Heath.

Center for Research on Criminal Justice. 1975. *Iron Fist in the Velvet Glove*. Berkeley, CA: Center for Research on Criminal Justice.

"Clinton Pushes $1.3 Billion More for COPS Programs." 1999. *Law Enforcement News*, February 14: 7.

Eck, J. E., and Rosenbaum, D. P. 1994. "The New Police Order: Effectiveness, Equity, and Efficiency in Community Policing." In D. P. Rosenbaum (ed.), *The Challenge of Community Policing: Testing the Promises*, pp. 3–23. Thousand Oaks, CA: Sage Publications.

Eck, J. E., and Spelman, W. 1987. "Problem-Solving, Problem-Oriented Policing in Newport News," *Research in Brief*. Washington, D.C.: National Institute of Justice.

Fleissner, D., and Heinzlemann, F. 1996. "Crime Prevention Through Environmental Design and Community Policing." *Research in Action*. Washington, D.C.: National Institute of Justice.

Frank, J., Brandl, S. G., and Watkins, R. C. 1997. "The Content of Community Policing: A Comparison of the Daily Activities of Community and 'Beat' Officers." *Policing: An International Journal of Police Strategies & Management* 20: 716–728.

Geller, W. A., and Swanger, G. 1995. *Managing Innovation in Policing: The Untapped Potential of the Middle Manager*. Washington, D.C.: Police Executive Research Forum.

Goldstein, H. 1979. "Improving Policing: A Problem-Oriented Approach." *Crime and Delinquency* 25: 236–258.

——. 1987. "Toward Community-Oriented Policing: Potential, Basic Requirements, and Threshold Questions." *Crime and Delinquency*, 33: 6–30.

——. 1990. *Problem-Oriented Policing*. Philadelphia: Temple University Press.

Hope, T. 1995. "Community Crime Prevention." In M. Tonry and D. P. Farrington (eds.), *Building a Safer Society: Strategic Approaches to Crime Prevention*, pp. 22–89. Chicago: University of Chicago Press.

Kelling, G. L., and Moore, M. H. 1988. "The Evolving Strategy of Policing." *Perspectives on Policing*. Washington, D.C.: National Institute of Justice.

Maguire, E. R. 1997. "Structural Change in Large Municipal Police Organizations During the Community Policing Era." *Justice Quarterly* 14: 547–576.

Maguire, E. R., Kuhns, J. B., Uchida, C. D., and Cox, S. 1997. "Patterns of Community Policing in Nonurban America." *Journal of Research in Crime and Delinquency* 34: 368–394.

Mastrofski, S. D., Worden, R. E., and Snipes, J. B. 1995. "Law Enforcement in a Time of Community Policing. *Criminology* 33: 539–561.

Moore, M. H. 1995. "Public Health and Criminal Justice Approaches to Prevention." In M. Tonry and D. P. Farrington, *Building a Safer Society: Strategic Approaches to Crime Prevention*, pp. 237–262. Chicago: University of Chicago Press.

Moore, M. H. and Stephens, D. W. 1991. *The Strategic Management of Police Departments: Beyond Command and Control*. Washington, D.C.: Police Executive Research Forum, p. 74.

Moore, M. H. and Trojanowicz, R. C. 1988. "Corporate Strategies for Policing." *Perspectives on Policing*. Washington, D.C.: National Institute of Justice.

"One Less Problem When It Comes to Problem-Solving," 1998. *Law Enforcement News*, April 30: 1, 9.

Osborne, D., and Gaebler, T. 1993. *Reinventing Government*. New York: Penguin.

❖ ❖ ❖ ❖

Paternoster, R., Brame, R., Bachman, R., and Sherman, L. W. 1997. "Do Fair Procedures Matter? The Effect of Procedural Justice on Spouse Assault." *Law and Society Review* 3: 163–204.

Police Executive Research Forum. 1996. *Themes and Variations in Community Policing: Case Studies in Community Policing.* Washington, D.C.: Police Executive Research Forum.

Reaves, B. A. and Goldberg, A. L. 1999. *Law Enforcement Management and Administrative Statistics, 1997: Data for Individual State and Local Agencies With 100 or More Officers.* Washington, D.C.: Bureau of Justice Statistics.

Rosenbaum, D. P., Lurigio, A. J., and Davis, R. C. 1998. *The Prevention of Crime: Social and Situational Strategies*. Belmont, CA: West/Wadsworth Publishing Co.

Scannell, J. 1988. *Community Foot Patrol Officer (CFPO) Guidelines and Procedures.* Towson, MD: Baltimore County Police Department.

Schwartz, A. T., and Clarren, S. N. 1977. *The Cincinnati Team Policing Experiment: A Summary Report.* Washington, D.C.: Police Foundation.

Sherman. L. W. 1997. "Policing for Crime Prevention." In L. W. Sherman, D. Gottfredson, D. MacKenzie, J. Eck, P. Reuter, and S. Bushway (eds.), *Preventing Crime: What Works, What Doesn't, What's Promising,* pp. 818–58. Washington, D.C.: National Institute of Justice.

Sherman, L. W., Milton, C. H., and Kelley, T. V. 1973. *Team Policing: Seven Case Studies.* Washington, D.C.: Police Foundation.

Skogan, W. G. 1994. "The Impact of Community Policing on Neighborhood Residents: A Cross-Site Analysis." In D. P. Rosenbaum (ed.), *The Challenge of Community Policing: Testing the Promises,* pp. 167–181. Thousand Oaks, CA: Sage Publications.

Skogan, W. G. and Hartnett, S. M. 1997. *Community Policing, Chicago Style.* New York: Oxford University Press.

Stevens, D. W. 1990. "Policing in the Future." *American Journal of Police* 9: 151–169.

Trojanowicz, R., and Bucqueroux, B. 1992. *Toward Development of Meaningful and Effective Performance Evaluations.* East Lansing: Michigan State University, National Center for Community Policing.

Tyler, T. 1990. *Why People Obey the Law.* New Haven: Yale University Press.

"Washington in COP Push," 1990. *Law Enforcement News,* January 15: 1, 6.

Wilson, J. Q., and Kelling, G. L. 1982. "Police and Neighborhood Safety: Broken Windows." *Atlantic Monthly,* March: 29–38.

Wycoff, M. A. 1995. *Community Policing Strategies*. Washington, D.C.: National Institute of Justice.

Wycoff, M. A. and Oettmeier, T. N. 1994. *Evaluating Patrol Officer Performance Under Community Policing: The Houston Experience.* Washington, D.C.: National Institute of Justice.

Zhao, J. and Thurman, Q. C. 1997. "Community Policing: Where Are We Now?" *Crime and Delinquency* 43: 345–357.

For a listing of websites appropriate to the content of this chapter, see "Suggested Websites for Further Study" (p. xv). ✦

Part II

Police Administration

Police Management

Chapter Outline

Key Terms	
arrest rates	fraternal organizations
bureaucracy	generalists
centralization	goals
chain of command	individual influences
classical principles of organization	job redesign
closed system	leading
Compstat	management
contingency management	manager's culture
controlling	open system
crime clearance rate	organization chart
crime index	organization design
decentralization	organizational influences
democratic model	organizing
environmental influences	paramilitary model
exceptional clearance	PPUs
flat structure	planning

Key Terms (continued)	
police union	systems theory
private world of policing	tall structure
public world of policing	TQM
socialization	Uniform Crime Reports
specialization	victim survey
street cop's culture	zero-tolerance policing
supervision	

Discussions in the chapters in part I indicated that the process of policing a democratic society is complex. Indeed, because of this complexity, a police department is probably one of the most difficult public institutions to manage effectively. Consequently, it is important to have a fundamental understanding of both the historical and present-day processes used in managing police departments. Not only are these processes critical to how the police operate and behave in society, but they also contribute to the type of individuals selected to become officers—the subject of chapter 6.

Management is directing individuals to achieve organizational goals in an efficient and effective manner. The functions carried out by police managers include organizing, leading, planning, and controlling; how well these functions are performed determines, to a large degree, how successful a department will be.

The Managerial Process

Although managers perform each of the functions described above, the time involved in each one varies according to the manager's level in the department. For instance, people at higher levels, such as assistant chiefs, spend a greater proportion of their time in organizing and planning; those at lower levels, such as sergeants, spend more time on **supervision**, which focuses primarily on leading and controlling. The time spent in various functions is also influenced by the size of the department. In a small police department, for instance, a sergeant may function both as an assistant chief and as a supervisor. Each managerial function is briefly described below.

Organizing is the process of arranging personnel and physical resources to carry out plans and accomplish goals and objectives. Organizational design or structure, job design, group working arrangements, and individual work assignments are subject to the organizing process. Although all managers are involved in organizing, once again the degree and scope differ, depending on their level within the department. While the patrol supervisor is more concerned with work assignments, the chief is more concerned with the overall distribution of personnel and physical resources.

Leading is motivating others to perform various tasks that will contribute to the accomplishment of goals and objectives. Motivating others is a difficult and complex process, especially in civil-service organizations, where managers have far less control over salaries and pay incentives than in the private sector. Accordingly, police managers must rely more on internal re-

Police executive must provide a leadership role within the community, as seen here addressing a town meeting. (Photo: Mark C. Ide)

wards to motivate employees, such as job satisfaction and feelings of accomplishment. This situation suggests that job design is a key ingredient in motivating police personnel (more on this later). It should be noted that the leadership role for top-level managers can also encompass managing the relationship between the police and the community, as well as other important organizations, including criminal justice and government agencies.

Planning is the process of preparing for the future by setting goals and objectives and developing courses of action for accomplishing them. The courses of action involve such activities as determining mission and value statements, conducting research, identifying strategies and methods, developing policies and procedures, and formulating budgets. Although all managers engage in planning, once again the scope and nature of the activity differ considerably, depending on the managerial level within the department. For instance, while a patrol supervisor may develop work schedules and operating activities for the upcoming week, police chiefs may plan activities and changes for the upcoming year. In general, the higher the managerial level, the broader the scope of planning and the longer the time frame for the plan.

Controlling is the process by which managers determine how the quality and the quantity of departmental systems and services can be improved, if goals and objectives are being accomplished, if operations are consistent with plans, and if officers follow departmental policies and procedures. Both efficiency (relationship between resources and outputs) and effectiveness (degree to which goals and objectives are accomplished) are key concepts in this phase of management. If goals or objectives are not realized, or plans, policies, and procedures are not being followed, managers must determine why and take action. Controlling may be the most troublesome managerial function because it may be difficult to determine why performance failures occur and what action to take to improve or correct them. For example, police corruption and brutality continue to be serious problems, despite frequent attempts to determine their causes and correct them.

As noted above, managers at various levels in the department perform their functions differently. Figure 4.1 depicts the various hierarchical levels found in medium to large police departments. Such organizational structures are termed pyramids because the number of personnel decreases as one goes up in the hierarchy (i.e., there are fewer at the top). At the same time, this diminishing group receives increased power, authority, and rewards.

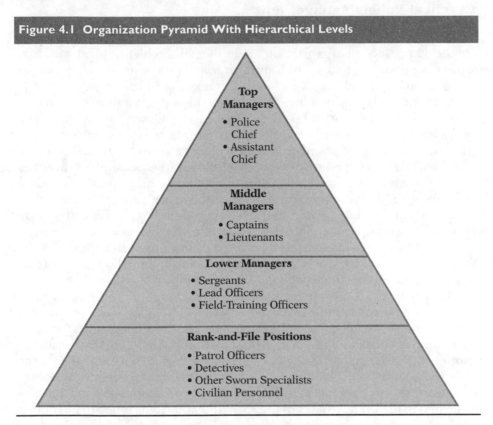

Figure 4.1 Organization Pyramid With Hierarchical Levels

Top Managers
- Police Chief
- Assistant Chief

Middle Managers
- Captains
- Lieutenants

Lower Managers
- Sergeants
- Lead Officers
- Field-Training Officers

Rank-and-File Positions
- Patrol Officers
- Detectives
- Other Sworn Specialists
- Civilian Personnel

In general, as shown in Figure 4.1, four separate levels of activities exist in larger organizations; smaller organizations may have only two or perhaps three levels. This hierarchical structure is known as the **chain of command,** where the higher the position, the greater the power, authority, and influence. The activities of personnel at each level are as follows: *top managers* conduct overall goal formulation and make policy decisions regarding allocation of resources; *middle managers* formulate objectives and plans for implementing decisions from above and coordinate activities from below; *lower managers* implement decisions made at higher levels and coordinate and direct the work of employees at the lowest level of the organization; and *rank-and-file personnel* carry out specific tasks.

The following discussion of the development of police management theory has relevance to how police departments have been traditionally structured and managed, and what impact contemporary developments are having on police management.

The Development of Police Management

The theory and practice of police management have evolved through three major developmental perspectives—classical, behavioral, and present-day. Each of these perspectives and its impact on police management are described below.

Classical Police Management

The early writers on police management emphasized what is known as a classical approach to organization, including a rigid hierarchical structure, strong centralized control, and authoritarian leadership styles. A cornerstone of this approach was Max Weber's concept of **bureaucracy**, a term he coined at the end of the nineteenth century to identify characteristics that organizations needed to operate on a rational basis. Following the introduction of the bureaucratic model, a number of writers started to develop what have become known as **classical principles of organization**, which were believed to be universal. Some of Weber's administrative principles that reflect this approach include **specialization** (division of work); authority and responsibility (right to command and require obedience); discipline (necessary for effectiveness); unity of command (employees are to receive orders from only one superior); scalar chain (hierarchy of authority); **centralization** (the extent to which decision making is retained by the top organizational levels); and small spans of control (the number of subordinates who report directly to a supervisor—the smaller the number, the greater the control).

Early police theorists, in an attempt to create a more professional police force, placed great emphasis on the classical principles. The result was a highly bureaucratic structure, managed and organized along military lines in an attempt to insulate the police from partisan politics. This **paramilitary model** emphasized a legalistic approach and authoritarian managerial practices intended to control officers' behavior in order to improve crime control and lessen corrupt practices. Influential writers promoting these ideals first appeared in the United States in the early 1900s and continued to be influential into the early 1950s. Some editions of the textbooks of these classical writers continued to appear into the 1980s and even the early 1990s and still have an influence on police managerial practices. In general, the classical police theorists differed little in their approaches for improving the police. For example, L. Fuld's *Police Administration* (1909) emphasized the need to eliminate partisan politics from police management; clearly defined police duties (including the elimination of "non-police" functions); and stressed strong supervision and discipline with clear-cut lines of authority, specialization, and improved selection and training of personnel. R. Fosdick, in his study of 72 American cities in *American Police Systems* (1915), discovered that police departments had not defined their function, had no established purpose, and clearly lacked capable leadership.

A work that had a major impact on police reform was B. Smith's *Police Systems in the United States* (1940). While addressing many of the earlier problems that had been identified, he also placed increased emphasis on his belief that not enough attention had been paid to the organizational structure and managerial practices of police departments. In a later edition, Smith

(1960) continued to emphasize that police departments could be significantly improved if they were properly designed and managed according to the "principles of organization," which had won wide acceptance in military and industrial circles. Another significant work that affected police practice was O. W. Wilson's *Police Administration* (1950), followed by later editions with R. C. McLaren as coauthor (Wilson and McLaren 1977). The early editions became known as the "bible" of police management, and the prescriptions set forth were, and to some extent still are, followed. Like Smith, Wilson and McLaren suggested that an effective crime-control organization should be designed and managed according to "fundamental" organizational principles, especially with respect to the chain of command and hierarchy of authority.

The legalistic model of policing relies heavily on classical theory for the development of organization and management. The principles of this approach were compatible with the aims of police reformers who wanted to reduce the politics commonly associated with police work by making police behavior more objective or bureaucratic and less personal in the political sense. Along with this bureaucratic approach to policing came an increased emphasis on law enforcement as the primary function of the police. This emphasis led to the police being judged primarily on their ability to control crime. (Such an approach may be resurfacing, see the section "Criticisms of the Paramilitary Design".)

Behavioral Police Management

Beginning in the early 1970s police management theorists began attacking the classical approach, with its emphasis on bureaucracy and hierarchical structure, authoritarian managerial practices, and narrow view of the police role. In line with the increased behavioral research (i.e., the scientific study of human behavior) of the 1950s and 1960s, which placed greater emphasis on worker participation and job satisfaction, these writers stressed a more flexible and democratic organizational model, along with a recognition of the complex nature of the police role.

By the 1960s, a considerable amount of behavioral research had also been completed on what police actually do on the job, indicating that the majority of police work was not directly related to law enforcement (20 percent or less), but rather to maintaining order and providing social services (e.g., see Bercall 1970; Cumming, Cumming, and Edell 1965; Goldstein 1968; Parnas 1967; and J. Q. Wilson 1968). Perhaps just as important, it was becoming clear that the police role was broader and more *complex* than many had originally suspected. This research provided the impetus for a new perspective on police work by suggesting that adherence to a legalistic and technical approach to the job would not be effective. In short, effective policing required qualified personnel who could *use discretion wisely* to deal with a wide range of complex problems and situations.

These findings had serious implications for the well-entrenched paramilitary model. As E. Bittner noted, "The core of the police mandate is profoundly incompatible with the military posture. On balance, the military bureaucratic organization of the police is a serious handicap" (1970, p. 51). Bittner viewed the proper use of discretion as central to the professional development of the police role, and he believed that overreliance on regulations and bureaucratic routine seriously inhibited such development. Furthermore, he suggested that although the paramilitary model helped to secure internal discipline, it continued to hinder the development of the police role, because "recognition is given for doing well *in* the department, not *outside* where all the real duties are located" (pp. 54–55). In other words, attention to a neat appearance and conformance to bureaucratic routine were more highly regarded than work methods and performance in the community (i.e., interacting and dealing with the public).

In response to these criticisms, J. E. Angell (1971) proposed a **democratic model** of policing, which is not hierarchical and has no formal ranks or supervisors. Police officers are generalists who work in teams and have considerable flexibility in work assignments; they specialize only when the need arises. The teams are expected to work closely with the communities they serve in solving problems. Such an organizational model emphasizes a broad service role for the police and is concerned about employee job satisfaction. Although this model was never adopted, parts of it were representative of the team policing approach of the early 1970s, as well as today's community policing model. Along these same lines, H. Goldstein (1977) suggested that the organizational climate in police departments must change if the objective is to retain highly qualified (and educated) officers and thus operate effectively in a democratic society. Officers should be more involved in policy making and in determining methods of operation; they should be able to realize their "full potential" in ways other than promotion. Although Goldstein agrees that a movement toward a more collegial model is in order, he does not believe that a police department should be run as a democracy. He emphasizes that some situations, such as mobilizing a large number of officers to deal with an emergency, will always require authoritarian management practices. What is called for, according to Goldstein, "is not a substitution of some radical new style of management, but instead, a gradual movement away from the extremely authoritarian climate that currently pervades police agencies toward a more democratic form of organization" (p. 264).

The "extremely authoritarian climate" noted by Goldstein had become a common characteristic of many police departments by the 1960s. The police were criticized for discriminatory behavior and ineffectiveness in responding to crime, and they were also considered to be using inappropriate management practices. It was suggested that there was even a connection between authoritarian management practices and authoritarian police behavior. Consequently, the knowledge gained from the behavioral science research of the period gradually began to influence the police and help them to understand the importance of increased employee involvement in decision making, of recognizing a broader police role, and of working in partnerships with the community. However, this new knowledge and the required managerial skills were not always readily embraced by the police, and in some instances are still not.

Modern Police Management

The increased level of sophistication and findings from behavioral science research led to the development of systems theory and contingency theory and the movement toward quality management. These developments allowed not only for improved managerial practices, but for an understanding of the importance of community relationships to the police.

Conceptually, **systems theory** means that all parts of a system (organization) are interrelated and dependent on one another. The importance of applying systems theory to police departments is that it allows managers to understand that any changes made in their unit will have a corresponding impact on other units. Thus, police managers should continually be in contact with one another to make sure that the activities of their units are in agreement with the overall needs and goals of the department.

Figure 4.2 illustrates the interrelated and dependent nature of several subsystems (divisions) within a police department—depicted by the two-way directional arrows—indicating that the actions of any part of a subsystem affect and, in turn, are affected by the other parts of the system. In this figure, the impacts of the training, communications, and patrol divisions on each other are depicted. For instance, if a department decided—for purposes of increased safety and limited officer liability—to adopt a more restrictive pursuit policy, this decision would have a significant impact not only on how officers are trained but also on communications (e.g., dispatching) and patrol (e.g., when to pursue) as well. In other words, in order to implement effectively such an important policy change, all three divisions would need to alter their policies, which, in turn, would have an impact on each of the other's operational practices.

Police managers should be aware that systems can be viewed as either open or closed. An **open system** interacts with, and adapts to, its environment; a **closed system** does not. In general, all organizations interact with their environment to some degree, but the degree of interaction varies greatly. Essentially, those systems that are more open function more effec-

Figure 4.2 Police Organization as a System

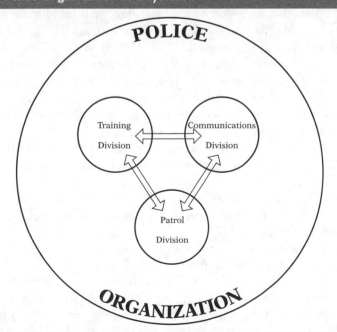

tively because of their environmental adaptability. The environment for police departments is essentially the community in which they operate; those departments that are relatively more open are more effective because they are aware of community needs and expectations and thus can adapt their practices accordingly. In the past, a lack of interaction with the environment, and thus a lack of understanding of community concerns, has led to serious problems in police-community relations. The early development of the community-policing model and, more specifically, the team-policing experiments, were the first serious attempts to involve citizens in identifying and solving crime and related problems in the community.

A complicating factor in this interaction between the police and the community is that a "single" community or constituency does not exist. Instead, in any particular jurisdiction served by the police, there are generally many different "communities," including people of varying ethnic, religious, class, or sexual orientation. Each community will undoubtedly have different and sometimes conflicting expectations concerning the police. Consequently, a department may need to operate differently in different areas within the same jurisdiction.

The police must also recognize that they are part of the criminal justice system and that their actions will have an impact on, and be affected by, the court and correctional subsystems. For example, if the police increase their number of arrests, an obvious impact will be felt by the courts and eventually by prisons and jails. Conversely, policy changes by the courts, such as rules of evidence, and by correctional institutions, such as early-release programs, ultimately will affect the police as well. Thus, the police need to adapt to changing conditions within the criminal justice system, as well as in the community at large. If police departments are not managed from an open-systems perspective, they cannot adapt to changing environmental influences and forces and thus will be ineffective, or certainly less effective, in their levels of operation. When this happens, the department will inevitably be forced to change, as external critics make demands that ultimately cannot be ignored. This point has been supported by J. Zhao's (1996) study of 228 police departments, in which he found that changes toward innovative community policing strategies were more likely to be forced on departments by external environmental demands (e.g., affirmative action programs and community makeup), rather than by consciously chosen internal considerations.

Two additional approaches are crucial to modern police theory: contingency management and total quality management (TQM). While neither of these approaches can be considered as distinct management theories, they are both highly relevant to the managerial process. **Contingency management** is based on open-systems theory and recognizes that there are many internal and external factors that influence organizational behavior. Because these factors differ according to different organizational circumstances, there is no one "best" way to organize and manage diverse types of police departments. The underlying theme for contingency management is that *it all depends on the particular situation.* For example, why does a certain type of leadership work in one type of a department but not in other types or in one part of a department but not in other parts? The answer is simply because situations differ. The task for managers then is to try to determine in which situations and at what times certain methods and techniques are the most effective.

In the late 1970s, R. R. Roberg (1979) applied contingency management to policing. He emphasized contingency concepts and the necessity of identifying *both* internal and external variables that affect police departmental behavior. Accordingly, such factors as the complex nature of the role, increasing educational levels of employees, and the relatively unstable nature of the environment (e.g., changing laws, cultural diversity, political influences) must be considered in attempting to determine the most effective police management methods. It has become obvious that when such factors are considered, "many of the simplistic classical prescriptions which have been applied to police organization design are clearly inadequate" (p. 190). It was concluded that a less bureaucratic, centralized design was necessary for police to perform effectively.

Total quality management was developed in Japan in an effort to help revitalize Japanese industries following World War II. The foundation for this approach lies in *quality-control* techniques and the process of *continuous improvement*. This management process helped turn around the entire Japanese industry, in which "Made in Japan" had become a symbol for inferior products, to become synonymous with the highest-quality products in the world. This impressive about-face resulted in a small nation—devastated by war—becoming a major economic power. Much of the credit for Japan's stunning turnaround goes to W. Edwards Deming (1986), whose work with quality efforts was so highly revered that today the Deming Prize is regarded as the highest honor for Japanese quality and improvement.

Total quality management (TQM), or quality management, is a customer-oriented approach that emphasizes human resources and quantitative methods in an attempt to strive toward continuous improvement. In order to maximize the use of human resources, quality management stresses the importance of employee participation, teamwork, and continuous learning and improvement. The quantitative dimension involves the use of research and statistical techniques to evaluate and improve the processes in an organization and to link those processes to results. First introduced in the private sector, this approach has spread rapidly to the public sector as well—including the police. It has been estimated that approximately 25 percent of governmental agencies use TQM in at least one functional area of management (West, Berman, and Milakovich 1994).

With respect to policing, in a survey of approximately 200 Texas police managers, L. T. Hoover (1996) indicated that various components of TQM were being utilized. For instance, he measured three primary concepts, including *culture* (i.e., are lower-level employees empowered, is there teamwork and cooperation, are rewards equitable, is there a sense of work ownership?); *customers* (i.e., are services to the customers measured with respect to what they want, including surveys and complaints?); and *counting* (i.e., are quality-versus-quantity indicators of police productivity being measured, such as problem solving versus arrests?). He found that the departments were making reasonable application of culture principles, moderate application of customer-orientation techniques, and sparse application of measurement efforts. Thus, although quality-management concepts are being implemented, work remains (especially with respect to implementing quality-performance measures) if police departments are to improve substantially.

Because of its emphasis on quality service to customers (citizens) and attention to continuous improvement, quality management should prove useful to police departments in the transition to community policing. Possibly the first department to utilize quality-management principles for this purpose was in Madison, Wisconsin. In *Quality Policing: The Madison Experience* (Couper and Lobitz 1991), the police chief of Madison at the time (D. C. Couper) and a colleague have written about the experiences of this department's change away from a highly traditional, bureaucratic organization toward a quality-oriented organization. The principles of quality management or "quality leadership" used by this chief in transforming the department are listed in Case Study 4.1.

Case Study 4.1

Principles of Quality Leadership in Madison

1. Believe in, foster, and support teamwork.
2. Make a commitment to the problem-solving process, use it, and let data (not emotions) drive decisions.
3. Seek employees' input before making key decisions.
4. Believe that the best way to improve work quality or service is to ask and listen to employees who are doing the work.
5. Strive to develop mutual respect and trust among employees.
6. Have a customer orientation and focus toward employees and citizens.
7. Manage on the behavior of 95 percent of employees, not on the 5 percent who cause problems; deal with the 5 percent promptly and fairly.
8. Improve systems and examine processes before placing blame on people.
9. Avoid "top down," power-oriented decision making whenever possible.
10. Encourage creativity through risk taking, and be tolerant of honest mistakes.
11. Be a facilitator and coach; develop an open atmosphere that encourages providing for and accepting feedback.
12. With teamwork, develop with employees agreed-upon goals and a plan to achieve them.

Source: D. C. Couper and S. H. Lobitz. 1991. *Quality Policing: The Madison Experience*. Washington, D.C.: Police Executive Research Forum, p. 48.

The process that the Madison Police Department went through in changing to a quality-oriented organization, emphasizing participation and teamwork, was time-consuming and demanding. It took approximately 20 years from the start of the change process in the department to reach a state of general implementation of community policing and quality management (Wycoff and Skogan 1993). If traditional paramilitary departments are to implement similar significant changes, this is the type of long-term sustained effort they must be willing to put forth.

Organization Design

Organization design is concerned with the formal patterns of arrangements and relationships developed by police management to link people together in order to accomplish organizational goals. It was traditionally assumed by the classical school of thought that a pyramidal design was the most appropriate for police departments. Even today, some departments that are moving toward community policing, which requires a less bureaucratic approach, steadfastly cling to a pyramidal design.

The classical design, characterized by many hierarchical levels and narrow spans of control (i.e., a small number of employees per supervisor), allowing for close supervision and control of employees and operations, is known as a **tall structure**. Conversely, a **flat structure** is characterized by few hierarchical levels with wide spans of control (i.e., large number of employees per supervisor), allowing for greater employee autonomy and less control of operations. These differences between tall and flat structure are shown in Figure 4.3. It is easy to see that the tall structure has two extra levels of hierarchy and narrower spans of control for closer supervision and control over subordinates.

In general, organizations with tall structures attempt to coordinate their activities through centralization; that is, authority and decision making are retained by the top organizational levels. And, in general, organizations with flat structures tend to use **decentralization,** wherein authority and decision making are delegated to lower organizational levels, as a mechanism to control their activities. Police departments may also be centralized or decentralized geographically; that is, there may be one central headquarters (centralized) or a headquarters with substations (i.e., generally located in a building

Figure 4.3: Tall and Flat Organizational Structures

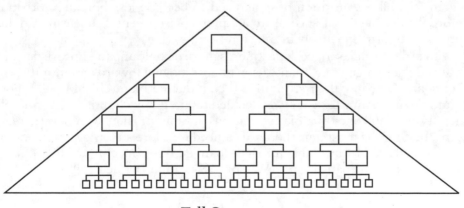

Tall Structure

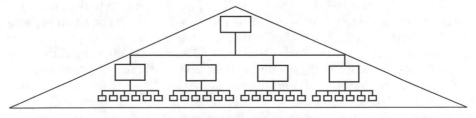

Flat Structure

with 24-hour operations and resources) or storefronts (smaller facilities with limited operations and resources). Police departments that are centralized in terms of decision making may be either centralized or decentralized geographically. Departments that practice decentralized decision making are most often decentralized geographically as well.

Tall structures also tend to have a greater degree of specialization with respect to the division of labor of personnel or the number of activities or tasks each individual performs. In other words, the fewer the number of tasks performed, the greater the level of specialization; conversely, the greater the number of tasks performed, the lower the level of specialization. For example, in Figure 4.4, under the Operations Branch, many types of specialized activities can be observed that are supportive of patrol work, including mounted patrol, detectives, response teams, canine units, and traffic. Patrol work itself can be recognized in terms of specialization; community-policing officers are known as **generalists** because they have a broad range of activities; traditional officers, who have fewer activities, are more specialized.

In one of the few examinations of police organization design, R. H. Langworthy (1992) argued that the type of design used depends on the nature of inputs to the police department. In other words, if police are viewed as ministers of the law or the local will, then a traditional, centralized model is most appropriate because it "curbs discretion and insures that either the law or local will is routinely served best" (p. 103). But if police are viewed more as professionals who are expected to use their discretion as well as their collective judgments in solving problems, then a community, decentralized model is more appropriate. With respect to these findings, it is important to recognize that because all present-day police environments are relatively unstable, essentially all organization designs need to become less bureaucratic and more flexible in order to be able to adapt to environmental concerns and, in turn, to perform effectively in the community.

In order to make police departments more flexible and to improve decentralized decision making, many departments moving toward community policing are flattening their structures (i.e., reducing hierarchical levels). For example, in Austin, Texas, it was decided to gradually eliminate the rank of deputy chief and one-third of the positions of captain. There were several reasons, but, for the most part there was a need for more street-level officers to handle calls and be available for the expanded-role concept (i.e., officers as generalists) of the patrol force (Watson, Stone, and DeLuca 1998).

Formal Organizations

One of the ways to learn about a police department is to look at how it is formally arranged or organized. This is most easily done through an **organization chart**, which depicts the intended functions, relationships, and flow of communication among designated groups. Such charts tell about the relative status of employees, the authority they have, the chain of command, the formal lines of communication, the job activities throughout the organization, and organizational values and priorities (e.g., is it bureaucratic [tall] or more democratic [flat], does it allow for decentralized decision making; is it highly specialized or more generalist?). For example, one can learn much about the Portland (Oregon) Police Department, which was adopting a community-policing approach in the mid-1990s, by examining its organization chart in Figure 4.4.

In its transformation toward community policing, the department made some conscious efforts to involve both community and employee participation with respect to "policy issues, public review, and setting priorities for community policing objectives (Williams 1995, p. 159). Thus, both a chief's

Figure 4.4   Organization Chart—Portland Police Department

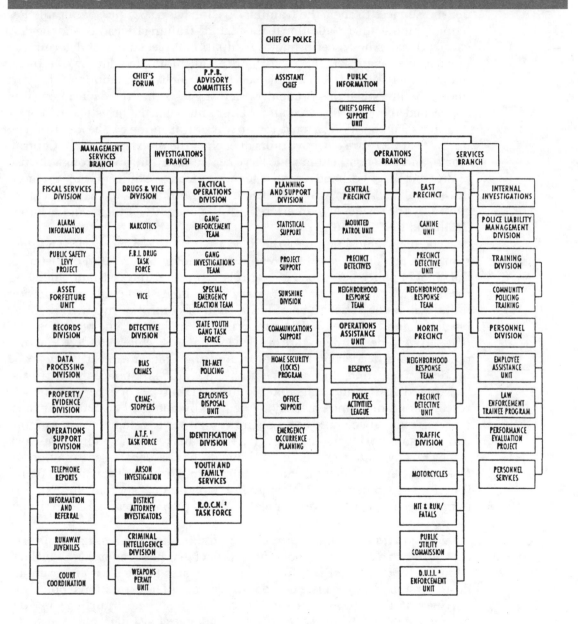

1. Alcohol, Tobacco and Firearms
2. Regional Organized Crime and Narcotics
3. Driving Under the Influence of Intoxicants

forum and an advisory committee unit, reporting directly to the chief, were added. There is also an assistant chief, with a support unit, who is responsible for the daily operation of the department. This arrangement allows the chief greater flexibility to interact with the public, as well as to manage internal change. A public information unit also reports to the chief, conveying additional input from the community.

Other organizational values and priorities—with a concern for community policing and a concern for the public—can be observed. For instance, under the Services Branch, the Training Division has a specific Community Policing Training unit (in addition to the regular Training Division), and the Personnel Division has a Performance Evaluation Project unit (for determining measurable "quality" police performance indicators); in addition, the Internal Investigations unit is under the Services Branch (it is traditionally located under the Investigations Branch), which suggests that the department was concerned about public perception of fair and impartial investigations of its members. Furthermore, a move toward decentralization can be identified by noting that there are detective units at each of the precinct stations (Central, North, and East), rather than one large centralized unit; and through the use of precinct neighborhood response teams, or teams of officers who "use nontraditional methods to focus on chronic neighborhood problems that are perceived by the residents to interfere with the livability of the neighborhood" (Williams 1995, p. 160).

The hierarchical nature of the department—lines of authority and division of responsibilities—is also readily apparent in Figure 4.4. For instance, the chief of police has a span of control of four (i.e., the assistant chief, and the heads of the chief's forum, advisory committees, and public information units), while the assistant chief has a span of control of five (i.e., the four branches and the chief's office support unit). In general, the branches (bureaus in some departments) are headed by captains, while most divisions and precincts are headed by lieutenants, and the units are most likely to be headed by sergeants. In many medium- and large-size police departments, however, divisions and units that require certain types of expertise, such as research and development, may be headed by qualified civilians. Furthermore, in many specialized units, such as employee assistance and communications, nonsworn personnel (civilians) may make up the bulk of the work force. Finally, organization charts indicate how a department may group tasks according to function and specialization. For example, while all patrol functions are under the same command (Operations), specialization occurs in mounted and canine patrols, neighborhood response teams, and motorcycle patrol.

Design changes and community policing. It is interesting to observe that although a community policing approach has been reported in Portland (Williams 1995), the organization chart indicates that a classic, pyramidal design is still in place. This is not too surprising, as large traditional police departments may allow for structural "tweaking" (e.g., decentralizing some operational activities), but major structural changes (e.g., flattening the structure by significantly reducing levels and command ranks) are far more difficult and time-consuming. This is not to suggest that the Portland department has not made progress toward community policing but rather to point out that a substantial, long-term effort is required for significant structural changes to occur One study by E. R. Maguire (1997), which analyzed the structural characteristics of 236 large municipal departments (with 100 or more sworn members), strongly supports this observation. Maguire found *no* significant structural differences among those departments that reported that they had adopted community policing (44 percent), those that reported they were in the planning or implementation stages (47 percent), or those that reported having no plans for community policing (9 percent).

These and other findings in the study draw attention to whether departments that *claim* to be doing community policing really are. It is one thing, of course, to report in a survey that one's department has implemented (or is implementing) community policing and quite another to be actually practicing it. For instance, is it being practiced throughout the entire department, or in part of the department, or in one unit made up of volunteers? Or, is a department reporting—perhaps even believing— that it is implementing community policing in order to gain professional status, community support, or even federal funding? (For example, some departments have used federal money to pay volunteer officers overtime in order to practice "community policing," with little or no additional training.) These are legitimate questions, but there really is no way of knowing for sure until a valid model of community policing is developed and tested on a large sample of departments (Maguire 1997). Nevertheless, Maquire's research will undoubtedly pique the interest of scholars who have suspected that at least some, if not many, of the reports of community-policing "adoptions" are premature or even manipulative. The following discussion on the continued strong influence of the paramilitary model and aggressive police tactics may only further muddy the debate on the "real" level of community policing practices.

Criticisms of the paramilitary design. As police departments attempt to move toward community policing, including the decentralization of operations and decision making, becoming less specialized, and flattening the hierarchy, the effectiveness of the classical, paramilitary design is increasingly being questioned. J. H. Auten (1981), for instance, suggests that the paramilitary organization treats the patrol officer like a *soldier* and thus is based on inappropriate assumptions about patrol work and democracy. He notes that soldiers are expected to obey orders and to show little, if any, initiative or discretion. They work as part of a larger unit; they perform tasks in a precisely prescribed manner; and they must be uniform in appearance, conduct, and behavior. The nature of the police role is quite different from these expectations. First, strict rules cannot be applied to policing because of the nature of the work. Second, orders are rarely required because most of the work by patrol personnel takes place on the street and out of the purview of supervisors. In addition, if the job is to be performed properly, a great amount of initiative and discretion are required.

Auten further explains that patrol officers seldom work in groups; rather, they perform most of their work alone or in pairs (thus, following the "book" cannot be enforced). He also criticizes the uniform appearance of patrol officers (patterned after soldiers), suggesting that it creates a mindset (we-they attitude) and rigidity on the individual officer's part. Such uniformity is depersonalizing, which may be appropriate for soldiers but is directly contrary to the police service goal. The decreased flexibility perpetuated by this system is also a problem—that is, there is a prescribed way for an officer (like a soldier) to act, even though most situations may be dissimilar. Finally, the managerial philosophy reflected by the paramilitary organization is characterized by an attitude of distrust, control, and punishment.

Although such criticisms and charges of ineffectiveness are not new and continue to grow, there has been surprisingly little research conducted either supporting or refuting them. However, a study conducted by V. Franz and D. M. Jones (1987) lends empirical support to the critics' charges. In this study, police officers were compared with employees in other city departments that had not been exposed to the paramilitary design. The researchers found that police employees perceived (1) greater problems with communications, (2) greater amounts of distrust, (3) lower levels of morale, and (4) lower levels of organizational performance. Franz and Jones concluded that "the data presented—seriously question the capability of the quasi-military police organizational model to meet today's needs" (p. 161).

Continued influence of the paramilitary design. Auten's analogy with the paramilitary model being based on inappropriate role assumptions about patrol work and the treatment of patrol officers like soldiers, is an interesting perspective when combined with some present-day research on the increasing emphasis on highly specialized **police paramilitary units (PPUs)**. PPUs are a generic term for units that have traditionally been known as SWAT (special weapons and tactics) teams and more recently referred to as SRTs (special response teams) and ERUs (emergency response units). This section will briefly describe the units, their activities, and how an even stronger paramilitary police culture and community presence may be developing.

These units function as military special-operations teams—often gaining expertise and training from the Navy's Seals and the Army's Rangers—and have as a primary function the threat or use of collective force, not always as a function of last resort. The teams generally wear black or camouflage battle dress uniforms (BDUs), with boots, body armor, and helmets, and are armed with submachine guns, sniper rifles, percussion grenades, tear gas, pepper gas, surveillance equipment, and sometimes employ armored personnel carriers. Two separate national surveys provide a developing picture on how these specialized units are increasingly being used. One study by P. B. Kraska and L. J. Cubellis (1997) consisted of small-locality police departments (municipal and county) serving jurisdictions having between 25,000 and 50,000 populations, with under 100 sworn officers; the second study by Kraska and V. E. Kappeler (1997) consisted of medium to large departments serving jurisdictions with populations exceeding 50,000, with over 100 sworn officers. The total sample included 473 small-locality departments and 548 medium to large departments.

By combining the data from both surveys, the results indicated that over 77 percent of police departments serving localities with more than 25,000 people had paramilitary units, an increase of 48 percent since 1985 (with a continued growth rate expected). The early formulation of SWAT teams in the 1970s and early 1980s was for the primary purpose of reacting to emergency situations *beyond the scope of patrol*, including civil disturbances, terrorism, hostage situations, and barricaded persons. Today, a much different perspective is emerging. The surveys documented 29,962 paramilitary deployments in 1995, a 939 percent increase over the 2,884 call-outs in 1980 (Kraska and Cubellis 1997, p. 620). The significant increase in PPU call-outs can be attributed to their increasing emphasis on executing search and arrest warrants and to their use as a proactive patrol force (often in full regalia) in high-crime areas. These activities consisted almost exclusively of proactive, no-knock raids, aggressive field interviews, and car stops and searches. Such activities are frequently carried out with a great deal of intimidation and often lead to increased police-community tensions. The authors conclude that PPUs are thus becoming a normal part of routine patrol work by moving away from their more traditional emergency roles and into more routine patrol activities.

Another study on the use of a PPU in a self-proclaimed community policing department (although its approach seemed to favor a paramilitary style) in the Southeast found similar results to those described above (Kraska and Paulsen 1997), that is, the increased use of the PPU as becoming a normal part of mainstream policing functions. Several themes emerged that are unique to these types of units, including a pronounced military culture, a preoccupation with danger, a high level of pleasure from engaging in paramilitary activities, and the viewing of the PPU team as a group of "elite" officers.

This integration of PPUs into patrol work appears to delineate a parallel trend with, but in opposition to, community policing: from less militaristic to more militaristic, from generalist to specialist, and from service- and problem-oriented to aggressive crime fighting. While the potential usefulness of PPUs in emergency conditions is well established, their use in mainstream policing appears unwarranted, especially in small-locality departments, which tend to be oriented toward crime prevention and service. Start-up and first-year costs of a 15-member unit (including training) were reported to be approximately one-quarter of a million dollars, not an insignificant amount for a small department and community to support (Kraska and Cubellis, 1997, p. 611).

Countering a common-sense argument that this buildup and increased use of PPUs simply reflects a rational response to crime-rate changes, Kraska and Cubellis compared call-out rates with the rates of violent crimes (i.e., homicide, robbery, and rape) from 1980 through 1995 for each small-locality jurisdiction and found no significant relationship between violent crime and call-outs. Therefore, they concluded that changes in the rate of violent crime were not an important factor in explaining the increased level of PPU activities. Instead, they argued that

> . . . we must first recognize that the specter of the military model still haunts the real world of contemporary policing, despite the recent rhetoric of democratic reforms. . . . [W]e find strong support for the thesis that the military model is still a powerful force guiding the ideology and activities of American police. This should not be surprising considering the war/military paradigm remains an authoritative framework for crime-control thinking and action by politicians, bureaucrats, the media, and much of the public. (1997, p. 622)

It seems clear that the military model still "haunts the real world of contemporary policing," where PPUs may operate in a normalized fashion alongside a community policing model. For example, in New York City (which acknowledges doing community policing), a tough anticrime program known as **Compstat** (an acronym for compare statistics) has been adopted where aggressive and sometimes intimidating police tactics may be used. In general, these include what has become known as **zero-tolerance**

Police utilizing aggressive tactics to take back the streets. (Photo: corbisimages.com)

policing in which officers make many stops and arrests for minor violations of traffic laws, ordinances and misdemeanors, regardless of public sentiment (see discussion in chapter 7). Although most experts agree that this get-tough, "take back the streets" strategy has played a role in reducing crime, questions are being raised as to whether or not it comes at an unacceptable price (especially in predominately minority neighborhoods). For instance, within approximately two years after implementation of the program, complaints of police abuse to the city's civilian review board rose by more than 50 percent (Reibstein 1997). Clearly, there needs to be a proper balance between law enforcement, democratic principles, and citizen rights. Law enforcement activities, and even "aggressive" patrols, which under certain conditions can be appropriate, must be carried out without unnecessary intimidation or abuse of civil rights.

It is noteworthy that due to the increased complaints and publicity by the community over New York's aggressive enforcement program, a new police chief (Howard Safir) implemented a policy directed at improving officer behavior, known as "courtesy, professionalism, and respect," or CPR. This new code of behavior may be working as citizen complaints filed against NYPD officers dropped 21 percent in the first half of 1997, compared with the same period of a year earlier. More specifically, complaints of police brutality dropped 20 percent (from 1,278 to 1,021) and complaints of abuse of authority fell almost 29 percent (from 1,166 to 829). In addition, charges of discourtesy fell 32 percent, and charges of profanity by police dropped almost 40 percent. These drops are impressive; nevertheless, some observers (such as the New York Civil Liberties Union) suggest that while CPR might be working, it could also mean that citizens have lost confidence in the Civilian Complaint Review Board and simply do not complain anymore ("Good News Just Gets Better" 1997, p. 18). Whatever the cause, it is important to note that the department is taking steps to improve officer behavior and is keeping track of the situation in order to determine the progress being made. It is further apparent, however, that with complaints numbering in the thousands in New York, community-police interactions require continuous attention and improvement. Inside Policing 4.1 takes a closer look at the potential problems of this aggressive approach to policing.

Compstat was developed as a process that utilizes current crime data to analyze crime patterns and to respond quickly with "appropriate" resources and crime strategies. It allows top-level police managers to share information

Inside Policing 4.1
New York's Aggressive Police Tactics

Diane Saarinen regularly hosted community forums at which police officials described how they were fighting drug dealers who had sometimes taken over entire blocks. As crime began to drop, she wrote strong letters of support to the local police, thanking them for their work. Now, however, she is writing a different kind of letter, strongly complaining of police abuse. She says she has heard too many stories of overly rough police conduct, including dragging people out of cars at gunpoint, of abusive tactics, of roughing up people who do not speak English, and of shooting civilians. "In the beginning we all wanted the police to bomb the crack houses," she says, "but now it's backfiring at the cost of the community. I think the cops have been given free rein to intimidate people at large."

Although most experts agree that the NYPD's aggressive zero-tolerance style has played a role in lowering the crime rate, the question remains whether or not this style of policing comes at too high a price. Opinion polls indicate that most New Yorkers approve of the crime strategy (of course, most citizens are not experts in police tactics or civil rights), but in some communities the heavy-handedness is straining already poor relations with young African Americans and Hispanics. In New York, for example, the city's civilian review board has reported a 50 percent increase in complaints over the past two years. That appears to be true in other cities that are implementing similar aggressive police tactics; for example, in Pittsburgh residents voted to establish a civilian review board and Charlotte, N.C., is expected to do the same, following a rash of complaints and disputed shootings.

Are increased complaints an appropriate trade-off for reduced crime? William Bratton, the former New York police commissioner who implemented the aggressive strategy, believes it is not surprising that complaints would increase, as the police are making more arrests and coming into contact with more citizens. He acknowledges that some police go too far, but contends that the reduction in crimes and victimizations is worth it. "In a city of 7.5 million people, 30 million tourists, and 38,000 police, is the level of complaints an appropriate trade-off?" he asked. "I think so, and the people seem satisfied." However, critics wonder if that sort of trade-off is appropriate in a democracy. If there is zero tolerance for lower-level street crimes, why is there not zero tolerance for heavy-handed cops? And the critics are not just from the criminal class or certain neighborhoods. For instance, George Kelling, the Rutgers University professor of criminal justice who coauthored the broken windows theory and helped Bratton implement it, is worried that his ideas are not being implemented appropriately. "There's an enormous potential for abuse," he says. He criticizes departments that demand IDs from residents or conduct neighborhood drug sweeps, indiscriminately stopping and frisking people, often using excessive force. This push for increased arrests may also lead police to "making guesses, and quite often they are wrong," adds James Fyfe, a Temple University professor of criminal justice.

It is interesting to note that in some cities, such as Seattle and Chicago, the police seem to have managed to increase enforcement while maintaining or improving relationships with the community. The key appears to be to make sure that the police are intimately familiar with their neighborhood and its residents. In Chicago, for example, the percentage of black and Hispanic officers has more than doubled, to 36 percent of the force. The Charlotte and New York departments have both developed training programs designed to alter excessive behavior, including ethnic-sensitivity lectures and community meetings. New York labeled its program CPR, for "courtesy, professionalism, and respect," and is holding its commanders accountable for citizen complaints in a similar manner to the way that it holds them accountable for the crime rate. It is hoped that through such tactics increased levels of enforcement can be applied but without the excesses of abusive behavior.

Source: Adapted from L. Reibstein. 1997. "NYPD Black and Blue." *Newsweek*, June 2: 66, 68.

about crime (both inside and outside the department) and essentially holds them accountable for the crime rate in their jurisdictions. Although it makes sound managerial sense to use a Compstat-type strategy to analyze crime, to share information about crime (and related problems), to respond to identified crime patterns, and to hold managers responsible for officer performance, it is potentially troublesome to hold command personnel totally responsible for crime rates. Since there are a number of complex social and economic factors affecting crime that are outside the purview of police, the police *by themselves* generally have a short-term impact on crime. (That is why establishing a partnership with the community and other social and governmental agencies—including police—is the foundation for true community policing efforts; *together*, these institutions can have a long-term impact on crime.) In addition, holding police managers accountable for the crime rate can lead, and in the past has led, to the manipulation of crime statistics (i.e., to underreport crime). Underreporting could be especially troublesome in departments where upper-level police managers are rewarded or punished on how well they keep the crime rate down; Inside Policing 4.2 provides an example of such data juggling by police executives.

It is interesting that Compstat, which started out as an innocuous computer file to compare crime statistics, is now a label for a strategic process that has been described as the NYPD's "all out, attention getting war on

---

Inside Policing 4.2
The Case of Doctored Statistics in New York

The *New York Times* reported that several high-ranking police officials in the department were forced to retire or were demoted for either committing or tolerating statistical manipulations designed to exaggerate the decrease in violent felonies. Due to the potential problem of manipulating crime data, the police commissioner created a special squad to review the accuracy of crime statistics in the department in 1997.

The statistical manipulations, carried out by the transit police, who were merged with the main police department in 1995, have possibly spanned a 20-year period. In some cases, transit commanders sent detectives and officers to re-interview crime victims, in an attempt to reclassify subway incidents as street-crime incidents. "It was out of control," said a supervisor, who has been interviewed by Internal Affairs and spoke on condition of anonymity. "Some guy who was pickpocketed would get these transit cops on his doorstep, grilling him. How do you know it happened in the subway? Did you check your pocket when you entered the station? Couldn't it have happened on the street?"

It was acknowledged that some officials believe a pattern of deception may have developed because city government became so focused on crime statistics that commanders feared they would be punished unless they produced the proper numbers. Former Police Commissioner William Bratton began holding weekly meetings (Compstat) of police supervisors that forced commanders to explain crime-fighting strategies in their precincts, and if crime rates had increased, they were often bitterly criticized in public. Although even critics of the department concede that crime has dropped markedly over the past several years, the department has also been the target of repeated charges that commanders intentionally undercount crime. For example, in 1995, the commander of the 41st Precinct in the Bronx was forced to retire after he was caught underreporting assaults.

Source: Adapted from D. Kocieniewski. 1998. "Police Official's Ouster Sought in Case of Doctored Statistics." *New York Times*, February 28: A11.

crime, fear and disorder" that "some believe will eventually be the *dominant approach* to policing in the United States" (Dodenhoff 1996, p. 4; emphasis added). Undoubtedly, the continued analogy in American society of police work to "wars" on crime and drugs helps strengthen the hold of the paramilitary organization and its influences on the police. As R. R. Roberg and J. Kuykendall (1997) have noted elsewhere, traditional departments have a hard time fighting the allure of incident-based enforcement actions (i.e., reactive versus preventive measures). Whereas such actions are appropriate in some situations, departments will "drift" toward this paramilitary approach unless checked. This type of response provides the most immediate gratification, is more "romantic," and is more in keeping with the "dangerous and dramatic" self-image of many police officers, as well as the expectations of many in the community (including politicians). Although this image is more myth than reality for most officers, it is still very powerful and seductive.

Due to the continued dominance and influence of the paramilitary model and its stereotypes about traditional policing (e.g., that it is exciting, dangerous, quasi-military), it is not difficult to understand why it is easy to drift toward a predominately authoritarian and coercive approach to policing. The following chapter will discuss the strategies that are used by some departments practicing community policing to sustain change, and in effect, ward off this "drift toward paramilitarism."

Police Goals

Like all organizations, police departments are oriented toward the attainment of goals. In a democracy, it is crucial that police managers, employees, and private citizens have an understanding of what these goals are and how they are to be accomplished (measured). As described in chapter 1, **goals** are general statements of long-term purpose. Goals are often used to identify the role of the police, for instance, to prevent crime, maintain order, or help solve community problems. They are also often used in mission statements. Goals are important because they help to identify expectations of what the police are doing and how productively they perform. Unrealistic and unreasonable goals make the job of managers and employees more difficult and can even ensure failure. When police over-promise or claim to be able to reduce crime or to solve problems that are largely outside police control, the public is usually disappointed and critical. When employees fail to behave in accordance with unreasonable managerial expectations, managers are often critical and employees are resentful and may even become less productive. These unreasonable expectations can and often do create an adversarial relationship between the police and the community and between managers and employees (e.g., see the discussion on managers' and street cops' cultures in the next section).

Three major influences affect the development of police goals: environmental, organizational, and individual. **Environmental influences** consist of the legal framework in which police function and the community's input into departmental priorities. As has been stressed, however, there is no such thing as a "single" community constituency. Police managers, therefore, must be aware of the various communities they serve and their differing expectations. Thus, departments within a heterogeneous geographic area, or

❖ ❖ ❖ ❖ even precincts or units within the same department, may need to establish different goals or use different methods to attain goals. **Organizational influences** are those of powerful members, especially top-level managers, who seek certain goals, primarily for the efficiency and perpetuation of the department but also to satisfy its members. Finally, **individual influences** generally benefit members (e.g., job security, pay, or fringe benefits).

It is clear, as the expectation-integration model discussed in chapter 1 suggests, that the closer police managers come to integrating individual and community (environmental) goals with those of the department (organizational), the more likely it is that the goals will be accomplished. Integration can be accomplished by police managers continually monitoring individual and community expectations and mixing them with those of the department.

Measuring police goals. The performance levels of police departments are, in general, difficult to measure. Performance indicators, such as making arrests, maintaining order, solving problems, providing services, and using discretion, are difficult to define in a meaningful and valid manner. That is to say, that although it may be relatively easy to count (*quantify*) the number of arrests that are made by the police, it is much more difficult to get a handle on how "good" the arrests are (*quality*). For example, was the arrest necessary, was there violence prior to the arrest that could have been prevented, did the arrest lead to a conviction, and so on? To date, the police have made very little effort to develop qualitative measures of performance. Therefore, officers may be performing activities that are supported within the department, while incurring the wrath of the community. In addition, because police departments operate in unstable environments, goal priorities are likely to change over time, thus creating new measurement challenges. Nevertheless, if goals are carefully and clearly defined, they can be measured in both a quantitative and qualitative manner.

To properly evaluate a police department's overall effectiveness, both external and internal goals should be assessed. From an external perspective, the department needs to know the extent to which it is satisfying the community it serves. For instance, are there conflicts between departmental and community goals? If the goals are similar, are the methods used to accomplish the goals acceptable? From an internal perspective, the department needs to know whether its goals are compatible with those of its employees. Is there conflict between what employees think the goals should be and what the department actually stresses, or do conflicts exist between operating units in the department? If they are to be meaningful, these goals need to be honest enough to be achievable and specific enough to be measurable. In general, attainable and generally satisfactory evaluation methods for the police include four major areas:

1. *Crime and Disorder Measures*. Crime and disorder statistics should be compared over time (in order to establish reliable trends and patterns). Criminal statistics may include the Uniform Crime Reports and victimization surveys. Measures of community disorder can be taken from the department's calls for service (e.g., complaints about noise, domestic violence, prostitution, or same-location repeat calls).

2. *Community Measures*. Community measures may include surveys, interviews, and feedback from community meetings re-

garding such factors as identifying and solving important community problems relative to crime, fear of crime, and general satisfaction with the police. In addition, representative community boards and police advisory committees that participate in departmental goal setting and performance feedback can be included.

3. *Employee Measures*. The opinions of employees can be measured by surveys and interviews regarding goal emphases, operating procedures and policies, and concerns with management.

4. *Performance Measures*. Evaluation of individual employees and group performance should include teamwork and cooperation.

With respect to crime and disorder, police departments often rely solely on the FBI's **Uniform Crime Reports** (Part I crimes, or **crime index**) as their crime-rate measure. This crime index is the rate per 100,000 population of eight common violent and property crimes, including murder and non-negligent manslaughter, forcible rape, robbery, aggravated assault, burglary, larceny or theft, motor vehicle theft, and arson, reported to the police. UCRs, however, are not a very precise measure of actual crime rates, with estimates of less than 50 percent of criminal acts being reported. The FBI is redesigning the program to help improve the quality and accuracy of the statistics (Bureau of Justice Statistics 1997). Another source of crime data that has become a part of many departments' assessment of crime is the use of **victim surveys,** in which scientifically selected samples of the population are asked about being victims of crime. Victimization data tend to provide a more accurate reflection of a community's incidence of crime. Currently the most widely used and extensive victim survey is the National Crime Victimization Survey, which asks a national sample of approximately 120,000 individuals over 12 years of age specific questions regarding criminal victimizations.

Other performance measures that police departments traditionally use to record crime levels include arrest rates and the crime clearance rate. **Arrest rates** are calculated as the number of persons arrested for all crimes known to the police. Arrest rates are an extremely poor measure of performance for several reasons. For example, they rely on UCR measures of crime known and police discretion of when to make arrests (officer levels of quality and quantity of arrests vary significantly). A further problem is that police make substantially more arrests for minor violations than for serious violations, whereas the crime rate is essentially based on serious crime. A final problem is the fact that much police work—perhaps the majority—does not even involve law enforcement activities, including arrests. The **crime clearance rate** is calculated as the number of Part I crimes reported to the police divided by the number of crimes for which the police have arrested a suspect. The crime clearance rate is another poor indicator of police performance for several reasons. For instance, the police usually consider a case to be "solved" even if the suspect is acquitted of the crime charged; furthermore, multiple crimes are often "cleared" by associating them with an arrested suspect who has admitted to similar or other felonies. Additionally, crimes can be solved by **exceptional clearance**, when the police claim to know who committed the crime but cannot make an arrest; for example, in a murder-suicide where the suspect is no longer alive. In any event, because clearance rates are determined entirely by the police (with no independent review), they are easily subject to internal manipulation.

Attributes of healthy police departments. The above discussion on police goals and measurement provides a framework for what a police department needs to do to become and remain healthy in a democratic society. The following list, put together by a panel of experts for the National Institute of Justice, examines this concept further by describing six attributes that a healthy police department would incorporate into its operational practices:

Attribute One. The healthy police organization knows what it wants to accomplish. It has articulated goals that can be expressed in an operational form, not as general as "To serve and protect." These goals can be appreciated by the people—certainly middle-management supervisors and especially the rank and file—who have to carry them out. The goals can be assessed, meaning that there are measures of things that are reflective of the goals.

Attribute Two. The healthy police organization needs to know its citizens. Are they getting what they want? What they are entitled to? These citizens are not just those who call and complain, who summon the police, but residents in a neighborhood, businesses, and so on. Finally, there are those whom we often think of as the objects of police control—the offenders—they, too, are people who need to be considered in terms of their experiences with the police. There are a variety of user surveys that could measure transactions with citizens, for example, periodic citizen surveys of the community. It is important to break them down into units that matter. Oftentimes, the breakdown will be for patrol officers, for example, at the beat level.

Attribute Three. The healthy police organization knows its business, the demands that are placed upon it. Calls for service are a readily available source of information in this regard. The department needs to know why "business" is increasing or decreasing, and knowing more about business is not be limited to relying on calls for service. There are a variety of other ways that business comes to police. Special efforts would have to be made in terms of measuring proactive efforts by officers, particularly trying to capture programmatic efforts. For example, problem-oriented policing requires not just random responses or responses to individual incidents but responses that are planned and coordinated to accomplish some objectives.

Attribute Four. The healthy police organization knows what it's doing about the demands of business. It has the ability to monitor resource allocations and officer activities. In terms of community policing, it knows what other agencies and organizations are doing that are pertinent to problems it's trying to deal with.

Attribute Five. A healthy police organization knows its people. Things that would tell us what people get from jobs, what they are looking for from their jobs, what motivates them about their work, and what demoralizes them. Knowing these things would help drive decisions about supervision, training, recruitment, and job design. The obvious implication in terms of measurement here is conducting surveys within the organization.

Attribute Six. The healthy police organization feeds back information to people and groups who need to know. To do this, you need to know what they need to know, what they want to know, and how they need to get it. Whether it's neighborhood groups that need to know more about the kind of service that they're getting, whether it's victim groups, or whether it's constituents within the organization. They are all users of information. (Travis and Brann 1997, pp. 4–5)

Job Design   ❖ ❖ ❖ ❖

Just as police departments have been criticized for overreliance on the traditional, paramilitary organization design, so too has the traditional design of police jobs. Historically, many police departments have tended to stress a narrow perspective on the role of the police and the community and have consequently designed their jobs from a narrow, legalistic perspective. As the complexity of the police role has become recognized, however, and as police have become better educated, and as community policing has developed, it is clear that traditional job designs are often not meeting the needs of police personnel, the department, or the community.

Because many aspects of police work involve community service, problem solving, and maintaining order, it is apparent that the job "requires a whole set of human relations and problem-solving skills that can be applied to the wide range of complex situations which police confront daily" (Sandler and Mintz 1974, p. 460). Along with this recognition of a more complex and broadened role concept has come an emphasis on the recruitment of more highly educated officers. Even so, as Goldstein has observed:

> Without changes in the function and working environment of the police, the potential contribution that these officers could make to policing has not been fully realized. Furthermore, the very qualities we have sought in more educated officers have been smothered in the atmosphere of traditional policing. (1987, p. 28)

Research on the personal-growth needs (self-actualization, esteem, and autonomy) and job satisfaction of highly educated officers suggests that these needs are not being fulfilled through the traditional design of police jobs and that these officers are often not satisfied with their work (for example, see Cacioppe and Mock 1985; Cordner 1978; Griffin, Dunbar, and McGill 1978; Lefkowitz 1973, 1974; and Mottaz 1983). These results indicate that college-educated officers are more likely to terminate their careers in policing, suggesting they are less likely to tolerate highly structured jobs that are unfulfilling and unsatisfying. These findings are not surprising when the traditional narrow and legalistically oriented role conception, associated with a paramilitary organization, is considered. With such a job design, there simply has been little attempt to build potential growth and satisfaction needs of individual employees into the job.

Such findings provide a strong argument that the traditional job design has not been meeting the needs of many of those in policing for some time and may be dysfunctional for those with higher levels of education. In part, the move toward community policing is an attempt at **job redesign**; that is, an effort to enrich police work in order that the intrinsic rewards of increased growth and levels of satisfaction can be obtained from the job itself. The expanded role concept emphasized by community policing has the potential to enrich patrol work while improving officer satisfaction and performance. In attempting to enhance community livability through problem solving and crime prevention, jobs are substantially redesigned by increasing the use of officer discretion and decision making, especially with respect to using alternatives other than those available primarily through the criminal justice system. For instance, officers may need to use counseling, mediation, referral to social agencies, or services from other public and private agencies. The en-

❖ ❖ ❖ ❖   riched nature of a community police officer's day is described below; this day would include activities in addition to traditional law enforcement, such as patrol and responding to calls for service (Mastrofski 1992, p. 24):

- Operating neighborhood substations.
- Meeting with community groups.
- Analyzing and solving neighborhood problems.
- Working with citizens on crime prevention programs.
- Conducting door-to-door surveys of residents.
- Talking with students in schools.
- Meeting with local merchants.
- Making security checks of businesses.
- Dealing with disorderly people.

The research on the impact of community policing on enriched job designs is mixed. On the one hand, it does appear that in programs or units that are relatively well developed community policing activities can significantly increase levels of personal growth and job satisfaction, as well as with the department itself, supervision, and the community (see Hayeslip and Cordner 1987; Hornick, Burrows, and Phillips 1989; Wycoff and Skogan 1993; and Skogan and Hartnett 1997). On the other hand, in programs that were either partially or poorly implemented, officers' attitudes and job-satisfaction levels were not so positive, usually with no discernible differences between experimental and comparison groups (see Weisburd and McElroy 1988; McElroy, Cosgrove, and Sadd 1993; Rosenbaum, Yeh, and Wilkinson 1994; and Wilson and Bennett 1994).

Although one must be cautious with interpreting results from programs that were different with respect to implementation, assignment of personnel (especially with the use of volunteers who may be more motivated, satisfied, and supportive to begin with), and internal and external condi-

The redesign and enrichment of traditional police jobs, such as conducting surveys of citizens above, may improve officer satisfaction and performance. (Photo: Mark C. Ide)

tions, some encouraging results have been reported. The early results appear to suggest that officers with needs for high personal growth and job satisfaction (characteristic of more highly educated officers) benefit from a community policing-enriched job design; more traditionally oriented officers (with a more legalistically oriented role concept) most likely will not. As J. R. Greene has pointed out:

> Community policing for some officers may represent a personal growth challenge, the chance to meaningfully participate in work decisions, and the enlightened work environment suggested by these programs. But for other officers community policing can be something completely different; it can be more work to be done at the same pay, it can be added responsibility without commensurate authority or autonomy, and it can mean that officer autonomy is actually restricted by an observant and activated community. For officers who may value these concerns, community policing may be perceived as more detrimental than beneficial. (1989, p. 181)

Greene further adds that because innovative programs in policing have been criticized for "creaming" off the "better" officers, it is not clear that community policing will "work with all or even the majority of officers currently policing American communities" (p. 180). Although this topic has long-term implications for the field, which will be discussed elsewhere, the initial challenge for community-policing managers will be to attempt to place those officers who have the skill levels and are the most challenged into enriched, community-oriented jobs. Gradually, community policing could then be spread throughout the organization; most efforts at organizational change develop this way. Some departments, however, are utilizing a more specialized approach, in which officers perform either community-oriented or traditional policing roles. For example, in Chicago (discussed in the following chapter), officers are assigned to either community-policing teams or rapid-response teams, whose primary responsibility is to respond to calls for service, which allows the community teams to concentrate on their activities in the community. Officers are required to switch teams at predetermined intervals.

Managing Group Behavior

Police managers need to be well informed about managing group behavior and possible conflict between and among groups. Because today's police departments tend to be relatively diverse in cultural background and level of skills, it is natural that different groups will have different—often conflicting—demands on management levels. The remainder of this chapter will discuss the varied nature and impact of these groups—both formal and informal—on management and how management must constructively deal with them.

Police Subcultures

Although the organization chart in Figure 4.3 depicted the formal structure of a police department, how a department operates actually depends more on *informal* organizational arrangements. Individual beliefs, values, and norms in police departments are strongly influenced by group behavior, especially by experienced officers. As will be discussed in greater detail in

Police subcultures develop when younger, less experienced officers learn and inculcate the attitudes and behaviors of older, more experienced officers. (Photo: Mark C. Ide)

subsequent chapters, **socialization** in policing occurs when recruits learn the values and behavioral patterns of experienced officers. From this early socialization, police officers tend to develop a different view of their job from that of their managers. For example, E. Reuss-Ianni (1983), in her study of New York police, observed that these divergent views result in two distinct subcultures within the same organization, namely a **manager's culture** and a **street cop's culture**.

This differing perspective of the patrol officer's job develops because the manager's view is often shaped by experiences that remove him or her from the street reality of officers. One example common to police work is the ends-means dilemma. Police managers must be concerned with both ends (i.e., results) and means (i.e., how the results are achieved), whereas officers may be concerned primarily with ends (i.e., making an arrest is more important than protecting constitutional rights). Managers are concerned with departmental priorities, policies, and procedures, whereas officers are concerned with doing the job "according to the street," often acquired not from the department's view of reality but from the officer's perspective, determined by trying to "survive." These differing perspectives can result in an adversarial relationship, where street cops maintain their own "code," which can include the set of rules described in Inside Policing 4.3.

Because both the manager's and the street cop's cultures must relate to the expectations of the communities they serve, there is both a public and a private world of policing (Roberg and Kuykendall 1997). The **public world of policing** is presented to the public as the essence of police work: dedicated public servants performing dangerous work for our safety. Although the managers' and officers' perspectives of police work may differ, neither group tends to be completely candid, because both have a vested interest in maintaining an image that avoids controversy. For example, if officers use excessive force to make an arrest, they will probably not admit it because of the street-culture norm to be secretive about illegal or inappropriate behavior. Managers may attempt to uncover the inappropriate behavior, but they may not disclose it, or they may disclose only parts of it. There may be potentially serious adverse consequences to the department, or they may be willing to disregard illegal tactics if a desirable result is obtained. Police managers, if

---

Inside Policing 4.3
Street Cop's Code

1. Take care of your partner first, then the other officers.
2. Don't "give up" (inform on) another cop; be secretive about the behavior of other officers.
3. Show balls; take control of a situation and don't back down.
4. Be aggressive when necessary, but don't go looking for trouble.
5. Don't interfere in another officer's sector or work area.
6. Do your fair share of work and don't leave work for the next shift; however, don't do too much work.
7. If you get caught making a mistake, don't implicate anybody else.
8. Other cops, but not necessarily managers, should be told if another officer is dangerous or "crazy."
9. Don't trust new officers until they have been checked out.
10. Don't volunteer information; tell others only what they need to know.
11. Avoid talking too much or too little; both are suspicious.
12. Protect your ass; don't give managers of the system an opportunity to get you.
13. Don't make waves; don't make problems for the system or managers.
14. Don't "suck up" to supervisors.
15. Know what your supervisor and other managers expect.
16. Don't trust managers; they may not look out for your interests.

Source: Adapted from E. Reuss-Ianni. 1983. *Two Cultures of Policing: Street Cops and Management Cops.* New Brunswick, CT.: Transaction Books, pp. 13–16.

---

they are to be effective leaders, however, must be willing to deal with such situations, both formally and informally, as the need arises.

In general, the **private world of policing** has been characterized as politically conservative, closed, or secretive, with a high degree of cynicism and an emphasis on loyalty, solidarity, and respect for authority (Doyle 1980). Undoubtedly, this private world of the patrol officer's culture has the strongest influence on the socialization process throughout the department and most likely the greatest impact on police behavior. A significant problem for managers is when the behavior dictated by the worker's culture conflicts with both departmental and community interests. This conflict is most apparent when a certain degree of deviant behavior (e.g., excessive force, racism, free meals, or gratuities) becomes acceptable, or at least tolerated, at the street level. Police managers must be willing to deal strongly with such behavior from both ethical and legal perspectives. Accordingly, police managers need to be aware of group pressures—especially with respect to the street culture—and how they influence, either positively or negatively, officer behavior.

Employee Organizations

Historically, the best-known police employee organization has been the **police union**, which is made up of police officers and is their official representative in collective bargaining with the employer. Because police departments operate on a local level, there is no single national police union. Instead, local departments may belong to one of many national unions. The largest include the Fraternal Order of Police (FOP) and the International Union of Police Associations (IUPA), which is affiliated with the AFL-CIO. Other local police unions are affiliated with the Teamsters; the American Federation of State, County, and Municipal Employees (AFSCME); and other smaller national unions.

Although a union is an employee organization, not all employee organizations are unions. As S. Walker (1992) has pointed out, police officers have historically belonged to **fraternal organizations.** These groups are generally organized along ethnic lines. Nationally, for example, African American officers are represented by the National Organization of Black Law Enforcement Officers (NOBLE), Latino officers by the Latino Police Officers Association, and Asian officers by the Asian Police Officers Association. Employee groups may also form their own local organizations. In San Francisco, for example, the African American officers' association is known as Officers for Justice (OFJ); in San Jose, California, it is known as the South Bay Association of Black Law Enforcement Officers (SABLE).

As departments become more diverse in their makeup, additional employee organizations develop. For instance, many departments have women's organizations (e.g., the Women's Police Officer Association), and gay and lesbian officers are represented in California by the Golden State Peace Officers Association. Furthermore, police officers and supervisors are often represented by their own associations. It is apparent that if departments are to maintain a healthy work environment, police managers must deal effectively with the diverse needs, expectations, and conflicts of these employee organizations. In general, it is best to establish a working relationship with each group and to share with them the department's expectations. Then, if there are conflicts, they can be dealt with in an open and honest manner.

Police Unions

The police labor movement has gone through several stages. Police associations were evident as early as the 1890s but did not establish themselves until the mid-1960s. Two previous attempts made to unionize police employees failed. The first attempt failed after the Boston police strike of 1919, which created a backlash against police unions throughout the country. The second, between 1943 and 1947, failed because of unfavorable court decisions and strong resistance by police chiefs.

Since the mid-1960s, however, police unionization has had a great deal of success. Several developments contributed toward this success, including the following:

1. *Lagging Salaries and Benefits.* Officers were angry over the fact that their salaries and benefits had fallen behind those available in other equivalent positions.

2. *Poor Police Management.* Officers were angry and alienated over the way their departments were managed. At the time, police chiefs had virtually unlimited power in managing their departments, and many operated in an arbitrary and vindictive manner. Officers who were critical of management were often punished with frequent transfers and assignments to low-status jobs. Officer participation in any form of decision making was virtually nonexistent.

3. *Social and Political Alienation.* During the social unrest of the 1960s and 1970s, police officers felt that they were being attacked from all sides; for example, they resented accusations of discrimination from civil rights groups and felt that Supreme Court decisions were "handcuffing" them in fighting crime.

4. *A New Generation of Officers.* The movement toward unionization was led by a new generation of officers; they were generally younger and more assertive than the established leaders of police fraternal groups.

5. *The Law-and-Order Mood.* Unionization succeeded, in part, because unlike the earlier two periods, there was little opposition to them. Because there was great concern over "law and order," mayors and council members did not want to appear hostile toward the police; thus, they were less likely to become involved in matters of unionization.

6. *A New Legal Climate.* Unions also succeeded because the attitudes of the courts changed dramatically. Previously, they held that police and public employees had no right to unionize, but by the 1960s, they had adopted the position that employees did have that right. (Adapted from Walker 1992, p. 371)

The early development of police unionization was controversial and often shrouded in conflict, especially with police management. Once established, unions demanded higher salaries; better fringe benefits; more participation in how, when, and where officers worked; and more elaborate disciplinary procedures to protect employees. They also tended to fight back against the charges of critics. In many police departments, employee organizations have become a major obstacle in effecting change. What began as an attempt to improve the lot of the working police officer has often become a barrier to improving standards and performance. Of course, members of police unions may not agree with this perspective; from their point of view, they are simply acting to preserve "hard won" gains. In addition, some unions are vocal proponents of organizational change that will improve performance. In some cases, police unions may be more progressive than police managers.

The issues that are negotiated between police unions and management tend to fall into three categories: *salaries and benefits, conditions of work,* and *grievance procedures*. Salaries and benefits are influenced by a number of factors, including the economic health of a community, the inflation rate, salaries in comparable police departments (or in comparable positions in other occupations), management's resistance, the militancy of the union, and the amount of public support for either labor or management.

Conditions of work include a broad range of possible issues, many of which have traditionally been considered management prerogatives, such as the procedures used for evaluation, reassignment, and promotions; equipment and uniforms; number of officers assigned to a car or section of the community; how seniority and education will be used in assignments and promotions; hours worked and off-duty employment; and training and professional development. Critics argue that this kind of union activity is detrimental to the effective management of the department and the provision of quality services to the community (see Bouza 1985). Others, however, blame the poor management and treatment of employees for promoting such union activity; they view employee influence over management prerogatives in positive terms, potentially leading to improved managerial practices (see Kleismet 1985).

Grievance procedures are concerned with the process to be used in accusing an officer of a violation of departmental policies and procedures of law. Usually, this process involves an identification of officer rights (which may even be codified in state law), how the complaints must be filed, how evidence is obtained and processed, how disciplinary decisions will be made, and what appeals, if any, will be allowed. Quite often, police unions, in an effort to protect employees from arbitrary treatment by managers, will demand elaborate grievance mechanisms that frustrate attempts to respond to almost any type of inappropriate police behavior. However, grievance procedures may also be a useful way of clarifying work rules and of understanding and agreeing on performance expectations.

Significant input in the managerial process by police unions is here to stay. It is important to recognize that union leaders often have a strong informal influence over departmental members. Consequently, these leaders should be treated with respect by police managers, and they should be kept abreast of managerial decisions in order that they can share this information with the membership. To facilitate this process, union representatives should be encouraged to serve on task forces and participate in management meetings. An open and participative relationship with the union may help to avoid the costly and unpleasant effects that often result from strikes, job actions (i.e., work slowdowns or speedups), refusals to negotiate, media attention, and perhaps most important, create an improved working environment.

Summary

The managerial process is concerned with organizing, leading, planning, and controlling. The history of police management theory begins with the classical theorists, who stressed a bureaucratic, paramilitary approach to organizational design. Beginning in the early 1970s, behavioral theorists began attacking the classical approach, placing greater emphasis on worker participation, job satisfaction, more flexible designs, and recognition of the complex nature of the police role. The final theoretical development, contemporary police theory, emphasized police departments as open systems and the use of contingency and quality-management approaches. Police organization design is depicted through an organization chart. There has been much criticism of the traditional paramilitary design, which continues to be influential.

It is important to establish realistic and measurable police goals, including both quantitative and qualitative indicators. In order to properly evaluate a department's overall effectiveness, both external (community) and internal (departmental) goals should be assessed according to six attributes. Because today's police departments are culturally diverse and vary widely with respect to skill levels, the managing of group behavior becomes important. From this perspective, both formal and informal groups (including police subcultures) are involved. Finally, police unions, despite a controversial development,

have improved benefits and job conditions. It is important for management
to develop a strong relationship with union leaders.

Discussion Questions

1. Briefly describe each of the managerial functions. Which function do you believe is the most important with respect to managing police departments? Why?

2. Describe the four separate hierarchical levels found in medium to large police organizations and the activities performed at each level.

3. Briefly discuss the contributions of several classical and behavioral theorists of police work. What were the major impacts of each of these theoretical orientations?

4. Describe the following concepts and how they relate to police organization and management: systems, open systems, contingency management, and total quality management (TQM).

5. Differentiate between tall and flat organizational structures. What advantages does a flat design have for police departments?

6. Briefly describe several criticisms of the traditional paramilitary organization design. What influence does this design still have on present-day policing?

7. Discuss several reasons why there is a need to redesign traditional police job descriptions.

8. If you were a police chief, how would you attempt to formulate and assess goals for your department?

9. Differentiate between the manager's and the street cop's cultures. How does this difference affect the police manager's job?

10. Briefly describe the development of police unions, and explain why it is important that managers form a strong working relationship with union leaders.

References

Angell, J. E. 1971. "Toward an Alternative to the Classic Police Organizational Arrangements: A Democratic Model." *Criminology* 9: 185–206.

Auten, J. H. 1981. "The Paramilitary Model of Police and Police Professionalism." *Police Studies* 4: 67–78.

Bercall, T. E. 1970. "Calls for Police Assistance." *American Behavioral Scientist* 13: 681–691.

Bittner, E. 1970. *The Function of the Police in Modern Society*. Washington, D.C.: U.S. Government Printing Office.

Bouza, A. V. 1985. "Police Unions: Paper Tigers or Roaring Lions?" In W. A. Geller (ed.), *Police Leadership in America: Crises and Opportunity*, pp. 241–280. New York: Praeger.

Bureau of Justice Statistics. 1997. *Implementing the National Incident-Based Reporting System: A Project Status Report*. Washington, D.C.: Department of Justice.

Cacioppe, R. L. and Mock, P. 1985. "The Relationship of Self-Actualization, Stress and Quality of Work Experience in Senior Level Australian Police Officers." *Police Studies* 8: 173–186.

Cordner, G. W. 1978. "Review of Work Motivation Theory and Research for the Police Manager." *Journal of Police Science and Administration* 6: 186–292.

Couper, D. C. and Lobitz, S. H. 1991. *Quality Policing: The Madison Experience.* Washington, D.C.: Police Executive Research Forum.

Cumming, E., Cumming, I., and Edell, L. 1965. "Policeman as Philosopher, Guide and Friend." *Social Problems* 12: 276–286.

Deming, W. E. 1986. *Out of the Crises*. Cambridge: MIT Center for Advanced Engineering Study.

Dodenhoff, P. C. 1996. "LEN Salutes its 1996 People of the Year, the NYPD and its Compstat Process." *Law Enforcement News, December*: 1, 4.

Doyle, M. A. 1980. "Police Culture: Open or Closed." In V. A. Leonard (ed.), *Fundamentals of Law Enforcement: Problems and Issues* pp. 61–83. St. Paul, MN: West.

Fosdick, R. 1915. *American Police Systems*. Montclair, NJ: Patterson Smith.

Franz, V. and Jones, D. M. 1987. "Perceptions of Organizational Performance in Suburban Police Departments: A Critique of the Military Model." *Journal of Police Science and Administration* 15: 153–161.

Fuld, L. 1909. *Police Administration*. New York: Putnam.

Goldstein, H. 1968. "Police Response to Urban Crisis." *Public Administration Review* 28: 417–418.

———. 1977. *Policing a Free Society*. Cambridge, MA: Ballinger.

———. 1987. "Toward Community-Oriented Policing: Potential, Basic Requirements, and Threshold Questions." *Crime & Delinquency* 33: 6–30.

"Good News Just Gets Better for NYPD." 1997. *Law Enforcement News* July/August: 18.

Greene, J. R. 1989. "Police Officer Job Satisfaction and Community Perceptions: Implications for Community-Oriented Policing." *Journal of Research in Crime and Delinquency* 26: 168–183.

Griffin, G. R., Dunbar, R. L. M., and McGill, M. E. 1978. "Factors Associated With Job Satisfaction Among Police Personnel." *Journal of Police Science and Administration* 6: 77–85.

Hayeslip, P. W. and Cordner, G. W. 1987. "The Effects of Community-Oriented Patrol on Police Officer Attitudes." *American Journal of Police* 6: 95–119.

Hoover, L. T. 1996. "Translating Total Quality Management From the Private Sector to Policing." In L. T. Hoover (ed.), *Quantifying Quality in Policing*. Washington, D.C.: Police Executive Research Forum.

Hornick, J. P., Burrows, B. A., and Phillips, D. M. 1989. "An Impact Evaluation of the Edmonton Neighborhood Foot Patrol Program," November. Paper presented at the annual meeting of the American Society of Criminology, Reno, NV.

Kleismet, R. B. 1985. "The Chief and the Union: May the Force Be With You." In W. A. Geller (ed.), *Police Leadership in America: Crisis and Opportunity*, pp. 281–285. New York: Praeger.

Kocieniewski, D. 1998. "Police Official's Ouster Sought in Case of Doctored Statistics." *New York Times*, February, 28: A 11.

Kraska, P. B. and Cubellis, L. J. 1997. "Militarizing Mayberry and Beyond: Making Sense of American Paramilitary Policing." *Justice Quarterly* 14: 607–629.

Kraska, P. B. and Kappeler, V. E. 1997. "Militarizing American Police: The Rise and Normalization of Paramilitary Units." *Social Problems* 44: 1–18.

Kraska, P. B. and Paulsen, D. J. 1997. "Grounded Research into U.S. Paramilitary Policing: Forging the Iron Fist Inside the Velvet Glove." *Policing and Society* 7: 253–270.

Langworthy, R. H. 1992. "Organizational Structure." In G. W. Cordner and D. C. Hale (eds.) *What Works in Policing?* pp. 87–105. Cincinnati, OH: Anderson.

Lefkowitz, J. 1973. "Attitudes of Police Toward Their Job." In J. R. Snibbe and H. M. Snibbe (eds.), *The Urban Policeman in Transition*, pp. 203–232. Springfield, IL: C.C. Thomas.

———. 1974. "Job Attitudes of Police: Overall Description and Demographic Correlates." *Journal of Vocational Behavior* 5: 221–230.

Maguire, E. R. 1997. "Structural Change in Large Municipal Police Organizations During the Community Policing Era." *Justice Quarterly* 14: 547–576.

Mastrofski, S. D. 1992. "What Does Community Policing Mean for Daily Police Work?" *National Institute of Justice Journal*, August: 23–27.

McElroy, J. E., Cosgrove, C. A., and Sadd, S. 1993. *Community Policing: The CPOP in New York*. Newbury Park, CA: Sage.

Mottaz, C. 1983. "Alienation Among Police Officers." *Journal of Police Science and Administration* 11: 23–30.

Parnas, R. 1967. "The Police Response to the Domestic Disturbance." *Wisconsin Law Review* Fall: 914–960.

Reibstein, L. 1997. "NYPD Black and Blue." *Newsweek*, June 2: 66, 68.

Reuss-Ianni, E. 1983. *Two Cultures of Policing: Street Cops and Management Cops*. New Brunswick, CT: Transaction Books.

Roberg, R. R. 1979. *Police Management and Organizational Behavior: A Contingency Approach*. St. Paul, MN: West.

Roberg, R. R. and Kuykendall, J. 1997. *Police Management, 2nd Edition*. Los Angeles: Roxbury.

Rosenbaum, D. P., Yeh, S., and Wilkinson, D. L. 1994. "Impact of Community Policing on Police Personnel: A Quasi-Experimental Test." *Crime & Delinquency* 40: 331–353.

Sandler, G. B. and Mintz, E. 1974. "Police Organizations: Their Changing Internal and External Relationships." *Journal of Police Science and Administration* 2: 458–463.

Skogan, W. G. and Hartnett, S. M., 1997. *Community Policing, Chicago Style*. New York: Oxford University Press.

Smith, B. 1960. *Police Systems in the United States*, 2nd ed. New York: Harper & Row.

Travis, J. and Brann, J. E. 1997. *Measuring What Matters, Part Two: Developing Measures of What the Police Do*. Washington, D.C.: National Institute of Justice.

Walker, S. 1992. *The Police in America: An Introduction, 2nd ed*. New York: McGraw-Hill.

Watson, E. M., Stone, A. R., and DeLuca, S. T. 1998. *Strategies for Community Policing*. Upper Saddle River, NJ: Prentice-Hall.

West, J. P., Berman, E. M., and Milakovich, M. W. 1994. "Implementing TQM in Local Government: The Leadership Challenge." *Public Productivity and Management Review* 17: 195–192.

Weisburd, D. and McElroy, J. E. 1988. "Enacting the CPO Role: Findings from the New York City Pilot Program in Community Policing." In J. R. Greene and S. D. Mastrofski (eds.), *Community Policing: Rhetoric or Reality?*, pp. 89–102. New York: Praeger.

Williams, E. J. 1995. *Implementing Community Policing: A Documentation and Assessment of Organizational Change*. Ph.D. dissertation. Portland, OR: Portland State University.

Wilson, D. G. and Bennett, S. F. 1994. "Officers' Response to Community Policing: Variations on a Theme." *Crime & Delinquency* 40: 354–370.

Wilson, J. Q. 1968. *Varieties of Police Behavior*. Cambridge, MA: Harvard University.

Wilson, O. W. 1950. *Police Administration*. New York: McGraw-Hill.

Wilson, O. W. and McLaren, R. C. 1977. *Police Administration, 4th ed*. New York: McGraw-Hill.

Wycoff, M. A. and Skogan, W. G. 1993. *Community Policing in Madison: Quality From the Inside Out*. Washington D.C.: National Institute of Justice.

Zhao, J. 1996. *Why Police Organizations Change: A Study of Community-Oriented Po-licing*. Washington, D.C.: Police Executive Research Forum.

For a listing of websites appropriate to the content of this chapter, see "Suggested Websites for Further Study" (p. xv). ✦

Change and Innovation

Chapter Outline

Key Terms	
change strategies	innovation
civil service commissions	learning organization
civil service regulations	negotiated job conditions
fraternal organizations	organizational change
group norms	police union
inertia	quality circle

❖ ❖ ❖ ❖

As discussed previously, the police have traditionally been organized and managed according to classical prescriptions. In other words, a department is structurally designed in a hierarchical, bureaucratic manner, where the leadership style is authoritarian and employees are tightly controlled. It is extremely difficult to make significant and sustained changes to such traditional, paramilitary departments. As past discussions have also indicated, a more flexible and democratic orientation allows a department to adapt more readily to both internal (employee) and external (community) concerns. The purpose of this chapter is to describe how the change process and police strategies, especially toward community policing, can be applied in a constructive manner. Furthermore, the importance of developing a climate of innovation (and learning) will be discussed; without such a climate, the amount of effort required to implement new programs cannot be sustained.

Police Organizational Change

Organizational change occurs when an organization adopts new ideas or behaviors (Pierce and Delbeq 1977). Usually, an innovative idea, such as a new patrol strategy or job design, is introduced and employee behavioral changes are supposed to follow. Consequently, the ultimate success of any organizational change effort depends on how well the organization can alter the behavioral patterns of its personnel—that is, change old behavior patterns to new behavioral patterns to "fit" the new strategy or method. Of course, the greater the degree of change required, the more significant will be the behavioral changes required. For instance, community policing requires a substantial change in the role and job design not only of police officers but also of their supervisors and managers. Thus, a transition toward community policing requires substantially greater behavioral changes of personnel than would simply changing a patrol tactic or procedure. The corollary to this behavioral change process is that the greater the degree of planned change, the greater will be the resistance to it. A discussion of how resistance to change develops in policing follows.

Obstacles to Change

Probably the most common characteristic of change is people's resistance to it. In general, people do not like to change their behavior. Adapting to a new environment or learning a new work method often results in feelings of stress and fear of the unknown (e.g., Will I like it; Will I be able to do it well?). The following is a discussion of the major reasons why resistance to change—using community policing as an example—is so common in police departments.

Inertia. A great deal of **inertia**, or "doing things as they have always been done," is strongly associated with paramilitary departments. People have what is known as "sunk costs" in their jobs and routines, including time, energy, and experience; these are powerful forces in resisting change. Individuals or groups with many such "investments" sunk into a particular department or job may not want changes, regardless of their merit. Community policing, for example, requires officers to do many of their old tasks in new ways and to take on new tasks with which they are not familiar. They may be "asked to identify and solve a broad range of problems; reach out to elements of the community that previously were outside their orbit; and put their careers at risk by taking on unfamiliar and challenging responsibilities" (Skogan and Hartnett 1997 p. 71). These expectations are often beyond the officers' capabilities and the traditional roles for which they were initially selected and trained (Lurigio and Rosenbaum 1994). There is little doubt that most officers would rather do what they believe they were hired for and what they perceive to be the "real" police role: crime fighting. Consequently, community policing is often dismissed as "social work," which takes important time away from their crime-fighting activities.

Management personnel will have the same inertia factor at work because they also have been selected and trained to do traditional policing. Although inertia occurs at all managerial levels, except possibly at the very top when a new police chief is brought in to implement community policing, the attitudes of sergeants are especially important. Because sergeants have the most direct influence over the day-to-day activities of street officers, it is crucial that they "buy into" the new program, promoting the department's new policies and procedures. In order to do so, sergeants will need to act as facilitators and trainers as well as supervisors. Mitigating against this facilitating and training role, however, is the newness of community policing; most sergeants have never experienced it themselves. They too must learn new skills and behaviors and what is expected of them. Another mitigating factor is that in "command and control" departments, supervision tends to be negative—relying primarily on sanctions for not "going by the book," that is, adhering strictly to departmental rules and regulations (Weisburd, McElroy, and Hardyman 1988). Of course, this attitude is antithetical to community policing, in which innovation in solving community problems is of primary concern. However, as W. G. Skogan and S. M. Hartnett note:

> little is supposed to happen in police departments without general orders that detail how it is to be done.... working life.... is dominated by the need to reconstruct or redefine what actually happens in the field, so it appears to fit the model. This helps ensure that top managers downtown "don't know what really happens on the street"—a derisive charge that rolls easily off the lips of street officers and helps legitimate their resistance to strategies devised at headquarters. (1997, p. 73)

It should be added that not only does such a managerial approach add to the resistance of new programs and strategies, but it helps contribute to the police culture as well, where the relationship between street cops and management cops is adversarial. Completing the circle, adversarial relationships between street officers and management contribute to resistance to management's attempts at change.

Misunderstandings. Resistance to change is likely to occur when officers do not clearly understand the purpose, techniques, or consequences of a planned change because of inadequate or misunderstood communication. A major problem concerns the uncertainty about consequences of change. If employees are not told how they will be affected by change, rumors and speculation will follow, and resistance and even sabotage may be strong enough to severely limit the change effort. When change is imposed on officers, instead of occurring as a result of their participation, misunderstandings are more likely.

When police departments are attempting to move to community policing, they frequently make the mistake of not clearly articulating what new roles will be created and the effect of those new roles on all involved. For instance, in Houston when evaluators interviewed officers who were assigned to the neighborhood-oriented policing (NOP) program (often referred to by the officers as "nobody on patrol"), they discovered that officers frequently had no idea what the program was about or what they should be doing differently (Sadd and Grinc 1994). In addition, departments often do not allow officers to participate in the planning and development of the new program. While rumors may abound, the first official announcement they hear about it is when the program is unveiled at a downtown press conference by the chief, surrounded by politicians. Because they have not been kept abreast of program development and expectations, what they see from their perspective is an increased workload that will be hard to maintain, that is, more social-work activities, while maintaining their current work schedule. In such instances, it is little wonder that the officers feel that the program is being forced upon them—creating a situation that is not conducive to cooperation.

Group norms. As discussed in the previous chapter, groups have an important impact on the behavior and attitudes of their members. **Group norms**, or expected behavior from group members, can be a powerful factor in resistance to change. If individual officers follow the norms strictly (e.g., that only law enforcement activities are important), they will not easily perceive the need for change. If significant departmental changes are to occur, police managers must consider group norms and influences and involve group consensus and decision making in planning for change. The major way to achieve such involvement is to allow for participatory management. For example, in Madison, Wisconsin, where participatory management practices (referred to as quality management) produced more satisfied workers, the planners believed that it was a necessary condition for the implementation of community policing (Wycoff and Skogan 1994; see Case Study 5.1). There is also little doubt that by allowing general participation, the adversarial relations between street cops and management cops will diminish and thus increase the chances for successful change.

Balance of power. Changes that are perceived to threaten the autonomy, authority, power, or status of a group or unit will most likely encounter resistance, regardless of their merit. For instance, such resistance was well documented in the team-policing experiments of the 1970s, when departments attempted to decentralize their operations into neighborhood teams (see Sherman, Milton, and Kelley 1973). Because this approach provided more control and autonomy for lower-level management (sergeants), middle management (lieutenants and captains) resisted the change (by subverting and, in some cases, sabotaging the plans) for fear that they would lose authority, power, and status. Because the failure of most team-policing efforts can be traced, at least in part, to the lack of support by mid-level managers, it is crucial that police executives plan for their role in the change process. It has been suggested that whether middle managers are part of the problem or part of the solution in changing to community policing will depend on such factors as (1) involving them in planning for change to increase their credibility with subordinates; (2) linking rewards to performance in implementing desired changes; (3) making a serious commitment to train them in the skills necessary to adjust to their new roles; (4) articulating and adhering to a consistent vision for the department; (5) allowing them to make honest and constructive mistakes; and (6) ensuring that community policing strategies have a long-term commitment and will prevail (Geller and Swanger 1995).

Inside Policing 5.1 provides a glimpse as to the reasons officers resisted change in New York in that city's attempt to make a transition to community policing. Notice how virtually every reason overlaps, to some degree, with the major reasons for resistance discussed above. These reasons for resistance would be similar in most, if not all, traditional, paramilitary police departments in the country.

Inside Policing 5.1
Resistance to Organizational Change in New York

The following are examples of reasons that some police officers in the New York City Police Department resisted change toward a community policing philosophy. These examples are based on informal discussions with officers. It should be noted, however, that these examples appear to be fairly representative in police departments attempting major organizational change. [Author's note: The department reduced its emphasis on community policing, at least in part, because of this resistance.]

Misunderstanding of purpose. Early in the process of implementing community policing, many officers do not truly understand (or wish to understand) the philosophy and purpose behind it.

Failure to see the need for change. Some officers believe that community policing is merely a result of the commissioner (chief) wanting to try out his ideas in New York. They see this as a grand management experiment attempted at their expense.

Confusion over new roles and fear of the unknown. Many officers do not fully understand their new roles or what the department expects of them. Some officers perceive a conflict between their new role, where they are asked to "serve the public," and their traditional role, in which they exerted coercive control over the community. Officers ask, "How can you expect people to work with me to solve their problems when they know I may have to enforce the law against them because their behavior is, at times, someone else's problem?" Some supervisors are also uncertain as

to their new roles and what the department expects of them.

Fear of loss of status, security, and power. Many officers in New York believe they are doing a credible job in controlling crime and see themselves as having achieved a reasonable status in society; they have earned this status by being brave. Community policing, with its reduced emphasis on adventure and bravery and its enhanced focus on public service, has some officers fearing that their status will be diminished. Some also feel that once they align themselves with the community, they will lose much of their power. After all, how can they exercise power over people they must befriend and be accountable to?

Lack of involvement with change. Some officers feel that they are simply being told this is the new philosophy and have no sense of participation in the decision. One superior officer stated after a training seminar, "Community policing is the new train—get on or get off." This attitude encourages the feeling that this program is being forced upon them, and they have no more intention of changing their philosophy of policing because the commissioner tells them to than they would change their political philosophy if the president told them to.

Vested interest in the status quo. In order to bring back the beat cop in dramatic numbers—a hallmark of community policing—some cops will have to be pried out of their radio cars. They do not like walking a beat, especially in cold or inclement weather. Some believe that after working hard for several years they have earned the right to ride comfortably in radio cars. Others still view foot patrol negatively because it was once used as punishment or as an assignment for rookies.

Threat to existing social relationships. While foot patrol officers are getting acquainted with merchants and other citizens who live and work in their assigned communities, the radio car cops are busy responding to calls and, as they say, "busting their butts." They are beginning to resent the department's preferential attitude toward the beat cops, and to resent the beat cops themselves, who they feel are not pulling their load and spend their time "schmoozing" with the public. One officer explained, "While I'm out here doing all the grunt work and risking my life, they're playing with the neighborhood kids or attending some community meeting."

Conflicting personal and organizational objectives. The police department is interested in getting officers to work with the citizens toward solving social problems, thereby improving the quality of life and making their streets safer. Some officers believe, however, that many of the problems brought forth by the public are not worthy of police attention and have little to do with crime. Although proponents of community policing believe that resolving such problems will create an environment less conducive to crime and thus lower the crime rate, to many officers this is a waste of their time, since the causes of crime go far beyond esthetic fixes to the immediate neighborhood. Some officers are also candid about their aversion to performing what they perceive as "social work." And they complain that after a while, other officers do not see them as "real cops."

Source: Adapted from S. L. Pisani. 1992. "Dissecting Community Policing: Part 2." *Law Enforcement News*, May 31: 8, 10. Reprinted with permission from *Law Enforcement News*, John Jay College of Criminal Justice, New York City.

From Traditional to Community Policing

One of the most successful transitions from traditional to community policing is the Madison (Wisconsin) Police Department. The use of participatory (quality) management smoothed the transition process and helped to overcome initial resistance to the new developments. It is important to understand that this department was one of the early leaders in the movement toward community policing. The change process started in earnest within the department in the early 1980s, well before most of the present-day knowledge gained through research and evaluation was available. Thus, much of what the department accomplished in the way of change was groundbreaking. At the time, the department had approximately 280 commissioned personnel serving a community of approximately 175,000. The organizational change process utilized in Madison is presented in Case Study 5.1.

Case Study 5.1

Organizational Change in Madison

In the early 1970s, with the appointment of a new chief, the Madison Police Department was operating on a high-control, central-authority model. This traditional style of police management continued through the early years of the chief's tenure but not without a cost to the department and its members in terms of a high degree of distrust, grievances, complaining, stress, and confrontations. In 1981, after a four-month leave of absence, the chief decided that something had to be done regarding the department's internal problems. After discussions with rank-and-file officers, it became clear that a "lack of communication" was a primary concern and that a new management or leadership style was necessary. Consequently, the chief

decided to let employees participate more in organizational decisions and to take on the role of facilitator for himself. This decision led to the establishment of the Officers' Advisory Council (OAC) to provide advice to the chief.

The Officers' Advisory Council

The development of the OAC was critical in clearing the way for a major change in leadership style within the department. The council consists of 12 peer-selected employees who serve for a two-year period. The group was originally made up of two officers elected from each patrol shift, two detectives, one sergeant, and one officer-at-large. A majority of the council agreed that all departmental employees should be represented. The OAC became a top priority and over a period of time was given increased organizational decision-making powers. The members meet at least monthly and attempt to develop new ideas and support them with research. They have learned that if they obtain data that support their recommendations, they are likely to see those recommendations put into practice. It is believed that the OAC's actions now reflect the problem-solving and research orientation of the department's quality-improvement effort.

Committee on the Future

In 1984 a Committee on the Future was formed to look at trends and how they might affect the department in the coming years. The committee was composed of a diverse group of department members who had at least 15 years of service remaining. The intent was to have committee members who had a vested interest in the future direction of the department. A member of the OAC was appointed to serve on this committee in order to link the two groups. After a year of meeting two to four times a month, the committee released a report on the results of its findings and made three major recommendations:

1. Get closer to the people we serve.
2. Make better use of available technology.
3. Develop and improve health and wellness in the workplace.

The report helped the department to establish a vision for the future and become aware of the importance of long-range planning. This thinking about the future caused the department to re-examine its structure, internal practices, and the direction in which it was moving.

The Experimental Police District

The decision was made to develop a prototype of a new design in one part of the department before attempting to reshape the entire organization. The result was the experimental police district (EPD), the first decentralized police facility in the department. Opened in 1988, the EPD housed approximately one-sixth of the department's personnel and served approximately one-sixth of Madison's population. The charge of the EPD was to promote innovation and experimentation in three areas:

1. Employee participation in decision making about the conditions of work and the delivery of police service.
2. Management and supervisory styles supportive of employee participation and of community-oriented and problem-oriented policing.
3. The implementation of community-oriented and problem-oriented policing.

Planning for the EPD was done by a team of persons representing all areas and ranks of the department. A captain from the chief's office was asked to become an ad hoc member and to serve as a link to the chief's office and the management team. Other links to the group included a patrol officer who was a member of the OAC, a union board member, a woman detective, and a minority (male) patrol officer. This was the first time that management actively involved the union in the development of a major program. The chief reserved the right to choose a team leader and name a team facilitator. Additionally, he established a project-coordinating team to act as a steering committee and assist the project team.

Employee and Citizen Involvement

As a first step in the planning process, project-team members identified depart-

☞ mental problems that they thought needed to be corrected, such as lack of meaningful involvement with the community, lack of teamwork among officers, inflexible management styles and resulting loss of creativity, and lack of communication and information exchange among ranks. Project-team members also conducted department-wide interviews, in which they met in small groups with all employees to find out what they thought needed to be corrected. The top preferences were voted on by the group and published in an EPD newsletter and sent to all employees. This was the first time that management had allowed employees to survey other employees on issues that heretofore were considered to be strictly management's concern.

To get citizens involved, the project team held eight community meetings in the project area, two in each alderman's district. The first set of meetings in each district was for people whom the department and alderman designated as community leaders. The second set of meetings was open to all concerned citizens. At the meetings, citizens were questioned about their knowledge of and satisfaction with police services and neighborhood problems and concerns and how they felt police could work with them in responding to problems. The group process used at the meetings resulted in a listing of problems rated by priority.

Operation of the EPD

The goals of EPD managers are to become coaches and teachers who allow and encourage creativity and risk taking among officers. They have given officers substantial latitude to decide their own schedules, their own work conditions, and how to address neighborhood problems. In other matters, the managers consider the input of employees before making decisions. They try to encourage problem solving by offering ideas, information, and scheduling alternatives. Though things moved slowly at the beginning, the managers began to see increased use of problem solving as a tool.

Sources: Adapted from D. C. Couper and S. H. Lobitz. 1991. *Quality Policing: The Madison Experience*. Washington, D.C.: Police Executive Research Forum, pp. 15–22, 33, 36–37; M. A. Wycoff and W. G. Skogan. 1993. *Community Policing in Madison: Quality From the Inside Out*. Washington, D.C.: National Institute of Justice, December, pp. 20–22, 26–28.

Obstacles to Change Outside of Management's Control

In addition to the obstacles to change described earlier, there are several additional obstacles outside the control of management that have a direct influence on management's ability to implement organization change. First, there are **civil service regulations**, which control matters relating to personnel, including selection and promotion. Police managers have very limited, if any, control over the limits of these regulations; for example, with respect to requiring higher educational standards in selection or emphasizing seniority over ability in promotions. Such regulations undoubtedly hinder progress toward change and may need to be dealt with by management, even to the point of lobbying to modify or eliminate them. However, since such regulations often state directives, it is difficult for a single local department to get attention. Concomitantly, many police departments are also accountable to **civil service commissions**, which may also have authority over officer discipline and dismissals. The authors know of several instances in which a police chief has terminated an officer for cause, only to have the civil service commission overrule the decision. In reality, there is little that can be done with respect to the civil-service commission's decisions, except possibly to wait until some new members are appointed.

Other factors that may affect management's efforts at change include police unions and fraternal organizations. Several primary objectives of **police**

An organization of police supervisors meets regarding work conditions. (Photo: Mark C. Ide)

unions include union recognition, improvements in wages and benefits, clear disciplinary procedures, and better job conditions. **Fraternal organizations** primarily seek recognition and benefits for their members, and these goals may differ from the goals of union or other fraternal units. With respect to wages and benefits, it is clear that if primary emphasis is placed on money issues, rather than employee satisfaction, change can be made more difficult. It is not suggested that unions should not attempt to increase salaries and benefits, but in those departments where pay and benefit packages are already attractive and competitive, management and labor leaders should work together to improve employee levels of satisfaction in the work environment. The research is clear that satisfied workers are more productive workers. Under the right circumstances, changes toward community policing can significantly improve officer satisfaction, especially through enrichment (i.e., broadening the police role). Finally, attempts by unions to limit or severely impede the disciplinary process can have a detrimental impact on management's attempts to change the department's culture, as well as to change the work of officers. It is crucial that management work with union leadership to preserve or to establish a fair yet firm approach to discipline.

Negotiated job conditions may also play a vital role in how much control management has over changing the content of jobs and even job assignments. As noted in the last chapter, it is becoming common for unions to negotiate matters that were once the traditional province of police managers, including personnel assignments and allocation of resources. How negotiated job conditions can affect management control with respect to departmental change can be illustrated by a San Francisco-Bay Area department that was attempting to implement community policing (see also: Case Study 5.2). One of the foundations of the approach was the "stable" beat area assignment of a team of officers in order that they could become familiar with

the residents and their needs. One popular team sergeant—with both resi- ❖ ❖ ❖ ❖
dents and officers—had served a certain amount of time on the beat and,
based on his seniority under union contract, was eligible to transfer to another beat. The sergeant applied for a transfer and was turned down by the
chief, because in the chief's view the sergeant's leadership and popularity
were too important to the community policing effort at that time. The sergeant promptly filed a grievance with the union, which immediately ordered
the transfer. Reluctantly, the chief allowed the transfer, lamenting that such
liberal transfer policies would need to be renegotiated in the next union contract if community policing were to succeed. Although the sergeant's right to
transfer in this case was unquestionable, the point is that implementing major organizational change is complicated and must be well planned, including negotiations with the department's union leaders.

Overcoming Obstacles to Change

The research to date provides some important lessons to help police managers overcome obstacles to organizational change in moving to community
policing. For instance, in a national survey of more than 1,600 agencies (National Institute of Justice 1995), police chiefs and sheriffs were asked about
the lessons they learned from their experiences with community policing.
They most frequently mentioned four such lessons: (1) the need for pre-im-
plementation training of personnel, (2) the importance of taking a long view
of the change process, (3) the need for support from elected officials and
other city agencies, and (4) the importance of listening to and involving the
community. In addition, 48 percent thought that implementation would require major changes in departmental policies or goals, 56 percent anticipated
that rank-and-file employees would resist such changes, and 83 percent
strongly supported the need for training in community policing and believed
that existing training efforts were inadequate.

Evaluations of major programs in New York and Houston, in which attempts at community policing failed, and the concept has been
deemphasized, provide evidence of the difficulty of attempting to implement
significant change—especially in large departments. Even after 10 years of
experience with various aspects of community policing in New York, many
officers "contended that there was little support among the rank and file"
(Sadd and Grinc 1996, p. 8). In Houston, an independent report by Cresap
Management Consultants pointed out a number of operational problems including officers being torn between immediate reports of crime and preventive work required by community policing, officers being unprepared for
their new tasks, and skepticism, even hostility, of many officers about the program's aims. The report further pointed out that it was unlikely that the department could recruit enough officers with the level of complex skills required to do community policing, particularly at current pay levels. The president of the Police Officers' Association stated that "most officers feel it's a
hoax, renaming things and using a lot of buzz words and the like," and that "a
lot of officers probably feel they're expected to be more like social workers
than police officers" ("Study Criticizes Community Policing" 1991, p. B2).

Other major cities have also encountered critical problems in their attempts to implement community policing. For example, in both Los Angeles

❖ ❖ ❖ ❖   and Atlanta, officers could not sustain community-oriented projects unless they were freed from the draining effects of responding to frequent, and unpredictable, 911 calls. It takes a considerable amount of time and effort to set up and meet with the public, help define and research problems, and coordinate community and interagency involvement in attempting to solve defined problems. In Los Angeles, community policing officers were also dissatisfied over the conflict between what they were told to do (which was new) and how their performance was actually evaluated (by the old standards, including how many arrests they made) (Booz, Allen & Hamilton 1992). Common implementation problems with community policing have been documented in a study of eight jurisdictions (Sadd and Grinc 1994, 1996), known as innovative neighborhood-oriented policing (INOP). These common implementation problems are discussed in Case Study 5.2.

Although implementing community policing is a strenuous and often arduous process, given enough effort, and under the right leadership and conditions, it *can* be done. As M. A. Wycoff and W. G. Skogan (1994, p. 88–89) found in their evaluation of Madison, "It is possible to change a traditional, control-oriented police organization into one in which employees become members of work teams and participants in decision making processes." With this in mind, some of the lessons learned in Madison in overcoming implementation problems include the following:

1. It is possible to implement participatory management in a police department, and doing so is very likely to produce more satisfied workers. Many managers and employees in Madison believe that such an approach, which they call quality leadership, is a necessary condition for the implementation of community policing. Some of the possible advantages of a participatory style of management include (a) employees whose input is valued learn to value the input of others (e.g., citizens); (b) employees who are invited to work in team relationships to solve internal problems learn to work in this way with citizens; (c) people closest to the problems (officers and citizens) have the most information about them, and their input is critical for problem definition and resolution; and (d) organizational change tends to be more readily accepted by employees who participate in the process of creating it.

2. Decentralization contributed significantly to the creation of the new management style. It also contributed to the development of team spirit and processes, conditions that should facilitate community policing. Officers who work in the experimental police district (EPD) believe the decentralized station improved relationships with the public; they report increased numbers of contacts with citizens in the community and an ever-increasing number of citizens who come to the station for assistance. The scale on which decentralization occurred was important, as the small physical space of the EPD station made close interaction among officers, detectives, supervisors, and managers unavoidable, thus increasing the flow of information.

Case Study 5.2   ❖ ❖ ❖ ❖

Innovative Neighborhood-Oriented Policing: Implementation Challenges

The innovative neighborhood-oriented policing programs evaluated were Hayward, California; Houston, Texas; Louisville, Kentucky; New York; Norfolk, Virginia; Portland, Oregon; Prince George's County, Maryland; and Tempe, Arizona. The INOP jurisdictions varied greatly, as did the prior experiences of each department with community policing. After one year of operation (which may have been insufficient time for significant results to appear), their overall effectiveness was only minimal. Perhaps the most important contribution of the findings, however, was that each of the sites experienced common implementation problems that hampered their ability to have the desired impacts. These problems included the following:

1. There was minimal involvement of police officers, city agencies, and community residents in program design; consequently, knowledge of the structure and goals of the program and of community policing in general was lacking in all of these groups. As a result, there was considerable resistance on the part of officers to the substantial role changes required. Many officers were critical of the program's community outreach and social-work role and criticized it as not involving "real" police work.

2. Similarly, community residents were generally unaware of the goals of the INOP projects, and their involvement was limited in scope (i.e., in some sites "involvement" simply meant providing their police with information about crime). In other words, the community did not become truly involved in community policing. Furthermore, it was not clear that the police knew what the community wanted from the program.

3. Often, community policing is defined and implemented solely as a police initiative to the virtual exclusion of other city agencies and to the communities it hopes to serve. One of the most important findings of the INOP research is that the education and training of community residents regarding their roles in community policing is almost nonexistent. This suggests that without meaningful involvement of the community in the planning process, community policing will fail to realize its potential.

4. The INOP research suggests that among the most difficult tasks of implementation are (a) educating and training police officers and administrators about the goals and techniques of community policing, (b) obtaining the cooperation of other city agencies in the community policing effort, (c) building trust between the police and residents of communities (particularly where there is a history of antagonistic relationships), and (d) stimulating from the outset community involvement in the planning and implementation of community policing.

The experiences of the eight INOP sites clearly indicated that in attempting to implement community-policing programs, departments (and their jurisdictions) need to pay particular attention to three critical issues: (1) overcoming patrol officer resistance, (2) generating interagency support (city or county-wide if possible), and (3) building community involvement . These common problems reflect the reality of attempting to implement community policing programs and the need for a sustained, long-term effort.

Source: Adapted from S. Sadd and R. Grinc. 1996. *Implementation Challenges in Community Policing: Innovative Neighborhood-Oriented Policing in Eight Cities*. Washington, D.C.: National Institute of Justice.

3. The managers of the Madison Police Department also thought that the best way to move toward decentralization and community policing was to change one part of the organization (i.e., the EPD) before proceeding with department-wide implementation.

Furthermore, it was evident that special attention paid to one part of the department did not block change elsewhere (i.e., other changes in the department were not affected by the attention received by the EPD).

4. During the long time frame of undergoing change and experimentation (some 20 years), Madison continued to make efforts to recruit highly educated officers whose backgrounds, life experiences, and attitudes increased the likelihood that they would be supportive of change. This may be an important observation as a caution against unrealistic expectations for departments attempting major change efforts whose personnel are not relatively highly educated. (Adapted from Wycoff and Skogan 1994, pp. 89–90).

Based on the research reviewed above, it appears that the bottom line with respect to the successful implementation of community policing can be tied directly to the amount of change made toward the following: (a) decentralized organization, (b) participatory management, (c) higher educational standards, (d) redefinition of the police role (including training, reward, and promotional practices), and (e) involvement of a representative body of citizens.

Planning for Large-Scale Change

In light of the previous discussion, this section will take an inside look at the overall plan for change, as well as the change strategies, used by the Chicago Police Department in its attempt to move to community policing. Chicago's attempt at organizational change has been the largest-scale effort to date (Skogan and Hartnett 1997). The experimental program consisted of five of the 25 police districts in the city, including 54 experimental beats; the

Successful organizational change toward community policing requires the involvement of a representative body of citizens. (Photo: Kathy McLaughlin/The Image Works.)

experimental districts were referred to as prototypes, since the program would eventually be expanded to include all police districts. The program became labeled as the Chicago Alternative Policing Strategy (CAPS), thus giving the department and city its own style of community policing. A total of 1,500 police personnel of all ranks went through orientation and skill-building sessions, and close to 700 beat meetings, attended by 15,000 people, were held during the first year and one-half of the program.

Laying the Foundation

In the early going, the department developed a mission statement and a 30-page supporting report describing the basic philosophy of community policing and identifying, step by step, many of the key components of change that were needed for the program to succeed. The report opened with a "rationale for change" that reviewed the limits of the traditional model of policing and argued for a "smarter" approach that would capitalize on the strengths of the city's neighborhoods. It further argued that the department had to be "reinvented" in order to form a partnership with the community, one that stressed crime prevention, customer service, and honest and ethical conduct. The report was mailed to every departmental member and to help ensure that it would be read it was included on the reading list from which questions would be drawn for the next promotional exam. It became the basis for planning the eventual citywide implementation of CAPS.

It should also be mentioned that the department had a traditional paramilitary structure with many managerial levels; this top-heavy bureaucracy was one of city hall's sources of frustration with the department. The mayor favored the idea of compressing the rank structure and freeing up more personnel for street-level work; he once exclaimed to the researchers, "Captains! Nobody can tell me what they do!" (Skogan and Hartnett 1997, p. 34). Ultimately, the rank of captain was eliminated, thus flattening the hierarchy by one level. Such a flattening of the rank structure parallels the need to decentralize community-policing departments, thus helping to push decision-making authority down to the street and neighborhood level.

Key Elements to Change

The organizational change process incorporated six key elements, briefly described below:

1. *The entire department and the city were to be involved.* Rather than forming special community-policing units, the whole department would change. Thus, community-policing roles were developed for all of the units, including the detective, tactical, gangs, and narcotics divisions, rather than just for uniformed officers. Only patrol would be utilized, however, until the program had proven to be effective. The commitment to citywide involvement was reflected in the decision to use diverse districts spread throughout the city as prototypes for the program (several of which had high rates of crime), as well as to use existing personnel in the districts. In some experimental community-policing departments, both the districts and the personnel (oftentimes

volunteers) were carefully selected. As one executive put it, the department did not "stack the deck in favor of success."

2. *Officers were to have permanent beat assignments*. In order to develop partnerships with the community and to learn about the neighborhood, officers had to be assigned to one place long enough for residents to know them and learn to trust them. Additionally, officers had to have enough free time to allow them to engage in community work. In attempting to resolve the conflict between working with the public and responding promptly to calls for service, officers in each district were divided into beat teams and rapid-response units (see Case Study 5.3). Beat teams were to be dispatched less frequently in order to have time to work on community projects. The rapid-response units and other teams that worked throughout the district were to be assigned to other calls.

3. *The department was to have a strong commitment to training*. The department invested a significant effort in training officers and their supervisors in the skills required to identify and solve problems in working with the community. Training was considered essential in promoting officer understanding and commitment to the program and in providing direction to officers and supervisors in their new roles. The lesson learned from other cities that did not pay proper attention to a strong training component was that those cities never developed serious community policing programs. It was also believed that by emphasizing training, a message would be sent to the rank and file that community policing was real and that upper management was committed to the program.

   The initial training program consisted of orientation sessions followed by skill-building sessions. During follow-up training, it was thought that officers needed to be evaluated on what they had learned. A test would be administered at the end of the training program, which they had to pass; participants who did not pass would have to repeat the course. This appeared "to have a salutary effect on their attentiveness" (Skogan and Hartnett 1997, p. 101).

4. *The community was to play a significant role in the program*. The foundation of CAPS was the formation of police-community partnerships, focused on identifying and solving problems at the neighborhood level. This cannot be accomplished without the cooperation of the community and public and private agencies. One of the major problem-solving roles for the police was to engage community resources by drawing other city agencies into identifying and responding to local concerns. This community involvement was developed in two ways. First, beat meetings began, usually monthly, involving small groups of residents and beat officers. The meetings were held in church basements and park buildings throughout the city. Second, advisory committees were formed at the district level to meet with upper management

and district staff; committees included community leaders, school council members, ministers, business operators, and other institutional representatives.

5. *Policing was to be linked to the delivery of city services.* Community policing inevitably involves the expansion of the police role to include a broad range of concerns that are outside the scope of traditional policing. Such expansion was considered necessary by management because they realized that although the police could put a lid on many crime-related problems, they could never eliminate them. They wanted to develop problem-solving systems that could keep the lid on even after they had moved on. In addition, the delivery of city services in the prototype districts was linked to community policing through the use of service-request forms. The requests for service generated by officers were closely tracked by city hall, which developed a system to prioritize and track each case.

    The primary concerns of the residents in beat meetings included a broad range of problems, most of which were *not* the types of crimes traditionally associated with the police; for example, predatory and violent crimes were identified by residents only 3 percent of the time and fear of crime only 2 percent. The four categories of problems that comprised over 75 percent of all beat meeting discussions were (1) social disorder (28 percent), including disturbances and drunkenness, prostitution, truancy, gun fire, and gang problems; (2) physical decay (23 percent), including abandoned cars and buildings, litter, graffiti, and vandalism; (3) police performance (15 percent), including harassment and insensitivity, response time to 911 calls, traffic stops, and neighborhood patrols; (4) drug problems (11 percent), including drug use or sale, and use of pay phones.

6. *There was to be an emphasis on crime analysis.* The geographic analysis of crime was considered a key element of the program. It was to provide the knowledge base that would drive the problem-solving process on the beat. Computer technology was to be used to speed up the collection and analysis of data, which would be used to identify crime problems in the beat area. A user-friendly crime-mapping system was developed for use on computers, with printouts to be distributed at beat meetings and made accessible to the public at each district station. Other planned analytic tools included "beat planners," which were beat officers' notebooks filled with local information. New roll-call procedures were also developed to encourage officers on various shifts to share information about their beats and community resources.

In addition to the six key elements developed in the organizational plan, Chicago also used a number of **change strategies**—methods or techniques used to facilitate the change process—throughout the department. The main change strategies are discussed in Case Study 5.3.

Change Strategies in Chicago

Management knew that there could be no real change without the support of rank-and-file members at the bottom of the organization. This became known as the "winning hearts and minds" (WHAM) component of organizational change. In order to win the hearts and minds of street officers, the following change strategies were used.

Changing the Job

Jobs were changed for the officers who served each prototype district, by dividing them into beat teams and rapid-response teams. The department took this approach rather than forming what is known as a split-force of community policing officers and regular ("real") policing officers into separate units; such an approach has been shown to create tension between the two units and ultimately to undermine community policing. By using beat teams, a majority of their time could be spent within their assigned geographical area. This new beat integrity, including the freedom from responding to 911 calls, was accomplished by increasing the number of officers who served in the prototype districts by about 13 percent. In addition, a radio-dispatch plan was implemented that allocated selected calls to beat teams. Beat officers were to work with schools, businesses, and residents to identify and solve problems and to serve as coordinators for service requests to other city agencies. They attended various neighborhood meetings to work with existing community organizations, as well as regularly held public beat meetings, to increase communications between residents and beat officers. Over time, officers would alternate between beat work and rapid-response cars in order to ensure that community policing did not become confined to special units.

Changing Supervision

The role of sergeants was crucial to CAPS, as prototype beat officers needed direction and mentoring in their new roles; sergeants were also responsible for supervising rapid-response officers as well. Although the sergeants were given some initial CAPS training, it soon became apparent that their role was not clearly defined, and they often felt unsure about what was expected of them. The prototype sergeants were told that their job was to coach officers in their new community roles, but, in reality, they knew as little as the street officers about what that entailed. They soon became disgruntled and felt overworked. Additional training attempted to alleviate this role confusion; it was designed to encourage them to become teachers, coaches, and mentors. These were all new roles in the department and a far cry from the traditional supervisory role of giving orders and signing forms. The additional training consisted of several skill-building sessions with respect to leadership styles, building partnerships, problem solving, and team building.

Avoiding the Social-Work Image

One of the lessons learned from other cities was that separate community policing units did not work. Members of these units inevitably were looked down on by their colleagues as "empty holsters" doing "wave-and-smiling" policing. The prototype districts that were selected joined the program as a unit, "warts and all"; they were not staffed by volunteers, or specially selected officers, supervisors, or even district-level managers (two of whom—out of five—never supported the program). Officers on all three shifts, not just the day shift, made up a beat team. The teams received no special privileges, such as selecting their own working hours or days off. (In New York, for example, the beat officers used flexible schedules to work only the day shift—Monday through Friday—which got the program into significant trouble both internally and externally.) Management also made a concerted effort to assure all sworn personnel that community policing was not a "soft on crime" approach. They stressed that officers would not become social workers, but rather, referral specialists who could help solve problems at the neighborhood level. In addition, it was emphasized that traditional police work would continue to be impor-

☞ tant and would be rewarded, with a strong emphasis on making arrests where appropriate.

Dealing With the Union

Employee organizations played major roles in departmental policy making in Chicago. Officers were represented in bargaining by the Fraternal Order of Police. There were also unions that represented the department's civilian employees and associations that separately represented sergeants, lieutenants, and captains, who were not allowed to form unions. The program had to be consistent with the union contract; assignments were closely regulated by union contract based on seniority and were renewable each year through a bidding procedure. Thus, only assignments to specific tasks—for instance, either to beat teams or to rapid-response cars—were under the control of management. As a result, management could not attempt to match officer skills with specific district conditions or guarantee that officers would remain in any job or beat for more than a year. During CAPS' first year, a new FOP president was elected and he was included on a policy-planning committee for the future of policing in the city. He was widely consulted, as were representatives of the civilian employees' unions. Later in the development of CAPS, the FOP's executive committee took the unique step of endorsing the program.

Source: Adapted from W. G. Skogan and S. M. Hartnett. 1997. *Community Policing, Chicago Style*. New York: Oxford University Press, pp. 89–95.

Results in Chicago

An early evaluation of the program found evidence of CAPS-related success with physical decay problems in three of the five experimental districts, a decline in gang and drug problems in two districts and a decline in major crimes in two districts (Hartnett and Skogan 1999). The most notable initial effects were found in Englewood district, one of the highest crime districts in the city. All four major problems identified by the community (trash in vacant lots, abandoned buildings, gang violence, and street drug dealings) decreased during the 16-month period after CAPS was introduced, while three of the four problems increased—especially gang violence—in a comparison district.

The evaluation also found that CAPS was helping to promote better relationships between police and residents in some of the city's poorest communities. Citizens reported seeing more community-oriented policing activity, and in two districts there was a decline in perceptions of excessive aggressiveness by the police. Satisfaction with police responsiveness to neighborhood problems went up in four of the five prototype districts. Perceptions of the quality of police service went up significantly among African Americans and whites, but not among Latinos. Since the development of CAPS citywide, surveys of all major groups indicate steady increases in satisfaction with the quality of police services. As one resident in the 10th district put it: "You have a sense of camaraderie and cooperation between beat officers and community residents; you lose that sense of fear." His point was reiterated by a senior command staff member: "I can't see policing any other way. When I was growing up, there was a real separation between the citizens and the police. Now there's a genuine trust that's come because they know us, and they know we can effect change together" (Hartnett and Skogan 1999, p. 7).

Changes in police management, however, remain problematic. The department continues to gather and distribute the same activity counts as before (calls answered and arrests made); there are no measures of the extent to which officers are involved in problem solving and no indicators of their success. It has proven difficult to develop workable performance measures and incentives that reflect the new mission. As one watch commander has stated:

> Nothing has been implemented—new disciplinary procedures, efficiency ratings. Good officers get disciplined the same as bum officers. Honest mistakes are judged the same as intentional mistakes. They promised a new promotional process—we haven't seen it. It's hypocritical. They wrote it, but they don't abide by it. (Hartnett and Skogan 1999, p. 10)

Lessons Learned From Madison and Chicago

Two of the most comprehensive organizational change efforts, from traditional policing to community policing, have been in Madison and Chicago. Many of the reasons for the success of these departments overlap, especially with respect to the internal environment. Both departments, for example, relied on a department report developed by departmental personnel to lay the foundation for change and to guide the change process; Chicago also relied on the input from outside consultants. Improving communication with rank-and-file officers was crucial to both programs. Madison, however, spent significantly more time developing a true participatory (quality) leadership style, including a comprehensive committee structure staffed with personnel from throughout the department, whose recommendations were generally adopted. This level of true employee participation in policing is unparalleled. Both departments also had strong support from their cities' top political leadership. In Madison, quality improvement was a citywide movement, whereas in Chicago, the mayor used the CAPS program to shore up city hall's provision of services throughout the city. Both cities recognized the importance of, and relied heavily upon, the training of their personnel. Finally, both cities started with experimental programs, which, over time, were expanded throughout the department.

One significant difference was that Chicago used regular officers and supervisors ("warts and all") in its prototype districts, whereas Madison selected personnel who were "interested" in the program (effectively volunteers), in its experimental police district; EPD personnel could also decide their own schedules and work conditions. An important point to be made about using regular officers, supervisors, and established beats is that the experimental or prototype programs will not be as likely to generate a "we versus they" mentality between experimental and regular officers. Such an approach can go a long way toward reducing the types of resistance to change discussed earlier and documented in Inside Policing 5.1.

One additional caveat should be noted. In Madison, a concerted effort had been made for approximately two decades to recruit highly educated officers who would be more likely to support change. If a true commitment to community policing is to take place, and if the police role is to be significantly broadened to carry it out, the level of higher education required for police must undoubtedly be raised. It appears that the history of promoting higher education in Madison contributed in no small part to establishing a more conducive atmosphere for large-scale organizational change.

Although both departments sought input from the external environment, the level of participation from each community differed significantly. Madi-

❖ ❖ ❖ ❖

son developed feedback mechanisms only (mainly surveys), whereas Chicago took the development of citizen communication and input to a new level for police departments. The involvement of beat officers who were geographically stable and generally free from 911 response calls allowed them to work closely with the community in problem solving. By meeting with various community organizations and attending regularly scheduled public beat meetings, they could get a sense of what residents considered to be the important problems in their areas. Although levels of organized participation were not significantly higher in the prototype areas than in comparison areas, there was evidence that both awareness and participation by residents were more widely distributed within the prototype districts. Furthermore, although the meetings were too frequently run by departmental community relations specialists—instead of beat officers—emphasizing a narrow law enforcement perspective, 50 percent of the participants responded that the meetings were very useful for improving the community's relationship with the police and 38 percent felt that they were very useful for finding solutions to neighborhood problems (Skogan and Hartnett 1997).

It would appear that both departments have made significant progress toward implementing community policing, but they have done it in different ways. In Madison, employee participation in the change process was a strong point, whereas in Chicago, the development of partnerships with the community through beat teams was the strong suit. Possibly the quintessential approach to community policing would be to mix the best practices from both Madison and Chicago, while at the same time raising educational standards for recruits.

Innovation

If constructive and timely change is to take place in police departments, mid-level and top-level managers must develop an organizational climate that fosters and encourages innovation. **Innovation** refers to the development and use of new ideas and methods. Such a climate should be relatively open, trustworthy, and forward looking. In their study on police innovation in six American cities, J. H. Skolnick and D. H. Bayley (1986) made several recommendations for improving police effectiveness. As you read the recommendations, try to keep in mind how each does or does not apply to the experiences of Madison and Chicago.

First, and most important to successful innovation, is effective and energetic leadership from the office of the chief. Although executive leadership is vital to any enterprise, it is essential to traditional paramilitary police departments. Because such departments tend not to be democratically run, most members are aware of the chief's preferences, demands, and expectations. It is not enough, however, simply to espouse certain ideals and values; the chief must become an active, committed exponent of them.

The second requirement for successful innovation is that the chief must be able to motivate (and sometimes manipulate) departmental personnel into supporting the values that the chief espouses. Some resistance from the old guard, who have strong ties to the status quo, is likely. Because these individuals may retain much influence, police executives often attempt to keep or enlist their support. As a result, chiefs may actually affirm conflicting norms, telling different audiences what each wants to hear. Consequently, nobody in the department knows what the chief stands for and everyone is confused. Preferably, a majority of the officers can be persuaded that the new values are superior. Persuasion is seldom easy, however, especially in departments that have associations and unions resistant to change. Nevertheless, innovatively inclined chiefs should be able to work with such associations and unions in order to gain the support of the rank and file.

Skolnick and Bayley noted that one of the ways of potentially lessening resistance from the old guard is first to implement change in one part of the department. In this way, the department can learn how best to change with the least amount of disruption, and those who are resistant have a chance to observe the potential benefits of the change. If the change is ultimately considered not to be beneficial for the entire department, it would not be implemented throughout the department.

A third requirement is that the integrity of innovation must be defended. Once a new value system (one dedicated to the development of new concepts and methods) has been established, it will need to be protected from the pull to return to the status quo. Such protection is especially necessary in policing, because police departments tend to be heavily tied to the traditional ways of doing things.

The fourth requirement for innovation is public support. Innovative crime-prevention programs that are implemented with community input enjoy strong, often unexpected, support from the public. If properly introduced and explained to the community, police innovations will most likely be widely supported.

As Skolnick and Bayley pointed out, the need to sustain or defend innovation is critical, as regression toward the traditional way of doing things is strong. What methods can police managers use to keep the department on the path toward innovation? Case Study 5.4 examines several types of management techniques that the Madison Police Department employed to gain momentum and sustain innovation in its organizational change process.

Case Study 5.4

Sustaining Innovation in Madison

In promoting and sustaining innovation, a vision was created for the department, asking what it wanted to be, how it could get there, and how it would know when it was making continuous improvement. In carrying out the plan, the department's managers attempted to follow these steps:

1. They listened carefully to their employees and their citizen-customers.
2. They tailored a leadership style to meet those needs.
3. They trained all employees in the new philosophy.
4. They empowered and coached managers and supervisors to be quality leaders.
5. They promoted, praised, and gave key assignments to the quality "champions" in the department.
6. They settled in for the long term; they took risks and continually tried to practice what they were preaching.

Some of the techniques used in carrying out the plan are described briefly below. ☞

☞ **Training**

The management team completed seven days of quality-productivity and quality-leadership training; during the last hour of each training day the chief appeared in order to answer questions and address concerns. Thus, he showed support for the new philosophy and served as a role model for the new leadership style. This training was followed by three similar six-day sessions for sergeants. Quality-improvement training then began for all departmental employees, both civilian and commissioned. A three-day training session covering systems thinking, group skills, interpersonal skills, and quality leadership was developed. The department also reserved four or five seats in each of the training sessions for other city employees, establishing the importance of teamwork among city agencies. At the end of the final training day, the chief and deputy chief were on hand to answer questions and clarify some of the principles of quality leadership.

Promotions

The first effort beyond training to start running the department in accord with the new philosophy involved implementing a new promotion policy. This was an important step because who is promoted sends a stronger message than any words from management. Consequently, the chief sent out a memorandum establishing the importance of the new promotion policy, which stated, in part:

> I strongly believe that if we are to "practice what we preach" in our Mission Statement to achieve excellence (i.e., teamwork, respect, problem solving, openness, sensitive and community-oriented policing), . . . we will have to alter the way in which we lead. . . . The promotions I make from now on are going to people who have strong interpersonal and facilitative skills and who can adjust and adapt to the new needs and demands. . . . In addition to being totally committed to the Mission of the organization [supervisors and managers] will have to be able to work in a team, become coaches, accept feedback, ask and listen to others in the team, and facilitate their employees' input and growth in the workplace.

Accordingly, subsequent promotions went to those officers who were peer-group leaders and who wished to adopt a quality-leadership style. Some of those promoted would not have been selected in the past; thus, new leaders who would help to implement and sustain innovative policing were being selected.

Customer Surveys

In order to establish base-line data and to assess the quality and customer satisfaction of the department, a survey was developed. The survey asks citizens to rate police services from poor (1) to excellent (5) in seven areas: (1) concern, (2) helpfulness, (3) knowledge, (4) quality of service, (5) solving the problem, (6) putting citizens at ease, and (7) professional conduct. An open-ended question at the end asks: How can we improve? About 25 percent of the responses include feedback on this question.

Surveys are mailed each month (with a stamped, self-addressed return envelope) to all persons identified in every 50th case-numbered report, including victims, witnesses, complainants, and arrestees. Approximately 160 surveys are mailed out each month with a return rate of about 35 to 40 percent, all of which are read by the chief. The results are periodically published in the department's newsletter, in which both positive and negative comments regarding improvement are summarized. The newsletter also provides statistical results for the seven areas, including demographic data on respondents, and tabulates satisfaction levels in relationship to the age, race, income, and gender of the respondent.

Managing by Wandering Around

The department believes that leadership involves being seen, and that leaders cannot be seen very well if they spend all their time behind a desk. Accordingly, the department has found that a very simple technique of managing by walking around (MBWA) is a powerful one. For most police managers, MBWA means getting out on the "street" (where the action is) and observing and asking or answering questions. ☞

> In this way, managers learn what their employees need from them to do a quality job, as well as letting them know that managers care about quality work and are looking for ways to improve conditions and processes.
>
> Source: Adapted from D. C. Couper and S. H. Lobitz. 1991. *Quality Policing: The Madison Experience*. Washington, D.C.: Police Executive Research Forum, pp. 59–60, 63, 66–68, 80.

Quality Circles

As most of the research and the case studies have revealed, police chiefs can help promote innovation by more directly involving line officers in department decision making and problem solving. In this way, the officers develop a greater understanding of the possible need for innovation and are more likely to become active participants in the change process. Originally developed in Japan in the mid-1950s to accentuate the Japanese emphasis on participatory management and decentralized decision making in business, the use of quality circles has grown in U. S. organizations, including the police. A **quality circle** consists of a group of employees from the same work area who meet on a regular basis for the purpose of identifying and solving common work problems.

The use of quality circles in policing can be illustrated by the Dallas Police Department (Melancon 1984), which originally had one of the most extensive programs in the country. Team leaders, generally sergeants, attend seminars to learn about the philosophy, techniques, and fundamentals of the operation. Team members are volunteers from various work groups, who must attend several meetings prior to determining if they wish to participate. Members attend meetings in both on-duty and off-duty status and may drop out at any time. The department has had 15 to 18 quality circles in operation at any one time, covering many units, including patrol, detectives, traffic, dispatching, property, records, legal services, community services, training, personnel, and tactics (Hatry and Greiner 1986). D. D. Melancon (1984) reported improved morale and worker satisfaction for participating employees. A survey of team leaders indicated that quality circles were beneficial in solving problems in the work area and that management supported the program. The survey further discovered that officers felt that through the program the department exhibited more openness, trust, and support toward the employees.

An early national survey of 300 police departments found that 48 (16 percent) were using quality circles (Hatry and Greiner 1986). One interesting finding was that although police departments with paramilitary structures and authoritarian managerial styles were more likely to have problems implementing quality circle programs, a surprising number of police executives were willing to try participatory techniques. The researchers concluded that management style may be less of a problem than was originally anticipated (this appears also to be true for those departments moving toward community policing). While quality circles appeared to improve employee morale, there was no significant improvement in department performance. It was believed this situation was due, in part, to the selection of topics that were too narrow in scope and, in part, because the circles involved only a small proportion of the work force in any one department. Finally, it was suggested that if quality circles spent more time emphasizing substantive service-delivery problems confronting individual police work units, their impact on departmental performance and long-term viability would be greatly strengthened.

Police Departments as Learning Organizations

The discussion of quality-management principles in the last chapter included the concept of continuous improvement. Continuous improvement cannot be accomplished without continuous learning, which is another way to sustain innovation in police departments. In other words, if management can develop an environment that promotes continuous learning, the department (and its members) would benefit from its own and other's experiences, including both success and failure. Such a learning environment leads to a **learning organization,** which is able to process what it has learned and adapt accordingly. According to W. A. Geller (1997), there are many structural and process ideas that would help police departments to become learning organizations. One idea is to create an R&D unit that actually does research and development, instead of only statistical descriptions of departmental inputs and outputs. In order to have such a unit, it must be run by someone who understands R&D and is supported by a respectable budget (also not the norm). Such a unit might help foster an appreciation for the practical benefits of prior research in the field. It is virtually impossible to be a learning organization if the use of recent research findings is not part of departmental processes.

Another idea along these lines is to continue to expand police-researcher partnerships, such as those sponsored by the National Institute of Justice. Such partnerships allow the department to get involved in a research project without all the necessary expertise or budget restraints, while learning something about themselves. The innovative neighborhood-oriented policing (INOP) project discussed previously would be an example of how such a research project might work. The training and technical assistance provided to the INOP police departments funded by the National Institute of Justice is documented in Inside Policing 5.2. Additionally, if a department finds a researcher it really trusts, it could contract with him or her part-time to serve as a research "broker," helping the department to become a better consumer and user of research. Some police departments have acquired this kind of capacity by hiring a criminologist to head their planning or R&D units.

Inside Policing 5.2
Innovative Neighborhood-Oriented Policing:
Training and Technical Assistance

To build knowledge and to develop skills in organizing, strategy development, leadership, and other areas, a systematic program of training and technical assistance was carried out as an integral part of INOP.

Needs Assessment

The assistance, which was tailored to the specific needs of each of the eight sites, was preceded by assessments conducted to identify these needs. Input for the assessments came from individuals at each site—representatives of the community, the police, and other agencies and organizations. A range of needs was identified, but two appeared to dominate the agenda: strengthening collaboration among agencies and developing citizen mobilization/leadership for both

❖ ❖ ❖ ❖   ☞

active and prospective community leaders. In Hayward, California, for example, the police expressed the desire that the current collaboration of the department with the building inspector's agency, a community preservation group, and the city attorney be expanded to other groups, including schools and churches.

Leadership development might require training in such skills as chairing a meeting and in the roles and responsibilities of tenants' organizations. Citizens were also interested in receiving training that was more directly related to crime reduction and control. They wanted to find out, for example, the effects of various illicit substances and how to locate prevention programs geared to young people and to substance abuse that could be replicated in their area.

The police departments also identified training needs in the areas of crime control, management, and information systems support. For example, they wanted training in innovative narcotics-abatement strategies and in CPTED, as well as in strategic planning, problem identification and analysis, and the development of computer-based information systems.

Training and Technical Assistance Received

Assistance focused on the areas identified in the needs assessment: building and sustaining interagency collaboration and community partnerships, mobilizing citizens and empowering them to address crime and crime-related problems and, for both the police and citizens, improving problem-solving capabilities. In Tempe, for example, citizens were taught how to implement strategies to prevent drug abuse and how to build and maintain positive police-community relationships and relationships with public and private agencies. Hayward received training in team building and conflict resolution, problem solving, and resource allocation. In Louisville, training in cooperation between the police and other agencies focused on where to go for what type of assistance both *outside* and *inside* the police department.

Typically, participants included representatives of local governments and government agencies, businesses, representatives of religious organizations, and community residents, as well as sworn and civilian police personnel. In Hayward, for example, the mayor, the deputy police chief, religious leaders, business people, and residents were among those taking part. In Louisville, staff from the city's public housing authority, other community agencies, and the schools were trained, as were patrol officers, first-line supervisors, and two district commanders.

Source: Adapted from S. Sadd and R. M. Grinc. 1996. *Implementation Challenges in Community Policing: Innovative Neighborhood-Oriented Policing in Eight Cities.* Washington, D.C.: National Institute of Justice, p. 9.

An idea that would help foster learning would be to organize police work around problem solving and to take seriously the SARA process for confronting problems. Managers and groups of problem-focused officers, who would be working with the community, could develop procedures to guide their work. For example, checklists could be developed for both police supervisors and community organizers to help ensure that corners are not cut and that the most viable solutions are sought.

Another process to foster learning could involve the use of senior police officials to help reduce turf battles between departmental units. For example, in its Compstat process, the New York Police Department holds monthly meetings to discuss progress against crime and disorder patterns throughout the city. Senior officials representing any unit that could reasonably be held accountable for attacking a particular crime problem attend each meeting. A senior executive with authority over all the represented units, attends the monthly meetings, and can, if necessary, take action against the leaders of units who unjustly hoard information or expertise.

Officers meeting to discuss progress against crime. (Photo: Mark C. Ide)

One interesting structural suggestion is to use middle managers to facilitate critical thinking. Since middle managers in police departments (i.e., lieutenants and captains) are continually coming under fire in reorganization plans as being unproductive and even counterproductive, it may be constructive to give them something useful to do. Because they are between the policymakers above and the policy implementers below, why not charge them "with facilitating critical thinking about the efficacy of policies and implementation?" (Geller 1997, p. 6). If departments were to do this (assuming proper training and ability levels), the performance ratings of middle managers might reflect how well they lead their units and the community constructively to criticize and improve departmental operations. A concomitant idea would be explicitly to include, as part of individual and unit performance ratings, employees' accomplishments with respect to industry standards and helping to promote organizational progress.

This last idea of matching police performance levels to present-day industry standards and to promoting organizational progress is an interesting concept whose time may have already arrived. For example, one municipal police chief (in Scottsdale, Arizona, at least), supports the idea that every community should require a "stockholders'" report of its local police department. The report would focus on 12 fundamental questions that should be asked by the community and answered by the department (Heidingsfield 1996). Inside Policing 5.3 takes a look at these questions.

Inside Policing 5.3
Community Stockholders' Report on Local PDs

Question 1. Has your police department been willing to examine its inner workings by comparing the local way of doing business with the most progressive national standards of the law enforcement industry? This is the rigorous three-year process of national accreditation, in which less than 3 percent of the nation's police departments have been accredited. ☞

Question 2. Does your local police department have a simple, easily understood statement of values that are known throughout the department and embody the fundamental notion of ethical behavior and principled decision making?

Question 3. Has your police department been rigorous in its effort to diversify itself by representing community cultures and instilling broad confidence in the police services being delivered?

Question 4. Has your police department embraced the concepts of community policing that imply openness, citizen partnership, and joint responsibility for public safety, and is the department recognized for its success in this regard?

Question 5. Does the leadership of your local police department consistently and passionately carry the message to the community and its police officers that disparate treatment for individuals, heavy-handedness and racism are absolutely not tolerated?

Question 6. Is the maintenance of dignity and respect a theme that is recurrent throughout the police department's culture?

Question 7. Is the police department willing to be formally evaluated by the community on its ability to deliver service in the best manner possible?

Question 8. Has your local department embarked on an organizational campaign to reinforce the concepts and premises of ethics in policing, in order to reaffirm the trust that law enforcement enjoys in the community?

Question 9. Does your police department have in place an open, formal system to ferret out misconduct and to deal with it decisively and promptly?

Question 10. In its hiring standards, does your department highly value college education and community service, as well as commitment to ideals and strength of character?

Question 11. Does your police department consistently enjoy the nonpartisan support of its elected and appointed leadership, and is public safety recognized as part of the necessary fabric of the community?

Question 12. Does your impression and assessment of your community's police officers include characterizations such as compassionate, skilled, proud and willing to serve, fair, committed to the principles of good public safety, available, and open?

When you as a citizen can answer yes to these questions, you then have a dramatic statement about a community's relationship with its police department—one that speaks of properly placed confidence, mutual respect, vigilance, and reassurance.

Source: Adapted from M. J. Heidingsfield, 1996. "Pointed Questions About Your Police Agency." *Law Enforcement News*, September 30: 8.

Summary

The process of organizational change in policing requires the development of a culture that encourages innovation. The primary obstacles to change include inertia, misunderstandings, group norms, and the balance of power. Obstacles to change that may be outside the control of police managers include civil-service regulations and police unions, especially with respect to negotiated job conditions. Each of these obstacles makes the change process more difficult and requires a sustained effort by management if it is to be overcome. In general, ways to overcome obstacles to change in the direction of community policing include taking a long-term view of the change process, preliminary training of personnel, gaining support from elected officials and city agencies, and involving the community.

Two relatively successful examples of large-scale organizational change efforts are Madison and Chicago. Many of the reasons for the success of these departments overlap; for example, both improved communication with their personnel; both had political support; both relied on training; both started out with experimental or prototype districts; and both involved the community, especially in Chicago, where regularly scheduled beat meetings were held. Unique to Madison was its concentrated effort to recruit highly educated officers who were believed to be more supportive of change. Two examples of techniques that can be used to sustain innovation include the use of quality circles and the development of a learning environment.

Discussion Questions

1. Discuss four reasons why police officers tend to resist organizational change.

2. Briefly describe the change process used in Madison. Why do you think the process was successful?

3. Discuss several obstacles to change that may be outside of management's control.

4. Discuss four lessons that were learned in overcoming obstacles to organizational change regarding community policing as noted by police chiefs and sheriffs in a national survey.

5. Describe the key elements used in Chicago's plan for organizational change. What key strategies were used?

6. Discuss the lessons learned from the Madison and Chicago large-scale change efforts. Which change process do you believe will be more effective in the long run, and why?

7. What is innovation, and why is it important to organizational change?

8. Briefly describe the major management techniques used to sustain innovation in Madison.

9. What is meant by a learning organization? Discuss several ideas that would help police departments to become learning organizations.

10. With respect to the 12 questions listed in the Stockholders' Report on Local Police Departments (Inside Policing 5.3), what do you believe to be the strengths and weaknesses of your local department? What could be done to improve it?

References

Booz, Allen & Hamilton, Inc. 1992. *Improving Police Service: Summary of Findings To-Date*. Consulting report for the city of Chicago.

"Community Policing Strategies." 1995. *Research Preview*. Washington, D.C.: National Institute of Justice.

Couper, D. C. and Lobitz, S. H. 1991. *Quality Policing: The Madison Experience*. Washington, D.C.: Police Executive Research Forum.

Geller, W. A. 1997. "Suppose We Were Really Serious About Police Departments Becoming 'Learning Organizations'?" *National Institute of Justice Journal*, December: 2–8.

Geller, W. A. and Swanger, G. 1995. *Managing Innovation in Policing: The Untapped Potential of the Middle Manager*. Washington, D.C.: Police Executive Research Forum.

Hartnett, S. M. and Skogan, W. G. 1999. "Community Policing: Chicago's Experience." *National Institute of Justice Journal*, April: 3–11.

Hatry, H. P. and Greiner, J. M. 1986. *Improving the Use of Quality Circles in Police Departments*. Washington, D.C.: National Institute of Justice.

Heidingsfield, M. J. 1996. "Pointed Questions About Your Police Agency." *Law Enforcement News*, September 30: 8.

Lurigio, A. J. and Rosenbaum, D. P. 1994. "The Impact of Community Policing on Police Personnel: A Review of the Literature." In D. P. Rosenbaum (ed.), *The Challenge of Community Policing*, pp. 147–166. Thousand Oaks, CA: Sage.

Melancon, D. D. 1984. "Quality Circles: The Shape of Things to Come?" *The Police Chief*, November: 54–55.

Pierce, J. L. and Delbeq, A. L. 1977. "Organization Structure, Individual Attitudes and Innovation." *Academy of Management Review* 2: 27–37.

Pisani, S. L. 1992. "Dissecting Community Policing: Part 2." *Law Enforcement News*, May 31: 8, 10.

Sadd, S. and Grinc, R. M. 1994. "Innovative Neighborhood Oriented Policing: An Evaluation of Community Policing Programs in Eight Cities." In D. P. Rosenbaum (ed.), *The Challenge of Community Policing: Testing the Promises*, pp. 27–52. Thousand Oaks, CA: Sage.

——. 1996. *Implementation Challenges in Community Policing: Innovative Neighborhood-Oriented Policing in Eight Cities*. Washington, D.C.: National Institute of Justice.

Sherman, L. W., Milton, C. W., and Kelley, T. V. 1973. *Team Policing: Seven Case Studies*. Washington, D.C.: Police Foundation.

Skogan, W. G. and Hartnett, S. M. 1997. *Community Policing, Chicago Style*. New York: Oxford University Press.

Skolnick, J. H. and Bayley, D. H. 1986. *The New Blue Line: Police Innovation in Six American Cities*. New York: Free Press.

"Study Criticizes Community Policing," 1991. *New York Times*, August 8: B2.

Weisburd, D., McElroy, J. and Hardyman, P. 1988. "Challenges to Supervision in Community Policing." *American Journal of Police* 7: 29–50.

Wycoff, M. A., and Skogan, W. G. 1993. *Community Policing in Madison: Quality From the Inside Out*. Washington, D.C.: National Institute of Justice, December.

——. 1994. "Community Policing in Madison: An Analysis of Implementation and Impact." In D. P. Rosenbaum (ed.), *The Challenge of Community Policing: Testing the Promises*, pp. 75–91. Thousand Oaks, CA: Sage.

For a listing of websites appropriate to the content of this chapter, see "Suggested Websites for Further Study" (p. xv). ✦

Selection and Development

Chapter Outline

Key Terms	
andragogy	pedagogy
assessment center	Police Cadet Corps
BFOQ	police image
career path	race norming
cognitive employment tests	recruitment strategies
community-service officer (CSO)	reliability
disparate impact	resident officer programs
education	screening in
field-training officer (FTO)	screening out
four-fifths rule	specialized training
in-service training	supervisory training
job analysis	training
job related	validity
lateral entry	virtual reality training
management training	

As noted in the previous chapters, the nature of policing and police departments is changing—becoming more complex and challenging—necessitating the importance of hiring and developing the highest-quality personnel available. Although the quality of police personnel has always been important, with the increased complexity of the police role and the movement toward community policing, the quality of personnel has perhaps become the *key* element in the effective operation of police.

The debate over the meaning of "quality," however, is not easy to resolve. For instance, does an individual need a certain level of intelligence, and how is that measured? Are certain physical characteristics a factor? Should higher education be required? What about ethical values? Considerations of quality also suggest that departments should select personnel, including women, who are representative of the communities they serve because they help provide a greater understanding of issues related to gender, race, and ethnicity. Cultural diversity in policing is discussed in chapter 12.

Police selection and development are also influenced by a city or county civil service system. For instance, civil service requirements may have a significant impact on a department's criteria for selection, promotion, and discipline. Civil service provisions were enacted in 1883 with the passage of the Pendleton Civil Service Act, which tried to eliminate the spoils system, in which politicians could simply hire and fire police personnel based on their political affiliation or friendship. By establishing hiring standards that had to be met by all applicants, police departments gained considerable autonomy and freedom against political influence. But civil service also had a number of negative side effects. For instance, O. W. Wilson and R. C. McLaren, who were early critics of the civil service, believed that civil service rules provided too much security for "incompetent and untrustworthy" officers, who are virtually impossible to "weed out" (1977, p. 28). Today, although it is possible to terminate incompetent or dishonest police employees, as a result of civil service provisions it is an onerous and time-consuming effort.

A police department makes essentially three selection decisions: entry, reassignment, and promotion. Decisions about police entrance are usually for the lowest level position (patrol), but supervisory and managerial-level entry is also possible. A few departments recruit for lower-level and middle-level managers (e.g., sergeants, lieutenants, and captains) from outside the department; this practice is known as lateral entry (discussed in the final section of this chapter). Some departments also select their chief of police from the outside. Because most sheriffs are elected, potential candidates may include persons outside the sheriff's department or even outside the law enforcement field.

All states have created statewide standards for parts of the personnel process (e.g., selection, training, and promotion). For example, many states now have an organization called Peace Officer Standards and Training (POST). There is still considerable variation among states, however, and some departments do not adhere to the personnel standards that are established because they are not obligated by law to do so.

Hiring recruits who can become effective patrol officers is the primary purpose of the selection process. The importance of this process cannot be overstated, since after a probationary period, officers essentially receive tenure and may be with the department for 20 years or longer. Although incompetent or dishonest officers can be disciplined, reassigned, or in some cases, terminated, it makes more sense to start by hiring high-quality personnel who will be contributing members of the department throughout their careers.

If high-quality police recruits are to be chosen, the selection process should be designed to screen in, rather than screen out, applicants. **Screening out** identifies applicants who are unqualified and removes them from consideration, while leaving all those who are minimally qualified still in the applicant pool. Recruits who may not be well qualified for police work are then selected from this pool. **Screening in** applicants, in contrast, identifies only the best-qualified candidates for the applicant pool. The department will select its recruits from these applicants, thus ensuring a relatively high-quality candidate. Interestingly, many police departments still rely on screening out applicants, but the process has been under attack since at least 1973, when the National Advisory Commission on Criminal Justice Standards and Goals noted:

> The selection of police personnel should be approached positively; police agencies should seek to identify and employ the best candidates available rather than being content with disqualifying the unfit. The policy of merely eliminating the least qualified results in mediocrity because it allows marginal applicants to be employed along with the most qualified. The benefits of a positive selection policy are seen in a lower rate of personnel turnover, fewer discipline problems, higher morale, and better community relations. (1973, p. 20)

Recruitment

The initial step in the selection process is recruiting well-qualified candidates. The relationship of the number of applicants to those who qualify for positions is often a major factor in the quality of the personnel employed. The most common recruitment methods in policing include (1) advertisement, including brochures, newspapers, television, radio, mass mailings, and journals; (2) requests to special interest groups, including neighborhood, social, political, and minority groups; (3) public announcements, including public-service announcements on television and radio; (4) requests to university career-planning and career-placement offices (campus recruiting is essential if educational requirements are to be increased); and (5) referrals from current employees (Chapman 1982; International City Management Association 1986; Langworthy, Hughes, and Sanders 1995). In addition, many police departments maintain a home page on the Internet containing recruitment information and materials, and some maintain a toll-free 800 number for their recruiting division (TELEMASP 1996). In some police departments, officers are given such incentives as extra days off or a pay bonus if they recruit someone into the department. In some cases, departments send their recruiters to other cities and states in an attempt to enlarge the applicant pool.

One of the major problems with advertising has been the **police image** that has been portrayed. Advertisements often present only the most favorable self-image of both the department and the police role, especially highlighting an ethnically and sexually diverse organization that continually performs adventurous and exciting work. Although this image, from a recruitment perspective, may be effective, it may also be deceitful. The recruits' perception of reality in the department after employment rarely matches the advertised image. There is a strong possibility that such discrepancies lead to employee disenchantment and frustration. Consequently, although the department needs to present an effective image for recruitment purposes, that image should be accurate and realistic.

When attempting to recruit the best-qualified applicants, it is important that departments recognize that different **recruitment strategies** may be necessary. For example, M. S. Meagher and N. A. Yentes (1986) compared men and women from two Midwestern police departments regarding their reasons for entering law enforcement. They found a high degree of consensus between male and female officers in their personal reasons for entering policing; for instance, the top two choices for both groups were helping people and job security. Women, however, were found to be substantially less interested in "fighting crime" than were men. These findings suggest that although recruitment strategies for both men and women can be essentially the same, to attract women candidates, recruiters should emphasize the helping nature of the role, including community service and problem-solving activities. In a national study of recruitment, selection, and training practices (Langworthy, Hughes, and Sanders 1995), based on 60 departments with over 500 sworn personnel, 52.5 percent responded that they use recruiting strategies to target women.

Another study, by H. R. Slater and M. Reiser (1988), was a replication of a 1966 study of police recruits in the Los Angeles Police Department. The 1988 study is particularly meaningful because it breaks down responses not only by gender but also by ethnic groupings. In comparing the results with the earlier study, two significant differences were found with respect to the reasons for becoming officers: (1) responsibility increased from 16 percent in 1966 to 52 percent, and (2) adventure and excitement rose from 13 percent in 1966 to 47 percent. This is an interesting finding in that police work apparently is viewed as being both a responsible and an exciting job. Although this reputation certainly adds to the enticement of the occupation, departments should attempt to educate recruits regarding the reality of police work. Although adventure and excitement can be a part of the job, the media hype of a continually dangerous, physically demanding role is simply not accurate. It is necessary that police officers be able to function in this capacity, but it should not dominate thinking about the job. Therefore, it is important that people be recruited into policing with as accurate an impression of the police role as possible; that is, expectations about the police role need to be shared. In this way, the type of individual that is required for policing a democratic society can be attracted.

The findings indicated some differences with respect to ethnic groups regarding reasons for entering policing. The three main reasons selected by each group in rank order were as follows: Blacks—variety, serve the public, responsibility; Hispanic—variety, responsibility and pay, serve the public; Asian—responsibility, serve the public, variety; Caucasian—variety, adventure, responsibility (see Table 6.1). These findings suggest that departments may need to vary their recruitment efforts somewhat, depending on the particular group targeted. The national study cited above (Langworthy, Hughes, and Sanders 1995) indicated that 90 percent of the surveyed departments use recruitment strategies to attract minorities.

Table 6.1	Factors in Deciding to Choose a Police Career, by Ethnic Groupings				
	Black	**Hispanic**	**Asian**	**Caucasian**	**Total**
Variety	65.5%	62.8%	46.2%	81.8%	68%
	(19)	(27)	(6)	(54)	(106)
Rank	1	1	3	1	
Responsibility	51.7%	51.2%	61.5%	53%	51%
	(15)	(22)	(8)	(35)	(80)
Rank	3	2.5	1	3	
Serve Public	62.1%	48.8%	53.8%	43.9%	48%
	(18)	(21)	(7)	(29)	(75)
Rank	2	4	2	4	
Adventure	27.6%	44.2%	30.8%	60.6%	45%
	(8)	(19)	(4)	(40)	(71)
Rank	6	5	5	2	
Security	41.4%	37.2%	38.5%	51.5%	43%
	(12)	(16)	(5)	(34)	(67)
Rank	4	7	4	10	
Pay	37.9%	51.2%	38.5%	40.9%	41%
	(11)	(22)	(5)	(27)	(65)
Rank	5	2.5	4	5	
Benefits	24.1%	39.6%	38.5%	34.8%	33%
	(7)	(17)	(5)	(23)	(52)
Rank	7.5	6	4	7	
Advancement	24.1%	30.2%	23.1%	37.9%	31%
	(7)	(13)	(3)	(25)	(48)
Rank	7.5	8	6	6	
Retirement	20.7%	22.3%	15.4%	25.8%	22%
	(6)	(10)	(2)	(17)	(35)
Rank	9	9	7	8	
Prestige	3.4%	16.3%	15.4%	19.7%	15%
	(1)	(7)	(2)	(13)	(23)
Rank	10	10	7	9	

H. R. Slater and M. Reiser. 1988. "A Comparative Study of Factors Influencing Police Recruitment, 1988." *Journal of Political Science and Administration*, pp. 16, 171. Reprinted by permission.

In order to improve recruitment practices in today's competitive market, departments may need to consider nontraditional recruitment methods. For example, in New York the use of a **Police Cadet Corps** is designed to attract college students as well as minority and women applicants. Since the Cadet Corps recruits through the City University of New York's campuses, candidates are representative of the city's racial and cultural makeup; more than 60 percent of the cadets are African American or Latino. The Cadet Corps program is a joint venture between the City University of New York and the New York Police Department; applicants must reside in New York, have no more than 30 credits, and be full-time students in good standing. While attending college, cadets selected for the program receive specialized police training and gain practical experience by serving in a social-service setting (e.g., victim or youth services). The cadet is then assigned to a precinct where he or she will work with a community-service officer. After completing the two-year program, the cadet is promoted to police officer status while completing a college degree (Zecca, 1993).

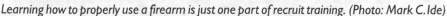

Learning how to properly use a firearm is just one part of recruit training. (Photo: Mark C. Ide)

In general, **community-service officers** (CSOs) are assigned support duties that do not require sworn authority or a weapon. The Sacramento Police Department in California uses CSOs to help attract minority candidates out of high school, who, after graduating from the police academy, attend college while working for the department. After completing the required number of college credits, the CSO is eligible to become a sworn officer (Carter, Sapp, and Stephens 1989).

Another recruitment strategy that departments are using to attract minorities, women, and college graduates is granting special entry conditions for these groups. Such conditions may include lower fitness and education standards, exemptions from examinations, faster promotion, higher pay, and waiting list preferences. In their national study, R. Langworthy, T. Hughes, and B. Sanders (1995) reported that approximately 40 percent of the surveyed departments have special entry conditions for minorities, 32 percent for women, and 28 percent for college graduates.

Selection

Following recruitment, the selection process attempts to determine which candidates are best suited to the needs of the department. The process must decide whether candidates have the requisite skills and abilities to perform effectively. In order to make such judgments, various selection criteria are used, including preemployment standards and preemployment testing, to establish a ranking system from which candidates are hired. It is crucial that these standards and tests be valid and reliable indicators of job performance. **Validity** is the degree to which a measure actually assesses the attribute it is designed to measure. For example, is the physical-strength and agility criterion traditionally used for selection related to the ability to perform the job satisfactorily? If not, it is not a valid criterion for selection. **Reliability** is a measure's ability to yield consistent results over time. In the physical-strength and agility example, the measure would be reliable if a candidate taking the test on more than one occasion received the same or a similar score. Departments attempt to use criteria that are both valid and reliable; of course, it is possible to have selection criteria that are valid but not reliable, or reliable but not valid. For instance, although a physical-strength score may be reliable, it may not be a valid criterion if it cannot be shown to be job related.

In addition, validity is important because invalid criteria may have an adverse impact on groups that are protected by equal employment opportunity (EEO) laws and regulations. The Equal Employment Opportunity Act of 1972 extended to public agencies the "antidiscrimination in employment" provision of Title VII of the 1964 Civil Rights Act. Title VII prohibits any discrimination in the workplace based on race, color, religion, national origin, or sex. In *Griggs v. Duke Power Company* (1971) the Supreme Court held that an employer's requirement of a high school diploma and two standardized written tests for a position disqualified a higher percentage of blacks than whites and could not be shown to be related to job performance. Consequently, the standards had a **disparate impact** on Griggs specifically and on blacks in general. A selection method can be considered to have a legally disparate impact when the selection rate of a group is less than 80 percent of the most successful group; this is also known as the **four-fifths rule**. Prior to *Griggs*, selection standards could be used as long they did not intentionally discriminate; after *Griggs*, standards could not be used that were intended to be impartial but in fact were discriminatory in practice.

In another important decision, *Albemarle Paper Company v. Moody* (1975), the Supreme Court found that selection and promotion tests or standards must be shown to be related to job performance; that is, the standard must be **job related**. This decision had far-reaching implications for police selection, because all selection criteria must be shown to be related to on-the-job performance. It is important to note, however, that departments can require a standard, even though it may have a disparate impact, if the standard can be shown to be a valid predictor of job performance. For example, in *Davis v. City of Dallas* (1985), the Supreme Court upheld the Dallas Police Department's requirement of 45 hours of college credit, even though it discriminated against minorities, because of the professional and complex nature of police work. Legal precedent for higher educational requirements had previously been established by other professions. Such a job-related standard, known as a **bona fide occupational qualification (BFOQ)**, is permissible under Title VII, even though it may exclude members of a protected group.

Police departments, of course, should attempt to use selection methods that not only are valid but also have no adverse impact. This means that departments must commit resources to validating their selection and testing methods, a task usually accomplished through a job analysis. A **job analysis** identifies the behaviors necessary for adequate job performance. Based on such identification, the knowledge, skills, and abilities (KSAs) required for on-the-job behaviors are formulated; procedures (e.g., tests and interviews) are then developed to identify candidates who meet these requirements. The procedures are tested relative to their effectiveness in predicting job performance (B. Schneider and N. Schmitt 1986). Because job analysis can be quite complex, it is often conducted by an industrial or organizational psychologist or some professional with similar qualifications. Although the job-validation process is a rigorous undertaking for any department, it should not be looked upon merely as a legal obligation; selection systems that can be scientifically shown to produce high-quality candidates in a fair manner will withstand legal scrutiny and produce candidates most likely to serve the community effectively (Sauls 1995, p. 31).

Preemployment Standards

Candidates are measured against a department's view of what is required to become an effective police officer. A number of minimum standards are established that must be met prior to employment. These standards are usually quite rigid and establish certain finite qualifications, which, if not met, will most likely eliminate the candidate from further consideration. Such standards may include age, vision, height and weight, physical agility, residency, education, background, psychological condition, and medical condition. Although not all departments have all of these requirements, they are common to many. The standards themselves, however, vary considerably.

Age, vision, height and weight, and physical agility standards. Traditionally, police departments allowed applicants to be between the ages of 21 and 32 to 38, with some accepting applicants as young as 18. Many police experts and police managers believe that 18- to 21-year-olds are not mature enough to perform police work satisfactorily and if hired should be assigned service duties only, much like the Police Cadet Corps and CSO programs described above. There have been legal challenges to age requirements, primarily at the upper limits. The Age Discrimination in Employment Act (ADEA) of 1967 and the amendment of 1974 have extended equal employment opportunity to apply to age, specifically to people 40 or older. Police departments have traditionally set maximum age limits for hiring because they also had mandatory retirement ages; many departments were temporarily exempt from the ADEA and were allowed to retain minimum-maximum age policies for a period of time (March 3, 1983 to December 31, 1993). Since January 1, 1994, however, this exemption has not applied, and today departments must be in compliance with the ADEA. Any recruiting or hiring practices that tend to discourage persons over 40 from applying might be deemed discriminatory. Without a BFOQ, for example, terms such as "recent graduate" or "young" cannot be used for advertising for police officer positions (Rubin 1994, p. 7). In compliance with the ADEA, departments are now hiring recruits over 40 and even 50. For example, there have been news stories regarding the Los Angeles Police Department's hiring of a 59-year-old male recruit ("Rookie Cop, 59 . . ." 1994) and of the Metro-Dade (Miami) Police Department's hiring of a 56-year-old female recruit (Robles 1997).

Stringent minimum and maximum height and weight requirements were standards for most departments in the past. As with age requirements, however, these requirements have been changing over the past several decades due to legal challenges. For instance, minimum height requirements have been challenged successfully as being discriminatory against both women and minority groups, especially Asians and Hispanics. For example, in *Vanguard Justice Society v. Hughes* (1979), the court noted that a 5-foot, 7-inch height requirement excluded 95 percent of the female population but

Stringent height and weight requirements in policing have been declared discriminatory. (Photo: Mark C. Ide)

only 32 percent of the male population, and found this to be evidence of sex discrimination. Because of such rulings, the general standard has now become weight in proportion to height. According to one national survey, fewer than 4 percent of municipal departments still maintain minimum height or weight requirements (J. Fyfe 1987). Vision requirements were also traditionally very stringent, ranging from 20/20 to 20/70 uncorrected in both eyes. This standard too has been relaxed over the years, because such a requirement cannot be job validated and eliminates otherwise potentially strong candidates. Virtually all police departments, however, still maintain certain corrected and uncorrected vision requirements.

Testing of physical agility and strength has been related to an assumed need for physical strength and endurance. For example, candidates would be required to perform a number of sit-ups, push-ups, and chin-ups, possibly perform a rope climb, and run a certain timed distance (a half-mile to two miles); if they fell below a certain minimum, they would be eliminated. Again, because many of these standards could not be shown to be job related, they were found to be discriminatory. Accordingly, some departments have changed their physical requirements to meet job-related criteria, such as climbing a fence or dragging a body (using a dummy or sack of sand); due to the difficulty of distinguishing between who can and cannot perform the job, physical testing is moving toward health-based testing rather than specific physical standards (L. K. Gaines and V. E. Kappeler 1992). A number of departments examine applicants' cardiovascular capacity, body fat composition, flexibility, and dynamic and absolute strength (D. L. Schofield, 1989). Tests are developed to measure these attributes, and a passing cut-off score is determined based on population norms, generally at the 50th percentile in one's age and sex groups.

Residency. Whether or not a department has a residency requirement has a strong impact on those who may be recruited. There are essentially two types of requirements: (1) an applicant must reside within a geographic area (state, county, or city) for a specific period of time (one year is common), prior to application (preemployment), and (2) an applicant must relocate after he or she is selected (postemployment). A 1995 national survey conducted by the Bureau of Justice Statistics (Reaves and Goldberg, 1999) of approximately 700 state and local police departments with 100 or more full-time sworn personnel found that of the 49 state police agencies, 92 percent had some type of residency requirement for new officers. About 60 percent of the local police departments in the survey had a residency requirement.

Proponents of such a requirement argue that it is important for individuals to have an understanding of the community in which they work and that those who live in the community have a greater stake in and concern for the community. Opponents of residency requirements argue that they unnecessarily restrict the applicant pool because the best candidates may not live within the geographic limits; they can also have a negative impact on minority recruitment. It seems clear, however, that if departments wish to hire the best available personnel, then it makes little sense to establish policies that severely restrict the applicant pool; thus, departments should not have preemployment residency requirements. However, if a residency requirement is necessary, a postemployment policy that allows the recruit a reasonable period of time to relocate appears to be reasonable.

One interesting development has been the increased interest by some departments in providing officers with rent-free or low-rent housing or low-interest loans to purchase rehabilitated homes in low-income or high-crime areas. These are known as **resident officer programs** (ROPs). Officials believe that resident officers provide a high-profile presence that helps to prevent crime while improving relationships with their neighbors. The federal government is also starting its own ROPs by giving a 50 percent discount to 2,000 police officers to buy federally foreclosed homes in 500 low-income neighborhoods in 24 cities across the country ("A Place to Call Home" 1997). This is potentially a very attractive fringe benefit for recruiting officers, especially in cities where rent and housing prices are high.

Education. Advances in raising educational requirements for police have been slow and sporadic. Until the 1980s, in many police departments an officer with a college degree was often viewed with contempt or resentment; it was not understood why anyone with a degree would want to enter policing. Although times have changed considerably, college requirements for the job have not kept pace. A national study in 1993 conducted by the Bureau of Justice Statistics (Reaves 1996) of more than 3,000 state and local police departments, serving communities of all sizes, indicates that overall only 1 percent of departments require a college degree for employment, whereas 86 percent of the departments require only a high school diploma.

The Bureau of Justice Statistics study further indicated that in some jurisdictions the figure for requiring a college degree is higher than 1 percent; for example, the figure is 7 percent for departments in jurisdictions having more than 100,000 in population but less than 250,000. Furthermore, 17 percent of departments in jurisdictions having more than 50,000 residents but less than 100,000 require a two-year degree. In addition, a more recent Bureau of Justice Statistics survey (Reaves and Goldberg 1999) of 700 police departments indicated that between 1993 and 1997 the percent of police departments requiring new officers to have a two- or four-year degree increased with state agencies averaging from 14 percent to 20 percent, and for local agencies from 6 percent to 8 percent (see Table 6.2).

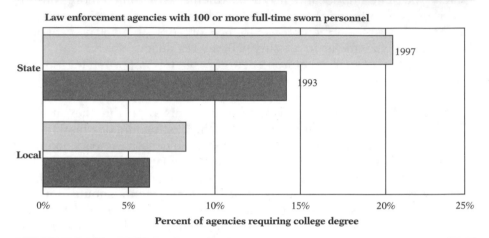

Table 6.2   Percent of Law Enforcement Agencies That Required New Officers to Have a 2-Year or 4-Year College Degree, 1993 and 1997

Source: Reaves, B.A. and A.L. Goldberg. 1999. *Law Enforcement and Admisistration Statistics, 1997*. Washington, D.C.: Bureau of Statistics, p.v.

Two other national studies have reported that although college degree requirements for initial selection are low, many officers later obtained degrees. A 1988 study of almost 500 departments (Carter, Sapp, and Stephens 1989) found that approximately 23 percent of the officers had obtained a college degree following employment. A 1994 study of 60 departments with more than 500 sworn officers (Sanders, Hughes, and Langworthy 1995) reported that approximately 28 percent of the officers were college graduates. These results are noteworthy, since they suggest that although college degree requirements, in general, remain low, approximately 25 percent of today's officers have graduated from college (for further discussion, see chapter 11).

Given the increasing numbers of college-educated officers in the field, such slow progress in developing higher educational standards is perplexing, especially in view of the fact that the preponderance of evidence indicates that, in general, college education has a positive effect on officer attitudes, behavior, and performance. Some of the reasons given for not raising educational standards have to do with fear of being sued over the job relatedness of higher education and possible discrimination toward minorities. Chapter 11 reveals that neither of these fears has been realized. In addition, tradition and inertia undoubtedly continue to play a role in this area, as well as the fear of some smaller departments that they will not be able to attract college graduates. In reality, there is much a department can do to recruit college graduates. For instance, in a study of 37 Texas police departments (TELEMASP 1996), it was found that the median number of recruiting trips to college campuses was six, that 21 departments (56 percent) have educational-incentive pay, providing additional pay for officers who have attained certain levels of higher education. In addition, some departments grant bonus points on hiring tests or use an accelerated career ladder for those with college education. Still others provide tuition-assistance programs and flexible duty shifts for officers who are still working on their degrees. One of the departments reported that it has had some success in recruiting college-educated officers through participation in a college internship program.

General Suitability

Departments usually conduct an extensive investigation of an applicant's past experience, behavior, and work history in an attempt to assess his or her character and general suitability for police work. In general, this process is composed of a background investigation and a polygraph examination.

Background investigation. A thorough background investigation, based on the extensive personal history provided by the candidate, is one of the most important aspects of the selection process. The investigator attempts to determine if the person is honest and reliable and would make a contribution to the department. Family background, employment and credit history, employment and personal references, friends and neighbors, education records, criminal and possibly juvenile records, drug use, and when appropriate, military records, are all checked to develop a general assessment of the person's lifestyle prior to applying for police work. B. Cohen and J. M. Chaiken (1972), in their study of New York police applicants, found that applicants who were rated as excellent by the background investigators had the lowest incidence of misconduct (some 36 percent had personal complaints filed), whereas the applicants rated as poor had the highest incidence of misconduct (some 68 percent). Because these investigations are time-consuming and expensive, some police departments, especially smaller ones with limited resources, may not be very thorough. Nevertheless, because the background investigation appears to be a good predictor of future police behavior, no shortcuts should be taken at this stage. Of course, these findings further suggest that poorly rated applicants should not be hired (i.e., screening in versus screening out).

Two important aspects of the background investigation relate to a candidate's criminal record and history of drug usage. Generally, a criminal record does not automatically disqualify one from police service. One survey found that 96 percent of departments would reject an applicant with a felony conviction and that 90 percent would reject one with a juvenile felony conviction (Eisenberg, Kent, and Wall 1973). With respect to misdemeanor convictions, departments vary widely, but the trend is to examine the type and extent of violations and make a determination based on the candidate's overall record. Some research suggests that preemployment use of illegal drugs is one of the best indicators of postemployment drug use by police officers (Kraska and Kappeler 1988). Several court cases have laid the foundation for what is a permissible drug use standard for police employment practices. For instance, a Dallas Police Department standard requiring police applicants not to have recent or excessive histories of marijuana use was upheld (*Davis v. City of Dallas*, 1985). In *Shield Club v. City of Cleveland* (1986), the court upheld drug-testing requirements and the rejection of applicants who tested positive for narcotics, amphetamines, or hallucinogenics. In both these rulings, the courts indicated that such requirements were job related and therefore not discriminatory. It is also important to note that each of the departments utilized an objective testing system that prevented any form of individual discrimination. Thus, it would appear that stringent drug-use standards can be used as a selection criterion, as long as that standard is applied objectively to all police candidates.

The 1995 Bureau of Justice Statistics survey (Reaves and Goldberg 1999) of 700 large police departments found that over 80 percent required applicants to take a drug test, indicating the importance currently placed on this requirement. Interestingly, this is the only testing requirement from the BJS study that differed significantly from an earlier study on selection standards by Langworth, Hughes and Sanders (1995); see Table 6.4. Inside Policing 6.1 discusses various departments' prior drug-use policies.

Inside Policing 6.1
Police Departments Becoming More Lenient Regarding Past Drug Use

Prior use of drugs by recruits has been a prickly subject for law enforcement departments for at least the last 10 years, when *Law Enforcement News* first examined the prior-use policies of a handful of medium and large police departments nationwide and discovered that some had implemented flexible, even lenient policies regarding applicants' drug histories. A recent reexamination of prior-use policies in those departments originally surveyed in 1986 has found that many continue to permit some latitude in this area, usually depending on the particular drug used, frequency of use, and time of last use. Some of the specific policies used in departments are excerpted below:

- In Baltimore County, Maryland, more than 50 percent of the department's successful candidates have had some type of drug experimentation in their past. However, there is an automatic rejection of those who admit to using any hallucinogenic drug, such as LSD or PCP, or of those who admit to selling or distributing any controlled substance. A one-time user of cocaine is not necessarily disqualified.

- In Fairfax County, Virginia, brief experimentation with marijuana is generally allowed (i.e., fewer than 20 times), but use of any drugs within 12 months of application would most likely be a disqualifier.

- In San Jose, California, applicants will not necessarily be disqualified for using any particular drug once, including cocaine and heroin. The effect of a history of prior drug use on an applicant's chances of employment is determined on a case-by-case basis.

- The Metro-Dade Police Department, Florida, allows for one-time use and some juvenile drug experimentation but bars outright all Schedule I drugs (e.g., heroin, LSD, mescaline) and Schedule II drugs (e.g., opium, cocaine, and barbiturates).

- The FBI has one of the more stringent prior-drug-use standards, banning illegal drugs, other than the experimental use of marijuana. Applicants who have used drugs in the past but have stopped—who have been rehabilitated, in the language of the FBI guidelines—may be considered for employment under certain conditions. Recruits who have used any illegal drugs within the past 10 years, other than experimental use of marijuana within three years prior to their application, will not be hired "absent compelling mitigating circumstances." ☞

> ☞   Furthermore, FBI guidelines stipulate that an applicant will not be hired "who used drugs while employed in a law enforcement or prosecutorial job or a post of high responsibility or public trust; or those who misrepresented their drug history or had sold drugs."
>
> - Most departments surveyed, including the FBI, use polygraph examinations to elicit or verify information about drug-use history from applicants, along with questionnaires and urine tests, which are usually administered in the latter phases of the recruit process.
>
> - Several departments declined to disclose their current policies on prior drug use by recruits and others did so reluctantly; it is feared by some that once such policies are made public, recruits can say they never used a specific drug (e.g., cocaine or a hallucinogenic) since they know it is part of the department's rejection criteria.
>
> ---
>
> Source: Adapted from "Getting the Inside Dope." 1996. *Law Enforcement News*, October 31: 1–14. Reprinted with permission from *Law Enforcement News*, John Jay College of Criminal Justice, New York City.

Polygraph examination. The polygraph, or lie detector, is used to check the accuracy of background information and to determine if there has been any inappropriate behavior, past or present, on the applicant's part (e.g., criminal acts, illegal drug use). Although the polygraph has been touted by some as an effective tool in discovering problems with applicants, some research has suggested that it is not a reliable method to determine truth or falsehood of an individual's statements (see Hodes, Hunt, and Raskin 1985; Kleinmuntz and Szucko 1982; Rafky and Sussman 1985). One problem with the polygraph is the amount of stress it puts on a candidate and the resulting false positives that result, that is, when a candidate is falsely accused of lying. Therefore, some jurisdictions have made such testing illegal. Furthermore, some departments still ask questions about an applicant's lifestyle or sexual practices that are private matters. If a polygraph examination is administered, all questions relating to the applicant's background should be job related. Finally, the polygraph should never be used as a substitute for the background investigation but only as a supplement to it.

Psychological Standards

Psychological screening to determine a candidate's suitability for police work has become more common in recent years; this screening may be written, oral, or both. The most commonly used written tests are the Minnesota Multiphasic Personality Inventory (MMPI) and the California Personality Inventory (CPI) (Johnson 1990). In 1980 the Inwald Personality Inventory (IPI) was developed specifically for police screening and is gaining some popularity with police psychologists and consultants (TELEMASP 1994). After the tests are administered, they are usually scored by a psychologist, who is looking for serious emotional problems that would disqualify a candidate, or for a profile of a person who would make a "good" police officer. In either case, the candidate will be disqualified if he or she does not meet the psychologist's criteria. There is considerable controversy surrounding the use of psychological testing for police screening; for example, research has indicated that some tests are racially biased (Winters 1989), and not job related (Dwyer, Prien, and Bernard 1990). After reviewing the literature, E. Burbeck and A.

Furnham (1985) suggested that such tests may be useful for selecting out people suffering from some mental abnormality but not for predicting job performance.

Because of these problems with psychological testing, it has been argued by some critics (e.g., Dwyer, Prien, and Bernard 1990) that until such time that predictors identifying job relatedness are developed, clinical assessments for screening police candidates should be eliminated. In the interim, it is suggested that because the best predictor of future behavior is past behavior, background investigation should be more thorough in order to identify candidates with tendencies toward morally unacceptable or violent behavior. Police departments should consider increasing their utilization of and scope of background investigation for screening purposes and rely less on clinical judgments.

Part of the problem of selection revolves around the changing nature of policing (i.e., toward community policing) and the perception of what makes a good officer (Grant and Grant 1995). For instance, the Independent Commission on the LAPD (1991) found that prior violent behavior of applicants appeared not to be a negative factor in selection in the Los Angeles Police Department. Such a finding suggests, at least at that time, that a "rough and aggressive" demeanor was perceived to be an asset to police performance rather than a warning signal for potential abusive violent behavior. Of course, if the majority of officers selected by a department had these types of attitudes, it is not difficult to understand why such a department would be constantly in conflict with the community regarding overly aggressive behavior.

Medical Standards

Virtually all police departments have certain medical requirements that an individual must meet before being hired. A medical examination is given by a physician either designated by the department or chosen by the candidate. The exam attempts to determine the general health of the candidate and identify specific conditions, such as heart, back, or knee problems. In general, any "weaknesses" that may be aggravated by the requirements of police work will eliminate the candidate from further consideration. The reason is that the costs of losing an officer to injury or illness, often with long-term disability compensation or a lawsuit, are too great. If a department requires some form of drug testing, it usually takes place during this phase of the process.

Preemployment Testing

The preemployment standards for police departments, and the legal justifications, change periodically. This is an area in which departments need specific, and the most current, information in order to select the best qualified candidates. Although preemployment standards are usually scored on a pass-fail basis and are used to eliminate candidates, preemployment tests are generally used to place candidates in order of rank. The two most commonly used tests are some form of written test and the oral interview. Some departments use the written test simply as a qualifier (i.e., on a pass-fail basis) and the oral interview as the only criterion for rank order.

Written and cognitive tests. Traditionally, departments have used some types of written and cognitive tests, usually some form of standardized intelligence test or jurisdictionally specific knowledge test to screen and rank order candidates. Few attempts were made, however, to determine if these tests had any impact on the applicant's ability to be a successful police officer. Although it is easy to argue that police officers should be intelligent and knowledgeable, it is difficult to determine what kind of intelligence or knowledge is being measured and what level should be required. Inside Policing 6.2 provides an example of one city's belief that an officer can be too intelligent for the job.

Inside Policing 6.2
Too Intelligent To Be a Cop?

In a time when intelligent, highly educated police recruits are in greater demand than ever, it might seem hard to believe that an applicant could be rejected for scoring too high on an IQ test, but that's just what a prospective officer in New London, Connecticut, claims happened to him.

In a complaint filed in U.S. District Court in New Haven, Robert Jordan, 46, claims the city of New London violated his constitutional rights by discriminating against him based on his intelligence. Jordan claims the assistant city manager who oversees the hiring of city employees told him, "We don't like to hire people that have too high an IQ to be cops in this city." According to the Associated Press, city officials reportedly have said in the past that candidates who score too high on intelligence tests would become easily bored with police

work and would leave the department shortly after being hired, sticking the city with the $25,000-per-officer training costs.

Jordan scored a 33 on the intelligence exam, described as a short-form IQ test that measures a person's ability to learn and solve problems. Under a policy said to have been in effect for at least five years, candidates who score above or below the 20–27 range generally are not interviewed for positions. The average national score for police officers is 21–22, the Associated Press said, the same as for bank tellers, salespeople, and office workers.

Source: Adapted from "Dumb-da-dum-dum." 1997. *Law Enforcement News*, June 15: 4. Reprinted with permission from *Law Enforcement News*, John Jay College of Criminal Justice, New York City.

It has also been found that minorities tend to score lower on police-entry exams. For example, C. F. Sproule (1984) and L. K. Gaines, P. Costello, and A. Crabtree (1989) found that minorities score on average at least one standard deviation below other applicants. If a simple rank ordering of candidates is used, it will generally create an adverse impact. These problems have led to attempts to validate police written tests empirically since at least the late 1970s (e.g., see Crosby, Rosenfield, and Thornton 1979), and for departments to seek exams which are more objective and job related (Law Enforcement Assistance Administration 1973).

This validation process is critical because the practice known as **race norming**, or using different cutoff scores on employment-related tests on the basis of race, color, religion, sex, or national origin, has been prohibited by the Civil Rights Act of 1991 (Public Law 102–166). Section 703(1) of the act bans setting differential standards or test scores designed to benefit protected-class members by equalizing work opportunities (Pynes 1994). This provision would appear to invalidate the Equal Employment Opportunity

Commission's testing guidelines, which have permitted employers to use different cutoff scores for both minorities and nonminorities, when lower scores for one group are just as predictive of job ability as higher scores are for the other group. Setting differential test scores to benefit protected classes is permitted, however, for programs that were in accordance with affirmative action laws prior to the passage of the 1991 act (Pynes 1994).

Although written tests have limitations, departments must have a way of distinguishing among a large pool of candidates and therefore will continue to use such testing. A primary concern is that the tests be objective. Objective testing standards can be defined as measures of relevant knowledge, skills, and abilities used in a neutral manner without regard to the individual's membership in any group (Pynes 1994). There also appears to be a consensus building in that **cognitive employment tests** (i.e., tests of the ability to synthesize and analyze material) are an important selection criterion and are equally valid for virtually all jobs (Schmidt 1988). J. Hunter (1986), for instance, found the following with respect to cognitive-ability tests: (1) general cognitive ability predicts performance ratings in all lines of work, although validity is higher for complex jobs than for simple jobs; (2) general cognitive ability predicts training success at a uniformly high level for all jobs; (3) data on job knowledge show that cognitive ability determines how much and how quickly a person learns; and (4) cognitive ability predicts the ability to react in innovative ways to situations in which knowledge does not specify exactly what to do.

Oral interview. Almost all police departments use some form of oral interview, usually at the end of the selection process. The interview allows police representatives (and sometimes community members) to observe the candidates directly with respect to their suitability for the department and to clear up any inconsistencies that may have developed in the earlier stages of the process. Candidates are measured on attributes that generally are not measured elsewhere, including motivation, verbal skills, confidence, potential for violence, decision-making skills, and overall demeanor. The interview is not usually substantive, that is, with specific questions about police policy or the department, but it can be. Typical questions might include these: Why do you want to be a police officer? How have you prepared yourself for a career in law enforcement? What types of books or magazines do you read? Why do you want to work for this department? There will usually be a few questions about hypothetical situations and how the person would respond (i.e., make decisions) to them; for example, What would you do in a particular crisis situation or if you knew your partner was involved in a criminal activity? Some departments, especially those moving toward community policing, are becoming more problem oriented in their formats and are replacing "how would you" questions with "describe what you did" questions. For example, the Redmond Police Department in Washington asks this question of its candidates: "Describe a problem that existed within your department or community that prodded you to develop solutions and take steps necessary to implement those solutions. Describe the net result of your efforts." The type of response the department is looking for includes the seriousness of the problem and whether or not the candidate accurately assessed the situation and initiated procedures that led to a solution (Krieble 1994).

Interviews should be conducted by well-qualified boards, rather than by individuals, who should be well trained in interview techniques and the type of questions asked. The same types of questions and evaluation criteria should be used for all candidates to attempt to make the interview procedure valid. Although police oral boards vary considerably, they should include members who are outside the police department. For instance, one type of oral board that is used includes a departmental representative (e.g., a police officer with the rank of sergeant or above), a civil-service representative, and a representative from the community. Generally, a score is assigned to each candidate, which when combined with the written score, provides a total score; candidates are then rank ordered with respect to hiring priority (though some departments may assign more weight to either the written test or the oral interview).

Some departments use only the oral interview to rank order candidates. This method has been useful in helping departments to overcome the potentially adverse impact of other selection criteria and to increase the employment of women and minorities. Although the interview is more flexible, it is more subjective, and there is no strong evidence that it is a useful predictor of future police performance (Burbeck and Furnham 1985). Other research indicates that the validity of the oral interview is also suspect and that the characteristics of the raters influence the ratings and ultimately the rankings of the candidates (Falkenberg, Gaines, and Cox 1990). Methods that help to improve the validity of the oral interview include using only those rating factors that are critical components of the job, training the raters so that they clearly understand the process and how responses should be graded, and using set standards that raters can compare with candidate responses (Gaines and Kappeler 1992).

Table 6.3 presents a summary of the general steps of the police selection process and the most important concerns at each step.

Table 6.3   Police Selection—Process Summary

Steps	Related Issues
Recruitment	Advertising, requests, and referrals
Selection criteria	Age, height, weight, vision, criminal record, and possible residency requirement
Written examination	General intelligence or job content
Physical examination	Agility and endurance
Oral interview	Communication skills, interpersonal style, and decision-making ability
Psychological testing	Emotional stability and psychological profiles
Background investigation	Character, employment/credit history, education, references, and criminal record
Polygraph examination	Character and background information
Medical examination	General health and specific problems

Source: R. R. Roberg and J. Kuykendall. *Police Management, 2nd ed.* Los Angeles, CA: Roxbury, 1977, p. 246.

Table 6.4 represents the findings of a national survey of police department recruitment, selection, and training practices (Langworthy, Hughes, and Sanders 1995), comparing a 1994 sample of 60 departments with a similar sample of 72 departments surveyed in 1990. The sample departments

❖ ❖ ❖ ❖   were given a list of 13 possible selection procedures and asked to identify which they used. As expected, over 90 percent of the departments required a written test, oral interview, background check, and medical exam. Significant increases were reported for intelligence tests, psychological interviews, written references, and practical tests. Such changes are not surprising in light of legislation regarding fair hiring practices. With an increased use of practical tests, "these departments appear to be moving toward selection methods which have been shown to test the skills which are necessary in performing the police job" (Langworthy, Hughes, and Sanders 1995, p. 29).

Table 6.4 Percent of Departments Using Various Selection Steps			
	1990 (N=71)	1994 (N=59)	Change (N=58)
Background check	98.6	96.6	-1.7
Medical exam	95.9	98.3	3.4
Written test	94.3	96.6	1.7
Oral interview	94.3	98.3	3.4
Physical-agility test	80.3	84.7	5.2
Psychological interview	83.1	91.5	12.0*
Intelligence test	76.1	94.5	15.5*
Polygraph	69.0	69.5	3.4
Written references	57.7	71.2	17.2*
Psychometric tests	56.4	55.9	-6.9
Drug test	23.9	22.2	-7.1
Handwriting analysis	11.2	10.2	-3.4
Practical tests	7.0	28.8	22.4*

* Significant increase ($p < .05$)
Source: Adapted from R. Langworthy, T. Hughes, and B. Sanders. 1995. *Law Enforcement Recruitment, Selection and Training: A Survey of Major Police Departments in the U.S.* Academy of Criminal Justice Sciences—Police Section, Highland Heights: KY, p. 26. Reprinted with permission.

The selection of candidates for police departments is time-consuming and expensive. Given the costs, the steps of the process are normally arranged from the least costly and most likely to eliminate the most candidates to the most expensive. Accordingly, the written and physical-agility tests are usually given at the beginning, followed by the medical exam, polygraph examination (if used), psychological testing (if used), background investigation, and finally the oral interview. The passage of the Americans with Disabilities Act (ADA) in 1990, however, will have a substantial impact on this traditional sequencing.

Americans With Disabilities Act

The purpose of the ADA is to eliminate barriers to equal employment opportunity and to provide equal access to individuals with disabilities to the programs, services, and activities delivered by government entities (Rubin 1994). Thus, the ADA prohibits discrimination against *qualified* individuals with a disability; it does not mean that by having a disability, one is entitled to protection under the law, but if a person meets the selection criteria for a job and has a disability, he or she cannot be discriminated against for the job. Generally, blanket exclusions of individuals with a particular disability are not permissible. For instance, to exclude all persons with diabetes would ignore the varying degrees of severity and the ability to control the symptoms (Rubin 1994). Also, standards that tend to screen out individuals or groups of individuals on the basis of disability must be related to functions that are essential to the job.

The ADA requires that applicants be given a conditional offer of employment *prior* to taking an exam or a test that may be disability related, including background investigations, psychological and medical exams, and polygraph tests. A good rule of thumb is that questions that would disclose information regarding a disability, whether asked on an application or during an interview, may be construed as a disability-related inquiry. That holds true for any selection procedure that would disclose information regarding a disability. If any of these tests are to be administered prior to a conditional offer of employment, no questions may be asked relating to disabilities unless they are essential to police performance. Although the full impact of the ADA on police selection is complicated and ongoing, departments will need to change many of their current procedures to ensure that selection criteria that screen out persons with disabilities are job related and that questions relating to disabilities (unless job related) are asked only after a conditional offer of employment has been made. In effect, the ADA is advancing the trend toward more job-related screening exams and tests to predict better which candidates are best suited to police work and will perform most effectively once hired.

Once candidates are selected, they are usually rank ordered and employed based on need. This ranking lasts for a given period, usually from six months to two years, before re-testing is undertaken. Once selected, candidates start their developmental phase by attending a recruit training program.

Development

Development of a police department's human resources for successful careers in police work begins with the training of the newly hired recruits, moves to a second phase of field training and evaluation, and continues into a third phase of long-term development, or career growth.

Recruit Training

The initial training of the recruit is generally conducted through a police training academy where the program content is determined by a state standards organization, often known as Peace Officer Standards and Training (POST). Although all police departments must meet minimum standards, some departments provide substantially more training than is minimally required. Larger departments often maintain their own academies, whereas smaller departments tend to send their recruits to regional or county academies.

Some states now require that people complete one of these basic training programs prior to being considered for employment. As a result, the department hires an already trained employee and does not have to pay for the cost of the training, including the recruit's salary while attending the academy. Another recent development in preemployment screening is testing for literacy. Because literacy skills in police applicants have been markedly declining, and written civil-service tests do not adequately screen for literacy, some states (e.g., Michigan and California) require all candidates to pass one of any number of tests designed to measure reading and writing skills before they begin the academy (Clark 1992). Since 1988, for example, the regional training center for Miami-area police departments has required participants in its pre-service program to take a test to make sure that they can read at a 10th grade level. The requirement was imposed because, according to the training center, earning a high school diploma does not guarantee that the graduate can read beyond the junior high school level (Clark 1992). Such a low-level reading standard is reflective of a limited concept of role, suggesting that police work is essentially a low-status, low-skill occupation. Most likely, such low standards produce many marginal employees who later have a difficult time adjusting to the rigors of police work and thus become troublesome. Because the Miami example is undoubtedly reflective of a national concern, the arguments for moving toward requiring a college degree become even more evident.

Until the late 1950s, training was primarily the responsibility of cities and counties and a few colleges and universities; curriculum and amount of training, if any, varied widely. Today, the amount of time devoted to recruit training varies from a low of around 400 hours to a high of more than 1,000 hours, especially in the West (Thibault, Lynch, and McBride 1990). This increased length of training time has been the result of the increased knowledge base about the police role, which, in turn, has led to a greater diversity in subject matter and training methods utilized in the academy.

Recruit training is influenced by program design and delivery. Some of the more important considerations in the design and delivery of a recruit training program include program orientation, philosophy and instructional methods, course content, and field training.

Program orientation. One of the important issues in police training is whether the orientation should be stressful or nonstressful. Stressful training is like a military boot camp or basic training; nonstressful training has a more academic environment. Many recruit programs continue to be a stressful orientation, expecting recruits to be obedient and subjecting them to both intellectual and physical demands in a highly structured environment. Discipline and even harassment have been an integral part of many of these programs. For in-service training (i.e., training after employment) with more experienced officers, a more academic environment is the norm.

Although stressful recruit training has a long tradition, no evidence exists that this approach is a valid way to train recruits (Berg 1990) or that it is any more or less effective than a nonstressful approach. Probably the most comprehensive study in this area (Earle 1973) indicates that nonstressful training produced officers who received higher performance evaluations, liked their work more, and got along better with the public. Given the trend toward community policing, problem solving, and higher educational requirements, a stress-oriented approach is likely to be counterproductive and should be eliminated from training programs, replaced by a more academic approach.

Philosophy and instructional methods. The philosophy of a program revolves around two primary approaches: training and education. **Training** can be defined as the process of instructing the individual *how* to do the job by providing relevant information about the job; **education** can be defined as the process of providing a general body of knowledge on which decisions can be based as to *why* something is being done while performing the job. Training deals with specific facts and procedures, whereas education is broader in scope and is concerned with theories, concepts, issues, and alternatives. Many police training programs are heavily oriented toward teaching facts and procedures to the exclusion of theories, concepts, and analytical reasoning. A strict reliance on this approach is problematic, because so much police work requires analysis and reasoning instead of application of specific procedures that supposedly fit all circumstances. Therefore, many academies are attempting to increase the percentage of time spent on an educational approach by employing professionals in the social sciences, especially criminal justice and criminology, psychology, and sociology, as instructors. With the ever-increasing recognition of the complexity of the police role and hence the necessity to utilize both training and education to prepare police recruits adequately, the traditional distinction between the two approaches has become less significant.

Another important aspect of program development is the type of instructional methods to be used. In large part, this is determined by what teaching philosophy is going to be emphasized. Two contrasting teaching philosophies are pedagogy and andragogy (Knowles 1970). **Pedagogy** involves a one-way transfer of knowledge, usually in the form of facts and procedures, from the instructor to the student (recruit). The primary concern is to promote "abso-

An instructor presents an idea in this example of pedagogical training in a typical recruit training class. (Photo: Mark C. Ide)

lute solutions" to particular situations. An alternative teaching philosophy, which promotes the mutual involvement of students and instructors in the learning process and stresses analytical and conceptual skills, is known as **andragogy.**

Where pedagogy involves lectures, use of visual aids, student note taking, rote memorization, and taking factual tests, andragogy involves problem analysis, role playing, group discussion and projects, independent student learning, and exercises requiring recruits to "act out" required skills in simulated situations. Recently, there has been a significant increase in the use of role playing, simulations, and problem analysis in recruit training. However, conceptual understanding and insight development (based on theory) are rarely emphasized; even in the more progressive programs training tends to be oriented toward how to do the job rather than toward general knowledge on which to base decisions while performing the job. As administrators continue to recognize the complex nature of the police role and the need to use discretion wisely, increased emphasis should be placed on using andragogical methods of instruction (Roberg 1979). At the same time, pedagogical teaching methods are also necessary, especially with respect to those activities that require memorization (e.g., laws and policies) and behavioral techniques (e.g., traffic stops and approaching a suspect).

Course content. Police training programs and curricula should be based on two common assumptions: first, the programs should incorporate the mission statement of the department and ethical considerations, and second, training should be based on what an officer actually does on a daily basis (Alpert and Smith 1990; Bayley and Bittner 1989). The subject matter should be based on a task analysis of the jobs to be performed by the recruits; such task analysis, however, still tends to be more the exception than the rule, with

The increased use of role playing in police training should help to improve decision making in dangerous situations. (Photo: Mark C. Ide)

training based more on legal requirements and experience. Nevertheless, some departments have tried to identify police tasks that are important to the job and to base their training on them. Some states have conducted comprehensive task-analysis studies of several police positions (e.g., entry-level and various managerial positions).

The importance of basing training on what an officer actually does cannot be overstated: that is, to what degree is reality presented and discussed? What image of the police is presented? Traditionally, training has underrepresented order-maintenance and social-service aspects of the police role while overrepresenting law enforcement activities; such an emphasis has undoubtedly contributed toward a macho view of policing that is still evident. Of course, the particular image presented can have a significant impact on the way recruits view their role as police officers. Because the training program is seen as representing the department's view of police work, an unrealistic presentation of policing will not only send the wrong message to recruits but most likely make initial occupational adjustments more difficult as well.

As the complex nature of the police role has become recognized (Roberg 1976), training requirements, including the number of hours trained and the number of subjects covered, has increased significantly. According to the Bureau of Justice Statistics national survey of 3,000 state and local agencies of all sizes (Reaves 1996), 90 percent of local police departments (which employ 99 percent of all local police officers), require new recruits to complete formal training (see Table 6.5). Nearly all departments (95 percent) serving a population of 2,500 or more required training; 83 percent of the departments in towns of under 2,500 had a training requirement. On average, departments required 640 training hours for new recruits, including 425 classroom hours and 215 field-training hours. Training requirements were higher in larger jurisdictions than in smaller ones—ranging from more than 1,100 hours in departments serving jurisdictions with populations of 100,000 to 250,000 to under 500 hours in jurisdictions with fewer than 2,500 residents.

By comparison, the more recent (1997) Bureau of Justice Statistics national survey of some 700 state and local agencies with over 100 sworn personnel (Reaves and Goldberg 1999) found, at least among the nation's larger agencies, a significant increase in the number of training hours required. The median number of hours of classroom training required of new officers was highest in state police agencies with 823 hours, followed respectively by county law enforcement with 760 hours, municipal police with 640 hours, and lastly, sheriff's department's with 448 hours. The median number of hours required for field training was 480 for county and municipal police, 436 for sheriff's departments, and 360 for state police. This survey is important because it describes differences among types of departments; for example, training requirements were highest for county police with 1240 total hours, followed by state police with 1183, municipal police with 1120, and sheriff's departments with 884. On average, the nation's larger police departments required 1107 training hours for new recruits, including 668 in the classroom and 449 in the field.

Table 6.5	Training Requirements for New Officer Recruits in Local Police Departments, by Size of Population Served, 1993		
Population served	Percent of agencies requiring training	Average number of hours required	
		Classroom	Field
All sizes	90%	425	215
1,000,000 or more	100%	865	311
500,000–999,999	100	757	396
250,000–499,999	100	727	551
100,000–249,999	99	630	498
50,000–99,999	100	494	435
25,000–49,999	100	492	393
10,000–24,999	100	468	305
2,500–9,999	93	455	405
Under 2,500	83	352	105

Note: Computation of average number of training hours required excludes departments not requiring training.
B. A. Reaves (1996). *Local Police Departments, 1993*. Washington, D.C.: Bureau of Justice Statistics, p. 5.

An example of the diverse topics covered in present-day recruit training can be seen in California's curriculum (mandated by POST), which includes 41 topics (domains). These are to be covered in a minimum of 599 hours of training—larger departments require more hours—with an additional 65 hours of testing. The testing includes both scenarios (where simulated field situations are presented and recruits respond to them) and written exams. In addition, once a recruit becomes a sworn officer, he or she must also complete a minimum of 24 hours of POST-certified training once every two years. Table 6.6 provides a list of the topics covered and the minimum number of hours required on each topic.

Table 6.6	California Police Academy Training Curriculum Content and Minimum Hourly Requirements	
	Domain Description	**Minimum Number of Hours**
01	History, Professionalism, and Ethics	8
02	Criminal Justice System	4
03	Community Relations	12
04	Victimology/Crisis Interventions	6
05	Introduction to Criminal Law	6
06	Crimes Against Property	10
07	Crimes Against Persons	10
08	General Crimes Statutes	4
09	Crimes Against Children	6
10	Sex Crimes	6
11	Juvenile Law and Procedure	6
12	Controlled Substances	12
13	ABC (Alcohol, Beverage Code) Law	4
14	Laws of Arrest	12
15	Search and Seizure	12
16	Presentation of Evidence	8
17	Investigative Report Writing	40
18	Vehicle Operations	24
19	Use of Force	12

Table 6.6	California Police Academy Training Curriculum Content and Minimum Hourly Requirements (continued)	
	Domain Description	**Minimum Number of Hours**
20	Patrol Techniques	12
21	Vehicle Pullovers	14
22	Crimes in Progress	16
23	Handling Disputes/Crowd Control	12
24	Domestic Violence	8
25	Unusual Occurrences	4
26	Missing Persons	4
27	Traffic Enforcement	22
28	Traffic Accident Investigation	12
29	Preliminary Investigation	42
30	Custody	4
31	Physical Fitness/Officer Stress	40
32	Person Searches/Baton, etc.	60
33	First Aid and CPR	21
34	Firearms/Chemical Agents	72
35	Information Systems	4
36	Persons with Disabilities	6
37	Gang Awareness	8
38	Crimes Against the Justice System	4
39	Weapons Violations	4
40	Hazardous Materials	4
41	Cultural Diversity/Discrimination	24
	Minimum Instructional Hours	599

Types of Testing	**Hours**
Scenario Tests	40
POST-Constructed Knowledge Tests	25
Total Minimum Required Hours	646

Source: Adapted from Commission on Peace Officer Standards and Training. 1995. *Bulletin 95–9: Regular Basic Course Required Minimum Hours Increases From 560 to 646.* Sacramento, CA: POST, May 12.

Whether recruit training is based on task analysis or experience, the department must determine what subject matter is most important, because most (if not all) programs are constrained by time and resources. The amount of time devoted to any particular subject emphasizes to recruits the importance attached to that subject by the department. Table 6.6 shows the varying amounts of hours devoted to certain topics, with a low of four hours to a high of 72 hours. It should be noted that in police training there will always be debate regarding what topics should be covered and for how much time. For example, given its importance to effective and just policing, should the area of professionalism and ethics receive more time? What about the use of force? If such topics were expanded, however, would other topics need to be dropped or cut back? Answering such questions is the reason why it is so important that the training for any particular job be based on task analysis; the importance attached to the subject matter is then based on scientific evidence rather than on a few individuals' experience, intuition, or guesswork.

For instance, in one national survey on police ethics of 874 members of the International Association of Chiefs of Police (IACP 1998), it was found that while 83 percent of the departments provided some form of ethics training for their recruits, 71 percent provided four classroom hours or less of programming. Only 17 percent provided eight hours of training for ethics. For supervisors, although 65 percent of the departments provided some kind of ethics training, it was generally for four hours or less. The report concluded that although most saw a high need for ethics training, the amount of time earmarked for it was far less than might be expected. Clearly, the implications of ethical behavior in policing a democratic society should make ethics a primary topic in training.

Another topic that appears in need of significant expansion, especially in relation to the development of community policing, is the *deescalation of force* to reduce violence between police and citizens. While some departments may cover this area briefly under a Use of Force topic, G. P. Alpert and M. H. Moore (1993) propose that nonaggressive behavior that reduces violence needs to be reinforced, rewarded, and established as the model for other officers to copy. Such training would need to recognize and emphasize the use of nonaggressive behavior that, when appropriate, does not lead to an arrest. This understanding would in turn lead to the recognition that many problems in the community can be solved without the use of force.

As new developments occur in policing, they must be added to the curriculum. For example, such areas as cultural diversity, victimology, crisis intervention, crimes against children, domestic violence, persons with disabilities, and gang awareness were not adequately addressed or even discussed a decade or two ago, and still are not in many recruit training programs. Furthermore, as the laws become more complex, officers need additional training in these areas. The scope of the Americans with Disabilities Act, for example, is likely to expand further as a result of a recent legal ruling that municipalities must train police to differentiate between people who are drugged or drunk and those who are disabled (Clark 1994).

It will be necessary for those departments that are moving seriously toward community policing to incorporate basic research methods and skills into their curricula to give officers a rudimentary understanding of how to evaluate the effectiveness of new policies and programs, community needs and expectations, and identifying and solving problems. Training content would most likely follow the pattern of a course developed in the Greater Manchester (England) Police Department, which offers a user-friendly introduction to quantitative research, with an emphasis on the design, distribution, and analysis of questionnaires, as well as the general research process (Seagrave 1992).

Finally, one interesting breakthrough that may have implications for policing is the developing area of **virtual reality training**. Although this type of training is essentially untapped, it would appear that it has great potential as far as providing a safe training experience. It works by programming data into computers to generate three-dimensional images to create virtual (lifelike) environments. These are usually viewed through a head-mounted device (goggles or a helmet), providing users with a sense of depth. Users remain stationary and use a joystick or track ball to move through the environment; they may wear a special glove to manipulate objects or employ virtual weapons to confront virtual aggressors. Recruits can make decisions and act on them without risk to themselves or others; these actions can then be critiqued, allowing trainees to learn from their mistakes. It appears that virtual reality can offer law enforcement benefits in a number of areas, including pursuit driving, firearms training, high-risk-incident management, incident re-creation, and processing crime scenes (Hormann 1995).

How effective is the training provided to the recruits? One means of evaluating it is to follow up on field performance to determine the areas in which recruits are having the most difficulty; methods used can include observation of recruits, the evaluation of recruit performance, and surveys of recruits, trainers, and supervisors. In general, the validity of the measurement will be higher if more than one of these methods is used. Once problems are identified, a determination can be made as to how to improve the program. In addition, as new knowledge and skills become available, they should be incorporated into the program.

Field Training

After successfully completing their work at the academy, recruits generally go through a final field-training program to prepare them for the real world of policing. This on-the-job, or apprentice, training has been an integral aspect of the recruit training process for some time but it has become much more sophisticated since the mid-1970s. The traditional assignment of new officers being broken in by experienced old timers is giving way to highly structured programs using **field-training officers (FTOs)**, that is, well-qualified, experienced officers especially trained to act as mentors for new recruits. In a national survey of 588 police departments of all sizes, M. S. McCampbell (1986) found that 64 percent (183) had a formal field-training program, while 36 percent (105) still did not use such programs. Major advantages of field-training programs include a reduced number of civil liability suits, standardization of the training process, and better documentation of recruit performance, thus improving the department's ability to make informed decisions about recruit retention (McCampbell 1986), as well as helping to determine the effectiveness of academy training. Interestingly, however, a national study of recruitment, selection, and training practices (Langworthy, Hughes, and Sanders 1995) found that only 56 percent of departments expected FTOs to communicate training needs to the academy.

The importance of FTOs cannot be overstated because they will have a significant impact not only on the training of the recruit but on imparting the department's culture as well. The national study cited above observed that the mean number of years required to become an FTO in those departments surveyed had decreased significantly from 1990 to 1994 (from 2.6 to 1.9 years). The study suggested that this decrease "may be because departments are having difficulty recruiting officers for the FTO assignment and have lessened their standards to fill training slots" (Langworthy, Hughes, and Sanders 1995, p. 39).

Much can be learned about the importance of maintaining high standards in the selection of FTOs from the Christopher Commission's report on the Los Angeles Police Department in the wake of the Rodney King beating. Case Study 6.1 is an excerpt from the report regarding the process then in use by the Los Angeles Police Department to select and train FTOs. As the commission notes, not only should rigorous selection standards be established,

Los Angeles Police Department: Selection and Training of FTOs

Upon graduation [from the academy] the new officer works as a "probationary officer" assigned to various field-training officers. The FTOs guide new officers' first contacts with citizens and have primary responsibility for introducing the probationers to the culture and traditions of the department. The commission's interviews of FTOs in four representative divisions revealed that many FTOs openly perpetuate the siege mentality that alienates patrol officers from the community and pass on to their trainees confrontational attitudes of hostility and disrespect for the public. This problem is in part the result of flaws in the way FTOs are selected and trained. The hiring of a very large number of new officers in 1989, which required the use of less-experienced FTOs, greatly exacerbated the problem.

Any officer promoted to Police Officer III by passing a written examination covering departmental policies and procedures is eligible to serve as an FTO. At present there are no formal eligibility or disqualification criteria for the FTO position based on an applicant's disciplinary records. Fourteen of the FTOs in the four divisions the commission studied had been disciplined for use of excessive force or use of improper tactics. There also appears to be little emphasis on selecting FTOs who have an interest in training junior officers, and an FTO's training ability is given little weight in his or her evaluation.

The most influential training received by a probationer comes from the example set by his or her FTO. Virtually all of the FTOs interviewed stated that their primary objective in training probationers is to instill good "officer safety skills." While the commission recognizes the importance of such skills in police work, the probationer's world is quickly divided into "we/they" categories, a division exacerbated by the failure to integrate any cultural awareness or sensitivity training into field training.

The commission believes that, to become FTOs, officers should be required to pass written and oral tests designed to measure communication skills, teaching aptitude, and knowledge of departmental policies regarding appropriate use of force, cultural sensitivity, community relations, and nondiscrimination. Officers with an aptitude for and interest in training junior officers should be encouraged by effective incentives to apply for FTO positions. In addition, the training program for FTOs should be modified to place greater emphasis on communication skills and the appropriate use of force. Successful completion of FTO School should be required before an FTO begins teaching probationers.

Source: Adapted from Independent Commission on the Los Angeles Police Department. 1991. *Report of the Independent Commission on the Los Angeles Police Department.* Los Angeles: California Public Management Institute, pp. xvi–xvii.

but officers with an aptitude for and interest in training junior officers should be encouraged to apply.

With FTO programs, the probationary period is usually a highly structured experience, in which new officers must demonstrate specific knowledge and skills. Frequent evaluations are made of the recruits' performance, usually by several FTOs who supervise their work in different areas and different shifts. In general, there are three phases in an FTO program (McCampbell 1986, p. 4–5):

Phase 1: The first weeks (eight to 20 or more) are for regional academy training; if the recruit passes, there may be additional weeks of classroom training provided by the department.

Phase 2: In the second phase (12 or more weeks), the recruit is assigned to the first FTO for several weeks, followed by a second FTO on a different shift, and then a third FTO on another shift. The officer then returns to the original FTO. During each tour, there are daily observation reports by the FTOs and weekly evaluation reports by supervisors (usually sergeants). At the end of this phase, the recruit moves on to the third phase, is given remedial training, or is dismissed. Figure 6.1 is an example of the San Jose, California, Police Department's Daily Observation Report form, which is used to rate the daily performance of recruits. Extensive training is provided to FTOs in how to evaluate and provide guidance to recruits.

Figure 6.1   San Jose Police Department's Daily Observation Report Form

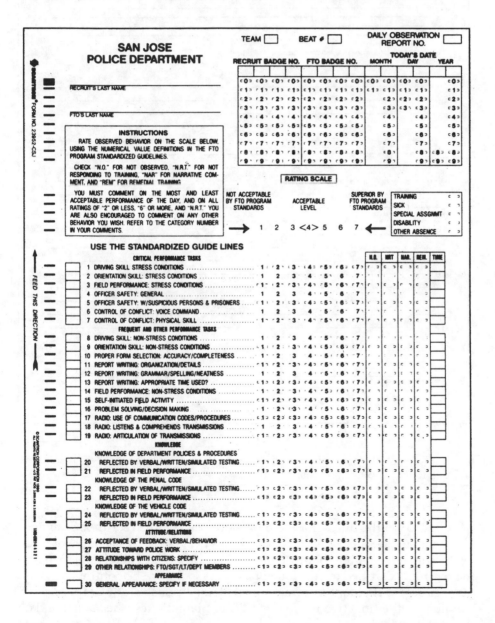

THE MOST ACCEPTABLE AREA OF PERFORMANCE TODAY WAS RATING CATEGORY NUMBER _____
A SPECIFIC INCIDENT WHICH DEMONSTRATES TODAY'S PERFORMANCE IN THIS AREA IS: _____

THE LEAST ACCEPTABLE AREA OF PERFORMANCE TODAY WAS RATING CATEGORY NUMBER _____
A SPECIFIC INCIDENT WHICH DEMONSTRATES TODAY'S PERFORMANCE IN THIS AREA IS: _____

DOCUMENTATION OF PERFORMANCE AND COMMENTS:
CAT. NO.

RECRUIT OFFICER SIGNATURE   TRAINING OFFICER SIGNATURE

Source: Reprinted by permission of San Jose Police Department, San Jose, Calif., and Scantron Corporation, Tustin, Calif.

Phase 3: In the third phase (16 or more weeks), the recruit is assigned a solo beat outside the training district and is evaluated every couple of weeks by the supervisor. After about 10 months, a review board determines whether the recruit is certified to continue Phase 3; if so, he or she continues to work the solo beat (with monthly evaluations); if not, he or she returns for remedial training. In the final two weeks, an FTO in plainclothes rides along and ob-

serves the recruit. At the end of this phase, the recruit is certified as a perma-   ❖ ❖ ❖ ❖
nent employee, Phase 3 is extended, or he or she is dismissed.

FTO programs have not always been as effective as was hoped. Although
monetary incentives and special training are generally provided, many officers believe that being an FTO is both burdensome and stressful. Evaluation
is undoubtedly one of the most difficult managerial tasks to perform, and
many managers do not do it well. FTOs frequently engage in evaluation activity on a daily basis. Their evaluations may be challenged, and if a trainee is
terminated, the FTO may be sued. Unless the stress of being an FTO is lessened substantially, it may be difficult to encourage the best officers to participate. The authors believe that FTOs should not only be paid more but that selection to the position be considered as a promotion. In addition, evaluations
should be conducted less frequently and, for the most part, determined by a
group of FTOs, rather than by an individual. In other words, recruits should
work with several FTOs over a period of several weeks or months, and a group
evaluation of each recruit's performance should be used instead of the daily
evaluations by individual FTOs. Of course, each FTO should still give daily
advice and guidance to the recruit, while keeping a daily evaluation log that
would be used in determining group FTO evaluations. Such a procedure
should not only increase the validity of the evaluation but also help to reduce
FTO stress as well.

After the recruit has passed the FTO program, he or she may become a
permanent, sworn police officer or work for an additional period in the field
on probationary status. During this time, officers are evaluated several more
times, and if their performance is acceptable, they become permanent employees.

Career Growth

Once a person is recruited, selected, and trained and completes probation in a police department, his or her career begins, and career growth becomes important. Career growth can be for individual development as well as
for a specific position within the department; it can involve training within or
outside the department, and it attempts to match the needs of the individual
with those of the department.

Departments must not only be upgraded regarding knowledge and skills
of officers in their current positions, but they must plan to incorporate officers' interests with **career paths** that involve position enhancement, new assignments, and promotion. For instance, assume Officer Nancy Brown has
worked in a medium-to-large police department for 25 years and has the following career path:

- Assigned to patrol for five years.

- Transferred to traffic unit for two years, where she worked as an enforcement specialist.

- Promoted to sergeant and transferred back to patrol for two years.

- Transferred to detective unit for three years, where she worked as a
  robbery and homicide investigator.

- Promoted to lieutenant and transferred to a training unit, where she supervised for three years.

- Promoted to captain and supervised the patrol division for three years.

- Transferred to the detective unit again and placed in charge for three years.

- Promoted to assistant chief and served for four years prior to retirement.

An effective career-path program must be able to provide for the improvement of the officer's knowledge and skills in each area of assignment. There is also a need to develop career-path programs that will financially reward officers for staying in patrol and performing well. In many departments, the only way to obtain a pay increase after five or six years of service (other than cost-of-living adjustments) is to be promoted or transferred to a specialized position. This is not an effective system, because good performers, even though they may wish to stay in patrol, think that they need to be promoted or become specialists to receive adequate compensation. Since the 1970s, the Los Angeles Police Department, for example, has had a career-path program that builds in several career-path levels below the rank of lieutenant, each with its own pay scale. This program allows officers to pursue police careers below the command level. All police departments should have overlapping pay scales in which patrol officers and investigators, if highly competent, could be paid at levels equal to those of management. Such a system would encourage many excellent officers to stay in patrol and investigations. This is the system in academe, for example, where the most highly regarded professors are often paid more than their managers (e.g., chairs and deans) and possibly even more than the college president.

Advanced training. Police officers and managers must be kept up to date on changing laws, community needs and expectations, and police methods and technologies, and must be prepared for reassignment or promotion. Large departments often have sufficient resources to allow them to develop and maintain their own advanced training programs. Mid-sized and smaller departments usually must find outside programs. Many states, as a result of statewide training and standards commissions, have developed extensive career-growth programs for the police. For instance, it is often possible for these departments to send their officers to programs that assist in preparing them for almost any assignment or promotion. Many departments also use private trainers or consultants, as well as university programs to upgrade their personnel, and many departments allow for flexible schedules or provide incentives for officers to attend college. In general, experienced older officers and managers want to be treated more as peers than as students and usually prefer a more academic approach to a stress-related one. This fact suggests that experienced officers would most likely prefer, and benefit from, an andragogical approach to training.

In-service training. The primary purpose of **in-service training** is the regular updating of all members of the department in a wide variety of subjects. It usually involves subject matter that all department members must know in order to function well. For example, officers must continually be aware of changing laws and ordinances, newly developed techniques, operating policies and procedures, and departmental changes and expectations. Departments moving toward community policing must incorporate the concepts of this approach in their training. The San Diego Police Department, for example, has developed an eight-hour training program called *problem-oriented policing* (POP), that has been used throughout California. The training emphasizes the history and methods of community policing and problem solving, a problem-solving model with case studies and scenarios, barriers and benefits from adopting POP, peer support and guidance to promote POP, and the examination of expectations and concerns about implementing POP (San Diego Police Department 1993).

Another area of training that has become increasingly important to the police, especially in cities that have a high degree of ethnic and racial diversity, is cultural diversity. Many police departments have underestimated the significance of the relationship between cultural sensitivity and police-community relations; it may take only a few insensitive, noncaring acts by the police to create a negative police image. Consequently, progressive departments have incorporated cultural sensitivity not only into their recruit training but also as an integral part of their in-service training. Inside Policing 6.3 provides several examples of the needs and types of cultural-sensitivity training provided by police departments throughout the San Francisco Bay Area.

Inside Policing 6.3
Police Striving for Cultural Sensitivity

After arresting a young, recently immigrated Asian boy, Fremont police detective Chris Mazzone received a surprising request from the boy's mother. She asked Mazzone to shake her husband's hand. "She wanted me to show respect for him. I had just been talking to her because she was the only one who spoke English. In their culture it was disrespectful to ignore the male," explained Mazzone, who shook the man's hand.

With an increasingly diverse population, the chances of a police officer in the Bay Area needing to cope with cultural barriers or language difficulties are high. In the past decade, the Asian population grew by 255 percent in Fremont, 157 percent in Union City, and 106 percent in Newark. And in San Jose, the Hispanic population—now 208,000—nearly doubled while the Asian community increased 191.4 percent.

To avoid misunderstandings, police throughout California are learning to avoid conflict in classes designed to heighten their cultural sensitivity. They are being taught that in the Asian community, beckoning to someone with a finger is offensive. Touching someone on the head can be insulting. And among some people, distrust of law enforcement stems from bad experiences in their homeland. "Officers encounter these problems almost daily," Mazzone said.

Some big-city departments—including Fremont's and San Jose's—have conducted cultural-sensitivity classes for years. But under a plan recently approved by the legislature, all of California's 35 police academies will be required to teach cultural awareness. The new requirement, experts say, was prompted in part by the police beating of Los Angeles motorist Rodney King.

"We try hard to make police sensitive to cultural issues because they're going to have to go out onto the street someday and deal with them head-on," said Ron L. Havner, dean of Evergreen Valley College's Criminal Justice Training Center, the academy that teaches recruits for Santa Clara County's 13 police departments. "There are 120 dialects and cultures in this valley, with 60,000 new immigrants coming into the state this year," Havner said. "The bottom line is to understand their value systems."

In San Jose, it took three hours and a Polish translator, but Officer Greg Sancier finally coaxed a frightened motorist into rolling down his window and signing a traffic ticket. "That's all I wanted him to do, but he didn't understand English," Sancier said. "You could see real fear in his face. I found out later that he once was imprisoned in Siberia after getting tricked into signing some paper." Sancier was lucky. It was a quiet day and he was able to spend time with the motorist, averting what could have been a messy, and confusing, argument.

Training of Officers

In San Jose, police officers who already have been through the academy also are required to take periodic training seminars that focus on cultural awareness. They often learn basic foreign phrases and discuss interpersonal communication, body language, and perceptions about others—all to get a better handle on their own attitudes and behavior.

Philip Nguyen, an employee of Child Protective Services, teaches San Jose officers a few language basics, such as "hello" or "come here," and offers simple tips on approaching wary people. "Sometimes it's hard to explain what's going on even when you both speak the same language," Nguyen said. "Officers have to listen more and try to show that they care and are interested in the person's problem."

Police officers want to do that, said Lt. Tom Wheatly, head of San Jose's training unit. That's why the department offers cultural-awareness classes. "Out on the street, there is no one to interpret for us," Wheatly said. "There's just us and them. So it's better that we learn to understand."

In Fremont, the police department began mandatory cultural-sensitivity training for all of its employees four years ago. It proved so successful that the city launched its own program that is now required for all employees. "We have such a tremendous diversity of cultures that we have to know some of the nuances," Fremont police captain Mike Lanam said.

Source: Adapted from B. Romano and S. Gonzales. 1991. "Police Striving for Cultural Sensitivity." *San Jose Mercury News,* November 10: B1, B2. Reprinted by permission.

Specialized training. **Specialized training** attempts to prepare officers for specific tasks (e.g., stakeouts or decoy work) or for different jobs throughout the department (e.g., homicide investigator or supervisor). Specialized training is essential if officers are to perform effectively outside the role of patrol officer.

Officers promoted to first-line supervisory positions (i.e., sergeant) should be provided with some form of **supervisory training**. Such training may be in-house or external and usually includes topics on leadership behavior, specific job requirements, and policies and procedures. Once an officer is promoted to a managerial or executive-level position (e.g., lieutenant or higher), additional **management training** is necessary. The role of the police manager is even more complex than that of first-level supervisor and requires not only increased knowledge regarding management's role in the department but also long-range planning, policy development, and resource allocation. In California, for example, each of these types of training is required: Police chiefs must complete an 80-hour executive-development course within two years of appointment; captains must complete an 80-hour management course within 12 months; lieutenants must complete an 80-hour management course (different in content from the captain's course) within 12 months; and sergeants must complete an 80-hour supervisory course within 12 months.

In addition, in those departments using community policing, some training relating to the concepts, processes, and new role requirements for managers is necessary. In San Diego, for example, a 16-hour POP training program for supervisors has been implemented. The course includes the basic course in POP (eight hours), issues and concerns for supervisors regarding the analysis of problems, supervision of problem solving, and performance evaluations. The department also has an executive-level POP orientation course (four hours), which emphasizes the history and methods of community and problem-solving policing and discusses the issues and concerns of implementation and operational strategies. Finally, the department has developed training courses in POP for investigators (eight hours) and for trainers (40 hours) (San Diego Police Department 1993).

One national survey of l44 police departments, including the two largest in each state, found that 97 percent provided in-house supervisory training and that 78 percent make the training mandatory (Armstrong and Longenecker 1992). This training was conducted prior to, or at the time of, promotion by 51 percent of the departments; 49 percent provided the training following the promotion. The subjects most frequently taught included supervisory techniques (95 percent), use of the disciplinary process (92 percent), counseling techniques (80 percent), employee evaluation and review (79 percent), and motivational techniques (73 percent). Other topics included management theory (68 percent), handling employee grievances and complaints (64 percent), EEOC guidelines and affirmative action (62 percent), and department personnel-harassment policy (52 percent).

Management training was provided by 81 percent of the departments. Of those, 37 percent offered the training in-house, and the remaining 63 percent sent their managers outside the department (e.g., to state agencies, contract agencies, or the FBI). The most common subject areas included management strategy (77 percent), budgeting (70 percent), management by objectives (63 percent), labor negotiations and contract administration (63 percent), administration of discipline (58 percent), police planning (52 percent), and work-force allocation and patrol strategy (45 percent). Finally, the departments reported that fully 90 percent of the police managers receiving management training considered it to be a worthwhile experience.

One of the most troublesome aspects of supervisory and management training for police is the evaluation procedure, or lack thereof. Although recruit training is often rigorously evaluated, training for experienced officers and managers rarely includes any meaningful evaluation. Thus, it is unlikely that an experienced officer will ever be "washed out" or required to improve, regardless of how inadequate his or her performance might be. This lack can be a serious problem because many of the participants may not take the training seriously and thus will not attain the skills and knowledge necessary to be effective. Consequently, departments should require all training programs to include meaningful performance evaluation, because only in this way can they be sure that their future supervisors and managers are effectively trained for their new roles.

Promotion and assessment centers. Promotion in police departments is usually based on one or more of several evaluative criteria, including an officer's (1) time on the job (seniority) or time in rank, (2) past performance, (3) written examination, (4) oral interview, and (5) college hours or degrees. In general, a percentage weight is assigned to each evaluative criterion used and an overall promotional score is assigned. As openings at the next level of rank occur, individuals are promoted according to their score. Which criteria are used and what weight is assigned varies by department, according to what the department or civil-service commission regards as the most important. Often, police departments use only one or two of these criteria, even though the criteria may have little, if any, relationship to the supervisory or managerial position for which the candidate is applying. Such a process can easily lead to the selection of the wrong candidate for the position, which may have a long-term negative impact on the department and the officers being supervised. Because it is difficult to measure supervisory or managerial potential based on these criteria alone, many departments are now using an assessment-center approach, which is perhaps the most promising method for selecting officers for promotion.

An **assessment center** involves a process that attempts to measure a candidate's potential for a particular managerial position. It uses multiple assessment strategies, typically spread over a two- or three-day period, which include different types of job-related simulations and possibly the use of interviews and psychological tests. Common forms of job simulations include in-basket exercises (e.g., carrying out simulated supervisory or managerial assignments such as writing memos or reports and responding to letters or personnel matters), simulations of interviews with subordinates, oral presentations, group discussions, and fact-finding exercises (Filer 1977). The candidate's behavior on all relevant criteria is evaluated by trained assessors, who reach a consensus on each participant. The primary advantage of this approach is that it evaluates all candidates in a simulated environment under standardized conditions, thus adding significantly to the validity and reliability of the selection process.

Lateral entry. **Lateral entry** refers to the ability of a police officer, at the patrol or supervisory level, to transfer from one department to another, usually without losing seniority. This concept is viewed by many as an important step toward increased professionalism through the improvement of career growth. Lateral entry is not a new concept, having been strongly endorsed by the 1967 President's Commission *Task Force on Police*:

> To improve police service, competition for all advanced positions should be opened to qualified persons from both within and outside of the department. This would enable a department to obtain the best available talent for positions of leadership. . . .. If candidates from within an agency are unable to meet the competition from other applicants, it should be recognized that the influx of more highly qualified personnel would greatly improve the quality of the services. (1967, p. 142)

Implicitly, this recommendation increases the competition for leadership positions; if those already within the department are not as well qualified, they will need to upgrade their skills and educational levels. Of course, this need is one of the primary obstacles to implementing lateral entry; older officers within the department feel that they should be provided the opportunity for advancement, not an "outsider." Although this resistance can be a problem, probably of greater significance are the restrictions of civil-service limitations, including retirement systems, which generally are not transferable. Because of these restrictions, and lack of departmental support, lateral entry is still used sparingly today. Some legislative reforms that contribute to its implementation have been made; before lateral entry can become widely adopted, however, individual departments will need to become its proponent.

Undoubtedly, the expanded use of lateral entry would increase the quality of the applicant pool for most police departments, thus improving the selection of police supervisors and managers.

The next chapter will discuss the results of the selection and development process—namely, police field operations. These include primarily patrol and investigative work. Generally, recruits are assigned to patrol after leaving the training academy, whereas veteran officers, at some point in their careers, may choose to become detectives and specialize in investigations.

Summary

With the increasing complexity of the police role and the movement toward community policing, the quality of police personnel has become perhaps the key factor to the effective operation of police departments. Thus, screening in, as opposed to screening out, candidates should be used in order that only the best qualified are selected for the applicant pool. Candidates must meet a number of preemployment standards that attempt to depict a department's view of what is required to become an effective officer, for example, physical agility; educational, psychological, and background qualifications; and polygraph examinations. Preemployment selection tests are also used and usually include written tests, oral interviews, or both. Some departments, however, also require reading exams because the reading ability of applicants has declined in recent years. The Americans With Disabilities Act prohibits discrimination against qualified individuals with a disability. This act will have a substantial impact on the traditional sequencing of selection steps, because applicants must be given a conditional offer of employment prior to taking any tests or exams that may be disability related.

In preparing recruits for the job, decisions must be made about program orientation, philosophy, instructional methods, course content, and program evaluation. Following academy training, recruits generally go through an on-the-job field-training program prior to job assignment; many departments use a field-training officer (FTO) program for this purpose. The career growth of officers is important, because they must be prepared for changes not only in their current jobs but also changes in job assignments and promotions. Departments should establish career paths that allow for employees at all levels to remain motivated throughout their careers. Finally, because promotions have long-term implications for the departments, administrators should carefully analyze the process and criteria used. Assessment centers may offer the greatest potential in this area.

Discussion Questions

1. Describe the meaning of "quality" with respect to police personnel. Explain what you consider to be the most important criteria with respect to quality in police recruits.

2. Explain the process of screening in applicants versus screening out applicants. Why is this process important?

3. Describe several different recruitment strategies and nontraditional methods of recruitment. Explain why such practices might be necessary in police recruitment.

4. Describe three preemployment standards that you consider to be the most important in the selection process and explain why.

5. Explain the meaning and importance of disparate impact and bona fide occupational qualification (BFOQ) with respect to police selection.

6. Discuss several important implications of the philosophy and structural methods used in recruit training.

7. Discuss what you believe to be the five most important topics in recruit-training curricula and why.

8. Discuss what you believe to be the most important criteria in the selection of FTOs. How would you assure that those selected meet these criteria?

9. Describe several types of advanced-training programs and why departments must make such training available.

10. Discuss why assessment centers are perhaps the most promising method for selecting officers for promotion.

References

"A Place to Call Home." 1997. *Law Enforcement News* July/August: 1, 17.

Albermarle Paper v. Moody. 1975. 10 FEP 1181.

Alpert, G. P and Moore, M. H. 1993. "Measuring Police Performance in the New Paradigm of Policing." In *Performance Measures for the Criminal Justice System*, pp. 109–140. Washington, DC: Bureau of Justice Statistics.

Alpert, G. and Smith, W. 1990. "Defensibility of Law Enforcement Training." *Criminal Law Bulletin* 26: 452–458.

Armstrong, L. D. and Longenecker, C. O. 1992. "Police Management Training: A National Survey." *FBI Law Enforcement Bulletin* 61: 22–26.

Ash, P., Slora, K., and Britton, C. F. 1990. "Police Agency Selection Practices." *Journal of Police Science and Administration* 17: 258–269.

Bayley, D. and Bittner, E. 1989. "Learning the Skills of Policing." In R. Dunham and G. Alpert (eds), *Critical Issues in Policing: Contemporary Readings*, pp. 87–110. Prospect Heights, IL: Waveland Press.

Bayley, D. and Mendelsohn, H. 1969. Minorities and the Police. New York: Free Press.

Berg, B. L. 1990. "First Day at the Police Academy: Stress-Reaction-Training as a Screening-Out Technique." *Journal of Contemporary Criminal Justice* 6: 89–105.

Burbeck, E. and Furnham, A. 1985. "Police Officer Selection: A Critical Review of the Literature." *Journal of Police Science and Administration* 13: 58–69.

Carter, D. L., Sapp, A. D., and Stephens, D. W. 1989. *The State of Police Education: Policy Direction for the 21st Century*. Washington, DC: Police Executive Research Forum.

Chapman, S. G. 1982. "Personnel Management." In B. L. Garmire (ed.), *Local Government Police Management, 2nd ed.*, pp. 241–273. Washington, DC: International City Management Association.

Clark, J. R. 1992. "Why Officer Johnny Can't Read." *Law Enforcement News*, May 15: 1, 16–17.

——. 1994. "Sweep of Disabilities Act Widens As Court Mandates More Police Training." *Law Enforcement News*, November 30: 1, 6.

Cohen, B. and Chaiken, J. M. 1972. *Police Background Characteristics and Performance*. New York: Rand Institute.

Commission on Peace Officer Standards and Training. 1995 (May 12). *Bulletin 95-9: Regular Basic Course Required Minimum Hours Increases From 560 to 664*. Sacramento, CA: POST.

Crosby, A., Rosenfield, M., and Thornton, R. F. 1979. "The Development of a Written Test for Police Applicant Selection." In C. D. Spielberger (ed.), *Police Selection and Evaluation*, pp. 143-153. New York: Praeger.

Davis V. City of Dallas. 1985. 777 F.2d 205 (5th Cir.).

"Dumb-da-dum-dum." 1997. *Law Enforcement News* June 15: 4.

Dwyer, W. O., Prien, E. P., and Bernard, J. L. 1990. "Psychological Screening of Law Enforcement Officers: A Case for Job Relatedness." *Journal of Police Science and Administration* 17: 176–182.

Earle, H. H. 1973. *Police Recruit Training: Stress vs. Non-Stress*. Springfield, IL: C. C. Thomas.

Eisenberg, S., Kent, D. A., and Wall, C. 1973. *Police Personnel Practice in State and Local Government*. Washington, DC: Police Foundation.

Falkenberg, S., Gaines, L. K., and Cox, T. C. 1990. "The Oral Interview Board: What Does It Measure?" *Journal of Police Science and Administration* 17: 32–39.

Filer, R. J. 1977. "Assessment Centers in Police Selection." In C. D. Spielberger and H. C. Spaulding (eds.), *Proceedings of the National Working Conference on the Selection of Law Enforcement Officers*. Tampa: University of South Florida.

Fyfe, J. 1987. *Police Personnel Practices*. Washington, D.C.: International City Management Association.

Gaines, L. K., Costello, P., and Crabtree, A. 1989. "Police Selection Testing: Balancing Legal Requirements and Employer Needs." American Journal of Police 8: 137–152.

Gaines, L. K. and Kappeler, V. E. 1992. "Selection and Testing." In G. W. Cordner and D. C. Hale (eds.), *What Works in Policing: Operations and Administration Examined*, pp. 107–123. Cincinnati, OH: Anderson.

"Getting the Inside Dope." 1996. *Law Enforcement News* October 31: 1, 14.

Grant, J. D. and Grant, J. 1995. "Officer Selection and the Prevention of Abuse of Force." In. W. A. Geller and H. Toch (eds.), *And Justice for All: Understanding and Controlling Police Abuse of Force*, pp. 151–162. Washington, DC: Police Executive Research Forum.

Griggs v. Duke Power Company. 1971. 401 U.S. 424.

Hodes, C. R., Hunt, R. L., and Raskin, D. C. 1985. "Effects of Physical Countermeasures on the Physiological Detection of Deception." *Journal of Applied Psychology* 70: 177–187.

Hormann, J. S. 1995. "Virtual Reality: The Future of Law Enforcement Training." *Police Chief* July: 7–12.

Hunter, J. 1986. "Cognitive Ability, Cognitive Aptitude, Job Knowledge, and Job Performance." *Journal of Vocational Behavior* 29: 340–362.

Independent Commission on the Los Angeles Police Department. 1991. *Report of the Independent Commission on the Los Angeles Police Department*. Los Angeles: California Public Management Institute.

International Association of Chiefs of Police. 1998. "Ethics Training in Law Enforcement." *Police Chief* January: 14–24.

International City Management Association. 1986. *Municipal Yearbook*. Washington, D.C.: International City Management Association.

Johnson, E. E. 1990. "Psychological Tests Used in Assessing a Sample of Police and Firefighter Candidates: An Update." <MI>American Journal of Police 9: 85–92.

Kleinmuntz, B. and Szucko, J. J. 1982. "Is the Lie Detector Valid?" *Law and Society Review* 16: 105–122.

❖ ❖ ❖ ❖   Knowles, M. S. 1970. *The Modern Practice of Adult Education: Andragogy Versus Pedagogy*. New York: Association Press.

Krasken, P. B. and Kappeler, V. E. 1988. "Police On-Duty Drug Use: A Theoretical and Descriptive Examination." *American Journal of Police* 7: 1–28.

Krieble, J. 1994. "Selection, Training, and Evaluation Ensure Success." *The Police Chief* 62: 26–29.

Langworthy, R., Hughes, T., and Sanders, B. 1995. *Law Enforcement Recruitment, Selection and Training: A Survey of Major Police Departments in the U.S.* Highland Heights, KY: Academy of Criminal Justice Sciences—Police Section. 1995.

Law Enforcement Assistance Administration. 1973. *Equal Employment Opportunity Program Development Manual*. Washington, D.C.: U.S. Government Printing Office.

McCampbell, M. S. 1986. *Field Training for Police Officers: State of the Art*. Washington, D.C.: National Institute of Justice.

McNamara, J. H. 1967. "Uncertainties in Police Work: The Relevance of Police Recruits' Background and Training." In D. J. Bordua (ed.), *The Police: Six Sociological Essays*, pp. 207–215. New York: Wiley.

Meagher, M. S. and Yentes, N. A. 1986. "Choosing a Career in Policing: A Comparison of Male and Female Perceptions." *Journal of Police Science and Administration* 14: 320–327.

National Advisory Commission on Criminal Justice Standards and Goals. 1973. *Report on Police*. Washington, D.C.: U.S. Government Printing Office.

President's Commission on Law Enforcement and Administration of Justice. 1967. *Task Force Report: The Police*. Washington, D.C.: U.S. Government Printing Office.

Pynes, J. E. 1994. "Police Officer Selection Procedures: Speculation on the Future." *American Journal of Police* 13: 103–112.

Rafky, J. and Sussman, F. 1985. "An Evaluation of Field Techniques in Detection of Deception." *Psychophysiology* 12: 121–130.

Reaves, B. A. 1996. *Local Police Departments, 1993*. Washington, D.C.: Bureau of Justice Statistics.

Reaves, B. A. and Goldberg, A. L. 1999. *Law Enforcement Management and Administrative Statistics, 1997: Data for Individual and Local Agencies with 100 or More Officers*. Washington, D.C.: Bureau of Justice Statistics.

Roberg, R. R. (ed.) 1976. *The Changing Police Role: New Dimensions and New Perspectives*. San Jose, CA: Justice Systems Development.

——. 1979. "Police Training and Andragogy: A New Perspective." *Police Chief* 46: 32–34.

Roberg, R. R. and Kuykendall, J. 1997. *Police Management, 2nd ed.* Los Angeles, CA: Roxbury Publishing Co.

Robles, F. 1997. "Line of Duty Calls for Woman: a Miami Rookie Cop—at 56," *Valley Times* February 14: 1A, 16A.

Romano, B. and Gonzales, S. 1991. "Police Striving for Cultural Sensitivity," *San Jose Mercury News*. November 10: B1, B2.

"Rookie Cop, 59, Can't Escape Media." 1994. *San Jose Mercury News* November 29: 3B.

Rubin, P. N. 1994. *The Americans With Disabilities Act and Criminal Justice: Hiring New Employees*. Washington, DC: National Institute of Justice.

Sanders, B., Hughes, T. and Langworthy, R. 1995. "Police Officer Recruitment and Selection: A Survey of Major Departments in the U.S." *Police Forum*. Richmond, KY: Academy of Criminal Justice Sciences.

San Diego Police Department, 1993. *Neighborhood Policing*. San Diego, CA: San Diego Police Department.

Sauls, J. G. 1995. "Establishing the Validity of Employment Standards." *FBI Law Enforcement Bulletin* August: 27–32.

Schmidt, F. 1988. "The Problem of Group Differences in Ability Test Scores in Employment Selection." *Journal of Vocational Behavior* 33: 272–292.

Schneider, B. and Schmitt, N. 1986. *Staffing Organizations, 2nd ed*. Glenview, IL: Scott, Foresman.

Schofield, D. L. 1989. "Establishing Health and Fitness Standards: Legal Considerations." *FBI Law Enforcement Bulletin*, June: 25–31.

Shield Club v. City of Cleveland, 1986. 647 R.Supp. 274 (N.D. Ohio).

Seagrave, J. 1992. "Community Policing and the Need for Police Research Skills Training." *Canadian Police College Journal* 16: 204–211.

Slater, H. R. and Reiser, M. 1988. "A Comparative Study of Factors Influencing Police Recruitment." *Journal of Police Science and Administration* 16: 168–176.

"Solid Corps for Policing's Future." 1994. *Law Enforcement News* April, 15: 4.

Sproule, C. F. 1984. "Should Personnel Selection Tests be Used on a Pass-Fail, Grouping, or Ranking Basis?" *Public Personnel Management Journal* 13: 375–394.

TELEMASP. 1994. "Background Investigation and Psychological Screening of New Officers: Effect of the Americans With Disabilities Act." Texas Law Enforcement Management and Administrative Statistics Program. October.

——. 1996. "Recruitment Practices." Texas Law Enforcement Management and Administrative Statistics Program. September.

Thibault, E. A., Lynch, L. A., and McBride, R. B. 1990. *Proactive Police Management, 2nd ed*. Englewood Cliffs, NJ: Prentice-Hall.

Vanguard Justice Society v. Hughes. 1979. 471 F. Supp. 670.

Wilson, O. W. and McLaren, R. C. 1977. *Police Administration, 4th ed*. New York: McGraw-Hill.

Winters, C. A. 1989. "Psychology Tests, Suits, and Minority Applicants." *Police Journal* 62: 22–30.

Zecca, J. M. 1993. "The CUNY/NYPD Cadet Corps." *ACJS Today* May/June: 5.

For a listing of websites appropriate to the content of this chapter, see "Suggested Websites for Further Study" (p. xv). ✦

Chapter Seven

Field Operations

Chapter Outline

❏ The Patrol Function
   Historical Development
   Patrol Methods
   Use of Patrol Resources
      Resource Determination
      Resource Allocation
      Computerized Crime Mapping

❏ Selected Research on Patrol Operations
   Random Patrol
   Response Time
   Management of Demand
   Directed Patrol
   Proactive Arrests
   Crackdowns
   Guns, Violence, and Gangs
   Zero-Tolerance Arrests
   Reactive Arrests
   Covert Patrol
   Police Pursuits

❏ Patrol Development Guidelines

❏ Selected Patrol Issues
   Special Populations
   Bias Crimes
   AIDS

❏ The Investigative Function
   Historical Development
   Resource Determination and Allocation

❏ Selected Research on Investigative Operations
   Investigative Effectiveness
   Career Criminal Programs
   Detective-Patrol Relationships
   Enticement and Entrapment

❏ Summary

❏ Discussion Questions

❏ References

Key Terms	
announcement effect	computerized crime mapping
beat	covert patrol
bias crime	crackdown
community policing model	crime repression

Key Terms (continued)	
domestic violence (misdemeanor)	police field operations
detective	police legitimacy
deterrence decay	police pursuit
due-process revolution	political model
enticement	preliminary investigation
entrapment	proactive approach
follow-up investigation	random patrol
generalist	reactive approach
hot spots	residual deterrence
hot times	ROP
ICAM	shift
investigators	specialist
legalistic model	sting operation
management-of-demand system	zero-tolerance arrests

Police field operations consist of two primary functions: patrol and investigations. Although most departments have other operational activities (e.g., traffic, vice, juvenile affairs, criminalistics, crime prevention), a substantial majority of all police work involves either patrol or investigations. These two operational units deal with the greatest diversity of problems and have the most influence on the public's perception of the police. Accordingly, the focus of this chapter is on patrol work, the "backbone" of policing, and secondarily on investigative or detective work.

In relatively small departments, patrol and investigations typically do not exist as separate units because the police are generalists. A **generalist** is an officer who performs a variety of activities—for example, conducting investigations that result from calls while on patrol, that otherwise could be assigned to a **specialist**. In contrast, most medium or large departments tend to *specialize* their investigative activities. In these departments, once a patrol officer is dispatched to the scene of a crime, he or she may conduct a preliminary investigation and then call in the detectives for follow-up and further case development. In highly specialized departments, the patrol officer may call in the detectives as soon as it is ascertained that an investigation is necessary; once the detectives arrive, the officer returns to patrol duty.

As described in chapters 3 and 4, in those departments moving toward community policing, the patrol job is being redesigned to define police work more broadly (i.e., to be more general), with increased decision-making powers and problem-solving and investigative capabilities. It should be noted, however, that there will always be a need for detectives in policing. Patrol officers simply cannot receive enough training or have enough time to investigate highly complex and specialized crimes such as homicides, serial killings, or terrorist acts. Even small departments attempt to train a few officers to become proficient in investigating such crimes. When a crime occurs that is out of their realm of expertise, such departments may use investigators from other departments.

The Patrol Function

Police patrol has been classified as the "backbone of policing" (Wilson 1972) because the vast majority of police officers are assigned to patrol and thus provide the greatest bulk of services to the community. In most police departments, the patrol force is the largest unit, accounting for over 50 percent (Garmire 1977) and frequently up to 60 or 70 percent of the sworn personnel. Because patrol officers are also the most highly visible personnel in the department, the patrol unit forms the public's primary perception of any particular department. Thus, it is clear why patrol work is considered to be the backbone of policing.

As discussed earlier, the police role is highly diversified and complex; consequently, there are many ways to classify the goals of policing. Based on workload analysis of police officers, the primary goals of patrol include (1) crime prevention and deterrence, (2) apprehension of offenders, (3) creation of a sense of community security and satisfaction, (4) provision of non-crime-related services, and (5) traffic control. For departments practicing community policing, another important goal is (6) identifying and solving neighborhood problems with respect to crime and disorder. It should also be kept in mind, as described in chapter 2, that officers tend to utilize four main strategies, including presence, enforcement, education, and community building, either formally or informally, in attempting to accomplish these goals.

As discussed in chapter 2, patrol activities can also be grouped into law enforcement, order-maintenance, and service functions. *Law enforcement* involves problems in which police make arrests, issue citations, or conduct investigations. *Maintaining order* may or may not involve a violation of the law (usually minor), during which officers tend to use alternatives other than arrest. Examples include loud parties, teenagers consuming alcohol, or minor neighborhood disputes. *Service activities* involve taking reports and providing information and assistance to the public. Deterrence, prevention, and apprehension are related to the law enforcement category. The creation of a sense of community security and satisfaction and provision of non-crime-related services are related to the order-maintenance and service functions. Traffic control can fall under any of the activity categories; although traffic enforcement would be a law enforcement activity, directing traffic at the scene of an accident would be a service activity. The final goal of analyzing and solving problems could also fall under any of the activity categories; for example, planning with the community to open a recreation center to keep at-risk juveniles off the street could be considered either as maintaining order or providing service, but it may relate to law enforcement (through deterrence and prevention activities) as well. Based on one of the few observational analyses of patrol work, Case Study 7.1 provides a description of the complex nature of a patrol officer's job.

Historical Development

Two of the most important activities of patrol officers are *watching* and *being watched*. In preindustrial societies, watching took place as a means of social control. The night-watch system was originally the responsibility of the private citizen, who served as a form of community obligation. Even-

❖ ❖ ❖ ❖

Police Patrol: A Job Description

This behavioral analysis of a patrol officer's job provides one of the few empirical descriptions of the complex and varied demands of patrol work. Based on extensive field observations, the findings are reported as a list of the attributes that are required for successful performance in the field. Although completed over two decades ago, the findings appear to conform well to patrol activities of today . The researchers concluded that a patrol officer must do the following:

1. Endure long periods of monotony in routine patrol yet react quickly (almost instantaneously) and effectively to problem situations observed on the street or to orders issued by the radio dispatcher.

2. Gain knowledge of the patrol area, not only of its physical characteristics but also of its normal routine of events and the usual behavior patterns of its residents.

3. Exhibit initiative, problem-solving capacity, effective judgment, and imagination in coping with the numerous complex situations he or she is called upon to face, e.g., a family disturbance, a potential suicide, a robbery in progress, an accident, or a disaster.

4. Make prompt and effective decisions, sometimes in life-and-death situations, and be able to size up a situation quickly and take appropriate action.

5. Demonstrate mature judgment, as in deciding whether an arrest is warranted by the circumstances or a warning is sufficient, or in facing a situation where the use of force may be needed.

6. Demonstrate critical awareness in discerning signs of out-of-the-ordinary conditions or circumstances that indicate trouble or a crime in progress.

7. Exhibit a number of complex psychomotor skills, such as driving a vehicle in normal and emergency situations, firing a weapon accurately under extremely varied conditions, maintaining agility, endurance, and strength, and showing facility in self-defense and apprehension, as in taking a person into custody with a minimum of force.

8. Adequately perform the communication and record-keeping functions of the job, including oral reports, formal case reports, and departmental and court forms.

9. Have the facility to act effectively in extremely divergent interpersonal situations. A police officer constantly confronts persons who are acting in violation of the law, ranging from curfew violators to felons. He or she is constantly confronted by people who are in trouble or who are victims of crimes. At the same time, the officer must relate to the people on the beat—businessmen, residents, school officials, visitors. His or her interpersonal relations must range up and down a continuum defined by friendliness and persuasion on one end and by firmness and force at the other.

10. Endure verbal and physical abuse from citizens and offenders (as when placing a person under arrest or facing day-in and day-out race prejudice) while using only necessary force in the performance of his function.

11. Exhibit a professional, self-assured presence and a self-confident manner in his conduct when dealing with offenders, the public, and the courts.

12. Be capable of restoring equilibrium to social groups, e.g., restoring order in a family fight, in a disagreement between neighbors, or in a clash between rival youth groups.

13. Be skillful in questioning suspected offenders, victims, and witnesses of crimes.

14. Take charge of situations, e.g., a crime or accident scene, yet not unduly alienate participants or bystanders.

15. Be flexible enough to work under loose supervision in most day-to-day patrol activities and also under direct supervision in situations where large numbers of officers are required. ☞

16. Tolerate stress in a multitude of forms, such as meeting the violent behavior of a mob, coping with the pressures of a high-speed chase or a weapon being fired, or dealing with a woman bearing a child.

17. Exhibit personal courage in the face of dangerous situations that may result in serious injury or death.

18. Maintain objectivity while dealing with a host of special-interest groups, ranging from relatives of offenders to members of the press.

19. Maintain a balanced perspective in the face of constant exposure to the worst side of human nature.

20. Exhibit a high level of personal integrity and ethical conduct, e.g., refrain from accepting bribes or "favors" and provide impartial law enforcement.

Source: Adapted from M. E. Baehr, J. E. Furcon, and E. C. Froemel. 1968. *Psychological Assessment of Patrolman Qualifications in Relation to Field Performance.* Washington, D.C.: Department of Justice, pp. II–3 to II–5.

tually, the citizen watcher became the paid watchman, who became the nineteenth-century patrol officer. Patrol officers in the political model were dispersed throughout the community in the hopes of preventing crime. However, given their availability, the lack of other government services, and political expediency, the patrol function was expanded beyond crime prevention to become an all-purpose governmental service. Even today, patrol remains the least specialized and the most diverse function of police work.

In the **political model**, the patrol officer was essentially a "neighbor," although how good a neighbor remains a subject of controversy. One image is the "friendly neighborhood cop," who knew and was known by the people on his beat or in his area. Supposedly, officers became friendly with family members and gained a great deal of knowledge regarding who was and was not trustworthy. Officers also were more concerned with quality-of-life problems, such as vandalism and disruptive juvenile behavior, and with providing a sense of neighborhood security rather than being preoccupied with crime-fighting and law enforcement activities. A less favorable, less romanticized version of the neighborhood cop was that he was inefficient, indifferent to basic responsibilities, and often dishonest. This is the neighbor who was a lazy, dishonest, and discriminatory bully. More recently, however, the possible positive aspects of the neighborhood patrol officer have been stressed as a basis for suggesting a reorientation for patrol officers' behavior and a return to foot patrol in neighborhoods (discussed in a later section).

The **legalistic model**, which gradually replaced the political approach, produced a patrol officer who functioned as a soldier, in sharp contrast to the often undisciplined "neighborhood cop." This model was an attempt to professionalize the police by providing a more disciplined approach to police problems and citizens, especially with respect to crime control. The legalistic approach further attempted to lessen the political nature of the police by making them more impersonal and more responsive to organizational authority. This process was enhanced by two critical developments in the 1930s (Walker 1984): (1) the greatly increased use of the patrol car and (2) the development of the Uniform Crime Reports. By adopting the UCRs (i.e., Part I Crimes reported to the FBI) as their primary measurement of performance, the police tended to stress the crime-fighting dimension of their role and became less interested in what they defined as noncrime-related activities.

These two developments, along with the influence of O. W. Wilson's bureaucratic or paramilitary approach to police management, led to the new professionalized police department. This increased level of professionalization was concerned with portraying a proper police image and running things by the book—literally, Wilson's influential *Police Administration* (1950). The image of the patrol officer was one of a nonpolitical, noncorruptible fighter of crime—in other words, an image that could not be confused with the political model of the past. It was felt that the increased use of the car would increase police efficiency through **crime repression**, which had traditionally been regarded as the most important patrol function. In other words, because more area could be covered and response time would be shortened, crime could be better controlled or suppressed. According to Wilson and R. C. McLaren, patrol procedures should be designed to create the impression of a police "omnipresence," which would eliminate "the actual opportunity (or the belief that the opportunity exists) for successful misconduct" (1977, p. 320). The increased use of patrol cars, however, further isolated the officer from the community. A series of anonymous "beat assignments" replaced officers' intimate knowledge of neighborhoods. Interestingly, some of the more "professionalized" departments took extra measures to depersonalize policing. For example, one strategy adopted to combat corruption was the frequent rotation of beat assignments (Walker 1984).

As the legalistic model became increasingly influential in the twentieth century, the informal watching of citizens and neighborhoods by police began to change. The nature of watching from a patrol car is different from watching while walking. As L. W. Sherman notes, "What the . . . officer sees is familiar buildings with unfamiliar people [while] what the public sees is a familiar . . . car with an unfamiliar officer" (1983, p. 149). Consequently, it is likely that because they do not have intimate contact with the community, officers will not develop the neighborhood contextual knowledge that helps them determine who is doing what to whom and when they are doing it.

The development of the radio and the telephone also had a strong impact on the relationship between the police and the community. Being able to call police and dispatch them to help citizens changed patrol from essentially watching to prevent crime to waiting to respond to crime, that is, from a **proactive** (police-initiated) to a **reactive** (citizen-initiated) **approach**. As a result, citizens tended to request police assistance more often (the relatively recent development of an emergency telephone number—911—has significantly contributed to this tendency), and this reinforced the all-purpose service orientation of the patrol function. Because police have often become deluged with 911 calls—many of which are not emergencies and do not necessarily require the response of an officer—some cities are developing and promoting the use of a 311 nonemergency number. In Baltimore, for example, the use of the 311 number is credited with a 25 percent drop in unnecessary calls to the 911 number, and the number of calls requiring a police response declined by 6 percent—the first decrease since 1990 ("Flush With Success" 1997a).

Poor people, in particular, began to use the police as lawyers, doctors, psychologists, and social workers. As Walker notes, "While the patrol car did isolate the police in some respects, the telephone brought about a more inti-

❖ ❖ ❖ ❖   mate form of contact between police and citizen by allowing the police officer to enter private residences and involving him in private disputes and problems" (1984, p. 88). What this meant was that the "soldiers" of the professional model were forced to work in a manner similar to a neighborhood patrol officer, but they knew less about the neighborhoods and people, were often ill-equipped to perform noncrime-related functions, and did not tend to like the order-maintenance and public-service aspects of police work (Sherman 1983; Walker 1984).

From the above discussion, it is not difficult to conclude that patrol work has come full circle and is attempting once again to regain knowledge and awareness of the neighborhood context, although in a much more sophisticated fashion than in the past. As discussed in chapter 3, a transition toward a **community policing model** is developing, which requires an intimate knowledge of, and cooperation with, neighborhood citizens. In this model, patrol officers must become intimately aware of the neighborhood context by working with citizens and community groups in the coproduction of public safety to identify and solve crime and disorder problems. Some practitioners in the field (Stephens 1996) believe that working with the community to solve problems is so vital to the effective role of policing that an officer's (or detective's) time should eventually be evenly split—at a minimum—between traditional police activities (i.e., responding to calls, administrative activities, and criminal investigation) and working with the community to solve problems. Along with this change in role emphasis, it is further suggested (Stephens 1996) that attitudes must change concerning the amount of time police spend on calls, including taking the time to ask a different set of questions on each crime report: Have we been here before? What is causing this situation to occur or reoccur? How can it be prevented? What should the police do? The callers? The victims? The community? The government? In this way, the police change their emphasis from incident oriented to problem oriented and from responding to problems to solving problems that cause crime.

Patrol Methods

The two most dominant methods of patrol are by automobile and by foot. As noted, the automobile had a revolutionary impact on policing. Because it offers the greatest coverage and most rapid response to calls, it is also usually considered to be the most cost-effective method of patrol. Along with this increased coverage, however, came a trade-off in terms of isolation from the community. All of a sudden, police officers lost contact with citizens in nonconflict and nonadversarial situations. The police, in the name of efficiency, essentially became "outsiders" in the communities they served. The urban riots of the early 1960s emphasized the problems that had developed in police-community relations. For instance, the President's Commission on Law Enforcement and Administration of Justice suggested that "The most significant weakness in American motor patrol operations today is the general lack of contact with citizens except when an officer has responded to a call" (1967, p. 53).

When automobiles first began to be used for patrol purposes, two or more officers were often assigned to a car. Since the 1940s, however, many departments have begun to use single-person cars. There has been consider-

❖ ❖ ❖ ❖

In recognition of the loss of contact with the community, there has been an increase in the use of foot patrol, especially in downtown districts. (Photo: Mark C. Ide)

able controversy surrounding this issue. Do one- or two-officer cars do more work? Which method is safer for the officer? Which is safer for the citizen? The most comprehensive study on this debate was undertaken in San Diego in the mid-1970s (Boydstun, Sherry, and Moelter 1977). The findings indicated that one-person units produced more arrests, filed more formal crime reports, received fewer citizen complaints, and were clearly less expensive. A second study replicating the San Diego analysis (Kessler 1985) found the same results and further indicated that two one-officer cars responded to the scene of an incident faster than one two-officer car. One-officer units also had a safety advantage. Even considering the danger of the area and shift assignment, one-officer units had fewer resisting-arrest problems and about an equal involvement in assaults on officers.

In recognition of the loss of contact with the community, there has been a resurgence of foot patrol in the 1970s and 1980s, especially in downtown areas. The development of the portable walkie-talkie radio vastly improved the capabilities of foot patrol officers, because they can now be in constant communication with headquarters regarding conditions on their beat. Of course, foot patrol officers are severely limited in terms of mobility and response to calls. Consequently, they are sometimes paired with other forms of patrol, such as car, horse, or motor scooter. Some departments use a combination of foot and car or foot and motor scooter together; that is, they allocate approximately one-half of their time to walking their beat and the other half to motor patrol. Departments that utilize such a patrol method feel that they are getting the best out of both forms of patrol—that is, a greater degree of citizen contact than provided by motor patrol and greater mobility than provided by foot patrol.

Two comprehensive evaluations of foot patrol, or "walking a beat," revealed that although foot patrol may effect a slight reduction in crime, it also

Patrol on bicycles offers good mobility and inter-action with the public, and is increasingly being used in departments implementing community policing. (Photo: corbisimages.com)

reduces citizens' fear of crime and changes the nature of police-citizen interactions—toward more positive and nonadversarial exchanges. The major studies were the Newark Foot Patrol Experiment, which included data on foot patrol in Newark and 28 additional cities in New Jersey (Police Foundation 1981), and the Neighborhood Foot Patrol Program, which was conducted in 14 neighborhoods of Flint, Michigan (Trojanowicz 1982). Later reports of the Flint study (Trojanowicz and Banas 1985a) discovered a decrease in the disparity between black and white perceptions of crime and policing and an increased positive acceptance of the program and confidence in police services by black members of the community.

In general, it appears that for foot patrol to be successful, it must be implemented in areas in which officers can interact with citizens—shopping centers, neighborhoods, or areas with businesses or outside citizen activity—and be able to see those citizens frequently. The size of a foot-patrol beat should be small enough that it can be covered at least once or twice per shift. Research has indicated that such coverage is necessary in order to obtain the benefits of improved police-community interaction and a reduction in the fear of crime (J. R. Greene 1987; Payne and Trojanowicz 1985; Trojanowicz and Banas 1985a; and Sherman 1983).

Departments may use numerous other patrol methods, depending on their particular needs and budgetary constraints. The more typical of these include the use of motorcycle, motor scooter, three-wheeled vehicles, bicycles, airplanes (both fixed-wing and helicopter), horses, and boats. Snowmobiles and dog sleds are also used in isolated, snowbound areas, where other forms of patrol are impracticable. In deciding what form of patrol should be used, police managers need to consider speed, access, density of population, visibility, cost, and community support.

In general, motorcycle patrol is used for traffic control in highly congested areas. One of the major problems with this form of patrol, however, is that it is extremely dangerous to the officer; just about any type of accident tends to cause harm to the rider. O. W. Wilson and R. C. McClaren stated that the hazard of motorcycle operation "is sufficient to condemn its use, and fairness to the officer and his family forbids it" (1977, p. 33). Motor scooters and three-wheeled vehicles are primarily used for traffic enforcement and in parks; they may also be used as part of "park and walk" programs, thus extending officers' mobility. Bicycles are often used in parks and beach areas and in conjunction with stakeouts; they offer good mobility and interaction with the public. Because of these assets, bicycle patrols have increased in departments implementing community policing. During the 1960s horse patrol was used mainly for crowd control but today is being increasingly used in both downtown and park areas. Planes and helicopters are used primarily for traffic control, surveillance, and rescues; their mobility and observation is great, but so is their cost. Cities surrounded by large bodies of water use boat patrol for the enforcement of boating rules, emergency assistance, and other law enforcement activities, including surveillance and narcotics control.

Table 7.1 indicates the differences in patrol allocation methods in selected, large police departments. This table shows departments' diverse attempts to meet needs (e.g., parks, lakes, downtown areas, freeways) with different patrol staffing levels and types of patrol; for example, Detroit and Los Angeles staff over 60 percent of their patrol units with two officers, while Atlanta and Baltimore have no two-officer units. In addition, Atlanta, Chicago, and Houston commit over 25 percent of their officers to patrol per 24 hours, while the remaining cities commit less than 20 percent. In addition, there are vast differences with respect to how departments use different types of patrol; for instance, while 50 percent of the departments assign 80 to 90 percent of their patrol resources to automobiles, Los Angeles, New York, and Seattle (with only 42 percent) assign 60 percent or less. Leaders in other types of patrol include: motorcycle patrol (Seattle, 14 percent and Los Angeles, 6 percent), foot patrol (New York, 39 percent; Chicago, 15 percent; and Atlanta 14 percent); bicycle patrol (Seattle, 16 percent and Los Angeles, 15 percent); horse patrol (Seattle, 4 percent); and marine patrol (Detroit, 4 percent and Seattle, 3 percent).

Table 7.1	Patrol Allocation in Selected, Large Police Departments, 1997							
	Departments Using Patrol Type and Percent of All Patrol Units Accounted For						Percent of Officers on Patrol Per	Percent of Units With
Department	Auto	Motorcycle	Foot	Bicycle	Horse	Marine	24 Hours	Two Officers
Atlanta	R 77%	R 1%	R 14%	R 3%	R 1%	— 0%	31%	0%
Baltimore	R 96	R 1	R 2	S 0	R 1	R 0	16	0
Chicago	R 82	R 1	R 15	R 1	R 0	R 0	26	52
Detroit	R 84	R 1	R 7	R 3	R 1	R 4	16	68
Houston	R 95	R 1	R 1	R 1	R 1	R 0	27	11
Los Angeles	R 64	R 6	R 5	R 15	S 0	S 0	19	63
New York City	R 54	R 1	R 39	R 5	R 1	R 0	19	57
Seattle	R 42	R 14	R 8	R 16	R 4	R 3	16	31

Note: The codes for patrol use are as follows:
R = Patrol type is used on a routine basis
S = Patrol type is used for special events only
— = Patrol type is not used
Source: Adapted from B. A. Reaves and A. L. Goldberg. 1999. *Law Enforcement Management and Administrative Statistics, 1997*. Washington, D.C.: Department of Justice, pp. 71–80.

Use of Patrol Resources

This section discusses how police resources are used, including resource determination (how many officers a department should have), resource allocation (how officers should be distributed), and computerized crime mapping (how to concentrate patrol activities).

Resource determination. Essentially two methods are used to determine the "appropriate" number of police personnel for a city: intuition and comparison. The *intuitive* approach is little more than an educated guess by police managers of how many human resources a department needs to police a city "effectively." Today, the figure arrived at is usually based on tradition (i.e., personnel numbers from past years) and increased by a certain percentage deemed appropriate to keep up with the increasing crime rate or level of services provided. As noted earlier, with the implementation of the Uniform Crime Reports, most police departments tied their levels of effectiveness to the index crimes. This development created a vicious cycle: When crime is going "down" (according to the UCRs), departments take the credit for reducing crime, and when it is on the increase, they ask for additional personnel with which to "fight crime" more effectively.

Probably the most frequently used method for resource determination is the *comparative* approach, which involves comparing one or more cities, using a ratio of police officers per 10,000 population unit; if the comparison city(ies) has a higher ratio of police-to-population, it is assumed that an increase in personnel is justified, at least to the level of the comparison city. For example, if a city of 50,000 (5–10,000 population units) has a police department with 100 police employees, the ratio is 20 officers per 10,000 persons. If the ratio for the comparative city was 22, the disparity would be 10 officers (i.e., 22–20=2 x 5=10). Table 7.2 indicates the significant differences in police-resident ratios between selected major cities. Although comparison is frequently used, it is not a valid indicator of needed strength, since individual cities are extremely diverse in their needs for police services, expectations, and crime rates. In addition, police departments vary widely in managerial effectiveness, use of technology, competency of officers, and policing styles. For example, because Washington, D.C., has nearly three times the police protection of Seattle, and over four times as much as San Jose, one might assume that it would be the safest of the three cities, which is not the case.

Table 7.2 Police–Population Ratios of Selected Major Cities, 1997	
City	**Sworn Officers per 10,000 citizens**
District of Columbia	67
Chicago	49
Atlanta	40
Baltimore	46
Detroit	41
New York	52
Houston	31
Los Angeles	27
Seattle	23
San Jose, Calif.	16

Source: Adapted from B. A. Reaves and P. Z. Smith. 1999. *Law Enforcement Management and Administrative Statistics, 1997.* Washington, D.C.: Department of Justice, pp. 1–10.

It should be noted that the comparison method is perhaps most useful to a department and the community's political structure as a yearly gauge for its own needs and progress. In other words, compared with last year's (or several years ago) level of police services provided to the city, how does the department measure up? If, for example, it can be shown that a department significantly increased its services to the community, a strong case could be made to the mayor or city manager and the city council that the ratio, and thus the resources for the department, should be increased.

In the final analysis, given the number of possible tasks to be performed and the time and effort that can be spent on them, police work is virtually a bottomless pit of human resource needs. Consequently, police departments, using any resource determination method they choose, rarely have difficulty justifying additional resources.

Another area of debate over police resources is whether or not adding more police has an impact on the crime rate. The Violent Crime Control and Law Enforcement Act of 1994, for example, authorized $9 billion for the hiring of an additional 100,000 police officers for community policing and, ostensibly, to reduce crime. A review of 36 studies found little evidence that more police reduce crime (Marvell and Moody 1996). The same authors, however, provided their own 20-year analysis of 56 cities of over 250,000 population and of 49 states. Using complex statistical techniques, they found consistent results that as the number of police in a jurisdiction increased, the level of crime was reduced the following year. Since this study is the most sophisticated to date—even though its findings are contradictory to an overwhelming majority of the research—it provides the clearest indication that modest increases in police numbers do appear to affect the crime rate. Interestingly, the authors' analysis also indicates that the prevention effect of more officers is greater in higher-crime cities than across the country in general. Why might this be? Possibly in larger cities, where the population density is greater, additional patrol officers may have a greater preventive capability due to their increased visibility.

Additional experimental research on this topic is necessary, however, before too much emphasis is placed on the quick fix of adding more police to reduce crime, even though it may be the most politically expedient thing to do. The above discussion clearly shows that police-to-population ratios, have little, if any, direct impact on crime rates. In general, managerial effectiveness, competency of officers, policing methods, and technology all appear to be factors in how the police affect crime. Accordingly, how the police are used and what they do are probably more important than adding a limited number of new officers to a department.

Resource allocation. Traditionally, police resources have been allocated equally over a 24-hour time period of three 8-hour shifts—for example, day shift: 8 A.M. to 4 P.M.; evening or "swing" shift: 4 P.M. to midnight; and "graveyard" shift: midnight to 8 A.M. During these shifts, officers patrolled geographic areas of approximately equal size. Of course, such an allocation method does not take into account the fact that police calls vary by time of day, day of week, area of the community, and even time of year. For instance, the swing shift tends to have the heaviest workload with respect to calls for police service (see Figure 7.1). The graveyard shift usually has a heavy workload for the first several hours (normally until 2:00 A.M. or 3:00 A.M.) and then is reduced to almost zero activity. The day shift falls in between the other two; although it is usually busy, the calls are often minor and nondangerous.

Figure 7.1 Typical Distribution of the Call for Service Workload

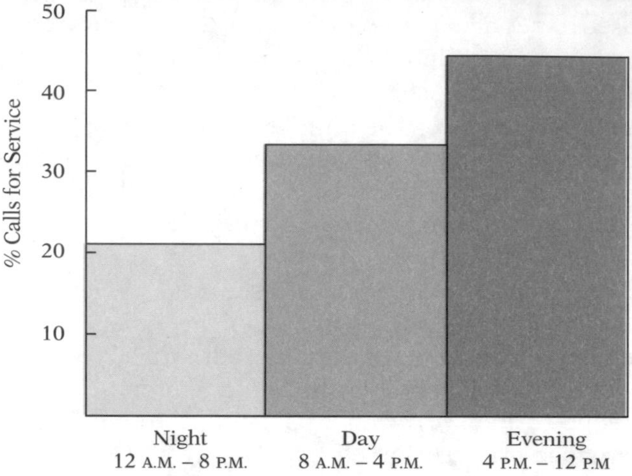

% Calls for Service

| Night 12 A.M. – 8 P.M. | Day 8 A.M. – 4 P.M. | Evening 4 P.M. – 12 P.M |

Source: W. G. Gay, T. H. Schell, and S. Schack. 1977. *Improving Patrol Productivity. Vol. 1: Routine Patrol*. Washington, D.C.: U.S. Government Printing Office, p. 25.

Because the workload distribution is not equal across time periods, days, or patrol areas, it is apparent that the equal allocation of police resources would mean that some officers were being overused (some would say overworked) while others were being underused. Such an arrangement presents operational problems, not only in attempting to respond to calls for service but also in not being able to perform directed or preventive patrol duties. Underused officers are quite likely to become bored and unmotivated to perform well.

Officer attitudes appear also to be affected by unequal workloads. One study (Brooks, Piquero, and Cronin 1994) of workload influence in two departments calculated workload rates by using official data that reflected the average number of Part I and Part II Crimes and total calls-for-service incidents that each officer engaged in over a one-year period. The study found that officers assigned to work in slower areas tended to view their role, their department, and their community in a more positive light than did their colleagues who worked in busier areas. Of course, such attitudes most likely also have an impact on performance levels. In recognition of these problems, professional departments have established allocation plans based on need rather than resource equalization.

In these plans, the two most important variables for determining allocation are *location* and *time*. Knowing the location of problems assists departments in dividing up a community into **beats** (sectors or districts), or geographic areas, of approximately equal workload. Time of occurrence is critical because it determines how officers will be grouped into working time periods, or **shifts**. As a general rule, the greater the number of problems or calls for service, the *smaller* the size of the beat and thus the more concentrated the resources. The time it takes to service a call is also important, since the re-source being allocated is a skilled officer's time, which needs to be managed as effectively as possible. Once data on these variables have been collected and analyzed, beat boundaries, number of officers, and shift times are deter-mined. Because of population shifts and changes in demand for service, it is important that departments continually reevaluate patrol beat boundaries and assignment of personnel.

To overcome the inherent problems in the equal allocation of resources, many medium- and large-size departments have adopted a 4-10 scheduling plan; smaller departments generally do not have adequate personnel to uti-lize this schedule. With such a plan, officers work four days a week, 10 hours per day, with three days off in a row. Officers tend to like the 4-10 plan because it allows for increased leisure time, while the department gains increased coverage due to overlapping shifts, normally assigned during peak workload periods. Another method that has been used to increase patrol coverage is the creation of an additional permanent shift or platoon. This fourth platoon is assigned as an overlapping shift during high workload periods, say from 7 P.M. to 3 A.M. or 8 P.M. to 4 A.M. Although such a method provides significant ad-vantages to a resource allocation plan based on need, it may be difficult to im-plement due to personnel needs (officers may want day shifts or weekends off) or union opposition. Proponents of such methods point out, however, that various accommodations can be made by devising a fair and equitable rotational system.

Computerized crime mapping. One of the more important recent break-throughs with respect to resource utilization has been the development of **computerized crime mapping** to assist officers in where to concentrate their patrol activities. Data obtained through a department's computer-aided dispatch and records-management systems (which store and maintain calls for service, records of incidents, and arrests) are matched with addresses and other geographic information such as beats and districts; maps can then be computer generated for a geographic area to be overlaid with specific infor-mation (Rich 1996).

In conjunction with the Chicago Police Department's development of its community policing strategy (see chapter 3) where beat officers focus on problem solving, a crime-mapping system known as **ICAM (information collection for automated mapping)** was developed to help beat officers fo-cus on problem solving. The system was developed from the beginning to be user-friendly in order that *all* officers throughout the department could have access to the system and to provide information to help them better under-stand the problems in their assigned areas and develop strategies to address them. Officers also share the ICAM maps with residents through their beat meetings, thus giving them a chance to help the police cut down on crime through joint problem-solving efforts (Rich 1996).

The ICAM main screen is depicted in Figure 7.2 and appears automati-cally when the computer is turned on. ICAM can perform two main tasks, in-dicated in the boxes containing the "Do It" buttons: (1) it can produce a map of reported offenses of a particular type in an area, or (2) it can generate a list of the 10 most frequently reported offenses in a beat.

The ICAM program also allows a user to select additional information through a few additional mouse clicks. As Figure 7.3 indicates, a user can specify one or more secondary classifications of the primary offense, change

❖ ❖ ❖ ❖   the geographic area, change the date and time range, or specify a particular type of location.

Figure 7.2 ICAM's Query Screens

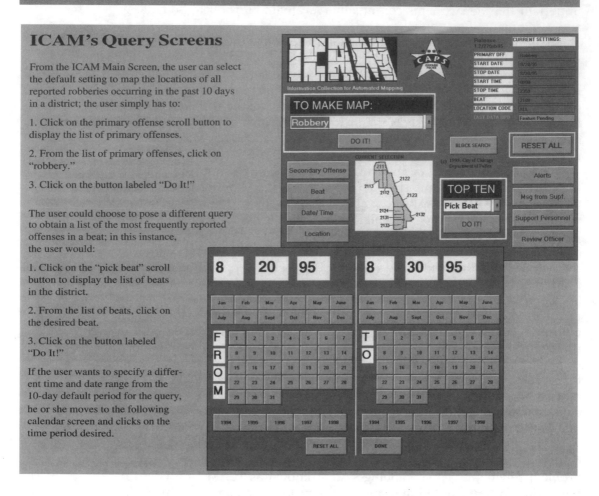

Source: T. F. Rich. 1996. *The Chicago Police Department's Information Collection for Automated Mapping (ICAM) Program.* Washington, D.C.: National Institute of Justice, p. 7.

Although no determinations can be made regarding the number of crimes ICAM has helped to resolve, some anecdotes of ICAM's effectiveness as a crime-solving tool for Chicago are available (see Inside Policing 7.1). ICAM also helps officers to make decisions regarding their work plans. For example, one beat officer in the 24th District said she uses ICAM as an aid in deciding where to concentrate her foot-patrol activities (Rich 1996). It would appear that the use of computers by patrol officers for problem solving and crime analysis (see also Inside Policing 3.2) is going to become more sophisticated and more widespread.

Figure 7.3   ICAM's Mapping Features Components

Components	Options
Primary Offense	Only one primary offense can be selected per map.
Secondary Offense	For the selected primary offense, up to 10 secondary classifications can be selected. For example, if robbery is the primary offense and the secondary offenses are "with a knife" and "with a gun," then only robberies with a knife or a gun are mapped.
Geographic Area	The choices are the entire district, one sector, or one beat. The default selection is the entire district.
Date Range	Both a start and end date are selected. The default selection is the last 10 days.
Time of Day Range	Both a start and end time are selected. For example, if the user is only interested in offenses occurring during the day shift, 800 to 1600 would be selected. The default selection is all day.
Type of Location	The type of location includes those categories listed on the CPD General Offense case report—examples include on a bus, in an apartment, at a business, and at a church. If "in an apartment" is selected, then only offenses occurring in apartments would be mapped. The default selection is all types of locations.

Source: T. F. Rich. 1996. *The Chicago Police Department's Information Collection for Automated Mapping (ICAM) Program.* Washington, D.C.: National Institute of Justice, p. 8.

Inside Policing 7.1
ICAM in Action

Anecdotes of how the Information Collection for Automated Mapping program has been used to help solve crimes include the following:

- In the 10th district three officers caught three teenagers in the act of burglarizing a home. The surrounding area recently had experienced a rash of burglaries, and the officers suspected that the teenagers were responsible for many of them. The teenagers confessed to committing several of the burglaries but could not remember the addresses of the homes. The officers used ICAM to generate a map and a list of all burglaries occurring in the past six months in the general vicinity where they were operating. The officers then drove the teenagers to specific homes to determine which ones they had burglarized. With just a few hours' work, 11 burglaries were cleared, and residents were able to recover their stolen property, which had been stored in the home of one teenager.

- In the 22nd District, officers learned of a rash of burglaries occurring at schools and used ICAM

☞ to map the exact locations of these burglaries and determine patterns about the times they were occurring. Officers then established surveillance at the appropriate times and locations and soon arrested a burglar as he was fleeing a school.

- In the 7th District, an ICAM map showed that the locations of recovered stolen vehicles were clustered around specific abandoned buildings. Armed with this information, police officials worked with the city's Department of Planning to expedite demolition of the buildings.

Source: T. F. Rich. 1996. *The Chicago Police Department's Information Collection for Automated Mapping (ICAM) Program.* Washington, D.C.: National Institute of Justice, p. 12.

Selected Research on Patrol Operations

Prior to the 1960s, there was only a limited amount of research about the patrol function. During the last four decades, however, a significant amount of research has been conducted on various aspects of patrol, much of it containing important policy implications. Except for team policing and community policing, covered in chapter 3, some of the better controlled, important studies are discussed in this section.

Random Patrol

Possibly the most influential early study on police operations, both for its breakthrough in initiating large-scale experimental research in police departments and the general impact of its findings, was the *Kansas City Preven-*

An officer using a laptop computer; the use of such computers by patrol officers is going to become more sophisticated and widespread in the near future. (Photo: Mark C. Ide)

tive Patrol Experiment (Kelling, Pate, Dieckman, and Brown 1974). Up until this time, police departments had little interest in scientific observation or intellectual inquiry; many, in fact, were anti-research (Caiden 1977). The purpose of the one-year experiment was to determine the effect of **random patrol** (i.e., officers patrolling "randomly" in their beats when not on assignment) on crime rates and citizens' feelings of security. For study purposes, one part of the city was divided into 15 areas, which were randomly divided into five beats, each containing three groups. Each group was matched with respect to crime data, population characteristics, and calls for service and assigned different levels of patrol as follows: *reactive beats* had no preventive patrol activities; *proactive beats* were assigned two to three times the normal number of patrol units; and *control beats* maintained the normal level of patrol (i.e., one car per beat). Figure 7.4 is a schematic representation of the 15-beat experimental area.

Figure 7.4   Kansas City Preventive Patrol Experiment: Fifteen-Beat Area

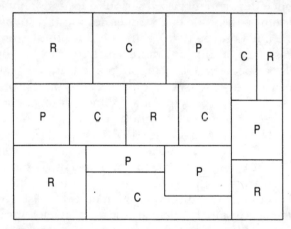

P = Proactive
C = Control
R = Reactive

G. L. Kelling, T. Pate, D. Dieckman, and C. E. Brown, 1974. *The Kansas City Preventive Patrol Experiment.* Washington, D.C.: Police Foundation, p. 9.

The results indicated that the three patrol conditions appeared not to affect crime rates suppressible by patrol (burglaries, auto thefts, larcenies involving auto accessories, robberies and vandalism), citizens' attitudes toward police, feelings of security, or rates of reported crime. Since most police departments had routinely based decisions on requests for personnel and resource allocation on having a certain percentage of an officer's time devoted to random patrol (normally 40 to 60 percent), this research raised important questions about the effectiveness of routine preventive patrol and the resource needs of police. The conclusions of the Kansas City study suggested that traditional preventive patrol was not effective and adding a minimum number of patrol officers would not diminish crime. The experiment indicated that the effectiveness of patrol could be improved if activities were more directed and less random. The research provided the impetus for police departments to question the effectiveness of traditional patrol procedures and to search for innovative and improved patrol methods.

The experiment, however, was not without critics. For example, R. C. Larson (1975) noted that because patrol cars entered reactive beats to respond to calls, they created a police presence; how did this differ from random patrol in the eyes of citizens or potential criminals? S. E. Feinberg, L. Kinley, and A. J. Reiss, Jr. (1976) suggested that the statistical methods used were not powerful enough to detect large percentage differences in crime as not due to chance. It should be noted that all social science studies of this magnitude can be criticized on the basis of their designs and statistical analyses, but they are still meaningful if they are well designed and the best available evidence at the time.

Response Time

Shortly after the preventive-patrol study, a follow-up investigation in the Kansas City Police Department raised serious questions about another common assumption of patrol: the effectiveness of rapid response times (Pate, Bowers, Ferrara, and Lorence 1976). Until this time, the assumption was that the faster the response to calls, the more satisfied citizens would be and the more likely that suspects would be apprehended. Based on these assumptions, police departments have spent considerable money in attempting to reduce response times by introducing new technology (e.g., the 911 telephone number, vehicle-location console monitors, and computer-aided dispatchers and sophisticated beat models (Caiden 1977). Overall, the results found that because the average citizen waits so long (approximately six minutes) to call the police—he or she often calls a friend or relative first—there is virtually no chance to make an arrest at the crime scene, regardless of how quickly police respond. Furthermore, it was discovered that citizen satisfaction with police departments depends less on quick response than on knowing approximately when the officer will arrive. Other studies have found similar results (Spelman and Brown 1982; Sherman 1983).

The impact of this study was that the police began to realize that they could respond differentially to calls; that is, because not all calls have the same level of importance, they can be assigned different priority levels. For example, noncritical calls can be responded to less quickly than critical call. As long as citizens are informed of approximate arrival times, their satisfaction levels with the police remain high, even though they may not actually see an officer for an extended period of time or, in some cases, not at all. Of course, for critical calls (e.g., crimes in progress, injuries), it remains important for the police to respond as quickly as possible.

Management of Demand

The findings about response time led to investigations attempting to determine how the police can best manage demand for services. Essentially, managing demand requires categorizing requests for service and matching those requests with differential police responses. Which calls for service require an immediate response and which can wait? Can some calls be handled by persons other than sworn officers? Which calls can be answered by telephone or mail or by asking the citizen to come to the police station? M. F. Cahn and J. Tien (1981), in their study of the Wilmington (Delaware) Police Department's **management-of-demand system**, which utilized alternative response strategies, found that residents continued to be satisfied with the department, crime did not increase, and patrol resources were freed up considerably to perform other activities. Another similar study of three departments in cities with populations over 100,000 (Cohen and McEwen 1984) found essentially the same results as the Wilmington study; citizens expressed an overall willingness to accept alternatives other than immediate dispatch of a patrol unit for nonemergency calls. The most acceptable alternative in all the cities was setting an appointment; the least acceptable was mailing in a report. In general, the evaluation of attempts to manage demand of calls for police service has been positive. Time can be saved for crime prevention, patrol, and other activities without loss of citizen satisfaction or an increase in crime. In the long term, there may be considerable savings because fewer personnel may be required (McEwen, Connors, and Cohen 1986).

Directed Patrol

Directing what officers do rather than allowing the random use of uncommitted patrol time became increasingly popular after the Kansas City experiment. The development of computerized crime analysis and, more recently, computerized mapping allows the police to identify more precisely patterns of crime and disorder. This increased precision allows patrols to be directed to primary crime areas at primary crime times. As such, directed patrol is more proactive, uses uncommitted time in specified activity, and is based on crime and problem analysis. Of particular importance is the proactive dimension of the directed activity, be it making arrests, issuing citations, conducting field interrogations, or educating the public about crime. Proactivity produces more information, heightens citizen awareness of police, perhaps creates an impression of greater police watching, and most certainly requires police to be more alert and active.

It is important to point out, however, that with increased proactivity, there can be serious side effects within the community, if not handled properly. As noted previously, such an increase in police "aggressiveness" can result in a lessening of public support, especially in minority communities where citizens believe they are the targets of police suspicion and intervention (Sherman 1986). One early study on police field interrogations, the San Diego Interrogation Experiment, discovered not only that field interrogations had some apparent crime prevention effects, but perhaps just as important, that if the field interrogations were conducted with civility and an explanation of the reason, there was no adverse impact on citizen attitudes, even in minority communities (Boydstun 1975). Thus, with respect to crime prevention, focusing on police "style" may be as important as focusing on police "substance" (Sherman 1997).

Targeting **hot spots** of crime developed out of research analyzing 911 calls in Minneapolis (Sherman, Gartin, and Buerger 1989) in which it was discovered that 5 percent of the addresses in the city accounted for 64 percent of all 911 calls. Thus only a few locations, which were labeled hot spots, were requiring a highly disproportionate amount of police time and resources. Following this research, the Minneapolis Hot Spots Patrol Experiment was designed to test the crime-prevention effects of extra patrol officers directed at hot spots for crime during **hot times** for crime over a one-year period (Sherman and Weisburd 1995). Increased police presence was directed to a randomly selected 55 of the worst 110 hot spot street corners in the city. The remaining 55 received normal patrol coverage, primarily in response to citizen calls for service. Results indicated that increased police presence had a "modest" deterrent effect, with fewer calls for service and lower rates of observed crime and disorder in the areas with extra patrol (4 percent versus 2 percent). In addition, a pre- and post-measurement study of community attitudes (Shaw 1995) indicated that the proactive police methods received strong support and that residents perceived an improvement in the quality of life in the experimental areas measured (attitudes of persons stopped by the police were not measured).

Further analysis of the hot spots patrol data (Koper 1995) found that the longer the police stayed, up to a certain point, the longer the hot spot was free of crime or disorder after the police left. The police presence was effective for about a 15-minute interval, at which point a negative effect developed. Thus, it would appear that the best way to use police visibility at hot spots may be to travel from hot spot to hot spot, remaining for about 15 minutes at each one.

The SMART (specialized multi-agency response team) program in Oakland, California, used a multi-agency task force targeting 321 drug hot spots. Coordinated visits were made to nuisance drug locations by the police and representatives from agencies such as housing, fire, public works, and Pacific Gas and Electric to inspect the location and, where necessary, to enforce local housing, fire, and safety codes. A training program for landlords was also initiated, which helped them to screen prospective tenants and evict those who violated the rules. In addition, the police increased their patrol presence around the sites, especially through field contacts and arrests. An evaluation (Green 1995) of SMART found that not only did it reduce the level of drug activity, but it also had a "diffusion" effect of improving (cleaning up) the areas surrounding the most targeted locations. It appears that the key component of this program was the combination of increased police activity and the cooperative working arrangement with agencies to enforce civil-code violations.

Proactive Arrests

Similar to directed patrol, proactive arrests, initiated by the police, focus on a narrow set of high-risk targets. The theory is that a high certainty of arrest for a narrowly defined set of offenses or offenders will have a greater deterrent effect than will low certainty of arrest for a broad range of targets (Sherman 1997).

Crackdowns

One of the most widespread developments in the use of proactive arrests in the mid-1980's was the use of police crackdowns. **Crackdowns** can be defined as intensive, short-term increases in officer presence and arrests for

❖ ❖ ❖ ❖

specific types of offenses or for all offenses in specific areas. Drunk driving, public drug markets, street-walking prostitutes, domestic violence, illegal parking, and even unsafe bicycle riding have all been targets for publicly announced crackdowns (Sherman 1990a). The theory behind this approach is that the use of such crackdowns make the risks of apprehension far more uncertain than in any fixed level of police-patrol activity. Most of the controversy centers on the effectiveness of the crackdown; that is, are they worth the increased cost and public inconvenience (Sherman 1990a).

One of the early investigations of crackdowns covered 18 case studies of various target problems and attempted to analyze what is known to date regarding crackdowns (Sherman 1990b). The evidence appears to support the notion of an initial deterrent effect on some offenses, as well as support for the notion of **residual deterrence**; that is, some crime reduction continues even after the crackdown is ended. Interestingly, the case studies revealed that short-term crackdowns suffered less from **deterrence decay** (i.e., a lessening of crime deterrent effect) than did longer-term crackdowns. This suggests that the use of crackdowns might be more effective if they are limited in duration and rotated across crime targets or target areas. With respect to deterrence decay, the cost-effectiveness of crackdown strategies should also be evaluated. For example, in an experimental study in raids on crack houses (Sherman and Rogan 1995), it was found that although crime on the block dropped sharply after a raid, the deterrent effect decayed after only seven days. Due to the labor-intensive nature of drug crackdowns, the strategy appears not be cost-effective in the long run.

Research has also indicated that an **announcement effect** may take place with certain types of crackdowns—that is, the publicity surrounding the crackdown appears to cause people initially to alter their behavior, which returns to normal as soon as the publicity surrounding the crackdown subsides. This seems to be especially true with crackdowns on drunk drivers, who appear to be particularly susceptible to short-term behavioral changes but whose behavior is not sustained over time. This appears to be because both the risk of arrest is extremely low in an enforcement crackdown and people believe that their chances of being arrested if they drive when drunk are low (Walker 1997).

Guns, Violence, and Gangs

Several proactive arrest strategies have been applied to the impact of increased police presence and activity on reducing guns, gun crimes, and gang violence.

The *Kansas City Gun Experiment* (Sherman, Shaw, and Rogan 1995) indicated that increased seizures of illegal guns in a high-crime precinct can reduce violent gun crimes. The experimental area contained extra gun-unit officers, working overtime shifts, who concentrated on detecting and seizing illegally possessed guns, while a control area had only regular levels of activity. Over a 29-week period, the gun unit had seized 29, while regular patrol officers in the experimental beat seized an additional 47 guns. The number of gun crimes in the experimental area declined by 49 percent but by only 4 percent in the control area. There appeared to be little evidence of a displacement effect to neighboring beats. The results are likely due to one or more of the following factors: (1) the removal from the area of guns that could not then be used in crime; (2) the incapacitation of violent criminals, who were arrested and imprisoned; or (3) a deterrent effect where people contemplating violent crimes became aware of the risks of apprehension. While these results appear promising, such a program is extremely expensive and may not be able to be maintained by a department.

In Boston, an effort known as the *Boston Gun Project* (Kennedy, Piehl, and Braga 1996) is an approach in which the police use a mix of strategies in an attempt to prevent gun violence, especially by gang members and probationers. The key components of the project include the following:

- A focus on gun-trafficking to and from gang-involved youth.

- A comprehensive and immediate interagency response when gang violence breaks out.

- Explicit warnings to gangs that violence will bring a swift and punitive response by police and prosecutors.

- Urging gangs to explore nonviolent means of resolving conflicts.

- Preventing and eliminating outbreaks of gang violence before they turn deadly. (Clark 1997)

What became known in Boston as the Ceasefire strategy was an attempt to *deter* the particular problem of gang-related violence (i.e., the strategy could focus on some other criminal justice problem) and was not an anti-gang strategy per se. In other words, if gangs refrained from violent activity but committed other crimes, the normal approach of police, prosecutors, and the rest of the criminal justice system came into play. If the gangs hurt people, however, Ceasefire members got involved (Kennedy 1998). This strategy included joint patrols of police and probation officers (who teamed up to make sure convicted young adult offenders were not roaming the streets and were abiding by the law), federal and local prosecutors, school police, and youth corrections. Joint ventures were carried out with various federal agencies, including the Bureau of Alcohol, Tobacco and Firearms (ATF)—which can help track firearms linked to violent crimes and determine patterns that could lead to suppliers of illegal guns—the Drug Enforcement Administration (DEA), and the Immigration and Naturalization Service (INS).

Direct meetings between gang members and authorities also took place, with warnings of severe sanctions if violence continued, while at the same time educational and employment opportunities were made available. Community centers, the clergy, and gang-outreach workers also played a role in spreading the antiviolence message to young offenders and attempted to help them to enter mainstream society. The early results were startling, with gang and gun-related homicides in the 24-and-under age category cut by 70 percent from 1990 to 1995; during one 28-month period there were no homicides in this age group (Clark 1997).

The apparent success of the program likely rests on the deterrent effect of identifying and focusing on a particular problem and sustaining a cooperative effort among federal and local criminal justice and public social-service agencies. Because of the initial positive results, other police departments have become interested in adopting or replicating the Ceasefire deterrence strategy. Inside Policing 7.2 takes a look at two such departments.

Inside Policing 7.2
Shared Interest in Replicating Boston

Minneapolis launched its version of the gun project last spring, with results that were beyond most people's expectations—the city's homicide rate fell by 80 percent during the summer months. Taking a page from Boston's experience, Indianapolis police most likely will focus their efforts on the gang-involved, repeat violent offenders aspect of the program. The first replication of the Boston effort, the Minneapolis Homicide Reduction Project, was launched in May, 1997, with the goal of reducing homicides across-the-board, and not just those stemming from gang killings, which represent a significant portion of the city's murder rate. Analyzing the city's murder rate from 1994 to May, 1997, it was found that:

- Nearly 45 percent of all city homicides appear to be gang related.

- Forty percent of the murder victims were in the 14-to-24 age bracket, as were over 60 percent of the suspects and arrestees.

- Firearms were used in two-thirds of the killings, which were clustered in a few neighborhoods.

- Nearly a quarter of the victims and one-third of suspects and arrestees had probation histories, while more than 40 percent of the victims and nearly 75 percent of the suspects had arrest records.

Armed with this data, officials went to work, setting up joint police-probation officer patrols; increasing collaboration between federal, state and local law enforcement agencies; beefing up foot patrols in high-crime beats; and aggressively enforcing quality-of-life crimes as well as the city's curfew. Authorities also spread the word to members of the city's 30 known criminal gangs that it would no longer be business as usual. Police rounded up key players of the Bogus Boyz, a renegade group held in contempt by other gangs because of its refusal to play by the "rules," and charged them with murder, firearms violations, robbery, and assault.

It has also not gone unnoticed that in addition to making the city safer and reducing fear among residents, it has also increased police morale. Officers have not been this excited about their jobs in 20 or 25 years; they feel they're actually saving lives by intervening when an incident is about to happen. Due to its apparent success, the program will remain in place indefinitely. Officials are so heartened by the decline in violence that elements of the project will most likely be adapted to drug enforcement operations as well.

Source: J. R. Clark. 1997. "LEN Salutes Its 1997 People of the Year, the Boston Gun Project Working Group." *Law Enforcement News*, December 31: 1, 4, 5. Reprinted with permission from *Law Enforcement News*, John Jay College of Criminal Justice, New York City.

Zero-Tolerance Arrests

Another strategy of proactive arrests has become known as **zero-tolerance arrests**, based on the broken-windows theory (Wilson and Kelling 1982) of crime causation (i.e., one broken pane, if not fixed, is likely to lead to more broken panes). In practice, this theory suggests that if police concentrate their activities on minor quality-of-life crimes (e.g., panhandling, public urination, rowdy behavior), the improvement in the quality of life in an area will indirectly lead to a lower rate of serious crime (Kelling and Coles 1996).

Chapter 4 described New York City's aggressive, zero-tolerance policies, which accompany its Compstat program, where, in designated areas, many stops are made for minor violations of traffic laws, ordinances, and misdemeanors. Although crime has decreased in New York, questions remain with respect to how much of this reduction can be attributed to zero-tolerance arrests and whether the cost was worth it (citizen complaints of police abuse increased 50 percent). Upon closer scrutiny, the evidence suggests that crime had been decreasing, sometimes as dramatically but without the use of zero-tolerance arrests and tactics, in other major cities over the same time period. Many criminologists believe that at least two important social factors are primarily responsible for this downturn in crime rates. First is demographics, in which the population is simply aging out of the volatile, crime-prone years between 15 and 24. Second is the lessening and "maturing" of the crack market; crack use has decreased significantly, the violence over turf battles have been fought, territories have been established, and peaceful ways to resolve conflict have been found (Witkin 1998). Clearly, the decrease in crime rates is much more complex than simply the implementation of zero-tolerance arrests, although such policies undoubtedly have some impact. The important question is one of cost-effectiveness, especially with respect to community satisfaction.

L. W. Sherman (1997) suggests that the larger concern about zero-tolerance policing is its long-term effect on people arrested for minor offenses. Even while massive increases in arrests, like those in New York, may reduce violence in the short run—especially gun violence—they may also increase crime in the long run (as arrestees may become more defiant and aggressive). Furthermore, the effects of an arrest experience over minor offenses may permanently lower **police legitimacy**, or the public confidence in the police as fair and equitable—both for the arrested person and for his or her social network of family and friends. Consequently, Sherman points out that zero-tolerance programs should be evaluated in relation to long-term effects on those arrested, in addition to short-term effects on community crime rates. In addition, program development to foster greater police legitimacy in the course of making the arrests is suggested, for example, providing arrested minor offenders an opportunity to meet with a police supervisor who would explain the program to them, answer questions about why they are being arrested, and give them a chance to express their views.

Reactive Arrests

Reactive arrests are made in response to citizen complaints, are random, and are generally for minor offenses. Although little value is given to the general preventive nature of reactive arrests, one set of studies looked at the specific effects of arrest for misdemeanor **domestic violence** (i.e., assault on or battery of a domestic partner).

The *Minneapolis Domestic Violence Experiment* (Sherman and Berk 1984) was the first study on the use of arrest in misdemeanor domestic violence, comparing arrest responses to nonarrest responses (either mediation or separation). The results indicated that suspects who were arrested were significantly less likely to become violent over the next six months. Subsequent replication studies, however, produced mixed, and often confusing, results. For example, in Omaha, Charlotte, and Milwaukee, arrests appeared actually to increase domestic violence; also in Omaha, arrest warrants issued for offenders who fled the scene had a substantial deterrent effect. The results were mixed in two other cities, Colorado Springs and Miami, although some evidence of a deterrent effect of arrest was found. All four of the experiments that analyzed data by employment status of offenders found that arrests increase assaults among unemployed offenders while reducing it among employed offenders. Other research (Marciniak 1994) has indicated that the type of community in which one lives may have an impact as well.

In response to the Minneapolis results and political pressure—especially from women's groups—police departments across the country implemented mandatory-arrest polices in cases of misdemeanor domestic violence. The replication experiments indicate clearly, however, that such a response was premature (ironically, in the past the police have not paid enough attention to important research findings; in this case, they may have paid too much). Taken as a whole, these experiments have produced several findings that should be considered in formulating arrest policy in cases of domestic violence: (1) arrest generally increases violence among unemployed suspects while decreasing it among employed suspects; (2) arrest increases violence, regardless of individual employment status, in communities with high levels of unemployment and single-parent households; and (3) offenders who flee before police arrive (approximately 50 percent) are substantially deterred when warrants are issued for their arrest.

Covert Patrol

Working undercover or covertly has always been a police activity. Patrol officers (and detectives) wearing civilian clothes designed to blend into the environment can walk, ride bicycles or motorbikes, or drive around in unmarked cars. They can focus on specific types of crime or in certain areas, act as a possible decoy in hopes of being victimized, or look for or follow individuals suspected of criminal activity. Each of these activities can be accomplished in either a random or a directed manner.

Such **covert-patrol** tactics have had mixed results. They tend to be widely utilized by police departments; although some programs have had positive results in increasing arrests, which is their primary purpose, there has been minimal impact on crime rates. This approach is costly and there is the possibility of an increased number of injuries and deaths among police officers and citizens (Caiden 1977; Sherman 1983; and Webb 1977). It is clear that covert activities should be used sparingly and then only when there is a very strong likelihood that they will significantly benefit the community.

Police Pursuits

Police can chase suspects either on foot or by motor vehicle. There is little information on foot pursuits; consequently, only pursuits involving automobiles will be addressed. A **police pursuit** is an event in which a suspect attempts to flee from police in order to avoid arrest. G. P. Alpert and L. Friedell (1992) suggest that a pursuit is at least as dangerous to the public as the use of a firearm. Estimates on the number of police pursuits yearly run as high as 50,000 with the number of injuries they cause at approximately 20,000 (Charles, Falcone, and Wells 1992). A national survey of some 436 police departments (Alpert 1997), which also included case studies of approximately

1,250 pursuits in three departments (Metro-Dade, Miami; Omaha, Nebraska; and Aiken County, South Carolina), found that most pursuits are initiated for traffic violations; in Miami, 45 percent (448), in Omaha, 51 percent (112), and in Aiken County, 36 percent (5). A large percentage of pursuits, however, were also initiated for felonies; for example, in Miami, 35 percent (344), in Omaha, 40 percent (89), and in Aiken County, 43 percent (6).

In addition, the national survey indicated that 41 percent of the chases in Miami ended in personal injury (428) whereas 20 percent ended in property damage (213); in Omaha,14 percent ended in personal injury (31) and 40 percent in property damage (91); in Aiken County, 12 percent ended in personal injury (2) and 24 percent in property damage (4). Arrests were made in 75 percent of the chases in Miami (784), 52 percent in Omaha (118), and 82 percent in Aiken County (14). Finally, in separate studies, it was found that pursuits led to deaths of at least one person in 0.7 percent of all chases (a little less than one in a hundred chases) in the Miami area (Alpert and Dunham 1988) and 0.2 percent in Minnesota (Alpert and Friedell 1992).

These are significant numbers and suggest that the police must pay careful attention to the development of proper policy, training, and enforcement of guidelines. In this regard, the national survey revealed that while 91 percent of the responding departments had written policies governing pursuits (meaning nearly 10 percent did not), many of them were implemented in the 1970s. Forty-eight percent of the departments reported having modified their pursuit policy within the past two years, with most of those (87 percent) making the modifications more restrictive than previously. The strong effects of policy changes were evident in the findings from both the Metro-Dade and Omaha departments. In1992 Metro-Dade adopted a "violent felony only" pursuit policy, and the number of pursuits decreased by 82 percent (from 279 to 51) the following year. In 1993 Omaha changed to a more permissive policy, allowing pursuits for offenses that were previously prohibited, and pursuits increased over 600 percent the following year (from 17 to 122).

Although most departments reported that routine follow-ups to pursuits were mandated (89 percent), most also indicated that they were either informal supervisory reviews (33 percent) or incident reports prepared by pursuing officers (47 percent). With respect to training, while 60 percent of the departments reported providing entry-level driver training at their academies, virtually all the training focused on the mechanics of defensive and pursuit driving rather than on questions of when or why to pursue. The findings of the national survey included the following implications for state and local departments:

1. Create and maintain systems to collect information on pursuit driving.

2. Review and update pursuit policies.

3. Evaluate the need for pursuit-specific training.

4. Support written policies with training and supervision. Require that officers justify their actions or have a supervisor evaluate the pursuit (i.e., after-action reports and meaningful discipline for problem pursuits).

The national study concluded that a balance needs to exist between the need to enforce the law and the safety of the public, and that an appropriate policy balancing these perspectives would limit chases to the pursuit of violent felons. G. P. Alpert, the author of the study, believes that officers need more training and direction through policy in order to know when they can and cannot pursue. He suggests that pursuit policies should be similar to shooting policies, in which it has become reasonably clear when one can and cannot fire a weapon ("NIJ Study Sees . . . Police Pursuit Policies Changing" 1997b, p. 14).

A study of statewide police agencies in nine Western states by the Pursuit Management Task Force (PMTF) (1998) based on 419 questionnaires filled out by law enforcement line officers, indicated that the officers strongly supported reasonable pursuits and effective supervision of such pursuits. The officers also expressed a preference for using spiked strips (tire deflating devices) and electrical vehicle-stopping technologies. PMTF found that more than 50 percent of all pursuit collisions in their survey occurred during the first two minutes of a pursuit, and that more than 70 percent of all collisions occurred before the sixth minute of a pursuit. This suggests the importance of training (whether to pursue and how to pursue) and that any pursuit technology (e.g., electrical or mechanical) must be able to be deployed very rapidly to have any significant impact in preventing pursuit-related collisions. Several recommendations from the task force included:

1. A national model for collection of pursuit statistics should be developed for the purpose of encouraging and facilitating research and to expand the body of knowledge relating to pursuits.

2. States should consider legislation that ensures that fleeing from a lawful attempt at detention/arrest in a motor vehicle is a serious crime with significant penalties.

3. The federal government should use the influence and expertise of its offices to further public education about pursuits.

4. Research should be conducted to determine methods to improve interagency tactical communications technology.

Patrol Development Guidelines

Based on the research to date, it appears that the patrol function in a police department can be most effective if developed according to the following 10 guidelines:

1. Directed patrol is preferable to random patrol; therefore, police departments need to have a capability to systematically analyze community problems and criminal activity. Increased proactivity must be handled properly, however, with respect for procedural safeguards, civility, and explanations, if necessary. Otherwise, there may be a lessening of police legitimacy, which in itself may hinder crime prevention.

2. Police departments need to have the capability to respond differently to noncritical calls for service; such responses, however, should not ignore citizen satisfaction in favor of other police objectives. Citizens should be informed of approximately when an officer will arrive or what alternative will be used.

3. Police should target crime hot spots with increased police presence and activity, traveling from hot spot to hot spot, and remaining for approximately 15 minutes at each. With respect to drug hot spot sites, police should increase their presence and activity and work with public agencies to enforce civil-code violations.

4. Proactive arrest strategies focusing on reducing guns and gang violence appear effective. Particularly promising is the use of mixed strategies targeting gun carrying among juveniles and the cooperative working arrangements among criminal justice and public agencies. Crackdowns on drug abuse and drunk drivers have short-term deterrence effects and thus are not cost-effective; however, drunk-driver crackdowns may be useful during high-consumption periods (e.g., holidays). Zero-tolerance arrests also may not be cost-effective, especially in terms of public support; this strategy should only be used when officers are highly trained in respect to civility and can communicate effectively.

5. Reactive arrests focusing on reducing misdemeanor domestic violence are situational; however, departments should always issue arrest warrants when suspects flee before the police arrive.

6. There should be a mix of overt and covert patrol activity, with an emphasis on the overt. Police stakeouts and decoys should be used only as a last resort because they are too dangerous to justify the questionable results obtained in increased arrests and reductions in crime.

7. Police pursuits are dangerous—to the officer, the suspect, and innocent bystanders. Policy should balance the needs of enforcing the law with public safety, suggesting that an appropriate policy would limit chases to pursuit of violent felons.

8. Although adding police officers to a department may have an impact on crime—especially in larger, higher-crime cities—how officers are used and what they do have more impact on crime than adding a limited number of new officers to a department.

9. Foot patrol, in the form of small, walking beats, should be established in neighborhoods with a dense population or an active citizenry (i.e., businesses, outside social interaction, and recreational activities).

10. As a general rule, one-officer cars should be utilized; the exception would be in high-crime or isolated areas when officer safety may become an issue.

The differences between a police department that follows these guidelines and one that does not will most likely be reflected in a substantial impact in citizens' fear of crime and citizen satisfaction toward the police, a slight-to-moderate increase in number of arrests, and a minor-to-moderate drop in the overall crime rate; however, major declines in certain targeted crime categories may be possible. It should again be emphasized that police should not engage in patrol activities and strategies that may be destructive to community expectations or concerns; citizen satisfaction should be the highest priority. The coproduction of public safety with the community, will, in the long run, probably have the most significant impact on crime.

Selected Patrol Issues

Throughout the past decade, several issues that have a vital impact on community health and safety have received increased attention. Below is a brief discussion of some of these issues: special populations (including the mentally ill, public inebriates, the homeless, and culturally diverse communities), hate crimes, and AIDS.

Special Populations

In recent years, requests for the police to assist in handling people who are mentally ill, drunk in public, or homeless have increased substantially. To help police lessen the burden of handling these special populations, some jurisdictions have attempted to share the responsibility by creating formal networks between law enforcement and social-service agencies. A National Institute of Justice study of such network arrangements in 12 jurisdictions (Finn and Sullivan 1988) indicated that benefits accrue not only to the agencies involved but also to individuals who need help. Table 7.3 identifies the target groups and agencies involved in the twelve networks in the study.

Table 7.3	Selected Features of Twelve Law Enforcement-Social Service Agency Networks					
	Birmingham	**Boston**	**Erie**	**Fairfax County**	**Galveston County**	**Los Angeles**
Target groups	Mentally ill — —	— Inebriates Homeless	Mentally ill — —	Mentally ill — —	Mentally ill — —	Mentally ill — —
Lead agencies	Police department	Shelter and police department	Private mental health emergency service	Community mental health center	Sheriff's department	Police department and county department of mental health
Law enforcement agencies	City police	City police	City police	County police	Sheriff's department and others	City police

Table 7.3	Selected Features of Twelve Law Enforcement-Social Service Agency Networks (continued)				
	Madison	**Montgomery County**	**New York/ Jersey City**	**Portland**	**San Diego**	**Washtenaw County**
Target groups	Mentally ill Inebriates —	Mentally ill — —	— — Homeless	— — —	— Inebriates —	Mentally ill Inebriates —
Lead agencies	Police department	Private, nonprofit psychiatric hospital	Quasi- private transporta- tion authority	Detoxifica- tion center	County Alcohol Program	Sheriff's department and county mental health center
Law enforcement agencies	City police	52 police agencies	Transporta- tion author- ity police	City police and others	City police and others	County sheriff

P. E Finn and M. Sullivan, "Police Response to Special Populations." 1988. *Research in Action*. Washington, D.C.: National Institute of Justice, p. 2 .

Networks that focus on the mentally ill all have special units, on duty or on call 24 hours a day, that screen individuals for the most advisable disposition, identify the most appropriate facility to refer them to, and provide on-scene emergency assistance when necessary. These units consist either of specially trained police officers or social workers hired by the department to perform these functions; in addition, some networks utilize a social-service agency to provide the special unit. In some jurisdictions, the special unit assists with all encounters between law enforcement personnel and the mentally ill; in other communities, patrol officers are trained to handle routine cases and are instructed to call on the unit only in emergencies.

With respect to public inebriates and the homeless, most networks have made arrangements directly between the police department and one or more detoxification facilities or homeless shelters. The parties involved have typically agreed to strict referral and admission procedures (Finn and Sullivan 1988).

Another emerging special population that requires modification in the approach taken by the police is culturally diverse communities. A national assessment survey including police chiefs and sheriffs from all 50 states and 411 counties (McEwen 1995) found that strategies for working with culturally diverse communities were widespread, with 89 percent of police chiefs and 73 percent of sheriffs adopting one or more of them. The most common strategies included (1) recruiting police from culturally diverse backgrounds, (2) recruiting bilingual officers, (3) training officers to communicate with people whose backgrounds were different from their own, and (4) offering foreign-language training. The need for bilingual officers was so high (about 80 percent for chiefs and 75 percent for sheriffs—see Table 7.4) that some departments helped meet their needs by offering higher pay (called "bilingual pay") as a recruitment incentive and to encourage officers to learn a second language (McEwen 1995).

Table 7.4   Need for Bilingual Officers in Police and Sheriff's Departments

	Major Increase Needed	Some Increase Needed	No Increase Needed
Police Chiefs	24.5%	55.6%	13.0%
Sheriffs	23.8%	50.8%	15.0%

Note: The percentages add up to less than 100 because some respondents indicated "not applicable." These respondents represented communities with small minority populations and therefore did not feel bilingual officers were needed.
Source: T. McEwen. 1995. "National Assessment Program: 1994 Survey Results." *Research in Action*. Washington, D.C.: National Institute of Justice, p. 9.

Bias Crimes

Although there is little accurate information regarding **bias crimes** (i.e., crimes that are racially or sexually motivated), it is a continuing problem for the police. Blacks, Hispanics, Jews, homosexuals, and other minority groups that are targets of criminal activity because of their race, ethnicity, or sexual orientation are included in this category. Police departments need a mechanism to identify these crimes, record them, and develop a specific response. The training of officers about the possibility of such "hate" crimes is an important first step. When such crimes occur, the department must make a concerted response that involves traditional patrol and investigative methods and also includes communication with the group that has been the target of the crime.

One study on bias crimes (Garofalo and Martin 1995) found that clearances were higher in departments where special police responses to bias crime emphasized investigations and arrest. It was further suggested that departments must provide some type of motivation for inducing patrol officers to recognize and report bias crime when they encounter it. Concerning the manner in which bias crimes are handled, a study by S. Walker and C. M. Katz (1995) found that of 16 police departments in the central United States that were surveyed, 4 (25 percent) had separate bias crime units with written procedures for handling bias crimes. Six of the departments (37.5 percent) did not have a separate bias-crime unit, but either designated specific officers in an investigative unit to handle bias crimes or had special policies and procedures that all officers would follow. Six of the departments (37.5 percent) had neither a special unit nor special procedures. Of the 12 departments that did not have a special bias-crime unit, eight provided no special training regarding hate crimes. Projecting the findings from this sample to the national level, it was estimated that special bias-crime units exist in only about 13 percent of municipal police departments. Clearly, more effort needs to be exerted in this area of law enforcement.

AIDS

As the number of people who have acquired immunodeficiency syndrome (AIDS) has increased, so too have the concerns of police officers, especially patrol officers, who have the most exposure to AIDS. AIDS involves high-risk behavior and is transmitted through unprotected sexual contact, sharing of needles, or any activity that includes the exchange of vaginal secretions, semen, or blood. Although it may be possible for AIDS to be transmitted through other means (e.g., bites, urine, feces), research indicates that it is highly unlikely and no such cases have thus far been reported. Police departments should provide training in this area, develop necessary procedures, and provide proper equipment that will lessen officer concerns. For example, officers should protect any wound on their own bodies, cover open wounds on victims, use rubber gloves when necessary, and use masks/airways when giving cardiopulmonary resuscitation (Hammer 1987).

The Investigative Function

Investigators, or **detectives** (the terms can be used interchangeably), are essentially specialists in responding to crimes serious enough to warrant an investigation. The primary goal of the criminal investigation is to increase the number of arrests for crimes that are prosecutable and that will result in a conviction. As by-products of this goal, detectives recover stolen property and produce information that may be useful in other crimes, often through the development and manipulation of informants (Cawley, Miron, and Araujo 1977; Forst 1982; Waegel 1982; and Wycoff 1982). As discussed previously, crime investigation is usually divided, especially in medium to large police departments. Patrol officers conduct the initial, or **preliminary investigation**, which is generally for the purpose of establishing that a crime has been committed and for protecting the scene of the crime from those not involved in the investigation. Once this has been done, detectives generally conduct **follow-up investigations** and develop the case. In some jurisdictions, the development phase involves working with the prosecuting attorney to prepare a case for trial. In others, this phase is the responsibility of investigators employed by the prosecuting attorney's office.

The basic responsibility of the detective is to establish a case, identify and locate a suspect, possibly obtain a confession, and then dispose of the case (Sanders 1977). The disposal phase may or may not involve a prosecution or a conviction. Investigations can be terminated if the police determine that no crime has been committed, if they have insufficient evidence to proceed, or if there is no longer a suspect available (e.g., a murder-suicide).

Historical Development

Investigative work did not become primarily a public function until the early 1900s. Until that time, private detectives were hired to recover stolen property, often in unscrupulous ways, rather than to apprehend criminals. The transition to a public policing activity took place because of a desire to prosecute suspected criminals and a general disapproval of the methods employed by private detectives. In addition, the emergence of insurance companies tended gradually to lessen the victim's concern about the return of stolen property.

Police detectives in the early 1900s were like "secretive rogues," and often their methods were as unscrupulous as those of the private detectives preceding them. Although some of their exploits were romanticized, the detectives were mostly inefficient and corrupt. They often had a close association with criminals, used and manipulated stool pigeons, and even had "deadlines" that established areas of a city in which detectives and criminals agreed that crime could be committed. Nineteenth- and early-twentieth-century detectives believed that their work should be essentially clandestine. They were considered to be members of a "secret service," whose identity should remain unknown lest the criminal become wary and flee. Some detectives wore disguises, submitted court testimony in writing, and even used masks when looking at suspects. Although they did investigate crimes, detectives functioned primarily as a nonuniformed patrol force. They tended to go where persons congregated (e.g., beer gardens and steamboat docks) to look for pickpockets, gamblers, and troublemakers.

Just as police reformers of the early twentieth century hoped to replace the "neighbor" patrol officer with the "soldier" crime fighter, they also hoped to replace secretive rogues with a scientific criminal investigator. The detective's relationships with criminals and stool pigeons were criticized as corrupting and undesirable for a professional police officer. It was further believed that the use of science would make such relationships unnecessary. The reformers stressed the importance of the detective as a perceptive, rational analyst, much like Sherlock Holmes; they also emphasized reorganization of departments to improve efficiency.

Like their colleagues on patrol, detectives gradually began to be more reactive than proactive. By the 1920s and 1930s, detectives were mostly investigating crimes after the fact rather than using clandestine tactics. Although many were ill prepared to utilize the newly developed scientific methods, this was less of a problem than it first appeared because the use of scientific evidence proved to be of value in only a few cases and rarely aided the police in identifying suspects. Consequently, the information that became most important in making arrests and ensuring successful prosecutions was derived from witnesses, informers, and suspects. As detectives stopped being secre-

Detectives begin an investigation of a crime scene. Today, the detective's primary role is that of a case processor.

tive rogues, they gradually became inquisitors, who often coerced information from suspects to make cases.

By the 1960s, important changes in criminal procedural laws (e.g., search and seizure, evidence, Miranda)—known as the **due process revolution**—and the continuing emphasis on reorganization and efficiency in police departments had created a detective who had become essentially a bureaucrat, or case processor. Although some detectives continued to work undercover, the majority were reactive and infrequently identified suspects who were not obvious. These detectives spent a greater proportion of their time processing information and coordinating with other criminal justice agencies than looking for suspects.

All the elements of the detective's role described above are present to some degree today. Some detectives are secretive, some are skillful in obtaining confessions without coercion, and all must invest considerable time in processing information. While the emergence of the legalistic model of policing tended to produce a detective who was more bureaucrat than sleuth, subsequent approaches and models of policing (e.g., team and community) tend to have a broader view of the detective's role. As a result of crime-analysis techniques, the detective has continued to evolve, becoming somewhat less reactive (since the 1960s) and more proactive, with an emphasis on criminals rather than on crimes. Of course, this is not a new role for the detective, and thus far police departments have been able to make these changes without the extensive corruption problems historically associated with them (Kuykendall 1986).

Detectives today have multifaceted roles: they work undercover, they may operate sting programs, they may be involved in career-criminal programs, they may be involved in breaking up organized gang activity, and they may be involved in intelligence-gathering operations. Detectives involved in such activities, however, constitute a relatively small percentage of those involved in investigative work, with the substantial majority functioning more as bureaucrats than sleuths. To characterize the detective as a bureaucrat is not intended to demean the role but rather to suggest the perspective from which most detectives should be viewed. They are primarily information processors, not Sherlock Holmeses or Dirty "Make My Day" Harry's.

Resource Determination and Allocation

The ideal number of personnel to be assigned to investigative units has never been precisely determined. Traditionally, many departments have used a "10 percent of total sworn personnel" criterion; the range in medium-to-large-sized police departments is from 8 percent to approximately 20 percent of sworn personnel. The criteria most often used to determine a department's needs for investigative personnel include whether detectives work in pairs or alone; the extent of patrol participation in investigations; level of training, experience, and competency of investigators; and the technological assistance available.

One-person assignments, as in patrol, generally appear to be the most appropriate for the vast majority of investigative work. Exceptions include particularly dangerous assignments, some interrogations, and meeting suspicious informers. Even in these areas, however, as in investigations in general, there is less direct evidence concerning the relative effectiveness of one- and two-person assignments in criminal investigation (Bloch and Weidman 1975).

The investigative workload generally requires some degree of specialization in medium- to large-sized departments. The most common specialization is to have separate detective units for crimes against persons (e.g., homicide, robbery and assault, sex crimes, vice, and narcotics) and crimes against property (e.g., arson, auto theft and burglary and larceny) (Greenwood and Petersilia 1975). Many departments today also have specialized detective units for juveniles, gangs, intelligence, arson, computer, and bias crimes.

Selected Research on Investigative Operations

Several important investigative issues are discussed in this section, including investigative effectiveness and how investigative work can be improved, career criminal programs, detective-patrol relationships, and the twin issues of enticement and entrapment as applied to covert operations.

Investigative Effectiveness

In the mid-1970s, as a result of an in-depth study by P. Greenwood and J. Petersilia (1975), investigative units were criticized as ineffective and inefficient. In this study, operations in 25 detective units were observed and surveys were completed in 156 units. The major findings of this study indicated that (1) most serious crimes are solved through information obtained from victims rather than through leads developed by detectives; (2) in 75 percent of the cases, the suspect's identity is known or easily determined at the time the crime is reported to the police; and (3) the major block of detective time is devoted to reviewing reports, documenting files, and attempting to locate and interview victims on cases that experience has shown are unlikely to be solved but are carried out to satisfy victims' expectations. M. William and J. Snortum (1984), who replicated the study, reported similar findings but concluded that detectives make a valuable contribution to the investigative process through skilled interrogation and case-processing techniques.

In an extensive study of burglary and robbery investigations, J. Eck (1984) found that preliminary investigations by patrol officers and follow-up investigations by detectives are equally important for solving crimes. He further discovered that even in situations where the preliminary investigation by patrol officers did not develop any leads, detectives were able to identify a suspect in approximately 14 percent of the cases and make an arrest in 8 percent. Thus, Eck concluded that investigators do, in fact, make a meaningful contribution to the solution of criminal cases. To improve the effectiveness of investigations, it was recommended that increased emphasis be placed on collecting physical evidence at the scene of a crime, identifying witnesses, using informants, and utilizing police records. It was further noted that successfully disposing of a case can be improved if (1) patrol officers carefully gather evidence at the crime scene and communicate that information to the detectives on the case; (2) cases are more carefully screened for further development (i.e., deciding which cases can be ignored or given only minimal attention); (3) productivity measures are developed to ascertain if individual detectives or detective units are meeting their goals; and (4) investigations are targeted (e.g., toward career criminals, who are known to have engaged in the behavior under investigation).

Finally, D. J. Farmer (1984) maintains that a broader approach to the study of the investigative function is needed. He notes that "the notion of case clearance as the sole objective of detective work is as inadequate as is the idea that the principal function of a detective is to solve crime" (p. 49). In addition, there is proactive investigative work to be considered: "Investigators may pursue other equally important goals to aid citizens—including increasing citizen satisfaction, reducing fear, counseling victims, and deterring further crime" (p. 50). In line with this reasoning, Eck suggests that criminal investigation can be improved by detectives focusing on justice and crime prevention: "If detective work were more than tracking down and arresting offenders, detectives would have to interact with communities . . . work more with other sections of the police force and other public and private groups to achieve their objectives" (1996, p. 181). Eck suggests four guiding principles to improve investigative effectiveness:

1. Abandon crime control through apprehension as a principal goal of investigations. There is little evidence that increased apprehensions by detectives make much of a difference in crime levels, except under special circumstances (see below).

2. Detectives should focus on justice. Offenders should be arrested because they violated the law. Detectives should find out who the offenders are and bring their evidence forward.

3. The special circumstances mentioned in item 1 are clear crime patterns. Obviously, arresting a repeat rapist or killer prevents crimes. As noted in point 4, focusing on patterns allows detectives to combine enforcement powers with many other techniques.

4. Crime prevention through problem solving should be emphasized. Detectives should look for patterns of crimes, determine why the patterns exist, and implement programs that stop the patterns. Criminal apprehension is one technique that may be useful, but there are other techniques (see Case Study 7.2) that can be used in conjunction or as substitutes. (pp. 177–178)

Career Criminal Programs

Some police departments have begun implementing programs that attempt to arrest, prosecute, and convict repeat offenders (career criminals) at a significantly higher rate than normal police practices would allow. The theory behind such programs is that since a small proportion of criminals commit a disproportionate number of crimes, if these offenders are convicted and subsequently incarcerated, there will be a significant reduction in the crime rate.

One of the most highly developed programs of this type is the repeat offender project **(ROP)** of the Washington, D.C. Police Department. The proactive ROP unit, consisting of approximately 60 officers, would target a small number of career criminals believed to be committing five or more In-

Case Study 7.2

Improving Criminal Investigation Through Problem Solving

Although problem solving has generally been related to patrol officers, there have been many cases in which detectives have applied this approach. Because detectives are not tied to a radio and have more control over how their time is used, they may find it easier to address problems than would patrol officers. Problem solving requires the examination of crime patterns, of which there are three basic types: (1) *common offenders*, the most usual approach to applying crime analysis to investigations; (2) *common victims or targets*, how are they similar and how do they differ from nonvictims and nontargets; and (3) *repeat places*, which asks the question, why are crimes occurring here instead of at other, similar places. Two examples of how detectives have used problem solving are described below.

Domestic Homicides

In Newport News, Virginia, one of the homicide detectives felt that as satisfying as it was to solve murders, it would be more satisfying to prevent them from occurring. He noticed that half of the homicides the department had investigated in the previous year were related to domestic violence, and in half of these cases, the police had previously been to the address. This suggested the possibility of attempting early intervention with the couples involved.

The detective brought together representatives from many public and private organizations, including the prosecutor's office, women's advocates, hospitals, the local newspaper, the military, and others. In cooperation they developed a program that forced the couples involved in domestic violence into mandatory counseling. When certain conditions were present in an assault case (e.g., serious injury or presence of a gun), an arrest was mandatory. In such circumstances, it was decided that the prosecutor would not drop charges unless the abuser and the victim entered into counseling. If they completed counseling and if the victim agreed, the charges would then be dropped. Although no formal evaluation of this program has been conducted, the department reports that both domestic homicides and repeat domestic violence declined in the first years following implementation.

Gas Station Robberies

In Edmonton (Alberta, Canada), a robbery detective noted that one particular chain of gas stations had a very high robbery rate. Because of a high cigarette tax in Canada, there is a large black market for cigarettes, and cigarette theft can be lucrative. By reviewing crime reports, the detective noted that many of the robberies only involved the theft of cigarettes. He visited those stations and found that there was a single attendant in a small booth stocked with cigarettes, candy, and other small items. The detective worked with the managers of the gas station chain, and they identified a number of simple changes that could be made to the booth itself, to cigarette displays, and to various operating procedures. The gas station chain made the recommended changes. Since the changes were made, the police department reports a major decline in the robberies of this chain of gas stations.

Source: Adapted from J. E. Eck. 1996. "Rethinking Detective Management." In L. T. Hoover, ed., *Quantifying Quality in Policing*. Washington, D.C.: Police Executive Research Forum, pp. 178–180.

dex crimes a week. To arrest persons not wanted on a warrant, ROP officers had to develop evidence about specific crimes in which their targets had participated. This effort involved a number of activities, including "buy and bust" techniques, cultivating informants, investigating tips, and placing targets under surveillance.

Prior to program implementation, ROP's proposed procedures were evaluated by the local American Civil Liberties Union (ACLU). The ACLU was concerned that ROP would be used as a "dragnet" operation that harassed and entrapped people. These concerns were alleviated when it was explained that ROP would use no formulas or "profiles" for target selection. Furthermore, the department made it clear that places where citizens have a right to privacy would be put under surveillance only with court permission (Epstein 1983). Target selection for ROP was based on informal understandings about what makes a "good" target. Common characteristics included the target's "catchability," deservedness, and longer-term yield (Martin and Sherman 1986).

A two-year evaluation of the program concluded that by most measures used, the ROP unit achieved its goals of selecting, arresting, and contributing to the incarceration of repeat offenders. Although the ROP program appears to have been successful, the authors of the study are cautious in their interpretations of the findings (Martin and Sherman 1986). They suggest that before other departments implement such programs they should recognize the potential side effects and dangers of "perpetrator-oriented proactive policing." For instance, the program is extremely costly in terms of time, resources, and expenses to equip the unit; thus, it may not be cost-effective in the long term. Additionally, ROP decreased its officers' arrest productivity and most likely other aspects of police service as well, especially with respect to reduced order maintenance. The unorthodox tactics used by ROP-type programs further create potential dangers to civil liberties. Although due to careful program planning and supervision such problems appear to have been avoided by ROP, other departments would need to be just as cautious in their development of similar programs.

Detective-Patrol Relationships

The relationship in a police department between detectives and patrol officers is both extremely important and a source of potential conflict. This potential conflict must be addressed by the department because effective communication between the two is vital to the success of many investigations. It is crucial that investigators make an effort to develop and maintain a good rapport with patrol officers. This relationship should be based on frequent personal contacts, the acknowledgment of patrol officers' contribution to investigations, seeking out patrol officer advice when appropriate, and keeping officers informed as to the status of cases.

One of the major problems that continues to exist in many departments is related to the different status of detectives and patrol officers. Investigators tend to dress in civilian clothes, are often perceived to have more status in the department, and may even be of a higher rank or receive a higher salary. There are several ways to address this problem. One possible solution relates to the basic structure of the department—that is, using a community model of policing, in which detectives and patrol personnel work together as a team. Another solution is to create a personnel system that gives equal status and financial rewards to both patrol officers and investigators. Rotating personnel through various investigative slots, so that the position is not thought of as being "owned" by anyone, is also a constructive approach. Police departments must be alert to the manner in which detectives and patrol officers are treated. It is essential that patrol officers not be given the impression that, when compared to investigators, they are second-class citizens (Bloch and Weidman 1975).

Enticement and Entrapment

In the course of using covert or undercover investigations, the police must be extremely careful that they do not violate citizen rights and therefore harm police-community relations even though they increase arrest rates. Do certain investigative activities involve **enticement**? That is, by their existence do these activities encourage the commission of crimes? When does **entrapment** occur? That is, when are individuals provided by the police with both the opportunity and the intent to commit a crime? Whether the police play the role of victim or criminal, covert activities have the potential of both enticing and entrapping.

In **sting operations** undercover detectives set up their own fencing outlets and encourage thieves to sell them stolen merchandise; the transaction is generally videotaped for later use in court. Can such programs actually result in more victims? If criminals can easily sell stolen property for a competitive or higher price, will they steal more while the outlet is available? Does the cost-to-benefit ratio of such programs (e.g., more arrests, more useful information, or the development of informants) outweigh the potential hazards? What about a police officer playing an inebriated decoy on the street, waiting to be mugged? Can this practice encourage an individual, who otherwise might not be inclined to steal, to take advantage of such an easy mark? Do career-criminal programs unfairly target certain individuals or groups for arrest? Does the random selection of targets for the undercover selling of drugs provide the intent to buy drugs? These are some of the questions that police departments face with respect to undercover operations. Extensive legal guidelines provide the framework for acceptable policies and procedures, but, once again, the importance of community satisfaction should play an integral role in determining the extent and type of undercover activities a police department should use.

Although the results of enticement or entrapment cannot be precisely measured, these activities create political issues of potentially serious consequences. There may be an adverse community reaction to any police action or inaction that is believed to result in more victims. It seems plausible, if not probable, that sting operations may do precisely that. To prevent improprieties, sting undercover operators should (1) never pay more than the going rate for stolen property, (2) never encourage suspects to steal specific items, and (3) actively discourage repeat business. This final recommendation may be difficult to follow, but it is necessary to keep criminals from stealing primarily because they have somewhere to sell what they steal.

Summary

The primary goals, activities, and historical development of police field operations are patrol, the "backbone of policing," and investigative work. Recent research has indicated that patrol activities related to law enforcement are more substantial than research over the past few decades has indicated, whereas detective work is primarily concerned with information processing rather than sleuthing. Patrol work is attempting to regain the neighborhood contextual knowledge that was lost in an attempt to "professionalize" the police in the early 1960s and 1970s, working with citizens and community groups in the coproduction of public safety to identify and solve problems of crime and disorder. Since the 1960s, as a result of crime-analysis techniques, investigative work has become more proactive, with an emphasis on criminals rather than on crimes. Patrol methods are chiefly by foot or automobile. Resources are determined by intuition and comparison. A new method of allocation is by computerized crime mapping.

Selected research on patrol and investigative operations emphasizes effectiveness relating to cost and crime reduction. Selected patrol issues include special populations, bias-related crimes, and AIDS. Although research suggests that some patrol strategies are effective in reducing crime, they may also produce negative community relations. Thus, the more sensitive of these strategies should be carefully implemented but not without community acceptance. For example, differential response, directed patrol, different types of proactive arrests, covert patrol, and career criminal programs must have strong community support if they are to be of mutual benefit to both the police and the public.

Discussion Questions

1. Describe the primary goals of patrol, including community policing departments, and provide an example of each.

2. What is computerized crime mapping? Provide several examples of how it might be used.

3. Briefly describe the Kansas City preventive patrol study; explain why this study was important to policing.

4. Discuss the research findings with respect to the impact on police patrol of response time and management-of-demand systems.

5. Describe how directed patrol and the targeting of hot spots are used. What does the research suggest regarding the effectiveness of these patrol methods?

6. Describe the Kansas City gun experiment and the Boston gun project. Why were these patrol strategies successful?

7. What is the theory underlying zero-tolerance arrests? Is this an effective patrol strategy? What are the possible concerns about the use of such a strategy?

8. With respect to the research on the use of arrest in misdemeanor domestic violence cases, what patrol policies would you formulate?

9. Discuss the general level of effectiveness of investigators; describe several ways their general effectiveness can be improved.

10. Describe several types of covert investigations; how can enticement and entrapment be avoided in such operations?

References

Alpert, G. P. 1997. *Police Pursuit: Policies and Training, May.* Washington, D.C.: National Institute of Justice.

Alpert, G. P. and Dunham, R. 1988. "Research on Police Pursuits: Applications for Law Enforcement." *American Journal of Police* 7: 123–131.

Alpert, G. P. and Friedell, L. 1992. *Police Vehicles and Firearms: Instruments of Deadly Force.* Prospect Heights, IL: Waveland Press.

Baehr, M. E., Furcon, J. E., and Froemel, E. C. 1968. *Psychological Assessment of Patrolman Qualifications in Relation to Field Performance.* Washington, D.C.: Department of Justice.

Bloch, P. B. and Weidman, D. R. 1975. *Managing Criminal Investigations.* Washington, D.C.: U.S. Government Printing Office.

Boydstun, J. E. 1975. *San Diego Field Interrogation: Final Report.* Washington, D.C.: Police Foundation.

Boydstun, J. E., Sherry, M. E., and Moelter, N. P. 1977. *Patrol Staffing in San Diego.* Washington, D.C.: Police Foundation.

Brooks, L. W., Piquero, A., and Cronin, J. 1994. "Workload Rites and Police Officer Attitudes: An Examination of Busy and Slow Precincts." *Journal of Criminal Justice* 22: 277–286.

Cahn, M. F. and Tien, J. 1981. *An Alternative Approach in Police Response: Wilmington Management of Demand Program.* Cambridge, MA: Public Systems Evaluation, Inc.

Caiden, G. E. 1977. *Police Revitalization.* Lexington, MA: Lexington Books.

Cawley, D. F., Miron, H. J., and Araujo, W. J. 1977. *Managing Criminal Investigations: Trainer's Handbook.* Washington, D.C.: University Research Corporation.

Charles, M. T., Falcone, D, N., and Wells, E. 1992. *Police Pursuit in Pursuit of a Policy: The Pursuit Issue, Legal and Literature Review, and an Empirical Study.* Washington, D.C.: AAA Foundation for Traffic Safety.

Clark, J. R. 1997. "LEN Salutes Its 1997 People of the Year, the Boston Gun Project Working Group." *Law Enforcement News* December 31: 1, 4, and 5.

Cohen, , M. and McEwen, J. T. 1984. "Handling Calls for Service: Alternatives to Traditional Policing." *NIJ Reports* September: 4–8.

Cawley, D. F., Miron, H. J. and Araujo, W. J. 1977. *Managing Criminal Investigations: Trainer's Handbook.* Washington D.C.: University Research Corporation.

Eck, J. 1984. *Solving Crimes.* Washington, D.C.: Police Executive Research Forum.

——. 1996. "Rethinking Detective Management." In L T. Hoover, (ed.), *Quantifying Quality in Policing*, pp. 167–184. Washington, D.C.: Police Executive Research Forum.

Epstein, A. 1983. "Spurlock's Raiders." *Regardies* 3: 41–42.

Farmer, D. J. 1984. *Crime Control: The Use and Misuse of Police Resources.* New York: Plenum.

Federal Bureau of Investigation 1991. *Uniform Crime Reports, Crime in the United States.* Washington, D.C.: Department of Justice.

Feinberg, S. E., Kinley, L., and Reiss, Jr., A. J. 1976. "Redesigning the Kansas City Preventive Patrol Experiment." *Evaluation* 3: 124–131.

Finn, P. E. and Sullivan, M. 1988. "Police Response to Special Populations: Handling the Mentally Ill, Public Inebriate, and the Homeless." *Research in Action.* Washington, D.C.: National Institute of Justice.

"Flush with Success, 311 System Due for Expansion in Maryland." 1997. *Law Enforcement News* November 30: 1, 10.

Forst, B. 1982. *Arrest Convictability as a Measure of Police Performance.* Washington, D.C.: U.S. Government Printing Office.

Garmire, B. L., ed. 1977. *Local Government, Police Management.* Washington, D.C.: International City Management Association.

Gay, W. G., Schell, T. H. and Schack, S. 1977. *Improving Patrol Productivity, Volume I: Routine Patrol*. Washington, D.C.: U.S. Government Printing Office.

Garofalo, J. and Martin, S. E. 1995. *Bias-Motivated Crimes: Their Characteristics and the Law Enforcement Response*. Carbondale, IL: Southern Illinois University.

Green, L. 1995. "Cleaning Up Drug Hot Spots in Oakland, California: The Displacement and Diffusion Effects." *Justice Quarterly* 12: 737–754.

Greene, J. R. 1987. "Foot Patrol and Community Policing: Past Practices and Future Prospects." *American Journal of Police* 6: 1–15.

Greenwood, P. and Petersilia, J. 1975. *The Criminal Investigation Process*. Santa Monica, CA: Rand.

Hammer, T. M. 1987. "AIDS and the Law Enforcement Officer." *NIJ Reports*. Washington, D.C.: National Institute of Justice, pp. 2–7.

Kelling, G. L. and Coles, C. M. 1996. *Fixing Broken Windows*. New York: Kessler Books.

Kelling, G. L., Pate, T., Dieckman, D., and Brown, C. E. 1974. *The Kansas City Preventive Patrol Experiment: A Summary Report*. Washington, D.C.: Police Foundation.

Kennedy, D. 1998. "Pulling Levels: Getting Deterrence Right." *NIJ Journal* July, pp. 2–8. Washington, D.C.: National Institute of Justice.

Kennedy, D., Piehl, A. M., and Braga, A. A. 1996. "Youth Gun Violence in Boston: Gun Markets, Serious Youth Offenders, and a Use Reduction Strategy." *Law and Contemporary Problems* 59: 147–196.

Kessler, D. A. (1985). "One-or Two-Officer Cars? A Perspective From Kansas City." *Journal of Criminal Justice* 13: 49–64.

Koper, C. S. 1995. "Just Enough Police Presence: Reducing Crime and Disorderly Behavior by Optimizing Patrol Time in Crime 'Hot Spots': A Randomized, Controlled Trial." *Justice Quarterly* 12: 625–648.

Kuykendall, J. (1986). "The Municipal Police Detective: An Historical Analysis." *Criminology* 24: 175–201.

Larson, R. C. (1975). "What Happened to Patrol Operations in Kansas City? A Review of the Kansas City Preventive Patrol Experiment." *Journal of Criminal Justice* 3: 267–297.

Marciniak, E. 1994. *Community Policing of Domestic Violence: Neighborhood Differences in the Effect of Arrest*. Unpublished Ph.D. dissertation. College Park: University of Maryland.

Martin, S. E. and Sherman, L. W. 1986. *Catching Career Criminals: The Washington, D.C. Repeat Offender Project*. Washington, D.C.: Police Foundation.

Marvell, T. B., and Moody, C. E. 1996. "Specification Problems, Police Levels and Crime Rates." *Criminology* 34: 609–646.

McEwen, J. T. 1995. "National Assessment Program: 1994 Survey Results." *Research in Action*. Washington, D.C.: National Institute of Justice.

McEwen, J. T., Connors, E. F., and Cohen, M. I. 1986. *Evaluation of the Differential Response Field Test*. Washington, D.C.: U.S. Government Printing Office.

"NIJ Study Sees Police Pursuit Policies Changing as Appreciation of Danger Rises." 1997. *Law Enforcement News* July/August: 1, 14.

Pate, T., Bowers, R. A., Ferrara, A. and Lorence, J. (1976). *Police Response Time: Its Determinants and Effects*. Washington, D.C.: Police Foundation.

Payne, D. M. and Trojanowicz, R. C. (1985). *Performance Profiles of Foot Versus Motor Officers*. East Lansing, MI: National Neighborhood Foot Patrol Center, Michigan State University.

Police Foundation. 1981. *The Newark Foot Patrol Experiment*. Washington, D.C.: Police Foundation.

President's Commission on Law Enforcement and Administration of Justice. 1967. *Task Report: The Police*. Washington, D.C.: U.S. Government Printing Office.

Pursuit Management Task Force. 1998. *Pursuit Management Task Force: A Summary of the PMST's Report on Police Pursuit Practices and the Role of Technology.* Washington, D.C.: Department of Justice.

Reaves, B. A. and Goldberg, A. L. 1999. *Law Enforcement Management and Administrative Statistics, 1997: Data for Individual State and Local Agencies with 100 or More Officers.* Washington, D.C.: Department of Justice.

Rich, T. F. 1996. *The Chicago Police Department's Information Collection for Automated Mapping (ICAM) Program.* Washington, D.C.: National Institute of Justice.

Sanders, W. (1977). *Detective Work.* New York: Free Press.

Shaw, J. W. 1995. "Community Policing Against Guns: Public Opinion of the Kansas City Experiment." *Justice Quarterly* 12: 695–710.

Sherman, L. W. 1983. "Patrol Strategies for Police." In J. Q. Wilson (ed.), *Crime and Public Policy,* pp. 145–163. San Francisco: Institute for Contemporary Studies Press.

——. 1986. "Policing Communities: What Works." In A. J. Reiss and M. Tonry (eds.), *Crime and Justice,* 8, Chicago: University of Chicago Press, pp. 366–379.

——. 1990a. "Police Crackdowns." *NIJ Reports* March/April: 2–6. Washington, D.C.: National Institute of Justice.

——. 1990b. "Police Crackdowns: Initial and Residual Deterrence." In by M. Tonry and N. Morris (eds.), *Crime and Justice: A Review of Research,* pp. 1–48. Chicago: University of Chicago Press.

——. 1997. "Policing for Crime Prevention." In L. W. Sherman, D. Gottfredson, D. MacKenzie, J. Eck, P. Reuter, and S. Bushway (eds.), *Preventing Crime: What Works, What Doesn't, What's Promising,* pp. 8/1–8/58. Washington, D.C.: Office of Justice Programs.

Sherman, L. W. and Berk, R. A. 1984. "The Specific Deterrent Effects of Arrest for Domestic Assault." *American Sociological Review* 49: 261–272.

Sherman, L. W., Gartin, P. R., and Buerger, M. E. 1989. "Hot Spots of Predatory Crime: Routine Activities and the Criminology of Place." *Criminology* 27: 27–55.

Sherman, L. W. and Rogan, D. P. 1995. "Deterrent Effects of Police Raids on Crack Houses: A Randomized, Controlled, Experiment." *Justice Quarterly* 12: 755–781.

Sherman, L. W., Shaw, J. W., and Rogan D. P. 1995. *The Kansas City Gun Experiment.* Washington, D.C.: U.S. Government Printing Office.

Sherman, L. W. and Weisburd, D. A. 1995. "General Deterrence Effects of Police Patrol in Crime 'Hot Spots:' A Randomized. Controlled Trial." *Justice Quarterly* 12: 625–648.

Spelman, W. and Brown D. K. (1982). *Calling the Police.* Washington, D.C.: Police Executive Research Forum.

Stephens, D. W. 1996. "Community Problem-Oriented Policing: Measuring Impacts." In Hoover, L. T. (ed.), *Quantifying Quality in Policing,* pp. 95–129. Washington, D.C.: Police Executive Research Forum.

Trojanowicz, R. C. 1982. *An Evaluation of the Neighborhood Foot Patrol Program in Flint, Michigan.* East Lansing, MI: National Neighborhood Foot Patrol Center, Michigan State University.

Trojanowicz, R. C. and Banas, D. W. 1985a. *The Impact of Foot Patrol on Black and White Perceptions of Policing.* East Lansing, MI: National Neighborhood Foot Patrol Center, Michigan State University.

Trojanowicz, R. C. and Banas, D. W. 1985b. *Job Satisfaction: A Comparison of Foot Patrol Versus Motor Patrol Officers.* East Lansing, MI: National Neighborhood Foot Patrol Center, Michigan State University.

Waegel, W. B. (1982). "Patterns of Police Investigation of Urban Crimes." *Journal of Police Science and Administration* 10: 452–465.

——. 1984. " 'Broken Windows' and Fractured History: The Use and Misuse of History in Recent Police Patrol Analysis." *Justice Quarterly* 1: 57–90.

Walker, S. 1997. *Sense and Nonsense About Crime and Drugs: A Policy Guide.* 4th ed. Belmont, CA: West/Wadsworth.

Walker, S. and Katz, C. M. 1995. "Less Than Meets the Eye: Police Department Bia-Crime Units." American Journal of Police 16: 29–48.

Webb, K. W. 1977. *Specialized Patrol Projects*. Washington, D.C.: U.S. Government Printing Office.

William, M. and Snortum, J. 1984. "Detective Work: The Criminal Investigation Process in a Medium-Size Police Department." *Criminal Justice Review* 9: 33–39.

Wilson, J. Q. and Kelling G. L. 1982. "Broken Windows: The Police and Neighborhood Safety." *Atlantic Monthly* 249: 29–38.

Wilson, O. W. 1950. *Police Administration*. New York: McGraw-Hill.

Wilson, O. W. and McLaren, R. C. 1977. *Police Administration*. 3rd ed. New York: McGraw-Hill.

Witkin, G. 1998. "The Crime Bust." *U.S. News and World Report* May 25: 28–36.

Wycoff, M. A. (1982). "Evaluating the Crime Effectiveness of Municipal Police." In J. R. Greene, (ed.) *Managing Police Work*, pp. 15–36. Newbury Park, CA: Sage.

For a listing of websites appropriate to the content of this chapter, see "Suggested Websites for Further Study" (p. xv). ✦

Part III

Police Behavior

Chapter Eight

Police Behavior

Chapter Outline

❏ Perspectives of Police Behavior
    Universalistic Perspectives
        Sociological Perspective
        Psychological Perspective
        Organizational Perspective
    Particularistic Perspectives
    Socialization Versus Predisposition
        Socialization Theory
        Predispositional Theory

❏ Studies of Police Behavior
    'Our Lawless Police'
    'Violence and the Police'
    'Justice Without Trial'
    'Varieties of Police Behavior'
    'City Police'
    'Observations on the Making of Policemen'
        Pre-entry Choice
        Admittance: Introduction
        Change: Encounter
        Continuance: Metamorphosis
    'Police: Street-corner Politicians'
    'Working the Street: Police Discretion'

❏ Decision Making and Police Discretion
    Organizational Variables
        Bureaucratic Nature
        Work Periods and Areas
    Neighborhood Variables
    Situational Variables
        Mobilization
        Demeanor and Attitude
        Race
        Gender
        Victim-compliant Relationship
        Type of Offense
        Location
        Presence of Others
    Individual (Officer) Variables
        Education, Age, and Experience
        Race
        Gender
        Career Orientation and Family Situation

❏ Police Deviance
    Types of Deviance

Key terms	
abuse of authority	police culture
avoiders	police deviance
clean-beat crime fighters	police misconduct
code of silence	police violence
culture	predispositional theory
danger signifiers	professional-style officers
discretion	reciprocators
economic corruption	rotten-apple theory of corruption
enforcers	service style
grass eaters	service-style officers
gratuity	slippery-slope theory
in-group solidarity	socialization theory
legalistic style	subculture
meat eaters	subjugation of defendant's rights
noble-cause corruption	symbolic assailant
occupational deviance	systemic theory of corruption
old-style crime fighters	universalistic perspectives
particularist-perspectives	use corruption
peer group	watchman style
police corruption	

This chapter provides an introduction to police behavior. It will look at many different perspectives on the conduct of the police, both in terms of the way police make decisions and in the factors that motivate their decisions. It is concerned with a general discussion of both appropriate and inappropriate (deviant) police behavior. Two particular forms of deviance are considered in this chapter: the acceptance of gratuities and police corruption. Chapter 9 will address other forms of police deviance that are related to the exercise of police authority and the use of coercion. Issues and strategies for controlling police behavior will be discussed in Chapter 10.

Perspectives of Police Behavior

Police behavior may be described from universalistic or particularistic perspectives. **Universalistic perspectives** look at the ways officers are similar. They are widely used by police researchers because they provide ways to distinguish police work from other occupations. **Particularistic perspectives** emphasize how police officers differ one from another.

Universalistic Perspectives

A wide variety of research has sought to explain police behavior in universalistic terms. This research takes three perspectives: sociological, psychological, and organizational (Worden 1989).

Sociological perspective. The sociological perspective emphasizes the social context in which police officers are hired and trained and in which police-citizen interactions occur. Police officers, as a result of their training and work experience, tend to view situations in a certain manner and act accordingly. Most of the research in this area has attempted to identify external or contextual factors that influence an officer's discretion (Black 1980). Research on women in policing has discussed the absence of roles for female officers and the problems women have adapting to male expectations (Martin 1990).

Psychological perspective. The psychological perspective is concerned with the nature of the "police personality." Officers may have a certain type of personality prior to employment or their personality may change as a result of their police experience. One of the enduring issues in research on police behavior is whether the values and attitudes of police officers stem from their backgrounds and upbringing or are the result of the experience of police work. Between the 1970s and the 1990s, researchers considered experience in police work as the most important determinant of the police personality. Recently research, however, is questioning this assumption, contending that predispositional factors (discussed later) may be more important than previously thought (Caldero 1997).

Organizational perspective. The organizational perspective suggests that organizational (departmental) factors—formal, informal (cultural), and institutional—play an important role in police behavior. Research on the influence of formal factors looks at the ways the department structures police activity. For example, J. R. Greene and C. B. Klockars (1991) studied the caseloads of officers to assess the overall importance of law enforcement, order maintenance, and service activity in the daily work of the police. (See Chapter 2 for a discussion of problems associated with activity and task analysis.) They discovered that police spend more time on law enforcement than had been previously thought. Some research in the 1960s and 1970s had stated that law enforcement accounted for only 10 to 20 percent of line officers' workloads. Greene and Klockars, however, found that police officers spend about 43 percent of their time on law enforcement, only 21 percent on maintaining order, and 8 percent on service. The second-largest category, traffic, accounted for 24 percent of their time.

Research on the informal factors studies police culture. In some ways, policing is both a culture and a subculture. As **culture,** police work is characterized by its own occupational beliefs and values that are shared by officers across the United States—for example, police everywhere value their assigned beats—their territories, and the way they deal with their territories, defines to a great extent their reputation in the department (Herbert 1997). Each department has its own local culture as well, a variation of the broader occupational culture (Manning 1977, 1989). As a **subculture**, police work has many values imported from the broader society in which officers live. For example, the conservative character of many police officers reflects the types of individuals drawn to police work from society.

Research on institutional factors is concerned with how the department adapts to its environment. Institutional theory recognizes that concerns over efficiency and effectiveness are secondary to values carried by important actors such as a mayor or city council member. J. Crank and R. Langworthy (1991) discuss the ways in which various police practices reflect broader values and how the department acts on the values. In several papers, S. Mastrofski and his colleagues (Mastrofski and Ritti 1996; Mastrofski and Uchida 1993) have discussed institutional processes affecting the behavior of police departments.

Particularistic Perspectives

Instead of emphasizing similarities among police, particularistic perspectives focus on decision-making differences among officers. Particularistic perspectives include typologies, which are perspectives that identify different officer types or styles of policing.

R. Worden's (1989) research on police behavior suggests that officers, contrary to conventional wisdom, are not psychologically homogeneous—that is, they are not always intensely loyal to one another nor preoccupied with order. Nor are they all suspicious, secretive, cynical, or authoritarian. The police socialization process does not necessarily result in officers having the same outlook.

Worden identified five ways that police officers are different from one another. First is their view of human nature. Cynical police, for example, tend to be pessimistic, suspicious, and distrustful. The important issue here is the extent to which a person is cynical prior to employment, how that cynicism changes over time, and how it influences his or her behavior.

Second, officers have different role orientations. Some see themselves as crime fighters who deter crime by making arrests and issuing citations. Others believe that the police role involves not only fighting crime but problem solving, crime prevention, and community service.

Third, officers have different attitudes toward legal and departmental restrictions. Some officers think that the ends justify the means in policing, often because they think that legal and policy guidelines are too restrictive, resulting in a criminal going free and thereby increasing crime and the suffering of victims. In addition, some officers believe that the criminal justice system is not punitive enough, and it is up to them to guarantee punishment through "street justice."

Fourth, officers' clientele influences their beliefs and their behavior. Preferences of particular judges, for example, or pressure on patrol enforcement practices from Mothers Against Drunk Driving can influence patterns of police enforcement. The influence of particular groups can lead to selective enforcement of particular laws and alienate other groups with whom the police interact.

Fifth is the relationship between management and peer group support. Theoretically, police departments reward desired behavior and punish undesired behavior. Many observers, however, have noted that police departments are punishment oriented. They do not have many ways to reward good behavior, so they tend to control the behavior of line officers by setting up elaborate standard operating procedures and punishing officers for infractions. Consequently, officers often turn to their **peer group** members for aid—that is, to other officers of the same rank in the department. The peer group is very influential in policing. Officers depend on it for physical protection and emotional comfort. This dependency in turn can result in increased secrecy in the department.

Socialization Versus Predisposition

As it enters the twenty-first century, police work is in the midst of broad change. The most visible changes are occurring under the umbrella of community policing, which emphasizes police discretion, decentralization of authority, and community involvement. Departments are increasingly seeking personnel who have the attitudes, values, and skills for community policing.

Community-policing concerns about hiring the "right" kind of officer have rekindled the debate about where officers' attitudes and values come from. If they come from the way officers adapt to their occupational environment, then commanders will have to change the department or the way it does its work. If they come from the background characteristics of officers, then administrators will have to change their hiring policies. These two ways of thinking about police officers' values and attitudes are called the socialization theory and the predispositional theory.

Socialization theory. Beginning in the 1960s, as the body of knowledge about police behavior increased, social scientists suggested that police behavior was determined more by work experiences and peers than by preemployment values and attitudes. This was called the **socialization theory**—that is, individuals are socialized as a result of their occupational experiences. If a police officer becomes corrupt, it is because the police occupation contributes in some way to weaken values; in other words, corruption is

learned within the department. This theory applies to any type of police behavior, good or bad.

Two socialization processes take place in a police organizations. *Formal
socialization* is the result of what transpires in the selection process, the training program, what is learned about policies and procedures, and what officers are told by supervisors and managers. *Informal socialization* takes place
as new recruits interact with older, more experienced officers. One's peers
play an important role in determining behavior, not only in the police occupation but in other jobs as well. An understanding of informal socialization processes is important because what one learns on the job and from one's peers
may contradict what is learned during the formal socialization process.

In many police departments the selection process attempts to eliminate
individuals who may be prone to unnecessary violence or dishonest behavior.
Therefore, police behavior—both good and bad—is seen as a consequence of
behavior that is learned after employment. The police experience, and how
individuals adjust to that experience, is the most important consideration in
determining how "good" police behavior is to be achieved and how "bad" police behavior is to be avoided.

Predispositional theory. In recent years there has been a renewal of interest in the **predispositional theory**, which suggests that the behavior of a
police officer is primarily explained by the characteristics, values, and attitudes that the individual had before he or she was employed. If an officer is
dishonest or honest, brutal or temperate in the use of force, he or she probably had those positive or negative traits before being hired.

The predispositional theory received early support from M. Rokeach,
M. Miller, and J. Snyder (1971), who found that police held similar conservative political values. Individuals who wanted to become officers had a particular value focus: belief in the importance of authority together with a high
emphasis on professional fulfillment.

M. Caldero (1997) extended Rokeach's research to three additional police
departments. Surprisingly, he found no differences between Rokeach's 1971
findings and the views of respondents in his research in the early and mid
1990s. Caldero's research consequently offers support for the predispositional theory. The central principles of both research efforts are presented below.

1. Police have distinctively different values from other groups in
   American society.

2. Police values are highly similar to the values of the groups they
   are recruited from.

3. Police values also are determined by particular characteristics of
   their personality, which sets police officers apart from the
   groups from which they are recruited.

4. Police values are unaffected by occupational socialization.

5. The values carried by police officers are stable over time.

6. Regardless of racial or ethnic differences, police officers hold
   similar values.

7. Education has little impact on values held by police officers.

8. The police socialization process has little effect on the values of individual officers.

This research was discussed by J. Crank and M. Caldero (1999), who found that values consistent with police culture were already in place when police were hired. Moreover, after hiring, police values were little changed over an individual officer's career. Finally, screening processes insured that police recruits held similar values, regardless of their ethnicity or gender. The perspectives developed by Crank and Caldero can be described as a "subcultural" theory of police attitudes and behavior, meaning that police values in general are not learned on the job but are already learned when a recruit applies for police work. Police work selectively accents some of these values; for example, working-class values are reflected and intensified in the strong loyalties officers have for one another.

Studies of Police Behavior

This section will review important studies on police behavior. Many of these studies were written many years ago. Why then, you might wonder, if police work is changing so dramatically, are these old studies discussed here?

These studies are as important today as they were when they were written. In many ways, the fundamental issues facing the police, the problems they confront on their beats, and the people that they must work with have not changed a great deal. Indeed, one of the fundamental problems is that, in spite of truly staggering organizational changes that have occurred over the past half-century, what officers do on the street has changed little. Put an officer into walking beat and he or she will view that work pretty much as officers did 100 years ago, spiced up only technological gadgets. Keep in mind that it is not the dates that the studies were written that is important; it is the currency of the ideas.

Police officers encounter a break-in. (Photo: corbis-images.com)

'Our Lawless Police'

In the early part of the twentieth century, reformers were concerned with police misbehavior. As a result of this concern, E. J. Hopkins wrote *Our Lawless Police* (1931) in order to explain why police officers engaged in illegal behavior. He developed what he called a "war theory of crime control," suggesting that police believe they are waging a "war" on crime and that any means is justified to win that war. The police perceive themselves as being pressured by the public to get results, and the consequences of that pressure include a tendency to settle matters "in the streets." In effect, these officers believed that illegal behavior (police brutality) was necessary if law and order were to be maintained. This study continues to be important today because it shows how police can be corrupted if they think the cause is noble enough. Corruption issue for the sake of a noble cause may be the most important corruption facing the police today (Crank and Caldero 1999; Human Rights Watch 1998).

'Violence and the Police'

The first social-science oriented study of the police, *Violence and the Police* (1970), was conducted by W. A. Westley in Gary, Indiana, in 1950. He identified the importance of socialization as a significant factor in police behavior. He found that old timers indoctrinated recruits with the belief that if the recruits were to be good cops, they must take charge of situations in which they became involved. Being in charge of a situation meant that citizens, particularly those in the lower classes, had to show the officer respect. If a citizen failed to show respect or challenged an officer's authority, officers felt compelled to react. Officers believed that they could not back down when faced with challenges to their authority. To do so only encouraged citizens to challenge the police more often, thus making the police officer's job more difficult. Many of the officers in Gary stated that it would be appropriate to "punish" the citizen by using some type of physical force.

Westley also found that the police in Gary believed that the public did not support them. They felt isolated from the public and did not believe that the public could be trusted. Consequently, many police officers were secretive about their daily routines. The police hated "stoolies," police officers who took problems outside the department and "washed their dirty linen" in public. A concern for secrecy and protecting fellow officers was grounded in the fundamental belief that the public could not be trusted to fairly evaluate the appropriateness of police behavior.

Westley's research and analysis underscore the importance of in-group solidarity. **In-group solidarity,** or closeness and loyalty among officers, results from a perception that the public cannot be trusted. In-group solidarity and officer secrecy make it difficult to determine what police officers actually do. Solidarity is often accompanied by a code of silence in which officers will not discuss inappropriate police behavior or may lie about it in order to protect a brother officer.

'Justice Without Trial'

The important study *Justice Without Trial* (1966), by J. H. Skolnick, was an analysis of two police departments, and it provided many important insights about the activities and behavior of police officers. One of these was related to the *production orientation* of a police department, meaning that police behavior was influenced by the goals or objectives that the department emphasized. For example, if a department was concerned about making arrests and issuing traffic citations, then officers were likely to be aggressive in making arrests and issuing tickets.

Skolnick discussed the significance of danger in police work. He coined the phrase **symbolic assailant** to represent the person the police officer thinks is potentially dangerous or troublesome. Who is a dangerous person? Those "types" of people with whom the officer has the most dangerous or troublesome experiences become, in effect, that officer's "symbolic assailant." From their experience and services told by other officers, police develop a repertoire of **danger signifiers** such as a person's actual behavior, language, dress, area, and in some situations, age, sex, and ethnicity.

Such signifiers can be interpreted by the police as challenges to their authority. The person who is perceived to challenge their authority may be verbally or physically abused. Of course, such abuse confirms an officer's belief that a particular kind of person or a particular area is troublesome or potentially dangerous. And, it convinces the person abused, and others who witness the abuse, that the police are repressive and brutal.

'Varieties of Police Behavior'

Perhaps the most important study of police behavior conducted in the 1960s was James Q. Wilson's *Varieties of Police Behavior* (1968). Wilson studied eight police departments and reported that in many respects they were quite different. He discussed these differences in terms of three styles of policing. Since Wilson's study, there have been many other attempts to identify different styles of police behavior in terms of both departments and individuals.

Wilson found that there were two general categories of problems confronting police departments: Law-enforcement problems were those behaviors considered serious enough to warrant a citation or arrest, such as serious traffic violations and most felonies and major misdemeanors. Order-maintenance problems involved less serious violations of the law such as misdemeanors or problems that police usually handled without resorting to issuing citations or making arrests.

Wilson stated that differences in policing styles were found primarily in how order-maintenance problems were handled. He identified three different styles: the watchman, the service, and the legalistic. To illustrate, assume that police discover a group of teenagers drinking beer in a public park, a problem in maintaining order.

In the **watchman style**, police officers are given a great deal of latitude in how they handle such problems. Often there are no policies or procedures to guide them. Consequently, each officer is free to devise his or her own response or solution. The officers might take the beer and tell the teenagers to go home, providing they were not drunk. They might even provide a lecture about excessive drinking or they might do nothing at all. And if different officers observed the same problem, there would probably be several different responses to that problem.

In the **service style**, police see themselves as providing a product that the community wants. Such departments tend to be found in homogeneous communities with a common idea of public order. They train officers in what to do and how to do it. The police intervene frequently, but many do so informally, and an arrest is not an inevitable outcome. The officers might refer the beer-drinking teenagers to a department program involving teenage drinking or to a community program. Or, they might call the parents to come and get their son or daughter. Of course, police in the service style do not do this with all order-maintenance problems but for those problems the community or the department considers important.

In the **legalistic style**, police try to enforce the law—write a citation or make an arrest—if possible. Police view themselves as law enforcers. They would probably arrest the teenage beer drinkers. Of course, police in the legalistic style do not always make arrests, but they tend to make more arrests and issue more citations than police do in the other two styles.

'City Police'

Another important study of police behavior was conducted by J. Rubinstein, who wrote *City Police* (1973). Rubinstein, who worked as a patrol officer in Philadelphia, provided numerous important insights about police activity and behavior. His findings support Skolnick's contributions regarding the importance of the perception of danger in police behavior. Rubinstein suggested that a patrol officer's most important concern was physical control of those individuals with whom he or she interacted. Of course, officers do not perceive all persons as requiring physical control, but in general they tend to watch a suspect's hands, are always alert to the possibility of weapons, and may even stand close to suspects to limit their ability to lash out with a swing or a kick.

Rubinstein's research emphasizes the importance of an officer's working environment as a critical factor in police behavior. Officers learn on the job from other officers about what is important and what is not, the types of situations and people that are potentially dangerous, and how to respond to them. The police department can substantially influence how the officer responds, but much is left to the individual officer. Rubinstein's experience provides support for the socialization theory of police behavior.

'Observations on the Making of Policemen'

Also in 1973, J. Van Maanen reported on his experiences in law enforcement in "Observations on the Making of Policemen." He attended a police academy and then participated in a limited role as a police officer for six months in a small city in California. One of his most interesting findings concerns the process by which an individual is initiated into a police department. He identified four stages, which are briefly described below.

Pre-entry choice. Most individuals who choose a police career select it from among a variety of career choices. They tend to go into police work believing they are entering an elite occupation. Many already know someone or something about police work and already tend to identify with the goals and values of the police, at least as they understand them. Their motivation for entering police work is often related to doing something important in society.

Admittance: Introduction. The second stage is the police academy experience. All officers, after being hired, must take some form of academy training, where they learn the necessity of adhering to the rules and regulations of the department. The academy Van Maanen attended had a military atmosphere in which officers followed a rigid routine and were punished for deviating from it (e.g., being late). Officers spent much time studying the technical aspects of police work, and instructors elaborated on these aspects with police experiences, or "war stories." These stories provided important insights about the traditions and values of the department and what was considered to be "good" police work. Recruits learned that they must stick together and protect one another. Today, academy training is less stress oriented, yet many of the lessons Van Maanen described are applicable today.

Change: Encounter. Once the police academy has been completed, new officers enter the third stage, going to work in the patrol division, each being assigned to a training officer. Once they are in the field, they are taught what the work is really like. It is also during this phase that the new officers are "tested" by the older officers. Can they perform? Can they operate the equipment effectively? Do they have "common sense?" Are they willing to take risks? Officers are always tested about their willingness to "back up" other officers. Perhaps the most crucial "test" an officer must pass is related to his or her dependability in helping fellow officers when they are in trouble.

Officers back up each other, preparing for a potentially dangerous situation. (Photo: corbisimages.com)

Continuance: Metamorphosis. In the final stage, new officers adjust to the reality of police work. In effect, this reality involves a large number of routine problems and bureaucratic tasks, with only an occasional exciting or adventurous activity. For some officers, however, the possibility of an exciting or adventurous "call" continues to be an important motivating factor. As they progress in police work, many officers learn that the public does not understand or support them. And, they often decide that the police system—meaning managers and supervisors and how they enforce rules and regulations—is unfair. Perhaps the most common adjustment made by officers, at least in the city Van Maanen studied, was to "lie low and hang loose." That is, they did as little work as possible in order to avoid getting into trouble.

'Police: Street-corner Politicians'

Another important study of police behavior was conducted in Oakland (he called it Laconia) in the 1970s by W. K. Muir. The result was a book titled

Police: Streetcorner Politicians (1977). Muir considered two issues central to police ethical development: (1) the degree to which the officer understood the nature of human suffering, that is, the degree of compassion displayed by the officer; and (2) how the officer responded to the contradiction of achieving just ends with coercive means—that is, how comfortable the officer was in exercising authority.

❖ ❖ ❖ ❖

The four styles identified by Muir are the professional, the reciprocator, the enforcer, and the avoider. **Professional-style officers** are both compassionate and comfortable with their authority. When necessary, these officers will use coercion to accomplish their work. Yet they view coercion from a perspective that would prefer to find other outcomes. Professionals recognize that coercion is sometimes a necessary means, but they will seek other means first.

Enforcers tend to use force when they have the opportunity. They recognize the need to use force, but they lack the "common touch," a sense of sharing a common destiny with those that they police. Enforcers have not integrated their use of force into a philosophy of life. Force is simply the simplest way to solve problems that they confront.

Reciprocators are compassionate but not comfortable with their authority. These officers try to persuade individuals to cooperate without relying on coercion. These officers understand the responsibilities that go with police work but are uncomfortable with coercion, even in circumstances where there are no alternatives.

Avoiders are neither compassionate nor comfortable with their authority. They tend to avoid difficult situations and problems. They lack the maturity of perspective to use coercion in a responsible way, and they also lack compassion for ordinary people. Most often, avoiders are officers who have decided the best way to avoid trouble is to do as little work and take as few risks, as possible.

'Working the Street: Police Discretion'

M. K. Brown's *Working the Street: Police Discretion* (1981) was a study of policing styles conducted in three southern California cities. Individual officer styles, Brown suggested, depended on a combination of their aggressiveness and selectivity of crime problems. Aggressiveness was the degree to which they actively seek out problems. Selectivity was the extent to which they were concerned only about serious crime problems.

Using these two variables, Brown identified four styles of police behavior: **Old-style crime fighters** are very aggressive and tend to be selective, concentrating primarily on felonies. These officers develop extensive knowledge of the area in which they work, use informants, and tend to be coercive. They are sometimes willing to act illegally to get "results." **Clean-beat crime fighters** believe in the importance of legal procedures. These officers are proactive and legalistic but do not tend to be selective. Almost all violations of the law are considered to be significant. **Service-style officers** do the minimum amount of work necessary to get by; that is, they are not aggressive but are selective. Only the most serious problems will result in their enforcing the law. Such officers tend to rely on informal solutions to problems rather than legalistic ones. Professional-style officers engage in limited proactivity and are not selective. They are situationally oriented, though "tough" when necessary, and at other times they may be service minded. Like Muir, Brown uses the term *professional* to denote the type of police officer that he considers to be the most desirable.

Crank's *Understanding Police Culture* (1998) is included here because it integrates a great deal of writing about police work and shows present-day trends in thinking about the police. It is an effort to develop a "middle-range theory" about the police and show how this theory can provide new insights into police work. Middle-range theory attempts to integrate findings from a broad body of research into a more general perspective.

Crank suggests that police culture emerges from the daily practice of police work. Culture, he argues, does not make the police different from the public. Rather, it humanizes the police by giving their work meaning. Rejecting the notion that police culture is a "dark force," he argues that culture is carried in police common sense, in the way in which everyday activities are celebrated, and in the way police deal with death and suffering. Consequently, to understand police culture, one must examine the physical setting in which police work occurs and the groups with which police interact, such as wrongdoers, the public, the courts, the press, and the department's administration. Because these groups tend to be similar everywhere, police culture tends to take on similar characteristics in different departments, and one can speak of a police culture generally.

Elements of police culture are organized around four central principles. The first and most central principle is *coercive territorial control*. The police are trained formally and socialized informally to view their work in terms of the use of force to control specific territories to which they are assigned. Police learn about the use of force, both in terms of use-of-force continuum (see Chapter 9) and in terms of informal tactics that enable them to control the public in police-citizen encounters. The use of force is more than a set of skills, however. Force is acted out as a moral commitment to control their assigned territories.

The second principle is *the unknown*. Police activity routinely puts officers in circumstances that are unpredictable and may have an outcome beyond their control. Such unpredictability makes police work interesting. The common unpredictability of everyday encounters may mask significant danger. Police officers have a wide repertoire of skills to insure that unknown situations do not deteriorate into dangerous life-threatening encounters.

The third principle is *solidarity*, or the intense bonding and sense of occupational uniqueness that officers feel for one another. It is produced by the dangers and unpredictability of their work and from the intense individualism that is part of the police ethos. Central to solidarity is conflict with other groups: police officers often feel alienated from the courts and the public and from outsiders and different ethnic groups. The greater the conflict with outside groups, the greater the degree to which the police feel united in a sense of solidarity.

The fourth principle is *loose coupling*, the idea that police develop strategies and tactics to protect themselves when department goals and policies are perceived to undermine their ability to do their work. At the core of the police morality is the idea that they have to do something about "bad guys." Efforts by administrators to control police behavior, as well as by the courts to hold them accountable for due process, are often met with distrust by line officers when such efforts interfere with their sense of occupationally driven morality. Lying in court, keeping information from administrators, and circumventing due process all are ways some police officers carry out their work in spite of administrative rules limiting what they are permitted to do.

This section has provided brief summaries of some of the more important studies about police behavior from the 1930s to the 1990s. Inside Policing 8.1 presents quotes of police officers regarding their own behavior. Their statements indicate the importance of some of the variables that are identified in this section.

❖ ❖ ❖ ❖

Inside Policing 8.1
Police Officer Quotes

Commitment to the Public. "I know it sounds corny as hell, but I really thought I could help people. I wanted to do something good in the world, you know?" (Baker 1985, p. 9)

Street Craziness. "The cabby had picked up the naked prostitute and now she couldn't pay. All four of them were screaming at each other. The cabby was screaming for his money, the naked prostitute was screaming that she had been raped by a john, and the other two prostitutes were yelling that the cabby should have known that she had no money when he picked her up naked." (McNulty 1993 p. 285)

Street Standards. "You have all the instructors up there teaching you the penal law, the study of minority groups. . . . psychology, . . . sociology. Then you got the [other cops]—telling you, 'that's all bullshit. It's either you or him out in the street. Go for the eyes. Kick them in the groin.'" (Baker 1985 p. 12)

The Perception of Danger. From a training class on actions to take inside a house. "On the page below, you'll see JDLR. That's *Just Don't Look Right*. Refer to GTHO, p. 5. Turn to p. 5. It says *Get the Hell Out*."(Crank 1996, p. 413)

Unpredictability. "The situations that seem to be the most unlikely to be dangerous are the ones that erupt into the most violent. The most tragic incidents have always come from the smallest incidents, usually traffic. . . . When you walk up to a car with a little old lady sitting in it and she pulls a sawed-off shotgun on you, you're completely surprised. Who you're stopping is always the joker in the deck." (Fletcher 1991, pp. 12–13)

Advice to young officers. "Don't drive faster than your guardian angel can fly." (Crank 1996, p. 415)

Supporting Fellow Officers. "It's a contact sport and if you don't watch my back for me, there's no one else I can count on. If you're not looking out for me, I'm going to get hurt." (Baker 1985, p. 210)

Fear. "I'd be lying between my teeth if I said I never get scared. I wouldn't want to work with a police officer who said he's never scared. That macho act—can't nothing hurt me, can't nothing touch me—that's all it is, an act. (Fletcher 1991, p. 276)

Survivors and Police Distrust of Media. "I had just finished shopping when I heard the chilling report of a police shoot-out on the car radio. The reporter was the one who informed me that it was my husband that had been killed. My neighbors found me, crying hysterically, parked in the middle of the road several blocks from home." (Sawyer 1993, p. 4)

Sources: Adapted from M. Baker. 1985. *Cops: Their Lives in Their Own Words*. New York: Simon and Schuster; C. Fletcher. 1990. *What Cops Know*. New York: Pocket Books; C. Fletcher. 1991. *Pure Cop*. New York: St. Martin's Press; E. McNulty. 1993. "Generating Common Sense Knowledge Among Police Officers." *Symbolic Interaction* 17: 281–294; S. Sawyer. 1993. *Support Services to Surviving Families of Line-of-Duty Deaths*. Camdenton, MO: Concerns of Police Survivors; J. Crank. 1996. "The Construction of Meaning During Training for Parole and Probation." *Justice Quarterly* 31: 277.

Decision Making and Police Discretion

Police officers make decisions that affect the public in important ways. Yet scholarly knowledge about the way police make decisions is limited. When scholars talk about decision making, they generally mean decisions involving citizens and questionable behavior. When police see something that is "out of kilter," two important decisions must be made: (1) whether to intervene in a situation (this is not a choice if the officer is sent by the department) and (2) how to intervene (Wilson 1968). What kinds of decisions are available for an officer who makes a routine traffic stop? D. H. Bayley and E. Bittner (1989, p. 98) note that officers have 10 actions to select from at the initial stop (for example, order the driver out of the car), seven strategies appropriate during the stop (for example, give a roadside sobriety test), and 11 exit strategies (for example, release the driver with a warning). From start to finish, this represents a total of 770 different combinations!

Decision making is different from the use of discretion. The circumstances above represent decision making regarding when and how to intervene in situations. **Discretion** is more narrowly defined. The most commonly used definition is the decision not to invoke legal sanctions when circumstances are favorable for them (Goldstein 1998). In encounters with suspects, for example, police may be presented with a situation in which they have the legal basis for an arrest. They do not, however, always make an arrest. The decision not to make an arrest when it is legally justifiable is sometimes called non-enforcement discretion.

Discretionary decisions not to arrest occur often in police work. An officer may witness a person drinking beer in a park, which is a violation of local codes. This situation might be handled with a warning rather than a citation or an arrest. Why did the officer not make an arrest? The officer might feel sympathy for the suspect. Or the officer might be waiting to see how the suspect reacts, prepared to arrest him if the suspect resists or gets "smart-mouthed." The officer might view this situation as a problem that can be easily handled without going to the trouble of arresting the suspect. The officer might be about to go off duty and not want to spend time doing paperwork at the end of the shift. Or arrest might be inconsistent with an officer's "style;" that is, she or he simply does not arrest beer drinkers in parks. Many factors affect officers' decisions about whether they should intervene, and what they should do after intervening, and whether they should make an arrest even when legal circumstances are favorable.

As Inside Policing 8.2 shows, discretion not to enforce the law is not legally authorized. J. Goldstein (1998) presents discretion as a special case of enforcement. Police officers in most jurisdictions are responsible for the enforcement of the criminal code. They are not permitted by law to enforce the law selectively, a principle that most people would view as a kind of favoritism. Their standard is full enforcement, which means (1) investigation of every disturbing event, (2) an effort to discover its perpetrators, and (3) presentation of all information collected to the prosecutors. Goldstein points out that, at a practical level, full enforcement of the law is unrealistic. For a variety of reasons, many factors prevent the police from fully enforcing the law. The difference between full enforcement and actual enforcement is the use of discretion not to invoke the criminal justice process (see Inside Policing 8.2).

Inside Policing 8.2
Discretion in the Criminal Justice System

Figure 8.1

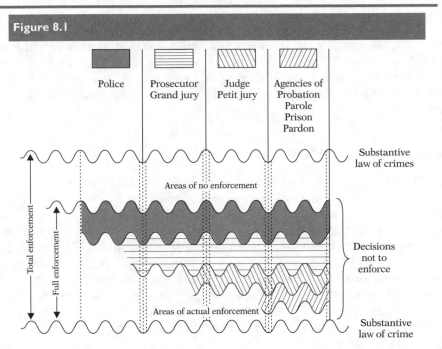

The figure above provides several kinds of information. First, it shows an "area of no enforcement." This area refers to the circumstances of crimes where enforcement is unreasonable or illegal. For example, due process on police procedures may limit the capacity of the police to make an arrest. Adultery crimes require that the spouse complain. Thus, there are areas where enforcement will simply not occur because it is prohibited or not possible.

Second, is the "area of full enforcement." This may appear to be a contradiction, since we have suggested that police sometimes use discretion to enforce the law. However, it should be recognized that, in the area of full enforcement, police are not provided the statutory authority *not* to enforce the law. Discretion consequently represents a decision not to enforce where enforcement is mandated by ordinance, state statute, or department rules and regulations.

Decisions by the police not to enforce occur within the band of full enforcement. How often do police not make an arrest, when the opportunity for an arrest is present? Donald Black (1980) as-sessed arrest decisions with a complainant and suspect present—circumstances seemingly optimum for invocation of arrest. He found that a police arrest occurred in 58 percent of the felony encounters and 44 percent of the misdemeanor encounters. In other words, decisions not to enforce, even though not permitted by statute or policy, occur in roughly half of the "full enforcement" area.

Finally and importantly, we can see that discretion is not unique to the police but characterizes all agencies involved in the criminal justice process. This tells us that the police are not acting in a way inconsistent with the criminal justice system but are in fact making the same kinds of discretionary judgments that other people in the justice system use. In other words, the discretionary behavior of the police is a normal aspect of the criminal justice process.

Source: Adapted from Joseph Goldstein. 1998. "Police Discretion Not to Invoke the Criminal Justice Process." In G. Cole and M. Gertz, ed., *The Criminal Justice System.* Belmont, CA: West/Wadsworth. Publishing Co. p. 89.

If the police are not using full enforcement but instead are selectively enforcing the law, it is reasonable to ask under what conditions arrests are actually made. Do police use their discretion arbitrarily, or are there principles or rules of thumb that guide their behavior?

There has been a considerable amount of research concerning variables that influence police decision making and discretion. Both L. W. Sherman (1985, pp. 183–195) and L. W. Brooks (1989, pp. 121–145) have analyzed research in this area. Their observations are grouped into five categories of variables: organizational, neighborhood (or community), situational, officer, and individual.

Organizational Variables

There are several organizational (departmental) variables.

Bureaucratic nature. The bureaucratic nature of a police department is an important factor affecting police behavior, as discussed in Chapter 4. It should be emphasized that the purpose of bureaucratic procedure is to guide and direct police behavior (Alpert and Smith 1998; Auten 1988). And, as R. Wasserman (1992) observes, without written policy, departments relinquish policy decisions to the idiosyncratic judgments of street officers. Nevertheless, various researchers have questioned the effectiveness of the bureaucratic "control principle" (Alpert and Smith 1998). G. Cordner (1989) challenged the notion that written policy always contributes to the quality of police service. The discretionary demands of street activity may undermine bureaucratic efforts to control behavior (Adams 1990). Bureaucratic controls can backfire, contributing to police secrecy and undermining bureaucratic control. For these reasons, the effectiveness of bureaucracy as a way to stimulate some behaviors and dampen others is certainly limited. Highly bureaucratic departments also tend to be impersonal and may overemphasize punitive discipline in an attempt to control officers' behavior. This tendency may result in officers doing as little as possible in an effort to avoid getting into trouble.

Work periods and areas. Another important organizational variable is the frequency with which officers change work periods (or shift or tour) and the areas (beat or district or sector) in which they work. The more frequent these types of changes, the more distant the relationship between citizen and officer. That there may be less communication and less understanding about community problems. Also important is the size of the area in which the officer works; the smaller the area, the more likely that a service rather than an enforcement orientation will prevail (Mastrofski 1981). A small area with a high quantity of serious crime, however, is more likely to have a law enforcement style (Brooks 1989, pp. 126–130).

Neighborhood Variables

To what extent do characteristics of neighborhoods affect police performance? Clearly the kind of beats police patrol affect the work they do. As early as 1968, Wilson noted that, in watchman-style departments, officers adapted their work to the kinds of problems that characterized their beats. This practice resulted in uneven delivery of service. J. Q. Wilson and G.

Kelling (1982) extended this idea to argue that police *should* tailor their work to the kinds of problems they encounter, a theme expanded by Skolnick and Bayley (1986).

Characteristics of neighborhoods may also affect police behavior. One of the most interesting characteristics is racial composition. Research tends to support the view that the police write more reports, make more arrests, engage in more abusive behavior, and receive more citizen requests for police intervention in minority areas. As a result of this increased activity, police get to know the people in these areas better than in other areas. In addition, police tend to view minority areas as places where violent crimes are more likely to occur and where they are more likely to have their authority challenged. As a result, police are more suspicious and alert and more concerned for their own safety. Data consistently show that police arrest more individuals in minority areas than in other areas, though arrest rates are highly correlated with criminal activity (Sampson and Lauritsen 1997).

Another aspect of neighborhoods is their racial and ethnic heterogeneity. The greater the racial and ethnic diversity, the more likely the police will become involved in encounters with citizens whom they think are troublesome. Police tend to exercise a great deal of discretion in these areas, may tend to feel more insecure, are often more aggressive, and tend to make more arrests. They are much more likely to arrest and threaten use of force in racially mixed neighborhoods (Smith 1980).

Situational Variables

Many elements in a situation affect police behavior.

Mobilization. The manner in which the police are mobilized, or enter into a situation, is important in determining their conduct. In proactive, or police-initiated encounters, officers are more likely to face antagonism from citizens. Proactive police behavior is more intrusive and less likely to be supported by victims and bystanders. As a result of the increased likelihood of a negative citizen response, police are more likely to make arrests and treat citizens harshly (Sherman 1985, p. 187). Consequently, proactive encounters are more likely to result in police-citizen antagonisms and conflict.

Demeanor and attitude. The characteristics of both suspects and complainants are important variables in the discretion of police officers. As Case Study 8.1 shows, perhaps the most important of these is the demeanor of the suspects. Disrespectful or uncooperative suspects are more likely to be arrested than suspects who are not. The socioeconomic status of individuals is also an important situational factor. Individuals in a lower socioeconomic status are more likely to be treated harshly by the police, and suspects in that status are more likely to be arrested. In contrast, D. Klinger (1994) contends that legal factors, specifically the criminal conduct of suspects *after* coming into contact with police, outweigh demeanor considerations.

The attitude of the complainant is another widely cited factor influencing police decisions to arrest, according to the research of D. Black (1980), D. Smith (1987), Worden (1989) and others. Black, for example, observed that arrests were more likely to occur in both felony and misdemeanor situations when the complainant wanted the suspect to be arrested. But officers are less likely to do what the complainant wants if the complainant shows disrespect.

The Mobilization of the Law

The most important early study of police discretion was conducted by Donald Black. Under what social conditions, Black asked, do the police decide to mobilize the law? The most important determinant of arrest was whether or not a law had been broken. Legal factors, Black observed, were more important than extralegal factors in determining the decision to make an arrest. Black observed, however, that even when conditions were favorable for an arrest—both the complainant and the suspect were present—an arrest often was not forthcoming. Why did officers decide sometimes not to make an arrest under such favorable circumstances?

First, police were more likely to make an arrest if the crime was serious. Although this may appear obvious, it is not. A large body of criminal code tends to go relatively unenforced, and the police are making personal decisions about the criminal code instead of acting impartially to enforce it. Felony crimes were more likely to result in arrest than misdemeanor crimes. Yet, under some circumstances officers didn't make arrests in felony encounters. The attitude of the complainant was the second factor. When the complainant was not interested in pursuing the case, or was disinterested, police often did not make arrests, even in felony cases. A third factor was the relationship between the victim and the suspect. Police were less likely to make an arrest when the relationship was close than when the relational distance was distant. For example, an arrest was less likely to occur if a woman was sexually assaulted by her husband than if she was sexually assaulted by a stranger.

Finally, Black considered the demeanor of the suspect. Belligerent suspects were more likely to be arrested than cooperative ones. When he initially wrote his theory of discretion, Black concluded that the apparent effects of race on arrest decisions were overshadowed by the demeanor of the suspect. However, in later work he stated that the role of race was more important than he had first thought. Race and demeanor are intertwined phenomena, he observed. On the one hand, belligerence may account for the greater frequency of minority arrests. However, their belligerence may stem from a long history of racist behavior on the part of the police. Moreover, belligerence is itself an extralegal factor, suggesting that the police are not weighing only legal factors in the decision to arrest.

The strength of Black's work lies not only in the findings but in his recognition of their implications. The police, Black notes, are moral filters through which the will of the public is converted into a decision to arrest. The police are disinclined to arrest in close familial circumstances, although the law may compel them to do so. And they don't want to arrest if the complainant is not interested. This, Black concludes, is intensely democratic. It is the will of the people acted out in the decision to arrest, when the law provides the necessary criteria for the arrest to occur.

Source: Adapted from D. Black. 1980. *The Manners and Customs of the Police*. New York: Academic Press.

The demeanor of suspects and attitude of complainants may interact with individual officer styles. For example, a widely cited "test" that many police officers apply to suspects is called the attitude, or personality test. Many officers believe that they cannot allow a citizen to challenge an officer's authority. The challenge can include a question about being stopped, too many questions in general, criticism of the officer, or failing to comply promptly to a police request for information. Of course, any physical resistance would also be included. Research suggests that citizens who flunk such tests are more likely to be verbally and physically abused or given a traffic citation or arrested (Van Maanen 1978).

Family disturbances require high levels of police discretion. (Photo: Mark C. Ide)

Race. Research on the importance of race in police behavior is mixed. A large body of research supports the contention that African Americans are treated more harshly than whites or are more likely to be arrested (Kappeler, Sluder, and Alpert 1994; Chambliss 1997; Maurer 1993). Some researchers contend that this situation is the result of the fact that African Americans, and possibly other minorities, may be more likely to resist police authority or display a "bad" attitude, from a police point of view. Others respond that hostility to the police derives from a history of police mistreatment. Inside Policing 8.3 concerns an issue of contemporary importance that has stirred a great deal of controversy—whether police make routine traffic stops based on race.

Inside Policing 8.3
DWB

The acronym DWB is increasingly entering public discourse. DWB means "driving while black." The police are being increasingly charged with making automobile stops based on the race of the driver, a practice known as racial profiling. The charge of racial profiling was frequently heard in the late 1990s. Consider the following cases:

Case 1. Eleven black motorists have filed a lawsuit in federal court, charging the Maryland State Police with using race as a factor in automobile stops and searches. The lawsuit charges that the police, in their zest to find illegal drugs and weapons, are selectively stopping automobiles because they believe that African Americans are more likely to be involved in crime. A federal judge had ruled the previous April (1998) that a police barrack in northeast Maryland targeted African-American motorists along I-95 in a "pattern and practice of discrimination."

Case 2. A local business in an Indiana community provided its minority employees with stickers to place on their automobiles. This practice was carried out because the business believed that local police officers disproportionately pull over African Americans. These stickers inform police officers that these individuals are ☞

gainfully employed by the business. Reminded that similar credentialing practices were used to identify employed Jews in Nazi Germany, the business abandoned the practice.

Case 3. Racial profiling emerges as a problem in New Jersey. A 1996 state court finding observed that although nearly all drivers exceed the 55 miles per hour speed limit, troopers pull over a disproportionate number of minorities. Maryland statistics indicated that 73 percent of motorists stopped and searched along I-95 were African American, although they made up only 14 percent of all motorists. In an incident on April 23, 1999, New Jersey state police were accused of using racial profiles in a routine stop of a van with minority occupants. African American and Hispanic men were shot in this incident, in which the police and the vehicle's occupants gave sharply different accounts of events. The incident is under investigation and has fueled concerns about stops for DWB.

Case 4. On Mercer Island, Washington, African Americans say that they are routinely stopped by police officers even when no crime has been committed. The chief noted that officers are taught to stop and investigate whenever they observe anything unusual. Unfortunately, on Mercer Island, being black is unusual—there are 300 African Americans in a population of 21,000 residents, and they find themselves the object of police inquiries. The problem is so bad that teachers in the school district gave officers a poster with the janitor's photograph (an African American) with the words "Not Wanted."

Case 5. In California in 1998, Assemblyman Kevin Murray had just won the Democratic nomination for a California senate seat. On the way to his victory party, he was stopped and ordered out of his car. He contended that the stop was the result of DWB. He has since submitted a bill, called the "California Traffic Stops Statistics Act," to control DWB stops.

Why does racial profiling occur? There are many reasons, some objectively reasonable, some not. Many police officers believe that minorities are disproportionately involved in drug activity and therefore that increasing the number of minority automobile stops will improve their chances of a career-building arrest. Local departments often receive a proportion of any monies received in drug arrests. Supreme Court decisions that permit profiling practices provide officers who have racist predispositions with the opportunity to act them out under the guise of "good police work." Given the current tendencies of the court to relax due-process concerns in favor of effectiveness, the principal resistance to racial profiling will come from civil litigation following critical incidents.

In December 1998, U.S. District Judge Nancy Gertner departed from federal sentencing guidelines because a black defendant's criminal history indicated multiple instances of arrest for DWB. In the case, the defendant had pleaded guilty to illegal possession of a firearm. Judge Gertner stated, however, that his criminal history was mostly of charges resulting from traffic-related incidents. The judge asked rhetorically, "What drew the officer's attention to Leviner [the defendant] in the first place?" Rigidly applying sentencing formulas, based as they are on previous record, would subvert the intent of the guidelines. The outcome of this case will ultimately affect race-based profiling practices.

Sources: Adapted from "On Wealthy Island, Being Black Means Being a Police Suspect." 1998. *New York Times*, May 10: 14; "ACLU Lawsuit Alleges Racial Bias." 1998. *New York Times* on the Web, June 5; "Maryland Troopers Stop Drivers by Race, Suit Says." 1999. *New York Times* on the Web, June 5; "The Spillover Effect of Driving While Black." 1999. *Bergen Record Corporation*, April 11; D. Ehrlich. 1998. "Driving While Black or Brown—Is This Cause for Arrest in California?" *American Civil Liberties Union*, August 20.

Gender. The effects of gender on police behavior regarding arrests are relatively unstudied. The masculine predispositions of police departments are widely cited (Martin 1980, 1990). Yet, the extent to which these predispositions affect police-citizen encounters is unclear. P. Kraska and V. Kappeler (1995) suggest that sexual violence by the police may be more widespread than previously thought. Opportunity, power, authority, and isolation increase the likelihood of sexual harassment of citizens (Sapp 1994). Attractive women are also more likely to be stopped by police officers for traffic violations, and the intent is not to issue a traffic citation but to make personal contact (see Kappeler, Sluder, and Alpert 1994). As the number of policewomen have increased, it may be that female officers become more likely to stop males they consider attractive.

Victim-complainant relationship. Another interesting situational variable is the relationship between the suspect and complainant. In general, if the relationship is close, the police may be reluctant to take official action (i.e., make an arrest) because they believe that it would be difficult to gain testimony from the victim in the courts. But the relationship has been, and remains, influential in the manner in which some police departments respond to calls about violence or a family fight. In addition, when the relationship between the complainant and suspect is close, the complainant may not wish the police to take official action. The preference of the complainant has a substantial influence on the officer's decisions. Although officers do not always do what complainants want, they are more likely to take official action, such as writing a report, if the complainant requests such action.

Type of offense. The type of offense also has an impact on police discretion. The more serious the crime, the greater the possibility of a formal response. Violent crimes are more likely to result in an arrest for a simple reason—the victim is a witness to the crime. Consequently, about 50 percent of all violent crimes result in an arrest; only about 20 percent of property crimes do so. Police are more likely to arrest in felony encounters than in misdemeanor situations. This fact may seem like common sense, but it is not (Friedrich 1980). As Black (1980) noted, the legal decision to arrest is based on probable cause, not the seriousness of the act.

Location. Police are also influenced by the location—public or private—of the call. Police are more likely to respond harshly in public settings than in private settings. This difference is the result of several factors: the type of crime (usually more serious crimes), the need to appear in control of the situation in public, and the fact that there are more police-initiated or proactive calls in public. As noted above, proactive police interventions with citizens are more likely to result in arrests and citizen resistance than are reactive police responses. Proactive interventions are usually the result of the police witnessing illegal behavior, usually at the misdemeanor level. Thus, as Black observed, police tend to be more proactive when a crime is not legally serious.

Presence of others. The presence of other police officers and bystanders has a slight influence on what police officers do (Parks 1982). If an officer thinks other police officers expect him or her to be harsh or punitive, or to write a report, or to make an arrest, then the officer is inclined to do so. Behaving in a manner that other officers believe to be appropriate is an important part of being accepted into the police "brotherhood." Crank and Caldero (1999) suggest that officers who "wolf-pack" stops, that is, congregate in high numbers during routine stops, are more likely to create a variety of problems for managers. These problems include due-process violations, violence, and increased levels of line-level secrecy.

Officers who work alone also tend to behave differently from officers who work in pairs. There is some support for the belief that officers working by themselves are more likely to make arrests because they are more concerned about taking control of a situation when working alone. Although two-person units may be less likely to make arrests, they are more likely to treat suspects harshly, possibly because each officer is concerned about what his or her partner will think, particularly if a suspect challenges police authority (e.g., asks questions, talks back, fails to follow police direction, fights) (Brooks 1989, pp. 134–137; Sherman 1985, pp. 189–192).

All the above variables have some influence on police behavior, but some are more important than others. Inside Policing 8.4 identifies those variables associated with both the suspect and complainant that appear to have a *reliable* influence on police behavior—that is, they are found to be influential in several studies.

Inside Policing 8.4 Critical Variables Influencing Police Behavior

| | Role of Citizen | |
Variables	Suspect	Victim
Race	x	o
Demeanor	x	x
Relation to victim	x	o
Social class	x	o
Age	x	o
Sex	x	o
Complainant's preference	o	x
Public/private setting	x	x
Number of citizens present	x	x
Proactive/reactive	x	o
Number of officers present	x	o

Key: x - consistent relationship found; o - no consistent relationship found
Source: Adapted from L. W. Sherman. 1985. "Causes of Police Behavior: The Current State of Quantitative Research" In A. S. Blumberg and E. Niederhoffer, eds., *The Ambivalent Force.* 3rd ed., pp. 183–195. New York: Holt, Rinehart and Winston.

Discretionary decisions are difficult to bring under departmental control. The ability of the police to use discretion enables them to adapt their responsibilities to the characteristics of public-order problems on their beat (Sykes 1986) and efforts to control discretion have sometimes backfired, creating line-level resistance and secrecy (Crank 1998). Perhaps the best to be hoped for is stated by D. Guyot (1991, p. 96): "The challenge for departmental leadership is to reduce the vindictive decisions and increase the wise ones."

Individual (Officer) Variables

Many individual factors influence police behavior.

Education, age, and experience. Education is discussed at length in Chapter 11. It is difficult to separate age and experience because most individuals entering police work are young, typically in their 20s, and grow older as they are gaining experience. In general, younger officers may work harder and are more aggressive and more punitive than older officers. However, the quality of the older officers' work may be superior. While some older, more seasoned officers may do less work and become less punitive, others may actually become more punitive if they become excessively cynical. Older police officers may become frustrated with the department and the legal system and engage in illegal behavior, including the use of excessive force.

Race. The race of the officer is also important. The bulk of the research on race has been about African American officers. Some evidence indicates that they are more respected by the African American community, but they may also be stricter in dealing with African American citizens. When compared with Anglo officers, African American officers tend to be more aggressive and to make more arrests in African American neighborhoods (Brooks 1989, pp. 138–140). There are also important race-related considerations concerning the police use of force. These are discussed in the next chapter.

Gender. The gender of the officer is also influential in the exercise of police discretion. There is some evidence to suggest that women are less aggressive. The studies that support this observation, however, were conducted in the first decade of women's involvement in patrol work (see Martin 1989, pp. 312–330, for a summary of these studies). One study found that women were less likely than men to use force (Grennan 1988, pp. 78–85). If women as a group tend to be less aggressive or use force less often than men, this finding may either be desirable or undesirable, depending on one's preference in policing styles. For the most part, however, the less aggressive (i.e., less forceful and abusive) the police, the more likely they are to have a positive relationship with the community.

Career orientation and family situation. Other important variables that influence the exercise of an officer's discretion are career orientation and family situation. W. F. Walsh's study (1986), conducted in the New York City Police Department, found that officers in high arrest categories were ambitious and believed that making arrests increased their chance of being promoted, or they believed that making felony arrests was an important part of police work. Some officers made numerous arrests because it gave them an opportunity to work overtime, which resulted in a higher salary. One of the reasons some of the high-arrest officers wanted to work overtime was because their wives did not work and they needed the money. Conversely, some of the officers in low-arrest categories had "outside work," or their wives worked and supplemented the family income.

The degree to which all these variables influence individual officers varies, but in general the decisions officers make to stop someone, to behave in a certain way when interacting with citizens, and to select a way to solve a problem, are determined by numerous factors other than the legality of a citizen's behavior. Yet, in spite of a great deal of research, scholars know little about the relative importance of extralegal factors. All that can be said for certain is that, in some circumstances, the police will make arrests based in part on factors other than whether the law is broken. Yet, even the law is highly interpretive, and officers have wide discretion in the application of punishments for misdemeanors. The contribution of extralegal factors consequently continues to be a topic in need of thoughtful research.

Police Deviance

Unfortunately, not all police behavior is legal. Sometimes police officers engage in acts that are inappropriate, and occasionally they do things that are illegal. Many people believe that police officers should be held to a higher standard than ordinary citizens. They hold the police as symbols of the moral fabric of society and their behavior as a standard for the public to emulate. Consequently, the police must display the image as well as the substance of propriety. They not only must be above reproach, they must also appear to be above reproach.

Police deviance is behavior that does not conform to the standards of norms or expectations. How are such standards determined? There are three major categories: ethical, organizational, and legal. *Ethical standards* are principles of appropriate conduct officers carry internally. Ethical behavior is an expression of personal values. *Organizational (departmental) standards* can be both formal and informal; they are derived from policy, procedures, rules, and regulations of the department (formal) and from the expectations of one's peers (informal). *Legal standards* are represented by the laws officers are sworn to uphold and by due process which establishes the means officers may use to achieve good ends.

Clearly, many of these standards carry the potential to conflict with others. Formal departmental policies may clash with informal cultural norms. The expectations surrounding the enforcement of the law may conflict with principles of due process. And, a police officer's personal values may be different from ethical principles established by the department. In short, the standards expected of a police officer are extraordinarily complicated, and deviance, in one form or another, is almost impossible to avoid.

It is very difficult to determine how frequently police engage in deviant behavior. It is difficult because people are not always forthcoming about their own inappropriate behavior and because, at times it is difficult to distinguish between inappropriate and appropriate behavior. Given the many conflicting expectations facing police, it is likely that deviance is widespread. Few police officers work even one shift without engaging in some form of behavior that is deviant by one standard or another. In fact, many police departments have so many rules and regulations that it is difficult not to violate some of them. Many of the violations are minor—for example, a requirement that officers wear their hat when not in a car.

T. Barker and D. Carter (1994) provide an interesting discussion of different types of police deviance. They state that police deviance is "a generic description of police officer activities which are inconsistent with the officer's legal authority, organizational authority, and standards of ethical conduct" (1994, pp. 4–5). Various dimensions of deviance and their implications are discussed below.

Types of Deviance

Barker and Carter divide police deviance into two categories: abuse of authority and occupational deviance. **Abuse of authority** is defined as "any action by a police officer without regard to motive, intent, or malice that tends to injure, insult, tread on human dignity, manifest feelings of inferiority, and/

or violate an inherent legal right of a member of the police constituency." **Occupational deviance** is deviant behavior—criminal and noncriminal—committed during the course of normal work activities or committed under the guise of the police officer's authority (1994, p.6). There are two subcategories of occupational deviance: police misconduct and police corruption.

Police misconduct is related to the violation of departmental guidelines (i.e., policies, procedures, rules, and regulations) that are created to define both appropriate and inappropriate conduct for officers. **Police corruption,** is "any forbidden act which involves the misuse of the officer's official position for actual or expected material reward or gain" (Barker and Carter 1994a, p. 56). Material rewards might be bribes, free dry cleaning, or discounted products. Various scholars' perspectives on police deviance are given below.

V. E. Kappeler, R. D. Sluder, and G. Alpert (1994) identify four general kinds of police deviance:

1. *Police crime.* Police crime is different from criminal acts; not all criminal acts committed by the police are police crime. Police crime is the "officer's use of the official powers of his or her job to engage in criminal conduct" (p. 21). In other words, an officer uses police authority to engage in violations of the criminal code.

2. *Occupational deviance.* Occupational deviance is activity that does not conform to standards and committed during the course of normal work activities or committed under the guise of the police officer's authority (p. 22; see also Barker and Carter 1994a, p. 6). It is not, that the deviance was just job related, but that the deviant act was substantially facilitated by being a police officer.

3. *Police corruption.* Corruption involves the use of police power and authority for personal gain (see also Sherman 1978; Goldstein 1977). Barker's study of police ethics is instructive here. He defines police corruption as follows: "Whatever the officer receives through the misuse of his or her authority must be of some material reward or gain. Material reward or gain must be some tangible object, either cash, services, or goods that have cash value" (1996, p. 25).

4. *Abuse of authority.* Finally, Kappeler and his colleagues observe that Carter's (1985, p. 22) definition of the term *abuse of authority* contains three different elements:

   a. Officers may physically abuse others through the use of excessive force.

   b. Officers may psychologically abuse citizens through the use of verbal assault, harassment, or ridicule.

   c. Officers may violate a citizen's constitutional, federal, or state rights. (Kappeler, Sluder, and Alpert, 1994, p. 24)

A similar typology was developed by M. Punch (1985), who identifies four kinds or categories of corruption:

1. *Straightforward corruption* is done for some reward. In this arrangement, the police may be linked to organized crime and selectively fail to enforce some crimes.

2. *Predatory corruption* occurs when the police stimulate crime, organize graft, or actively extort money. Here, the police themselves are the organized crime.

3. *Combative corruption* occurs when the major goal is to make arrests, obtain convictions, and get long sentences. It includes the following practices (see Manning 1980):

   Flaking: planting evidence on a suspect.
   Padding: adding evidence to strengthen a case.
   Verbals: words attributed to a suspect that are actually created by the police to help incriminate the criminal.
   Intimidating witnesses.
   Scoring on informants: shaking down informants for money, drugs, and other goods.
   Burning: revealing the identity of an informant.
   Paying informants with illegally obtained drugs.

4. *Perversion of justice* includes lying under oath, intimidating witnesses, and planting evidence on a suspect. It is distinguished from item 3 above by the motive of the police officer. In combative corruption, the motive was to do justice, although it is a "police" conception of justice. Here the motive is revenge.

Punch's typology differs from the others in two ways. First, his category "perversion of justice" recognizes that police behavior can carry sentiments of revenge against felons. Second, his category "combative corruption" clearly recognizes corruption for a noble cause—that is, revision of legal means for perceived good ends. Punch's model is consequently an important contribution to the literature on corruption.

Barker (1996) argues that assessments of police corruption should focus specifically on those activities for which there is a monetary reward. He identifies eight patterns of corrupt practices, which are reproduced in Inside Policing 8.5.

Stages of Deviance

Deviance can be described in terms of stages, each stage representing an increasingly deviant act. Sherman (1988) has described police deviance in terms of progressive corruption, a process he calls "getting bent." The process is comprised of different stages, each more serious than the previous:

1. *Minor "perks."* These can include free coffee, meals, or free dry cleaning.

2. *Bar closing hours.* Officers stay in bars until they close. They receive free drinks. In turn, the bar owner receives free protection.

3. *Regulative crimes.* On a routine speeding stop, an officer finds a $100 bill folded beside the motorist's driver's license. He takes the $100 and wishes the motorist a good day.

Inside Policing 8.5 Patterns of Police Corruption

Pattern	Acts	Degree of Organization
Corruption of authority	Free meals, liquor, discounts, rewards	None
Kickbacks	Money, goods, and services from those who serve clients of the police	High
Opportunistic theft	Thefts from arrestees, victims, crime scenes, and unprotected property	None
Shakedowns	Money, goods, or other valuables from criminals or traffic offenders	None
Protection of illegal activities	Protection money from vice operators or companies operating illegally	Often high
Fixes	Quashing of prosecution proceedings or disposing traffic tickets; fixers could be on payroll	Medium, fixers, could be on payroll
Direct criminal activities	Police officers engaged in such crimes as burglary, robbery, etc.	Low, small groups
Internal payoffs	Sale of work assignment, off-days, evidence and promotions	Low to high; depending other forms of corruption present

Source: Tom Barker. 1996. *Police Ethics: Crisis in Law Enforcement*, Table 7-1, pp. 38. Springfield, IL: Charles C. Thomas.

4. *Gambling*. If an officer is accepted by other officers "on the pad," that is, taking regular gambling payoffs, they might cut him or her in on a percentage of the "nut," or amount received from the operation.

5. *Prostitution*. Officers accept bribes from prostitutes, pimps, or brothel operators.

6. *Narcotics*. Officers use, buy, and sell narcotics. They may steal narcotics or cash from dealers during drug raids.

Officers who undertake a "bent" career do so because they are socialized into an atmosphere of corruption, and becoming corrupt is the path of least resistance. The process is subtle. For example, an officer may buy a drink at a bar. When she or he offers to pay for it, the manager might say, "It's OK. On the house for our best customers." Consider Barker's observation on a restaurant robbed by "gang-bangers:"

> In my letter [to the local newspaper], I stated that there was something wrong with police officers accepting free or discounted meals. . . . I

pointed out that his department had a policy against accepting any gratuities. . . . Several weeks after my letter was printed, this very fast food restaurant and a number of customers were robbed by a group of "gang-bangers" from a nearby metropolitan area. An unnamed police captain was quoted as saying "If they hadn't stopped the free meals, there would have probably been a cop in there when it happened." In my opinion, that statement is pure and simple extortion. No free meals, no protection. (Barker 1996, p. 29)

At any stage, an officer has the opportunity to resist, though doing so may cost her or him the esteem of her or his colleagues. Resistance is difficult because officers associate with other officers in the police culture. When they resist, corrupt officers they may break this affiliation and isolate the honest ones.

A bent career is also a **slippery slope**— that is, officers who have become corrupt at one level have already accustomed themselves to being corrupted. Having been corrupted at a lower level, it is easier to "give in" and commit a more serious kind of illegal activity. The hidden complexity of the slippery slope can be seen in the following section, which looks at the complex issues surrounding the acceptance of gratuities.

The Trouble With Gratuities

One of the most perplexing areas of police deviance concerns gratuities. A **gratuity** is the acceptance of something of value, such as coffee, meals, discount-buying privileges, free admission to athletic or recreational events or movies, gifts, and small rewards. Most commonly it is coffee, beverages, or meals free or at reduced cost. Gratuities do not seem to be harmful, and they are often offered under the friendliest of circumstances. A beer "on the house" is, for many young people, an indication of their social worth, that they are valued by their friends and colleagues. Yet an officer who accepts gratuities may unknowingly undermine the legitimacy of her or his police department, endanger a future promotion, and possibly lose the job.

Though acceptance of gratuities is a common practice in many police departments, it is considered to be unethical by the International Association of Chiefs of Police. Although many departments have an explicit policy that precludes accepting gratuities, these policies are frequently ignored by officers. Many police managers view violations of such policies to be a minor problem and may not enforce departmental regulations against them. Consider the following arguments in favor of gratuities:

1. They are a gesture of friendship and support from an appreciative public.

2. It is discourteous to refuse such gifts of appreciation.

3. Gratuities can be a "building block" for the development of positive social relationships (Kania 1988, p. 37).

4. The police deserve such considerate treatment because theirs is a dangerous and difficult job.

5. Business establishments that give gratuities like the police to "drop by" more often.

6. Gratuities are not solicited but are given voluntarily.

Arguments against gratuities are equally fervent. Consider the following: ❖ ❖ ❖ ❖

1. The public perceives the giving of free tokens to public servants as unfair.

2. The intent of the giver of the gratuity may be selfish and may take away needed protection from other businesses. Or the giver may expect to be treated differently by the police.

3. Such treatment encourages the police to think that they are "special," deserving of benefits that others are not.

4. Some police experts believe that acceptance of gratuities is the first step on a "developmental ladder" (or slippery slope) that may lead to more serious forms of corruption (Sherman 1985, p. 259).

Although a police officer may enjoy gratuities at first, they have a way of unpleasantly complicating life. For example, in a survey of citizens in Reno, Nevada, a majority of citizens polled did not think police should accept any gratuities. Almost half of the respondents stated that if they provided a gratuity they would expect special consideration (e.g., extra patrol, warning instead of a citation if stopped for a traffic violation) by police officers (Sigler and Dees 1988, pp. 16–17).

The following examples come from the authors' personal experiences. A police officer was standing in line at a restaurant to pay for his meal, which was charged at half price. When the next person in line saw the officer's bill, she insisted on paying only half of her bill. Clearly she did not think officers should be treated differently. In addition, the restaurant where this happened was part of a large motel complex. The officers who received discounted meals were expected to handle certain calls (e.g., for disturbances or prostitution) according to the manager's wishes.

The practice of accepting gratuities can become complicated. One department created a policy that allowed gratuities at certain restaurants for some food items but required each restaurant to keep a record of the food and beverages provided. Officers who did not accept gratuities but who did not wish to offend those establishments left payment at the table or counter. The food server then kept the money and marked the bill for separate distribution.

In some restaurants that give gratuities, only certain food items may be provided. In another circumstance, police officers received free meals, but they had to order the daily special. A dilemma occurred when an officer requested something other than the special. Under the informal rules shared by the officers and the restaurant management, he was not permitted to order it. Under pressure from a senior officer, he was not allowed to pay for a meal he wanted but had to eat a "free" meal he did not enjoy.

Business owners may offer gratuities in order to encourage the police to spend more time at their establishment. Assume, for example, that an officer goes to the same restaurant every day to eat because a free meal is provided. The value of the meals, over a month's time, is equal to about $180. The restaurant owner likes having police officers around because she thinks it will decrease the likelihood of a robbery or unruly customers. However, if the owner offered to give the officer $180 in cash every month to spend the equivalent amount of time at the restaurant, the officer would probably not accept the money and the police department would most certainly consider the acceptance of money to be a more serious problem than acceptance of the free meals. But there is no real difference in the two acts; both involve giving something of value for the express purpose of obtaining a private service—extra police protection or preferential treatment—from a public official.

Of course, many people consider this perspective too extreme. They believe it is possible to allow officers to accept gratuities without causing undue ethical problems. The authors disagree. If enough officers take gratuities, the departmental culture can easily become tolerant of other "minor" deviant acts, and ultimately, perhaps, even more serious types of problems will develop. The problem is not only the gratuity itself but an attitude about what is and is not appropriate police behavior. The acceptance of gratuities by many officers can create a departmental climate of grass eaters, individuals who are passive participants in crime but whose secrecy about their activities permits more serious types of criminality to emerge. Such organizational permissiveness can bring out the most secretive aspects of police culture.

Deviant Officers

Police officers vary in their vulnerability to corruption. Most officers do not become involved in corrupt activities. They are morally committed to their work and are not psychologically capable of illegal activity. Only a small percentage become "bent" to the extent that they commit illegal activity. What should society think about those who do?

One of the more important insights into police corruption was presented by the Knapp Commission, which conducted an investigation into the activities of the New York City Police Department in the late 1960s and early 1970s. Inside Policing 8.6 provides a summary of its findings, which remain comprehensive and influential.

Inside Policing 8.6
The Knapp Commission

The Knapp Commission was established in May 1970 by Mayor John V. Lindsay as a result of an article that appeared in the *New York Times* on April 25, which stated that there was widespread corruption in the New York City Police Department. The commission was given the task of determining the extent and nature of police corruption. Judge Whitman Knapp was appointed to head the investigation, which issued its final report in 1972.

The investigation found corruption to be widespread in the police department and many officers, both investigators and patrol officers, to be involved. Corruption was most extensive among investigators (what the commission called plainclothes officers) in the area of gambling. The plainclothes officers partici-

pated in what was known as a "pad." For example, each illegal gambling establishment in a precinct would contribute a certain amount of money (as much as $3,500 per establishment once or twice a month) to the officers. The total amount collected would be divided among the officers, each one receiving his "nut" (which was usually $300 to $400 per month, but at least one precinct had a "nut" of $1,200 per officer). Newly assigned officers had to wait two months before receiving a "nut," but all plainclothes officers who left the precinct were given two months' severance pay.

Corruption in the narcotics area was less organized but was also extensive. Many of the payments came from "shakedowns" of narcotics dealers. Such payments were known as "scores"; ☞

the highest payoff uncovered was $80,000. There was some evidence to suggest that such large payments to police officers were not uncommon. [Since the 1980s, corruption scandals in police departments have been primarily related to narcotics].

Other plainclothes officers not involved in gambling and narcotics were engaged in other corrupt activities. They attempted to obtain money by engaging in "shakedowns" of the criminals with whom they interacted, for example, auto thieves.

Uniformed patrol officers did not receive the large sums of money that went to plainclothes officers, but many patrol officers were involved in corrupt activities. Some participated in small gambling "pads" and often collected money from construction sites, bars, grocery stores, parking lots, and other business establishments. They could also get money from traffic violators, tow trucks (for business given to the company), prostitutes, and defendants who wanted their court cases "fixed." These types of businesses were subject to a number of city laws, which, if violated, could result in a fine. In order to get around some of these laws, patrol officers were paid to "look the other way." Most often, the payoffs were $20 or less, but many officers were able to collect a large number of such payoffs in a month, adding substantially to their salary.

Ranking officers, sergeants, lieutenants, and even others above this level, participated in corrupt activities, but the evidence was difficult to obtain, above the level of lieutenant. This is because when ranking officers were involved they used a "bagman," usually a patrol officer, to collect the payoffs. He received a percentage of the payoff. If he was discovered, he had to be willing to take the fall.

The commission divided the corrupt police officers into two types: the "grass eater" and the "meat eater." The meat eater aggressively seeks out the corruption opportunities. This officer will look for prostitutes or gamblers or narcotics sellers with the explicit purpose of extracting money from them. The grass eater is less aggressive but will accept payoffs if they come his way. The grass eaters were more numerous and also made the problem of corruption more difficult to resolve. There were so many of them that it made the acceptance of payoffs seem respectable. They also contributed to the development of a code of silence about the corrupt practices. The commission noted that it was easier for a new officer to become corrupt than to remain honest because corrupt behavior was so widely practiced that it was a norm of the department.

Although the Knapp Commission was careful to point out that not all police officers in New York City were corrupt, those who were not aware of the corruption problems and, for the most part, did nothing about them.

Source: Adapted from Knapp Commission. 1972. *Report on Police Corruption.* New York: George Braziller, pp. 1–11.

Of particular importance in the inset is the description of grass eaters and meat eaters. **Grass eaters** are police officers who accept graft when it comes their way but do not actively solicit opportunities for graft. **Meat eaters** are officers who actively solicit opportunities for financial gain and are involved in more widespread and serious corruption (Knapp Commission 1972).

A casual reader might think that meat eaters are a more serious problem than grass eaters. They certainly commit more serious crime. Yet that is not so. The Knapp Commission found that the grass eaters were a more significant problem. They outnumbered meat eaters by a considerable margin, and even though they did not solicit illegal opportunities, they took advantage of them when opportunity provided. Their illegal involvement created a wall of silence behind which meat eaters could operate with impunity. The problem confronting efforts to clean up corruption, the commission found, was the **code of silence**, which they could not penetrate. The code of silence is the secrecy that line-level officers maintain about their activities, both from the public and from police administrators.

Barker (1996) expanded the Knapp Commission's typology of deviant officers, identifying five types. *White knights* are totally honest and may take an extreme stance in ethical issues. These officers are in the minority and are not deviant. *Straight shooters* are honest but willing to overlook some of the indiscretions of other officers. They suffer in silence or seek out corruption-free assignments. *Grass eaters* engage in corrupt activities if the opportunity arises. *Meat eaters* actively seek out opportunities for corruption. Finally, *rogues,* at the far end of the scale, are considered an aberration even by meat eaters. They engage directly in criminal activities and in high-visibility shakedowns of citizens.

The Persistence of Corruption

Corruption has been and continues to be one of the most frequent problems faced by police departments in the United States. In describing early twentieth-century America, R. M. Fogelson says:

> The police did not suppress vice; they licensed it. From New York . . . to San Francisco, and from Chicago . . . to New Orleans . . . , they permitted gamblers, prostitutes, and saloon keepers to do business under certain well understood conditions. These entrepreneurs were required to make regular payoffs [to the police]. (1977, p. 32)

Consider the New York City Police Department. It was found to have serious corruption problems in 1895 (by the Lexow Committee), in 1900 (by the Mazet Committee), in 1913 (as a result of the Curran investigations), in 1932 (by the Seabury Committee), in 1942 (as a result of the Amen investigation),

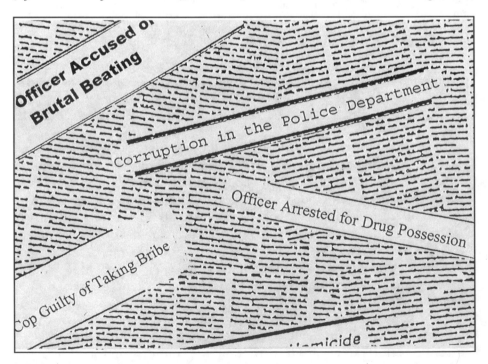

Police misconduct is frequently in the newspapers.

and in 1952 (by the Brooklyn Grand Jury) (Caiden 1977, p. 159). The Knapp
Commission followed with a fresh new corruption exposé in the 1970s. In the
mid-1980s, the department was rocked by the Buddy Boys scandal ("Drug
Corruption" 1986, p. 1). In 1993 the Mollen Commission noted widespread
drug extortion among members of the 75th Precinct.

New York City has a large department, with approximately 37,000 officers. It is unreasonable to assume on the one hand that all these officers will
be honest or on the other that any particular incident indicates that the entire
department is tainted. Yet New York displays the persistence of corruption
that characterizes many American police departments, large and small.

It is remarkable that many police departments have been as successful as
they have at controlling corruption problems. As S. Walker (1984) observed,
in the 1800s corruption *was* the business of many police departments. Today,
although many have periodic scandals, they are usually less pervasive than in
the past. Generally, present-day investigations tend to uncover only a small
number of deviant police officers. They rarely uncover all the corrupt officers, nor do they reveal the officers who know what is taking place and say
nothing.

Why does corruption continue to recur in police departments? There are
essentially four reasons: First, police officers are very powerful. By virtue of
their authority they encounter widespread opportunities for corruption.
They are constantly exposed to situations in which the decisions they make
can have a positive or negative impact on a person's freedom and well-being.
Citizens may try to influence this discretion by offering free coffee and meals,
money, sex, property—any item of value that will result in a favorable decision. Sometimes an offer can be extraordinarily tempting. The Knapp Commission identified payoffs as high as $80,000 in drug cases, and that was in
the late 1960s. Once officers begin to accept payoffs, they may become "addicted"— that is, they begin to depend on the extra income and spend accordingly. Some officers may become aggressive in seeking out corruption opportunities (Goldstein 1977, p. 200).

Second, the community and political environment are influential in establishing attitudes toward corrupt activities. Corruption in other government agencies, among prominent politicians, and in the business world enables police officers to rationalize their own behavior. P. V. Murphy and G.
Caplan make this point in the following statement:

> Operating in this larger environment, it is not surprising that police be-
> come cynical about their work and feel that "nothing is on the level."
> When they meet citizens from every walk of life who are willing to pay
> them to overlook the law ... some officers come to see themselves as "oper-
> ating in a world where [money is] constantly floating about, [and they
> would be] ... stupid and ... fainthearted ... not to allow some of [that
> money] to stick to their fingers." (1991, p. 248)

In police departments there are often many standards of behavior for officers to follow. In fact, there are so many standards that it is difficult to adhere to all of them. This multiplicity is also true of society in general. There
are many laws, some of which are often violated by citizens, particularly traffic laws. Officers see instances of such behavior all around them, in both the
public and private sector, among both the poor and the rich. Many officers
even come to believe that if they are to be good police officers (e.g., to help
people, maintain order, keep citizens from being afraid, make arrests, insure

a successful prosecution), they have to violate some of the rules they are supposed to follow.

Third, there is a widespread tolerance among citizens for some kinds of police deviance. Citizens encourage the police to violate due process and citizens' rights in order to arrest felons. Television regularly displays "good" policing as that which inflicts pain on suspected felons, even when their guilt or innocence is as yet undecided. Businesses encourage small corruptions by giving officers gratuities and other perks for preferential treatment. In sum, it is unclear whether citizens always want police to "play fair," thus encouraging their moral and economic corruption.

Fourth, patterns of deviance can themselves become standards of behavior. Officers may be introduced by their training officers, for example, to restaurants that provide meals discounted for police. When standards encompass deviant behavior, line officers become secretive. Enormous pressure is put on all officers not to discuss police behavior outside police ranks. Even nondeviant officers will not break the code of silence for fear of reprisal. This belief can carry over to the chief executive and managers in the department. In addition, executives and mangers may be blamed and lose their jobs if the deviance is exposed, even if they are not involved. G. E. Caiden (1977, p. 165) has identified characteristics of departments that have had widespread corruption problems. He refers to such departments as being systematically corrupt. These characteristics are presented in Inside Policing 8.7.

Inside Policing 8.7
Characteristics of Corrupt Police Departments

1. The department's professional code of ethics is contradicted in practice.

2. Police mangers and officers encourage, aid, and hide illegal and unethical behavior.

3. Nonparticipants in corrupt activities are penalized because they do not receive any of the benefits of corruption, and they may have to endure the displeasure of corrupt officers.

4. When corrupt officers are investigated, they will be protected; or if they are found guilty of corrupt practices, they will not be punished severely.

5. Officers who do not like the corruption in the department have no one to assist them within the department, and if they complain to someone outside, they may not be believed.

6. Officers who consider exposing the corrupt practices of other officers may be intimidated, even terrorized, in order to "shut them up." In some cases, such officers may actually have to be protected from bodily harm.

7. The officers who are corrupt develop rationalizations for their behavior. These include the arguments that "everyone else is doing it," that others [attorneys and judges] are corrupt, that police officers deserve "something extra" because they risk their lives or because the public doesn't appreciate them and pay them enough.

8. Eventually corrupt officers accept their behavior as "normal," as a way of doing business in police work. If and when they are exposed, they may be genuinely surprised that their corrupt behavior is considered deviant. They may even argue that they are being unfairly singled out because such behavior is commonplace for many officers.

9. Those responsible for investigating corruption tend to suggest, in effect, that the corrupt officers are only a few "rotten apples." ☞

10. Following a corruption scandal, efforts to reform the police department have only minimal influence in changing the attitudes of officers toward corruption, and the reforms are intended only to convince the public that something is being done to correct the problems.

Source: Adapted from G. E. Caiden. 1977. *Police Revitalization.* Lexington, MA: D.C. Heath and Company.

Caiden argues that real progress in dealing with corruption was made in the 1950s and 1960s because the police began to understand that the basic problem was systemic, not just the result of a few "rotten apples" (pp. 169–171). The **systemic theory of corruption** is that corruption stems from the nature of police work, and if anticorruption protocols are inadequate, corruption will spread throughout a police department. The **rotten-apple theory of corruption** is that corruption is limited to a small number of officers who were probably dishonest prior to their employment. The term *rotten apple* stems from the metaphor that a few rotten apples will spoil the barrel; in other words, a few bad officers can spoil a department. It was the most prevalent theory of corruption prior to the 1960s and 1970s. This explanation is compatible with the predispositional theory of police behavior. A systemic theory of corruption tends to support the sociological perspective of police behavior.

Caiden may be too optimistic about the extent to which police corruption has been controlled. The drug "wars" begun in the 1960s have significantly increased the opportunities for corruption, with the possibility of financial payoffs that far exceed other forms of corruption. And, there is some evidence that the rotten-apple theory is still influential. J. Dorschner's (1989) description of the Miami Police Department linked corruption to a rapid expansion in the number of personnel and an inadequate screening process. Yet, as he notes, the police department had extensive problems with political corruption even prior to its rapid expansion. Its political atmosphere provided the environment for the development of systemic corruption.

Some research has found support for the rotten-apple theory. Lersch and Mieczkowski (1996) suggested that particular kinds of officers are more likely to be involved in questionable use-of-force incidents. They noted that 7 percent of sworn personnel in a large Southeastern police department accounted for over one-third of the use-of-force complaints from 1991 to 1994. These officers were younger than their peers and had less experience. And, the incidents were more likely to result from proactive contacts with citizens.

The Prevalence of Police Deviance

It is difficult to gauge the extent of deviant behavior among the police. This is not surprising: People who commit illegal acts tend to keep them secret. In police departments, where peer support and loyalty are high, assessments of the extent of deviance will always be difficult to conduct and are likely to underestimate its true extent.

A few authors have assessed the prevalence of deviance in particular departments. Barker (1994) looked at five categories of deviance in what he called "South City." Using a questionnaire, he asked each officer to judge the extent to which individuals in the department engaged in or had engaged in each of the five patterns. His findings are presented in Case Study 8.2.

Case Study 8.2	
Perceived Extent of Police Occupational Deviance in South City	
Deviant Pattern	**Perceived Extent (%)**
Sleeping on duty	39.58
Police brutality	39.19
Sex on duty	31.84
Police perjury	22.95
Drinking on duty	8.05

A review of Case Study 8.2 shows that deviance in some categories was quite high. Four of 10 officers were thought to be sleeping on duty by their fellow officers and the same number to be indulging in police brutality. Slightly over one in five were believed to engage in police perjury. It is not reasonable to assume that these numbers represent police everywhere: generalizing from one research setting to the entire population is bad science. Barker's findings, however, because they represent a seemingly normal department, are troubling. And, there is evidence that other forms of deviance may be widespread.

Crank (1998) discussed two surveys to assess police deviance in one department in Illinois (Knowles 1996) and two in Ohio (Martin 1994). His overview presents two types of deviance not yet considered: racial and sexual harassment. Crank's discussion extends G. Sykes' (1996) analysis of these two surveys. Officers were asked in both surveys whether they had seen another officer harass citizen based on race or gender (see Case Study 8.3).

Case Study 8.3

Perceived Extent of Racial and Sexual Harassment in Illinois and Ohio

Racial Harassment

One out of every four officers in the Illinois survey (26.2 percent) and one in six in the Ohio survey (14.9 percent) stated that they had witnessed racial harassment by their fellow officers. If one extrapolates these percentages back to the base populations from which they were drawn, one can appreciate the magnitude of the harassment and its potential for the alienation of minority citizens. According to the 1994 crime reports, Ohio has 18,721 sworn "local," or municipal, officers, and Illinois, outside the Chicago Police Department (which declined to participate in the Illinois survey), has 16,131. Certainly not all of these officers are active on the streets. One can allow a generous estimate that 50 percent of a police department is in administrative support. This reduces the street-officer populations to 9,360 in Ohio and 8,065 in Illinois. Calculating the population estimates from these reduced figures, one arrives at 2,113 instances of police harassment in Illinois and 1,395 in Ohio in a single year's time, and excluding the largest department in either state. . . . Thus, in the two typical states, dominated by smaller police departments but with a sprinkling of big-city departments as well, police racism is by any reasoning a pervasive phenomenon. Nor are these figures in some way inflated by groups that har-

☞ bor ill will against the police: Keep in mind that these are numbers that the police are reporting about themselves.

Sexual Harassment

Six percent of the officers surveyed in Ohio stated that they had witnessed sexual harassment, and 8.6 percent of the respondents in Ohio agreed. These percentages sound relatively small until one recognizes that they are incidents where one officer (1) witnesses another officer display this behavior, and (2) is willing to tell an interviewer they he or she has witnessed the behavior. In other words, situations where officers won't come forward, and incidents where officers acted alone—a more likely occurrence . . .—aren't reported. Extrapolating back to the original populations, one begins to appreciate the magnitude of this activity. These numbers represent approximately 1,520 incidents in Ohio and 3,175 in Illinois, not including estimates by the state police or the city of Chicago.

Source: Adapted from John Crank. 1998. *Understanding Police Culture*. Cincinnati: Anderson Publishing Co., p. 212.

When these three surveys are considered together, they present a disturbing picture of police deviance. In all three departments, the findings suggested that deviance was widespread. In all three, there appeared to be strong peer support to cover up deviant activities. Finally, all three departments were typical—none had a particularly negative record of police corruption. These findings, when compared with findings presented in the previous discussion, suggest that police corruption may indeed be diverse in its types, widespread across departments, and hidden behind the secretive screen of department loyalties.

Police Sexual Misconduct

The research cited above provides insight into a poorly understood area of police behavior, sexual deviance. A similar view is provided by Kappeler (1993). In a review of litigation on police sexual misconduct, he found that the police lost 69 percent of the cases brought against them, a high number when one considers the average 10 percent for all other forms of civil litigation.

Many police have argued that much of this litigation stems from misunderstandings about police work. Many departments tend to justify sexual misconduct as a boys-will-be-boys attitude among their male personnel (see Sapp 1994). Others argue that sexual activity is consensual, a view sharply challenged by Kraska and Kappeler (1995). The image of consensuality, they contend, is an illusion. The substantial power differential that police have in exchanges with the public results in an image of consensuality, when in fact sexual relations may stem from a citizen's fear of the consequences if she or he fails to submit to an officer's implied or direct demands.

Drug Wars and Police Deviance

Deviance is a persistent problem. Unfortunately, some forms of deviance may be intensifying. Drug corruption, in many different forms, appears to be on the increase among police in the United States. As a new century begins, the United States is deeply involved in a drug war, carried out by municipal police, federal police, and military troops, aimed at controlling the use and distribution of illegal narcotics. The authors are not going to debate the merits of drug legalization here—suffice it to say that there are persuasive arguments for both the legalization and the criminalization of illegal substances. Our concern is with the negative impact of the current drug interdiction on U.S. police.

Kappeler, Sluder, and Alpert (1994) identify four types of drug corruption: (1) When officers use drugs, it is called **use corruption**. Kraska and Kappeler (1988) found that about 20 percent of the officers they studied in a medium-size department admitted that they smoked marijuana. (2) **Economic corruption** occurs when officers seek personal gain. Officers might, for example, keep drug money confiscated from dealers. Kappeler and his colleagues identify two additional types of corruption: (3) **police violence**, for example, which is the use of force to extract confessions, and (4) the **subjugation of defendant's rights** to obtain drug convictions. This includes police perjury and "flaking," the planting of drugs on a suspect by a police officer in order to acquire evidence.

Use of violence and subjugation of rights have been described by Crank and Caldero (1999) as **noble-cause corruption**, which occurs when police abandon ethical and legal means in order to achieve so-called good ends (see also Delattre 1996, pp. 190–214; Klockars 1983). Both violence and subjugation of rights may be used by police who are more concerned about the noble cause—getting bad guys off the streets, protecting victims and children— than about the morality of "technically" legal behavior. Noble-cause corruption occurs when officers break the law to do something about the drug problem.

According to Crank and Caldero, noble-cause corruption and economic corruption may be inversely related. They argue that police departments during the twentieth century have been somewhat successful in combating economic corruption among the police. This success has been accomplished in large part by instilling police with a mission to do something about crime. The consequence is that, as police economic corruption decreases, noble-cause corruption seems to increase. Police today may be less likely to commit crime for personal gain, but they also may be more likely to commit crime in order to carry out ends-oriented justice.

Two examples of drug corruption occurred in Philadelphia and Miami in the mid-1980s, as described in Case Study 8.4. In these examples, the reader can see the presence of both economic and noble-cause corruption. The severity of some of the corrupt activities, including murder, emphasizes why drug corruption has emerged as a critically important problem in law enforcement.

Since the Knapp Commission proceedings, New York has experienced another cycle of corruption and scandal. This time, however, the problems were different from those cited in preceding scandals because of their linkages to drugs. The Mollen Commission, established in 1993, also sought to identify the presence of police corruption. Kappeler, Sluder, and Alpert summarize the commission's findings as follows:

> Witnesses told the commission of systematic corruption that was strikingly similar to the [mid-1980s] Buddy-Boys case. Michael Dowd, a former officer in the 75th precinct, bluntly described how he and his peers routinely robbed

❖ ❖ ❖ ❖

Case Study 8.4

Examples of Corruption

Corruption in Philadelphia

In 1985, Mayor W. Wilson Goode stated that "The Philadelphia Police Department is in crisis." The attorney for the federal government who was involved in the investigation said that corruption was "entrenched" in the police department. A federal investigation of corruption in the 7,000-person department began in the early 1980s (the city also had corruption scandals in the 1920s, 1930s, and 1970s). By 1985, eight ranking officers and 26 officers had been arrested. A deputy commissioner of police was sentenced to 18 years in prison because he had used his office to establish a citywide extortion ring. An officer in the police department, who was involved in the investigation, participated in 500 instances (over two years) in which payoffs to police officers were either videotaped or recorded. Unlike previous corruption scandals, when the major problems had been related to gambling, prostitution, and liquor, the most serious problem in the current scandal involved narcotics.

Corruption in Miami

In the 1980s, the Federal Bureau of Investigation began a broad investigation into the Miami Police Department. The FBI believed that there was pervasive corruption in the department. This concern was the result of numerous incidents of illegal police activity, including charges of police officers murdering drug dealers, firing their weapons at drug dealers' homes, conspiring to sell police radios and badges, and being involved in "big time dope dealing." The unit charged with narcotics enforcement had $150,000 and several hundred pounds of marijuana stolen from its safe. By the mid-1980s, 75 police officers had been arrested. The most infamous of these were the seven officers called the Miami River Cops. Three of them were charged with the murder of a drug dealer. All were charged with being involved in selling drugs, including selling drugs from their police cars.

Sources: Adapted from *Law Enforcement News*. 1985. October 21: 1 and 5; and *Law Enforcement News*. 1986. December 30: 1 and 7.

---

crime victims, drug dealers, and arrestees of money, drugs, and anything else of value. Dowd revealed that many officers were receiving substantial sums for protecting illegal drug operations; Dowd's share amounted to $4,000 each week. Dowd told of officers routinely using drugs and alcohol while on duty, informing the Commission that he regularly snorted lines of cocaine off the dashboard of his police cruiser (Frankel 1993). Other witnesses told of extensive use of excessive force culminating in the physical and psychological brutalization of many citizens (Frankel and Stone 1993). (1994, p. 202)

Summary

Universalistic perspectives of police behavior are sociological, psychological, and organizational. Two particularistic theories are predisposition and socialization. The former explains police behavior in terms of the type of individual employed, while the latter is concerned with what happens after employment. Some of the more important studies of police behavior were made by Westley, Banton, Skolnick, Wilson, Muir, and Brown. These studies tend to support the importance of the socialization theory, because the influential factors that they have identified are all related to the experiences of being a police officer. More recent research has suggested that predispositional factors are also important.

There have also been attempts to relate police behavior and discretion to a number of specific variables: organizational, neighborhood, situational, and officer. Legal factors tend to determine the decision to arrest, but extralegal factors also sometimes play a role. In spite of a great deal of research on extra-legal factors, their actual contribution to the use of police discretion is unclear.

Police deviance includes abuse of authority and deviant acts (contrary to standards) committed in the normal course of the job. The latter can be misconduct in terms of rules or corruption, such as accepting gratuities, which the authors consider inappropriate. Police corruption is marked by periodic scandals in some departments, and corruption involving drugs appears to be increasing.

Discussion Questions

1. Define and give examples of the predispositional and socialization theories of police behavior.

2. Discuss the contributions of William Westley to the understanding of police behavior.

3. What is Van Maanen's perspective on police behavior?

4. Explain the three styles of policing identified by James Q. Wilson.

5. Identify and discuss Black's conditions under which officers decide to make an arrest.

6. Discuss organizational (departmental) and neighborhood variables considered important in police behavior.

7. What are meat eaters and grass eaters? Which is the greater problem in controlling police corruption? Why?

8. What is a police gratuity? Discuss the reasons why some individuals considered the acceptance of gratuities appropriate. Discuss the potential problems in the acceptance of police gratuities.

9. What is meant by noble-cause corruption? Provide an example.

10. What are the four kinds of drug corruption described by Kappeler, Sluder and Alpert? By Punch? How do the kinds described by Kappeler and his colleagues compare with those of Punch?

References

Adams, T. 1990. *Police Field Operations*. Englewood Cliffs, NJ: Prentice-Hall.

Alpert, G. and Smith, W. 1998. "Developing Police Policy: An Evaluation of the Control Principle." In L. Gaines and G. Cordner, eds. *Policing Perspectives: An Anthology.* pp. 353–362. Los Angeles: Roxbury Publishing Co.

Auten, J. 1988. "Preparing Written Guidelines." *F.B.I. Law Enforcement Bulletin* 57: 1–7.

Baker, M., 1985. *Cops: Their Lives in Their Own Words*. New York: Simon and Schuster.

Banton, M. 1965. *The Policeman in the Community*. New York: Basic Books.

Barker, T. 1996. *Police Ethics: Crisis in Law Enforcement*. Springfield, IL: Charles Thomas Publishers.

Barker, T. 1994. "Police Deviance Other than Corruption." In T. Barker D. and Carter, eds. *Police Deviance*, 3d ed., pp. 123–138. Cincinnati: Anderson Publishing.

Barker, T. and Carter, D. 1994. "A Typology of Police Deviance." In T. Barker and D. Carter, eds. *Police Deviance*. 3d ed., pp. 3–12. Cincinnati: Anderson Publishing.

Bayley, D. H. and Bittner, E. 1989. "Learning the Skills of Policing." In R. G. Dunham. G. P. Alpert, eds. *Critical Issues in Policing: Contemporary Readings*, pp. 87–110. Prospect Heights, IL: Waveland Press.

Black, D. 1973. "The Mobilization of Law." *Journal of Legal Studies, The University of Chicago Law School*, 2: 125–144.

——1980. *The Manners and Customs of the Police*. New York: Academic Press.

Brooks, L. W. 1989. "Police Discretionary Behavior: A Study of Style." In R. G. Dunham and G. P. Alpert, eds. *Critical Issues in Policing: Contemporary Readings, pp. 121–145. Prospect Heights, IL: Waveland Press.*

Brown, M. K. 1981. *Working the Street: Police Discretion*. New York: Russell Sage Foundation.

Caiden, G. E. 1977. *Police Revitalization*. Lexington, MA: D.C. Heath.

Caldero, M. 1997. "Value Consistency Within the Police: The Lack of a Gap." Paper presented at the annual meeting of the Academy of Criminal Justice Sciences, Louisville, KY., March.

Carter, D. 1985. "Police Brutality: A Model for Definition, Perspective, and Control." In A. S. Blumberg and F.. Niederhoffer, eds. *The Ambivalent Force*. pp. 321–330. New York: Holt, Rinehart and Winston.

Chambliss, W. 1997 "Policing the Ghetto Underclass: The Politics of Law and Law Enforcement." In B. Handcock and P. Sharp, eds. *Public Policy: Crime and Criminal Justice*. pp. 146–165. Upper Saddle River, NJ: Prentice-Hall.

Cordner, G. 1989. "Written Rules and Regulations: Are They Necessary?" *F.B.I. Law Enforcement Bulletin*. July: 17–21.

Crank, J. P. 1996. –The Construction of Meaning During Training for Parole and Probation." *Justice Quarterly* 31(2): 401–426.

Crank, J. P. 1998. *Understanding Police Culture*. Cincinnati: Anderson Publishing.

Crank, J. and Caldero, M. 1999. *Police Ethics: The Corruption of Noble Cause*. Cincinnati: Anderson Publishing.

Crank, J. and Langworthy, R. 1991. "An Institutional Perspective of Policing." *Journal of Criminal Law and Criminology* 8: 338–63.

Delattre, E. J. 1996. *Character and Cops: Ethics in Policing*. 3d ed. Washington, D.C.: American Enterprise Institute.

Dorschner, J. 1989. "The Dark Side of Force." in R. G. Dunham and G. P. Alpert, eds. *Critical Issues in Policing: Contemporary Readings*, pp. 250–270. Prospect Heights, IL: Waveland Press.

"Drug Corruption—The Lure of Big Bucks." 1986. *Law Enforcement Journal*, December 30: 1,4.

Fletcher, C. 1990. *What Cops Know*. New York: Pocket Books.

——. 1991. *Pure Cop*. New York: St. Martin's Press.

Fogelson, R. M. 1977. *Big-City Police*. Cambridge, MA: Harvard University Press.

Frankel, B. 1993. "Ex-NYC Officer Tells Stark Tale of Cops Gone Bad." *USA Today*, September 28: A-3.

Frankel, B. and Stone, A. 1993. "You'll Be in the Fold" by Breaking the Law." *USA Today*, September 30: A1, A2.

Friedrich, R. J. 1980. "Police Use of Force: Individuals, Situations, and Organizations." *Annals* 452: 82–97.

❖ ❖ ❖ ❖   Goldstein, H. 1977. *Policing a Free Society*. Cambridge, Mass: Ballinger Books.

Goldstein, J. 1998. "Police Discretion Not to Invoke the Criminal Justice Process: Low Visibility Decisions in the Administration of Justice." In G. F. Cole and M. G. Gertz, eds., *The Criminal Justice: Politics and Policies*, 7th ed., pp. 85–103. Belmont, CA: Wadsworth Publishing Co..

Greene, J. R. and Klockars, C. B. 1991. "What Police Do." In C. B. Klockars S. Mastrofski, eds. *Thinking About Police: Contemporary Readings, pp. 273–285. New York: McGraw-Hill.*

Grennan, S. A. 1988. "Findings on the Role of Officer Gender in Violent Encounters with Citizens," *Journal of Police Science and Administration* 15: 78–85.

Guyot, D. 1991. *Policing as Though People Matter*. Philadelphia: Temple University Press.

Herbert, S. 1997. *Policing Space: Territoriality and the Los Angeles Police Department*. Minneapolis: University of Minnesota Press.

Hopkins, E. J. 1931. *Our Lawless Police*. New York: Viking.

Human Rights Watch. 1998. *Shielded From Justice: Police Brutality and Accountability in the United States*. New York: Human Rights Watch.

Johnson, D. R. 1981. *American Law Enforcement*. St. Louis: Forum Press.

Kania, R. 1972. "Police Corruption in New York City." In A. W. Cohn and E. C. Viano, eds. *Police Community Relations: Images, Roles, Realities*, pp. 330–341. New York: J. B. Lippincott.

———. 1988. "Should We Tell the Police to Say 'Yes' to Gratuities?" *Criminal Justice Ethics*. 7: 37–48.

Kappeler, V. E. 1993. *Critical Issues in Police Liability*. Prospect Heights. IL: Waveland Press.

Kappeler, V. E., Sluder, R. D., and Alpert, G. 1994. *Forces of Deviance: Understanding the Dark Side of Policing*. Prospect Heights, IL: Waveland Press.

Klinger, D. 1994. "Demeanor on Crime: Why 'Hostile' Citizens Are More Likely to be Arrested." *Criminology*. 32-3: 475–493.

Klockars, C. 1983. "The Dirty Harry Problem." In C. Klockars, ed. *Thinking About Police: Contemporary Readings*, pp. 428–38. New York: McGraw-Hill.

Knapp Commission of Police Corruption. 1972. *Report on Police Corruption*. New York: George Braziller.

Knowles, J. J. 1996. *The Ohio Police Behavior Study*. Columbus, OH: Office of Criminal Justice Services.

Kraska, P. B. and Kappeler, V. E. 1988. "Police On-Duty Drug Use: A Theoretical and Descriptive Explanation." *American Journal of Police* 7 (1): 1–28.

———. 1995. "To Serve and Pursue: Exploring Police Sexual Violence Against Women." *Justice Quarterly* 12–1: 85–112.

———. 1999. "Exploring Police Sexual Violence Against Women." In L. K. Gaines and G. W. Cordner, eds. *Police Perspectives: An Anthology,* pp. 324–341. Los Angeles: Roxbury Publishing.

Lersch, K. and Mieczkowski, T. 1996. "Who Are the Problem-Prone Officers? An Analysis of Citizen Complaints." *American Journal of Police* 15(3): 23–44.

Manning, P. 1980. *The Narc's Game*. Cambridge, Mass: MIT Press.

———. 1989. "The Police Occupational Culture in Anglo-American Societies." In L. Hoover and J. Dowling eds. *Encyclopedia of Police Science*. New York: Garland Publishing.

———. 1997. *Police Work: The Social Organization of Policing*. 2d ed. Prospect Heights, IL: Waveland Press.

Martin, C. 1994. *Illinois Municipal Officers' Perceptions of Police Ethics*. Chicago: Illinois Criminal Justice Information Authority, Statistical Analysis Center.

Martin, S. E. 1980. *Breaking and Entering: Policewomen on Patrol*. Berkeley: University of California Press.

——. 1989. "Female Officers on the Move?" In R. G. Dunham and G. P. Alpert, eds. *Critical Issues in Policing: Contemporary Readings*, pp. 312–330. Prospect Heights, IL: Waveland Press.

——. 1990. *On the Move: The Status of Women in Policing*. Washington, D.C.: Police Foundation.

Mastrofski, S. 1981. "Policing the Beat: The Impact of Organizational Scale on Patrol Officer Behavior in Urban Residential Neighborhoods." *Journal of Criminal Justice* 4: 343–358.

Mastrofski, S. and Ritti, R. 1996 "Police Training and the Effects of Organization on Drunk Driving Enforcement." *Justice Quarterly* 13 (2): 291–320.

Mastrofski, S. and Uchida, C. 1993 "Transforming the Police." *Crime and Delinquency* 30–3: 330–358.

Maurer, M. 1993 *Young Black Men and the Criminal Justice System: A Growing National Problem*. Washington, D.C.: The Sentencing Project. U.S. Government Printing Office.

McNulty, E. 1993 "Generating Common Sense Knowledge Among Police Officers." *Symbolic Interaction*. 17: 281–294.

Muir, W. K. 1977. *Police: Streetcorner Politicians*. Chicago: University of Chicago Press.

Murphy, P. V. and G. Caplan. 1991. "Fostering Integrity." In W. A. Geller, ed. *Local Government Police Management*, pp. 239–271. Washington, D.C.: International City Management Association.

Niederhoffer, A. 1967. *Behind the Shield*. New York: Doubleday and Co.

Parks, R. 1982. "Citizen Surveys for Police Performance Assessment: Some Issues in Their Use." *Urban Interest* 4: 17–26.

"Philadelphia Unveils Anti-corruption Plan." 1985. *Law Enforcement News*, October 21: 1, 5.

Plitt, E. 1983. "Police Discipline Decisions." *Police Chief*, March: 95–98.

Punch, M. 1985. *Conduct Unbecoming: The Social Construction of Police Deviance and Control*. London: Tavistock Publications.

Rokeach, M., Miller, M., and Snyder, J. 1971. "The Value Gap Between Police and Policed." *Journal of Social Issues* 27–2: 155–171.

Rubinstein, J. 1973. *City Police*. New York: Farrar, Straus, and Giroux.

Sampson, R. and Lauritsen, J. 1997. "Racial and Ethnic Disparities in Crime and Criminal Justice in the United States." In M. Tonry, ed. *Ethnicity, Crime, and Immigration: Comparative and Cross-National Perspectives*, pp. 311–374. Chicago: University of Chicago Press.

Sapp, A. D. 1994. "Sexual Misconduct by Police Officers." In T. Barker and D. Carter, eds. *Police Deviance*, 3d edition, pp. 187–200. Cincinnati: Anderson Publishing.

Sherman, L. W. 1978. *Scandal and Reform: Controlling Police Corruption*. Berkeley: University of California Press.

——. 1985. "Causes of Police Behavior: The Current State of Quantitative Research." In A. S. Blumberg and E. Niederhoffer, eds. *The Ambivalent Force*, 3d ed., pp. 183–195. New York: Holt, Rinehart and Wilson.

——. 1988. "Becoming Bent." In A. Elliston and M. Feldbert, eds. *Moral Issues in Police Work*, pp. 253–265. Totowa, NJ: Rowan and Allanheld.

Sigler, R. T. and Dees, T. M. 1988. "Public Perception of Petty Corruption in Law Enforcement," *Journal of Police Science and Administration*. 6, 14–19.

Skolnick, J. and Bayley, D. 1986. *The New Blue Line: Police Innovation in 6 American Cities*. New York: The Free Press.

Skolnick, J. H. 1966. *Justice Without Trial*. New York: John Wiley and Sons.

Smith, D. 1987. "Police Response to Interpersonal Violence: Defining the Parameters of Legal Control." *Social Forces* 65: 767–782.

——. 1980. "The Neighborhood Context of Police Behavior." In A. Reiss and M. Tonry, eds. *Communities and Crime*. Chicago: University of Chicago Press.

Sykes, G. 1986. "Street Justice: A Moral Defense of Order-Maintenance Policing." *Justice Quarterly* 3(4): 467–512.

❖ ❖ ❖ ❖

———. 1996. "Police Misconduct: A Different Day and Different Challenges." Subject to Debate: A Newsletter of the Police Executive Research Forum. March, April. 10–3: 1,4–5.

Van Maanen, J. 1973. "Observations on the Making of Policeman," *Human Organization.* 32, 407–418.

———. 1978. "The Asshole". In P. K. Manning and J. Van Maanen, eds. *Policing: A View From the Streets*, pp. 221–238. Santa Monica, CA: Goodyear Publishing.

Walker, S. 1984. " 'Broken Windows' and Fractured History: The Use and Misuse of History in Recent Patrol Analysis." *Justice Quarterly* 1: 57–90.

Walsh, W. F. 1986. "Patrol Officer Arrest Rates." *Justice Quarterly.* Vol. 3, 271–290.

Wasserman, R. 1992. "Government Setting." In G. Garmire, ed. *Local Government Police Management,* 2d ed. Washington, D.C.: International City Management Association.

Westley, W. A. 1953. "Violence and the Police," *American Journal of Sociology.* vol. 59, 34–42.

———. 1970. *Violence and the Police.* Cambridge, MA: MIT Press.

Wilson, J. Q. 1968. *Varieties of Police Behavior.* Cambridge, MA: Harvard University Press.

Wilson, J.Q. and Kelling, G. 1982. "Broken Windows: The Police and Neighborhood Safety." *Atlantic Monthly* 127: 29–38.

Worden, R. 1989. "Situational and Attitudinal Explanations of Police Behavior: A Theoretical Reappraisal and Empirical Assessment." *Law and Society Review* 23: 667–711.

For a listing of websites appropriate to the content of this chapter, see "Suggested Websites for Further Study" (p. xv). ✦

Force and Coercion

Chapter Outline

Key Terms	
abuse of authority	coercive approach
administrative search	command voice
anticipating danger	contact stage
assailant geographies	continuum of force
coercion	cultural themes

Key Terms (continued)	
deadly force	imperative approach
definitional approach	mere presence
deterrence	pain compliance
edge control	plain-view doctrine
excessive force	police brutality
exigent circumstances	processing stage
exit stage	stopping power
firm grips	symbolic assailants
fleeing-felon rule	third degree
force, or coercion	verbalization
impact techniques	working notions of normal force

Police departments represent the legitimate force of government in internal state matters. Their authority is derived primarily from law. The police are charged with enforcing substantive criminal laws, such as laws against robbery and rape, and they are expected to operate within procedural laws, such as having probable cause to make an arrest and advising suspects of their rights. In addition to these legal guidelines, the police are guided by departmental policies and procedures.

The use of force is central to the police craft. Police carry the legal authority to maintain order, to gain compliance, and to kill if need be. They are granted this authority in order to shield victims from dangerous felons; to control unruly, hostile, or physically abusive citizens; and to protect immediate threats to human life.

Use of force is the most controversial aspect of the legal authority of the police. Yet its necessity is inescapable. It is a skill, which means that it is a means to an end—the preservation of orderly social relations as society perceives them. Consequently, police use of force in the United States should be considered in the broader context of how it contributes to democratic relations among citizens.

Where does the right to use force come from? How can society reconcile the use of force with the democratic principle of equality? In 1970 E. Bittner, briefly discussed in Chapter 1, provided important insights into the use of force. According to Bittner, the use of force can be justified in two ways. The first is self-defense: people can use force to defend themselves if they have a realistic belief that they are in danger. The second is based on the inherent police power to address matters of health, welfare, order, and safety; that is, the police are a "mechanism for the distribution of situationally justified force in society" (1995, p. 129).

Why does society need a police mechanism for the distribution of force? Historically, U.S. society has moved from the use of force to the use of democratic, rational processes for solving problems and disagreements among citizens. Yet it is impossible to abandon altogether the use of force in the pursuit of democratic justice. In order to preserve democratic processes, society grants to police an exclusive right that is not permitted to citizens: the use of force to achieve democratic ends.

Many students of police behavior think that "force" is violent behavior by the police. That is incorrect. **Force, or coercion,** occurs any time the police attempt to have citizens act in a particular way. Force can be very mild, such as a simple request to see a driver's license. Even a request, though, is a use of force because it carries in it the authority of the state to back up the request with greater force and the implicit recognition, by citizen and officer alike, that "no" is not an acceptable answer. Because the police carry the governmental authority to intervene in a citizen's activities, all police-citizen interactions carry elements of force, even when officers are not consciously trying to be forceful. Consequently, this section will discuss police-citizen interactions in order to shed light on social contexts in which the use of force emerges.

Police use of force and its justifications are determined by two factors. The first is formal training according to the state code and limits on the use of force determined by local departmental regulations and by due-process constraints. The second factor is local police cultures, which represent understandings of police territorial responsibilities, danger, and the control of unpredictable situations.

The chapter will then turn to excessive use of force. At what point does force become excessive, even brutal? Many observers contend that the excessive use of force is increasing in the United States today, although others believe that police are encountering increasing problems that require it. The chapter will review literature on overuse of force and then discuss its most controversial aspect, the use of deadly force.

Police-Citizen Interactions

How often do encounters between police and citizens become situations in which force is used? Information is provided by a number of scholarly studies and by a questionnaire provided by the Bureau of Justice Statistics.

Context of Force

One of the most extensive and important studies of police-citizen encounters was conducted by A. J. Reiss (1967). He reported on more than 5,000 observations of police-citizen interactions that took place in areas that were racially diverse and had different crime rates. About 86 percent of the encounters were reactive, resulting from citizen requests. About 14 percent of the encounters were proactive, initiated by police officers. Police were more likely to experience antagonism or injury in proactive encounters, primarily because, unlike reactive situations, the person or persons they stopped did not request assistance from the police.

Reiss also found that approximately 60 percent of citizens behaved in either a detached or civil manner toward police, about 20 percent were agitated (mildly upset), and about 10 percent were antagonistic. Almost all such antagonism came from suspects. Officers behaved in a businesslike or routine manner in about 74 percent of the encounters, were personal (jovial, or humorous) in about 15 percent, and were hostile or derisive in about 11 percent. Police were more likely to be hostile or derisive when citizens were agitated or antagonistic. Reiss also noted that police behavior was closely related to citizen behavior; if a citizen was antagonistic, the officer would most likely respond in the same manner. The importance of a citizen's attitude in the exercise of police discretion was noted in Chapter 8.

Of the 5,000 plus encounters, the police made only 225 arrests, less than 5 percent. About 50 percent of the persons arrested openly challenged police authority; the challenge, however, was more likely to be verbal than physical. Of those arrested, 98 (42 percent) were treated "firmly," while only 21 (9 percent) were handled with "gross" force. These figures means that in all the police-citizen encounters observed, only about 2 percent involved any type of physical force. None involved the use of lethal, or deadly, force.

Reiss' research suggested that police-citizen encounters were most likely to result from citizen requests for help and that, in most cases, police treated citizens in a businesslike or routine manner. Most encounters were like those of any business providing a service to a client; they involved exchanges of information in a friendly or civil manner. Police were rarely antagonistic toward citizens, and when they were, it was typically in response to citizen-initiated hostilities. Overall, police officers infrequently made arrests, and when they did, they rarely used physical force.

Another important study of police-citizen encounters was conducted by R. E. Sykes and E. E. Brent (1983), who analyzed more than 3,000 police-citizen encounters. They identified several different types of situations. Three of the most important are listed below:

1. *Hazardous*: Calls that officers believe are potentially risky and personally rewarding but possibly depressing. *Examples*: assaults and purse snatchings.

2. *Annoying*: Calls that are neither risky nor personally rewarding but possibly depressing. *Examples*: unwanted guests, loud parties, disturbances involving children, and failure to pay a bill.

3. *Boring*: Calls that are neither risky nor rewarding but possibly slightly depressing for some officers. *Examples*: taking reports and persons drinking.

Sykes and Brent found that the most common initial police response was definitional, occurring about 83 percent of the time. Police almost always spoke first when dealing with citizens; thus, they had the opportunity to direct the discussion with their questions. The second most common initial response was imperative, occurring in about 17 percent of encounters. Researchers did not find the coercive response used initially in any police-citizen encounter. It was eventually used, however, if citizens did not cooperate with the officers. Even then, the most common officer response was to repeat the initial approach one or more times in order to obtain cooperation.

From Sykes and Brent's research, it is clear that officers first try the definitional approach and if a citizen does not cooperate, will frequently repeat it. If cooperation is not forthcoming or the citizen's behavior becomes threatening or too abusive, officers will become imperative and coercive. What is not clear, however, is how this sequence should proceed in a given situation. Should the department provide specific guidance or should it be left to an officer's discretion? For instance, if one officer used the definitional approach several times with an uncooperative citizen, is this officer "better" than one who uses it only once before making threats or using force? How can one judge which approach is better?

D. H. Bayley (1986) studied police interactions with citizens in Denver. He focused on two types of situations in which officers made tactical choices about appropriate actions—domestic disturbances and traffic stops. This discussion will focus only on the traffic stops because of recent changes in the manner in which many police departments respond to domestic violence calls. Bayley divided police-citizen interaction into three stages: The **contact stage** describes tactical choices made when the officers first approach citizens. The **processing stage** is concerned with decisions made during the interaction between contact and exit. The **exit stage** describes strategies used to end contact with the citizen.

Bayley identified several contact actions by police officers in traffic stops. In some situations, more than one action was used. These actions are listed in Case Study 9.1. Many are similar to the findings of Sykes and Brent.

Asking drivers or passengers questions or for documents (**definitional approach**) was the initial police action in a large majority of times. Giving or-

---

Case Study 9.1
Actions at a Traffic Stop

Initial Actions of Police Officers at Traffic Stops

Action	Use (%)
1. Asked driver for documents	88.4
2. Explained reason for stop	28.0
3. Asked driver if he knew reason for stop	25.6
4. Had driver leave the vehicle	20.1
5. Allowed driver to leave vehicle	16.5
6. Asked passengers for documents	15.9
7. Allowed or ordered passengers out of vehicle	9.2
8. Ordered driver and/or passengers to remain in vehicle	4.2

Processing Actions of Police Officers at Traffic Stops

Action	Use (%)
1. Checked whether vehicle and driver were wanted	59.1
2. Discussed nature of traffic violation	27.4
3. Searched vehicle from outside or inside	25.0
4. Gave roadside sobriety test	12.8
5. Body-searched driver and/or passenger	7.3
6. Questioned drivers and/or passengers	3.7

Exit Actions of Police Officers at Traffic Stops

Action	Use (%)
1. Issued traffic citation	43.3
2. Gave admonishment or warning only	20.7
3. Arrested driver (DUI or other offense)	15.8
4. Released without admonishment or warning	13.8
5. Issued citation and gave warning	12.8
6. Completed "contact" card (recorded information about driver)	9.8
7. Transported or arranged transportation for driver	2.4
8. Impounded vehicle	1.8
9. Insisted driver proceed on foot	1.8
10. Arrested passenger	1.8

Totals do not add up to 100% because more than one alternative was used in many traffic stops. In addition, some categories have been combined.

Source: D. H. Bayley. 1986. "The Tactical Choices of Police Patrol Officers." *Journal of Criminal Justice* 14: 329–348.

ders (**imperative approach**) was sometimes used. Bayley's findings revealed the complicated nature of police-citizen transactions. In the three areas—contact, processing, and exit—officers used at least 28 different actions. By carefully reviewing the first actions, one can see how the use of coercion is part and parcel of police work, even when not directly used. The initial acts all involve various levels of coercion, from the relatively mild, "asked passengers for documents", which is not coercive but carries the potential for a stronger response, to the more significant "ordered driver to remain in vehicle." Under processing actions, coercive behavior includes "body search." Exit actions range from the mildly coercive "gave admonishment" to the quite serious "arrested driver." Moreover, the original stop itself represents a seizure, an aggressive intervention of the state into the affairs of citizens.

This research gives some understanding how practical applications of force are integral to police work. This realization may be uncomfortable for citizens. Yet, if they fail to see how force is intertwined with the daily routines of police work, they will not understand what the police are about.

Bayley and J. Garofalo (1989) studied 62 police officers in New York City to determine the extent to which they used some type of violence, including verbal aggression. They identified 467 potentially violent situations, of which 168 were proactive. Of these situations, although reports suggested possible violence, such as a fight or the reported presence of weapons, only 78 (17 percent) actually involved visible conflict when the police arrived. In 70 of these cases, the violence was not physical but only involved verbal threats or gestures. Police used physical force against citizens 37 times, and citizens used it against the police 11 times. Police force was almost always limited to "grabbing and restraining." Police use of deadly force was not observed.

This study, like the preceding ones, indicates that police work rarely involves the use of violence, though the use or threat of force is ever present. However, a word of caution must be used in evaluating these studies. They all used researchers who observed officers' behaviors. It is possible that officers' behaviors were influenced by the presence of an observer.

The use of violence is one of the most important areas of study. The potential consequences to both the victim and officer can be severe, including emotional trauma and the possibility of either physical injury or death, particularly when the police use physical force.

The Police-Public Contact Survey

In 1995 the Bureau of Justice Statistics prepared the first national questionnaire designed to assess overall use of force by the police during police-citizen contacts (Greenfeld, Langan, and Smith 1997). The Police-Public Contact Survey was conducted of representative American households, who were asked about their contacts with the police during the 12 months prior to the interview. A total of 6,421 households were interviewed over three periods (May, June, and July, 1996), with one-third interviewed during each monthly period. The authors looked at the prevalence of citizen contacts with the police, reasons for citizen contacts, and police actions during citizen contacts. It estimated from the interviews found that 44.6 million citizens had a face-to-face contact with a police officer. In most instances, citizens initiated the contact. An estimated 1.2 million people were handcuffed. Although this number may seem large, it represents only 2.6 percent of the citizens police came into contact with. Survey findings are presented in Case Study 9.2.

As has been shown, the actual or potential use of force is a common occurrence in police-citizen encounters. Some uses of force are mild and may not be noticed by citizens or police officers. In conclusion, there are a wide variety of uses of force to control and direct different kinds of circumstances.

Case Study 9.2

Highlights From the Police-Public Contact Survey

Prevalence of Citizen Contact With Police

- An estimated 44.6 million persons (21 percent of the population age 12 or older) had a face-to-face contact with a police officer during 1996.

- Men, whites, and persons in their 20s were the most likely to have face-to-face contact. Hispanics and African-Americans were about 70 percent as likely whites.

- Nearly three in ten persons with a contact in 1996 reported multiple contacts with police during the year.

Reasons for Citizen Contact With Police

- An estimated 33 percent of residents who had contact with police had asked for or provided the police with some type of assistance.

- An estimated 32 percent of those who had contact with police had reported a crime, either as a victim or a witness.

- Reporting traffic tickets and being involved in traffic accidents were common reasons for police contacts.

- Just under one-third of those contacts were police initiated; for most, nearly one-half, the citizen initiated the contact. (The remainder were unclear from the data.)

- Teenagers were most likely to have a police-initiated contact, and persons age 60 or older were the likely.

- Persons age 60 or older were the most likely to have a citizen-initiated contact with the police, and teenagers were likely.

- Hispanics had a higher level of police-initiated contacts and a lower level of self-initiated contacts.

Police Actions During Contacts With Citizens

- An estimated 1.2 million persons were handcuffed during 1996, or about 0.6 percent of the population, aged 12 or older.

- Men, minorities, and persons under the age of 30 represented a relatively large percentage of those handcuffed.

- An estimated 500,000 persons (0.2 percent of the population aged 12 or older) were hit, held, pushed, choked, threatened with a flashlight, restrained by a police dog, threatened or actually sprayed with chemical or pepper spray, threatened with a gun, or experienced some other form of force. Of those, about 400,000 were also handcuffed.

Adapted from Source: Lawrence Greenfeld, Patrick Langan, and Steven Smith. 1997. *Police Use of Force: Collection of Statistical Data.* Washington, D.C.: Bureau of Justice Statistics.

The Use of Force

This section will look at two different but related ways police departments provide direction in the use of force. These ways are formal training in levels of force and informal, cultural standards about the use of force in routine encounters.

Training

Officers are trained to use a **continuum of force**, from the least to the greatest, to match the intensity of the suspect's resistance. Ideally an officer employs the least force necessary to solve a problem, restrain a suspect, or control a situation. J. Skolnick and J. Fyfe's (1993) description of levels of force (with authors' comments) is presented below.

Force Continuum

1. *Mere presence.* At the lowest level of force, the simple presence of an officer is usually enough to control most situations. Mere presence operates on the assumption that the visible authority of the state is sufficient to deter criminal wrongdoing. As a wide body of research has shown, however, the passive authority of the state alone is insufficient to deter illegal behavior or gain compliance. As J. Q. Wilson (1968) observed 30 years ago, officers have to get personally involved—they have to develop personal skills in the use of coercion in order to control some kinds of problems.

2. *Verbalization.* This stage is sometimes called verbal force. When officers speak, they are taught to do so persuasively. Officers verbalize their commands in "adult to adult" communications. That is, they communicate on the presumption that they are talking to adults who will understand and comply with their requests: Example: "Sir, would you please step out of the car."

3. *Command voice.* Command voice is more vibrant and is issued in the form of an order. Skolnick and Fyfe (1993) provide the following example: "Sir, I asked you for your vehicle papers once. Now I'm *telling* you to give them to me *now.*"

4. *Firm grips.* Physical grasps of the body direct a suspect when and where to move. They are intended to control a suspect's physical movements but are not intended to cause pain. They can be restraining, holding, or lifting. *Example:* Two persons are attempting to fight. An officer grabs one person to hold him back, or two or more officers working as a team may separate the two persons or may "swarm" one person.

5. *Pain compliance.* A suspect's compliance is gained by causing pain. Various techniques are taught that enable officers to cause pain without lasting injury. *Example:* A person the officer is attempting to handcuff pulls away, and the officer twists the suspect's arm in order to put on the cuffs.

❖ ❖ ❖ ❖

6. *Impact techniques.* Impact techniques involve physical contact between the suspect and an officer's body or nonlethal device. They are intended to knock down or incapacitate a dangerous suspect who has not responded to other techniques. Included among impact techniques are increasingly popular less-than-lethal weapons, including bean bags shot from a shotgun and O.C. pepper spray. *Example:* A suspect under the influence of drugs resists the police so vigorously that she cannot be controlled. She is struck with a baton, or is sprayed in the face, or stunned with an electrical weapon such as the Taser.

    Two new less-than-lethal weapons are currently being developed. Sticky foams may be fired from a large gun from 35 feet away. They act like contact cement, sticking the suspect to the floor or to whatever he or she touches. "Dazzler" light and laser weapons use brilliant pulses of light to distract, disorient, and control violent suspects and potentially violent crowds (Miller 1995, pp. 485–486).

7. *Deadly force.* The highest level is force that is capable of killing a suspect. The purpose is usually to incapacitate a suspect who presents an immediate and potentially deadly threat to another person, not to kill the suspect. Death, however, is a frequent by-product. Skolnick and Fyfe describe three uses of deadly force: the carotid hold (or sleeper hold), which induces unconsciousness in a suspect and can be deadly in practice; the bar arm-control hold, in which the forearm is squeezed against the neck to cut off the flow of air; and the use of a gun. *Example:* A suspect vigorously resists arrest, and the officer gets behind him and "chokes him out" in order to gain control of the suspect and to place him in handcuffs.

One type of nonlethal force available to the police is the baton. (Photo: Mark C. Ide)

In the continuum of force, death is indicated as a likely outcome at only the last two levels, but, of course, it can result from a wide range of circumstances. For example, citizens are sometimes killed when struck with a nightstick. These two levels of force are not intended to kill or seriously injure citizens; rather, the intent is only to control them.

As discussed earlier, there are often differences of opinion concerning what is and is not appropriate when police force is used. One important factor in determining appropriate use is the actual or perceived threat posed by the person resisting police authority. This threat potential is assessed not only in terms of the nature of the threat or actual resistance but also by the physical size of the person in question, whether he or she is under the influence of drugs or alcohol, or whether he or she has or might have a weapon. In addition, any prior knowledge about the person and his or her potential for danger would be important. Also, if the police officer is biased or has had "dangerous" experiences with members of a minority group, then certain types of minority persons (e.g., young, black men) may be perceived to be potentially more dangerous than other people.

Areas of Training

The training regimen for the use of force is elaborate. Particular areas of training related to the use of force are discussed below.

Firearms. For most police trainees, the most popular training is in firearms (Marion 1998). It is frequently the highlight of the academy. Traditional firearms training is gradually giving way to situationally based training, which includes simulated firearms scenarios and the use of mobile targets. "Shoot-don't shoot" scenarios are used to teach officers to use restraint in the use of deadly force. Among the most popular of these are FATS (Firearms Training Systems), which present trainees with scenarios whose outcomes are manipulated by a specialist. Scenarios are presented whose outcome is uncertain and typically call for the unholstering of a weapon. Many outcomes, however, do not call for the discharge of a weapon, and officers learn to react quickly in order *not* to shoot. When they shoot, a laser mounted on the weapon shows the number of target hits and locations of the hits.

OC spray. Officers are required to train in the use of OC (oleoresin) spray. Some departments require that trainees submit to being sprayed; in others, being sprayed is voluntary. OC's location on the force continuum also varies. In the continuum presented above, it is located at level 6 as an impact technique. Some departments, however, consider it less powerful than a baton. The North Carolina Police Department, for example, locates OC spray just above mace and below hard hands, the PR-24 (baton), and swarming techniques (Lamb and Friday 1997). According to this perspective, officers are taught to use OC spray when they think a person is about to become belligerent, in order to prevent the escalation of force (Trimmer 1993).

Self-defense. Officers are taught a variety of techniques for self-defense. N. Marion (1998) describes self-defense training as follows:

> Recruits may be taught some "come-along" or "hand holds" (Peak 1993) as well as pressure points. . . . By the end of the University Academy, recruits learn the Infra-Orbital [under the base of the nose], the Mandibular Angle [behind the ear] and the Hypoglossal [under the jaw] pressure

points (Faulkner 1994). They also learn take-downs and proper handcuffing techniques. The force continuum is stressed in self-defense training, where cadets are taught to use no more force than necessary to subdue a subject. But once again, officer safety is the primary concern of all the training. (1998, p. 68)

Officer survival. Central to many training programs are classes on "officer survival." Such classes deal with the major risks faced by police officers—officer stress, suicide, and threats. Officers are taught how to deal with the murder of a partner, about the police officers' memorial in Washington, D.C., and about the federal pension their spouse will receive if they are killed. They are exposed to the bureaucratic paperwork associated with death. Extremely violent encounters, though rare in practice, are central to training. Officer survival is also a component of many other classes. Classes on police procedure instruct officers that concerns over safety provide a legal justification for a wide variety of actions, including pat-downs. Finally, it is not unusual for officers to see training films emphasizing the hazards of police work.

Flashlights. A flashlight is infrequently thought of as a weapon, yet many officers use flashlights in just that way. As T. McEwen (1997) noted, policies on the use of flashlights are often ambiguous. Some departments provide policies forbidding the use of flashlights as weapons. When a flashlight is considered a weapon, it is regarded only in a backup capacity. The policy in one department McEwen assessed stated that "The department does not recognize the flashlight as a formal policy weapon." Recognizing that it may be needed in some circumstances, the policy further observed that "when a flashlight is utilized in an application of force, whether to restrain or to effect an arrest, or in defense against an attack, it will be considered a weapon and all requirements pertaining to the use of force and the reporting of such force will be applicable." McEwen concludes that flashlights will be used as less-than-lethal weapons and that policy needs to recognize this fact and bring flashlights under use of force policy (1997, p. 51).

Canines. An emerging area of interest in the use of force is the use of K-9 dog patrols. Many police departments use police canines for a number of purposes: to search for drugs, explosives, and individuals who might be trying to avoid or escape from the police and to control individuals and crowds. Many officers also believe that the use of dogs to search for suspects who might be armed reduces the possibility that the officers will be injured or killed. Although they are not trained to do so, some handlers permit their dogs to bite as a "reward."

The use of canines varies by department. Some departments do not recognize them as a level of force, others do. K-9's are listed by the North Carolina Police Department at a level just above swarm techniques and below deadly force (Lamb and Friday 1997). A. Campbell, R. Berk, and J. Fyfe (1998) argue that the widespread use of canines in some departments requires a revision in thinking about the use of force. In a study of the Los Angeles Police Department and the Los Angeles Sheriffs' Department, they found that the use of canines was routine, and encounters often ended with bites, many serious. Inside Policing 9.1 describes uses associated with canines.

Inside Policing 9.1
Canines and Police Use of Force

Should dogs be thought of as a kind of police use of force? Campbell, Berk, and Fyfe argue that they should. The use of dogs is common. Moreover, dog bites are frequently severe. Consider the following observations:

> The data show that using police dogs as a means of force has been common in the Los Angeles area. From the middle of 1990 through the middle of 1992, LAPD's (Los Angeles Police Department) police dogs (which varied in number between 13 and 15) bit 44 percent of the 539 suspects they helped to apprehend. A total of 37 percent (n-86) were bitten badly enough that they were admitted to hospitals. As far as we have been able to determine, this was a greater number of hospitalizing injuries than was caused by all the noncanine officers in the department combined during the period. In 1990 alone, this bite-to-use ratio—the LAPD term for the percentage of persons bitten among those apprehended after canines had arrived at the scene—was 81 percent. For the LASD (Los Angeles Sheriffs Department), the bite-to-use ratio was 36 percent

(119 bitten of 335 persons apprehended) over the slightly different period we studied. No deaths have resulted in Los Angeles, but some victims were permanently disfigured, whereas others have experienced persistent physiological and/or psychological problems. Indeed, survivors of police shootings in Los Angeles (and the vast majority do survive) typically have injuries less severe and less enduring than are suffered by the LAPD's canine bite victims. (1998, p. 543)

The study observes that the use of canines frequently lacks the rigor of policy that accompanies the use of other kinds of less-than-lethal and lethal weaponry. When policies were in place, they were enforced in an incomplete and perfunctory way. Moreover, minority-group members suffered a disproportionate number of dog bites, raising the specter that they might be used in a discriminatory way (see also Beers 1992). The authors concluded that because of the hazardous and injurious consequence of dog bites, the implementation and review of department policy regarding canines should be conducted in a rigorous manner with other uses of force.

Gear for Use-of-Force Encounters

M. R. Miller (1995) describes the proper uniform and equipment officers need for encounters with citizens that might require force. The most important item of uniform is their belt. A "Sam Brown" belt is the officer's support system because it contains the various systems that he or she is required to carry. The next most important piece of equipment is the duty weapon and holster. Departments have strict rules on what kinds of hand-guns can be carried. Officers also may carry backup weapons, which Miller observes are considered by officer-survival experts to be essential. The reloading system is also important. It should be effective for both weapons. Speed-loaders—rapid loading mechanisms for a handgun—are required in many departments.

Officers also carry a variety of nonlethal weapons. They carry a PR-24 (baton) or similar "tactical" baton for striking and throwing. The stems of PR-24s are sometimes fitted with lead. Chemical agents such as OC spray are carried. Officers typically carry two pairs of handcuffs; today many of these are plastic cuffing strips rather than traditional metal handcuffs. Some officers carry knives. Sometimes their leather gloves are fitted with lead powder in the knuckles. Finally, officers wear a ballistic vest. Vests are bullet resistant but vary in their ability to retard ballistic impact. Skolnick and Bayley capture the implications of dress and training for police work:

> Policing in the United States is very much like going to war. Three times a day in countless locker rooms across the land, large numbers of men and a growing number of women carefully arm and armor themselves for the day's events. They begin by strapping on flak jackets, designed to stop most bullets, under their regulation blue, white, or brown shirts. Then they pick up a wide, heavy, black leather belt and hang around it the tools of their trade: gun, mace, handcuffs, bullets. When it is fully loaded, they swing the belt around their hips with the same practiced motion of the gunfighter in Western movies, snugging it down and buckling it in front.

> Dressing them to kill, we expect them to keep order so that we may live in security. What a colossal act of faith on our part; what a tremendous responsibility on theirs. (1986, pp. 141–142)

The use of force is not a random exercise but occurs in specific settings under known circumstances. Consider the act of arrest as an example. Arrest is a circumstance where the likelihood of use of force is heightened. Simply put, citizens do not like to surrender their freedom. Inside Policing 9.2 gives insight into the use of force involved arrest and custody.

Inside Policing 9.2
Use of Force During Arrest

An officer can use whatever force is reasonable and necessary to make the arrest, to overcome resistance, and to prevent escape. The key is that force has to be reasonable. A suspect may legally counter the use of excessive force with force sufficient to fend off the officer's use of force. Further, the officer, the police chief, and the city may be sued. When a police officer encounters resistance, he or she is taught to use escalating levels of force until resistance is overcome. The officer must keep in mind that increasing levels of force have to be reasonable—a police officer cannot meet mild resistance with deadly force. The purpose of force is to effect an arrest. If an officer encounters a suspect who resists, the officer should not necessarily back down.

While it might make sense to back away and wait for assistance, the law says they don't lose their right to self-defense by the use of force to effect the arrest, overcome resistance, or prevent the suspect's escape. In almost every case, the suspect's actions will indicate the level of force used to arrest him. When a suspect arms himself with a deadly weapon, it is generally reasonable to respond with deadly force.

Even if an arrest may be later found to be unlawful, a suspect still has a legal obligation to submit to arrest. A citizen may only resist an excessive use of force. If a citizen resists an arrest, lawful or not, the suspect has committed a separate crime of resisting arrest.

Source: Adapted from Mark R. Miller. 1995. *Police Patrol Operations*. Placerville, CA: Copperhouse Publishing. 298–299.

Police Culture and the Use of Force

The use of force is also affected by informal standards of police culture. "Culture" refers to what E. Reuss-Ianni calls "precinct street cop culture," which carries the "values, and thus the ends, towards which officers individually and in task groups strive" (1983, p. 8). Although each department has its own culture, J. Crank (1998) has identified a wide variety of **cultural themes**, or building blocks of culture, that are so similar across departments that police officers generally can be described as participating in a police culture. As building blocks, these themes have two features. First, they are areas of activity. Second, according to E. McNulty (1994), they also carry with them ways of common-sense thinking about the activity. Several cultural themes affect how police officers use force. These themes are summarized in Inside Policing 9.3.

Inside Policing 9.3
Cultural Themes Affecting Police Use of Force

1. **Force**. Force is a theme as well as a subject of formal police training.

   Whether legal, questionable, or illegal, force is bound up in the day-to-day doing of police work. . . . Department policy reflects administrative rather than street imperative and is typically viewed as more organizational "bullshit." It's not that cops don't believe in the necessity of due process in a democracy or the imperatives of the administration, nor is it that, by nature, cops are authoritarian. It's just that when things get wild, when an officer has to maintain the edge and is burning with energy and fear, other considerations become irrelevant. (1998, p. 65)

2. **Stopping Power.** Stopping power is the symbolic and real importance of guns (handguns) to the police. Guns are central to police culture. Police officers have been raised in families where guns are normal fare, and guns symbolize their sense of traditional individualism. Guns bring to the foreground the idea of personal responsibility. They represent the apex of an officer's street skills and are used at the defining moments of a police officer's career: confrontation with an dangerous and armed offender.

3. **Edge Control**. Edge control means that an officer (1) makes sure that he or she has more firepower, skills, training, or backup than the bad guys and (2) brings decisive force to

bear on encounters with bad guys. The idea of always bringing a little more force to bear on encounters than is actually needed is described by C. Shearing and R. Erickson as "taking a four-foot leap over a three-foot ditch" (1991, p. 492).

4. **Deterrence.** Police view deterrence in a specific way. Their ability to halt an adversary comes not by using threats or reason but by using force. "Deterrence is immediate, slamming, final. Deterrence doesn't threaten to bring about punishment; deterrence ends the threat. Nothing else works; all else is weakness" (Crank 1996, p. 254).

5. **Anticipating Danger.** The anticipation of danger, or the scenting of trouble, is central both to police training and to the police culture (Kappeler, Sluder, and Alpert 1994). Skolnick (1994) describes the anticipation of danger in terms of **symbolic assailants**, people who give signs that they may be dangerous because of their dress, the way they walk, bulges in their clothes that might indicate a weapon, and the way they talk. Officers are leery of individuals who display these indications of trouble. There may be **assailant geographies**, public and private places that show signs of being as potentially perilous, such as playgrounds that appear safe but are known as areas where drugs are exchanged.

These cultural themes are interrelated. For example, if the anticipation of danger is linked to deterrence, it is easy to see how police will sometimes react too forcefully before all information about the potentially dangerous na-

❖ ❖ ❖ ❖   ture of a suspect is known, especially if the suspect is acting in a hostile way. By carefully considering the various themes presented here, the reader can begin to understand how the difference between justified force and excessive force, so important in legal and administrative reviews of police behavior after an incident, is balanced by the ways street officers confront danger and gauge forceful responses.

J. Hunt (1985) has also described how police rely on informal, cultural standards in the use of force. By focusing too much on legal definitions of force, society tends to overlook the "understandings and standards police officers actively employ in the course of their work" (p. 316). Hunt observed that police have **working notions of normal force**, which are standards of acceptable force learned on the street. They are different from what police learn in training; for example, that they should not hit a person on the head or neck because it could be lethal.

> On the street, in contrast, police conclude that they must hit wherever it causes the most damage in order to incapacitate the suspect before they themselves are harmed. New officers also learn that they will earn the respect of their veteran coworkers by not observing legal niceties in using force, but by being "aggressive" and using whatever force is necessary in a given situation. (1985, p. 319)

Force is normal, or acceptable, under two circumstances. First, it is normal because it is the natural outcome of strong, even uncontrollable emotions normally arising from certain routine sorts of police activities. Second, it is justifiable if it establishes police authority in the face of a threat or is morally appropriate for the type of crime encountered by the officer. When officers use too much force, or when they do not use enough, they are the subject of reprimand, gossip, and avoidance. Hunt described how normal levels of force are learned in day-to-day practice and the psychological mechanisms that justify the use of force.

Use-of-Force Conflicts

On occasion, the use of force by police officers may conflict with community standards, legal factors, or department policy. These three types of conflicts are considered below.

Type 1: Conflicts with the community. In Type I conflicts, the law and departmental policy may consider the police use of force appropriate, but a substantial segment of the community does not. Such conflict occurs most often in a minority neighborhood. The relationship between police and some minority citizens may be one of suspicion and distrust, so when the police, particularly officers who are not of that minority use coercion, they have a substantial burden placed on them to prove that the use was appropriate. In these circumstances, incidents of force, even seemingly minor ones, accumulate into a reservoir of grievances in which any additional incident, however justified, can provoke community violence, rioting, and other antipolice activity.

V. E. Kappeler, R. D. Sluder, and G. P. Alpert describe a case of Type 1 conflict that occurred in Miami in 1979.

> On December 17, 1979, Arthur McDuffie, an African American, was riding his motorcycle on the streets of Miami, Florida. The police officers gave chase and

[were] eventually joined by more than a dozen Miami patrol cars. Following a brief pursuit that allegedly reached speeds over one hundred miles per hour, McDuffie stopped his motorcycle. Officers converged on the scene, and at least six white officers jumped McDuffie. In a matter of minutes, McDuffie lay motionless on the ground with his head split open. He died four days later as a result of police-inflicted injuries. . . . As a result of inconsistencies uncovered by a departmental investigation, the officers were in-

---

Case Study 9.3

Use of Force, the Community, and Liability

According to an article in *Law Enforcement News* (1998), in 1998 the Washington, D.C. Metropolitan Police unveiled a new use-of-force policy. The policy was developed in response to an escalating number of shooting incidents in recent years. The Metropolitan Police had been involved in 640 shooting incidents during the five-year period from 1992 to 1997. This is more shootings than in either the Los Angeles or the Chicago Police Department for the same period, both of which have double Washington's manpower. Moreover, 85 people had been shot and killed since 1990. Eight police officers had also been shot since 1993. In 1997, three officers were killed in a three-month period.

The shootings had resulted in more than 300 civil suits against the District. One man, armed with a knife, was shot by SWAT team members 12 times and subsequently awarded $6.1 million dollars. Of particular concern was that police were shooting at a large number of cars. Since 1993, "54 cars have been shot at after officers said they had drove at them in 'vehicular attacks.' Nine people had been killed, all of them unarmed, and 19 wounded" (p. 1).

The following is an example of such an incident: A 16-year-old man, wanted for reckless driving and running red lights, was shot through his side window. In two other cases, one individual was shot while he sat at a roadblock. Another was shot while sitting in his vehicle during a traffic stop. Officers involved in these cases stated that they fired to stop a vehicular attack. However, all of these shootings were considered to be unjustified, and the city agreed to pay the families of the victims in out-of-court settlements.

In response to these problems, the police department revised its use-of-force policy, rewrote the continuum of force, and increased annual training requirements.

> Officers are trained to use certain measures to prevent an incident from escalating to brutal or deadly force. A suspect's body movement, for instance, will be met by a uniform presence. If a suspect is unresponsive, the officer may respond with verbal force. If threatening words or gestures are used, the officer assumes an escort position to lead the subject. To meet passive resistance, the officer may grab the suspect's wrists and pin his arms behind him. Responses to active resistance range from take-down techniques and pepper spray or other nonlethal weapons to the use of deadly force (p.10).

Nightsticks and the use of arms across the front of a person's neck to render the person unconscious were banned. Officers were also prohibited from shooting through doors or windows unless someone was clearly visible and from firing on fleeing cars. Officers were told to get out of the way of cars being used as deadly weapons.

A survey of officers found that 75 percent of those who had used their firearms failed to meet department standards. Consequently, firearms instruction was increased from 8 to 16 hours yearly, and training was expanded to focus on defensive tactics and judgment. Officers were taught how to de-escalate situations and reduce the need for deadly force. Finally, shooting review teams were to be sent to the scene of all shootings in order to thoroughly investigate them.

dicted for manslaughter and tried in Tampa. An all-white jury was selected to hear the charges; in May of 1980, the jury acquitted all of the officers.

> As a result of the jury's verdict, "one of the ugliest incidents of racial violence in the United States rocked Miami and sent shock waves across the whole country." (1994, p. 56)

The Miami incident resulted in 18 deaths and three days of rioting. As Kappeler and his colleagues noted, the police pledged to make changes in recruitment, selection, training, complaint management, and supervision (see also Alpert, Smith, and Watters 1992, p. 472).

Type 2: Conflicts with the law. A Type 2 conflict occurs when there are differences between law and department policy. For example, a department might decide to overlook illegal immigration because it thinks that enforcement will lead to loss of public support. Policy-law conflicts tend to involve the public. Some segments may favor the law, others the department. An area of considerable concern has to do with high-speed police chases. Consider a description of chase policy in Tampa, Florida.

> Since the 1980's, departments nationally are increasingly restricting high-speed pursuits. Chases are most troubling—they require a police department to balance public safety with law enforcement. Unfortunately, these two goals move at cross-purposes sometimes, and increases in law enforcement sometimes threaten the public safety. Chases are dangerous; the suspect, police officers, and innocent bystanders are sometimes injured and killed. Police chases are the "most deadly force" (Alpert and Anderson, 1986). Yet, many officers balk at the notion that they should withdraw from a chase and permit a suspected felon to escape. As Alpert (1989: 229) observes, "few would argue that police should not initiate a chase, but that is where the consensus disappears." Wide controversy exists regarding if and when a chase should be curtailed.
>
> Tampa, Florida, illustrates the issues surrounding high-speed chases. In 1994, over 11,000 cars were stolen. In 1995, officers began to chase car thieves, and the number of auto thefts was cut in half. Further, the rate of overall crime dropped by 25 percent, and officers attribute this to the use of stolen cars by felons to commit other crimes. However, police involved in chases have been involved in several accidents. In one of these, officers careened into a utility pole. In another, they knocked a house off its foundation. More troubling, a car driven by a suspect crashed into another car and killed the two German tourists inside. This accident happened less than three weeks after a suspected car thief, followed by another sheriff's deputy, hit a car and killed two occupants. (Navarro 1995, p. 18)

The consequences of a Type 2 conflict are usually twofold: Some segments of the community would pleased by the pursuit policy, other segments would not. In Tampa, residents facing higher insurance costs and economic loss supported the policy restricting pursuits. Within the police department, however, many officers would probably be angry and upset. M. F. Brown (1983), in his study of two large police departments, found substantial differences among officers concerning the appropriate policy for the use of deadly force. In fact, in cities in which organizational policies concerning the use of force are more restrictive than state law, officer morale may become an important issue.

Type 3: Conflicts between norms. In a Type 3 conflict, an officer's behavior meets the expectations of some segments of the community but is inconsistent with both law and departmental policy. For example, assume that two police officers are working in a neighborhood that has extensive drug problems. They decide to harass and physically abuse individuals suspected of drug dealing. Such action is clearly illegal and in violation of departmental policy, but it may be applauded by many persons in the neighborhood. In such a situation, the police department might discipline the officers, perhaps even terminate them, and possibly recommend criminal prosecution. But the residents of the neighborhood might protest the action of the department, perhaps vigorously.

Type 3 conflict is most likely to occur when the police department and officers get too "close" to residents in a particular area and begin to enforce what they consider to be "neighborhood norms" rather than following the law. Community-oriented policing could result in this type of conflict if not carefully monitored. It remains to be seen if the police can "resist" citizen pressure to "go outside the law to get the job done."

The examples provided in the three types of conflict illustrate important problems in determining the appropriateness of police behavior. Officers are sometimes required to make choices that will alienate part of their public. There are also many less dramatic examples concerning the exercise of police authority and the use of coercion. And there are many "gray areas." For example, a police officer might stop a citizen for a traffic ticket. If the citizen refuses to give the officer his or her driver's license, the officer must decide how to treat the citizen. At what point in this police-citizen encounter should the officer begin to use coercion? When should verbal threats be made? In many police departments the guidance provided to police officers in these areas is vague or nonexistent. Officers, police managers, and members of the community are likely to have opinions about appropriate behavior in these situations, and at times there will be conflicting expectations among these groups.

The recognition that some decisions will have no good outcome may be frustrating for young adults interested in a career in policing. Many individuals approach police work with a clear conception of "good-guy vs. bad-guy" fixed in their minds. Unfortunately, policing is not like that, nor can it be. In a democratic society, as J. Q. Wilson (1968) observed long ago, the use of force will always be controversial.

Inappropriate Force

In a democracy, police authority is constrained by democratic ideas of fair play. On the one hand, due-process laws provide the legalized *means* that police are permitted to use in order to pursue suspected crimes and to deal with citizens and suspects. Department policy provides the administrative means that police are supposed to follow in their day-to-day activities. On the other hand, many police officers are *ends* oriented. They are more focused on the ends of criminal justice—arresting dangerous felons or acquiring information about criminal activity—than on following legally acceptable means to achieve those ends. Also, police culture seems to give more emphasis to good ends than to legal means, and it sometimes justifies questionable means in the pursuit of good ends (Crank 1998; Klockars 1980).

The use of questionable and illegal force, as well as of unacceptably high levels of force and police brutality, has consequently been a problem for the police throughout the twentieth century. What is meant by inappropriate police behavior? What constitutes brutality? Clearly, these questions have to be at the center of any investigation into police misuse of force and abuse of authority.

Brutality and Excessive Force

Police brutality is difficult to define. It means different things to different people. Two approaches to defining brutality are recognized in this book. The first distinguishes between brutality and excessive force. R. R. E. Kania and W. C. Mackey (1977, p. 28) define **excessive force** as violence "of a degree that is more than justified to effect a legitimate police function." According to D. L. Carter, **police brutality** is excessive force but to a more extreme degree and includes violence that does not support a legitimate police function (1994, p. 270). An officer who beats a suspect who has already been handcuffed, for example, is committing police brutality.

This definition, however, does not fully address some aspects of police behavior that are widely seen as brutal but are not violently forceful. Carter, in dealing with this problem, focused on **abuse of authority**, which is the second approach to defining brutality. He defined abuse of authority with a three-part typology, depending on the nature and effects of police abuse.

> *Physical Abuse/Excessive Force.* Operationally, this classification includes (1) any officer behavior involving the use of more force than is necessary to effect an arrest or search, and/or (2) the wanton use of any degree of physical force against another by a police officer under the color of the officer's office. The key test is whether there was any physical force directly used against an individual with no distinction between injurious and noninjurious incidents with the proposition that the causal variables are the same.
>
> *Verbal/Psychological Abuse.* These are incidents where police officers verbally assail, ridicule, or harass individuals and/or place persons who are under the actual or constructive dominion of an officer in a situation where the individual's esteem and/or self-image are threatened or diminished. Also included in this category is the threat of physical harm under the supposition that a threat is psychologically coercive and instills fear in the average person.
>
> *Legal Abuse/Violation of Civil Rights.* This form of abuse occurs with greater frequency than the other categories. Legal abuse is defined as any violation of a person's constitutional, federally protected, or state-protected rights. Although the individual may not suffer any apparent psychological damage in the strictest sense, an abuse of authority has nonetheless occurred. In all cases of physical abuse and in many cases of verbal abuse, there will also be a legal question. However, legal abuse can—and does—occur frequently without the other forms. (Carter 1994, p. 273)

The underlying premise of the typology is that whenever police officers exercise their authority in a manner inconsistent with law or policy, they have abused their authority. Carter states that this model is useful because each of the different kinds of abuse has different causes, and each has to be treated differently, with different implications for policy.

Physical and Psychological Force

Both physical and psychological force were commonplace well into the 1930s. E. J. Hopkins (1931, pp. 212–215) reported on a study of the New York Police Department in 1930 that found in 166 cases (23.4 percent of the total cases studied) some type of physical force was employed. The most frequently used method was to strike the suspect one or more times with a fist (67 cases). Other methods included use of a rubber hose (19 cases) and black-jacks (12 cases). One suspect was "hung out the window, kicked and dragged by the hair" (1931, p. 215). J. A. Larson (1932, pp. 95–100) also discussed some of the coercive methods commonly used by police during this period. These methods became associated with the term **third degree**. Various third-degree methods historically employed by the police are listed in Inside Policing 9.4.

Most police officers of this period tended to deny any use of physical force. However, Bruce Smith, a prominent police consultant of that era, commented about the third degree in this regard: "In every police station in this

❖ ❖ ❖ ❖

Inside Policing 9.4
Historical Methods of Psychological and Physical Force Used by the Police

Psychological Force

- Suspects are placed on "The Loop"—that is, moved from station to station to deny them access to family, friends, and attorneys.

- Suspects are placed in very small, completely dark cells. Rats are placed in women's cells to "exhaust their nervous energy." A prisoner in an adjoining cell is told to "moan" and "yell" during the night. A large stove is placed next to a cell, and the stove is filled with items (e.g., bones, vegetable matter, old tires) designed to give off a foul odor and increase the heat in the cell to unbearable levels (i.e., to create a "sweat box").

- Suspects are interrogated for long periods under bright lights and without food or water, and/or they are denied access to substances like tobacco to which they are addicted. Suspects are threatened with various weapons; for example, a gun with blank shells is fired at the subject.

- Murder suspects are required to touch or hold the hand of the murder victim.

- Police pretend to beat prisoners in an interrogation room adjoining that of the suspect. One police officer is "hard" and "tough" and threatens the suspect; the other officer is sympathetic and supportive and pretends to protect the suspect from harm in exchange for information or a confession (also known as "good cop, bad cop" and the Mutt and Jeff technique).

- Police officers make false promises about what will happen to the suspect.

Physical Force

- Suspects are beaten on all parts of their body (usually except for the head) with rubber hoses, clubs, blackjacks, fists, telephone books, straps, brass knuckles, pistol butts, and whips. Arms and legs are twisted. Testicles are kicked, twisted, squeezed, and used to lift suspects upward, and testicles are also burned with acid. Suspects are tortured with electric shocks, dental drills, and lighted cigars. Suspects are dragged or pulled by their hair.

- Suspects are drenched with cold water from a hose, their heads are held under water, water is forced into their noses, they are hung out the window, they are choked with neckties and ropes, and they are required to go without shoes until their feet are bleeding. Chemicals such as tear gas, scopolamine, and chloroform are employed.

Sources: Adapted from J. A. Larson. 1932. *Lying and Its Detection*. Chicago: University of Chicago Press, pp. 95–121; E. J. Hopkins. 1931. *Our Lawless Police*. New York: Viking Press, pp. 25, 128, 215.

Police officers have used psychological coercion as a means to obtain confessions.

country about which I know anything, there is a room remote from the public parts of the building where prisoners are questioned" (Hopkins 1931, p. 195). The Wickersham Commission (National Commission on Law Observance and Enforcement, 1931), discussed in Chapter 3, found that the police use of such methods was widespread.

Continued problems with coercive psychological techniques resulted in the famous decisions of the Warren Court in the 1960s. In 1966 the *Miranda v. Arizona* Supreme Court decision observed that psychologically coercive techniques interfered with constitutional ideas of fair play. Consequently, the court issued its now famous requirement that suspects be advised of their right to an attorney and that the police right to question suspects be restricted except when that right has been waived or after an attorney has advised the suspect whether or not to talk to the police. The courts have limited the reach of Miranda, however. In *Illinois v. Perkins* (1990) an undercover officer, placed in a cell with a suspect, acquired information that the suspect had committed a murder. The U.S. Supreme Court ruled that undercover officers did not have to give Miranda warnings to incarcerated suspects prior to eliciting incriminating statements (Kappeler, Sluder, and Alpert 1994). As M. Vaugn (1992) has noted, other court rulings have expanded the rights of the police to use trickery and deception. By permitting open deception, however, several observers of the police have contended that the courts are encouraging the police to emphasize good ends over legal means (Skolnick and Fyfe 1993).

Police today continue to rely on deception, a form of psychological coercion, to secure information. Nor has the use of physical coercion been abandoned. For instance, in 1985 in New York City, several police officers employed stun guns (i.e., a weapon that shoots an electrical charge into a person) to secure confessions ("Stun-Gun Charges," 1985). This incident is described in Inside Policing 9.5. Similar incidents also took place in San Antonio, Texas, and Los Angeles in the 1980s (Berg 1992, p. 208).The following are examples of contemporary uses of deception:

Inside Policing 9.5
Modern Technology and Coerced Confessions

Five persons charged police officers in New York City with acts of brutality in the spring of 1985. As a result of these charges, several officers were indicted on criminal charges, and several police managers were either transferred or forced to retire.

The individuals who lodged the charges of police brutality were all members of a minority group, either black or Hispanic, and were suspected of selling small amounts of marijuana to undercover police officers. One of the individuals, a high school student, was arrested by six officers who were members of an elite street narcotics unit. The student was taken to the police station, given a "black eye," and burned with a stun gun. He screamed when he was being tortured and pleaded for the officers to stop. He was told that they would do it all night if he didn't confess. The suspect finally confessed when the officers threatened to use the stun gun on his testicles. Another suspect said he was jolted with a stun gun more than 10 times and beaten with a metal pipe in order to secure his confession.

The commissioner of the police department moved quickly to investigate the allegations, and the officers involved were suspended and later indicted on criminal charges. The investigation into the allegations brought other possible incidents to light, which were also investigated. However, the investigations have proven difficult because of the "blue wall of silence," which means that police officers are reluctant to provide information about the illegal activities of other officers. A police union representative maintained that the police department was overreacting because there were only a few isolated incidents and that the problem was not endemic to the whole department.

[The authors note that this is essentially the same position the union took during the Knapp Commission (1972) investigations discussed in Chapter 8 and is known as the rotten-apple theory of police deviance.]

Source: Adapted from "Stun-Gun Charges Shake NYPD to the Rafters." 1985. *Law Enforcement News*, May: 6, 13.

---

1. The person, or suspect, is not told the truth about why he or she is being questioned.

2. The suspect is not told that the person asking the questions is a police officer.

3. The suspect is told that he or she is being interviewed rather than interrogated and that he or she is free to leave at any time.

4. The police misrepresent the circumstances of the crime the suspect is alleged to have committed; for example, a suspect might be told there was an eye witness or that there is other available evidence that "ties" the suspect to the crime.

5. The police may make the crime seem more serious (carrying a more severe punishment) than it is in order to induce the suspect to make a bargain to confess to a less serious crime.

6. The police provide a justification to the suspect for the act, for example, "the victim got what she deserved."

7. The police may make some type of promise that later can be denied or modified.

Frequency of Excessive Force and Brutality

How widespread is police violence? T. Barker (1986) studied the extent of police brutality, along with other types of police deviant behavior, in a city of moderate size in the southern United States. Based on questionnaire responses from 43 (of 45) officers in that department, he found that about 40 percent used excessive force at times. Officers tended to believe that lying in court (committing perjury), sleeping on duty, and having sex and/or drinking on duty were more serious forms of police deviant behavior than was the use of excessive force. This was particularly true when the excessive force was used against persons in custody. Almost half the officers said they would rarely, if ever, report another officer if he or she used excessive force.

In another study, Carter conducted a survey of 95 police officers in McAllen, Texas. He found that 23 percent believed that excessive force was sometimes necessary to demonstrate an officer's authority, and 62 percent believed that an officer had a right to use excessive force in retaliation against anyone who used force against the officer. In the areas of verbal abuse, slightly over one-half of the officers believed that it was permissible to talk "rough" with citizens and that "rough" talk was the only way to communicate with some citizens.

R. J. Friederich (1980), in his comprehensive analysis of research on the use of force, found that police used force in only about 5 percent of encounters with offenders or suspects. In about two-thirds of these encounters, it was considered to be excessive. Because only a small percentage of all police-citizen encounters are with offenders or suspects and only about 5 percent of these types of encounters involve the use of force, his findings suggest that both the use of force and the use of excessive force are rare events in police work.

Because almost all use-of-force incidents involve suspicious persons, offenders, or suspects who resist police authority, any circumstances that result in an increase in the number of these types of police encounters will likely result in more incidents in which police use force, including excessive force. From the police point of view, the 1980s and the early 1990s were a period when the police were confronted with greater resistance to their authority and were at greater risk of being injured. Consequently, the police may be using excessive force more now than in the 1970s.

Excessive use of force may be either unintentional or deliberate. Force may be inflicted either to secure cooperation, to maintain the officer's authority, or to retaliate. When it is used, the officer believes that many, if not all, of the other officers (including supervisors and managers) who may be aware of this behavior will not report the brutality and will lie about the incident if it is investigated by the department or other individuals.

Perhaps the most infamous case of police brutality in recent years is the attack on Rodney King which took place in Los Angeles in 1991. Case Study 9.4 describes this incident and some of the subsequent events connected with it.

Interestingly, a comprehensive study of the Los Angeles police just prior to the King incident indicated widespread officer support for the values and management of the police department (Felkenes 1991). Furthermore, wide-

Case Study 9.4

The Rodney King Incident

Police officers beat and kick Rodney King as other officers look on. (Photo: AP/Wide World Photos)

On March 3, 1991, Rodney G. King was stopped for a speeding violation and trying to evade the police. What ensued between King and police officers was videotaped by a "home-camera buff." King did not immediately cooperate with police and may have resisted the attempts of officers to arrest him. Several officers hit him with police batons and kicked him over 50 times. Before the incident was over, 27 police officers (two of whom were black and four of whom were Latino), representing three different police agencies, were on the scene, and they stood by as King was brutally beaten and severely injured. The beating appeared to continue even after King had stopped making any meaningful effort to resist police authority. King received 11 skull fractures (including a shattered right cheek bone, shattered right eye socket, and fractured right sinus bones), a broken ankle, and numerous other injuries as a result of the beating. When the videotape was show on local and national television, it created tremendous outrage across the United States. Other citizens came forward with examples of how they had also been mistreated by the police.

The reports of the officers involved in the incident indicate that they may not have been truthful in describing the events in question. For example, some officers reported that King drove his car in excess of 100 miles an hour in order to avoid the police. However, a tape recording of the conversations between pursuing officers and one police department never indicated a speed in excess of 65 miles an hour. Two of the officers involved were, in fact, charged with submitting a false report.

An independent commission, headed by Warren Christopher, former deputy attorney general and deputy secretary of state of the United States, was appointed to investigate the King incident and related incidents in the department. Information revealed in the investigation indicated that some of the officers involved did not take the King matter seriously and even made jokes about it. One officer said after the incident that he hadn't "beaten anyone this bad in a long time." At the hospital to which King was taken, one police officer reportedly told King that "we played a little hardball tonight and you lost."

The attitudes of some Los Angeles police officers concerning race, excessive force, and the shooting of suspects are illustrated in the police officer statements listed below. These statements were taken from records of computer communications between patrol cars and between patrol cars and police headquarters. These statements are an example of 1,450 similar remarks made in the 16 months preceding the King incident. The language is reported as given, including the spelling errors of the officers. Although the number of such remarks is less than one-tenth of 1 percent of the total communication statements made during the period in question, the fact that such statements were made so openly indicates the possibility of both tolerance and support within the department for the values and beliefs represented by these remarks.

Statements Concerning Race

"Don't cry Buckwheat, or is it Willie Lunch Meat?"

"Sounds like monkey slapping time."

"Well . . . I'm back over here in the projects, pissing off the natives."

"If you encounter these Negroes shoot first and ask questions later."

"Just clear its [busy] out hear. This hole is picking up, I almost got me a Mexican last night but he dropped the dam gun to quick, lots of wit."

Statements Concerning Excessive Force

"I'm gonna bk my pursuit suspect . . . hope he gets ugly, so I can vent my hate."

"Capture him, beat him and treat him like dirt . . . Sounds like a job for the dynamic duo."

"After I beat him, what do I book him for and do I have to do a use of force [report]."

"Some of the suspects had big boot marks on their heads, once they were in custody."

"The last load went to a family of illegals living in the brush alongside the Pas frwy. I thought the woman was going to cry . . . so I hit her with my baton."

"I should shoot'em huh, I missed another chance dammmmmmm. I am getting soft."

Some of the other findings of the Christopher Commission and of research conducted by newspaper reporters are listed below:

1. Supervisors in the department were aware of a "significant number" of officers who used excessive force repeatedly and who also lied in reports about what they had done. Sometimes these officers were even praised by supervisors.

2. The messages sent via the computer that indicated prejudice and a tendency toward violence on the part of some officers were ignored by police supervisors and managers.

3. It was rare for the department to find in favor of citizens who complained about the police use of excessive force. In over 2,000 citizen complaints filed between 1986 and 1990, only 42 were resolved in favor of the complainant. For the same period, the department brought excessive-force charges against officers in 80 cases, and in 53 of these, officers were found guilty as a result of an internal affairs investigation. In some of these 53 cases, more than one officer was involved. In incidents involving several officers, all officers denied the allegations, and none of the officers who had been present at the incident reported another officer for the use of excessive force. The disciplinary action taken against officers for the use of excessive force varied. Some officers were sus-

☞

pended for more than 20 days, but some were treated more leniently than other officers who had been disciplined for kissing a girlfriend while on duty, for the unauthorized use of the department's copying machines, and for sleeping on duty.

The commission stated, however, that it believed that only a small percentage of officers, perhaps 3 to 5 percent, were responsible for most of the racial and excessive-force problems (this figure means that at least several hundred Los Angeles police officers may have engaged in this type of behavior). The Christopher Commission also found serious problems with the police department's management and suggested that the chief of police retire when his term of office was over.

As a result of the King incident, four officers were charged with criminal assault, among other things, and placed on trial. Their defense was that prior to the events depicted on the videotape, King, whom they considered to be a large and potentially dangerous person, violently resisted their attempts to arrest him. They indicated that they believed King was under the influence of liquor or drugs, and from their training and experience, this would make him very difficult to control. When they were unable to control him physically, they used the Taser, but even after he was shocked with electricity, King continued to refuse police orders to lie down in a prone position with arms and legs spread; he even got up and "charged" one of the officers. Consequently, the officers began to use their batons and some kicks, as they were trained to do in such situations. The officers tended to perceive every movement by King, even when he was on the ground, as an indication that he continued to pose a threat. Therefore, they continued to beat him until he complied with police orders. Only one of the four officers in question believed that what they had done was excessive or that it constituted "police brutality."

The jury in the criminal trial found the four officers not guilty on all criminal charges except one, on which the jury was divided. Many citizens, who believed that the videotape of the beating was sufficient evidence to convict the officers, were outraged at what they considered to be an unjust verdict. There was widespread violence (more than 50 persons were killed), extensive property damage (numerous buildings were burned down), and looting in Los Angeles and several other cities. Many elected officials expressed their concern and demanded that additional steps be taken to hold the officers accountable for their actions.

Two of the officers were subsequently convicted in federal court for the violation of King's civil rights. Both were sent to federal prison. King also sued the city of Los Angeles and was awarded $3.6 million.

Source: Adapted from "Inside View of L.A. Beating." 1991. *San Jose Mercury News*, March 19. 1A, 9A; "Doubt Shed on Cops Report in L.A. Beating." 1991. *San Jose Mercury News*, March 23: 1F, 4F; "L.A. Fires Only 1% of Officers." 1991. *San Jose Mercury News*, May 5: 4B; "Report Calls For Gates' Ouster." 1991. *San Jose Mercury News*, July 10: 1A, 6A. Used by permission.

spread support was found in both white and minority and male and female officers. It was found that, overall, all patrol officers were very satisfied with their jobs and would recommend that their friends consider a job with the department. This research also found that Los Angeles police officers were likely to have a professional outlook concerning their role in society. The conflict between the criticisms of the Los Angeles Police Department reported in Case Study 9.4 and the police officer support for the department reported in the Felkenes research vividly illustrates the differences that can exist between community and departmental expectations of the police role in society and the meaning of what is, and is not, police brutality.

Brutality at the End of the Century

The police professionalism movement, discussed in Chapter 10, has placed powerful administrative and ethical controls over the behavior of line officers. Throughout the twentieth century, it and subsequent reform movements have tried to control violent and brutal police behavior. Looking back over the past 100 years, can one say that police brutality has decreased? What are the trends in brutality? Is it a problem that society needs to be concerned about?

This section looks at two opposing views on police violence and brutality. The first argues that brutality is a significant problem in major American cities and is not being dealt with successfully. The second contends that brutality should be considered against the backdrop of increasing levels of violence among the citizenry.

View 1: Brutality is a problem. In 1998 the Human Rights Watch published *Shielded From Justice*, an assessment of brutality in major American cities. It looked at brutality and accountability procedures in 14 large cities, selected to represent different regions and to provide an overall picture of police behavior across the United States. Its assessment of brutality and lax accountability was a harsh indictment of big-city policing.

> Police officers engage in unjustified shootings, severe beatings, fatal chokings, and unnecessarily rough physical treatment in cities throughout the United States, while their police superiors, city officials, and the justice department fail to act decisively to restrain or penalize such acts or even to record the full magnitude of the problem. Habitually brutal offenders—usually a small percentage of officers on a force—may be the subject of repeated complaints but are usually protected by their fellow officers and by the shoddiness of internal police investigations. A victim seeking redress faces obstacles at every point in the process, ranging from overt intimidation to the reluctance of local and federal prosecutors to take on brutality cases. Severe abuse persists because overwhelming barriers to accountability make it all too likely that officers who commit human rights violations escape due punishment to continue their abusive conduct. (1998, p. 1)

Prosecution of cases has been infrequent and ineffective. Local prosecutors, the study argues, are frequently closely allied to police activities and are ineffective in efforts to prosecute police brutality. Indeed, most prosecutions conducted by the Human Rights Watch did not keep a log of police brutality cases. The criminal section of the Civil Rights Division of the U.S. Department of Justice is responsible for prosecution of civil rights violations. This includes the excessive use of force and police brutality. Yet the record of prosecution has been bleak.

> In fiscal year 1997, the Civil Rights Division received a total of 10,891 complaints, with thirty-one grand juries and magistrates to consider law enforcement officers leading to twenty-five indictments and informations, involving sixty-seven law enforcement agents; nine were convicted, nineteen entered guilty pleas, and four were acquitted. (1998, p. 102)

In other words, of over 10,000 complaints, only 28 convictions or pleas were achieved. This is a conviction rate of 2.6 per 1,000 cases. The data are clear: Citizens hoping for criminal remedies at the federal level for police brutality are virtually certain to be frustrated.

Federal data also show an alarming rise in reports of police brutality over recent years. In 1989, 8,953 cases were forwarded to the FBI. By 1996 the figure had risen to 11,721. Though the time interval is too short to make long-term inferences about trends, the data show an increase of 30 percent in reported cases over the seven-year period.

Human Rights Watch concluded that the most significant problem confronting big-city police departments was the lack of a system of effective accountability (discussed in Chapter 10).

Critics have countered that data collected by Human Rights Watch was derived primarily from high-profile cases. This is a selective bias that, outside of the FBI reports listed above, tells little about the ordinary cases encountered by police departments. Human Rights Watch responded to this concern by observing that it was difficult to obtain information from departments in instances that had not reached public attention and that prosecution for those cases was consequently even less common than the more visible cases that it discussed.

View 2: Brutality is not a problem. Not all observers of the police believe that there is a brutality problem. L. B. Sulc (1995) argued that restraint, rather than brutality, is typical of police behavior toward citizens. He contended that police brutality is less prevalent than it was 20 years ago. Citing the news magazine *New Dimensions,* he observed that

> while the FBI's civil rights division reports 2,450 complaints involving law enforcement officers in 1989, during the same period, 62,712 law enforcement officers were victims of assaults. In 1990, there were more than 71,794 assaults against law enforcement officers nationwide, according to the Uniform Crime Reports. Sixty-five officers were killed. (1995, p. 80)

Sulc attributes the widespread perception of police violence to media attention.

> Police violence, although unquestionably a matter of serious import, isn't as bad as it appears. It is exacerbated by warped media treatment both in fiction (network shows) and in reporting (network news). The unusual stress of police work contributes to the overreaction of cops—the overreaction of media and public to the cops contributes to the stress. (1995, p. 81)

W. Tucker (1995) argues that the public tends to look at complaints against the police and fails to consider whether the complaints are justified:

> The truth, however, is that most complaints are either frivolous or unjustified. This is borne out by the experience of the old New York City board, which the Vera Institute of Justice, a nonpartisan organization, found to be prejudiced neither for nor against civilians or police officers.

> In 1990, the Board's annual report showed a total of 2,376 complaints for "excessive force," 1,140 for "abuse of authority," 1,618 for "discourtesy," and 420 for "ethnic slurs." Among the 2,376 complaints for excessive force (presumably the most serious charge), injuries were documented in 267 cases. These involved 71 bruises, 92 lacerations requiring stitches, 30 fractures, 22 swellings, and 41 "other." In the 2,286 cases that were pursued, 566 were dropped because the complainant became uncooperative, 234 were dropped because the complainant withdrew the charge, and 1,405 were closed with less than full investigation, usually because the complainants became unavailable. Only 81 cases resulted in a finding against the policeman. (1995, p. 72)

The "no problem" perspective suffers from a tendency to blame police brutality on the behavior of their victims or on increases in crime, seeming to imply that police officers are not primarily responsible for their own behavior. Nor does the perspective acknowledge the very real problems victims of

❖ ❖ ❖ ❖   brutality face when they try to file reports—filing a report in a police department is frequently an intimidating experience, and full follow-up on reports
that are filed is not common in many departments. This perspective nevertheless raises important points that should not be overlooked. The following
six points summarize central policy issues confronting excessive force and
police brutality.

1. The presence of brutality cannot be gleaned only from "official"
   reports," which may be unsubstantiated. Individuals file brutality or excessive-force reports for a variety of reasons, and not all
   of the reports will accurately tap underlying instances of brutality. Also, scholars know from their studies of crime that official
   reports vary sharply from true levels, though that same argument suggests that brutality may well be higher than suggested
   by "official" reports.

2. Citizens may perceive behavior whose purpose is to ensure officer safety as acts of brutality. There is no question but that the experience of being arrested, searched, and cuffed is harsh and unpleasant. But it should not be dealt with in the same way as brutality, which is typically viewed by the public and police officials
   alike as inappropriate or illegal behavior.

3. The media are widely and correctly perceived to dramatize that
   which comes to their attention. This applies to the villainy of
   criminals, and it extends to the brutality of police as well. It
   should not assume that what is presented in the media is a thorough or accurate portrayal of the facts. Indeed, as S. Walker
   (1998, pp. 30–32) has pointed out, what we receive from the media is the exceptional, not the normal case. Unfortunately, bad officers are able to hide behind the protective veneer of police loyalty, and the media are frequently the only way that excessive
   force and brutality are brought to the attention of the public.

4. Police brutality emerges in the context of a police-citizen interaction, and it is unreasonable to believe that police can be wholly
   dispassionate in the conduct of criminal investigation and in
   dealing with rude individuals. Although dispassionate police
   work is a goal of police reformers, the ability to police without
   the expression of emotion, including anger, is improbable. It is
   important that police departments seek to control the angry or
   mean-spirited outbursts of officers against citizens, but it is also
   inconceivable that they will be wholly successful.

5. Research suggests that some officers exhibit single or rare instances of excessive force, and only a small percentage are
   rogues in their behavior, accounting for repeated violent acts.
   These two types of police officers should be dealt with in different ways, the rare or one-time offender subject to interdepart-
   mental review and the repeat offender decertified and prosecuted.

6. The public, widely supportive of a "war on crime" and aggressive
   anticrime efforts, has created an environment in which police of-

Police executives being interviewed after an incident. (Photo: Mark C. Ide)

ficers feel morally justified in the use of force. It is seemingly unfair to single out officers for the overuse of force when the message they frequently receive from powerful public, media, and political figures is to do just that.

Use of Deadly Force

The term **deadly force** is defined as that force used with the intent to cause great bodily injury or death. Such deadly force is almost always limited to those situations when police use firearms in encounters with suspects. As noted, there are certainly other times that citizens may be seriously injured or killed as the result of the use of other types of force, but that is rarely, if ever, the intent of the police. Some police scholars have suggested, however, that choke holds be defined as deadly force because deaths do occur when such holds are employed (Fyfe 1983). When the police engage in a high-speed pursuit that results in an accident and someone dies, this may be seen as use of force in which the outcome involved death. This fact does not mean that deaths that result from this and other police activities are not important but only that they are not included in the definition and therefore will not be considered.

Based on the definition above, there are three categories for which data are required if the extent of the use of deadly force is to be determined:

Category 1: Death. The police use a deadly weapon, and as a result, the person dies.

Category 2: Injury. The police use a deadly weapon, and the person is wounded but does not die.

Category 3: Noninjury. The police use a deadly weapon, but the person against whom it is directed is not injured.

A fourth possible category, but one that will not be addressed, relates to the total times the officer fires his or her weapon. A person who is shot at and killed, wounded or missed, may be fired at more than once. Research indicates that police officers miss with about 60 to 85 percent of the bullets they fire (Geller and Scott 1992). For example, on the one hand, an officer could shoot at a suspect five times and hit the suspect only once, causing either a death or an injury. Or, more than one bullet might strike the victim. On the other hand, an officer might shoot several times and not hit the intended person.

Category 1: Death. Sources of data for Category 1 use of deadly force can be found in three places: the National Center for Health Statistics, FBI reports, and the study of individual cities. The National Center for Health Statistics data are found in the volumes on mortality that are published annually and based on reports from coroners and medical examiners. Under the "homicide" cause-of-death category, there has been a "police or legal" intervention subcategory since 1949. These data provide a very rough estimate of the number of people killed by police as the result of the use of deadly force. In the 42-year period from 1949 to 1990, police killed approximately 13,000 people.

The estimate of 13,000 may be low. An analysis of the records of 36 large police departments conducted by L. Sherman and R. Langworthy (1979) suggests that the center's statistics are approximately 25 to 50 percent low because of reporting problems. This means that a more realistic estimate of citizen deaths from Category 1 use of deadly force is between about 16,000 and 20,000 since 1949. Although there is no accurate way to determine the number of citizen deaths that have resulted from the use of deadly force since the 1840s, when modern police departments were first established, it is not unreasonable to assume that 30,000 to 40,000 citizens, and possibly many more, have been killed by police officers in the United States.

The FBI does not provide data on the police use of deadly force unless requested. The data are based on what are called Supplemental Homicide Reports submitted to the FBI by police departments, and the submission of such reports is voluntary. Although the number of people reported killed by police may give an accurate picture of the use of deadly force in individual cities, the reports do not provide an accurate national overview.

One of the most comprehensive studies conducted in individual police departments was made by K. R. Matulia (1985), who studied citizens killed by the police in the 57 largest cities (250,000 population or higher) in the United States between 1975 and 1983. He found that the police had killed a total of 2,336 people, or an average of about 259 per year. He estimated that this figure represented about 70 percent of the total number of citizens killed by police each year in the United States. By using this estimate, the total number of citizens killed during this period would be about 370 per year. This figure is consistent with National Center data if Sherman and Langworthy's adjustment is taken into consideration.

Category 2: Injury. Category 2 data (i.e., a person is shot and injured) are more difficult to acquire for the entire United States because there is no national reporting requirement. Fyfe (1988), however, provides some interesting insights on this category of data. He summarizes the research of several studies conducted over varying time periods (two to nine years) from a total of 14 large cities in the United States. Although some variation exists among departments, these studies suggest that, in general, when the police shoot an individual, that person is approximately twice as likely to be wounded as killed. If this estimate is accurate for the entire United States, this means that for the period 1949 to 1990, police used deadly force that injured citizens between 32,000 and 40,000 times.

Category 3: Noninjury. Data for Category 3 (i.e., person is shot at but not injured) are even more difficult to obtain. However, there are some indications of the frequency of police actions in this area. In studies of four large cities, the frequency that officers shot and missed, as a percentage of total times they used their firearms, was 48.6 in Los Angeles during the period 1971 to 1975 (Fyfe 1978), 73.1 in Chicago for the period 1975 to 1977 (Geller and Karales 1981), and 74.1 in Detroit for the period 1976 to 1981 (Horvath and Donahue 1982). If these data are indicative of practices throughout the United States, it means that, depending on the city, police officers shoot at and miss two to four times as many people as they shoot at and either injure or kill.

The above discussion includes some very general projections about the use of deadly force in the United States. There is a need to determine how changes in training, departmental policy, programs (like community or problem-oriented policing), and new laws affect frequency of deadly-force incidents. For example, as a result of changes in the policies concerning the use of Category 1 deadly force, there was an apparent decline in the number of citizens killed in the early 1980s (Fyfe 1988; "Big Decline in Killings" 1986). These policy and legal changes will be discussed later.

R. Van Raalte's (1986) research identifies as many as 30,000 officers killed in the line of duty in the twentieth century. However, he does not separate those killed in accidents from those killed by citizens. Historically, there is about a 1:4 or 1:5 ratio when comparing officers killed to citizens killed; that is, about one police officer is killed by a citizen for every four or five citizens killed by the police (Kuykendall 1981).

In recent years, there has been substantial research concerning the police use of deadly force. Some of the more prominent authorities in this area are W. A. Geller (1983), J. J. Fyfe (1978, 1979, 1980, 1982, 1983, 1985, 1988), P. Scharf and A. Binder (1983), and M. Blumberg (1985, 1997), among others. The most important research findings for four areas—(1) environmental and departmental variations, (2) factors that influence officers, (3) racial considerations, and (4) changes in law and policy— are summarized below.

Environmental and Departmental Variations

The frequency with which police use Category 1 deadly force varies considerably across the United States. Matulia found that the rates per 1,000 police officers varied from 0.44 in Sacramento, California (about 1 incident for every 2,000 police officers), to 7.17 in Jacksonville, Florida. Overall, the mean rate was 2.24 citizens killed for each 1,000 officers for the period 1975 to 1983. Of the 57 largest cities studied, twenty-nine were below this rate and twenty-seven were above.

❖ ❖ ❖ ❖   Two categories of factors influence the frequency with which police use deadly force: environmental and organizational (departmental). Environmental factors—factors having to do with the community and neighborhood where the police do their work—are the homicide rate, the overall arrest rate, violent-crime arrest rate, and gun density (i.e., ratio of gun ownership to total population). Generally, the police are more likely to confront situations where they think the use of deadly force is necessary in areas with higher crime and more guns. In addition, in any area where there are higher poverty and divorce rates, often the police may be called on more to intervene in potentially dangerous situations (Fyfe 1980, 1988; Kania and Mackey, 1977; Sherman and Langworthy 1979). These factors do not by themselves, however, explain all of the variation that may exist.

Departmental values, policies, and practices of police leaders and managers also affect the frequency with which police use deadly force. Current research suggests that a more restrictive shooting policy would reduce the frequency with which deadly force is employed (discussed in more detail later). In addition, some evidence suggests that the leadership attitude in the department influences the frequency of use: The increase in the use of deadly force in Philadelphia in the 1970s appeared to be the result of the aggressive policing attitude of leaders in the city and the department. The training that officers receive may also be influential. Some departments may encourage officers to intervene aggressively in potentially dangerous situations rather than wait until adequate "backup support" is available. Officers, on their own initiative, may also engage in such behavior (Fyfe 1988).

What is not known about neighborhood and department variation is more striking than what is known. Scholars know that often deadly-force fatalities occur, but they do not know how many deadly-force incidents occur (Blumberg 1997). The proportion of deadly-force incidents, rates of justifiable homicide, and firearms discharge rates vary dramatically across jurisdictions (Geller and Scott 1992) and departments (Fridell 1989). Blumberg has made the following observations.

> The inescapable conclusion one must draw from the available evidence is that nobody knows how many times each year law enforcement officers in the United States fire their weapons at citizens, how many citizens are wounded, or how many are killed as the result of police bullets. (1997, p. 521)

Officer Factors

The decision by an officer to use deadly force appears primarily to be the result of his or her perception of whether or not a threat exists and the frequency with which he or she is exposed to threats. As used here, threat could mean any situation in which the department permitted the use of deadly force. An officer's assignment appears to be a much more important predictor of the use of deadly force than age, intelligence, and educational background. Officers with more risky assignments are more likely to use deadly force.

Off-duty officers are involved in many shootings. As many as 15 to 20 percent of incidents of the police use of deadly force involve an officer who is off-duty. The more aggressive the off-duty officer is in intervening in potentially violent situations, whether or not encouraged to do so by the department, the ❖ ❖ ❖ ❖ higher the rates for the use of deadly force.

The race of the officer also appears to be important, largely because of the assignment and living practices of officers. For example, African American officers are more likely to use deadly force and to be the victims of its use than are other officers because they are more likely to live in, frequent, and be assigned to areas with high crime rates. Therefore, they are exposed to more situations in which they might have to use deadly force or become its victim (Fyfe 1988; Geller and Scott 1992).

There is also some evidence that women may use deadly force less frequently than men because they may have no ego involvement with suspects. Men may tend to personalize violent encounters to such a degree that the encounter becomes a survival competition governed more by macho rules than by departmental training and policy (Grennan 1987).

Racial Considerations

African American and Hispanic minorities are more likely to be shot by the police than are whites. There are two explanations for this disproportion. The first is that such disparities in shooting incidents simply mirror ethnic and racial involvement in criminal activity. When compared with rates of police-citizen contacts, arrest rates, and resistance to or attacks upon the police, there is no apparent racial disparity in police use of deadly force. That is, in communities in which blacks are shot at a high rate on the percentage of their contacts with police, their arrest rates and the likelihood they will resist the police tend to be similarly high (Fyfe 1988; Geller and Scott 1992). The second explanation is that police disproportionately use deadly force against minority-group members. Fyfe, for example, found that police officers in Memphis were 15 times as likely to shoot at African American offenders in the area of property crime as at whites.

Because of the sensitivity of the racial issue in the use of deadly force, more restrictive policies have tended to reduce the number of African Americans who have been killed. L. W. Sherman and E. G. Cohn (1986) found that in the 15-year period between 1970 and 1984, the police use of deadly force declined substantially, largely because fewer African American citizens were killed by police. This fact suggests that prior to the adoption of more restrictive deadly-force policies by many police departments during this period, African Americans were more likely to be shot at in certain types of situations (e.g., running away from the scene of a crime) than were whites. Declines in racial disparities in deadly-force incidents today are associated with departmental efforts to control discretion in the use of deadly force (Sparger and Giacopassi 1992).

Legal and Policy Changes

Blumberg identifies five changes in present-day laws and departmental policy regulating the use of deadly force.

1. Many states have modified the fleeing-felon rule and have tightened the legal basis for use of deadly force.

2. The shooting of unarmed, nonviolent suspects has been ruled by the Supreme Court to be a violation of the Fourth Amendment of the Constitution.

3. Almost all urban police departments have enacted restrictive administrative policies regarding the use of deadly force.

4. The courts have made it much easier for a citizen to file a lawsuit and collect civil damages as a result of a police action.

5. Social-science research has facilitated the understanding of the reasons for, and policy implications of the use of deadly force. (1997, pp. 507–508)

As late as 1967, few police departments had policies to guide officers in the use of deadly force. The state laws that existed at that time and that still exist in many states tended to broadly define occasions when officers could use deadly force. Perhaps the broadest of these legal guidelines was the **fleeing-felon rule,** which authorized the use of deadly force when attempting to apprehend individuals who were fleeing from a suspected serious crime. This rule dates from the early Middle Ages, when almost all crimes considered to be felonies were punishable by the death penalty; consequently, to kill those fleeing from suspected felonies did not seem inappropriate.

An alternative to the fleeing-felon rule was first developed and tested in New York. The New York Police Department, responding to concerns over the high number of officer and civilian shootings, formulated a restricted policy, permitting use of deadly force only under circumstances of immediate danger to an officer or the public. The policy resulted in a nearly 30 percent reduction in shootings of citizens by officers. No increase in the number of officers shot was observed (Fyfe 1979).

Changes in departmental policies have had more influence than changes in the law in determining when police officers use deadly force. Once police departments began to develop policies in this area, they often were more restrictive than state law. Initially, departments limited the number of situations in which police could use deadly force; for example, a policy might indicate that a person who was fleeing from a certain property crime could no longer be shot at.

By the 1980s, more and more police departments began to adopt what is often called a defense-of-life shooting policy. Generally, such policies restrict the use of deadly force situations to those in which the officer's life, or another person's, is in jeopardy or to prevent the escape of a person who is extremely dangerous. In some departments, even under these circumstances, deadly force can be employed only when other, less deadly, means seem inappropriate (Geller and Scott 1992).

Since the adoption of more restrictive deadly-force policies, the number of citizens killed by police has declined. This decline is understandable when one considers that prior to the adoption of a defense-of-life policy, in some communities as many as 25 percent of the victims of police use of deadly force posed no threat to a police officer or another person when they were shot. Despite the fears of many officers, more restrictive guidelines have not resulted in an increased number of police injuries or deaths (Fyfe 1988). In addition, no evidence either confirms or refutes the belief of some police officers that more restrictive policies encourage suspects to try to run away from the police.

Summary

Force is an inherent part of police-citizen interactions. Police are trained to act in terms of levels of force. However, local police cultural standards for the use of force differ considerably from formal departmental policy and are more likely to support greater force than do formal training and policy.

Some use of force is legal, but some is questionable and illegal. The public frequently has different definitions of excessive force and brutality from those of the police. The frequency of illegal violence or brutality is low. There are two views of police brutality. The first is that brutality is widespread because rogue police officers are permitted to hide behind lax accountability mechanisms. The second is that brutality is not a problem and has to be considered in the context of overall high levels of violent crime.

Police use of deadly force has been extensively studied, but its frequency is still difficult to determine because of reporting problems. Research has examined the factors that contribute to the use of deadly force and attempted to explain why its frequency varies from community to community. In the last decade, policy guidelines for the use of deadly force have changed, and many police departments have adopted strict policies governing the use of such force. The result has been fewer citizens being killed by the police.

Discussion Questions

1. According to Bittner, why do police exist?

2. Using the research of Reiss and of Sykes and Brent, describe the type and nature of police-citizen encounters, particularly as they relate to the use of force by police officers.

3. Identify and explain the seven levels of the continuum of force and give examples for which each one would be both appropriate or inappropriate.

4. According to Crank, what are the police cultural themes having to do with force, and how do they influence an officer's use of force?

5. What does Hunt mean by normal force?

6. How frequent is the police use of illegal violence? Discuss the various perspectives used in the book to answer this question.

7. Identify and define the three categories of deadly force. What are the problems with each data source for the categories?

8. Identify and discuss the environmental, departmental, officer, and racial policy changes that influence the police use of deadly force.

9. Write an essay with two parts. In the first part, argue that "Police violence in the United States is increasing." In the second part, argue that "Police violence in the United States is not increasing."

References

Alpert, G. P. 1989. "Questioning Police Pursuits in Urban Areas." In R. G. Dunham and G. P. Alpert (eds.), *Critical Issues in Policing: Contemporary Readings*, pp. 216–229. Prospect Heights, IL: Waveland Press, Inc.

Alpert, G. P. and Anderson, P. 1986. "The Most Deadly Force: Police Pursuits." *Justice Quarterly* 2: 1–14.

Alpert, G. P., Smith, W. C., and Watters, D. 1992. "Implications of the Rodney King Beating." *Criminal Law Bulletin* 28 (5): 469–478.

Barker, T. 1986. "Peer Group Support for Police Occupational Deviance." In T. Barker and D. L. Carter (eds.), *Police Deviance*, pp. 9–21. Cincinnati: Pilgrimage.

Bayley, D. H. 1986. "The Tactical Choices of Police Patrol Officers." *Journal of Criminal Justice* 14: 329–348.

Bayley, D. H. and Garofalo, J. 1989. "The Management of Violence by Police Patrol Officers." *Criminology* 27: 1–12.

Beers, D. 1992. "A Biting Controversy." *Los Angeles Times Magazine*, February 9: 23–26, 43–44.

Berg, B. L. 1992. *Law Enforcement: An Introduction to Police in Society*. Heedham Heights, MA: Allyn & Bacon.

"Big Decline in Killings of Citizens by Police." 1986. *San Francisco Chronicle* October 20: 23.

Bittner, E. 1995. "The Capacity to Use Force as the Core of the Police Role." In V. Kappeler (ed.), *The Police and Society: Touchstone Readings*, pp. 127–137. Prospect Heights, IL: Waveland Press. Reprinted from *The Functions of Police in Modern Society*. Washington, D.C.: National Institute of Mental Health.

Blumberg, M. 1997. *Controlling Police Use of Deadly Force: Assessing Two Decades of Progress*. In R. G. Dunham and G. P. Alpert (eds.), *Critical Issues in Policing*, 3rd Edition, pp. 507–530. Prospect Heights, IL: Waveland Press.

Blumberg, M. 1985. "Research on the Police Use of Deadly Force." In The Ambivalent Force: Perspective on the Police, edited by Blumberg, A. S. and Neiderhoffer, E. pp. 340–350. New York: Holt Rinehart, & Winston.

Brown, M. F. 1983. "Shooting Policies: What Patrolmen Think." Police Chief 50: 35–37.

Campbell, A., Berk, R., and Fyfe, J. 1998. "Deployment of Violence: The Los Angeles Police Department's Use of Dogs." *Policing* 22 (4): 535–561.

Carter, D. L. 1994. "Theoretical Dimensions on the Abuse of Authority by Police Officers." In T. Barker and D. Carter (eds.), *Police Deviance*, 3rd Edition, pp. 269–290. Cincinnati, OH: Anderson Publishing Co.

——. 1985. "Police Brutality: A Model for Definition, Perspective, and Control." In A. S. Blumberg and E. Niederhoffer (eds.), *The Ambivalent Force: Perspective on the Police*, pp. 321–330. New York: Holt, Rinehart & Winston.

Chapman, S. G. and Crockett, T. S. 1964. "Gunsight Dilemma: Police Firearms Policy." In S. G. Chapman (ed.), *Police Patrol Readings*, pp. 311–321. Springfield, IL: Charles C. Thomas.

Crank, J. P. 1996. "The Construction of Meaning During Training for Parole and Probation." *Justice Quarterly* 31(2): 401–426.

——. 1998. *Understanding Police Culture*. Cincinnati: Anderson Publishing Co.

Crank, J. and Caldero, M. 1999. *The Corruption of Noble Cause: Police and the Ethics of Power*. Cincinnati: Anderson.

"Doubt Shed on Cops' Report in L.A. Beating." 1991. *San Jose Mercury News* March 23: 1F, 4F.

Faulkner, S. 1994. "A Ralph Nadar Approach to Law Enforcement Training." *Police Studies* 17 (3): 21–32.

Felkenes, G. T. 1991. "Affirmative Action in the Los Angeles Police Department." *Criminal Justice Research Bulletin* 6: 1–9.

Fridell, L. 1989. "Justifiable Use of Measures in Research on Deadly Force." *Journal of Criminal Justice* 17: 157–165.

Friederich, R. J. 1980. "Police Use of Force: Individuals, Situations, and Organizations." *Annals of the American Academy of Political and Social Sciences* 452: 82–97.

Fyfe, J. J. 1978. "Shots Fired: An Examination of New York City Police Firearms Discharges." Ph.D. dissertation, University of New York at Albany.

——. 1979. "Administrative Interventions on Police Shooting Discretion." *Journal of Criminal Justice* 7: 309–323.

——. 1980. "Geographic Correlates of Police Shooting." *Journal of Research in Crime and Delinquency* 17: 101–113.

——. 1982. "Blind Justice." *Journal of Criminal Law and Criminology* 73: 707–722.

——. 1983. "Enforcement Workshop: The Los Angeles Chokehold Controversy." *Criminal Law Bulletin* 1961–67.

——. 1985. Interview. *Law Enforcement News* June: 9–12.

——. 1988. "Police Use of Deadly Force: Research and Reform." *Justice Quarterly* 5: 165–205.

Geller, W. A. 1983. "Deadly Force: What We Know." In C. Klockars (ed.), *Thinking About Police*, pp. 313–331. New York: McGraw-Hill.

Geller, W. A. and Karales, K. J. 1981. *Split-Second Decisions: Shootings of and by Chicago Police*. Chicago: Chicago Law Enforcement Study Group.

Geller, W. and Scott, M. 1992. *Deadly Force: What We Know*. Washington, D.C.: Police Executive Research Forum.

Greenfeld, L., Langan, P., and Smith, S. 1997. *Police Use of Force: Collection of Statistical Data*. Washington, D.C.: Bureau of Justice Statistics.

Grennan, S. A. 1987. "Findings on the Role of Officer Gender in Violent Encounters With Citizens." *Journal of Police Science and Administration*, 15: 78–85.

Hopkins, E. J. 1931. *Our Lawless Police*. New York: Viking Press.

Horvath, F. and Donahue, M. 1982. *Deadly Force: An Analysis of Shootings by Police in Michigan, 1976–1981*. East Lansing: Michigan State University.

"How Much Force Is Enough." 1998. *Law Enforcement News*, November 30: 1, 10.

Human Rights Watch. 1998. *Shielded From Justice: Police Brutality and Accountability in the United States*. New York: Human Rights Watch.

Hunt, J. 1985. "Police Accounts of Normal Force." *Urban Life* 13(4): 315–341.

Illinois v. Perkings. 110 S.Ct. 2394 (1990).

"Inside View of L.A. Beating." 1991. *San Jose Mercury News*, March 19: 1A, 9A.

Kania, R. R. E. and Mackey, W. C. 1977. "Police Violence as a Function of Community Characteristics." *Criminology* 15: 27–48.

Kappeler, V. E., Sluder, R. D., and Alpert, G. P. 1994. *Forces of Deviance: Understanding the Dark Side of Policing*. Prospect Heights, IL: Waveland Press.

Klockars, C. 1980. "The Dirty Harry Problem." *Annals*, 452: 33–47.

Knapp Commission, 1972. *Report on Police Corruption*. New York: George Braziller.

Kuykendall, J. 1981. "Trends in the Use of Deadly Force by Police." *Journal of Criminal Justice* 9: 359–366.

"L.A. Fires Only 1% of Officers." 1991. *San Jose Mercury News* May 5: 4B.

Lamb, R. and Friday, P. 1997. "Impact of Pepper Spray Availability on Police Officer Use-Of-Force Decisions." *Policing* 20(1): 136–48.

Larson, J. A. 1932. *Lying and Its Detection*. Chicago: University of Chicago Press.

Marion, Nancy. 1998. "Police Academy Training: Are We Teaching Recruits What They Need to Know?" *Policing* 21(1): 54–79.

Matulia, K. R. 1985. *A Balance of Forces*, 2nd ed. Gaithersburg, MD: International Association of Chiefs of Police.

McEwen, T. 1997. "Policies on Less-Than-Lethal Force in Law Enforcement Agencies." *Policing* 20: 39–59.

❖ ❖ ❖ ❖

McNulty, E. 1994. "Generating Common-Sense Knowledge Among Police Officers." *Symbolic Interaction* 17: 281–294.

Miller, M. R. 1995. *Police Patrol Operations*. Placerville, CA: Copperhouse Publishing Company.

Milton, C. H., Halleck, J. W., Lardner, J., and Albrecht, G. L. 1977. *Police Use of Deadly Force*. Washington, D.C.: Police Foundation.

Miranda v. Arizona. 384 U.S., 436,466 (1966).

Muir, W. K. 1977. *Police: Streetcorner Politicians*. Chicago: University of Chicago Press.

National Commission on Law Observance and Enforcement. 1931. *Report on Lawlessness in Law Enforcement*, No. 11. Washington, D.C.: Government Printing Office, (Also known as the Wickersham Commission.)

Navarro, M. 1995. "The Debate over High-Speed Police Chases." *The New York Times National*, Dec. 17: 18.

Newman, D. J. and Anderson, P. R. 1989. *Introduction to Criminal Justice*, 4th ed. New York: Random House.

Peak, K. 1993. *Policing America: Methods, Issues, Challenges*. Englewood Cliffs, NJ: Prentice Hall.

President's Commission on Law Enforcement and the Administration of Justice. 1967. *Task Force Report: The Police*. Washington, D.C.: Government Printing Office.

Reiss, A. J., Jr. 1967. *The Police and the Public*. New Haven, CT: Yale University Press.

"Report Calls for Gates' Ouster." 1991. *San Jose Mercury News* July 10: 1A, 6A.

Reuss-Ianni, E. 1983. *The Two Cultures of Policing: Street Cops and Management Cops*. New Brunswick, NJ: Transaction Books.

Scharf, P. and Binder, A. 1983. *The Badge and the Bullet*. New York: Praeger.

Shearing, C. and Erickson, R. 1991. "Culture as Figurative Action." *British Journal of Sociology* 42: 481–506.

Sherman, L. W. and Cohn, E. G. 1986. *Citizens Killed by Big-City Police: 1974–1984*. Washington, D.C.: Crime Control Institute.

Sherman, L. and Langworthy, R. 1979. "Measuring Homicide by Police Officers." *Journal of Criminal Law and Criminology* 9(4): 317–331.

Skolnick, J. 1994. "A Sketch of the Policeman's Working Personality." In J. Skolnick (ed.), *Justice Without Trial: Law Enforcement in Democratic Society*, 3rd Edition, pp. 41–68. New York: Wiley.

Skolnick, J. and Bayley, D. 1986. *The New Blue Line: Police Innovation in Six American Cities*. New York: The Free Press.

Skolnick, J. and Fyfe, J. 1993. *Above the Law: Police and the Excessive Use of Force*. New York: The Free Press.

Sparger, J. and Giacopassi, D. 1992. "Memphis Revisited: A Reexamination of Police Shootings After the Garner Decision." *Justice Quarterly* 9(2): 211–225.

"Stun-Gun Charges Shake NYPD to the Rafters." 1985. *Law Enforcement News* May: 6, 13.

Sulc, L. B. 1995. "Police Brutality is Not a Widespread Problem." In P. Winters (ed.), *Policing the Police*, pp. 79–85. San Diego, CA: Greenhaven Press, Inc.

Sykes, R. E. and Brent, E. E. 1983. *Policing: A Social Behaviorist Perspective*. New Brunswick, NJ: Rutgers University Press.

Tennessee v. Garner. 471 U.S. 1,105 S. Ct. 1964 (1985).

Trimmer, R. 1993. "Pepper Spray After Concord: Legal Issues for Policy Makers." *North Carolina Justice Academy*. July.

Tucker, W. 1995. "Inner-City Crime is a Worse Problem than Police Brutality." In P. Winters, (ed.), *Policing the Police*, pp. 69–78. San Diego, CA: Greenhaven Press, Inc.

Van Raalte, R. 1986. Interview. *Law Enforcement News* March: 9–12.

Vaughn, M. 1992. "The Parameters of Trickery as an Acceptable Police Practice." *American Journal of Police* 11(4): 71–95.

Walker, S. 1998. *Sense and Nonsense About Drugs and Crime: A Policy Guide*, 4th edition. Belmont, CA: West/Wadsworth Publishing Company.

Wilson, J. Q. 1968. *Varieties of Police Behavior: The Management of Law and Order in Eight Communities*. Cambridge, MA: Harvard University Press.

For a listing of websites appropriate to the content of this chapter, see "Suggested Websites for Further Study" (p. xv). ✦

Controlling Police Behavior

Chapter Outline

❖ ❖ ❖ ❖

Key Terms	
accreditation	good-faith exemption
CALEA	good-faith defense
certification	internal-affairs unit
civil-liability suit	internal (departmental) review
civilian review board	intentional torts
consulting-modeling	negligent torts
decertification	process-criterion approach
deep-pocket theory	probable-cause defense
discretionary-act defense	reasonable certainty
ethical formalism	reliability
ethical relativism	scientific research
ethical utilitarianism	sudden-emergency defense
exclusionary rule	sustained complaints
exoneration	tort
external (citizen) review	unfounded complaints
false complaints	unsubstantiated complaints
Garrity interview	

The police are the visible representatives of criminal justice processes in the United States. Yet, in important ways, the police stand apart from society. Their special dispensation is the use of force so that citizens can live together in peace. Nevertheless, by virtue of the authority granted to them, using force they have the potential to undermine due processes of law (Skolnick 1994). This potential may be infrequently utilized, yet citizens are concerned about police abuse of authority.

The police are respected and feared at the same time. They are respected by many citizens who highly regard the commitment police make to their work, but they are also feared because of the enormous life-and-death authority that they carry. The accountability of the police to democratic processes has been and continues to be one of the central issues confronting the police throughout modern times (McMullan 1998).

To whom are the police accountable? One might be tempted to answer that they are accountable to elected and appointed officials, the general public, people who receive police service (e.g., victims, suspects), and other parts of the criminal justice system (e.g., prosecuting attorneys, judges). Yet this answer overlooks important issues of accountability. Do citizens understand police work well enough to judge the behavior of the police? Should police be responsible for assessing the behavior of their own officers? And what happens when the public encourages the police to break the law in order to do something about law-breaking people? In short, the issues of accountability are complicated, and there is little agreement on who has the authority to hold the police accountable, the means by which they should be held accountable, or for what they should be held accountable (Geller 1985).

The control of police behavior occurs in two fundamentally different ways. The first way is through mechanisms of oversight. These are based on the idea that if a police officer's behavior can be tracked, then illegal or inappropriate behavior can be identified, corrected, or punished. Oversight mechanisms are both internal and external to a police department. Internally, oversight is through departmental investigation and the restraints of bureaucratic organization and management. Externally, oversight occurs through citizen review and through legal remedies for police misconduct.

The second way is through standards, which will be considered in the second half of this chapter. According to this view, officers can be hired with, or trained in, standards of conduct by which they can gauge their behavior. Both professional and ethical standards of "right behavior" fortify them with an appropriate way of thinking about their work and thereby control their behavior.

Oversight Mechanisms Internal to the Police Department

Two oversight mechanisms within police departments will be considered here: managerial process and internal review.

Bureaucratic Organization and Management

The most important day-to-day source of accountability for police officers is in the way their department is organized and managed. Accountability is carried out through the design and operation of principles of bureaucratic organization, as extensively discussed in Chapter 4. This idea will be reviewed here primarily in terms of management-employee relations.

In police departments, bureaucratic standards are omnipresent. As G. Alpert and W. Smith observe, "Law enforcement is a paradigm of operational control. Virtually every aspect of policing is subject to some combination of either policy, guideline, directive, rule, or general order" (1999, p. 353). The organization of rules and regulations takes a specific language in a bureaucracy. Principal terms are listed below. These terms provide the statements that guide the behavior of the department and indicate the responsibility of officers within it.

1. *Departmental policies* are not, as often thought, rules but statements of guiding principles that should be followed. A policy should be thought of as a guide to thinking rather than a fixed outcome. A policy is a general statement that gives guidance to police officers as to the proper course of action (e.g., a use-of-force policy).

2. A *goal* is a general statement of purpose that is useful in identifying the role and mission of the police (e.g., to apprehend criminals).

3. An *objective* is a more specific and measurable statement of purpose that is related to a goal (e.g., make arrests in 25 percent of the burglary cases).

4. A *procedure* identifies a method or series of steps to be taken when performing a task or attempting to solve a problem (e.g., how to investigate a traffic accident).

5. Finally, a *rule*, or *regulation*, is a specific statement that identifies required or prohibited behavior by officers (e.g., all officers must dress in a certain manner). The terms *policy, rule,* and *regulation* are often used interchangeably.

Administrative guidance focuses on a wide variety of topics. Under principles of departmental supervision, managers' responsibilities aim at ensuring that officers' behaviors are consistent with bureaucratic policies and standards. Written directives, as D. Carter and T. Barker (1994, pp. 22–23) have observed, are important for the following reasons:

1. They inform officers of expected standards of behavior.

2. They inform the community of the department mission, goals, values, policies, procedures, and expected standards of officer behavior.

3. They establish a common foundation for the execution of the police process to enhance operational consistency, equal protection, and due process.

4. They provide grounds for disciplining and counseling errant officers.

5. They provide standards for officer supervision.

6. They give direction for officer training.

Responses to directives. Within a bureaucratic environment, standards exist in written terms of department policy and guidelines. Yet in a police department, managers may not follow policies and standards to the letter. In practice, managers may react in a variety of ways when officers deviate from those written standards. They may (1) ignore it, (2) act formally or informally, or (3) protect the officer.

A manager's formal responses include counseling or training (advising or teaching the person how to improve) or some type of disciplinary action (reprimand, suspension, demotion, or termination). The more public criticism there is of certain types of police behavior, the more likely managers are to use some form of punitive discipline. Some managers like to make an example of an employee in order to send a signal to other officers that certain types of behavior will not be tolerated. Employees, however, may consider this type of managerial response to be politically motivated and unfair. From the employees' point of view, they are being made a scapegoat to satisfy political interests.

If a manager believes a deviation exists but has insufficient evidence to act formally, he or she might respond informally, perhaps by transferring the employee to a new work area or assignment. Certain types of assignments can be used so often in a department that they become known as punitive assignments (e. g., the jail or foot patrol during the winter). Sometimes, for instance if the problem is related to the behavior of the officer when interacting with the public, the officer may be assigned to a job with minimal public contact. In addition, the manager may hope that this type of informal, punitive control will result in a resignation or retirement.

A manager may be aware of a deviation but elect to protect the officer for at least five reasons. The manager may (1) approve of the "deviant" activity or behavior, (2) believe that the most likely departmental response will be too punitive, (3) be influenced by the so-called code of silence in policing, (4) believe that acknowledging the deviation will result in criticism of the manager, or (5) simply want to avoid dealing with the problem by denying that it exists.

Too many directives? Policies, procedures, rules, and regulations, and objectives are written standards against which an officer's behavior is judged by supervisors. Officers are expected to conform to these standards. In many police departments, standards number in the hundreds and are printed in very thick manuals. Standards tend to accumulate over time as police departments are faced with a wide variety of situations. It is not uncommon for police officers to be unfamiliar with many of these standards because some are rarely used.

Why do police departments have so many policies? Part of the reason lies in the unpredictable nature of the police function. Police work is highly varied and carried out in a diversity of circumstances. Policies provide direction in unclear situations. J. Auten notes that the absence of policy leaves officers "in the dark in the expectation that they will intuitively divine the right course of action in the performance of their duties" (1988, pp. 1–2).

Policies, while providing a standard for behavior, suffer from significant limitations. In practice, they are sometimes rule-oriented and tell officers what not to do rather than suggest a possible course of actions. This can have an alienating effect on individual officers. Some researchers contend that the rigid bureaucracy characteristic of many police departments is principally responsible for the alienation of line officers and the intensification of more secretive elements of police culture. Consider the following statement P. K. Manning recorded during an interview:

> "140 years of fuck-ups. Every time something goes wrong, they make a rule about it. All the directions in the force flow from someone's mistake. You can't go eight hours on the job without breaking the disciplinary code . . . the job goes wild on trivialities." (1978, 79).

In sum, a written directive system is the cornerstone for administrative control (Carter and Barker 1994). It provides guidance and protects the department from liability. Many directives, however, are out of date, not clearly written, or not usable. It is important that departments periodically review their directives for currency and utility.

Internal Investigation

All police departments have some way of responding to citizen complaints or internal concerns about police behavior. In many small and moderate-size departments, this response may be the part-time responsibility of only one officer, probably a supervisor or manager. In larger departments, it has been the practice to establish a unit, often called **internal affairs,** to respond to complaints. Prior to studying the investigation process itself, this chapter will first consider the way in which complaints come to the attention of the police department.

In some communities, citizens do not complain about the police because they do not think it will do any good or because they are afraid the police will retaliate. Some departments make it difficult for citizens to complain by creating a cumbersome complaint process and by the negative (e.g., unfriendly,

Man voicing a complaint with officers. (Photo: Mark C. Ide)

rude, curt, discouraging) behavior of officers when citizens attempt to complain.

The political climate in a community may be particularly important in encouraging or discouraging complaints against the police. On the one hand, a new mayor or other elected official who calls for an aggressive "crackdown" on crime or who talks about the police as the "thin blue line" between citizens and criminal predators may be indicating to citizens that their concerns about police excesses will not be taken seriously. On the other hand, a new mayor or chief of police might encourage citizens to come forward with complaints about the police. Such encouragement, however, may result in an increase in frivolous as well as serious complaints.

A small number of officers receive a disproportionate number of complaints. For instance, K. Lersch and T. Mieczkowski (1996), in their study of a large police department in the Southeast, found that 2.9 percent of the officers in their study accounted for about 25 percent of the complaints. This finding may be explained by several factors. The officers' training may have been inferior. He or she may have had a more aggressive style of policing, which could result in more complaint-generating conflict with citizens. Finally, complaints may have been related to the area in which the officers worked—for instance, an area in which citizens are more likely to resist police authority (Toch 1995). Younger officers probably receive more complaints (Croft 1987) because more younger officers are assigned to patrol duties and, as a result, they are probably more likely that other officers to have disagreements with citizens. It should be noted that research on characteristics of officers receiving complaints is mixed: For example, Alpert (1989) noted that age had no effect on use-of-force problems; similarly, G. Hayden (1981) found that length of service also had no effect.

❖ ❖ ❖ ❖   ***The investigative process.*** When police officers are being investigated as suspects in a crime, they have the same legal procedural rights as any other suspect. But what rights should they have when they are being investigated by supervisors, managers, or internal affairs units? Although states vary in the rights afforded police officers facing discipline. California has enacted into law what is, in effect, a police officer's bill of rights. Inside Policing 10.1 provides a summary of these rights.

Inside Policing 10.1
Police Officer's Bill of Rights

When any police officer is under investigation and subjected to interrogation, which could lead to punitive action, the interrogation shall be conducted under the following conditions. These rights do not apply to an interrogation in the normal course of duty, which might involve counseling, instruction, or informal verbal admonishments.

1. The interrogation shall be conducted at a reasonable hour, preferably when the police officer is on duty, or during normal waking hours, unless the seriousness of the investigation requires otherwise. If the interrogation takes place during off-duty time, the officer shall be compensated in accordance with regular departmental procedures.

2. The persons to be present at the interrogation must be identified in advance, and the officer will not be interrogated by more than two investigators at one time.

3. The police officer will be informed of the charges against him or her prior to any interrogation.

4. The interrogation will be for a reasonable period of time.

5. The police officer shall not be subjected to any offensive language or threats of punitive action, except

that an officer refusing to respond to questions or submit to interrogation shall be informed that failure to answer questions that are directly related to the investigation may result in punitive action. There will be no promise or reward offered as an inducement to answer any question.

6. The interrogation may be recorded by either the persons conducting the interrogation or the officer under investigation or both. The officer in question is entitled to written or recorded copies of the interrogation if additional action is contemplated by the department or if there is to be a continuing investigation.

7. If prior to, or during, the interrogation it is decided he or she may be charged with a criminal offense, the officer will immediately be informed of his or her constitutional rights.

8. If a formal written statement of charges is filed against a police officer by the department, the officer has a right to request that a representative of his or her choice be present during any interrogation.

Source: Adapted from the *California Government Code*, Section 3303.

The process for investigating complaints against officers tends to be similar to other types of investigations. The steps used by many police departments are briefly summarized below (D'Arcy et al. 1990):

1. Review the complainant's allegation to determine what departmental standard(s) was violated.

2. Contact and interview all witnesses and reinterview the complainant if necessary.

3. Collect all other evidence, such as photographs, medical reports, police reports, and so on.

4. Obtain background information on the complainant (e.g., criminal history and any prior allegations against officers).

5. Obtain background data concerning the officer (e.g., prior complaints, personnel evaluations, prior disciplinary actions by the department).

6. Interview all departmental members who may be involved.

Although internal investigations and criminal investigations are similar, there are important differences. Carter (1994) identifies several pertinent differences in internal investigations:

1. Fourth Amendment guarantees apply to police officers at home and off duty, as they do to a citizen.

2. Lockers at the police station, a police car, and other elements of on-duty performance are unlikely to be protected by the Fourth Amendment.

3. If an unlawful search occurs, the fruits of that search may be used during a disciplinary hearing but not in a legal proceeding. This may not apply to departments that have elaborate policies on the internal-investigation process.

4. Under *Garrity v. New Jersey* (1967), statements compelled during an internal investigation cannot be used in a court of law. Compelled testimony for internal investigations is routine practice and is not protected by the Fifth Amendment. Such compelled testimony is typically referred to as a **Garrity interview**.

Complaint outcomes. Investigations into citizen complaints are typically classified in one of four possible ways: **Sustained complaints** are ones that, as the result of an investigation, are determined to be justified. **Unsubstantiated complaints** are ones that, in the opinion of those making the decision, have no supporting evidence and so cannot be considered either true or false. The majority of citizen complaints against officers are classified in this manner because it is often difficult to determine with **reasonable certainty** that the complainant's allegation is true. **Unfounded complaints** are those that the investigation determines did not occur as alleged by the complainant. **Exoneration** of an officer occurs when the investigation results in a finding that the alleged complaint is essentially true, but the officer's behavior is considered to be justified, legal, and within organizational policy (Perez 1994).

If an officer is found guilty of the complaint, she or he can appeal the outcome. If the complaint is sustained, the officer will receive some sort of punishment. Carter identifies several kinds of punishments.

1. *Termination of employment.* This is complete severance, including salary and benefits.

2. *Demotion/loss of rank.* Loss of rank is a significant action because it represents loss of salary and liability in career growth. It

may not include "grades," which are salary increments within ranks.

3. *Punitive suspension.* An officer is barred from work without salary for a designated period usually not exceeding four weeks. In many jurisdictions the officer cannot even work off-duty in positions that require police authority.

4. *Punitive probation.* An officer stays on duty with full salary and benefits. A subsequent sustained misconduct allegation may result in dismissal.

5. *Reassignment.* It is often used in conjunction with some other kind of punishment. An officer may be taken out of a specialized position or may be moved to another shift or location.

6. *Mandatory training.* An officer may receive training on the issue related to the misconduct.

7. *Reprimand.* An officer is officially admonished for his or her behavior. It is in written form, usually from a division commander, with a copy placed in the personnel file.

8. *Supervisory counseling.* This is a discussion with the officer concerning a problem usually related to some performance factor or procedure. It is intended to be both instructive and corrective. It does not typically become a part of the employee's personnel file. (1994, pp. 367–368)

Research concerning the number, types, and dispositions of complaints against police is limited. Several studies, however, provide useful insights. A summary (Independent Commission . . . 1991; Dugan and Breda 1991; "Younger NYC Cops" 1989; Petterson 1991; Walker 1998; Wallace 1990) is presented below:

1. Although less than 1 percent of citizens complain about police methods and behavior, as many as 10 to 15 percent may think that they have something to complain about—either what officers did or failed to do.

2. The rate of complaints varies among police departments, from about 6 to 81 complaints per 100 officers.

3. The percentage of sustained complaints also varies among police departments, from about 0 to 50.

4. Complaints concerning the excessive use of police force are usually sustained less often than other types of complaints.

5. It appears that a small number of police officers account for a disproportionate number of complaints. Although the research varies, a reasonable estimate is that approximately 10 percent of the officers in a police department receive at least 25 or 30 percent of the complaints by citizens.

6. It also appears that a disproportionate number of complaints are filed against younger, less-experienced officers. As many as two-thirds or more of all complaints in some departments may in-

volve officers who are 30 years of age or younger and who have five or less years of experience.

Case Study 10.1 presents the results of a survey of citizen complaints in 10 large cities. This table indicates the widespread differences between rates of complaints per 100 officers and the percentage of sustained complaints. The frequency of complaints varies sharply from city to city. To understand these differences, several factors must be considered.

Case Study 10.1

Citizen Complaints About Police Misconduct in 1988

City	Number of Complaints	Complaints per 100 Officers	% Sustained
San Francisco	1,146	81.4	1.2
Seattle	412	35.9	7.7
Boston	427	21.8	25.0
Cleveland	376	21.7	8.8
New York	4,179	15.7	2.4
Indianapolis	156	15.3	14.1
Miami	312	13.3	21.4
Los Angeles	702	9.1	17.1
San Jose	91	9.0	16. 4
Oakland	47	7.3	0.0

Source: Adapted from B. Wallace. 1990. "S. F. Watchdog Upholds Few Charges." *San Francisco Chronicle*, May 29: 1, 4–6.

The number and types of complaints against the police, in general, are the result of actual differences in police behavior, the perceived receptivity of a police department to accepting and acting upon complaints, and a political climate that either discourages or encourages citizens to complain.

The reasons for variations in sustained complaints are also related to the degree to which departments have well-defined standards for police behavior, take those standards seriously, and conduct thorough investigations into complaints. Low rates of sustained complaints may result from a departmental culture that implicitly encourages officers to engage in of aggressive police work.

Issues in Internal Investigations

There are several controversies concerning the internal investigation of police officers. These include the physical location of the internal-affairs unit, the personnel assigned to work in internal affairs, whether or not complaints should be encouraged, whether or not internal-affairs units should be proactive or reactive, what should be done about false complaints, the type and severity of discipline for officers who have sustained complaints, and whether the police can effectively police themselves.

Location and personnel. Does the location of internal-affairs units influence the number of citizen complaints? It is possible that a citizen who believes he or she has been abused by the police will be reluctant to go to the police department to file a complaint. As D. Perez observes,

> The uniforms, badges, guns, and paramilitary carriage of police officers at a station house might be too much to confront for more passive complaints. A system that requires complaints cannot be made exclusively for those citizens having the audacity to confront the government. (1994, p. 103)

As a result of this possibility, some police departments have placed the internal-affairs unit in another location away from police headquarters. This change of location may also have a positive impact on the public perception of the police, because citizens may believe that the police are taking their complaints seriously.

Most often the personnel who conduct internal investigations are sworn police officers, but some departments also use civilians for some investigations on the assumption that some citizens who want to complain will be more comfortable with a civilian than a police investigator. Also, the use of civilians creates the public perception that complaints will be taken more seriously and be more thoroughly investigated. In addition, because a substantial number of complaints are made by minority citizens, internal-affairs units may also be staffed with minority members. This use of minorities may even be necessary if the police department has no minority officers who can be assigned to the internal-affairs unit.

Assignment to internal affairs is often controversial. Internal-affairs investigators are rarely popular with other officers. The term headhunter or some other uncomplimentary nickname, is sometimes used by officers to describe internal-affairs investigators. As a result, some police chiefs and sheriffs have made it clear that assignment to, and effective performance in, an internal-affairs unit is a "fast track" to advancement.

Orientation of internal-affairs units. Should citizen complaints against the police be encouraged? Encouraging citizens to come forward—either openly or anonymously—has several possible consequences. On the one hand, it may increase the trust between police and citizens and provide managers with valuable information about officer behavior. On the other hand, it may also result in more complaints, justified or otherwise. Unfortunately, in departments that encourage complaints, a morale problem may develop as an increasing number of officers have to endure an investigation into a complaint. Whether or not complaints are sustained, internal-affairs investigations are often stressful for the officers involved and unpleasant for officers throughout the department.

Should internal-affairs units be reactive or proactive? A reactive unit investigates only those complaints that are brought to its attention. A proactive unit seeks out officers involved in deviant behavior. For example, an internal-affairs investigator might purposely commit traffic violations and, when stopped by an officer, offer a bribe to avoid a citation. If the officer takes the money, he or she is usually terminated and may be criminally prosecuted. Such a proactive approach may be strongly resented by officers because it creates a climate of mistrust between them and managers. Although some authorities recommend that internal-affairs units be proactive (Murphy and Caplan 1991, pp. 261–263), managers must be aware of the possible adverse consequences of such action.

Although it is not clear how often it occurs, citizens make **false complaints** about police officers. How should the police respond? In some jurisdictions, persons suspected of filing a false report can be criminally prosecuted. Police officers can also sue the person for defamation if he or she falsely accuses an officer of criminal conduct, misconduct, or incompetence.

Whereas the officer involved decides whether or not to file a civil suit against a person who made a false complaint, the police department decides whether to file criminal charges. Should they have that right? Although filing criminal charges may act as a deterrent against false complaints, it may also have a chilling effect on citizens with legitimate grievances, making this a most difficult question to resolve.

Sustained complaints. When complaints against officers are sustained, what should be done? The alternatives include counseling, retraining, verbal reprimands, written reprimands, demotions, suspension without pay, and termination. Unfortunately, there is no standard to follow. Generally, of course, the more serious the behavior of the officer, the more severe the punishment.

After their examination of 171 sustained complaints involving excessive force or improper police tactics in the Los Angeles Police Department, the Christopher Commission (Independent Commission 1991) concluded that the type of disciplinary measures taken against the officers were too lenient. Only about 12 percent of the officers were terminated, resigned, or retired. Approximately 58 percent were suspended without pay for a period of time, and the remainder received some type of reprimand.

Officers do not have to accept the recommended disciplinary action if they believe it is inappropriate. Many police departments have an appeal process that allows the officer in question to challenge the type of discipline recommended. Officers can challenge in court what they perceive to be extreme forms of discipline. Consequently, discipline may be based, at least in part, on an assessment of whether or not the officer will appeal. The authors of this book are aware of instances in which police managers knew of inappropriate behavior but took no action because they believed that the appeals process would undermine any effort to punish the officer.

Another factor affecting the complaint process is the likelihood of civil litigation (discussed later) if the complaint is sustained. Some departments may be reluctant to discipline officers for fear that it will be interpreted as an admission of negligence on the part of the department. In some instances, citizen complaints cannot be investigated because the complainant will not cooperate until the civil suit is resolved. Consequently, the investigation of a citizen complaint may not be completed for a long time, possibly a year or more.

Effectiveness of Internal Investigations

Can the police effectively regulate the behavior of their own? Historically, there has been a recurring debate on this question.

Proponents of **internal (departmental) review** argue that review is necessary to maintain police morale, that external review interferes with the authority of the chief executive, and that other methods (e.g., elected and appointed officials, the courts) are available to citizens if they are not satisfied.

In addition, many police officers do not believe that external review of police conduct is likely to be impartial. They believe that such reviews and recommendations for discipline will often be politically motivated. Furthermore, they belive that in general, those favoring internal review have been the police themselves and ideological supporters.

Proponents of the **external (citizen) review** of police behavior (to be discussed in the next section) include individuals with a liberal political ideology, civil rights organizations, minority-group members, and the media (West 1988). Proponents argue that the internal investigations of police complaints are the actions of a system closed to outsiders and favorably predisposed toward police officers. Furthermore, internal investigations may not be trusted by the public. If the public perceives that the police are unresponsive and unfair in their investigation of complaints, public confidence in the police will be eroded. Consequently, involving citizens in the complaints process has the capacity to restore trust and confidence in police-citizen relations (West 1988).

Oversight Mechanisms External to the Police Department

The second set of oversight mechanisms are those outside the police department. They have emerged primarily in response to concerns that police departments do not hold their members sufficiently accountable. Two external oversight mechanisms—citizen review and legal remedies are considered here.

Civilian Review

A **civilian-review board** is an effort to control police behavior by establishing an external form of review for allegations of police misconduct. It should be noted, however, that even in those communities that have some type of external review, the police department usually continues to conduct its own investigations of complaints.

Research indicates that about 17 percent of the 132 largest cities and 60 percent of the largest 50 cities in the United States have some type of external review of citizen complaints against the police (West 1988; Walker and Bumpus 1991). The creation of an external review board is usually related to a political perception that the police are out of control and typically follows in the wake of a police scandal.

A brief history of civilian review. Citizen participation in the review of complaints against the police can be traced to the Progressive Era, when reformers wanted to reduce the influence of corrupt politicians (Caiden 1977). Yet throughout the first half of the twentieth century, there was little progress in establishing citizen review. In its 1967 report, the President's Commission on Law Enforcement and Administration of Justice noted the problems faced by citizens when they tried to complain about police brutality. Such citizens might be arrested, or the police would file criminal charges against them for filing a false report. Many police departments had no formal internal investigations unit or procedure. The commission found that less than 10 percent of citizen complaints were substantiated, and even when they were, officers were infrequently or too lightly punished.

Both the National Advisory Commission on Civil Disorders (1968) and the National Commission on the Causes and Prevention of Violence (1969) reached similar conclusions. These studies found that police departments had inadequate investigative procedures and resisted efforts to make complaint procedures more meaningful.

R. J. Terrill (1991) divides the discussion about civilian review into three time periods which he calls "climates of opinion." The first era was the late 1950s and 1960s, in which various forms of civilian review boards were first suggested. These early proposals were politically controversial and were vigorously resisted by the police. Several cities, such as Chicago and New York, struggled to establish some form of civilian review; only Philadelphia established a review process that lasted for several years, but it too was eventually abandoned. Inside Policing 10.2 describes what happened in Philadelphia.

Inside Policing 10.2
Civilian Review in Philadelphia

In 1957 the American Civil Liberties Union called for the establishment of a civilian-review board because there was tension between the police and some citizens, particularly African-Americans, who criticized the police for discriminatory practices. Although the police department did have an internal-affairs unit, called the Board of Inquiry, few citizens filed complaints. When they did, officers were usually exonerated or the complaint was not sustained.

The mayor of Philadelphia, Richardson Dilworth, had been supported by blacks in the recent election. He introduced an ordinance to establish a civilian-review board, but the city council did not support the board, so the mayor established the Police Review Board by executive order. The board consisted of five members who were to consider complaints against the police involving brutality, false arrests, discrimination, or any other wrongful act against a citizen. After considering complaints, the board would recommend what they considered the appropriate disciplinary measure to the head of the police department (Police Commissioner).

The lack of political support for the board and its limited legal standing (i.e., the next mayor could eliminate it by executive order) placed the board in a difficult position. Even the mayor's commitment was questioned because he provided minimal guidance and gave the board only a limited budget. The board could not even afford to employ an investigator; rather, they used a police officer to investigate complaints. In addition, except for some minority-group leaders, there was little community support for civilian review of the police.

The police response to the board was negative. The Fraternal Order of Police (FOP) was the police union in the city. The FOP attacked the board on two fronts; they conducted a propaganda campaign and also took legal action. The FOP argued that civilians were incapable of judging the behavior of officers, that civilian review subverted the authority of the police commissioner, and that it had an adverse impact on officer morale. The union even hinted that civilian review might result in officers doing less and, therefore, citizens would be in greater danger of being victimized. Finally, the union argued that the movement toward civilian review across the United States was a communist plot designed to undermine law enforcement and make it easier to overthrow the government. The FOP's position was supported by the International Association of Chiefs of Police, who came out in opposition to civilian-review boards.

The first legal action taken in 1960 by the FOP was to request that an injunction be issued to keep the board from holding hearings. This was resolved when the board agreed to change some of its procedures. The FOP filed another suit in 1965 that questioned the legal ☞

standing of the board. They requested an injunction to keep the board from holding any hearings, and the court granted it for about six months. After the court lifted the injunction, the board resumed hearings. In 1967, however, the court found that the executive order that had created the board violated the Philadelphia Home Rule Charter, and the board was enjoined from holding any hearings or investigating complaints against the police. The city government appealed the decision, even though the new mayor, James Tate, did not support the board. The state supreme court overturned the lower court's decision, but Mayor Tate did not reactivate the board.

In the nine years in which the board existed, it received slightly more than 1,000 complaints, but only 21 percent of those were heard. The others were either dismissed or handled informally. Of the 207 cases heard, less than 25 percent resulted in any disciplinary recommendations, and not one officer was terminated. In contrast, during the same period, the internal-affairs unit of the police department investigated over twice as many complaints, sustained complaints at a much higher rate, and imposed much harsher discipline, including terminations.

Sources: Adapted from G. E. Caiden. 1977. *Police Revitalization*. Lexington, Mass.: D. C. Heath, pp. 189–191; R. J. Terrill. 1991. "Civilian Oversight of the Police Complaints Process in the United States." In A. J. Goldsmith, ed. *Complaints Against The Police: The Trend to External Review*, pp. 291–322 Avon, Great Britain: Bookcraft, Ltd.

The second era, the 1970s, was distinguished by increases in public concern about the criminal justice system. The urban riots, the civil rights movement, the President's Commission on Law Enforcement and Administration of Justice (1967), and the National Advisory Commission on Civil Disorders (1968) all called attention to troubling behavior on the part of the police. This period was marked by increased public support for civilian review.

Several communities (e.g., Detroit and Miami-Dade County, Florida) established some type of civilian oversight of the police. However, these civilian-review processes were not without problems and resistance. The city of Detroit, over the opposition of the Detroit Police Department, established a five-person Board of Police Commissioners, which continues today. Its role includes the development of policies and procedures in consultation with the chief of police and approval of the police budget. The board also created the Office of Chief Investigator, who was given a staff of both civilian and police investigators. The chief investigator is responsible for coordinating the investigation of complaints and disciplinary matters in the police department. The board has the authority not only to receive complaints but also to review the investigation of complaints undertaken by the police department, and either to affirm or change any disciplinary action taken against officers.

During the third era, the 1980s, several major cities established review processes, including the San Francisco Office of Citizen Complaints, the San Diego Police Review Commission, and the Dallas Citizens' Police Review Board. Police opposition to civilian review did not change, however, nor did their principal arguments. Although the police no longer considered civilian review to be part of a communist plot to overthrow the government as they had in the 1960s, police executives, departments, and unions continued to argue that it undermined managerial authority and the professionalism of the police. To strengthen their argument, many departments worked hard to improve the internal investigations of citizen complaints.

W. E. Petterson's survey (1991) of 19 communities with some type of civilian-review board indicates the diversity of approaches in this area. One of the boards was established in the 1960s, four in the 1970s, and 14 in the 1980s. Fourteen of the boards conduct their own investigations, whereas the others rely on investigations by the police department. Only one of the boards, however, is authorized actually to determine the discipline to be imposed on officers. The others can only recommend disciplinary measures that the police department may or may not follow.

Today, civilian-review boards encompass many different types of organizational designs and purposes. S. Walker and B. W. Kreisel (1996) identified five dimensions along which civilian-review boards vary. They are discussed in Inside Policing 10.3. Walker and Kreisel provide an understanding of the diversity of forms of external review in the United States today.

Inside Policing 10.3
Organizational Features of Citizen Review

The Nature of Citizen Input

How are citizens involved in the review process? There are three ways.

1. Citizens conduct the initial fact-finding investigation.
2. Citizens have input into the review of complaints but do not conduct the investigation.
3. Citizens monitor the process but do not review individual complaints.

The Complaint-Review Process

Review boards may have two purposes.

1. They review individual complaints. Virtually all boards do this.
2. They review department policies and make recommendations for changes. About 66 percent of the boards also do this.

Jurisdiction

Do boards monitor police officers only or are they also responsible for other public employees? Seventeen percent of the boards studied also set up other boards with the authority to monitor other public employees.

Organizational Structure

1. The majority (85 percent) had a multi-member board. Boards ranged in size from 3 to 24 members. Twenty-seven percent of these boards included sworn police officers. This structure deals with one of the most important questions affecting civilian review: Who has representation on the civilian review board? Many minority-group members, while seeking advocacy, are concerned with the issue of tokenism.
2. The remainder (15 percent) are administrative boards with a single administrative director. These boards presume that administrative procedure, rather than representation, is the best way to conduct review of police behavior.

Operating Policies

There are four different policies, each of which has direct implications for police accountability.

1. Independent investigative powers are held by about 33 percent of all review boards.
2. Subpoena power is held by 38 percent.
3. Public hearings are conducted by about half (46.2 percent).
4. About 32 percent provide legal representation for the officer, for the citizen, or both.

Each of these four policies may be described as a different element of a "criminal trial" model. Only 11 percent of the boards studied had all four elements. Two of the review boards had none.

Source: Adapted from S. Walker and B. W. Kreisel. 1996: "Varieties of Citizen Review." *American Journal of Police* 15: 65–88.

The limits of civilian review. The decision by a community to establish some form of civilian review of police behavior is usually based on the assumption that it will be more effective and fair than internal investigation by

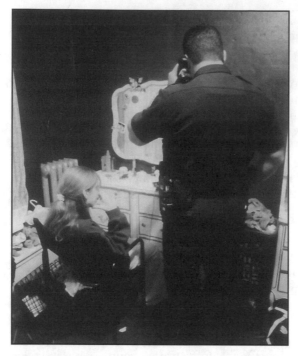

Officer searching a residence. The scope of his search is limited by the Fifth Amendment and related legal cases. (Photo: Mark C. Ide)

the police. The limited research in this area, however, tends not to support this assumption. G. E. Caiden (1977) concluded that attempts to institute civilian review in the 1970s failed because the police resisted such attempts and used both political and legal means to limit their potential effectiveness.

West found that complaint procedures (internal or external) were not related to the number of complaints filed or the seriousness of those complaints. But when complaints were encouraged by either the police or civilian-review boards, they were less likely to be sustained. It appeared that frivolous and minor complaints occurred more frequently when complaints were encouraged.

Perez (1994) has identified several problems associated with civilian review. First, civilian review boards do not tend to find problems occurring more frequently than internal affairs units do. He observes that

> No fair system will find the police guilty of misconduct very often because, in a legalistic sense, the police are not guilty of misconduct very often.

> One must also consider a sociological reality. Most civilian-review board members develop an appreciation for the police and for police work. Over time, they are less and less prone to be tough on officers, and they actually begin to find fault with complainants. (1994, p.146)

Consequently, civilian review is unlikely to change the efficiency or effectiveness of police review. Finally,

> Members of civilian-review boards . . . seem to have a sort of "boys will be boys" attitude toward truthfulness. . . . When a lie is discovered by civilian systems, it is considered to be a part of the "playing of the game," a natural product of a system designed to investigate misconduct. . . . Thus, while chiefs take lying very seriously, civilian review boards largely do not. (1994, p. 147)

Perez notes three additional limitations of civilian review. First, it is too far removed from the day-to-day existence of the line officer to understand and respond to the dynamics of illegal behavior. Second, civilian review can take away opportunities for the immediate supervisor to deal creatively with problems. Inadvertently, civilian review undermines the ability of the police department to "generate genuine humility and acceptance of error on the part of young, developing police officers" (p.161.) Finally, civilian review tends to discourage the use of internal socialization processes. Perez believes that the role of peers and their contribution to the socialization of recruits is an inevitable and essential part of police work. It should be encouraged, not discouraged.

❖ ❖ ❖ ❖

Legal Control

Criminal, civil, and administrative laws are important tools in the control of police. Like all citizens, the police are required to obey all substantive criminal laws. In addition, some states impose criminal penalties for officers who misuse the verification given them by standards commissions. Such officers can be decertified. Procedural laws, called criminal procedure or due process, provide legal guidelines for the police when enforcing substantive laws. They govern the process of investigating crimes and apprehending suspects. Police officers and departments may also be sued civilly if they fail to act in a responsible manner.

Criminal liability. Prior to 1937, there were few important procedural rulings by the Supreme Court. The individual safeguards found in the Bill of Rights had not yet been applied to the states. Between the 1930s and 1960, the Court began to selectively incorporate some of these safeguards into the procedural requirements that local police had to follow. Not until the 1960s did the "age of incorporation" or the "due process revolution" begin. During this decade, the Supreme Court increasingly applied provisions of the Bill of Rights to the states.

The 1960s were characterized by widespread support for the protection of the civil rights of individuals. The Warren Court of this period, named for Chief Justice Earl Warren, was associated with a liberal political philosophy because the majority of judges supported more legal restrictions on the police. From a politically conservative point of view (which included the views of a majority of police officers), the police were "handcuffed" in their ability to fight crime.

The criminal procedures established in the Warren Court era had little substantive impact on the ability of the police to make arrests or secure confessions (Walker 1998). But these new procedures did tend to reduce the psychological and physical coercion used by police to gain information from suspects (see Chapter 9). Procedures mandating due process also reduced the number of illegal searches conducted by the police.

The Warren Court is perhaps best known for the **exclusionary rule,** which provides a legal means for attempting to control officer behavior. It was a product of *Mapp v. Ohio* (1961). The Supreme Court stated in Mapp that "all evidence obtained by searches and seizures in violation of the Constitution is, by the same authority, inadmissible in a state court." This rule has been one of the most controversial legal rules that apply to the police, in spite of an increasing body of evidence that it has had no discernible effect on police practice involving violent and property crime. The possibility that evidence will be excluded from a criminal trial provides an incentive for officers to follow the correct criminal procedure. In practice, legal motions to suppress evidence are infrequently filed in criminal cases, and when they are, they are routinely denied. In addition, it appears that U.S. Supreme Court cases in the areas of search and seizure, the obtaining of confessions, and the threat of excluding evidence have had a positive impact on police behavior (Walker 1998).

When police officers violate a criminal law, they can be held for criminal prosecution in both state and federal courts. For example, a police officer engages in the use of force, which may be excessive, against a minority citizen but is exonerated by both the police department and the state criminal justice system. That is, he or she did not violate any state criminal law. Yet, despite being found not guilty, the officer could be prosecuted in federal court for a violation of the civil rights of the minority citizen. The officer could also be prosecuted in federal court even if he or she was not tried at the state level.

In contrast to the Warren Court, the subsequent courts under Burger (1969–1986) and Rehnquist have displayed decisions that are seen as "friendly" to the police. For example, the **good-faith exemption** to the exclusionary rule increasingly guided the court's assessments of the lawfulness of police searches. The good-faith exemption stated that police have acted in accordance with the Constitution if they have acted honestly or as in the case of *Leon v. California* (1984) their transgressions have been minor. One way to think about the difference between the Warren and the Burger courts is in terms of H. Packer's (1968) two models of criminal justice. The Warren Court exhibited more of a due-process model and the Burger Court a crime-control model. The Burger Court focused more on factual determinations of a person's guilt or innocence and presumed that police generally acted in good faith (Weddington and Janikowski 1996). The criminal justice system was conceived as a fact-finding body rather than as an arbiter of an adversarial contest between the government and citizens. The Rehnquist Court continued this trend—some observers have called it a counterrevolution following the Warren revolution (Decker 1992)—by focusing on speed, finality, and efficiency, particularly in habeas corpus decisions. In other words, the Rehnquist Court has continued to display characteristics of Packer's crime-control model.

Inside Policing 10.4 lists and briefly describes some of the more important Supreme Court cases that established procedural standards for the police. In addition to these decisions, each state also has procedural requirements for police that may be even more restrictive than those established by the Supreme Court. The cases noted also illustrate how procedural requirements can change. Supreme Court cases are influenced by the political beliefs of the judges on the court and the political climate in the nation. The Warren Court was considered to be politically liberal, while the Rehnquist Court is considered to be more conservative.

Criminal violations of civil rights. Police officers, like anyone else, can also be charged with criminal violations of civil rights, as defined in Title 242, Section 18 of the U.S. Code:

> Whoever, under color of any law, statute, ordinance, regulation, or custom, willfully subjects any inhabitant of any State, Territory, or District to the deprivation of any rights, privileges, or immunities secured or protected by the Constitution or laws of the United States, or to different punishments, pains, or penalties on account of such inhabitant being an alien, or by reason of his color or race that are prescribed for the punishment of citizens shall be fined not more than $1,000 or imprisoned not more than one year, or both; and if death results shall be subject to imprisonment for any term of years or life.

❖ ❖ ❖ ❖

Inside Policing 10.4
Selected Supreme Court Cases (1960 to present)

Mapp v. Ohio, 367 U.S. 643 (1961): The "exclusionary rule" used in federal trials is applied to the states. Evidence obtained illegally cannot be used in a trial or in subsequent proceedings.

Gideon v. Wainwright, 372 U.S. 335 (1963): The right-to-counsel provision of the Sixth Amendment is applied to the states.

Escobedo v. Illinois, 378 U.S. 478 (1964): If the defendant requests an attorney, police must comply before interrogating the defendant.

Miranda v. Arizona, 384 U.S. 436 (1966): In order to prevent police from coercing confessions, the court established a rule that a defendant must be informed of Fifth and Sixth Amendment rights and that the defendant must waive those rights prior to any police interrogation.

Katz v. United States, 389 U.S. 347 (1967): Fourth Amendment requirements for search and seizure apply to electronic surveillance even if there is no actual physical intrusion into the property of a defendant.

Terry v. Ohio, 468 U.S. 1 (1968): Police officers are authorized to "stop and frisk" suspicious persons in order to conduct a proper investigation and to protect the officer from possible harm.

Chimel v. California, 395 U.S. 752 (1969): When making arrests, police officers are allowed to search the defendant and the immediate area under the defendant's control (which, in effect, means that only the area within an "arm's length" distance could be searched).

Harris v. New York, 401 U.S. 222 (1971): Statements taken from a defendant that were not coerced, but that were obtained in violation of the Miranda ruling can be used to question the credibility of the defendant if he or she testifies in court.

Michigan v. Mosley, 423 U.S. 93 (1975): A second attempt to interrogate a defendant, after the defendant has refused to make a statement in the first interrogation, does not violate the Miranda ruling if the defendant waives his or her right to an attorney.

United States v. Ross, 456 U.S. 798 (1982): Where probable cause exists to believe that an automobile contains evidence in a criminal case, police may conduct a warrantless search, including searching any closed containers that may be in the automobile (e.g., luggage).

New York v. Quarles, 467 U.S. 649 (1984): Miranda rights do not apply when circumstances dictate to the police that "public safety" is an important and "immediate necessity." This means that under certain circumstances the police can ask incriminating questions of suspects prior to giving the suspect the Miranda warning. This is the "public safety" exception to the exclusionary rule.

Nix v. Williams, 467 U.S. 431 (1984): Illegally obtained evidence will not be excluded from a trial if it is "inevitable" that the evidence will be "discovered" anyway. This is the "inevitability of discovery" exception to the exclusionary rule.

United States v. Leon, 468 U.S. 897 (1984): Evidence obtained using a search warrant that a police office obtained from a "detached and neutral" judge can be used at trial even if it is later discovered that there was no probable cause to issue the warrant. This is one example of the good-faith exception to the exclusionary rule.

Moran v. Burbine, 475 U.S. 412 (1986): A request for an attorney must come from the defendant. If another party calls an attorney, and the attorney contacts the police about the defendant, the police are not obligated to delay or stop an interrogation of the defendant. And this attempted contact has no bearing on the admissibility of defendant's statement if the defendant waived his or her right to an attorney.

Maryland v. Garrison, 480 U.S. 79 (1987): When police officers conduct a warrant search at the wrong location, but their mistake is considered reasonable given the circumstances, there is no violation of the Fourth Amendment, and any evidence obtained will not be excluded in a criminal trial.

U.S. v. Sokolow, 490 U.S. 1 (1989): Sokolow was stopped by police as a possible "drug courier" when trying to ☞

smuggle drugs through the Honolulu airport. The Supreme Court ruled that probabilistic information describing characteristics of drug couriers provided a basis for an investigative detention in accordance with principles of reasonable suspicion.

Illinois v. Rodriquez, 110 S. Ct. 2793 (1990): If police enter a residence in good faith and observe drugs in plain sight inside the residence, the evidence thusly seized is acceptable in court.

Michigan Department of State Police v. Sitz, 110 S. Ct. 2481 (1990): This case upheld the constitutionality of a highway sobriety checkpoint.

Harmelin v. Michigan, 111 S. Ct. 2680 (1991): The court permitted imposition of a life term for a nonviolent first offense: possession of 650 grams of cocaine. Under federal law, the sentence would have been about 10 years. The court ruled that the Eighth Amendment would invalidate only grossly disproportionate sentences. Two justices stated that proportionality in sentencing, short of the death penalty, was irrelevant.

Florida v. Bostick, 111 S. Ct. 2382 (1991): This case expanded the meaning of "consent" in consensual searches. If an officer's request is not coercive and the passenger was free to refuse, the search satisfies consent, even if the passenger—Bostick, in this case, being on a bus—is not free to leave.

Holland v. McGinnis, 763 F. 2d 1044 (1992): The police lied to a suspect, telling him that his car had been seen at the scene of a crime. The suspect confessed. The courts ruled that the confession was admissible evidence.

Minnesota v. Dickenson, 113 S. Ct. 2130 (1993): A police pat-down of a suspect on the basis of reasonable suspicion that reveals drugs is admissible evidence. An officer's sense of touch justifies seizing contraband even when no other reason to suspect the presence of narcotics exists.

United States v. Hatchett, 31 F. 3rd 1411-1417 7th Cir. (1994) Officers investigating a crime do not have to list every detail in order for a warrant to be valid. Only those facts that provide a basis for probable cause are sufficient.

Arizona v. Evans, 63 LW 4179 (1995): Evans was arrested on a warrant that was outdated. Marijuana was found on the suspect at the time of arrest. The Supreme Court ruled that evidence cannot be excluded because of a clerical error.

Maxwell v. City of New York, 102 mF. 3rd 664, 666, 2nd Cir. (1996): Checkpoints constitute seizures, but they are lawful under the Fourth Amendment if the societal interest advanced by the checkpoint outweighs the intrusion of the individuals stopped. The checkpoint must be considered "reasonably" effective.

Maryland v. Wilson, 117 S. Ct. 882, 137 L. Ed. 2nd 347 (1996): Is a police officer's order of a passenger to exit a vehicle after a valid stop a legal seizure? When a passenger, Wilson, exited, drugs fell from his pocket. The court ruled that the officer's order did not constitute an unreasonable seizure.

Whren v. United States, 116 S. Ct. 1769, 135 L. Ed. 2nd 89 (1996): Does a pretextual stop (a stop made for a legally valid reason such as a taillight violation but whose underlying purpose was altogether different, such as to examine the vehicle for drugs) made by a police officer invalidate a subsequent legal vehicular search for drugs? The court ruled that the subjective intentions of police officers do not invalidate an objectively reasonable action.

County of Sacramento v. Lewis, 118 S. Ct. 1708 (1998): The Supreme Court hcld that, in a high-speed chase, a police officer does not deprive an individual of substantive due process by causing death through actions that indicate a deliberate disregard or a reckless disregard for the rights of others. Only arbitrary conduct is actionable.

It is difficult to prove beyond a reasonable doubt that a police officer committed a crime—either state or federal—as a result of the possible use of excessive or deadly force. To do this, it is usually necessary to establish that the officer had criminal intent to engage in the behavior. The prosecution has to establish that the officer knew and understood the nature and the consequences of his or her action, that the officer knew what he or she was doing was a crime and did it anyway.

Decertification. Another method of legal control involves the possible ❖ ❖ ❖ ❖
decertification of officers. About three-fourths of the states have some form
of decertification (Goldman and Puro 1987). In Florida, the Criminal Justice
Standards and Training Commission is authorized to "decertify" (or suspend
or put on probation) officers for (1) violating the legal rights of individuals;
(2) the "negligent deprivations of liberty or property"; (3) failing to maintain
the required qualifications for the job; (4) falsifying or misrepresenting information during the application process; and (5) "gross insubordination, gross
immorality, habitual drunkenness, willful neglect of duty, incompetence, or
gross misconduct." Between 1976 and 1983, the commission decertified 132
officers, suspended 14, and put two on probation. In 22 cases, the decertification was the result of behavior that involved criminal conduct; in the other
cases, it was for departmental or private misconduct (Goldman and Puro
1987, pp. 67–68).

Civil liability. One of the most common legal methods to control police
behavior is a **civil liability suit.** This means that a police officer, his or her supervisor, the chief, and the police (or at least the governmental unit, i.e., the
city of which the department is a part) can be sued for monetary damages for
negligent behavior.

It is increasingly common to sue the police for misconduct under federal
law. The most common statute for suing the police is Title 42 of the United
States Codes, Section 1983 (Meadows 1996). A Section 1983 suit can be filed
whether or not a criminal action has been filed, but it commonly follows
criminal cases brought against the police. There are two requirements for a
Section 1983 suit (Meadows 1996). First, the defendant must be acting under
the color of law. Second, there must be a violation of a federally protected
right. Meadows explains these principles as follows:

> The first requirement means that the on-duty officer is performing an act
> lawfully or unlawfully. Police officers who arrest without probable cause,
> or administer excessive force, are misusing their authority under the color
> of law. Committing unlawful acts (e.g., sexual assaults) can fall under this
> principle. The second requirement refers to violations of protected rights.
> Some examples are Fourth and Fifth Amendment violations or police ac-
> tions violating a person's due process rights. Thus, an officer who mali-
> ciously beats a prisoner or denies an arrestee needed medical treatment
> would fall under this principle. (1996, p. 105)

Police officers can be held liable in both state and federal courts. In states
this is done through the use of state tort law, or in some cases, through a
state's civil rights law. Under federal law a police officer can be held liable for
depriving an individual of her or his civil rights, conspiring to interfere with
someone's civil rights, or failing to protect a citizen's equal rights under the
law.

The emphasis in this section is on civil suits in state courts. It should be
emphasized, however, that civil suits in federal courts are increasingly common for these reasons. The suit may include a request for an injunction to
keep officers from engaging in inappropriate behavior. The time it takes to go
to trial is usually shorter than in state court. And it is easier for the plaintiff
(the person suing the officer) to get documents from the police department.
In addition, in federal court, if the plaintiff is successful, the defendant has to
pay the cost of the plaintiff's attorney (del Carmen 1991).

In state law, a **tort** is a civil wrong (not including a contract) in which the act of one person, in violation of a legal duty required by law, causes an injury to another person or damage to his or her property. There are two kinds of torts used in civil liability suits against officers: intentional and negligent.

Intentional torts are those in which the officer intends to cause some physical or mental harm. The most common type of legal actions against the police in this area are for excessive use of force, false arrest and imprisonment, assault and battery, wrongful death, intentional affliction of emotional or mental distress, misuse of legal procedure (e.g., a malicious prosecution), invasion of privacy, illegal electronic surveillance, and defamation.

Negligent torts involve a breach of lawful duty to act reasonably toward individuals by a police officer which might cause harm. Examples of a negligent tort would be the careless operation of a motor vehicle, failure to protect someone, or failure to respond to a call. The major difference between intentional and negligent torts is that, in the former, the officer's mental state is important, whereas in the latter it is not.

The types of monetary awards that can be granted for a successful civil suit include both actual (or compensatory) and punitive (or exemplary). **Actual damages** apply to the estimated actual costs of the damage caused, such as medical bills or lost wages. **Punitive damages** are designed to punish and make an example of an officer who engages in reckless or intentional misconduct or who displays a callous indifference to the rights of another individual (del Carmen 1991).

Police officers can use several defenses in civil-liability suits involving intentional torts. A **good-faith defense** is one in which the officer did not know that what he did was against the law. A **probable-cause defense** is based on the officer's reasonable belief that the action taken was legal.

There are other defenses in negligent tort cases: The **discretionary-act defense** is based on the decisions made by officers during required acts. An officer had discretion on the time, nature, and extent of the act. The **sudden-emergency defense** is based on the argument that in some situations an officer has to act from instinct due to lack of time to exercise reasonable judgment. When a plaintiff in a civil suit can be shown to have contributed to his or her injuries, the officer cannot be held liable. Finally, a police officer cannot be held liable if a citizen does something dangerous that he or she was warned not to do by the police; in effect, this person assumes the risk.

Not only can individual officers be subject to civil suits, so can their superiors in the police department. Supervisors and managers can be held liable if it is determined that they were negligent in the manner in which officers were selected, trained, assigned, supervised, or disciplined. It is quite common for citizens alleging negligence to sue not only the officer involved but also the immediate supervisor, the chief of police or sheriff, the police department, and even the elected officials of the community. This is known as the **deep-pocket theory** because it is assumed the officer may have limited financial resources, whereas the other parties in the suit may have "deep pockets" filled with money, usually taxpayers' money, to pay damages (del Carmen 1989).

Civil suits have become increasingly popular in the last two decades. Large police departments frequently have numerous civil suits filed against officers every year. In 1967 there were 1,741 such civil suits filed. By the mid-

1970s the number had increased to over 6,000 a year. I. Silver (1995) esti-   ❖ ❖ ❖ ❖
mates that currently the police face around 30,000 civil suits annually.

The amount of damages paid by the police tends to be larger if a jury decides the police are negligent and determines the amount. In 1982 the average jury award in a liability suit was about $230,000. In 1985 this average had
increased to about $2 million. Between 1966 and 1983 the number of jury
awards against the police that exceed $1 million went from 1 to 350. In Los
Angeles the total monetary damages paid increased from $7,000 in 1965 to $8
million in 1990. Detroit paid out $14 million in police-brutality suits between
1970 and 1980 (del Carmen 1991).

How effective are suits as a mechanism of police accountability? P.
Chevigny (1995), in his study of New York and Los Angeles, contended that
damage suits had little impact on police policy. Los Angeles, in 1990, aver-
aged $1,300 per officer in suits. Yet, that money was viewed as part of the cost
of doing business. Individual officers were rarely fined. Departments, in fact,
infrequently keep data on litigation (Pate and Fridell 1993). Moreover, damage actions, even when sustained, offer little basis for guiding policy. "The
nexus between police accountability and civil damage claims is generally
very weak almost everywhere in the country" (Chevigny 1995, pp. 104–105).
In other words, although suits carry the power to punish wrongdoing, they
seem to be an ineffective control mechanism.

The Human Rights Watch has also found that civil litigation was an ineffective control mechanism:

> Gannet News Service published a series of investigative articles in March
> 1992 examining the fate of police officers named in one hundred civil law-
> suits in twenty-two states in which juries ordered $100,000 or more to be
> paid to plaintiffs between 1986 and 1991. The awards from these lawsuits
> totaled nearly $92 million dollars. Of 185 officers involved in these cases,
> only eight were disciplined. No action was taken against 160, and seven-
> teen were promoted. (1998, p. 82)

In other words, the outcome of a civil litigation was twice as likely to be a
promotion as a disciplinary action.

> Perhaps most important, and consistently lacking, is a system of oversight
> in which supervisors hold their charges accountable for mistreatment
> and are themselves reviewed and evaluated, in part, by how they deal with
> subordinate officers who commit human rights violations. Those who
> claim that each high-profile case of abuse by a "rogue" officer is an aberra-
> tion are missing the point: problem officers frequently persist because the
> accountability systems are so seriously flawed. (Human Rights Watch
> 1998, p. 33)

It can be concluded from the research conducted by the Human Rights
Watch that the systemic problem confronting police is not brutality, which it
claims is typically carried out by a small percentage of rogue officers, but the
fact that inadequate accountability procedures protect line officers and administrators. Yet the central charge made by the Human Rights Watch cannot be easily ignored. Brutality becomes public knowledge only when it
reaches a scandalous level, as it frequently does. Because of shoddy investigation and intentional lapses in internal police review, underfunded and
undersupported citizen review, and lax local and federal prosecution, citi-

zens are fundamentally unable to find out the true extent of brutality in the United States.

Liability in community policing. As previously discussed, departments are increasingly adopting community policing. Yet liabilities associated with it have been infrequently assessed. J. Worrall and O. Marenin (1998) framed the liability question as follows: Are there particular aspects of community policing that increase the liability of police departments? Community policing, they suggest, may lead to changes in civil liability claims in three ways:

1. Advocates of community policing support the development of creative solutions to problems. This may lead to uneven delivery of police services, according to the needs of particular neighborhoods. V. Kappeler (1993) expresses the concern that uneven application of the law—one of the central tenets of police professionalism—may result in increased negligent claims against the police. Further, the police might find themselves in the anomalous position that they are sued for failing to come up with innovative solutions to neighborhood crime problems.

2. Community policing officers assimilate into their tasks activities previously accomplished by citizens and citizen organizations, particularly in crime-prevention and public-order problems. In doing so, they are acting in an official capacity in situations different from those that characterize the traditional law enforcement mandate. They may consequently lower the bar for the color-of-law threshold for Section 1983 filings (civil rights violations under color of law) by creating more opportunities for lawsuit vulnerability.

3. Community-oriented policing enlarges the definition of the job of the police and increases the number of approved encounters. It is consequently changing the standard of "legal duty." The standard of "legal duty" is already hazy and may be made more so by community-oriented policing.

Worrall and Marenin identify particular cases in which community-oriented policing (COP) practices have resulted in liability.

1. In *Sovary v. Los Angeles Police Department* (1986), the plaintiff argued that the LAPD failed to carry through with a bicycle and foot patrol at the level promised, hence not allocating sufficient resources to protect citizens.

2. In *J.H. by D.H. v. West Valley City* (1992), the West Valley City Police Department implemented a Law Enforcement Explorer Scout program. The officer in charge of the program turned out to be a child molester. Because he was involved in transporting children to and from the program, he was acting in an official capacity.

3. In *Loper v. New York City Police Department* (1992), the plaintiffs argued that the police department's enforcement of a loitering statute amounted to harassment of needy people.

Each of these examples reveals how an increased scope of police activity associated with community policing has the inadvertent consequence of expanding departmental liability. Worrall and Marenin conclude that "preemptive speculation and preparation" can reduce the chances that community policing programs will face unanticipated legal disruptions.

The Limits of Oversight Mechanisms

Oversight mechanisms, focused on punishment, are in many ways responsible for the development of the more secretive elements of police culture. J. P. Crank and M. A. Caldero (1999) explain police culture and its relationship to secrecy with the metaphor of an onion:

> Think of police culture as an onion. It has a heart that animates every police officer and gives meaning to police work. The heart is how police officers feel and think about their work, how they celebrate their victories and mourn their losses. It is how they do their work and how it is meaningful to them. The values most central to police, the heart of the onion, are encased by the first layer. . . . The outermost layers of the onion enable police to protect themselves from external influences, particularly the upper management levels of the organization itself, so that they can maintain their moral control over their territories and protect the inner "heart," the commitment to the noble cause.

Chapter 1 defined the organization culture as "the pattern of basic assumptions that a given group has invented, discovered, or developed in learning to cope with its problems of external adaptation and internal integration, [and] that have worked well enough to be considered valid" (Schien 1985, p. 9). The culture is made up of values that guide the behavior of police officers. This section will discuss these values.

M. Sparrow, M. Moore, and D. Kennedy (1990) have listed what they consider to be some of the most influential values of police officers. These values are summarized in Inside Policing 10.5.

Inside Policing 10.5
Building Blocks of the Police Culture

1. The public wants the police to be crime fighters, and that is what the police think of themselves as being, the primary crime-fighting organization in government.

2. No one other than another police officer understands the "real" nature of police work and what is necessary to do to get the job done.

3. Police have to stick together; loyalty to one another is more important than anything else because everyone else, including the public, politicians, and police managers, seems only to try to make the job of police officers more difficult. And these individuals are often unfair in their evaluations of the police.

4. Police cannot "win the war" on crime without violating legal, organizational, and ethical standards.

5. The public does not support or appreciate the police, and they expect too much of police officers.

Adapted from: M. Sparrow, M. Moore, and D. Kennedy (1990). *Beyond 911: A New Era for Policing* New York: Basic Books, p. 51.

The values that undergird police culture are derived substantially from daily work experiences. The most important elements of police culture reflect how officers adapt to their environment. Culture is the process of adaptation shared, discussed, and finally formed into habits. Cultural values are the meanings associated with those habits.

It is the type and frequency of problems confronted by the police—not the hopes of police reformers or administrators—that determines the way police do their work and what is important to them. Externally imposed control systems, often failing to understand this simple truth, backfire by intensifying resentment and secrecy. Police will not change unless their working environment is in some way changed. But they will become more secretive. As reformers and administrators intensify their efforts to hold the police accountable for an impossible mandate—to police a democracy—the strength of secretive elements of police culture will also increase (Manning 1998).

The next section will look at moral/ethical standards, as distinct from legal standards, which control behavior by providing officers with an internal gauge for their work. These standards are preventive because officers are expected to anticipate outcomes of their behavior before they act. They can be divided into professional standards and ethical standards.

Professional Standards

The concept of professionalism in policing is associated with the recurring attempts of reformers to ensure that police officers are honest. More specifically, an occupation, to be considered a profession, must adopt certain criteria. Recognition that such adoption is a prolonged process is called a **process-criterion approach**. As an occupation becomes a profession, one criterion is the learning of a systematic process that uses the scientific method (Cullen 1978; Geison 1983). Inside Policing 10.6 provides a list of the criteria the authors believe indicate that an occupation has reached professional status.

Inside Policing 10.6
Professional Criteria

1. Professionals are represented by professional associations, which serve the purpose of transmitting knowledge of the field.
2. Professionals are provided autonomy to perform their work. Even in organizations characterized by a bureaucracy, professionals are granted the opportunity to do their work with only limited control by supervisors.
3. A profession encompasses a unique body of knowledge, associated with research, which must be constantly updated.
4. Professionals require lengthy and

5. formal training.
6. Professionals require certification of quality and competence.
7. Professionals have a commitment to service on behalf of a clientele.

Sources: J. B. Cullen. 1978. *The Structure of Professionalism. Princeton*, N.J.: Princeton University Press; G. L. Geison. ed. 1983 *Professions and Professional Ideology in America.* Chapel Hill, N.C.: University of North Carolina Press; R. Hall 1968. "Professionalization and Bureaucratization." *America Sociological Review* 33: 92–104. and Bureaucracy.

The Police Professionalization Movement

Occupations that adopt the criteria presented in Table 10.6 are professionalized and are recognized as such by the public and other professional organizations. Their members believe in these criteria and are accorded the status of professionals (Hall 1968). As professionals, they are granted wide latitude to decide how to conduct their work. Even when they work in bureaucratic organizations, they have the autonomy to define problems in their area of expertise, to respond to those problems, and to gauge the success of their work. In a word, they are largely left alone by managers. Members of professions, such as doctors and lawyers, operate on these principles.

These conditions have not been true of the police. The police professionalization movement, undertaken in 1893 by the International Association of Chiefs of Police (IACP) and central to efforts to reform the police until 1968, sought to bureaucratize the police through specialization of function and intense control of line officers (Fogelson 1977). Rather than fostering independent decision making in line officers, the movement sought centralization of command under the authority of the chief. Individual officers were not admitted to the ranks of professionals but instead were controlled with ever tighter accountability (Fogelson 1977). Police departments, not police officers, became professionalized (Regoli et al. 1988).

As the police professionalization movement unfolded, officers were considered to be the product of a management system controlled by police executives. Police executives blended bureaucratic management and chain-of-command control to attempt to force line officers to go along with the reforms the executives wanted (Kuykendall and Roberg 1990). Consequently, police officers below the executive level were (and continue to be) rarely considered professional colleagues but only a group of individuals that had to be "managed". These police officers were left out of the professionalization process. One consequence of this trend was the development of sharply antagonistic relationships between line personnel and management (Reuss-Ianni 1983). Such antagonisms continued to be a critical issue at the end of the twentieth century.

Officers studying. (Photo: Mark C. Ide)

As subordinates, police officers have been told what not to do more often than what to do, and they have been laden with rules and policies seeking to control their behavior rather than to expand and sharpen their discretionary skills (Alpert and Smith 1999). Therefore, the professionalization movement itself, except for commitment to service (discussed later), did not contribute toward professionalization of policing. True professionalism did not begin until the professionalization movement declined and the community policing movement—with its emphasis on the decentralization of authority and empowerment of line officers—began to gain ground.

Criteria of Police Professionalization

Characteristics of policing as a true professional are described below.

Autonomy. The development of professional autonomy is a central criterion in the process of professionalization. Autonomy provides professionals with the discretion to carry out their work, and its presence shows that society acknowledges their professional status.

Police departments, as previously noted, have historically sought to control the behavior of line officers. The community-policing movement, however, emphasizes increased autonomy and with it the decentralization of authority and the use of creative techniques in solving problems. Each of these items expands the autonomy of police officers and thus represents movement toward professionalism.

Decentralization of authority occurs in two ways. One is the transfer of authority to make tactical decisions down the chain of command. For example, patrol officers may be given the authority to decide what kinds of crime problems they want to focus on. Line officers are expected to make decisions about tactics traditionally reserved for sergeants and lieutenants. The second way is geographic decentralization, meaning that officers are assigned to specific areas and take increased responsibility in solving the problems confronted in those areas.

Increased decision making is a relaxation of traditional constraints on the use of police discretion. J. Q. Wilson and G. Kelling (1982) argue that officers should be provided broad latitude in controlling common public-order problems on their beat. Such problems, if unaddressed, lead to neighborhood degradation and the onset of serious crime. By allowing officers wider latitude to deal with these problems, more effective long-term solutions to crime can be developed.

"Creative, customized police work," according to J. Skolnick and D. Bayley (1986), is important in finding creative solutions to recurring public-order problems. J. Goldstein (1998) suggests that officers engaged in problem-solving analysis redefine problems in non-criminal terms. Tailor-made responses, he contends, are a critical ingredient in finding effective solutions.

A unique body of knowledge. Another criterion of professionalism is that a profession has an area of unique expertise that only its practitioners are qualified to assess. Such expertise can be gained in three ways.

The first way, common especially before the 1960s, is to study the work of experts. These are well-educated, experienced practitioners, usually executives such as O. W. Wilson and August Vollmer, who lectured and wrote journal articles and books. Wilson's famous *Police Administration* contains many useful ideas about how to manage police departments. Many of his ideas were the result of his extensive experience, but some were taken from writers about general management principles. Many police today continue to depend almost exclusively on the knowledge of experts as a basis for their actions.

The second way to gain expertise is by **consulting-modeling.** In this method, the management and practices of a police department are analyzed by an expert or consultant who then compares the results to a model of what he or she considers to be desirable—for example, an effective way to select and train officers.

Models come from several sources. One source is the creativity and imagination of the expert or consultant. Another might be another police department that the consultant likes or considers to be progressive. If the consultant has been a police manager, the model might be his or her department. Or, models may come from books written by other experts in the field.

The third way to acquire expertise is by **scientific research,** Scientific research is empirical—that is, based on what can be observed. Two conditions apply to scientific observations. The first is that the observation has validity, meaning that the first is that the observation has validity, meaning that what the observer sees is what is actually going on. The second is that it has **reliability**, meaning that, if other observers conducted the research again in the same setting, they would be likely to come to similar (but not precisely the same) conclusions.

The research conducted by L. Sherman (1999) and by Sherman and his colleagues (1997), for example, shows how scientific research has had powerful effects on police knowledge. It has dramatically expanded knowledge about what works in policing. It has enabled scholars systematically to compare a wide variety of research on policing. And, it has provided a benchmark for thinking about the quality of police research.

Education and training. A further criterion of professionalism is formal preparation. Professionals typically undergo extensive training and education, followed by certification. Chapter 6 identified the types and extent of police training. Higher education is becoming increasingly important in all aspects of policing, as discussed in Chapter 11. Over the past three decades, the numbers of educated officers and in quantity of education that they possess have increased dramatically. Nevertheless, it does not yet approach the level expected in other professions.

Certification and accreditation. Professionalism also requires **certification** as a criteria of its members to ensure quality and competence. Usually state-level organizations give licenses or certifications. The legal profession, for example, has the state bar associations, and all lawyers must pass the bar examinations in their state in order to practice law there.

State standards organizations fulfill this function for the police. They set standards for the selection, training, and certification of police officers. Currently, all states have such organizations. Their titles vary. For example, in Arizona the state organization is called the Law Enforcement Officer Advisory Council; in Kentucky it is called the Department of Criminal Justice Training. Their central function is training, defined by B. Berg (1994) as learning the techniques for particular processes or procedures via example and through instruction.

The first standards organization, established in California in 1959, was the Commission on Peace Officer Standards and Training (POST). Its purpose is "to raise the level of competence of local law enforcement officers, to help improve the administration, management, and operation of local law enforcement agencies" (Commission on POST 1990, p. 4). In attempting to accomplish this mission, the commission engages in four activities (p. 4):

1. Develops minimum selection standards and minimum required knowledge and skill standards for the training of all levels of police officers (i.e., entry, supervisor, technical, managerial, and executive).

2. Develops and approves training programs that meet POST standards.

3. Provides management and research assistance and services to local law enforcement agencies.

4. Provides financial reimbursement to local agencies for officers who attend some POST-approved training courses.

Today POST exists in many states. It provides a wide diversity of training that focuses on skills, knowledge, cultural diversity, attitude, and ethics. Case Study 10.2 discusses areas of POST preparation.

Case Study 10.2

Are We Teaching Recruits What They Need to Know?

In a review of POST at the University Academy in Ohio, N. Marion (1999) asked a provocative question: Are recruits receiving training that practitioners and academics think will adequately prepare them for police work? To answer this question, she attended a POST class as a nonparticipant observer (a researcher who observes but does not participate). At the academy, students received 543 hours of training over 14 weeks. There was open enrollment, meaning that both employed police and nonemployed recruits alike could participate. The academy used about 30 instructors, who were retired or still active. Marion described course content as follows:

1. Knowledge. This area takes up the majority of hours.
   A. Students begin the first week with instruction on adult learning theory, including note taking, studying, and taking exams.
   B. Students spend a large section of time on the Ohio Revised Code.
   C. Civil liability is an important subject, on which officers spend six hours.
   D. Though ethics are recognized as an increasingly important part of police work, the academy has no classes on ethics.
   E. Special needs of problem groups are discussed. Of particular interest are gangs and practitioners of the occult. Recruits receive four hours of training on issues having to do with the disabled and mentally disturbed.
   F. Victims of crime are not generally dealt with.
   G. Victims of domestic violence are one of the mandatory subjects. Officer safety is the top priority during this training session.
   H. Cultural diversity requires 24 hours. Many students do not take it seriously, though the teaching is of high quality.
2. Skills.
   A. The most necessary and popular area of training is firearms. For many, it is the highlight of the academy.
   B. Self-defense tends to focus on unarmed tactics and includes use of pres-

☞ sure points and proper handcuffing technique. Use-of-force continuum is taught here.

C. The importance of physical conditioning is discussed on many occasions, but there are no formal classes on the topic.

D. Communications skills are taught so that recruits will know how to interview people effectively. Verbal judo is a major part of the training. Also emphasized is writing reports, taking field notes, and investigative form and content.

E. HAZMAT refers to hazardous materials. Cadets receive training in handling dangerous chemicals including how to notify the proper authorities and keep the community safe. The instruction also includes maintaining control during civil disorders, controlling crowds, the use of chemical agents, and an introduction to bombs.

F. Traffic-control skills are taught along with defensive driving and pursuit.

G. Cadets learn how to use the OC spray correctly. They have the option to have themselves sprayed.

H. Students are trained in the use of defensive weapons, such as the straight baton, the PR24 (one-sided baton), and the ASP. The primary concern of trainers is officer safety.

I. Several techniques for investigation are taught.

J. Training for patrol includes responding to crimes in progress, vehicle-patrol techniques, VIN reconstruction, prowler calls, vehicle stops, and techniques for officers' safety aid.

K. Cadets are trained in first aid so that they can provide preliminary first aid to themselves, other officers, victims of crime, and accident victims.

Marion concluded that the cadets generally received high-quality training. When comparing the training to the needs described by practitioners and researchers, she found that University Academy effectively covered the core topics. She noted that there was inadequate formal training in ethics and in procedures for dealing with victims and the elderly.

Marion expressed concern about the attitudes of instructors. Some instructors displayed views that she described as sexist. Others showed elitist attitudes, which contributed to a "we-them" view of the relationship between attitude regarding the police and the public. Yet overall, the trainers were doing well in providing the skills and knowledge that future officers would need.

An important aspect of licensing is **accreditation.** Professional organizations frequently provide for means of accreditation of member associations. Universities, for example, are periodically reviewed and accredited by regional accreditation boards. The purpose of accreditation for the police is to determine if a department meets general standards of policy and training. This determination is accomplished through self-assessment in an attempt to match national standards set up by the Commission on Accreditation for Law Enforcement Agencies **(CALEA)**. If a department is deemed to meet these standards, it is accredited by CALEA for a five-year period, which is renewable on reassessment if the department remains in compliance with the standards (Cole 1992).

CALEA was established in the early 1980s with 944 standards; this number was later reduced to 897 and then to the current 436 (Commission on Accreditation . . . 1995). Proponents of accreditation believe that self-assessment helps to identify departmental strengths and weaknesses and may reduce the exposure to liability. Departments in several states have been offered reduced insurance rates for completing the process (Williams 1989). Accreditation may help departments to develop the areas of administration issues and policy and perhaps by tightening up in these areas to become more professional and less exposed to liability (McAllister 1987). Nearly all of the accreditation standards, however, require that only a formal policy or procedure be established or that records be maintained. There is no monitoring system set up to determine the extent that CALEA-revised policies and procedures are actually implemented and followed.

The 436 standards set by CALEA are extensive, and if all are applied, it is likely that a department would become more, not less, bureaucratic. Also, most of the standards that apply to patrol work focus on law enforcement to the virtual exclusion of order maintenance and service (Mastrofski 1990). This situation is inconsistent with community policing. According to G. W. Cordner and G. L. Williams (1995, 1996), an examination of these standards regarding their applicability to community policing indicated, for the most part, that these standards are either silent or neutral on the subject. It appears that such standards could be constraining departments that are attempting to implement community policing, especially in the areas of officers' participation, encouraging risk taking in applications of discretion, and removing organizational barriers to creativity (Cordner and Williams 1996, p. 256). Cordner and Williams suggest that CALEA address the following concerns in the future:

1. Improve its research and development capacity and establish a more proactive posture toward contemporary changes in policing.

2. Play a more active role in big-picture issues affecting policing.

3. Pay more attention to accreditation issues and participate more actively in CALEA's direction and focus. (1996, pp. 378–379)

At this time, it seems prudent to suggest that, in relatively well-developed departments that are in transition to community policing, accreditation would impede managers' efforts to promote change (Oettmeier 1993; Sykes 1994). This conclusion would hold until the accreditation process places significant emphasis on problem solving, innovation, and community input, instead of focusing on bureaucratic rules and regulations. On the other hand, in less well-developed departments that have inadequate policies and procedures, accreditation may be beneficial.

Commitment to service. One of the most important criteria of a professional is a "commitment to service." Service is mean of a formal obligation to act on behalf of the professional's clientele to render service as needed. This is one area in which the police professionalism movement has contributed to the professionalism of individual officers.

One of the principal objectives of the movement was to instill a sense of calling in police officers. Early-twentieth-century reformers, concerned about the lax standards many recruits brought to police work, sought to instill officers with a commitment to law enforcement. To them, this meant a commitment to a belief in the contribution of police to society. The movement was successful in instilling this sense of commitment in police recruits. Chapters 3 and 4 discussed the service activities of police officers. Indeed, in many departments today, police work is mandated as a 24-hour obligation. In a reversal of direction, some reformers today are concerned about the overcommitment of police to their work, believing that police officers are overzealous in their pursuit of "bad guys" (Chapter 8).

Ethical Standards

The most effective method for controlling a person's behavior is for that person to believe in the standards of conduct he or she is supposed to follow. Ethical standards identify right and wrong behavior in any endeavor in life. Individual ethical standards about integrity, responsible behavior, use of coercion, and compassion provide officers with internal guides for their conduct. If officers do not have an internalized standard of ethics, they are more likely to engage in some form of deviant behavior (e.g., corruption brutality. Inside Policing 10.7 gives the code of ethics for police officers for the state of California. Part of this code was adopted from the IACP's code of ethics, which is utilized by many states (see Inside Policing 10.7).

Inside Policing 10.7
Law Enforcement Code of Ethics

The purpose of the police code of ethics is to ensure that all peace officers are fully aware of their individual responsibility to maintain their own integrity and that of their department. Every peace officer, during basic training, or at the time of appointment, must swear to abide by following code of ethics. The officer is also expected to abide by certain canons (rules) that embody those ethics.

Code

As a law enforcement officer, my fundamental duty is to serve humanity; to safeguard lives and property; to protect the innocent against deception, the weak against oppression or intimidation, and the peaceful against violence or disorder; and to respect the constitutional rights of all people to liberty, equality, and justice.

I will keep my private life unsullied as an example to all; maintain courageous calm in the face of danger, scorn, or ridicule; develop self-restraint; and be constantly mindful of the welfare of others. Honest in thought and deed in both my personal and official life, I will be exemplary in obeying the laws of the land and the regulations of my department. Whatever I see or hear of a confidential nature or that is confided to me in my official capacity will be kept ever secret unless revelation is necessary in the performance of my duty. I will never act officiously or permit personal feelings, prejudices, animosities, or friendships to influence my decisions. With no compromise for crime and with relentless prosecution of criminals, I will enforce the law courteously and appropriately without fear or favor, malice or ill will, never employing unnecessary force or violence and never accepting gratuities.

I recognize the badge of my office as a symbol of public faith, and I accept it as a public trust to be held so long as I am true to the ethics of the police service. I will constantly strive to achieve these objectives and ideals, dedicating myself to my chosen profession—law enforcement.

Canons

1. The primary responsibility of police officers and departments is the protection of citizens by upholding the law and respecting the legally expressed will of the whole community, not that of a particular political party or clique.

2. Police officers should be aware of the legal limits on their authority and the "genius of the American system," which limits the power of individuals, groups, and institutions.

3. Police officers are responsible for being familiar with the law and not

only their responsibilities but also those of other public officials.

4. Police officers should be mindful of the importance of utilizing the proper means to gain proper ends. Officers should not employ illegal means nor should they disregard public safety or property to accomplish a goal.

5. Police officers will cooperate with other public officials in carrying out their duties. However, the officer shall be careful not to use his or her position in an improper or illegal manner when cooperating with other officials.

6. In their private lives, police officers will behave in such a manner that the public will "regard [the officer] as an example of stability, fidelity, and morality." It is necessary that police officers conduct themselves in a "decent and honorable" manner.

7. In their behavior toward members of the public, officers will provide service when possible, require compliance with the law, respond in a manner that inspires confidence and trust, and will be neither overbearing nor subservient.

8. When dealing with violators or making arrests, officers will follow the law; officers have no right to persecute individuals or punish them. Officers should behave in such a manner so that the likelihood of the use of force is minimized.

9. Officers should refuse to accept any gifts, favors, or gratuities that, from a public perspective, could influence the manner in which they discharge their duties.

10. Officers will present evidence in criminal cases impartially because the officer should be equally concerned with the prosecution of criminals and the defense of innocent persons.

Sources: Adapted from California Commission on Peace Officers Standards and Training. 1990. *Administrative Manual*, p. c-5; and J. M. Pollock-Byrne. 1989. *Ethics in Crime and Justice*. Pacific Grove, CA: Brooks/Cole Publishing CO.

Ethical Perspectives

Attempts to identify appropriate ethical standards for the police have proven difficult. Different schools of thought, concerning what is and is not ethical "show the difficulty encountered by reformers concerned with police behavior."

Ethical formalism. The school of **ethical formalism** places moral worth in "doing one's duty." An officer who believes that police should "go by the book" is an ethical formalist. Legalistic policing is a kind of ethical formalism. An element of legalistic policing, as noted earlier, was that officers strive for the full enforcement of the law. Police legalism does not provide for fine distinctions in police discretion. On the contrary, legalistic departments justify their presence in terms of their capacity to enforce the law fairly among all groups.

Ethical utilitarianism. According to the school of **ethical utilitarianism,** it is the results of one's actions that determine what is moral or good. Behavior is judged not by the goodness of the acts, but by the consequences that they bring. For example, if an officer thought an illegal search was necessary in order to arrest a serious criminal, a utilitarian argument could be used to justify that search. An officer who says that she or he would sooner be "judged by 12 than carried by 6" is taking a utilitarian point of view—it is more important to use deadly force in an ambiguous though perilous encounter than it is to take a chance of being convicted of illegal behavior by a jury.

Ethical relativism. Perhaps the most complicated ethical position of all is **ethical relativism**. Relativism means that which is considered good varies with the particular values of groups and individuals. This perspective can be used to justify enforcing certain laws in some neighborhoods but ignoring them in others (Pollock-Byrne 1998, pp. 12–30). Police might object strenuously that they are not relative in their ethics. Yet, the idea of "full enforcement" of the law is neither realistic nor possible (Goldstein 1998). The discretionary nature of police work is widely cited. Consequently, an ethically relativistic approach to policing is probably a more realistic description of day-to-day police ethics than any other.

Inside Policing 10.8, adapted from J. M. Pollock (1997), displays in summary form several schools of ethics.

Inside Policing 10.8
Schools of Ethics

Religion

    What is good is that which conforms to God's will.

  How do we know God's will?

        Bible or other religious document.

        Religious authorities.

        Faith.

Ethical Formalism (deontological ethics)

    What is good is that which conforms to doing one's duty and the categorical imperative.

  What is the categorical imperative?

        Act in such a way that one would will it to be a universal law.

        Treat each person as an end and not as a means.

Utilitarianism.

    What is good is that which results in the greatest benefit for the greatest number.

    Act utilitarianism "weighs" the benefits of an act for just those people and just that incident.

    Rule utilitarianism "weighs" the benefits after determining the consequences of making that behavior a rule for the future.

Egoism

    What is good is that which results in the greatest benefit for me.

    Enlightened egoism, however, may allow one to reciprocate favors and may be practiced by a "good" person (because it benefits the self to be nice to others).

Source: Adapted from Joycelyn Pollock. 1997. *Ethics and Law Enforcement*. p. 348 in R. G. Dunham and G. P. Alpert (eds.), *Critical Issues in Policing*. 3rd Edition. Prospect Heights, IL: Waveland Press.

Elements of community policing are consistent with ethical relativism. One of the tenets of community policing is that community values should determine what is "good" in police work. But what a particular neighborhood considers to be "good" police work may result in the police tolerating certain types of illegal behavior or in officers engaging in illegal tactics to solve problems (e.g., conducting illegal searches of suspected drug dealers). Case Study 10.3 describes an incident in one Western city in which ethical relativism resulted in police officers tolerating illegal behavior.

Case Study 10.3

Ethical Relativism and the Law in Police Work

In Santa Ana, California, in the early 1980s, most of the people who frequented the downtown part of the city at night were "overwhelmingly Mexican." This area, in effect, became a *corso*, a customary part of Spanish life in which mariachi bands play and sing in cafes and bars and then come out onto the street, creating a festive atmosphere. Some of the persons participating in the *corso* were illegal aliens, but police officers made no attempt to determine the status of those individuals who frequented the area. In addition, officers did not usually provide assistance to agents of the Immigration and Naturalization Service (INS), whom many city residents called the "green gestapo" (referring to the green card that legal residents are supposed to have). In fact, the police department had a history of not cooperating with the INS because the police chief did not agree with the methods used by INS agents to identify and arrest illegal aliens (many of whom were otherwise law-abiding). Known prostitutes also frequented the downtown area at night. One prostitute, Sugar, was a drug addict who had four children. Sugar openly solicited young men to have sex. In one incident, Sugar met a young man on the street they engaged him in a short conversation, and then walked together with him around the corner of a building to a more private area. When the young man returned, a foot patrol officer called out in Spanish, "How was it?" The bystanders, who apparently knew what was going on, laughed at the young man's obvious embarrassment. The officer in question said: "We don't arrest these people [because] they are young men . . . who work hard [to] save up money to bring their families from Mexico . . . . They're gonna have sex. There just isn't any point in arresting people for having sex."

Source: Adapted from J. H. Skolnick, and D. H. Bayley, D. H. 1986. *The New Blue Line*. New York: The Free Press, pp. 40–43.

Notice that in this example, the community, meaning those individuals who frequented the downtown area at night, openly tolerated the practice of prostitution by drug addicts; consequently, the police ignored this illegal behavior as long as prostitutes did not appear to be under the influence of drugs at the time of the sexual activity. In addition, some officers undoubtedly thought it would be pointless to enforce laws against prostitution in such circumstances. This example also illustrates how community values can be in conflict with laws enforced by other government agencies such as the INS.

Ethical Dilemmas

Police confront profound ethical dilemmas. To fail to recognize this fact is to fail to understand the nature of policing. An ethical dilemma central to the craft of policing is the conflict between means and ends.

In their day-to-day practice, police confront what is widely called the Dirty Harry problem, that is, a conflict between means and ends. The end is so ethically right that they feel compelled to pursue it. Yet there are not legal means to do so. Should the officer use illegal or "dirty" means to pursue an unquestionably good end? Carl Klockars notes that police will justify dirty means if "what must be known and, importantly, known before the act is committed, is that it will result in the achievement of the good end" (1991, p. 414).

Klockars presented a compelling argument that the Dirty Harry problem is at the core of the police role. Police tend to think that they are dealing with people who are factually, if not legally, guilty. Consequently, an officer's belief in the certainty of guilt is not always determined by factual accuracy but by police cultural standards: "Dirty Harry problems," Klockars observes, "can arise wherever restrictions are placed on police methods and are particularly likely to do so when police themselves perceive that those restrictions are undesirable, unreasonable, or unfair" (1991, p. 414). In other words, Dirty Harry problems are probably more widespread, and less certain in the likelihood of factual guilt, than the police think that they are.

The particular ways that means vs. ends conflicts affect police work are expanded by Crank and Caldero. The core of police work, they argue, is the noble cause (see Chapter 8). This is the belief in the absolute rightness of doing something about criminals. It is a compelling commitment to "get bad guys off the street." Police, they note, not only dislike lawbreakers and troublemakers, but they identify intensely with victims of crime, and feel a moral responsibility for their assignments. The noble cause is corrupted when police consider it justifiable to break the law in order to apprehend or punish suspected wrongdoers. Noble-cause corruption means that officers are willing to violate legal means in order to achieve the noble end (Delattre 1996). Officers, Crank and Caldero contend, are hired into policing already morally committed to the noble cause. They are frequently hostile to due-process ideas at the time they are hired, and police culture reinforces this hostility. Only later in their career, as they move up the departmental ladder and gain broader perspective, do some officers begin to understand how the police are part of a broader system of competing moral values.

Noble-cause corruption takes many different forms. It includes testifying wrongly, or testimonial deception (Barker 1996), fluffing up evidence (Barker and Carter 1999), and in more extreme cases, drug corruption (Manning and Redlinger 1977). It encompasses all situations in which police bend the rules in order to sustain an arrest or get a conviction.

The Limits of Professional and Ethical Standards

The idea that codes of conduct can prevent misconduct seems reasonable. Yet prevention has proven to be difficult. First, although professional and ethical standards provide a good model of police work, they may have limited impact on its reality. They tend to be in written form, presented to satisfy external audiences, with little impact on day-to-day police behavior.

Second, the need for controls is driven to a certain extent by the people-based, unpredictable nature of police work. This same unpredictability, however, limits the effectiveness of those controls. And unpredictability cannot be removed from police-citizen interactions (Harmon 1995).

Third, the study of ethics can result in the development of arguments to justify deviating from established ethical or professional standards. Officers who belong to different ethical schools may use those schools to justify their behavior. It is not hard to review the research on police ethics, for example, to find adequate justification for breaking the law in order to get bad guys off the street, if that's what a police officer believes in.

Fourth, the manner in which officers carry out their day-to-day activities is affected as much by informal group ethics—the "ethics of the street"—as by any of the ethical schools discussed. The exercise of discretion, whether or not officers follow departmental standards or the law, or use force, or tell the truth or lie, or accept gratuities or engage in other corrupt practices, may be affected as much by peer group processes as formal ethical and professional standards.

B. R. Price sums up the challenge confronting the police in her essay on the quest for professionalism.

> Eradicating the excessive use of force and the scourge of police corruption are the most critical internal issues police face if they are to continue the long and arduous course toward professionalism. There have been many successes of late for law enforcement, especially in communications technology, forensics, information systems, interagency cooperation, and the development of a commitment to their peers, if not to professional conduct. But until attitudes of the police towards those they serve can be changed, they will continue to make their own jobs more difficult and more dangerous—and professionalism for the police will not come to pass. (1996, p. 87)

Summary

Police accountability is concerned with controlling line-officer behavior. Two kinds of accountability mechanisms are oversight (internal and external) and standards (professional and ethical). Internal oversight mechanisms are bureaucratic procedure and internal investigation. External mechanisms of accountability are citizen-review boards and legal control. Officers are controlled primarily through the administrative procedure. Internal investigations are usually associated with internal-affairs units; external review is usually associated with civilian-review boards. The legal methods to control the police include criminal prosecution in both state and federal courts, the exclusionary rule, decertification, and civil suits.

Two primary sources of standards for police officers are professional and ethical training. The police professionalization movement has historically represented efforts to make the police occupation a profession. However, with its preoccupation for the image of the department, it focused on controlling the behavior of line officers. Other trends in policing are consistent with ideas of professionalism at the individual level. These include efforts to expand and refine police discretion and advances in functional research. The expansion of police professional organizations, state standards organizations, and CALEA and accreditation all indicate increasing levels of police professionalism.

By considering different ethical schools of thought, one can see how officers facing the same problem might come to quite different solutions. The Dirty Harry dilemma, for example, is commonly confronted by police officers and has no solution.

Discussion Questions

1. What are the differences between an internal-affairs unit and a civilian-review board?

2. Should internal affairs be reactive or proactive? Which would be more effective? Why?

3. What are the principal issues in internal investigations?

4. What are the arguments for a civilian review board? What are the arguments for the police policing themselves? What type of officer review do you think is the most effective? Why?

5. How can criminal law and procedure be used to control police officers?

6. Explain civil liability and its importance to the control of police officer behavior.

7. What are the three ethical perspectives described in the chapter. Which one matches the Dirty Harry problem? Why?

8. What is the difference between an intentional and a negligent tort?

9. Is CALEA a hindrance to the community-policing movement? Justify your answer.

10. Explain the role of police culture in efforts to hold the police accountable for their behavior.

References

Alpert, G. 1989. "Police Use of Deadly Force: The Miami Experience." In R. Dunham, G. Alpert eds., *Critical Issues in Policing*, pp. 480–496 Prospect Heights, IL: Waveland Press.

Alpert, G. and Smith, W. 1999. "Developing Police Policy: An Evaluation of the Control Principle." In L. K. Gaines and G. W. Cordner (eds.), *Policing Perspectives: An Anthology*, pp. 353–362. Los Angeles: Roxbury Publishing Co.

Auten, J. 1988. "Preparing Written Guidelines." *FBI Law Enforcement Bulletin* 57: 1–7.

Barker, T. 1996. *Police Ethics: Crisis in Law Enforcement.* Springfield, IL: Charles Thomas Publishers.

Barker, T. and Carter, D. 1999. "Fluffing up Evidence and Covering Your Ass: Some Conceptual Notes on Police Lying." In L. K. Gaines and G. W. Cordner (eds.), *Policing Perspectives: An Anthology*, pp. 342–350. Los Angeles: Roxbury Publishing Co.

Berg, B. 1994. "Education v. Training." In A. Roberts (ed.), *Critical Issues in Crime and Justice.* Thousand Oaks, CA: Sage Publications.

Bittner, E. 1970. *The Functions of Police in Modern Society.* Boston: Northeastern University Press.

Bopp, W. J. 1975. "The Detroit Police Revolt." In J. H. Skolnick and T. C. Gray (eds.), *Police in America.* Boston: Educational Associates.

Burek, D. M. et al., eds. 1992. *Encyclopedia of Associations*, 26th ed. Detroit: Gale Research.

Caiden, G. E. 1977. *Police Revitalization.* Lexington, MA: D. C. Heath.

Carter, D. 1994. "Police Disciplinary Procedures: A Review of Selected Police Departments." In T. Barker and D. Carter (eds.), *Police Deviance*, 3rd ed., pp. 355–376. Cincinnati: Anderson Publishing Co.

D. Carter and T. Barker. 1994. "Administrative Guidance and the Control of Police Officer Behavior: Policies, Procedures, and Rules." In T. Barker and D. Carter (eds.), *Police Deviance*, 3rd ed., pp. 13–28. Cincinnati: Anderson Publishing Co.

Chevigny, P. 1995. *Edge of the Knife: Police Violence in the Americas.* New York: New Press.

Cole, G. F. 1992. *The American System of Criminal Justice*, 6th ed. Pacific Grove, CA: Brooks/Cole Publishing Co.

Commission on Accreditation for Law Enforcement Agencies. 1995. *Standards Manual*, 3rd ed. Alexandria, Va.

Commission on Peace Officer Standards and Training. 1990. *POST Administrative Manual*. State of California: POST.

Cordner, G. W. and Williams, G. L. 1995. "The CALEA Standards: What Is the Fit With Community Policing?" *National Institute of Justice Journal*, August: 39–49.

——. 1996. "Community Policing and Accreditation: A Content Analysis of CALEA Standards." In L. T. Hoover (ed.) *Quantifying Quality in Policing*, pp. 23–261. Washington, D.C.: Police Executive Research Forum.

——. 1999. "Community Policing and Police Agency Accreditation." In L. Gaines and G. W. Cordner (eds.), *Policing Perspectives: An Anthology*, pp. 372–379. Los Angeles: Roxbury Publishing Co.

Crank, J. P. 1995. "The Community Policing Movement of the 21st Century: What We Learned." In J. Klofas and S. Stojkovic. (eds.) *Crime and Justice in the Year 2010*, pp. 107–126. Belmont, CA: Wadsworth Publishing Co.

Crank, J. P. 1998. *Understanding Police Culture*. Cincinnati: Anderson Publishing Co.

Crank, J. P. and Caldero, M. A. 1991. "The Production of Occupational Stress Among Line Officers." *Journal of Criminal Justice* 19 (4): 339–350.

——. Forthcoming. *Police Ethics: The Corruption of Noble Cause*. Cincinnati: Anderson Publishing Co.

Crank, J. P. and Langworthy, R. 1992. "An Institutional Perspective of Policing." *The Journal of Criminal Law and Criminology* 83: 338–363.

Croft, E. 1987. "Police Use of Force in Rochester and Syracuse, New York: 1984 and 1985." *Report to the New York State Commission on Criminal Justice and the Use of Force*, Vol. 3. New York.

Cullen, J. B. 1978. *The Structure of Professionalism*. Princeton, NJ: Princeton University Press.

D'Arcy, S. et. al. 1990. "Internal Affairs Unit Guidelines." San Jose, CA: San Jose Police Department.

Decker, J. 1992. *Revolution to the Right: Criminal Procedure Jurisprudence During the Burger-Renquist Era*. New York: Garland Publishing.

del Carmen, R. V. 1989. "Civil Liabilities of Police Supervisors." American Journal of Police, 8: 107–136.

——. 1991. *Civil Liabilities in American Policing*. Englewood Cliffs, NJ: Brady.

Delattre, E. J. 1996. *Character and Cops: Ethics in Policing*, 3rd Edition. Washington, D.C.: American Enterprise Institute.

Dodenhoff, P. 1985. "Interview with Robert B. Kliesmet." *Law Enforcement News* January 21: 9–11.

Dugan, J. R. and Breda, D. R. 1991. "Complaints About Police Officers A Comparison Among Types and Agencies," *Journal of Criminal Justice* 19: 165–171.

Dunford, F. W. 1986. "The Role of Arrest in Domestic Assault: The Omaha Police Experiment," *Criminology* 28: 183–206.

Fogel, D. 1987. "The Investigation and Disciplining of Police Misconduct: A Comparative View," *Police Studies* 10: 1–15.

Fogelson, R. 1977) *Big-City Police*. Cambridge, MA: Harvard University Press.

Garrity v. New Jersey. 385 U.S. 483 (1967).

Geison, G. L. (ed.). 1983. *Professions and Professional Ideologies in America*. Chapel Hill: University of North Carolina Press.

Geller, W. A. (ed.). 1985. *Police Leadership in America: Crisis and Opportunity*. New York: Praeger.

——. 1991. *Local Government Police Management*, 3rd Edition. Washington, D.C.: International City Management Association.

Gibson, J. L., Ivancevich, J. M. and Donnelly, J. H. 1988. *Organizations: Behavior, Structure, Process*, 6th ed. Plano, TX: Business Publications.

Goldman, R. and Puro, S. 1987. "Decertification of Police: An Alternative to Traditional Remedies for Police Misconduct," *Hastings Constitutional Law Quarterly* 15: 50–80.

Goldstein, J. 1998. *Police Discretion Not to Invoke the Criminal Justice Process: Low Visibility Decisions in the Administration of Justice*. In G. F. Cole and M. G. Gertz (eds.), *The Criminal Justice: Politics and Policies*, 7th Edition, pp. 85–103. Belmont, CA: Wadsworth Publishing Co.

Hall, R.1968) "Professionalization and Bureaucratization." *American Sociological Review* 33: 92–104.

Harmon, M. M. 1995. *Responsibility as Paradox: A Critique of Rational Discourse on Government*. Thousand Oaks, CA: Sage Publications.

Hayden, G. 1981. "Police Discretion in the Use of Deadly Force: An Empirical Study of Information Using Deadly Force Decision Making." *Journal of Police Science and Administration* 9: 102–107.

Human Rights Watch. 1998. *Shielded from Justice: Police Brutality and Accountability in the United States*. New York: Human Rights Watch.

Independent Commission on the Los Angeles Police Department. 1991. *Report*. Los Angeles: California Public Management Institute. (Also known as the Christopher Commission.)

J.H. by D.H. v. West Valley City. 840 P. 2nd 115 (Utah 1992).

Kappeler, V. 1993. *Critical Issues in Police Civil Liability*. Prospect Heights, IL: Waveland Press.

Kerstetter, W. 1985. *Citizen Review of Police Misconduct*. Chicago: Chicago Bar Association.

Klockars, C. 1991. "The Dirty Harry Problem." In C. Klockars and S. D. Mastrofski (eds.), *Thinking About Police: Contemporary Readings*, pp. 428–38. New York: McGraw-Hill.

Kuykendall, J. and Roberg, R. R. 1990. "Police Professionalism: The Organizational Attribute," Journal of Contemporary Criminal Justice. 6, 49–59.

Lersch, K. and Mieczkowski, T. 1996. "Who Are the Problem-Prone Officers? An Analysis of Citizen Complaints." American Journal of Police 15(3): 23–44.

Loper v. New York City Police Department. 802 F. Supp. 1029, 1033 (S.D.N.Y. 1992).

Manning, P. K. 1998. *Police Work: The Social Organization of Policing*. 2nd Edition. Prospect Heights, IL: Waveland Press.

Manning, P. K. 1978. "Rules, Colleagues, and Situationally Justified Actions." In P. K. Manning and J. Van Maanen (eds.), *Policing: A View From the Street*, pp. 71–89. Santa Monica, CA: Goodyear Publishing.

Manning, P. K. and Redlinger, L. 1977. "Invitational Edges of Corruption: Some Consequences of Narcotic Law Enforcement." In P. Rock (ed.), *Drugs and Politics*, pp. 279–310. Rutgers, NJ: Society/Transaction Books.

Marion, Nancy. 1998. "Police Academy Training: Are We Teaching Recruits What They Need to Know?" *Policing: An International Journal of Police Strategies and Management" 21(1): 54–79.*

Mastrofski, S. 1990. "The Prospects of Change in Police Patrol: A Decade in Review." *American Journal of Police* 9: 1–79.

McAllister, B. 1987. "Spurred by Dramatic Rise in Lawsuits, Police Agencies Warm to Accreditation." *The Washington Post*. March 17: A7.

McMullan, J. 1998. "Social Surveillance and the Rise of the Police Machine." *Theoretical Criminology* 2(1): 93–117.

Meadows, R. J. 1996. "Legal Issues in Policing." In R. Muraskin and A. R. Roberts (eds.), *Visions for Change: Crime and Justice in the Twenty-First Century*, pp. 96–115. Upper Saddle River, NJ: Prentice Hall.

Murphy, P. V. and Caplan, G. 1991. "Fostering Integrity." In W. A. Geller (ed.), *Local Government Police Management*, pp. 239–271. Washington, D.C.: International City Management Association.

National Advisory Commission on Civil Disorders. 1968. *Report*. Washington, D.C.: U.S. Government Printing Office.

❖ ❖ ❖ ❖

National Commission on the Causes and Prevention of Violençe. 1969. *To Establish Justice, To Ensure Domestic Tranquility*. Washington, D.C.: U.S. Government Printing Office.

Nowak, J. E. 1983. "Criminal Procedure: Constitutional Aspects," In S. H. Kadis (ed.), *Encyclopedia of Crime and Justice*, II, pp. 527–536. New York: The Free Press.

Oettmeier, T. N. 1993. "Can Accreditation Survive the '90s?" In J. W. Bizzack (ed.), *New Perspectives on Policing*. Lexington, KY: Autumn House Publishing.

Packer, H. 1968. The Limits of the Criminal Sanction. Stanford, CA: Stanford University Press.

Pate, A. and Fridell, L. 1993. *Police Use of Force: Official Reports, Citizen Complaints, and Legal Consequences*. Washington, D.C.: Police Foundation.

Perez, D. 1994. *Common Sense About Police Review*. Philadelphia: Temple University Press.

Petterson, W. E. 1991. "Police Accountability and Civilian Oversight of Policing: An American Perspective." In A. J. Goldsmith (ed.), *Complaints Against The Police: The Trend To External Review*, pp. 259–289. Avon, England: Bookcraft Ltd.

Pfuhl, D. H. 1983. "Police Strikes and Conventional Crime." *Criminology* 21: 489–504.

Pollock-Byrne, J. M. 1998. *Ethics in Crime and Justice: Dilemmas and Decisions*, 3rd Edition. Belmont, CA: West/Wadsworth Publishing Co.

Pollock, J. M. 1997. "Ethics and Law Enforcement." In R. G. Dunham and Alpert, G. P. (eds.), *Critical Issues in Policing*, 3rd Edition, pp. 337–354. Prospect Heights, IL: Waveland Press.

Pomeroy, W. A. 1985. "The Sources of Police Legitimacy and a Model for Police Misconduct Review: A Response to Wayne Kerstetter." In W. Geller (ed.), *Police Leadership in America: Crisis and Opportunity*, pp. 183–186. New York: Praeger.

President's Commission on Law Enforcement and Administration of Justice. 1967. *Task Force Report: The Police*. Washington, D.C.: U.S. Government Printing Office.

Price, B. R. 1996. "Police and the Quest For Professionalism." In J. Sullivan and J. Victor (eds.), *Criminal Justice: Annual Editions 96/97*, pp. 86–87. Guilford, CT: Brown & Benchmark Publishers.

Regoli, R., Crank, J. P., Culbertson, R., and Poole, E. 1988. "Linkages Between Professionalization and Professionalism among Police Chiefs." *Journal of Criminal Justice* 16 (2): 89–98.

Reiss, A. J. 1968. "Police Brutality—Answers to Key Questions." *Trans-Action* 5: 10–19.

Reuss-Ianni, E. 1983. *Two Cultures of Policing: Street Cops and Management Cops*. New Brunswick, NJ: Transaction Books.

Rhoades, P. W. 1991. "Political Obligation: Connecting Police Ethics and Democratic Values," *American Journal of Police* 10: 1–22.

Roberts, M. 1985. "Lecture on Police Behavior," *Police Management Training Program*. San Jose, CA: San Jose State University.

Schien, E. H. 1985. *Organization Culture and Leadership*. San Francisco: Jossey-Bass.

Scogin, F. and Brodsky, S. L. 1991. "Fear of Litigation Among Law Enforcement Officers." *American Journal of Police* 10: 41–45.

Scott, E. J. 1981. *Calls for Service: Citizen Demand and Initial Police Response*. Washington, D.C.: U.S. Government Printing Office.

Sherman, L. W. 1991. "From Initial Deterrence to Longterm Escalation: Short Custody Arrest For Poverty Ghetto Domestic Violence," *Criminology* 29: 821–850.

——. 1999. "Policing for Crime Prevention." In C. Eskridge (ed.), *Criminal Justice: Concepts and Issues*, 3rd Edition, pp. 131–148. Los Angeles, CA: Roxbury Publishing Co.

Sherman, L., Gottfredson, D., MacKensie, D., Eck, J., Reuter, P. and Bushway, S. 1997. *Preventing Crime: What Works, What Doesn't, and What's Promising*. Washington, D.C.: U.S. Department of Justice.

Silver, I. 1995. *Police Civil Liability*. New York: Matthew Bender.

Skolnick, J. 1994. *Justice Without Trial: Law Enforcement in Democratic Society*, 3rd Edition. New York: John Wiley & Sons.

Skolnick, J. and Bayley, D. 1986. *The New Blue Line. Police Innovation in Six American Cities*. New York: The Free Press.

Smith, A. B. and Pollack, H. 1996. "The Bill of Rights in the 21st Century." In R. Muraskin and A. R. Roberts (eds.), *Visions for Change: Crime and Justice in the Twenty-First Century*, pp. 157–169. Upper Saddle River, NJ: Prentice Hall.

Sovary v. Los Angeles Police Department. 176 Cal. App. 3d 992 (1986).

Sparrow, M., Moore, M., and Kennedy, D. 1990. *Beyond 911: A New Era for Policing*. New York: Basic Books.

Steinman, M. 1988. "Anticipating Rank and File Police Reactions to Arrest Policies Regarding Spouse Abuse." *Criminal Justice Research Bulletin* 4: 1–5.

Sykes, G. W. 1994. "Accreditation and Community Policing: Passing Fads or Basic Reforms?" *Journal of Contemporary Criminal Justice* 10(1): 1–16.

Terrill, R. J. 1991. "Civilian Oversight of the Police Complaints Process in the United States." In A. J. Goldsmith (ed.), *Complaints Against The Police: The Trend To External Review* pp. 291–322. Avon, England: Bookcraft, Ltd.

Toch, H. 1995. "The 'Violence-Prone' Police Officer." In W. Geller and H. Toch (eds.), *And Justice For All: Understanding and Controlling Police Abuse of Force*, pp. 99–112. Washington, D.C.: Police Executive Research Forum.

Wadman, G. and Olson, R. 1990. *Community Wellness: A New Theory of Policing*. Washington, D.C.: Police Executive Research Forum.

Walker, S. 1977. *A Critical History of Police Reform*. Lexington, MA: Lexington Books.

———. 1985. "Setting the Standards: The Efforts and Impact of Blue-Ribbon Commissions on the Police." In W. A. Geller (ed.), *Police Leadership in America: Crises and Opportunity*, pp. 354–370. New York: Praeger.

———. 1998. *Sense and Nonsense About Crime and Drugs: A Policy Guide*, 4th Edition. Pacific Grove, CA: Brooks/Cole.

Walker, S. and Bumpus, V. W. 1991. *Civilian Review of the Police: A National Review of the 50 Largest Cities*. Omaha, NE: University of Nebraska.

Walker, S. and Kreisel, B. W. 1996. "Varieties of Citizen Review: The Implications of Organizational Features of Complaint Review Procedures For Accountability of the Police." *American Journal of Police* 15(3): 65–88.

Wallace, B. 1990. "S. F. Watchdog Upholds Few Charges." *San Francisco Chronicle*. May 29: 1, 4–6.

Wasserman, R. and Moore, M. H. 1988. "Values in Policing." *Perspectives on Policing*. Pamphlet. Washington, D.C.: National Institute of Justice.

West, P. 1988. "Investigation of Complaints Against The Police." *American Journal of Police* 8: 101–21.

Weddington, M. and Janikowski, W. 1996. "The Renquist Court—The Counter-Revolution That Wasn't, Part 2: The Counter-Revolution That Is." *Criminal Justice Review* 21-2: 231–250.

Whitebread, C. 1987) "The Counterrevolution Enters a New Era: Criminal Procedure Decisions During the Final Term of the Burger Court." *University of Puget Sound Law Review* 10: 571–590.

Williams, G. L. 1989. *Making the Grade: The Benefits of Law Enforcement Accreditation*. Washington, D.C.: Police Executive Research Forum.

Wilson, J. Q. and Kelling, G. 1982. "Broken Windows: The Police and Neighborhood Safety." *Atlantic Monthly* March: 29–38.

Worrall, J. and Marenin, O. 1998. "Emerging Liability Issues in the Implementation and Adoption of Community Oriented Policing." *Policing* 21(1): 121–135.

"Younger NYC Cops Comprise Bulk of Arrests for Misconduct." 1989. *Law Enforcement News* August 5: 1.

For a listing of websites appropriate to the content of this chapter, see "Suggested Websites for Further Study" (p. xv). ✦

Part IV
Contemporary Issues

Chapter Eleven

Higher Education

Chapter Outline

❏ The Development of Higher-Education Programs for Police

  Federal Programs and Support for Higher Education
  Quality of Higher-Education Programs

❏ Higher-Education Requirements for Police

❏ The Impact of Higher Education on Policing

  Police Attitudes and Performance
  Other Findings
  Police Executives' Views on Higher Education

❏ Validating Higher Education for Police

❏ Higher Education and Discrimination

❏ Policies Relating to Higher Education

❏ College Education as a Minimum Standard for Police Employment

❏ Summary

❏ Discussion Questions

❏ References

Key Terms	
BFOQ	Omnibus Crime Control and Safe
Crime-Control Act	Streets Act
COPS	Police Corps program
Educational incentive policies	PERF
Law Enforcement Assistance Act	scholarship and recruitment
LEAA	program
LEEP	Voilent Crime Control and Law
National Advisory Commission on	Enforcement Act
Higher Education for Police	
Officers	

❖ ❖ ❖ ❖

There has been a long-standing debate over whether a college education for police officers is desirable or even necessary. In present-day society, with the ever-expanding complexity of the police role and the transition toward community policing, this question is more significant than ever. Interestingly, the initial requirement of a high school diploma to enter the field of policing occurred at a time when most of the nation's population did not finish high school. Thus, a requirement of a high school education actually identified individuals with an above-average level of education. Statistics from the Department of Health, Education and Welfare, for instance, indicated that immediately after World War II, less than half of the 17-year-old population had earned a high school diploma in 1946 (National Advisory Commission 1973, p. 370). Although it is difficult to determine precisely when the high school diploma, or its equivalent, the general education diploma (GED), became a standard requirement for a majority of the country's police departments, it was a well-established trend following World War II.

Today, of course, the high school diploma has essentially been replaced by a college degree as the above-average level of educational attainment in the United States. Consequently, those police departments that have not raised their educational requirements for entry have failed to keep pace with their tradition of employing people with an above-average education. It should be noted, however, that most police departments with minimum educational requirements have employees who exceed that minimum. Additionally, police forces at different governmental levels have traditionally required different levels of education for employment. For example, most federal agencies such as ATF, DEA, or the FBI have required at least a college degree for quite some time, but only a minimal number of city and state police and sheriff's departments require one. Many others require a minimum two-year degree.

The debate over higher education, however, is much more complicated than determining whether or not police requirements are above or below national population norms. The development of higher-education programs and the ensuing debate is the focus of this chapter.

The Development of Higher-Education Programs for Police

The debate over higher educational requirements for police officers is not new. Starting in the early 1900s, Berkeley, California, Police Chief August Vollmer called for the recruitment of officers who were not only trained in the "technology of policing" but who also understood "the prevention of crime or confrontation through [their] appreciation of the psychology and sociology of crime" (Carte 1973, p. 275). Contrary to traditional practices of the time, Vollmer felt that such skills must not only be learned through on-the-job experience but first be taught in the classroom. The educational experience should include a strong liberal arts emphasis, combined with vocational training. Following this perspective, Berkeley police officers were required to be educationally well qualified before they joined the department.

Calling for the "very best manhood in the nation" to join the police profession (Carte 1973, p. 277), Vollmer campaigned strongly for police courses in higher education and the need for college-educated personnel throughout the police ranks. He was primarily responsible, along with the faculty, for the establishment of the first police school in higher education at the University of California-Berkeley, which he joined part-time in 1916 and full-time in 1932 after his retirement from the Berkeley Police Department (Caiden 1977). For his efforts to reform and professionalize the police, Vollmer eventually gained a reputation as the father of modern American policing.

Following Berkeley's lead, other programs emphasizing police education were developed at major universities. Between the early 1920s and mid-1930s, a number of schools established programs of study for criminal justice professionals, primarily the police. Although the majority of these programs lasted only a few years, several continue to this day, including those at the University of Chicago, Indiana University, Michigan State University, San Jose State University, and Wichita State University.

These early programs laid the foundation for higher education in criminal justice, which was typically labeled police science, police administration, or law enforcement. Such curricula were developed in selected four-year institutions and many community colleges through the mid-1960s. The focus of these programs was usually on administration and supervision issues in policing, as well as on the practical applications of the "science" of policing, including such topics as patrol procedures, traffic enforcement, criminalistics, criminal investigation, and report writing. Although the programs were established to make the field more professional, their curricula were frequently driven not according to any developing body of knowledge but instead on the perceived training needs of local police departments. It is interesting to note that during these years, most police departments had no formalized training programs; many of these programs were designed to fill this "training gap."

Even with the development of academic police programs, the concept of the college-educated police officer was strongly resisted by the majority of rank-and-file officers. Those who either had a degree or were attending college, the so-called college cops, were often viewed with suspicion and distrust. H. Goldstein aptly describes their plight during this era:

> The term itself implied that there was something incongruous about an educated police officer. College graduates, despite their steadily increasing number in the general population, did not seek employment with the police. The old but lingering stereotype of the "dumb flatfoot," the prevalent concept of policing as a relatively simple task, the low pay, and the limitations on advancement—all of these factors made it appear that a college education would be wasted in such a job. And the tremendous difference between the social status accorded a college graduate and the status accorded an officer made an anomaly of the individual who was both. (1977, p. 284)

The reasons listed by Goldstein—including (1) viewing the police role in simplistic terms, (2) the need to hire only low-quality personnel to perform the job, (3) low pay, (4) lack of advancement opportunities, and (5) low status—all continued to play a role in discouraging the concept of advanced education for the police. Two significant and interrelated events, however, took place in the mid-to late 1960s that required the country to take a hard look at the level of professionalism and quality of U.S. police forces as well as the rest of the criminal justice system. These two events played a major role in ushering in the "golden age" for higher education for the police (Pope 1987).

The first event was the enormous increase in the crime rate that began in the early 1960s leveled off in the early 1980s, and started moving upward again in the mid-1980s. In 1968, for the first time in three decades of opinion sampling, the Gallup poll found crime ranked as the most serious national issue (ahead of civil rights, the cost of living, and poverty), as well as the most important local issue (ahead of schools, transportation, and taxes). Furthermore, Gallup found that 3 persons in 10, and 4 in 10 for both women and residents of larger cities, admitted that they were afraid to go out alone at night in their own neighborhoods (Saunders 1970).

The second event was the ghetto riots, which occurred in the mid-1960s. The burning, looting, and general turmoil in many of the nation's major cities was the catalyst that spurred the public and the government into action. At this juncture, the "war on crime" began (Pope 1987).

"Crime in the streets" thus became a national issue in the 1964 presidential campaign. The following year Congress passed the Law Enforcement Assistance Act of 1965, a modest grant program that expressed a national concern about the adequacy of local police departments. Two years later, the President's Commission on Law Enforcement and Administration of Justice issued a comprehensive report titled *The Challenge of Crime in a Free Society* (1967) documenting the serious impact of crime on U.S. society. Although the report issued over 200 specific proposals for action involving all levels of government and society, a majority of the recommendations—either directly or indirectly—dealt with the police as the "front line" of the criminal justice system.

Serious and continuing problems between the police and the community, especially minority-group members, were a major concern of the commission. It was thought that without respect for the police or community participation in crime prevention, there could be little impact on the crime rate. Because much of this problem was associated with the low quality of police personnel, many of the commission's recommendations dealt with the need for "widespread improvement in the strength and caliber of police manpower . . . for achieving more effective and fairer law enforcement" (President's Commission 1967, p. 294). The commission thought that one of the most important ways to upgrade the quality of police personnel would be through higher education. Consequently, one of their most significant, and controversial, recommendations was that the "ultimate aim of all police departments should be that all personnel with general enforcement powers have baccalaureate degrees" (p. 109). Perhaps just as important, the commission further recommended that police departments should "take *immediate* steps to establish a minimum requirement of a baccalaureate degree for all supervisory and executive level positions" (p. 110, italics added).

Federal Programs and Support for Higher Education

Shortly thereafter, Congress passed the **Omnibus Crime Control and Safe Streets Act** of 1968, which created the **Law Enforcement Assistance Administration (LEAA)**. Through LEAA, the federal government poured literally billions of dollars into the criminal justice system—focusing on the police—in an attempt to improve their effectiveness and reduce crime. This money was initially earmarked for the research and development of "innovative" programs in policing, but it was instead used primarily to purchase additional hardware (e.g., cars and communications equipment, weapons) that departments could not afford on their own and secondarily for training. The result was that most police departments, rather than introducing new programs, instead operated from a perspective of "more of the same."

Under LEAA an educational-incentive program, known as the **Law Enforcement Education Program (LEEP),** was established in the late 1960s; it provided financial assistance to police personnel, as well as to others who wished to enter police service, to pursue a college education. The impact of LEEP on the growth of law enforcement programs in both two-year and four-year schools was nothing short of phenomenal. For example, it has been reported that in 1954 there was a total of 22 such programs in the country (Deutsch 1955, p. 213) but by 1975 the numbers had increased to more than 700 in community colleges and nearly 400 in four-year schools (Korbetz 1975).

In 1973 a highly influential *Report on Police* (1973) by the National Advisory Commission on Criminal Justice Standards and Goals, further advanced the higher-education recommendations made by the President's commission. The report included a graduated timetable that would require all police officers, at the time of initial employment, to have completed at least two years of education (60 semester units) at an accredited college or university by 1975, three years (90 semester units) by 1978, and a baccalaureate degree by 1982 (p. 369). In the same year, the American Bar Association issued another influential report, *Standards Relating to the Urban Police Function*, which recognized the demanding and complex nature of the police role in a democracy. The ABA further elaborated on the need for advanced education in order to meet the professional skills required by such a role:

> Police agencies need personnel in their ranks who have the characteristics which a college education seeks to foster: intellectual curiosity, analytical ability, articulateness, and a capacity to relate the events of the day to the social, political, and historical context in which they occur. (1973, p. 212)

More recently, the **Violent Crime Control and Law Enforcement Act** of 1994 (**Crime-Control Act**) is the most comprehensive federal crime legislation since the **Omnibus Crime Control and Safe Streets Act of 1968**. The crime-control act allocates approximately $30 billion to various criminal justice agencies, with almost $11 billion for state and local law enforcement, including almost $9 billion to hire an additional 100,000 police officers under the **community-oriented policing services (COPS)** program (U.S. Dept. of Justice 1994). These new officers are to be used by local departments to help further their community policing efforts. In addition, the legislation provides for federal funds to be used to establish a police corps and a scholarship and recruitment program for local police departments. This is the largest federal investment in education for law enforcement personnel since the creation of the Law Enforcement Education Program ("Dissecting the Crime Bill" 1994).

The **Police Corps** and the **scholarship and recruitment program** were established under Title XX of the Crime-Control Act of 1994 and are administered through the Office of the Police Corps and Law Enforcement Education, under the auspices of the Justice Department. Under the police corps program, full-time college students are eligible for up to $10,000 annual tuition reimbursements; they must agree to work in a state or local police force for at least four years after graduation (see Inside Policing 11.1). Participants who fail to meet service requirements will be required to repay all of the tuition reimbursements plus 10 percent interest; however, a community-service commitment can be substituted for police work if there is a physical or emotional disability or a "good cause" reason the participant cannot fulfill the original commitment ("Dissecting the Crime Bill" 1994).

Inside Policing 11.1
The Federal Police Corps

With Police Corps programs in operation in Maryland and Oregon, more programs are beginning to recruit college students who are willing to serve as police officers for four years in exchange for tuition reimbursement. The program is administered by the Justice Department's Office of Community Oriented Policing Services (COPS), which disburses funds to localities by states, which have broad discretion to develop the programs to meet the specific needs of local police departments. In 1996, six states—Arkansas, Maryland, Nevada, North Carolina, South Carolina, and Oregon—received funding and started to develop programs to provide positions for up to 200 participants. The nation's first class of 19 Police Corps Cadets took a 16-week training course at the Oregon State Police Academy. Once the cadets completed training, they went to work for the Portland Police Department and began receiving $10,000 annual tuition reimbursements up to a total of $40,000. In Maryland, the Police Corps program recruited up to 120 participants, who eventually went to work for the Balti-

more Police Department. "It's very exciting," said Lieutenant Governor Kathleen Kennedy Townsend. "It's an innovative way to recruit a number of young people into police work, some of whom will stay and be excellent police officers, while others will go out and be supporters of the police in their communities."

In Oregon, in order to get the program off the ground, college graduates were given the highest priority to apply for the program. In the future, however, new cadets will be selected from high school seniors and current college students. Cadets must complete the same selection process as regular officers, including a written exam and oral interview, on which they are scored on an overall point system.

Source: Adapted from "Surprise! The Police Corps Is Back—Not That It Ever Left." 1997a. *Law Enforcement News*, January 31: 1, 10. Reprinted with permission from *Law Enforcement News*, John Jay College of Criminal Justice, New York City.

The scholarship and recruitment program provides scholarships for higher education to in-service law enforcement personnel and to students who are juniors or seniors in high school, or who are enrolled in an institution of higher learning (who do not currently hold a law enforcement position) and are interested in pursuing a career in law enforcement. Priority is given to racial, ethnic, or gender groups whose representation in police departments is substantially less than in the population eligible for police employment in the state. Participants are required to work in a law enforcement position for one month for each credit hour for which funds were received, for a period of not less than six months or more than two years. If participants fail to meet program guidelines, they will be required to repay the entire scholarship ("Dissecting the Crime Bill" 1994).

Quality of Higher-Education Programs

The meteoric, unregulated rise of programs in police science or law enforcement led to serious questions about their academic rigor and viability.

The increase coincided with the infusion of federal moneys distributed through LEEP. In order to capture their fair share of the federal funds, many schools hurriedly spliced together programs to study the police. Due to a lack of qualified faculty, many part-time instructors, frequently selected from the local police or sheriff's departments, were employed to teach classes. Because instructors generally lacked proper academic qualifications, little attempt was made to introduce current research or critical analysis of contemporary issues and practices. Instead, instructors focused on training using readily available models from their own experience. They concentrated on their department's operating policies and procedures and offered "war stories" from their street experiences as examples of the "way things are." The students taking these courses were overwhelmingly in service, that is, full-time police or criminal justice employees returning to school through the provision of LEEP funds.

An example of a "typical" early law enforcement curriculum is highlighted in Table 11.1, which describes several courses of San Jose State College's Police School of the early 1960s. This school (now at San Jose State University) is one of the oldest in the nation. It was developed in 1930 as a two-year degree program and became a four-year degree program in 1936 (Kuykendall and Hernandez 1975). It is interesting that while the police program's courses were highly specialized and narrowly focused, the required courses outside of the major were broad based, providing the student with a well-rounded education. Examples of such "outside" courses included English composition and English literature, anatomy and physiology, accounting, statistics, two semesters of chemistry, and a number of courses in history, psychology, political science, and sociology (San Jose State College 1960, p. 270). It is apparent that despite the orientation toward training, the need for a broader-based education was recognized as well.

Table 11.1   Course Descriptions of Police School Curriculum 1960–1961, San Jose State College

Lower Division

General Administration of Criminal Justice. Purpose, function, and brief history of the agencies dealing with the administration of criminal justice.

Beginning Gunnery. Elementary use of all types of firearms; basic fundamentals of breathing and trigger squeeze, with actual use of firearms.

Criminal Identification. Theory and practice of fingerprint classification and its application to individual circumstances.

Advanced Gunnery. Gunnery especially adapted to practical police problems; participant must be able to maintain a minimum score of 245 at pistol course.

Upper Division

Elementary Criminal Law and Law of Arrest. Elements of criminal law; principles of constitutional law.

Law of Evidence and Court Procedure. How evidence is obtained; methods of presenting it in court; elementary rules; weight and value of various types.

Crime Prevention. Organization and functions of the crime-prevention division; techniques employed in the repression of delinquency and crime through preventive methods.

Traffic. Organization and functions of the traffic division; application of educational, engineering, and enforcement methods to traffic problems.

Table 11.1   Course Descriptions of Police School Curriculum 1960–1961, San Jose State College (continued)

Police Record Systems. Structure and functions of the record system; administrative aspect; criminal files; modus operandi; statistical method and prediction of significant trends.

Beginning Investigation. Fundamental principles and problems of an investigator; techniques of searches, observation, surveillance, and interrogation.

Police Organization and Administration (A). Introduction to principles of organization, administration, and territoriality: discussion of the principles as pertaining to service: e.g., training, transportation, communications, jail, and property.

Police Organization and Administration (B). Continuation of the principles of organization and administration as applied to field operation: e.g., patrol, traffic, and crime prevention.

Report Writing. Survey of police reports and police reporting. Prerequisites: Typing 30 w.p.m., or 20 w.p.m. composing; 10-minute test.

Police Department Field Work. Individual experience and cadet training in a city police department or other investigatorial organization.

Advanced Criminal Investigation. Critical examination of assigned cases and specified crimes; techniques and arts employed in conducting raids and undercover work.

Police Problems. The investigation of selected problems in police science and administration; practical demonstrations and participation by class or individually by assignment.

Source: Abbreviated descriptions adapted from San Jose State College. 1960. *General Catalog: 1960–61.* San Jose, CA.: San Jose State College, pp. 271–272.

Because they were narrowly focused, training-oriented programs were not traditionally found in a university setting, and it is not surprising that they encountered stiff opposition from the well-established, academic disciplines. This attitude was especially true throughout the decade of the 1960s, when a "liberal" perspective was very pervasive throughout college cam-

Uniformed San Jose State University Police Science students collecting evidence in the early 1960s. Notice that the students wore uniforms. (Photo: Spartan Daily, May 16, 1967)

puses. Curriculum content, as well as the quality of both the faculty and students, was viewed as inferior and not suitable to a university environment. It soon became clear that if police programs were to remain on college campuses, major changes would have to be made, especially with respect to the quality of the faculty and the curriculum. In the late 1960s and early 1970s, many of these programs began to broaden their focus, emphasizing the criminal justice rather than technical training. The titles of the programs began to change to reflect this broader approach; common new titles were Departments of Criminal Justice, Criminology, or Administration of Justice. Reflecting on these changes, C. E. Pope comments

> Curriculums became much less practice oriented (at least in the four-year institutions) and more academically based. Some criminal justice programs even took a more critical stance toward the criminal justice system, adding courses based on a radical perspective. Many programs eliminated courses on patrol, traffic and the like, or at least expanded offerings to include race, gender, victims and related issues. It was a period when criminal justice attempted to gain academic respectability and institutional support. (1987, p. 4)

A policy decision by LEAA to spend more money for research on crime and justice issues, and less on police hardware indirectly helped to advance the respectability of these programs. Scholars entering the field now had a chance to receive grants to study and evaluate criminal justice programs. Accordingly, the criminal justice faculty could more easily expand its research efforts and develop a research orientation (i.e., advancing knowledge of the field) similar to the more traditional disciplines. Another important development during this period was the emergence of doctoral programs in criminal justice, developed to supply faculty for the new criminal justice departments. At the same time, the nature of the student body was also changing from in-service students to pre-service students (Terry 1980).

Following a decade of tremendous growth, accompanied by severe criticism of police programs in higher education, the Police Foundation put together a commission of noted educators, police administrators, and public officials to evaluate the quality of these programs. Known as the **National Advisory Commission on Higher Education for Police Officers,** the commission spent two years conducting a national survey and documenting the problems of police education (Sherman and the National Advisory Commission 1978). The report was extremely critical of the state of the art of police education at the time. It recommended significant changes in virtually all phases of police higher education, including institutional, curriculum, and faculty. Among the more crucial recommendations, the commission proposed the following:

1. The majority of federal funds for police higher education should go to programs with broad curriculums and well-educated faculty rather than to narrowly technical programs.

2. No college credit should be granted for attending police department training programs.

3. Community colleges should phase out their terminal two-year degree programs in police education.

4. Colleges should employ primarily full-time police-education teaching staffs, seeking faculty members with Ph.D. degrees in arts and sciences.

5. Prior employment in criminal justice should be neither a requirement nor a handicap in faculty selection.

6. Government policies at all levels should encourage educating police officers before they begin their careers.

These recommendations struck at the heart of many police programs throughout the country and consequently were not well received by many. However, as discussed above, improvements had already begun.

The commission's call for eliminating terminal two-year degree programs in police education further emphasized the importance it attached to a broad-based education, enhanced by a campus setting where "greater student interaction with diverse kinds of people" could take place (p.115). According to the commission, the two-year terminal-degree programs, which focused on vocational training, produced a "paraprofessional caste" system, since they were often housed in the same academic units as programs in cosmetology and auto mechanics.

The changing nature of the criminal justice student was also significant, as the commission recommended that police should be educated *prior* to employment; this argument attacked the very basis of the LEEP program, which provided an overwhelming amount of its funds to in-service personnel only. This recommendation started a serious debate on whether police departments should place more emphasis on "recruiting the educated" or on "educating the recruited." The commission thought that the "occupational perspective" of full-time police work, "probably reduces the impact of college on students" (p. 13).

As the LEEP program was eventually phased out, so too were many of the weaker police programs in higher education. The stronger programs continued to recruit Ph.D.'s trained in criminal justice and other social sciences for their faculties, thus establishing a more scholarly approach toward teaching and research. The emphasis on a broader-based curriculum became firmly established, and the students became less vocationally and in-service oriented. For example, compare the nature and scope of San Jose State University's Administration of Justice Department's present-day curriculum in Table 11.2 with the law enforcement curriculum of the early 1960s in Table 11.1.

These changes in higher education in criminal justice, including faculty quality, student body makeup and curricular content, have allowed the field to mature quite rapidly and gain academic respectability; students of such programs are no longer viewed as second-class citizens of the university community. Today, on most college campuses where degree programs have become firmly established, program quality and student interest continue to increase.

Higher-Education Requirements for Police

Advances in raising educational requirements for police have been slow and sporadic. Until the 1980s, in many police departments, an officer with a college degree was often viewed with contempt or resentment; it was not un-

Table 11.2 Course Descriptions of Administration of Justice Curriculum 1998–2000, San Jose State University

Lower Division

Administration of Justice. Historical and philosophical development of administration of justice; analysis and evaluation of criminal justice agencies and the relationship between theory and practice.

Concepts of Criminal Law. Historical development of philosophy of law and constitutional provisions, legal definitions, classifications of crime, case law, and concepts of criminal law as a social force.

Criminal Evidence. Origin, development, philosophy, and constitutional basis of evidence; kinds and degrees of evidence; admissibility and judicial decisions interpreting individual rights and case studies.

Principles of Investigation. Principles, methods, and investigative techniques to locate, gather, document, and disseminate information, including the field of corrections; recognition and preservation of evidence.

Upper Division

Police and Society. A multidisciplinary study of law enforcement from the early 1800s to the present; focus on significant studies in relation to police role and analysis of current models and practices.

Courts and Society. Structure and function of the court system; emphasis on the roles of prosecutor, defense attorney, judge, jurors, and witnesses; and examination of criminal legislation and Supreme Court decisions.

Corrections and Society. Multidisciplinary study of corrections from the early 1800s to present; significant studies relating to the role of corrections and methods of community treatment and of current models and practices.

Justice Management. How to understand, manage, and apply skills concerning personnel development, motivation, leadership styles, policy planning, conflict resolution, and labor relations within the multifaceted fields of criminal justice.

Intervention and Mediation Methods. Review of related literature and study of mediation and intervention in family court, community disputes, juvenile court, and police settings.

Violence and the Justice System. Examination of the causes and prevention of criminal violence, ranging from the individual offender to mob and riot behavior; includes serial and mass murder, gangs, vigilantism, gun control, and related issues.

Nature of Crime. Analysis of the nature and extent of crime, including causation and prevention; criminal typologies and victim surveys and evaluation of various control and prevention strategies.

Narcotics and Drug Abuse. Narcotics, dangerous drugs, and people who abuse them; implementation, evaluation, and coordination of drug-control programs.

Women, Minorities, and the Law. History of legal issues and definitions of individual and institutional discrimination; laws related to women and minorities in education, employment, criminal justice, government, and social welfare.

Terrorism and the Criminal Justice System. Examination of terrorist organizations, activities, and threats posed to free society; policy choices and implications for justice system agencies.

Organized Crime. Examination of organized crime as a system; explanation of investigation techniques and impact on police, courts, and correctional agencies.

White-collar Crime. Growth and development of white collar crime in the United States; crimes at the workplace, computer fraud, swindles, embezzlement, bribery and graft at the corporate and governmental levels.

Senior Seminar: Contemporary Problems. Identification, discussion, and analysis of selected problems in the justice system.

Source: Abbreviated descriptions adapted from San Jose State University. 1998. *SJSU Catalog: 1998–2000.* San Jose, CA.: San Jose State University, pp. 50–51.

derstood why anyone with a degree would want to enter policing. Indeed, a college degree requirement is still virtually nonexistent. A national study conducted in 1993 by the Bureau of Justice Statistics (Reaves 1996) of more than 3,000 state and local police departments, serving communities of all sizes, indicates that only 1 percent of departments require a college degree for employment (see Table 11.3.).

Table 11.3	Minimum Educational Requirement for New Officer Recruits in Local Police Departments, by Size of Population Served, 1993				
	Percent of agencies requiring a minimum of:				
Population served	Total with requirement	High school diploma	Some college*	2-year college degree	4-year college degree
All sizes	97	86	4	7	1
1,000,000 or more	100%	75	25	0	0
500,000–999,999	100	85	11	4	0
250,000–499,999	98	73	13	9	2
100,000–249,999	100	81	9	3	7
50,000–99,999	100	72	11	17	1
25,000–49,999	100	78	9	9	4
10,000–24,999	98	84	5	7	3
2,500–9,999	100	90	2	7	1
Under 2,500	94	85	4	5	0

Note: Detail may not add to total because of rounding.
* Nondegree requirements
Source: B. A. Reaves. 1996. *Local Police Departments, 1993* Washington, D.C.: Bureau of Justice Statistics, p. 5.

Table 11.3 also indicates that in some jurisdictions the figure is considerably higher than 1 percent, for example, 7 percent for departments in cities serving more than 100,000 residents but less than 250,000. Furthermore, 17 percent of departments in cities having more than 50,000 residents but less than 100,000 require a two-year degree, and 25 percent of departments in cities of more than 1 million population require some college. An indication of how slow the development of the higher-education requirement has been is the fact that the highest total educational requirement for entry remains a high-school diploma at 86 percent of the departments.

Another survey on police higher education analyzed by the Bureau of Justice Statistics for 1997 (Reaves and Goldberg 1999) of 639 county, municipal, and state police and sheriff's departments with 100 or more officers provides another perspective on educational requirements. (see Table 11.4).

Table 11.4 Percent of Local and State Law Enforcement Agencies With Educational Requirement for New Officers, 1997				
	Type of agency			
	County police (n=30)	Municipal police (n=454)	Sheriff (n=167)	State police (n=49)
Percent of departments with educational requirement for new officers				
4-year college degree	3%	2%	1%	4%
2-year college degree	13%	7%	5%	16%

Source: Adapted from B. A. Reaves and A. L. Goldberg. 1999. *Law Enforcement Management and Administrative Statistics, 1997,* Washington, D.C.: Bureau of Justice Statistics, p. v.

By looking at the higher-education requirements for new officers based on type of police department in Table 11.4, it is clear that state police are the leaders in requiring advanced education, including a four-year degree (4 percent) and a two-year degree (16 percent). Interestingly, county police agencies are second in higher-educational requirements with both a four-year degree (3 percent) and a two-year degree (13 percent), followed by municipal police (2 percent and 7 percent respectively) and county sheriff's departments (1 percent and 5 percent respectively). This more recent data is especially important because it looks at more than just municipal police agencies (although all are large in size with over 100 officers) and thus provides a perspective of higher-educational requirements in different types of police departments.

Criminal justice curriculums (and textbooks) are more broadly based and scholarly than in the past, allowing for the rapid development of this emerging field of study.

Another national survey of 486 state, county, and municipal police departments, conducted for the **Police Executive Research Forum (PERF)** by D. L. Carter, A. D. Sapp, and D. W. Stephens (1989), found that the average educational level of the police increased only a little over a year in two decades, from 12.4 years (12.0 is equivalent to a high school diploma) in 1967 to 13.6 in 1989. However, 13.6 years does indicate that the average officer in the late 1980s had approximately one and one-half years of some type of college. Of even more interest was the discovery by the authors that officers actually *possessing* college degrees had increased substantially over approximately a 30-year period. As Table 11.5 indicates, officers with college degrees were nearly 23 percent in 1988 but only 2.7 percent in 1960, 3.7 percent in 1970, and 8.9 percent in 1974. Conversely, only about 35 percent of the officers in 1988 had no college, compared to 80 percent in 1960, 68 percent in 1970, and 54 percent in 1974. A 1994 national study of departments with more than 500 sworn officers (Sanders, Hughes, and Langworthy 1995) found that approximately 28 percent of the officers were college graduates. This finding supports the PERF findings and suggests that although college-degree requirements for initial selection remain low, in general, about 25 percent of today's officers have graduated from college.

Table 11.5 Changes in Police Education Level by Years*				
College Level	**1960**	**1970**	**1974**	**1988**
No College	80.0%	68.2%	53.8%	34.8
< 2 years	10.0%	17.2%	15.8%	20.5%
2–3 years	7.3%	10.9%	21.5%	22.1%
> 4 years	2.7%	3.7%	8.9%	22.6%

*Data for 1960, 1970, and 1974 taken from National Institute of Law Enforcement and Criminal Justice, 1978.
Source: D. L. Carter and A. D. Sapp 1992. "College Education and Policing: Coming of Age." *FBI Law Enforcement Bulletin*, January: 10.

Given the increasing number of college-educated officers in the field, such slow progress in developing higher-education standards is perplexing, especially considering the evidence that, in general, college education has a positive effect on officer attitudes, performance, and behavior (see following section). With such support for higher education, why have standards not been significantly raised by most police departments? The Carter, Sapp, and Stephens study discussed above found two common reasons: (1) fear of being sued because a college requirement could not be quantitatively validated to show job relatedness and (2) fear that college requirements would be discriminatory toward minorities. Each of these important issues will be discussed in later sections.

Just as the percentage of police officers holding college degrees has increased, so too has the number of police chiefs holding degrees. A study conducted by PERF ("Survey Says Big-City Chiefs Are Better-Educated Outsiders" 1998) of 358 city and county police chiefs in jurisdictions of 50,000 or more residents discovered that 87 percent held bachelor's degrees, almost 47 percent had master's degrees, and nearly 5 percent had law or doctoral-level degrees. In comparison, a 1975 International Association of Chiefs of Police (IACP) survey found that about 15 percent had bachelor's degrees and only about 4 percent had advanced degrees. This is an important finding because it suggests that with highly educated police chief executives as role models, higher education may now be emerging as an important part of the police culture. It is likely that these chiefs will begin to emphasize, and even require, higher education as part of their overall strategy to improve their departments, including promotional and hiring practices.

The Impact of Higher Education on Policing

If college is going to become a requirement for policing, it will be necessary to indicate to the courts the relevance of such a requirement to on-the-job performance. Over the past three decades, research on higher education and police officer behavior can essentially be classified into two major categories: (1) the relationship between education and police attitudes and (2) the relationship between education and police performance. Although the quality of the research and the consistency of the findings have varied tremendously, it appears that some important general trends and conclusions can be drawn.

Police Attitudes and Performance

Early research on the impact of college on police attitudes centered on comparing levels of authoritarianism of college-educated police to police with little or no college. For instance, it was shown that police with some college (Smith, Locke, and Walker 1968) and those with college degrees (Smith, Locke, and Fenster 1970), were significantly less authoritarian than their noncollege-educated colleagues. I. B. Guller (1972) found police officers who were college seniors showed lower levels of authoritarianism than officers who were college freshmen and of similar age, socioeconomic background, and work experience; this fact indicated that the higher the level of education, the more flexible or open one's belief system may be. A. F. Dalley (1975) further discovered that authoritarian attitudes correspond with a lack of a college education and increased work experience; he suggested that a more liberal attitude is more conducive to the discretionary nature of law enforcement.

Numerous other researchers have also found college-educated officers to be more flexible and less authoritarian (Parker, Donnelly, Gerwitz, Marcus, and Kowalewski 1976; Roberg 1978; and Trojanowicz and Nicholson 1976). Finally, some evidence indicates that college-educated officers are not only more aware of social and ethnic problems in their community but also have a greater acceptance of minorities (Weiner 1976) and are more professional in their attitude (Miller and Fry 1978) and ethical in their behavior (Tyre and Braunstein 1992).

Because police departments are so diverse, it is difficult to define performance measures; that is, what is considered to be "good" or "poor" performance may vary from department to department. The criteria used to measure police performance then are not clear-cut and are often controversial. Accordingly, research findings on police performance will usually be more useful if they are based on a wide variety of performance indicators. The research described next, on the relationship between higher education and police performance, is based on a number of different indicators, or measures, of performance.

Several studies have indicated that officers with higher levels of education performed their jobs in a more satisfactory manner than their less educated peers, as evidenced by higher evaluation ratings from their supervisors (Finnegan 1976; and Roberg 1978; Smith and Aamodt 1997). The Smith and Aamodt (1997) study, which consisted of 299 officers from 12 municipal departments in Virginia, found that the benefits of a college education did not become apparent until the officers gained some experience; this finding is not surprising and suggests that higher education is simply another tool, along with training and experience, that allows officers to become more effective performers.

Other researchers have found college to have a positive effect on numerous individual performance indicators. For example, several researchers have found college-educated officers to have fewer citizen complaints filed against them (Cascio 1977; Cohen and Chaiken 1972; Finnegan 1976; Sanderson 1978; and Trojanowicz and Nicholson 1976). Additional research has indicated that college officers tend to perform better in the academy (Sanderson 1978), have fewer disciplinary actions taken against them by the department, have lower rates of absenteeism, receive fewer injuries on the job, and are involved in fewer traffic accidents (Cascio 1977; Cohen and Chaiken 1972; and Sanderson 1977). There is even some evidence that better-educated officers tend to use deadly force (i.e., fire their weapons) less often (Fyfe 1988).

Some interesting findings with respect to the future development of police departments indicate that college-educated officers are more likely to attain promotions (Cohen and Chaiken 1972; Roberg and Laramy 1980; and Sanderson 1978), tend to be more innovative in performing their work (Trojanowicz and Nicholson 1976), and are more likely to take leadership roles in the department and to rate themselves higher on performance measures (Cohen and Chaiken 1972; Krimmel 1996; Trojanowicz and Nicholson 1976; and Weirman 1978). Finally, there is developing evidence that college-educated officers become involved in cases of "individual liability significantly less frequently than non-college officers" (Carter and Sapp 1989, p. l63), and that college-educated officers tend to have a broader understanding of civil rights issues from legal, social, historical, and political perspectives (Carter and Sapp 1990). Because lawsuits claiming negligence on behalf of police departments are on the increase (along with the amount of damages being awarded—often between $1 million and $2 million per case), this is an important area for future research. If a correlation between higher education and reduced liability risk can be established, the availability and cost of such insurance to police departments could be affected.

These findings suggest that, in general, college has a positive impact on police attitudes and behavior. Essentially, college is related to less authoritarian beliefs, greater tolerance toward others, and greater acceptance of minority groups. Additionally, college-educated officers tend to perform better than their non-college-educated colleagues. It would appear then, that more tolerant and flexible attitudes may have an impact on police performance, at least in certain areas.

One study that examined the relationship between attitudes and performance (as measured by supervisory ratings) found that "patrol officers with higher levels of education had more open belief systems (were less authoritarian) and performed in a more satisfactory manner on the job than those patrol officers with less education" (Roberg 1978, p. 344). Additionally, patrol officers with "college degrees had the most open belief systems and the highest levels of job performance, indicating that college-educated officers were better able to adapt to the complex nature of the police role" (p. 344). It was shown that age, seniority, and college major had no impact on the results, lending support to the notion that the *overall* university experience is important in broadening one's perspectives. It is important to note that all the college graduates in this research were from a major land-grant state university that could be considered to have high-quality academic programs. Thus, the *quality* of the educational experience may also be an important variable in determining the impact of higher education.

Other Findings

Of course, not all of the research findings on higher education and policing have been positive. There is some evidence that highly educated officers are more likely to terminate their careers in policing (Levy 1967; Cohen and Chaiken 1972; Stoddard 1973; and Weirman 1978), and to hold differing and more negative views of job satisfaction (Griffin, Dunbar, and McGill 1978; Mottaz 1983). It is possible, however, that such results may be related to the traditional bureaucratic nature of police departments. Since it appears that higher education affects authoritarian attitudes, it would follow that college-educated police would be less willing to work in, and be less satisfied with, authoritarian departments and managerial practices. If this is so, and police executives wish to attract and retain college-educated personnel, increased attention will need to be paid to how jobs are designed and the overall quality of police work environments. As noted in previous chapters, this change may already be taking place, as police departments begin to move toward community policing.

Some research has suggested that there is little, if any, relationship between higher education and police attitudes and performance. For example, in one large-scale re-analysis of survey findings in a 1977 study, R. E. Worden (1990) found that the effects of higher education on attitudes and performance were so small that they were not significant. Nevertheless, he did discover that supervisors found educated officers to be more reliable employees and better report writers, and citizens found them to be exceptional in their use of good judgment and problem solving. These are important performance advantages that should not be overlooked, especially for present-day policing and the continued development of community-policing models.

The conflicting findings on the impact of higher education on policing are not really surprising, because educational experiences are so varied and there are so many different types of attitudinal and performance measures. One should also keep in mind that due to the complexity of the subject matter, cause-and-effect relationships between higher education, attitudes, and performance will probably never be empirically established. At this time, however, the preponderance of evidence strongly supports the notion that higher education is a positive influence on policing and should be a *requirement* for the job. As the level of college-educated police chiefs rises, this view is likely to become more prominent as discussed in the next section.

Police Executives' Views on Higher Education

In Table 11.6, the advantages and disadvantages of college-educated officers, as reported by police executives throughout the country, are summarized. The findings of the PERF study (Carter, Sapp, and Stephens 1989),

where nearly 500 police executives were surveyed with respect to their opinions on higher education and policing, are consistent with most of the research findings discussed thus far. Citing the study, a resolution was passed
by the members of PERF (college-educated police chief executives) calling
for all police applicants to possess 30 semester units from an accredited college or university. This requirement was to be increased in increments of 15
units until the minimum requirement for employment in policing is the baccalaureate degree (PERF 1989).

Table 11.6 Police Executives Opinions: Advantages and Disadvantages of Police Officers with Higher Education

Advantages	**Disadvantages**
College-educated officers are more likely to:	College-educated officers are more likely to:
Communicate better with the public	Leave policing
Write better reports	Question orders
Perform more effectively	Request reassignment
Receive fewer citizen complaints	
Show more initiative in work performance	
Be more professional	
Use discretion more wisely	
Be promoted	
Make better decisions	
Show more sensitivity to racial or ethnic groups	
Have fewer disciplinary problems	

Source: Adapted from D. L. Carter, A. D. Sapp and D. W. Stephens. 1989. *The State of Police Education: Policy Directions for the 21st Century*. Washington, D.C.: PERF, pp. xxii–xxiii. Used by permission.

Reflecting on the advantages of higher education described above, the
police chief of Tulsa, Oklahoma, helped push through a policy requiring all
police recruits to have a college degree. Tulsa thus became the largest city in
the nation to require a college degree of all of its officers. Case Study 11.1 describes the reasoning behind Tulsa's degree requirement.

Case Study 11.1

No BS: Tulsa PD Rookies Required to Have Four-Year Degree

Beginning with the January 1998 class, recruits entering the Tulsa, Oklahoma,
police academy will have to have a four-year college degree after the City Council
unanimously endorsed a proposal by Police Chief Ron Palmer to increase the police department's college requirement from the current 108 credit hours. There are
only approximately 15 police departments nationwide with similar requirements.
The department is used to being on the cutting edge of higher education for police,
having required 108 credit hours since 1981. "It wasn't a quantum leap for us but
it's certainly something that's unusual for a city of our size, and it's unique among
major cities," observed Palmer, who has a master's degree.

Chief Palmer believes that college-educated officers are better grounded to meet
the demands of the job and are less likely to be the subjects of citizen complaints or
engage in misconduct. He also believes that officers with college degrees "come to
you a bit more mature, they're a little more aware of diversity issues, and they're

❖ ❖ ❖ ❖

☞   more prone to use their minds to problem-solve than one that doesn't have that type of background." Currently, about 73 percent of the department's 794 officers have college degrees, while an additional 20 percent have 60 hours or more of college credit. More than 40 sworn members have master's degrees, and the department has one member with a Ph.D. and three officials with law degrees. "We're a very well-educated department," Palmer notes.

At the same time, he points out, the requirement has not hampered the department's efforts to attract more minority recruits, as some thought might happen. "That doesn't appear to be the case," said Palmer. "We've hired [minorities] at the same level for the past two or three years, which was the result of a multicultural recruiting task force that partnered with the community. Coupled with this, we do a fairly strong recruiting effort not only in Tulsa, but outside the state, to get the numbers we feel will satisfy our goals."

Source: Adapted from *Law Enforcement News*, 1997b. "Men & Women of Letters: No BS: Tulsa PD Rookies to Need Four-Year Degrees." *Law Enforcement News*, November 30: 1. Reprinted with permission from John Jay College of Criminal Justice, New York City.

Validating Higher Education for Police

As the PERF study of police executives reported (Carter, Sapp, and Stephens 1989), one of the primary reasons departments had not embraced higher-educational requirements more vigorously was the dilemma of not being able to validate such a requirement for the job, thus opening the department to a court challenge. Establishing higher-educational requirements as a bona fide occupational qualification (BFOQ) for police work could be an important step in facilitating the use of advanced education as a minimum entry-level selection criterion. A brief discussion of higher education as a BFOQ for police work follows.

Interestingly, the courts in this country have continuously upheld higher educational requirements in policing to be *job related*. In *Castro v. Beecher* (1972), the requirement of a high school education by the Boston Police Department was affirmed, citing the recommendations of the President's Commission on Law Enforcement and Administration of Justice (1967) and the National Advisory Commission on Civil Disorders (1968). *Arnold v. Ballard* (1975) supported the notion that an educational requirement can be quantitatively job validated in stating that such requirements "indicate a measure of accomplishment and ability which . . . is essential for . . . performance as a police officer (p. 738). And, in *Davis v. City of Dallas* (1985), the court upheld a challenge to the Dallas Police Department's requirement of 45 semester units (equivalent to one and one-half years of college) with a minimum of a C average from an accredited university.

In *Davis*, the court's decision was based partially on the complex nature of the police role and the public risk and responsibility that are unique to it. Such a decision indicates that higher standards of qualification can be applied to the job because police decision making requires an added dimension of judgment. This logic has been applied by the courts to other occupations, such as airline pilots and health-related professions. Thus, the *Davis* decision can be viewed as the next logical step in increasing police professionalism and may provide further support for police executives to require higher education (Carter, Sapp, and Stephens 1988, p. 10).

To validate the need for higher-education requirements, possibly the best approach, one that has withstood the scrutiny of the courts, is to use national studies and commission reports (e.g., National Advisory Commission on Criminal Justice . . . 1973; President's Commission on Law Enforcement 1967; and others cited in this chapter) and the opinion of experts (including both police scholars and police executives). The PERF study recommended a preventive approach for a department that is going to require higher education for employment. This can be accomplished by having an expert prepare a policy support paper citing the "benefits and need of college-educated officers" (Carter, Sapp, and Stephens 1988, p. 16). The study further suggested that, although general studies and reports should be used, the policy support document should be specific to the individual department. The probability of litigation should be substantially lessened with such a document, and the educational program can also be based on the policies developed in the document.

Higher Education and Discrimination

A second area of concern reported to PERF by police executives was the potential impact the higher-education requirement might have on the employment of minorities. If minority-group members do not have equal access to higher education, such a requirement could be held to be discriminatory by the courts. Not only that, but there are also obvious ethical and social issues raised. Any educational requirements for policing, then, must not only be job related but also nondiscriminatory.

In the *Davis* case, the suit contended that higher-education requirements were discriminatory in the selection of police officers. According to Title VII of the Civil Rights Act, there cannot be employment barriers (or practices) that discriminate against minorities, even if they are not intended to do so. However, in *Griggs v. Duke Power Co.* (1971), the U.S. Supreme Court held that if an employment practice is job related (or a "business necessity," p. 853), it may be allowed as a requirement, even though it has discriminatory overtones. Thus, courts must base decisions on the balance between requirements that are necessary for job performance and discriminatory practices. In *Davis,* the city of Dallas conceded that the college requirements did have a "significant disparate impact on blacks" (1985, p. 207). As noted above, the court held that the complex requirements of police work (e.g., public risk and responsibility, amount of discretion) mitigated against the discriminatory effects of a higher-education requirement.

It would appear, then, that if certain requirements for the job can be justified, even though they may discriminate against certain groups, the benefits of such requirements may be judged to outweigh the discriminatory effects. Following this line of reasoning, if higher-educational requirements can be shown to be a **bona fide occupational qualification (BFOQ)**, such a requirement would be considered a business necessity and thus a legitimate requirement for successful job performance.

With respect to higher educational levels in policing and minority representation, the PERF study of some 250,000 geographically dispersed police officers throughout the nation reported some interesting findings. For instance, as indicated in Table 11.7, the average educational levels of the various racial and ethnic groups (12.0 years equals a high-school degree), as well as the overall minority representation, are not significantly different. Furthermore, the percentage of black and Hispanic officers with some undergraduate work, and also with graduate degrees, is greater than for white officers.

Table 11.7	Educational Levels by Race/Ethnicity and Minority Representation in Police Organizations					
Group	Mean Yrs.	% in Police	National %	No college	Some under-graduate work	Graduate degree
Black	13.6	12.3	12.1	28%	63%	9%
Hispanic	13.3	6.4	8.0	27%	68%	5%
White	13.7	80.3	76.9	34%	62%	4%
Other	13.8	1.0	3.0	19%	73%	8%

Source: Adapted from D. L. Carter, A. D. Sapp, and D. W. Stephens. 1988. "Higher Education as a Bona Fide Occupational Qualification (BFOQ) for Police: A Blueprint." *American Journal of Police* 7: 20; and D. L. Carter and A. D. Sapp. 1992. "College Education and Policing: Coming of Age." *FBI Law Enforcement Bulletin*, January: 11.

Another important PERF finding, reported in Table 11.8, indicates that the average educational level of women officers was a full year higher (14.6 years to 13.6 years) than that of their male colleagues, with almost one-third (30.2 percent) possessing graduate degrees. This extreme difference may exist for at least three reasons: (1) Women tended to believe that they must have stronger credentials to compete effectively for police positions, (2) police departments may have been more rigid in their screening of female applicants, and (3) many women entering law reinforcement tended to come from other occupations that required a college degree, such as teaching (Carter and Sapp 1992, p. 13).

Table 11.8 Educational Level of Police Officers by Gender		
	Male	**Female**
Mean years	13.6 years	14.6 years
No college	34.8%	24.1%
Some undergraduate work	61.7%	45.7%
Graduate degree	3.3%	30.2%

Source: Adapted from D. L. Carter and A. D. Sapp. 1992. "College Education and Policing: Coming of Age." *FBI Law Enforcement Bulletin*, January: 11.

These data clearly indicate that a trend toward higher education exists in policing and appears not to have the negative impact on minority-officer recruitment that was initially feared. The fact that the proportion of minorities employed by state and local departments is approximately equal to proportions in the national population is also encouraging. As Carter and Sapp suggest:

> It appears that a college requirement is not impossible to mandate as evidenced by both the legal precedent and empirical data. . . . A college educated

police force that is racially and ethically representative of the community can be achieved. This only serves to make a police department more effective and responsive to community needs. (1992, p. 11, 13)

❖ ❖ ❖ ❖

As discussed above, those departments that wish to establish higher-education requirements need to develop a sound policy-support document. Inside Policing 11.2 shows how the framework for such a policy might look.

Inside Policing 11.2
Developing a Higher-Education Policy for Police Departments

Each department should have a written policy defining college education as a BFOQ as it uniquely relates to the department, regardless of the requirements adopted. The department can then be fully prepared for any questions concerning the validity of any new educational requirements.

Policy development should include input from all levels of the department, particularly the local collective-bargaining organizations. This provision will lead to a common understanding of the rationale for the policy, enhance its acceptance, and expedite its implementation.

Promotional Requirements. If the entry-level educational requirements are raised, then the educational requirements for promotion should also be reviewed. As more highly educated officers enter policing, more highly educated supervisors, managers, and police executives will be needed.

Policy Standards. Educational policies should specify standards, especially that college credit and degrees be awarded from an accredited college or university. Acceptable credit should be based on a minimum grade average of "C," or 2.0 on a 4.0 scale. Other standards could include the requirement that college credits earned be directly in pursuit of a degree. This rule ensures that the student has a liberal arts background in addition to courses in a major area.

Departments should also require majors that directly relate to the practice of policing, such as criminal justice, criminology, public administration, business administration, sociology, or psychology. Graduate education should also be job related, especially with respect to management issues and skills. College credit should be given for police academy or advanced training only after an academic accreditation review of specific courses, for example, the FBI National Academy's proactive practice of awarding credit through the University of Virginia.

Women and Minority Candidates. Attracting qualified women and minority candidates continues to be a concern for police departments. It is increasingly evident, however, that there is no need to limit entry or promotional educational requirements for these groups so long as innovative and aggressive recruiting programs are in place.

Equal-opportunity plans must continue to be used for entry and promotion in order for police departments to achieve demographic parity with their respective communities. Such parity is possible without reducing educational or other substantive requirements but not without clear-cut policies and well-planned programs.

Source: Adapted from D. L. Carter and A. D. Sapp. 1992. "College Education and Policing: Coming of Age." *FBI Law Enforcement Bulletin*, January: 12.

Policies Relating to Higher Education

If college education is to become an entry-level requirement for policing, it is important that supporting policies also be established. As noted above, it is possible to offset the possible discriminatory effects of a higher-education requirement through an aggressive recruitment strategy (see also Chapter 12). Additionally, of course, it is helpful to have a competitive salary scale, good employment benefits, and high-quality working conditions. It is important to point out that over the past decade, most medium and large police departments have implemented highly competitive salary structures, in line with, and often substantially above, the starting salaries for college graduates in most public-sector and many private-sector jobs.

The PERF study found that most of the departments had developed one or more **educational-incentive policies** to encourage officers to continue their education beyond that required for initial employment. As Table 11.9 indicates, some of these include tuition assistance or reimbursement, incentive pay, shift or day-off adjustments, and permission to attend classes during work hours. Another study of 72 Texas police departments, representing more than half of the police officers licensed in the state (Garner 1998), indicated that 52 departments (72 percent) offered some type of incentive for obtaining a college education. Forty-two reported various forms of tuition reimbursement, while 32 provided higher pay for those with degrees. Other educational incentives offered by numerous departments included the use of vehicles for transportation to classes, time off to attend courses, and scheduling preferences to accommodate the college semester. Various departments used one or more of these incentives.

Table 11.9 Higher Educational Incentive Policies for Sworn Officers		
College incentive policy	**Number***	**Percentage**
Tuition assistance or reimbursement	302	62.1
Educational-pay incentive	261	53.7
Adjustments of shifts or days off	207	42.6
Permission for class attendance while on duty	115	23.7
Other programs or policies**	57	11.7
No educational incentives	43	8.8

*Based on sample of 486 departments.
**Includes tuition for POST-approved course only; leaves of absence for college; fellowship and scholarship programs; in-service training programs for college credit. Most agencies have more than one incentive.
Source: Adapted from D. L. Carter and A. D. Sapp. 1992. "College Education and Policing: Coming of Age." *FBI Law Enforcement Bulletin*, January: 13.

Another type of incentive to program relates to promotional opportunities. Once again, the PERF survey found a growing trend for departments to tie educational requirements to promotion. Some 20 percent of those responding indicated that they had either a formal or informal policy requiring some level of advanced education for promotion; 5 percent required a college degree. In addition, a notable number of police chiefs said they believed a graduate degree should be required for officers in command ranks. The Texas survey found that only five of the 72 departments reported that they had an educational requirement for promotion; this number, however, may be similar to the PERF findings, since it does not include informal departmental policies or practices.

College Education as a Minimum Standard for Police Employment

❖ ❖ ❖ ❖

In the final analysis it appears as though enough evidence (both empirical and experiential) has been established to support a strong argument for a college-degree requirement for entry-level police officers:

1. The benefits provided by a higher education, along with the changing nature of police departments and society, suggest that a college degree should be a requirement for initial police employment.

2. If educational and recruitment policies are appropriately developed, a higher-education requirement should not adversely affect minority recruitment or retention.

Recognizing that there are diverse types of police departments throughout the country, with differing styles of operation, levels of performance, and community needs, it is apparent that some can adapt to a college-degree requirement more readily than others. For the near term, perhaps some type of graduated timetable for college requirements—similar to those found in the National Advisory Commission on Criminal Justice Standards and Goals (1973)—would be appropriate for departments that find attracting college graduates more problematic. For example, it would seem reasonable to suggest that beginning in the year 2005, all police candidates must have completed at least two years of higher education (60 semester units) at an accredited college or university for initial selection, three years (90 semester units) by 2010, and a baccalaureate degree by 2015. In addition, all executive-level positions should have a minimum requirement of a baccalaureate degree by 2005 and an advanced degree by 2010.

Although some "growing pains" are to be expected, the advantages of such a requirement in today's fast-paced, ever changing society outweigh the disadvantages of waiting for additional "evidence" of its importance (see Inside Policing 11.3). The time has arrived to upgrade American policing through higher-education requirements, moving the occupation closer to a truly professional status.

Inside Policing 11.3
Support for College-Education Requirement for Entry-Level Police Officers

At least three significant changes support a college degree requirement for initial selection of police.

Organizational Changes. Today's police departments are very different from those that existed when LEAA and LEEP were begun in the 1970s. Many more police officers and managers have college degrees (and advanced degrees), and the police cultural bias against "college cops" has significantly declined. The challenges of community policing require officers to use more discretion in problem solving and decision making. At the same time, officers must be aware of cultural differences in, and sensitivity to the needs of, the community. Research has suggested that successful community policing is dependent on the quality of educated police officers.

Because of these changes, departments can now recruit college-educated officers and provide them with salaries ☞

commensurate to other entry-level occupations requiring degrees. Most police departments throughout the country provide incentives to officers to continue their education or to pursue a college degree. In some ways, even though few departments formally require a college degree, it has become a de facto requirement. With strong support from police chief executives for college education, they may give little credence to those applicants that hold only a high school diploma. Although once considered an indicator of some skill and education, today high school diplomas have lost value because some individuals receive them through social promotion rather than demonstrated competence. Many university professors contend, and research supports, that the communication and analytic skills of high school graduates are less developed than a decade ago. This important issue further supports the argument favoring a college education requirement for police officers.

Societal Changes. Today's police officers need to be culturally sensitive and willing to value ethnic differences. Most college degree programs offer courses in such areas as cultural diversity, ethics, and cross-cultural comparisons, and some even require a foreign language. In addition, courses in sociology, psychology, and other human-behavior courses (including criminal justice and criminology) all contribute to a better understanding of the complex society in which we live. Research has demonstrated that officers who are exposed to such an educational experience deal better with diverse community groups.

Police departments must also recognize that as members of the community are becoming more educated, their expectations of police service will also increase. Thus, police departments need to raise their educational requirements in order to represent the populations they serve.

Technological Changes. Today's police officer is faced with more modern technology than ever before. The field notebook has been replaced by the laptop computer. The Internet, World Wide Web, and e-mail have greatly expanded resources and data-collection techniques, and the emphasis on solution-oriented policing has placed greater demands on crime analysis, problem solving, and computer sophistication.

As innovative programs are developed to address crime and disorder, departments must have officers who can evaluate their impact with methodologically sound techniques. Because this level of sophistication was not part of the "increased educational equation" during the time when the presidential and national commissions were emphasizing the importance of a college education, it is all the more important now. Most college-degree programs require coursework (e.g., computer science, research methods, and math and statistics) that is beneficial in today's technologically sophisticated environment.

Source: Adapted from R. Garner. 1998. "Community Policing and Education: The College Connection." *Texas Law Enforcement Management and Administrative Statistics Program,* January: 7-9.

Summary

Berkeley police chief August Vollmer began a campaign for higher education for police that has continued to the present. Major universities developed programs for police education, despite the resistance of many street officers. Research has indicated that higher education can be job validated for police entry and that such a requirement should not have an adverse impact on minority recruitment or retention if innovative and aggressive recruitment policies are appropriately developed. To this end, police departments should develop a written policy defining college education as a BFOQ as it uniquely relates to the department.

The Police Cadet Corps and the scholarship and recruitment program established under the Crime Control Act of 1994 appear to expand further the importance and availability of higher education to both in-service and pre-service students. In general, college education for entry-level police officers can also be based on present-day change, including organizational changes, societal changes, and technological changes. In the final analysis, enough evidence has been established to support the requirement of a college degree for policing, even though a graduated timetable may be necessary for some departments.

Discussion Questions

1. Briefly describe Vollmer's influence on police higher education.

2. What two events ushered in the "golden age" for higher education in police work and criminal justice?

3. How were the President's Commission on Law Enforcement and Administration of Justice and the National Advisory Commission on Criminal Justice Standards and Goals important to higher education for police?

4. What was LEAA? In your opinion, was it successful?

5. List several significant recommendations made by the National Advisory Commission on Higher Education for Police Officers (1978) regarding proposed changes in higher education for police.

6. Briefly describe the programs established by the Violent Crime Control and Law Enforcement Act of 1994 and the impact you believe they may have on policing and on society in general.

7. Briefly describe the important empirical research on the impact of higher education on policing.

8. In your opinion, can higher education be supported as a BFOQ in policing? State specific reasons why or why not.

9. Is a higher-education requirement for entry into policing discriminatory? State specific reasons why or why not.

10. If you were a police chief, would you attempt to require higher education for entry-level positions or promotion? Discuss your reasons for both positions.

References

American Bar Association. 1973. *Standards Relating to the Urban Police Function*. New York: American Bar Association.

Arnold v. Ballard 390 F. Supp. (N.D. Ohio 1975).

Caiden, G. E. 1977. *Police Revitalization*. Lexington, Mass.: D. C. Heath.

Carte, G. E. 1973. "August Vollmer and the Origins of Police Professionalism." *Journal of Police Science and Administration* 1: 274—281.

Carter, D. L. and Sapp, A. D. 1989. "The Effect of Higher Education on Police Liability: Implications for Police Personnel Policy." *American Journal of Police* 8: 153–166.

❖ ❖ ❖ ❖   ——. 1990. "Higher Education as a Policy Alternative to Reduce Police Liability." *Police Liability Review* 2: 1–3.

——. 1992. "College Education and Policing: Coming of Age." *FBI Law Enforcement Bulletin*, January: 8–14.

Carter, D. L., Sapp, A. D., and Stephens, D. W. 1988. "Higher Education as a Bona Fide Occupational Qualification (BFOQ) for Police: A Blueprint." *American Journal of Police* 7: 1–27.

——. 1989. *The State of Police Education: Policy Direction for the 21st Century.* Washington, D.C.: Police Executive Research Forum.

Cascio, W. F. 1977. "Formal Education and Police Officer Performance." *Journal of Police Science and Administration* 5: 89–96.

Castro v. Beecher 459 F.2d 725 (lst Cir. 1972).

Cohen, B. and Chaiken, J. M. 1972. *Police Background Characteristics and Performance.* New York: Rand Institute.

Dalley, A. F. 1975. "University and Non-University Graduated Policemen: A Study of Police Attitudes." *Journal of Police Science and Administration* 3: 458–468.

Davis v. City of Dallas 777 F.2d 205 (5th Cir. 1985).

Deutsch, A. 1955. *The Trouble with Cops.* New York: Crown Publishers.

"Dissecting the Crime Bill: New Era for Law Enforcement & Higher Education." 1994. *Law Enforcement News* October 15: 1, 7.

Finnegan, J. C. 1976. "A Study of Relationships Between College Education and Police Performance in Baltimore, Maryland." *The Police Chief* 34: 60–62.

Fyfe, J. J. 1988. "Police Use of Deadly Force: Research and Reform." *Justice Quarterly* 5: 165–205.

Garner, R. 1998. "Community Policing and Education: The College Connection." *Texas Law Enforcement Management and Administrative Statistics Program Bulletin* January.

Goldstein, H. 1977. *Policing a Free Society.* Cambridge, MA: Ballinger.

Griffin, G. R., Dunbar, R. L. M. and McGill, M. E. 1978. "Factors Associated with Job Satisfaction Among Police Personnel." *Journal of Police Science and Administration* 6: 77–85.

Griggs v. Duke Power Co. 401 U.S. 432 (1971).

Guller, I. B. 1972. "Higher Education and Policemen: Attitudinal Differences Between Freshman and Senior Police College Students." *Journal of Criminal Law, Criminology, and Police Science* 63: 396–401.

Korbetz, R. W. (1975). *Law Enforcement and Criminal Justice Education Directory, 1975–1976.* Gaithersburg, MD: International Association of Chiefs of Police.

Krimmel, J. T. 1996. "The Performance of College-Educated Police: A Study of Self-Rated Police Performance Measures." *American Journal of Police* 15: 85–96.

Kuykendall, J. L. and Hernandez, A. P. 1975. "Undergraduate Justice System Education and Training at San Jose State University." *Journal of Criminal Justice* 3: lll–l30.

Levy, R. J. 1967. "Predicting Police Failures." *Journal of Criminal Law, Criminology, and Police Science* 58: 265–276.

"Men & Women of Letters: No BS: Tulsa PD Rookies to Need Four-Year Degrees. 1997. *Law Enforcement News* November 30: 1.

Miller, J. and Fry, L. J. 1978. "Some Evidence on the Impact of Higher Education for Law Enforcement Personnel." *The Police Chief* 45: 30–33.

Mottaz, C. 1983. "Alienation Among Police Officers." *Journal of Police Science and Administration* 11: 23–30.

National Advisory Commission on Criminal Justice Standards and Goals (1973). *Report on Police.* Washington, D.C.: U.S. Government Printing Office.

Parker, L. Jr., Donnelly, J., Gerwitz, J., Marcus, J., and Kowalewski, V. 1976. "Higher Education: Its Impact on Police Attitudes." *The Police Chief* 43: 33–35.

Police Executive Research Forum (1989). *A Resolution of the Membership of the Police Executive Research Forum.* Washington, D.C.: PERF.

Pope, C. E. 1987. "Criminal Justice Education: Academic and Professional Orientations." In R. Muraskin (ed.), *The Future of Criminal Justice Education*, Brookeville, NY: Long Island University.

President's Commission on Law Enforcement and Administration of Justice 1967. *The Challenge of Crime in a Free Society*. Washington, D.C.: U.S. Government Printing Office.

Reaves, B. A. 1996. Local Police Departments, 1993. Washington, D.C.: Bureau of Justice Statistics.

Reaves, B. A. and Goldberg, A. L. 1999. *Law Enforcement and Administrative Statistics, 1997*, p. v. Washington, D.C.: Bureau of Justice Statistics.

Roberg, R. R. 1978. "An Analysis of the Relationships Among Higher Education, Belief Systems, and Job Performance of Patrol Officers." *Journal of Police Science and Administration* 6: 336–344.

Roberg, R. R. and Laramy, J. E. 1980. "An Empirical Assessment of the Criteria Utilized for Promoting Police Personnel: A Secondary Analysis." *Journal of Police Science and Administration* 8: l83–l87.

San Jose State College. 1960. *General Catalog 1960–1961.*. San Jose, CA: San Jose State College.

San Jose State University. 1998. *SJSU Catalog 1998–2000*. San Jose, CA: San Jose State University.

Sanders, B., Hughes, T., and Langworthy, R. 1995. "Police Officer Recruitment and Selection: A Survey of Major Departments in the U.S." *Police Forum*. Richmond, KY: Academy of Criminal Justice Sciences.

Sanderson, B. B. 1977. "Police Officers: The Relationship of College Education to Job Performance." *The Police Chief* 44: 62–62.

Saunders, C. B. 1970. *Upgrading the American Police*. Washington, D.C.: The Brookings Institution.

Sherman, L. W. and the National Advisory Commission on Higher Education for Police Officers. 1978. *The Quality of Police Education*. San Francisco: Josey-Bass.

Smith, S. M. and Aamodt, M. G. 1997. "The Relationship Between Education, Experience, and Police Performance." *Journal of Police and Criminal Psychology* 12: 7–14.

Smith, A. B., Locke, B., and Fenster, A. 1970. "Authoritarianism in Policemen Who Are College Graduates and Non-College Graduates." *Journal of Criminal Law, Criminology, and Police Science* 6l: 313–315.

Smith, A. B., Locke, B., and Walker, W. F. 1968. "Authoritarianism in Police College Students and Non-Police College Students. *Journal of Criminal Law, Criminology, and Police Science* 59: 440–443.

Stoddard, K. B. 1973. "Characteristics of Policemen of a County Sheriff's Office." In J. R. Snibbe and H. M. Snibbe (eds.), *The Urban Policemen in Transition*. Springfield, IL: C. Thomas.

"Surprise! The Police Corps Is Back—Not That It Ever Left." 1997. *Law Enforcement News* January 31: 1, 10.

1998. "Survey Says Big-City Chiefs are Better-Educated Outsiders." *Law Enforcement News* April 30: 7.

Terry, W. C. 1980. "Criminal Justice Faculty and Criminal Justice Students." *Journal of Criminal Justice* 8: 287–298.

Trojanowicz, R. C. and Nicholson, T. 1976. "A Comparison of Behavioral Styles of College Graduate Police Officers v. Non-College-Going Police Officers." *The Police Chief* 43: 57–58.

Tyre, M. and Braunstein, S. 1992. "Higher Education and Ethical Policing." *FBI Law Enforcement Bulletin* June: 6–10.

U.S. Department of Justice. 1994. *The Violent Crime Control and Law Enforcement Act of 1994*. Washington, D.C.: U.S. Government Printing Office.

Weiner, N. L. 1976. "The Educated Policeman." *Journal of Police Science and Administration* 4: 450–457.

Weirman, C. L. 1978. "Variances of Ability Measurement Scores Obtained by College and Non-College Educated Troopers." *The Police Chief* 45: 34–36.

Worden, R. E. 1990. "A Badge and a Baccalaureate: Policies, Hypotheses, and Further Evidence." *Justice Quarterly* 7: 565–592.

For a listing of websites appropriate to the content of this chapter, see "Suggested Websites for Further Study" (p. xv). ✦

Cultural Diversity

Chapter Outline

Key Terms	
affirmative action plan	police culture
Civil Service, or merit, system	police*woman*
cultural diversity	*police*woman
defeminization	quid pro quo harassment
double marginality	reverse discrimination
empirical evidence	sexual harassment
hostile work-environment	structural characteristics
harassment	testimonial evidence

 One of the more critical issues facing policing today is the **cultural diversity**—especially in terms of race, ethnicity, and gender—of the force in a democratic society. A belief in the importance of diversity in policing has existed since the mid-l800s, when modern policing began in the United States. There have always been proponents of matching the cultural types of people being policed with the same cultural types of police officers. In the last several decades, the diversity of a police department has again become important for both political and performance reasons. Although it is clear that diversity has widespread political support in many communities, the actual difference that diversification makes in police effectiveness is less clear.

In general, it is believed that a diverse police department is more effective than one that is not. In fact, diversity has become so important that it is often considered to be a significant strategy to reform those departments with performance problems, particularly as they relate to police use of force and community fear and distrust of the police. The evidence regarding the impact of diversity on police effectiveness can be categorized as either testimonial or empirical. **Testimonial evidence** is based on the opinions of individuals who have strong political beliefs about the importance of diversity or whose experience (e.g., as citizens or police officers) has led them to believe that a diverse department is either more or less effective. In general, testimonial evidence about the effectiveness of diversity is usually favorable. **Empirical evidence** regarding the effectiveness of diversity based on data is derived from systematic study of one or more effectiveness criteria (e.g., crime rates, arrest rates, and citizen trust of police or fewer complaints, civil suits, and confrontations). There is no empirical evidence that, in the long term, diversity makes a measurable, sustained difference in the effectiveness of the police. There is some short-term evidence, however, that diversity can make a difference in some areas of police effectiveness. For example, it has been shown that African-American citizens in Detroit (Frank, Brandl, Cullen, and Stichman 1996) have a higher regard for the police than whites (Detroit employs a significant number of black police officers) and that citizens in New York who came into contact with female officers (when they were first put on patrol) had a higher regard for the police department than they had before (Sichel, Friedman, Quint, and Smith 1978).

Given all the possible factors that can influence the relationship between police and citizens, it is unlikely that a police department that is a "perfect cultural match" for a community will necessarily be more effective *for that reason alone*. In the long term, the integrity, competence, and style of the officer, and the philosophy, strategies, and methods of the department have the greatest impact on effectiveness. However, diversity continues to have substantial political support because many persons believe that it is equitable to employ minorities and women, given the discrimination they have experienced in the past.

Historically, police departments have systematically discriminated against minorities and women in employment, assignments, promotions, and social acceptance. In addition, many white men have not, and do not, consider minorities and women to be their equals in terms of either capabilities or competencies. Beginning in the 1960s, governmental intervention was required in order to eliminate discrimination in employment and promotion. Legally, and in terms of government policy, this intervention became known as affirmative action (discussed in a later section). As noted previously, during the early- to mid-1960s there were ghetto riots and campus demonstrations that were often "sparked" by police actions. These events further raised questions that went to the very core of the police role and operations in a democratic society: Are the police isolated from the community? How important is it to have community representation in police departments? How important to the community are the nonenforcement aspects of the police role? What type of individuals should be recruited as police officers? As has also been discussed, several national commission reports, addressing these and other fundamental questions about the police, cited the need to increase especially minority but also female representation throughout the police field. The following is a brief discussion on the history of minorities and women in policing.

Minorities in Policing

Very little has been written about the early development of minority police officers in this country. Virtually all the literature that is available concerns African Americans and makes it clear that blacks and other minority members, until recently, have had very little access to policing. For example, even though there were black police officers in Washington, D.C. as early as 1861 (Johnson 1947), by 1940 they represented less than 1 percent of the police population (Kuykendall and Burns 1980, p. 5). Since World War II, however, there has been a steady increase in the proportions of black officers, as well as other minorities, in policing. In general, although the proportions of blacks and other minorities reflect the available work force in some communities, most departments do not have minority personnel equal to their numbers in the available work force (see "Increasing Diversity in Police Departments" discussed later).

Minority representation of police grew in many cities only as a result of pressure from the black community. In Chicago, for instance, black citizens complained frequently of the "stupidity, prejudice and brutality" of white officers (Gosnell 1935, p. 245). After 1940, use of black police increased as a result of the emerging political participation of blacks. Organized movements were often supported by liberal whites (Rudwick 1962). Often a church or civic group would become concerned over crime rates, law enforcement in black areas, or race relations because of either racial tension or a desire for integration. Believing that the use of black officers to patrol in black areas would substantially reduce black hostility toward the police, community leaders would usually agree to make a few experimental appointments (Johnson 1947).

Unequal Treatment

Even though African Americans were increasingly being hired into policing, they were not treated equally in the ares of powers of arrest, work assignments, evaluations, and promotions. Frequently, black officers were allowed to patrol only in black areas and to arrest only other black citizens. If a white person committed a crime in a black neighborhood, a black officer would have to call a white officer in order to make the arrest. In a 1959 survey of 130 cities and counties in the South, 69 required black officers to call white officers in arresting white suspects, and 107 cities indicated that black officers patrolled only in black neighborhoods (Rudwick 1962). As recently as 1966, in a survey of Southern states, *Ebony* magazine found that 28 police departments reported restrictions on arrest powers (*Ebony* 1966). E. Elysee Scott, associated with the National Organization for Black Law Enforcement Executives, who grew up in a small Louisiana town in the 1950s, remembers that the black police officers rode in cars marked "Colored Police" and were allowed to arrest only "colored" people (Sullivan 1989).

Black officers also were frequently restricted in type and location of assignments, and performance ratings were negatively manipulated by superior officers. Dismissal because of race was also a possibility. In addition, black and white officers rarely worked together (Gosnell 1935); even as late as 1966, squad cars were not totally integrated in the Chicago Police Department (National Center 1967). Promotions also were rare for black officers. For example, S. Leinen (1984) found that in the mid-1960s only 22 police departments had promoted blacks above the rank of patrol officer. Even when promotions did occur, it was often a mixed blessing; blacks were not congratulated by whites and were not given duties involving active command. In at least one instance, black lieutenants were assigned to walk a beat as patrol officers (Gosnell 1935).

Performance of African-American Police

As noted above, the ghetto riots of the mid-1960s were a major reason that increased emphasis was placed on the role of minorities in policing. Because a large number of these riots were triggered by incidents involving white officers patrolling black ghetto areas, many people thought that community relations would be improved if there were African American officers in these areas. Several national reports came to the same conclusion. For instance, the President's Commission on Law Enforcement and Administration of Justice stated:

> Police officers have testified to the special competence of Negro officers in Negro neighborhoods. The reasons given include: they get along better and receive more respect from the Negro residents: they receive less trouble...; they can get more information; and they understand Negro citizens better. (1967, p. 162)

Another important commission, the National Advisory Commission on Civil Disorders (1968), issued a comprehensive report on the problem and placed a large part of the blame for the riots not only on the serious underrepresentation of blacks on police departments but also on the general level of racism that existed in society.

Historically, evidence to support the belief that black officers would perform more satisfactorily in black areas has been mixed. On the one hand, many black citizens wanted black officers because it would provide an opportunity for more public jobs, more understanding, less white police brutality, and more effective supervision of black criminals (Landrum 1947; Myrdal 1944). On the other hand, E. Rudwick (1960) has argued that blacks from lower socioeconomic classes preferred white to black officers. He found that poorer, uneducated blacks frequently asked for white officers when in need of help and were more likely to plead guilty to a charge made by a white officer (Rudwick 1962).

Some evidence indicates that black officers have actually been "harder" on black citizens than have white officers. In a study in Philadelphia in the 1950s, W. M. Kephart (1957) found that the majority of black officers believed it was necessary to be "stricter" with their "own" people than they were with non-blacks. N. Alex (1976) found that black officers were actually challenged more by young blacks and may have viewed themselves as protectors of the black community. In contrast, black officers needed to prove to the white officers that they were not biased and therefore treated black suspects equally, or more harshly, than white suspects. Alex, in his influential book *Black in Blue* (1969), termed this dilemma of black officers "double marginality."

This **double marginality** was evident by the mid-1960s, when the apparent desire of many black citizens for black police began to lose appeal. Studies conducted in San Diego and Philadelphia, for example, found that some black citizens felt that blacks who chose to become police officers were "selling them out." Of course, given the tenor of the times—police officers in general were viewed as enemies in minority communities—such a finding is hardly surprising. It is also interesting to note that while many still take the view that minority neighborhoods need minority patrol officers, others view such an approach as a form of segregation. It is ironic that many of those same people who, during the riots of the 1960s, demanded that black officers be sent into black areas, are now condemning the same practice as racist (Sullivan 1989, p. 342).

Today, as African-American officers become more self-assured and less likely to accept discriminatory practices (Alex 1976), double marginality is less of a problem. On the one hand, in one study conducted in the aftermath of the Miami riots of the early 1980s, B. Berg, E. True, and M. Gertz (1984) found that black police officers were far less detached and alienated from the local community than were white or Hispanic officers. On the other hand, some police officials believe that black officers have trouble relating to the community because they tend to identify with their white colleagues, who tend to have a limited understanding of cultural differences (Felkenes 1990; Georges-Abeyie 1984). Because so little data exist in this area of study, it is difficult to know how large an issue double marginality remains to minority officers. One thing seems clear, however; as long as there is tension between minority communities and police departments, minority officers will be caught in the middle. It is anticipated that as the degree of discrimination lessens, both within and outside police departments, the problem of double marginality will lessen accordingly.

Women in Policing

The historical record for women in policing is even weaker than for minorities. The first woman to hold full police powers was Lola Baldwin in Portland, Oregon, who in 1905 was hired in a social-work capacity with the responsibility for protecting young girls and women. Such a crime-prevention role was viewed as separate from the traditional police role; as S. Walker notes, "Once the police began to think in terms of preventing juvenile delinquency, they responded to the traditional argument that women had a special

A female police officer of the late 1940s. (Source: San Francisco Police Museum)

❖ ❖ ❖ ❖

capacity for child care" (Walker 1977, p. 85). Between 1905 and 1915, several police departments across the country copied Portland's example. The policewoman idea achieved the status of an organized movement in 1910 with the appointment of Alice Stebbins-Wells to the Los Angeles Police Department. Like Baldwin, Stebbins-Wells had a background in social work and was assigned to care for young women in trouble with the law and to prevent delinquency among juveniles of both sexes (Walker 1977). Stebbins-Wells became the national leader for the policewomen's movement, which lasted into the 1920s. Her appointment led to the appointment of women to similar positions (as police-social workers) in police departments in at least 16 cities by 1916 (Walker 1977). By 1925, 210 cities had women working in police positions, 417 as police-social workers and 355 as jail matrons (Owings 1925).

Between 1925 and 1965, both the numbers and functions of policewomen increased, but only minimally. For example, a 1967 survey of police departments in the nation's largest cities indicated that there were only 1,792 women with police powers (Berkeley 1969). When they were represented on the force, policewomen typically comprised less than 2 percent of the personnel (Eisenberg, Kent, and Wall 1973; Melchionne 1967) and were excluded from patrol duties. During this period, most police departments had policies that not only discouraged the hiring of women but often included quotas as well, usually 1 percent or less (Simpson 1977).

Unequal Treatment

Prior to the 1950s, the role of women in policing was restricted primarily to social-welfare assignments, including dealing with juvenile and family problems; being prison matron; detecting purse snatchers, pickpockets and shoplifters; investigating sexual assault; and clerical work (Eisenberg, Kent, and Wall 1973). During the 1950s their role was expanded to cover narcotics and vice investigations (Garmire 1978). During this period, it is ironic that the advocates for women in policing tended to argue that because of their "unique" contributions, including their skills with women and children, defusing domestic violence, and doing undercover work, they should be allowed to join the law enforcement profession (Melchionne 1967). Of course, such an argument most likely added to the prevailing view that women could handle specialist activities in "their areas" but were not suited for general police work. As J. Balkin notes, "It is an interesting if unanswered question why there was reluctance to demand simple equality for women in police work" (1988, p. 30). Undoubtedly, a large part of the answer lies in the strong tradition placed on the law enforcement, as opposed to social service, nature of the job. In addition, O. W. Wilson and R. C. McLaren, in their highly influential text, *Police Administration* (see Chapter 4), were firmly against the equal employment of women. They argued that while women could be of some value in specialized activities and units, they were not qualified to head such units. Men, they noted, were more effective administrators and "were less likely to become irritable and overly critical under emotional stress" (1963, p. 334).

Although these stereotypic images of women and police work were soon to be challenged, the major breakthrough for the equal treatment for policewomen on the job was the passage of the 1972 amendments to the Civil Rights Act of 1964 (see the discussion on equal employment opportunity in the next section). After this date, police departments were required, often under the threat of a court order, to eliminate such discriminatory practices of hiring and job assignment. The changes that followed were drastic. For example, in 1971 there were fewer than 12 policewomen on patrol in the United States; by 1974, this number was approaching 1,000 (Garmire 1978).

In 1968 the first women were assigned to patrol work in the Indianapolis Police Department (Milton 1972). Within five years, many of the nation's largest police forces, including those of New York, Philadelphia, Miami, Washington, and St. Louis, had women working in patrol (Sherman 1973). By 1979, the percentage of policewomen assigned to patrol was approximately 87 in city departments serving populations over 50,000 (Sulton and Townsey 1981). In a comprehensive survey for the Police Foundation of municipal departments serving populations ranging from 50,000 to over a million, it was shown that the integration of women into all police assignments has continued to grow at a steady pace. The data indicated that by 1986, 98 percent of the responding departments assigned women to patrol, and women were being assigned to field-operations units (including patrol, special operations, and traffic assignments) in slightly greater proportion than their overall representation in policing (Martin 1989a). Today, policewomen are assigned to virtually all police functions.

Performance of Women Officers

The evaluations of the first generation of women patrol officers found that they perform in a highly satisfactory manner. These findings are especially interesting because it was the argument that women could not handle the "physically demanding" job of patrol that barred them from patrol work. The first study of women on patrol was conducted in Washington, D.C., in 1973 (Bloch and Anderson 1974). A matched pair of 86 newly trained policewomen and policemen were placed on patrol and evaluated for one year. The results indicated that men and women performed in a generally similar manner. Women responded to similar calls and had similar results in handling violent citizens. Some interesting differences were also found: Women made fewer arrests but appeared to be more effective than men in defusing potentially violent situations. Additionally, women had a less aggressive style of policing and were less likely to be charged with improper conduct. The unmistakable conclusion drawn from these results was that female officers can perform effectively on patrol.

Two additional major studies closely followed the Washington study, both with similar conclusions. In 1975 L. J. Sherman conducted an evaluation of policewomen on patrol in the St. Louis County Police Department; the first 16 women put on patrol in the county were compared with a group of 16 men who had been trained with the women officers. The results indicated that the women were equally as effective as the men in performing patrol work. Once again, some interesting differences were noted: Women were less aggressive, made fewer arrests, and engaged in less "preventive" activities, such as car and pedestrian stops. Citizen surveys indicated that women were more sensitive and responsive to their needs and handled service calls, especially domestic disturbances, better than men.

The second study, conducted in New York City in 1976 by J. L. Sichel, L. N. Friedman, J. C. Quint, and M. E. Smith (1978), was comparable to the Washington study in methodological rigor and sophistication. Once again, comparison groups of 41 women and men officers with similar background characteristics were evaluated. Based on 3,625 hours of observation on patrol, and some 2,400 police-citizen encounters, the results indicated that both groups of officers performed in a similar manner. Again, however, women officers were judged by citizens to be more respectful, pleasant, and competent; furthermore, citizens who came into contact with women officers tended to have a higher regard for the police department. Similar findings on the effectiveness of policewomen on patrol have been reported throughout the 1970s in departments of widely divergent sizes and geographical locations (see Pennsylvania State Police 1973; Washington 1974; California Highway Patrol 1976; Bartlett and Rosenblum 1977; Kizziah and Morris 1977; and Snortum 1983).

A review of these studies by M. Morash and J. R. Greene (1986) pointed out that despite the generally favorable evaluations, gender biases were inherent in the study designs. For example, there was an emphasis on traits stereotypically associated with "maleness" and policing, and approximately two-thirds of the policing situations observed were related to direct or potential violence, even though such incidents are not frequently encountered. Also important, although the studies found differences in men's and

Today women perform virtually all police tasks, including bicycle patrol. (Photo: Mark C. Ide)

women's behavior, they did not consider the possibility that the women's policing style in resolving conflicts and disputes, rather than escalating incidents into unnecessary arrests, might have had a beneficial rather than a negative effect. Public policing may indeed benefit from police styles that play down the values of coercive authority, conflict, and interpersonal violence (Morash and Greene 1986, p. 249).

Another study of patrol teams in New York City (Grennan 1988) reported similar results with respect to male and female policing style differences: Women were found to be less likely to use a firearm in violent confrontations, were less likely to seriously injure a citizen, were no more likely to suffer injuries, and were more emotionally stable. This study debunked another male stereotype, that because women have less strength and are less capable of subduing a suspect physically, they will be more likely to use their firearms. The above findings suggest that women have adapted well to their increased presence and responsibilities in policing; it will be seen, however, there are still many obstacles to be overcome before they are accepted as equals on the force.

Affirmative Action

The National Advisory Commission's *Report on Police* stated that "When a substantial ethnic minority population resides within the jurisdiction, the police agency should take affirmative action to achieve a ratio of minority group employees in approximate proportion to the makeup of the population" (1973, p. 329). The National Advisory Commission on Civil Disorders (1968, p. 3l6) suggested that police departments should not only intensify their efforts on minority recruitment but should also increase the numbers of minorities in supervisory positions. Attempts to remedy past discriminatory employment and promotional practices are reflected in an **affirmative action plan**. In other words, the department tries to make an affirmative, or positive, effort to redress past practices and ensure equal employment opportunity. Such plans have been developed voluntarily, though often with political pressure, or by court order following legal action.

In one study of the nation's 50 largest cities, Walker (1989) found that affirmative action plans appeared to play an important role in police employment trends. Nearly two-thirds (64 percent) of the departments reported operating under an affirmative action plan at some point during the five-year period. Interestingly, 23 of the affirmative action plans were court ordered, and only 7 were voluntary. Clearly, much of the growth of both minorities and women in policing over the past several decades can be attributed to affirmative action plans and policies (see Case Study 12.l).

Equal Employment Opportunity

In general, the legal challenges to discrimination in employment are brought under either (1) the "equal protection of the laws" clause of the Fourteenth Amendment (which protects citizens of all states) or (2) the Equal Employment Opportunity Act of 1972, which extended to public agencies the "anti-discrimination in employment" provisions of Title VII of the 1964 Civil

---

Case Study 12.1

Dallas Police Department Reports Minority Officers Reflect City Makeup

Long a target of protests over its racial makeup, the Dallas Police Department is making progress in its efforts to make the ranks of its sworn employees reflect the increasingly diverse population it serves. For the first time, the number of black employees at the officer rank is virtually proportionate to the city's black population, according to statistics kept by the departments. In the near future, the share of Hispanic officers also will be proportionate to the city's Hispanic population.

As of early 1998, 29 percent of the department's 1,145 officers were black and 18.8 percent were Hispanic. The 1990 census, which the city uses to set hiring goals, showed Dallas had 29.5 percent black residents and 18.8 percent Hispanics. Asian Americans make up less than 1 percent of officers and senior corporals. The department, however, has a way to go before minorities are proportionately represented in its upper ranks. Whites, who make up 55.3 percent of the city's population, account for about 75 percent of the 1,697 senior corporals, sergeants, lieutenants, captains, and chiefs. While the department acknowledges the imbalance, it continues to make headway in improving promotional opportunities for all officers.

The figures on the number of minority officers are heartening in light of the tenuous, nearly incendiary police-minority relations that were the norm less than 10 years ago, a period in which the racial dynamics of the department were a major issue. To remedy the scant numbers of minorities on the force, the City Council adopted an affirmative action plan in 1988. Revised in 1993 and due to expire this September (1998), the plan stipulates that each new class of police recruits should be one-third black, one-third Hispanic, and one-third female. It also sets promotional goals for women and minorities in each rank.

In 1992, protesters massed outside the department, charging that the effort was moving too slowly in hiring and advancing minorities. Two years later, an internal audit concluded that in the early 1990s the department had fired dozens of officers with questionable credentials. Critics of the affirmative action plan, including the Dallas Police Association, charged that standards had been lowered, leading to the firing of unqualified applicants. The DPA still opposes affirmative action, particularly the practice of "skip promotions" allowing minorities who score lower on tests to rank higher on promotion lists than whites with better scores. The apparent progress made by the department shows that the time is near to dismantle the controversial practice, said the DPA's president, Glenn White: "If you continue to hire minorities and get them in, having an affirmative action program with skip promotions is not necessary. They'll make it on their own."

Other observers cautioned that progress does not mean police now can become complacent on the issue of minority representation in the upper ranks. "If we can reach the representation goal at the police officer level, why not at the senior corporal, sergeant, and lieutenant and above?" said Thomas Glover, president of the Texas Peace Officers' Association, a predominantly black organization.

Source: Adapted from "Dallas PD Says Black Officers Mirror City Makeup." 1998. *Law Enforcement News*, March: p. 7. Reprinted with permission from *Law Enforcement News*, John Jay College of Criminal Justice, New York City.

Rights Act. Title VII prohibits any discrimination in the workplace based on race, color, religion, national origin or sex. The Equal Employment Opportunity Commission (EEOC) was established in 1964 to investigate possible violations of the act.

T. K. Moran (1988, p. 274) suggests that much of the resistance to affirmative action litigation rests with the belief by many police executives that the **Civil Service, or merit system** is a fair and effective means of producing a professional force. This system generally involves selecting in rank order those individuals who obtained the highest combined score on an objective, multiple-choice, written exam (many of which have been shown to be culturally biased and not job related) and an oral interview. Additionally, candidates must meet several physical, medical, and personal requirements in order to qualify for appointment to the department. The problem with this "fair" and "effective" system is that it excluded women, except in some specialized positions, and many minorities from police work.

The federal courts began to recognize that many selection standards that appeared to be neutral in form and intent, in fact operated to exclude minorities and women. In general, the courts have indicated (Moran 1988, p. 275–276) that a police department must (1) establish that a selection procedure can be scientifically linked to job performance (i.e., "job validated"), or (2) restructure the selection process in a manner that does not discriminate against qualified minorities. The outcome of the affirmative action litigation has been that, from a scientific perspective, there was very little "merit" in the police-selection process. In fact, such standards as height, weight, age, and gender have not been correlated to job performance.

In the landmark decision in this area, *Griggs v. Duke Power Co.* (1971), the U. S. Supreme Court held that the use of a professionally developed examination (for intelligence) could not be used if it had a discriminatory effect. The Court pointed out that Title VII prohibited tests that are neutral in form but discriminatory in operation; that is, if a selection practice excludes minorities or women (even though not intended to do so) and cannot be shown to be job validated, it is prohibited. *Griggs* further found that once discrimination has been established, the burden of proof in establishing the validity of the practice shifts to the defendant (i.e., employer). In other words, once a police department has been judged to have engaged in a discriminatory practice, the department must indicate to the court that the practice (or requirement) is job related (Moran 1988).

In contrast, if a selection standard or requirement does not have a discriminatory impact, there is no need for validation. Furthermore, if a requirement can be shown to be a valid requirement for the job, *even if it may have a discriminatory impact*, it may be allowed to remain as a requirement. Chapter 11, for example, discussed how higher education may be shown to be a BFOQ for policing and thus be allowed as a requirement for initial selection.

Reverse Discrimination

Increasing the proportional representation of ethnic minorities and women in policing is an extremely complex undertaking that has important social, ethical, and legal implications. Although there is undoubtedly a need for the increase, the question is how to do so fairly. When affirmative action plans for selection and promotions (which may include the use of quotas, separate lists, and "skip" promotions—although often temporary, see Case Study 12.1) are put into practice, individuals who are not part of that plan—usually white men—often feel they have been discriminated against. This situation has become known as **reverse discrimination**. As with affirmative action policies, there has been much litigation in this area.

The idea of reverse discrimination is important because those who feel they are victims frequently develop a resentment (known as "white backlash") toward those who are helped most by affirmative action. This reaction should not be too surprising when the immediate effect may be either rejection or lack of promotion for whites who believe they are more "qualified" for the position based on the merit system. Even though the criteria used may not have been job validated, because the merit system has been used for so long, it is often difficult to get this point across when careers are seriously affected. For example, a study by J. Jacobs and J. Cohen (1978) indicated that white police officers view affirmative action programs as a threat to their job security. Additionally, if new criteria (i.e., not based on the old merit system) are used to further increase minority representation in a department, veteran officers often view the new process as "lowering standards" and, thus, the quality of police personnel.

Often, it is difficult for individuals, who may not be prejudiced themselves, to comprehend fully the depth of prejudice that has existed in the past, and which has not allowed minorities and women to compete equally for police jobs and promotions. Policing has been a traditionally white, male-dominated occupation, virtually unchallenged in its makeup, until the anti-discrimination in employment provisions of the Civil Rights Act were extended to the public through the Equal Employment Opportunity Act in 1972. Historically, of course, that is a very recent event. Although some form of remedial action for this past behavior is necessary, both sides of the controversy undoubtedly have misgivings and legitimate complaints regarding the best way to proceed.

The litigation in this area is as complicated as the issue itself. In 1974, for example, the Detroit Police Department voluntarily adopted a policy of promoting one black officer to sergeant for each white officer promoted. The Detroit Police Officers Association filed suit against the department, claiming that the policy discriminated against white males. In *Detroit Police Officers' Association v. Young* (1978), the court ruled that preferential treatment had been granted to blacks solely on the basis of race, and the policy therefore discriminated against all others. In a similar suit, *U.S. v. Paradise* (1987), the U. S. Supreme Court upheld racial quotas as a means of reversing past discrimination. The Alabama Department of Public Safety was ordered to promote one black officer to corporal for each white officer promoted to rectify "blatant and continuous patterns of racial discrimination" (the department had only four of 66 black corporals and no blacks at the sergeant level or above). Interestingly, the Court justified the ruling in that it did not impose an unacceptable burden on innocent third parties since the "one-for-one" requirement was *temporary* and would only postpone the promotion of qualified whites. Additionally, the promotion quota advanced blacks only to the level of corporal (not higher ranks) and did not require layoffs or dismissals of white officers.

As the above court interpretations indicate, rulings in this area are subject to changes by the judges who try the cases. Based on *Paradise*, however, it would appear as though the Supreme Court, in its attempt to balance equal employment opportunities is equally concerned about blatant racial discrimination as well as unacceptable injuries to innocent third parties.

Increasing Diversity in Police Departments

The number of women and minorities in police departments has consistently increased since the 1960s, even though their increase has been uneven. For instance, a survey of municipal police departments serving cities of 50,000 or more (Martin 1989a) indicated that in 1978 women made up 4.2 percent of sworn personnel and by 1986 they made up 8.8 percent. In local departments with 100 or more officers, about 99 percent have women officers, but fewer than 1 percent have 20 percent or more female representation. Furthermore, most of these departments are sheriff's departments where many women officers work in the jails (Carter, Sapp, and Stephens 1989). With respect to minorities, Walker (1989) reported that in the nation's 50 largest cities, between 1983 and 1988, nearly half (45 percent) made significant progress in the employment of black officers; however, 17 percent reported a decline in their percentage of African Americans. Forty-two percent of the departments reported significant increases in the percentage of Hispanic officers employed, while approximately 11 percent indicated a decline and 17 percent reported no change.

The 1993 survey of more than 3,000 police departments by the Bureau of Justice Statistics (Reaves 1996) provides the most comprehensive look at the cultural changes taking place in policing to date. The increasing percentages of women and minorities can be readily observed in Figure 12.1. Women comprised 8.8 percent of all full-time local police officers in 1993, compared to 8.1 percent in 1990 and 7.6 percent in 1987. Black officers accounted for 11.3 percent of the total in 1993, compared to 10.5 percent in 1990 and 9.3 percent in 1987. Hispanic officers made up 6.2 percent of the total in 1993, compared to 5.2 percent in 1990 and 4.5 percent in 1987. All minorities made up about 19 percent of the total in 1993, with an estimated 71, 244 officers, which was larger than the 61,710 in 1990 and the 51,872 in 1987. In contrast,

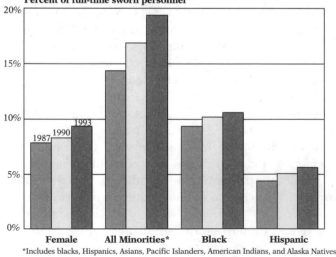

Figure 12.1 Women and Minority Local Police Officers, 1987, 1990, and 1993

Percent of full-time sworn personnel

*Includes blacks, Hispanics, Asians, Pacific Islanders, American Indians, and Alaska Natives

Source: B. A. Reaves. 1996. *Local Police Departments, 1993.* Washington D.C.: Bureau of Justice Statistics, p. 4.

the percentage of white male officers in 1993 was approximately 81 with an estimated 281,057, a decrease of about 20,000 from 1990 and about 22,000 from 1987 (Reaves 1996, p. 4).

The uneven increase of both women and minority officers in departments is represented in Tables 12.1 and 12.2. Although women comprised 8.8 percent of all local police officers in 1993, their percentages were highest in large jurisdictions, with 15 percent of officers in jurisdictions of 1 million or more in population and 12 percent in jurisdictions with at least 250,000 residents but fewer than 1 million (see Table 12.1).

Minority officers, who made up approximately 19 percent of the total, also had the highest percentages in large jurisdictions, with black officers making up approximately 18 to 21 percent in jurisdictions over 250,000 residents; Hispanic officers were the most represented in jurisdictions with populations over 250,000, making up 7 to 12 percent. Each of these groups had the highest percentage of officers in jurisdictions with over 1 million population (i.e., blacks with 18% and Hispanics with 12%). Other minorities, including Asians, Pacific Islanders, American Indians, and Alaska Natives, represented 1.5 percent of the total, with 1.2 percent in jurisdictions with over 1 million population; all other jurisdictions were under 6 percent representation (see Table 12.2).

Table 12.1 Gender of Full-Time Officers in Local Police Departments, by Size of Population Served, 1993

Population Served	All sworn employees		
	Total%	Male%	Female%
All Sizes	100	91.2	8.8
1,000,000 or more	100	85.4	14.6
500,000-999,999	100	87.6	12.4
250,000-499,999	100	88.1	11.9
100,000-249,000	100	91.0	9.0
50,000-99,999	100	93.0	7.0
25,000-49,999	100	94.8	5.2
10,000-24,999	100	95.0	5.0
2,500-9,999	100	95.6	4.4
Under 2,500	100	97.2	2.8

Note: Detail may not add to total because of rounding.
Source: B. A. Reaves. 1996. *Local Police Departments, 1993*. Washington, D.C.: Bureau of Justice Statistics, p. 3.

Three recent surveys of women in policing further point out their uneven development and continued gender-specific problems. The first survey of 800 police executives by the IACP reported that women make up 12 percent of the police officers but are not represented at all in nearly 20 percent of the departments ("Plenty of Talk ... " 1999). Furthermore, the IACP found that 91 percent of the departments have no women in policy-making roles, and 10 percent reported that gender bias was one of the reasons women are not promoted. It was also found that women have more than one-third of the lawsuits filed against departments charged with gender bias and sexual harassment. Based on the findings, the IACP recommended that police departments should implement fairer screening procedures, institute more rigorous polices against sexual harassment and increase recruiting drives designed to attract and retain more women in policing. The Albuquerque (New Mexico) Police Department was identified by police executives in the survey as a possible model for other departments with respect to women in policing; Case Study 12.2 describes why.

Albuquerque Police Department Identified as Model for Policewomen

The Albuquerque Police Department has been identified by police executives as a possible model for other departments regarding policewomen. In the past three years, women in the academy class have increased from just 8 percent to 25 percent. In the January 1999 class, the department reports, one-third of the recruits were women. Several years ago, however, despite participation in job fairs and a competitive salary, the department was still having problems recruiting female candidates. But significant changes seem to have turned the situation around. Those changes included (1) hiring a trainer to help women candidates pass the physical conditioning tests, (2) switching to weapons that were better suited to women's smaller hands, and (3) finding a body-armor manufacturer that was willing to construct bulletproof vests that accommodated bust sizes.

Officer Deedy Smith, an 18-year veteran of the APD, told *USA Today*: "For a long time, they tried their best to squeeze us into men. The uniforms, the vests, the whole thing. This has always been a man's job."

In addition, the department discovered that its in-house psychologists were disqualifying a disproportionate number of women whose employment histories did not include law enforcement experience or other work traditionally listed by male applicants. "We really don't know how many candidates we lost in that," said Lieutenant Vicky Peltzer, who assisted outside consultants in reviewing the APD's hiring practices.

Source: Adapted from *Law Enforcement News*. "Plenty of Talk, Not Much Action: IACP Survey Says PDs Fall Short on Recruiting, Retaining Women." 1999. January 15/31: 1, 14. Reprinted with permission from *Law Enforcement News*, John Jay College of Criminal Justice, New York City.

The second survey of some 700 state and local police departments with 100 or more full-time sworn officers by the Bureau of Justice Statistics (Reaves and Goldberg 1999) found that sheriff's departments employed the highest percentage of female officers (15 percent)—although many of those worked in the jails rather than on patrol—followed by county departments (11 percent), municipal departments (9 percent), and State agencies (5 percent). The third survey, by the National Center for Women and Policing (LEN 1998) of 100 local and state agencies, found that women held 11.6 percent of all sworn positions in 1997. The center further reported uneven employment with respect to type of organization, with state law enforcement agencies employing only 5.2 percent females, compared to 14 percent in municipal agencies and 13.1 percent in county agencies. The 10 lowest-ranked agencies were state police or highway patrols.

With respect to ethnicity and policewomen, Table 12.2 indicates that the proportion of minority women was related to city size—that is, as the size of the city increased, so too did the proportion of minority female representation. For example, minority women constituted 7.1 percent of women officers (white females made up 7.5 percent) in jurisdictions over 1 million and

6.3 percent (white women made up 6.1 percent) in jurisdictions over 500,000. Furthermore, minority women made up a disproportionately large share of women in policing—approximately 35 percent (3.0 percent out of a total of 8.7 percent) in 1993. It has been suggested that this large proportion of minority women officers—who are mostly black (2.2 of the 3.0 percent)—may be related to several factors (Martin 1989a). First, black women may view policing as an attractive occupational choice because they have a narrower range of options to choose from due to racial differences in education and job discrimination. Second, black women have historically worked in occupations involving physical labor and therefore may be less likely to be bothered by this aspect of the work than white women. Third, municipal departments may be disproportionately recruiting and hiring minority women in order to simultaneously meet affirmative action goals related to racial and sexual integration.

Table 12.2 Race and Ethnicity of Full-Time Officers in Local Police Departments, by Size of Population Served, 1993

| | | | | | | | Percent of full-time sworn employees who are: | | | | | | |
| | | White | | | Black | | | Hispanic | | | Other* | | |
Population served	Total	Total	Male	Female	Total	Male	Female	Total	Male	Female	Total	Male	Female
All sizes	100%	80.9%	75.2%	5.7%	11.3%	9.1%	2.2%	6.2%	5.5%	.7%	1.5%	1.4%	.1%
1,000,000 or more	100%	69.2%	61.7%	7.5%	17.7%	12.8%	4.9%	12.0%	10.0%	2.0%	1.2%	1.0%	.2%
500,000-999,999	100	66.2	60.1	6.1	21.0	16.1	5.0	7.0	6.1	.9	5.8	5.4	.4
250,000-499,999	100	71.9	64.5	7.4	17.7	14.3	3.4	9.0	8.2	.9	1.4	1.2	.4
100,000-249,999	100	80.6	74.2	6.3	12.4	10.4	2.1	5.4	4.9	.4	1.6	1.5	.1
50,000-99,999	100	86.3	80.7	5.5	7.2	6.3	.9	5.1	4.7	.5	1.4	1.3	.1
25,000-49,999	100	89.8	85.1	4.6	5.4	5.0	.5	4.3	4.1	.2	.6	.6	—
10,000-24,999	100	91.6	87.1	4.5	5.1	4.8	.3	2.6	2.5	.1	.6	.6	—
2,500-9,999	100	92.8	88.9	3.9	4.1	3.8	.3	2.6	2.4	.1	.5	.5	—
Under 2,500	100	91.7	89.3	2.3	5.3	5.0	.3	1.9	1.8	.1	1.2	1.1	—

Note: Detail may not add to total because of rounding.
—Less than .05%.
*Includes Asians, Pacific Islanders, American Indians, and Alaska Natives.
Source: B. A. Reaves. 1996. *Local Police Departments*, 1993. Washington, D.C.: Bureau of Justice Statistics, p. 4.

It is interesting to take a look at how the nation's largest jurisdictions and agencies are progressing with respect to diversity, since they tend to set the trends in policing. In 1997 full-time sworn officers in these departments, sometimes referred to as the "Big Six"—New York, Los Angeles, Chicago, Houston, Detroit, and Philadelphia—employed, on average, 17.8 percent female and 42.7 percent minority officers (Reaves and Goldberg 1999), up from 15.5 percent female and 36.8 percent minority officers in 1993 (Reaves and Smith 1995). Another way to view the progress of diversity is to look at those departments that have the largest percentage of women and minority representation. Table 12.3 presents the top five local police departments, with 100 or more officers, which have the largest percent of women, blacks, Hispanics, Asians/Pacific Islanders, and American Indian/Alaska Natives.

Table 12.3	Top Five Local Police Departments With Percent of Women and Minority Officers		
	Department	**No. of Sworn Officers**	**Percentage**
Women			
	Pittsburgh, PA	1,122	29
	Madison, WI	327	28
	Washington, DC	3,618	25
	Boulder, CO	137	24
	Bossier, LA	176	23
Blacks			
	Washington, DC	3,618	69
	East Orange, NJ	285	66
	Gary, IN	243	63
	Jackson, MS	417	62
	Atlanta, GA	1,612	58
Hispanics			
	Laredo, TX	269	100
	McAllen, TX	195	90
	Brownsville, TX	180	82
	El Paso, TX	1,013	66
	Santa Fe, NM	117	56
Asian/Pacific Islanders			
	Honolulu, HI	1,619	76
	San Francisco, CA	2006	14
	Berkeley, CA	199	12
	Vallejo, CA	141	11
	Culver City, CA	119	10
	Oakland, CA	617	10
	San Jose, CA	1,336	10
American Indians			
	Modesto, CA	248	10
	Tulsa, OK	800	6
	Long Beach, CA	838	5
	Duluth, MN	141	4
	Lawrence, KS	110	4

Source: Adapted from B. A. Reaves and A. L. Goldberg, 1999. *Law Enforcement Management and Administrative Statistics, 1997*. Washington, D.C.: Bureau of Justice Statistics, pp. 1–29.

The data from these tables indicate that many police departments are culturally diverse and becoming more so all the time. Even though this trend is uneven throughout the country, it is probable that within the next several decades half or more of local police officers in many police departments will be women and minorities. Such growth, however, assumes a continued emphasis on affirmative action and equal employment opportunity programs, which may be subsiding in some departments (see Chapter 14).

Promotional Opportunities

A comparison study of 290 police departments of women police supervisors (Martin 1989a) shows that women represented 2.2 percent of all municipal supervisory levels in 1978 and 7.6 percent in 1986 (including 3.7 percent at the sergeant level; 2.5 percent at the lieutenant level; and 1.4% above the lieutenant level). Another survey in the nation's 50 largest cities (Walker and Martin 1994) found that women comprised 7.1 percent of supervisory personnel, including 4.8 percent white women and 1.8 percent black women. Figure 12.2 represents the percent of women officers in eight nationally representative large departments and the percent holding supervisory ranks. Like the employment of female officers, progress with respect to promotions is uneven, depending on the department.

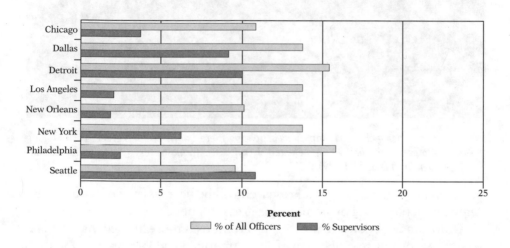

Figure 12.2 Percent of Female Officers in Representative Large Police Departments and Percent in Supervision, 1992

Source: Adapted from S. Walker and K. B. Turner. 1992. *A Decade of Modest Progress: Employment of Black and Hispanic Officers,* 1983-1992. Omaha: University of Nebraska at Omaha. Reprinted with permission.

A more recent study of 100 departments by the National Center of Women and Policing ("Rank Objections" 1998) found significantly higher percentages of women supervisors. The center reported that women held 16.2 percent of all supervisory positions, with 7.4 percent in top command positions (captain or above) and 8.8 percent in supervisory positions (lieutenant and sergeant). Women of color held 5.5 percent of all supervisory positions, including 2.4 percent of top commands and 3.1 percent of supervisory jobs. These data indicate that one out of every six police supervisors in America is a woman. The center's findings are intriguing in that they suggest that women have made significantly greater strides on the promotional front than previously indicated. The question remains why these data are so different from previous reports. The differences, at least in part, may be due to the types of departments that were surveyed (i.e., municipal, county, and state); previous studies have included only municipal departments. Another possibility is simply that the center's data is more recent and more women have in

Women are also being elected to top ranks in policing. Here, Laurie Smith is greeted after taking the oath of office as the first woman elected sheriff in California history. (Photo: Judith Calson/ San Jose Mercury News © 1999)

fact been promoted. Additional research will be necessary in order to have a clearer understanding of women's progress in police promotions.

Unfortunately, data on minority promotions is more limited than data on women. According to officials in African American and Hispanic national organizations, there is no agency that routinely and systematically gathers information about the promotion of minorities. Despite the lack of data, many affirmative action specialists claim that most minority officers are not promoted equally with white officers and remain essentially at the entry level (Sullivan 1989). As with woman officers, however, it is also true that because minority members, until recently, have not been well integrated into policing, they have not had a sufficient amount of time in which to be promoted. The type of progress being made in Dallas (see Case Study 12.1) may be indicative of departments adopting affirmative action plans; approximately 48 percent of the department's officers are minority, and about 25 percent account for supervisory or command positions.

As might be expected, wide variation exists in promotion practices among police departments. In general, it appears as though the departments with the best records of promoting minority officers are those in cities that have large minority populations and minority leadership in the mayor's office or at the top levels in the police department. Thus, as Sullivan (1989) has noted, promotions tend to be more likely for black officers in Chicago and Atlanta (or Detroit) or for Hispanic officers in Miami (or Los Angeles), than for their colleagues in cities with larger white populations and power bases. This can be observed, at least to some extent, in Figures 12.3 and 12.4, which show the percent of black and Hispanic officers in eight nationally representative large police departments and the percent holding supervisory ranks.

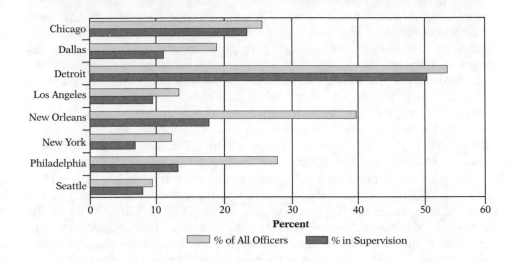

Source: Adapted from S. Walker, and K. B. Turner. 1993. *A Decade of Modest Progress: Employment of Black and Hispanic Police Officers, 1983–1992*. Omaha: University of Nebraska at Omaha. Reprinted with permission.

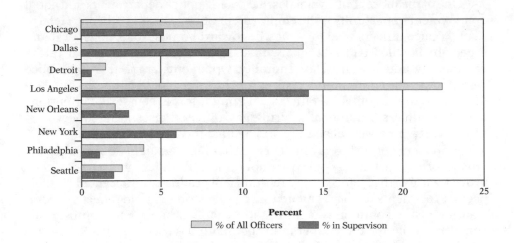

Source: Adapted from S. Walker, and K. B. Turner. 1992. *A Decade of Modest Progress: Employment of Black and Hispanic Police Officers, 1983–1992*. Omaha: University of Nebraska at Omaha. Reprinted with permission.

❖ ❖ ❖ ❖   The Supreme Court's ruling in *Paradise* also appears to set the direction in attempting to balance the need to rectify past discriminatory practices, while protecting innocent third parties from discrimination. Rulings such as *Paradise*, along with continued emphasis on minority recruitment and affirmative action plans, should contribute substantially toward a higher percentage of minority personnel in supervisory positions in the near future. One interesting dilemma has developed, however, with respect to minority promotions at the local level—namely, "federal raiders," who recruit away top minority candidates (Sullivan 1989). Because federal agencies usually require some previous enforcement experience prior to employment, federal agents often recruit their personnel from local police departments. Furthermore, because federal agencies tend to be viewed as more prestigious and may pay more, it is easy to understand why they are often successful in recruiting the best qualified personnel (especially minorities and women) that the local departments have to offer. Such "raiding" results in the loss to local departments of minority officers with the greatest potential for promotion.

As minority representation in policing has continued to increase, so has promotion of minorities to the highest position of police chief in major cities. In 1982 there were 50 black police chiefs, and in 1988 there were 130, an increase of 160 percent (Narine 1988). At one point in the 1990s, 6 of the 10 largest cities in the country, including the South, had a black chief (Narine 1988). For example, Lee Brown served as chief in Houston and New York City prior to his retirement and was appointed the nation's "drug czar." Beverly Harvard serves as the nation's first African-American woman chief of a major U.S. police department, Atlanta. Such appointments are important because these chiefs serve as role models and will be sensitive to the recruitment and promotion of minority officers.

Employment Opportunities for Homosexuals

One of the more controversial issues facing police departments and equal employment opportunity is the employment of homosexual officers. Heterosexual police officers tend to be hostile toward homosexuals in general and especially hostile in a traditionally male-dominated occupation that values masculinity and working-class morality. Opponents argue that gay police would lower the community's respect for the force, could not be counted on to come to the aid of fellow officers, and might force their sexual attentions on other officers. Additionally, hiring gay officers raises legal concerns in states where homosexual acts are still against the law (Shilts 1980).

Proponents of hiring gay men argue that homosexuality does not affect job performance, that gay police are not noticeably different, and that if they prove their worth as officers, gay recruits will gradually be accepted by their peers. Proponents further contend that a police force should reflect the composition of the community, and, in most major urban areas, homosexuals constitute a significant number in the population. While the Civil Rights Act does not specifically prohibit discrimination based on sexual identity, if gender is not a bona fide job-related requirement for police employment, then, proponents argue, it is also inconceivable to maintain that sexual orientation is a valid basis for exclusion. In any event, it is likely that homosexuals are already employed in most larger police departments throughout the nation, but they conceal their identity in order to avoid ridicule by their colleagues and loss of jobs (Shilts 1980). As gay-rights activists become more adamant about public-sector employment, this issue will become more sharply focused in the courts and in hiring policies. It should be noted that some movement in hiring practices is occurring; one prominent department on the West Coast is actively recruiting gays (see Inside Policing 12.2).

❖ ❖ ❖ ❖

Inside Policing 12.2
Police Chief To Personally Recruit Gays

San Jose (CA.) Police Chief Lou Cobarruviaz will become the first police chief in the nation to personally recruit gays and lesbians. He intends to recruit at the San Jose Gay and Lesbian Pride Celebration at the Santa Clara County Fairgrounds on June 13. "I will be there and have my recruiting team there," he said this week. It will be the first time San Jose police have actively recruited in the gay community and the first time any police chief has personally invited gays and lesbians to try to become officers, according to leaders of a statewide gay officer's group and the National Lesbian and Gay Task Force.

"As we move into community policing, I believe it's important I set an example for my officers," Cobarruviaz said. The move is part of the chief"s efforts to increase the diversity in his department and increase the trust in police of the various communities in San Jose. "Regardless of anyone's lifestyle or personal beliefs, if they are qualified for the department, I"m happy to have them join us," he said. "My only concern is that we have competent officers who can do the job."

Chief Understands Distrust

Many gays and lesbians traditionally have been distrustful and fearful of police, and until recent years they have rarely reported crimes directed against them according to watchdog groups. The chief says he understand this distrust. "It is difficult for any community to trust the department if they feel they are not represented on that department, so I will not hesitate to send my officers to any community," he said.

There are two openly gay officers among San Jose's 1,100, and Cobarruviaz called their coming out "an act of courage." The officers, both women, revealed their sexual orientation to their fellow officers at a mandatory sensitivity training session last summer. "It is a healthy thing to do what is appropriate and have the courage to get it out in the open," the chief said, adding that he was "very proud of the professionalism" of the other officers present.

No Hullabaloo

"There was no hullabaloo, not even a ripple," he said. "Some people even gave them a hug." The chief conceded there has been a change in climate in the department over the past few years that made it easier for the officers to come out of the closet. "We don't have the hostilities and animosities we had in years past," he said, recalling the difficulties Latinos once had in becoming police officers or getting promoted in the department. Cobarruviaz, who as a co-founder of the Latino Peace Officers Association helped knock down those barriers, compared gays' struggles for recognition with those of Latinos. But gay men in the department still have not come out to their fellow officers, the chief noted. "Perhaps [the women] will lead the way," he added.

Encouraging Crime Reporting

The change of climate, he noted, is promoting more and more gays to report crimes against them. Cobarruviaz added that police can serve the gay and lesbian community primarily in the area of hate crimes. He said his reaching out to gays will encourage them "to report to us directly and cooperate with us in identifying suspects."

Nationally, few police officers are openly gay. A few cities, such as San Diego, New York, and Los Angeles, have their own gay officer groups. California has a statewide group of law enforcement personnel called the Golden State Peace Officers Association with hundreds of members. Gay leaders have ☞

asked Cobarruviaz to appoint a liaison to their community. But the chief said he is planning instead to appoint an advisory board to the department representing "all the minorities—blacks, Hispanics, Asians, and gays."

Source: J. Dickey. 1992. *San Jose Mercury News*, "S. J. Police Chief Will Be First To Recruit Gays." February. 27: A1, A16. Reprinted by permission. Author's note: Chief Cobarruviaz retired from the department in 1997. (Permission from 1st ed.)

Integration of Minorities and Women Into Policing

From the preceding discussion, it is apparent that an increasing percentage and number of both minorities and women are entering the law enforcement field. Much of this increase, however, is due to the passage of the 1972 amendments to the Civil Rights Act of 1964. These amendments, and subsequent court decisions based on them, forced police departments to alter, rather radically in some instances, their selection and promotional practices. Hence, the question remains: How well are these "nontraditional" officers being treated once inside the department? This section takes a look at how well women and minorities appear to be integrating into the police work environment, as well as prospects for the future.

Because many male officers have been opposed to women in policing in general, and women on patrol in particular, (see Bloch and Anderson 1974; Sherman 1975; Martin 1980; Charles 1981; and Linden 1983), it is not surprising that women have had a particularly difficult time breaking into policing. Even though many departments are moving toward community policing, for the most part, they remain tradition-bound and masculine. As R. Linden (1983) points out, men tend to object to women on patrol because they fear that women will not be able to cope with physical violence and that the image of the police will suffer. For example, a survey of police departments in the Northwest (Brown 1994) indicated that only one-third of male patrol officers actually accept a woman on patrol and that more than half do not think that women can handle the physical requirements of the job as well as men. S. E. Martin (1980) further notes that women threaten to disrupt the division of labor, the work norms, the work group's solidarity, their insecure occupational image, and the sexist ideology that undergirds the men's definition of the work as "men's work" and their identity as masculine men.

Police Culture

The major underlying dilemma confronting women in policing is the **police culture**, which has as its foundation a sexist and macho perception of the role of police. As Martin has noted:

> The use of women on patrol implies either that the men's unique asset, their physical superiority, is irrelevant (as it is, on most assignments) or that the man with a female partner will be at a disadvantage in a physical confrontation that he would not face with a male partner. (1989a, p. 11)

As emphasized previously, in general, the police role is not physically demanding and requires a much stronger mental than physical capacity. In addition, no research has ever indicated that strength is related to police functioning, nor has there been any research to suggest that physical strength is related to an individual's ability to successfully manage a dangerous situation (Charles 1981).

As the earlier review of the research on the performance of policewomen indicated, women not only perform satisfactorily on patrol but tend to be exemplary in the less aggressive, nontraditional aspects of the role (e.g., interacting with citizens, handling domestic disturbances). This suggests that in many respects, women may actually be better suited for police work than men. In a sense, this was K. Van Wormer's argument in an article titled "Are Males Suited to Police Patrol Work?" (1981). In her article, she pointed out that men tend to be more prone to violence and unbecoming conduct. J. McDowell (1992) supports this view when she reports that the Christopher Commission (investigating the Los Angeles Police Department after the Rodney King beating) found that the 120 officers with the most use-of-force reports were all men, and that civilian complaints against women were also consistently lower. Policewomen, by contrast, tend to meet the public better, handle domestic violence better, and deal with rape victims better. The conclusion reached by Van Wormer was that the shortcomings of male officers could possibly be overcome through special selection and training.

Women face other hurdles in attempting to be accepted into the policing profession. For instance, the use of sexist language, sexual harassment, sexual jokes, and sex-role stereotyping all contribute to creating severe adjustment problems for women (Martin 1989a). Men frequently use language to keep women officers in their "place" by referring to them as "ladies" or "girls," suggesting that they need to be protected. Women who do not conform to sex-role stereotypes and are "tough" enough to gain respect as officers may be labeled as "bitches" or "lesbians" in an attempt to neutralize their threat to male dominance (Berg and Budnick 1986), a process referred to as **defeminization**. Men's cursing can also create problems for women, since men may feel inhibited—and resentful—about swearing in front of women, and yet men may lose their "respect" for women who swear.

Possibly due to the hurdles women face on entering policing, some research (Martin 1979) has suggested that two separate identities may develop: the **police*woman*** and the ***police*woman**. The former attempts to gain her male colleagues' approval by adhering to traditional police values and norms, with law enforcement her primary orientation; the latter attempts to perform her duties in a "traditionally feminine manner" by making few arrests, infrequently using physical activity, and placing strong emphasis on "being a lady." While Martin's research included only 32 female officers, seven of whom were classified as police*woman* and eight as *police*woman—with the rest in between—it is important that police departments promote policies and practices that allow female officers to be "themselves" and to utilize the particular strengths that many bring to the job. Some research (Belknap and Kastens Shelley 1992) suggests that in departments with a larger percentage of women officers (10 percent or more), women tend to view themselves as police officers first and women second; the opposite was found in departments with a smaller percentage of women officers. This finding suggests that peer support and familiarity may improve the working conditions of women officers. Different types of adjustments have been noted among black officers as well; some tend to align themselves with the black community, while others tend to align themselves with traditional police values (Alex 1969).

In general, research on policewomen suggests that they are still struggling for acceptance, believe that they do not receive equal credit for their work, and are often sexually harassed by their coworkers (Daum and Johns 1994). One study of over 500 women officers from nine Western states (Timmins and Hainsworth 1989) revealed that open sexual discrimination and sexual harassment were far more common today than expected, especially by supervisors and commanders, who not only tolerate such practices by others but frequently engage in such practices themselves. The survey also indicated that duty assignments were often based on one's gender. Martin (1989a) further notes that frequent sexual jokes and informal harassment cause many women to avoid interaction with men that might be viewed as having a sexual connotation. To maintain their moral reputation, they may sacrifice the opportunity to build close interpersonal relationships that are so necessary for gaining sponsors and mentors (i.e., an influential person who provides guidance and assistance). Without backing from the informal political network within the department, women are likely to have a more difficult time being promoted or gaining specialized job assignments.

This lack of access to the informal political network within a department also applies to minority officers. Although there are many reasons, some of which were discussed earlier, why minorities may not be assigned to specialized jobs or promoted equally with whites, P. S. Sullivan (1989) believes that the major reason is that minority networks usually do not reach the upper echelons of power and the existing white network. He suggests this is a "catch 22" situation—that is, minority promotions will increase only when more minority officers are promoted. Once again, it is important to recognize how important equal promotional opportunities are for both minority and female officers.

Structural Characteristics

Women also face problems relating to the **structural characteristics** or features of police departments (Martin 1989a). For example, most training academies place a strong emphasis on physical fitness. Once a certain level of fitness and performance has been achieved, however, it generally need not be maintained; that is, few departments require any testing of physical performance beyond that of the academy. Such an emphasis tends to magnify the importance of physical differences between the sexes, which, of course, tends to perpetuate the sex-role stereotype. This is not to suggest that police officers should not be physically fit but that fitness should be within the parameters of job-related standards. Furthermore, if physical standards are job related, then they certainly should be maintained throughout an officer's career, at least in those jobs where such a requirement is necessary.

Training academies also often fail to place the proper amount of importance on the development of *interpersonal skills* that are essential to effective police work. Such skills are usually more highly developed in women than men, and their absence from the training curriculum deprives women of excelling in an important job-relevant area. Consequently, as Martin has observed: "New women recruits enter male turf on male terms with little recognition of their own problems or strengths" (1989a, p. 12). Associated with the problem of not recognizing the importance of interpersonal skills is the performance-evaluation process itself. Despite the favorable response to the effectiveness of women on patrol, internal performance-evaluation criteria tend to have a gender bias favorable toward males. As noted previously, some research (Morash and Greene 1986) has discovered that such criteria tend to emphasize traits that are primarily associated with a male stereotype (e.g., forceful and dominant).

Pregnancy and Maternity

An important policy area concerning women officers is that of pregnancy and maternity or disability leave. As more women enter policing, and become pregnant, their treatment becomes important not only to the officer and her family but also to the department and the community. Title VII of the Civil Rights Act was amended in 1978 to add the Pregnancy Discrimination Act, which outlaws discrimination on the basis of pregnancy, childbirth, or any medical condition they might cause. Employers are thus required to treat pregnancy as they would any other temporary disability (Rubin 1995a).

Although there is no law that requires a department to provide paid maternity leave to employees, if a department has a paid-leave policy for temporarily disabled officers, it must afford pregnant officers the same leave. Leave policies that favor pregnant woman, however, may not be discriminatory. In *California Savings & Loan v. Guerra* (1987), the U.S. Supreme Court upheld a California law that requires employers to provide a pregnant employee with up to four months' maternity leave and to permit her to return to her original job unless it has been eliminated due to business necessity. The Court reasoned that although the law appeared to favor women, employers also could give comparable benefits to employees with nonpregnancy-related disabilities. In addition, the Family Medical Leave Act of 1993 (FMLA) requires employers with 50 or more employees to provide 12 weeks unpaid leave for employees to care for a newborn child, adopted child, or foster child. This requirement applies equally to men and women and requires the employer to offer employees taking leave the same or an equivalent job when they return (Rubin 1995a).

Although the research is scarce with respect to policies on pregnancy and maternity, one survey of 73 of the largest departments in each of the 50 states and the District of Columbia (Watson 1995) provides some initial information. All but eight of the departments provided some form of pregnancy leave for women line officers. In general, the policies involved combining types of leave, including sick leave, then annual leave, and then unpaid leave of 180 days to a year or more. Only a few departments required pregnant officers to begin leave at a specific point in their pregnancy. Nine required women to leave only when advised to do so by their doctors. Fitness was the key for others; three required leaves to begin when women were unable to perform the full range of duties, and one said when uniforms no longer fit. In general, in returning to work, officers were allowed to exhaust all permissible leave time, including unpaid leave to the limit that it was available. If this occurred, and if the officer had to be terminated, then she was given preference in applying for a vacancy when it occurred. Although such a termination violates the FMLA, the survey was conducted prior to its implementation. However, since

FMLA applies only to organizations with 50 or more employees, the act does not apply to a majority of the nation's police departments.

There also was consistent application to pregnant women of policies covering all employees who suffer disability from nonwork-related injuries or illness. The primary issue was that all employees must appear for duty in uniform, which for patrol personnel includes wearing a belt supporting a firearm, baton, handcuffs, and ammunition; such a policy undoubtedly shortens the time a pregnant officer may remain on duty. The majority of departments had provisions to transfer a pregnant officer to temporary or "light" duty in a manner consistent with other temporary transfers for medical disability. In most departments, women officers would not lose seniority or medical benefits while on maternity leave. A few departments made no distinction between men and women officers, although most paternity leave would have to fall under the categories of sick, annual, or emergency leave, (Watson 1995).

Although the FMLA of 1993 goes a long way toward establishing rights in pregnancy and maternity, it does not cover a majority of the nation's police departments; nevertheless, all departments should attempt to meet the FMLA requirements. In addition, based on *California Savings*, benefits for pregnant woman do not necessarily have to be equal—if departments wish to establish a favorable culture for women, they should establish maximum benefits in this area. For example, for many light-duty assignments, pregnant women may not need to wear their heavy belts (to be in uniform); this provision would allow them to work longer before initiating maternity leave. With the FMLA policies as a guide, a model policy needs to be developed to protect a woman officer's right to have children without damaging her career in policing. At the same time, policies regarding uniform and bulletproof vest sizes for women could also be addressed; most uniforms and vests are not made for women and fit improperly (Hale and Wyland 1993).

Sexual Harassment

The discussion on police culture above established that policewomen still face sexual harassment by their coworkers. If women officers are ever to gain equal treatment and status in police departments, sexual harassment must be taken seriously by the department and eliminated. Title VII of the Civil Rights Act prohibits sex discrimination. Sexual harassment is simply another form of sex discrimination. **Sexual harassment** in the workplace has been defined as

> Unwelcome sexual advances, requests for sexual favors, and other verbal or physical conduct that enters into employment decisions and/or conduct that unreasonably interferes with an individual's work performance or creates an intimidating, hostile, or offensive working environment. (Rubin 1995b, p. 1–2)

Sexual harassment applies to men as well as women and to same-sex harassment as well. In general, there are two forms of sexual misconduct:

Quid pro quo harassment requires the employee to choose between the job and the sexual demands. Once equal access to employment opportunities are blocked for refusing the demands, Title VII has been violated (Rubin 1995a). This type of harassment usually occurs between a supervisor and subordinate (Rubin 1995b).

If female officers are to gain equal treatment and status in policing, sexual harassment must be take seriously and eliminated. (Photo: corbisimages.com)

Hostile work-environment harassment occurs when unwelcome conduct is so severe or pervasive that it interferes with a person's job. Unlike quid pro quo harassment, which usually occurs as an isolated incident or single offending act, a hostile work environment usually includes repeated incidents or a series of events (Rubin 1995a).

It is crucial that police departments have a policy that defines and prohibits sexual harassment, because failure to have such a policy may be construed as *deliberate indifference,* exposing the department to claims of liability. Employees who claim sexual harassment will not have to prove economic or psychological injury in order to win a claim. Even when such a policy exists, the department may still be held liable. In addition, departments can also be held liable even if they did not know of the offending behavior if a court determines that they should have known of it. Departments are also generally liable for the acts of their supervisory personnel (Rubin 1995a). Accordingly, *every* complaint of sexual harassment should be taken seriously and acted on immediately with a follow-up investigation. Confidentiality should be maintained and every step of the investigation should be documented. Whenever harassment is found, swift remedial action—including warnings, reprimands, suspension, or dismissal—should be taken (Rubin 1995a). This action not only sends a message that sexual harassment will not be tolerated but further indicates (to the courts) that the department is seriously attempting to control it. Inside Policing 12.2 provides a primer on how departments can prevent sexual harassment.

Future Prospects

Over the past three decades substantial progress has been made in the recruitment and hiring of minorities and women in policing. However, although some departments have accomplished this voluntarily, others have been reluctant and were forced by the courts. This situation, combined with the traditional police culture, has created some serious problems for minorities and women with respect to integration and equal treatment within the field.

It is apparent that police departments will continue to struggle with the complex problems associated with minority hiring and promotion. If they are to increase or, in some instances maintain, their minority representation,

---

Inside Policing 12.2
Preventing Sexual Harassment

No matter how flawless the investigation or how quickly and fairly a complaint is handled by the department, *prevention* is still the best approach to sexual harassment. Departments should build their prevention programs around four areas: policy, training, supervision, and discipline.

Policy

Departments should have a policy that clearly prohibits any type of sexual harassment. Having a policy, however, is not enough; it must be effectively communicated to all employees and consistently and fairly enforced. The policy should be posted for a period of time in employee work areas, locker rooms, or break rooms. Copies should then be kept in accessible locations, and the policy should be included in any employee handbooks.

At a minimum, any sexual-harassment policy should include the following statements:

- That the department will not tolerate sexual harassment.

- That defines sexual harassment, including examples of quid pro quo and hostile work environment harassment.

- That advises employees of the department's grievance procedure and requires employees to report incidents immediately.

- That complaints will be taken seriously and investigated immediately.

- Of the penalty for violating the policy.

- That all employees are to treat one another professionally and with respect.

Training

Departments next must train employees to understand what sexual harassment is. Training should include the following: Identify and describe forms of sexual harassment and give examples. The American Law Institute and the American Bar Association endorse the following examples:

- Sexual propositions or advances.

- Touching, pinching, or patting.

- Insulting or suggestive sounds.

- Comments about a person's body or body parts.

- Sexually oriented jokes which degrade men or women.

- Cartoons, pinups, calendars, pictures, etc., of naked men or women of a sexual nature.

- Repeated flirtations or sexual comments.

- Turning work discussions into sexual topics.

- Repeated insults against men or women.

- Comments or behavior that promise benefits for sexual favors (Barker and Heckeroth 1997).

- Outline the department's grievance procedure, explain how to use it, and discuss the importance of doing so.

- Discuss the penalty for violating the policy.

- Emphasize the need for a workplace free of harassment, offensive conduct, intimidation, or other forms of discrimination.

Supervision

Supervisors should be taught how to build and maintain a professional work environment. Training should cover such matters as the following:

- How to spot sexual harassment

- How to investigate complaints, including proper documentation.

- What to do about observed sexual harassment, even when no complaint has been filed.

- How to keep the work environment as professional and nonhostile as possible.

Discipline

The department's grievance policy should be clearly communicated to all ☞

employees which must be strictly and promptly followed. When violations occur, proper disciplinary action should follow. This is important since courts look at the action taken by employers in determining liability. The following measures should be considered:

- Informing employees in advance of conduct that may result in immediate dismissal or in disciplinary action (describe the penalties involved).

- After an interval of time, following up on an incident to make sure the

problem has not returned.

- Counseling all parties and training (or retraining) all employees in cases where harassment has been alleged but cannot be determined.

- Repeating assurances that sexual harassment will not be tolerated.

Source: Adapted from P. N. Rubin. 1995b. "Civil Rights and Criminal Justice: Primer on Sexual Harassment." *Research in Action.* Washington, D.C.: National Institute of Justice, pp. 5–6.

they should pay particular attention to several areas (Sullivan 1989). First, agencies must continue to actively recruit among minorities while attempting to improve community relations and eliminating the reasons many minorities have had to distrust the police. Second, because studies have indicated that many of the entry-level paper-and-pencil tests are not job validated, it may be necessary to design a new series of tests that can more accurately measure potential police performance while ensuring they do not discriminate against racial or ethnic groups. Finally, because minority members may have been at a disadvantage prior to their police service, departments may need to initiate special programs to help these officers to develop needed skills and knowledge in order to perform effectively on the job. This final suggestion applies equally well to women candidates, especially with respect to the physical requirements of the hiring process.

In order to improve the recruitment and retention of women in policing, departments must attempt to accelerate change in the traditional, militaristic, male-dominated sexist police culture. Although some important strides have been made with respect to de-emphasizing the highly militaristic and masculine approach to police organization and management, especially by those departments moving toward community policing, such traditions are firmly entrenched and difficult to overcome. Of course, as more women enter the field and move into supervisory positions where they can have an impact on policy, the more quickly change is likely to occur. As with minority personnel, police departments must continue to eliminate those aspects of the selection process that are discriminatory toward women and that cannot be job validated.

It is important for departments to implement policies and practices that are not discriminatory. It is crucial that minorities and women personnel become fully integrated into police work. Only then can these officers become true role models and not merely "tokens" within their departments. Quite possibly the best recruitment "device" at a police department's disposal is its own personnel, who can act as sponsors and mentors for others who wish to enter the field.

Over the next decade, one important influence on minority and women recruitment is making police work attractive to them. Since these groups are recruited vigorously by other public-sector (including federal police departments) as well as private-sector agencies, the pool of qualified applicants may actually be shrinking. Accordingly, it may be even more difficult in the future to recruit qualified candidates. At least one study (Hochstedler and Conley 1986) has indicated that one major reason why blacks tend to be underrepresented in municipal police departments is that they simply choose not to pursue a career in policing. One thing is clear; if departments are to remain competitive for minorities and women in the future, they must have an active and innovative recruitment strategy, promote police culture that treats all employees equally and with respect, and, if necessary, have a well-developed affirmative action plan regarding selection, duty assignment, and promotional opportunity.

Summary

The development of cultural diversity in policing was traced in this chapter. Included in this analysis was how minorities and women, once they entered the profession, were treated unequally, even though their performance was, in general, satisfactory. There has been litigation regarding the impact of equal employment opportunity legislation and the use of the Civil Service, or merit, system. Reliance on the use of a nonjob-validated merit system for both selection and promotion in policing has lead to the belief by many police traditionalists that a form of reverse discrimination and "lowering of standards" is taking place. Although implementing affirmative action plans in policing is complex, such plans have played an important role in police employment trends, in some cases significantly increasing the number and percentage of minorities and women. Once inside the department, however, these "nontraditional" officers have not always been well received—in large part due to the traditional police culture. As more minority and women officers enter policing and are promoted to higher ranks, their integration and acceptance into the field should become easier. Whether or not police departments can continue to attract qualified minority and women personnel depends on the public's interest in the police occupation, an active recruitment strategy, departmental culture that treats members equally and with respect, and possibly a well-developed affirmative action plan.

Discussion Questions

1. Is cultural diversity important in policing? Explain why or why not.

2. Briefly discuss the types of unequal treatment received by minority and female officers when they first entered policing.

3. In general, how have minority and female officers performed on patrol?

4. Describe the two primary forms of legal remedy to employment discrimination in the workplace.

5. What is the Civil Service System? Is it discriminatory? Why, or why not?

6. Discuss the importance of the *Griggs* and *Paradise* decisions by the U.S. Supreme Court regarding affirmative action plans.

7. Discuss the meaning of reverse discrimination. Do you think it is a major concern today? Why, or why not?

8. Briefly discuss the growth of diversity in police departments over the past several decades. What is the significance of this growth?

9. Briefly describe several problems confronting women and minorities in attempting to integrate into the police work environment. What are the prospects for the future?

10. Discuss what is meant by sexual harassment in the workplace and to what degree it exists in policing. What steps can be taken to eliminate sexual harassment?

❖ ❖ ❖ ❖

References

Alex, N. 1969. *Black in Blue*. Englewood Cliffs, NJ: Prentice-Hall.

———. 1976. *New York Cops Talk Back*. New York: Wiley.

Balkin, J. 1988. "Why Policemen Don"t Like Policewomen." *Journal of Police Science and Administration* 16: 29–38.

Barker, A. M. and Heckeroth, S. E. 1997. "Deterring Sex-Harassment Liability: It Takes Proactive Policy and Commitment." *Law Enforcement News* April 15: 14–15, 18.

Bartlett, H. W. and Rosenblum, A. 1977. *Policewomen Effectiveness*. Denver, CO: Denver Civil Service Commission.

Belknap, J. and Kastens Shelley, J. 1992. "The New Lone Ranger: Policewomen on Patrol." *American Journal of Police* 12: 47–72.

Berg, B. and Budnick, K. 1986. "Defeminization of Women in Law Enforcement: A New Twist in the Traditional Police Personality." *Journal of Police Science and Administration* 14: 314–319.

Berg, B., True, E., and Gertz, M. 1984. "Police, Riots, and Alienation." *Journal of Police Science and Administration* 12: 186–190.

Berkeley, G. E. 1969. *The Democratic Policeman*. Boston: Beacon.

Bloch, P. and Anderson, D. 1974. *Policewomen on Patrol: Final Report*. Washington, D.C.: Police Foundation.

Brown, M. 1994. "The Plight of Female Police: A Survey of NW Patrolmen." *The Police Chief* 61: 50–53.

California Highway Patrol. 1976. *Women Traffic Officer Project: Final Report*. Sacramento, CA: California Highway Patrol.

California Savings & Loan v. Guerra. 479 U.S. 272 (1987).

Carter, D. L., Sapp, A. D., and Stephens, D. W. 1989. *The State of Police Education: Policy Direction for the 21st Century*. Washington, D.C.: Police Executive Research Forum.

Charles, M. T. 1981. "Performance and Socialization of Female Recruits in the Michigan State Police Training Academy." *Journal of Police Science and Administration* 9: 209–223.

Daum, J and Johns, C. 1994. "Police Work from a Woman"s Perspective." *The Police Chief* 61: 46–69.

Detroit Police Officers Association v. Young, 446 F. Supp. 979 (1978).

Dickey, J. 1992. "S. J. Police Chief Will Be First To Recruit Gays." *San Jose Mercury News* Feb. 27: A1, A16.

Ebony Magazine. 1966. *The Negro Handbook*. Chicago: Johnson Publishing.

Eisenberg, T., Kent, D. A., and Wall, C. R. 1973. *Police Personnel Practices in State and Local Government*. Washington, D.C.: Police Foundation.

Felkenes, G. T. 1990. "Affirmative Action the Los Angeles Police Department." Criminal Justice Research Bulletin 6: 1–9.

Frank, J., Brandl, S., Cullen, F., and Stichman, A. 1996. "Reassessing the Impact of Citizens' Attitudes Toward the Police: A Research Note." *Justice Quarterly* 13: 321–334.

Garmire, B. L., ed. 1978. *Local Government, Police Management*. Washington, D.C.: International City Management Association.

Georges-Abeyie, D. 1984. "Black Police Officers: An Interview with Alfred W. Dean, Director of Public Safety, Harrisburg, Pennsylvania." In D. Georges-Abeyiue, (ed.), *The Criminal Justice System and Blacks*, pp. 161–165. Beverly Hills, CA: Sage.

Gosnell, H. F. 1935. *Negro Politicians: The Rise of Negro Politics in Chicago*. Chicago: University of Chicago Press.

Grennan, S. 1988. "Findings on the Role of Officer Gender in Violent Encounters with Citizens." *Journal of Police Science and Administration* 78–85.

Griggs v. Duke Power Co. 40l U.S. 432 (197l).

Hale, D.C. and Wyland, S. M. 1993. "Dragons and Dinosaurs: The Plight of Patrol Women." *Police Forum* 3: 1–8.

Hochstedler, E. and Conley, J. A. 1986. "Explaining Underrepresentation of Black Officers in City Police Agencies." *Journal of Criminal Justice* 14: 319–328.

Jacobs, J. and Cohen, J. 1978. "The Impact of Racial Integration on the Police." *Journal of Police Science and Administration* 6: 168–183.

Johnson, C. S. 1947. *Into the Mainstream: A Survey of Best Practices in Race Relations in the South*. Chapel Hill: University of North Carolina Press.

Kephart, W. M. 1957. *Racial Factors and Urban Law Enforcement*. Philadelphia: University of Pennsylvania Press.

Kizziah, C. and Morris M. 1977. *Evaluation of Women in Policing Program: Newton, Massachusetts*. Oakland, CA: Approach Associates.

Kuykendall, J. L and Burns, D. E. 1980. "The Black Police Officer: An Historical Perspective." *Journal of Contemporary Criminal Justice* 4: 4–12.

Landrum, L. W. 1947. "The Case of Negro Police." *New South* 11: 5–6.

Leinen, S. 1984. *Black Police, White Society*. New York: New York University Press.

Linden, R. 1983. "Women in Policing—A Study of Lower Mainland Royal Canadian Mounted Police Detachments." *Canadian Police College Journal* 7: 217–229.

Martin. S. E. 1979. "Policewomen and Policewomen: Occupational Role Dilemmas and Choices of Female Officers." *Journal of Police Science and Administration* 7: 314–323.

——. 1980. *Breaking and Entering: Policewomen on Patrol*. Berkeley: University of California Press.

——. 1989a. "Women in Policing: The Eighties and Beyond." In D. J. Kenney (ed.), *Police and Policing: Contemporary Issues*, pp. 3–16. New York: Praeger.

——. 1989b. "Female Officers on the Move? A Status Report on Women in Policing." In R. G. Dunhan and G. P. Alpert (eds.), *Critical Issues in Policing: Contemporary Readings*, pp. 312–330. Prospect Heights, IL: Waveland.

McDowell, J. 1992. "Are Women Better Cops?" *Time* 132: 70–72.

Melchionne, T. M. 1967. "Current Status and Problems of Women Police." *Journal of Criminal Law, Criminology and Police Science* 58: 257–260.

Milton, C. 1972. *Women in Policing*. Washington, D.C.: Police Foundation.

Moran, T. K. 1988. "Pathways Toward a Nondiscriminatory Recruitment Policy." *Journal of Police Science and Administration* l6: 274–287.

Morash, M. and Greene, J. R. 1986. "Evaluating Women on Patrol: A Critique of Contemporary Wisdom." *Evaluation Review* 10: 231–255.

Myrdal, G. 1944. *An American Dilemma: The Negro Problem and Modern Democracy*. New York: Harper & Brothers.

Narine, D. 1988. "Top Cops: More and More Black Police Chiefs are Calling the Shots." *Ebony* May: 130–136.

National Advisory Commission on Civil Disorders. 1968. *Report of the National Advisory Commission on Civil Disorders*. Washington, D.C.: U.S. Government Printing Office.

National Advisory Commission on Criminal Justice Standards and Goals. 1973. *Report on Police*. Washington, D.C.: U.S. Government Printing Office.

National Center on Police and Community Relations. 1967. *A National Survey of Police and Community Relations, Field Survey V*. Washington, D.C.: U.S. Government Printing Office.

Owings, C. 1925. *Women PoliceMd. New York*: F. H. Hichcock.

Pennsylvania State Police. 1973. *Pennsylvania State Police Female Trooper Study*. Harrisburg, PA: Pennsylvania State Police Headquarters.

"Plenty of Talk, Not Much Action: IACP Survey Says PDs Fall Short on Recruiting, Retaining Women." 1999. *Law Enforcement News* January 15/31: 1, 14.

Police Foundation. 1990. *Community Policing: A Binding Thread Through the Fabric of Our Society*. Washington, D.C.: Police Foundation.

President"s Commission on Law Enforcement and Administration of Justice. 1967. *Task Force Report: The Police*. Washington, D.C.: U.S. Government Printing Office.

"Rank Objections: Study Calls Growth of Women in Policing 'Alarmingly Slow.' " 1998. *Law Enforcement News* May 15: 1, 10.

Reaves, B. A. 1996. *Local Police Departments, 1993*. Washington, D.C.: Bureau of Justice Statistics.

Reaves, B. A. and Goldberg, A. L. 1999. *Law Enforcement Management and Administrative Statistics, 1997: Data for Individual State and Local Agencies with 100 or More Officers*. Washington, D.C.: Bureau of Justice Statistics.

Reaves, B. A. and Smith, P. Z. 1995. *Law Enforcement Management and Administrative Statistics, 1993. Data for Individual State and Local Agencies with 100 or More Officers*. Washington, D.C.: Bureau of Justice Statistics.

Rubin, P. N. 1995a. "Civil Rights and Criminal Justice: Employment Discrimination Overview." *Research in Action*. Washington, D.C.: National Institute of Justice.

———. 1995b. "Civil Rights and Criminal Justice: Primer on Sexual Harassment." *Research in Action*. Washington, D.C.: National Institute of Justice.

Rudwick, E. 1960. "The Negro Policeman in the South." *Journal of Criminal Law, Criminology and Policed Science*, 11: 273–276.

———. 1962. *The Unequal Badge: Negro Policemen in the South, Report of the Southern Regional Council*. Atlanta: Southern Regional Council.

Sherman, L. J. 1973. "A Psychological View of Women in Policing." *Journal of Police Science and Administration* 1: 383–394.

———. 1975. "Evaluation of Policewomen on Patrol in a Suburban Police Department." *Journal of Police Science and Administration* 3: 434–438.

Shilts, R. 1980. "Gay Police." *Police Magazine* Jan.: 32–33.

Sichel, J. L., Friedman, L. N., Quint, J. C., and Smith, M. E. 1978. *Women on Patrol— A Pilot Study of Police Performance in New York City*. New York: Vera Institute of Justice.

Simpson, A. E. 1977. "The Changing Role of Women in Policing." In D. E. J. MacNamara (ed.), *Readings in Criminal Justice*, pp. 71–74. Guilford, CT: Dushkin.

Snortum, J. R. 1983. "Patrol Activities of Male and Female Officers as a Function of Work Experience." *Police Studies* 6: 36–42.

Sullivan, P. S. 1989. "Minority Officers: Current Issues." In R. G. Dunham and G. P. Alpert (eds.), *Critical Issues in Policing: Contemporary Readings*, pp. 331–345. Prospect Heights, IL: Waveland Press.

Sulton, C. and Townsey, R. A. 1981. *Progress Report on Women in Policing*. Washington, D.C.: Police Foundation.

Timmins, W. M. and Hainsworth, B. E. 1989. "Attracting and Retaining Females in Law Enforcement." *International Journal of Offender Therapy and Comparative Criminology* 33: 197–205.

U.S. v. Paradise. 107 U.S. l053 (1987).

Van Wormer, K. 1981. "Are Males Suited to Police Patrol Work?" *Police Studies* 3: 41–44.

Walker, S. 1977. *A Critical History of Police Reform.* Lexington, MA: Lexington Books.

——. 1989. *Employment of Black and Hispanic Police Officers, 1983–1988: A Follow-Up Study.* Omaha, NE: Center for Applied Urban Research, University of Nebraska at Omaha.

Walker, S. and Martin, S. E. 1994. "Through the Looking Glass Ceiling: Patterns in Hiring and Promotion by Race, Ethnicity and Gender in American Policing, 1982–1992." Paper presentation, Annual Meeting of the American Society of Criminology, Miami, FL, November.

Walker, S. and Turner, K. B. 1993. *A Decade of Modest Progress: Employment of Black and Hispanic Police Officers, 1983–1992.* Mimeo. Omaha, NE: University of Nebraska at Omaha.

Washington, B. E. 1974. Deployment of Female Police Officers in the United States. Washington, D.C.: Police Foundation.

Watson, P. S. 1995. "Maternity-leave for Cops—it"s a Mother." *Law Enforcement News* December 15: 10, 15.

Wilson, O. W. and McLaren, R. C. 1963. *Police Administration.* 3rd. ed. New York: McGraw-Hill.

For a listing of websites appropriate to the content of this chapter, see "Suggested Websites for Further Study" (p. xv). ✦

Chapter Thirteen

Stress and
Officer Safety

Chapter Outline

❏ The Concept of Stress

❏ Occupational Stress

❏ Historical Overview of Stressors

   Police Stressors

   Emerging Sources of Stress

❏ Categories of Stressors

   Line of Duty and Crisis Situations

   Posttraumatic Stress Disorder

   Social Supports and Police Stress

   Shift Work

❏ Stress and Emotional Problems

   Alcohol Abuse

   Drug Abuse

     Narcotics

     Anabolic Steroids

   Suicide

   Marital and Family Problems

   Policies and Programs

❏ Officer Safety

   Danger and Police Work

   Improving Safety and Reducing Fatalities

❏ Summary

❏ Discussion Questions

❏ References

Key Terms	
actual danger	police stressors
acute stress	posttraumatic stress disorder
chronic stress	(PTSD)
critical-incident debriefing	potential danger
distress	psychological stress
eustress	sensitization training
peer-counseling program	situational danger
perceived danger	social-supports model
person-initiated danger	stressor-outcome model
physiological stress	suicide prevention training

Although negative effects of stress on society in general have been well documented by both the medical and social science professions, certain occupations, by their very nature, inflict more stress than others. Police work entails unique stressors (sources of stress) that are nonexistent or not as prevalent in many other occupations. Some of these include departmental practices, shift work, danger, public apathy, boredom, and exposure to human misery. In addition, officers are expected to be in control at all times, yet they encounter people at their very worst, often on a daily basis. This demand of ongoing restraint, coupled with a set of unique job stressors, may lead to high levels of stress and, concomitantly, poor performance or dysfunctional behavior. This chapter will take a look at the concept of stress and stressors unique to police work, stress and emotional problems, policies and programs to help cope with stress, and officer safety.

The Concept of Stress

Stress is a highly complex concept because of the overlap of both physiological and psychological processes. **Physiological stress** deals with the biological effects on the individual, including such factors as increased heart disease, high blood pressure, ulcers, and so on. **Psychological stress** is much less clear and more difficult to evaluate. According to R. E. Farmer (1990), most psychologists prefer to use the term *stress* to refer to the physiological changes that can be determined and the term *anxiety* to capture the psychological effects. This book will use the more popular conception of stress, which includes anxiety within its scope.

Although stress is difficult to define, one of the more accepted interpretations comes from the pioneering work of H. Selye, who suggests that "the body's non-specific response to any demand placed on it" can cause stress (1974, p. 60). In other words, a person can be considered under stress when he or she is required to adapt to a particular situation. Selye further identifies two main types of stress: **eustress**, which is positive, and **distress**, which is negative. Some stress then, is considered to be positive or pleasurable—for example, the stress produced by a challenging sporting activity. Police stress, by contrast, relates to those aspects of police work that lead to negative feelings and consequences.

Basically, two forms of stress (distress) may affect police behavior (Farmer 1990). The first of these is **acute stress,** which represents high-order emergency or sudden stress, such as shootings or high-speed chases. The second type is **chronic stress,** low-level, gradual stress that includes the day-to-day routine of the job. Each type of stress is important to police work, but acute stressors require large amounts of physical and psychological adaptation; chronic stressors do not. In studying the possible effects of stress, there are several key concerns:

1. *Stress, like beauty, is in the eye of the beholder.* One person's experiences of stress may have little or nothing in common with another person's.

2. *Stress is cumulative.* Minor stresses may pile up to produce a major stress that leads to a heart attack or actual physical or mental breakdown.

3. *Prolonged emotional stress.* Stress that is a part of the everyday work environment can produce wear and tear on the body, with effects that may prove irreversible if not treated in time.

4. *When it comes to stress, there are no supermen or superwomen.* Stress-tolerance levels may vary from person to person, but everyone is susceptible to the ravages of stress. (Territo and Vetter 1981, p. 7)

Occupational Stress

How stressful is police work? In general, there has been a tendency to give an alarmist answer, which is interesting in that existing research does not unanimously support this conclusion (Terry 1981, 1985; Malloy and Mays 1984). W. C. Terry has suggested that the reason for the push to support policing as a high-stress occupation may lie in an attempt to develop professional recognition and create a professional self-image.

> The concept of stress ... provides a tidy symbolic representation of the crime control and order maintenance functions of police work as well as providing a ready link to other professional occupations that bear responsibility for other people's lives. (1985, p. 509)

This perspective is interesting, especially in light of the fact that some of the earlier research does not support this view. For instance, in a comparative study of 23 white-collar and blue-collar occupations by J. R. P. French, it was discovered that "policemen ... were not an extreme group, but they were higher than average on some stresses and lower than average on other stresses" (1975, p. 60). In another study of occupational groups, including skilled, semiskilled, and unskilled workers, W. Richard and R. Fell found that "police have an incidence of health problems which is somewhat greater than other occupations" (1975, p. 78).

In a more recent study, M. Pendleton, E. Stotland, P. Spiers, and E. Kirsch (1989) compared the stress and strain levels of police officers, firefighters, and government employees and found that government workers experienced the greatest stress and firefighters the least, with police falling in the middle. Thus, they concluded that contrary to popular belief, the police as a work group do not experience more health and social problems than all other occupations. The study urged caution, however, in that the research could not control for the possibility that police work could be more stressful and that those officers selected for the job might simply be better able to manage stress and avoid strain. In a study of more than 500 officers of an Australian police department (P. M. Hart, A. J. Wearing, and B. Headey 1995) discovered that, compared with other groups, police display relatively high levels of psychological well-being and concluded that collectively, their findings indicate that policing is not highly stressful. This more recent research suggests that policing may not be as stressful as previously believed.

Nevertheless, policing can be a dangerous occupation. For example, officers are killed while on the job at a rate second only to taxi drivers, although the rate has been dropping steadily, from a high of 134 in 1973 to fewer than 80 per year in the 1990s (Friedell and Pate 1997; see the last section of this chapter). With respect to nonfatal violence, a Bureau of Justice Statistics survey from 1992 to 1996 found that police officers had the most hazardous job with 306 nonfatal attacks per 1,000 officers, with private security guards second (218 per 1,000), and taxi drivers third (184 per 1,000) (Lardner 1998). Not too surprisingly, on the one hand, the potentially dangerous nature of the job, especially in large urban departments, can be stressful. On the other hand, most fatal encounters are initiated by the police themselves and occur in situations that the police know to be dangerous. The implications suggest that while police work is sometimes dangerous, it could be considerably less so based on the officer's own actions.

Some research suggests that levels of stress vary by job assignments. For example, P. A. Wallace, R. R. Roberg, and H. E. Allen (1985), in a study of five police departments, found that narcotics investigators had significantly higher job-burnout rates than either former narcotics investigators or patrol officers. In another comparative study of job burnout and officer assignment, Roberg, D. L. Hayhurst, and Allen (1988) discovered that although narcotics investigators had the highest levels of burnout, civilian dispatch personnel exhibited significantly higher levels of occupational stress than did either former narcotics investigators or patrol officers. The conclusion is that although patrol work may be stressful, other job assignments (including civilian dispatchers) may actually be more stressful. Accordingly, while appropriate actions to prevent or reduce stress for patrol officers are certainly warranted, it should be recognized that all police personnel should be afforded appropriate stress-reduction programs.

Historical Overview of Stressors

In their review of the literature of police stress, J. M. Violanti and F. Aron (1995) discovered that two major categories of **police stressors** emerged: departmental practices and the inherent nature of police work. *Departmental practices* may include the authoritarian structure of the department, lack of administrative support, minimal participation in decision making affecting work tasks, and perceived unfair discipline. Stressors inherent in *police work* include rotating shift work, boredom, danger, public apathy, and exposure to human misery, including death or injury to fellow officers.

Police Stressors

Based on the above, Violanti and Aron ranked 60 police stressors of 103 officers in a large police department in New York state. The top 15 stressors are ranked by their mean scores in Table 13.1. The top two stressors were "killing someone in the line of duty" and "fellow officer killed." Although these incidents occur infrequently, they have a significant psychological impact on the individuals involved. It is further interesting to note that eight of the top 15 (i.e., killing someone, officer killed, physical attack, chases, use of force, auto accidents, aggressive crowds, and felony in progress) are stressors related to potentially dangerous aspects of the work. Shift work was also reported as a major stressor because sleep patterns, as well as eating habits and family relationships, may be affected by rotating shifts. "Inadequate department support" (by supervisors) was another high-ranking stressor, due to the paramilitary structure of the department that minimizes interpersonal relationships between supervisors and subordinates. Other findings indicated that officers with work experience of six to ten years had higher mean stressor scores than those with work experience of one to five years. This fact may be because newer officers with less work experience may remain challenged and may still cling to idealism, whereas the more experienced officers may be less enchanted with police work and thereby find it more stressful and frustrating.

Table 13.1 Police Stressors Ranked by Mean Scores

Stressor	Mean score
Killing someone in line of duty	79.4
Fellow officer killed	76.7
Physical attack	71.0
Battered child	69.2
High-speed chases	63.7
Shift work	61.2
Use of force	61.0
Inadequate department support	61.0
Incompatible partner	60.4
Accident in patrol car	59.9
Insufficient personnel	58.9
Aggressive crowds	56.7
Felony in progress	55.3
Excessive discipline	53.3
Plea bargaining	52.8

Note: Overall mean score of 60 ranked stressors = 44.8.
Source: Adapted from J. M. Violanti and F. Aron. 1995. *Journal of Criminal Justice* 23, p. 290.

The most significant early study attempting to identify police stressors was that of W. H. Kroes, B. L. Margolis, and J. L. Hurrell (1974), whose research design was similar to the Violanti and Aron study. The researchers interviewed 100 male officers in the Cincinnati Police Department and asked them what they considered to be the most "bothersome" aspects about their job (it was assumed that "bothersome" and "stressful" were synonymous terms). Table 13.2 indicates the 12 categories into which the responses fell and the frequency of the responses.

Table 13.2 Bothersome Aspects of Police Work

Category	Definition	Number of responses
Courts	Court rulings and procedures	56
Administration	Administrative policies/procedures; administrative support of Officers	51
Equipment	Adequacy/state of repair of equipment	39
Community relations	Public apathy/negative reaction to and lack of support of policemen	38
Changing work shifts	28-day rotating shift schedule	18

Table 13.2 Bothersome Aspects of Police Work (continued)

Category	Definition	Number of Responses
Relations with supervisor	Difficulties in getting along with supervisor	16
Nonpolice work	Tasks required of officer which are not considered to be police responsibility	14
Other policemen	Fellow officers not performing their job	8
Bad assignment	Work assignment that the officer disliked	6
Other	Stresses that did not readily fit into the above categories	5
Isolation/boredom	Periods of inactivity and separation from social contacts	3
Pay	Adequacy or equity of salary	2

Note: As officers may mention more than one stressor, the overall total can exceed 100.
Source: Adapted from W. H. Kroes, B. L. Margolis, and J. L. Hurrell, Jr. 1974. "Job Stress In Policemen." *Journal of Police Science and Administration* 2: 145. Reprinted by permission.

Court leniency with criminals and the scheduling of court appearances on "off days" were the highest stressors. The second-highest stressors were administrative policies regarding work assignments, procedures, and personal conduct and a lack of administrative support. The third most significant stressor was the inadequacy and poor state of repair of equipment. The fourth stressor was poor community relations, including apathy and negative responses exhibited by the public toward officers.

The most striking difference between the 1974 and 1995 studies is the dangerous stressors of the job listed in the 1995 study but not listed in the earlier study. Although society, and the police, may be more concerned about violent crime today, it is important to note that one of the reasons for the differences in these stressors may be in how the surveys were completed. The 1995 study used a 60-item check-off (listing potential dangerous stressors); the 1974 study asked officers to list those aspects of policing that were "bothersome" to them. In this study, crisis situations that might affect officer health and safety were categorized under "Other" because so few officers mentioned them. Kroes, Margolis, and Hurrell suggest there may have been two reasons for such a surprising finding. First, officers may not think of such situations as merely "bothersome" so much as threatening and dangerous. Second, officers may not consciously think about physical dangers at work, in order to maintain their psychological well-being. A similar finding was reported in the J. P. Crank and M. Caldero study discussed below, where concerns over occupational danger were among the least frequently cited stressors. As one officer commented, "The stress caused by work on the street is nothing compared to the stress caused by the administration in this department" (1991, p. 336). In addition, as the Crank and Caldero research also suggests, it is likely that larger, urban police departments contend with higher crime rates, and thus the perception of danger is most likely higher than in medium or small departments.

In contrast, the 1974 study ranked court leniency as the highest stressor. Since the 1960s and early 1970s are known as the age of judicial activism (i.e., the Warren Court era), it is likely that the number of decisions expanding criminal "rights and procedures" influenced police stress as officers had to adapt their behavior accordingly; "restrictive court decisions" and "court leniency" were not ranked in the top 20 on the 1995 study. Inadequate department or administrative support and shift work ranked very high in both studies; clearly, these issues need to be addressed. Lastly, equipment failure and poor community relations were high stressors in the 1974 study but much lower in the 1995 study; "inadequate equipment" ranked 18th and "public criticism" and "public apathy" were not in the top half. The state of repair of equipment may always be a problem to some degree in policing because of hard use, although it appears no longer to be the problem it once was. Since the improvement in community relations, especially through community policing, has become a top priority in many police departments during the 1990s, poor community relations are viewed as less of a stressor today.

A survey conducted by Crank and Caldero (1991) studied 167 line officers in eight medium-size municipal departments in Illinois. Responses were categorized into five areas: organization, task environment, judiciary, personal or family concerns, and city government. More than two-thirds of those responding (114 officers, or 68 percent) identified the department as their principal source of stress, especially problems relating to management and supervisors (70 officers, or 42 percent), followed by shift changes (28 officers, or 17 percent). The second most frequently cited source of stress (27 officers, or 16 percent) was the task environment, with citizen contact as the primary source in this category (8 officers or, 29 percent), concerns regarding potential danger were second (6 officers or, 21 percent). The judiciary was the third ranked source (12 officers, or 7 percent); the primary concern related to the court's failure to prosecute criminals adequately. Personal or family concerns were ranked fourth (6 officers, or 4 percent) while city government was ranked fifth (5 officers, or 3 percent).

The findings of this 1991 study are similar to those of the 1974 and 1995 studies regarding stress relating to inadequate department support and shift work. The difference in the dangerousness of the work is most likely due to the size of the department; larger departments tend to have to contend with higher levels of crime. Interestingly, with respect to the courts or judiciary, both of the 1990s findings had relatively low rankings (third out of five in 1991 and in the 30s out of 60 in the 1995) compared with the 1974 findings (first). It is likely that in the years since the Kroes study, officers have learned more about and adapted to court decisions with which they may not agree. In addition, it is likely that departments have improved courtroom training to ensure that officers meet certain requisites when testifying in court. Such training should emphasize the importance of thorough reports and documentation, evidence, courtroom behavioral tactics, interface with the prosecution, case review, and prior mental rehearsal. It is likely that improved courtroom demeanor and presentation by police officers can help to curtail "unfavorable" court decisions.

Emerging Sources of Stress

P. Finn and J. E. Tomz (1997), in their interviews with approximately 100 people, including law enforcement administrators, union and association officials, mental-health practitioners, and 50 line officers and family members from large and small departments, discovered that today's police are encountering new emerging sources of stress. As an example, although community policing has produced increased job satisfaction among many officers, others have found the transition to be stressful. V. B. Lord (1996) in his study of the Charlotte-Mecklenburg Police Department, which was attempting to move to community policing, also found increased levels of stress among officers and sergeants, particularly with respect to role conflict and role ambiguity. Moreover, some officers felt that the higher expectations of solving community crime problems enhanced job pressure and burnout. Furthermore, certain officers experienced reactions of disdain from those not involved in community policing. Community policing requires attributes that some officers may not possess nor have been screened for: interpersonal, verbal, and problem-solving skills. Therefore, the transition to community policing may be difficult and require adequate training and communication in order to circumvent this emerging form of stress.

Many respondents thought that there had been a rise in violent crime and that they no longer had the upper hand; heavily armed criminals and increased incidents involving excessive violence and irrational behavior created added tension. Additionally, they thought that the violent crime issue had been exacerbated because many departments had not increased the number of officers and in some instances had downsized. Thus, police employment has not increased commensurately with respective rises in the population and crime rates in some locations. With respect to violent crime, these findings would appear to be consistent with the Violanti and Aron study, where "killing someone in the line of duty," "fellow officer killed," "physical attack," "use of force," and "insufficient personnel" were ranked relatively high.

Another newer form of stress involves what officers perceive as negative media coverage, public scrutiny, and prospective litigation. Many officers felt

Dealing with large crowds, which may become aggressive, is one of the top stressors in police work. (Photo: The Feminist Majority Foundation)

stressed by negative publicity such as that surrounding the Rodney King incident, the Branch Davidian incident in Waco, Texas, police corruption scandals, and other dubious police incidents. Generally, the media focus attention on offenders' rights as opposed to victims' rights or officers' rights which was resented by officers. More important, respondents demonstrated an increased fear of lawsuits, both civil and criminal, and consistently worried about the use of force as endangering their lives.

Another emerging stressor was fear of both air-borne and blood-borne diseases (e.g., AIDS, hepatitis B, and tuberculosis). Cultural diversity and political correctness caused stress for some white officers, who perceived reverse discrimination in hiring, training, and promotional practices and excessive sensitivity to their behavior and language.

Categories of Stressors

Based on the research findings presented above as well as on some earlier research (e.g., Grencik 1975; Roberts 1975; Stratton 1978), police stressors can be categorized into four major types, as indicated in Table 13.3.

Table 13.3 Stressors in Police Work

External Stressors
Frustration with the criminal justice system
Lack of consideration in scheduling officers for court appearances
The perception of inadequate public support and negative public attitudes
Negative, biased, and inaccurate media coverage

Internal Stressors
Policies and procedures that officers do not support
Inadequate training and career development opportunities
Inadequate recognition and rewards for good work
Inadequate salary, benefits, and working conditions
Excessive paperwork
Inconsistent discipline
Favoritism regarding promotions and assignments
Politically motivated administrative decisions

Police Stressors
The unhealthy consequences of shift work
The potential role conflict between law enforcement and serving the public
Frequent exposure to human suffering
Boredom interrupted by the need for sudden alertness
Fear and danger involved in certain situations
Being responsible for protecting other people
Too much work to do in time allotted

Officer Stressors
Fears regarding job competence and success
Fears regarding safety
The possible need to take other jobs to support family or to pursue education
Altered social status in the community

Source: Adapted from R. M. Ayers and G. S. Flanagan. 1992. *Preventing Law Enforcement Stress: The Organization's Role*. Washington, D.C.: Bureau of Justice Assistance, pp. 4–5.

In addition, because policing has been primarily a white, male-dominated occupation, there are additional stressors affecting minority and women officers. As T. Eisenberg (1975) points out, minority officers face the additional stresses of rejection and skepticism by members of their own race and may not be accepted into the "police family," a source of support, camaraderie, and occupational identity. In support of Eisenberg, Harr and Morash (1999) found in their national survey of over 1,000 officers in 24 departments that African American officers were significantly more likely than Caucasians to use as a coping strategy for stress the bonding with officers whom they share a racial bond. For female officers, the stressors include her own feelings of competence; how she is perceived; how her peers, particularly males, view her competence; and reluctant acceptance within the police culture.

As discussed in the previous chapter, additional sources of stress for both minority and women officers can also entail discriminatory practices with respect to job assignment and promotions and a lack of acceptance into the field. Another category of stressors is the *sexist culture* in policing, along with the overt sexist attitudes of many colleagues. Both W. G. Wexler and D. D. Logan (1983) and M. Morash and R. Harr (1995) provide examples including a lack of acceptance as officers; denial of information, sponsorships or mentors, and protection; and both sexual harassment and language harassment (i.e., the deliberate use of profanity and telling of sexual jokes). Once again, in support of these previous findings, Harr and Morash (1999) in their study of gender, race and occupational stress, discovered that women officers were 48 percent more likely to belong to a high-stress (versus a low-stress) group.

Line of Duty and Crisis Situations

The continual potential for crisis situations in the line of duty is what tends to differentiate police work from most other occupations. On the one hand, the level of "routine" patrol activities can be extremely busy, emotionally draining, and potentially dangerous. On the other hand, the routine can become extremely boring and uneventful. The reason this situation may be so stressful is the idea of the "startle" response—that is, when the police officer must respond rapidly, at any point in time, to any number of extreme situations. The amount and type of "activity" on any particular patrol depends on many factors, including the type of city, beat, and shift. In some departments, especially in larger cities, officers are becoming more and more immersed in a continuous round of serious calls dealing with violence, drugs, and gang warfare. In such patrol areas there can be little doubt that the high workload, combined with intense emotional demands and potential physical harm, is conducive to high levels of stress and strain. For an up close look at an officer's patrol duties in one such high-crime area, see Case Study 13.1.

Posttraumatic Stress Disorder

The psychological stress caused by frequent or prolonged exposure to crises or trauma can lead to a condition known as **posttraumatic stress disorder (PTSD)**. Although officers may not suffer physical injury, the emotional trauma may be catastrophic and could result in PTSD. While some officers

San Francisco Cops' Toughest Duty

Situated at Third and 20th streets in the police department's oldest and most dilapidated building, the Potrero station house was once a place where arrests of burglars, marijuana users, and petty thieves were big deals. Now, vicious thugs and kids too young to shave are routinely hauled in toting military assault weapons and sawed-off shotguns under their jackets. The explosion of crack cocaine and gang-related shootings has spawned another change in the Potrero district: cops punch the clock every day at the station house wondering whether they will live through their shifts. "When I drive in over the Bay Bridge, I look out over at the hill and I wonder if tonight will be the night I get it," said Jimmy Lewis, who has worked in the Potrero Station for two years. "Every call you go on could be your last one."

Huge Arsenals

Part of the fear comes from the knowledge that the outlaws far outgun the good guys. Sometimes, the sheer size of the arsenals they find on the streets shakes up the cops. "A couple of months ago we got a tip that there was going to be a gang fight out by Candlestick" (since renamed 3 Comm stadium), said Officer Lea Militello, a seven-year police veteran. "Four of us responded and found about 40 kids in a few cars. I collected seven automatic rifles, about eight to 10 revolvers, Molotov cocktails—the works. I started shaking. It was incredible." To even the odds a bit, most officers pack second guns along with their standard issue .38-caliber service revolvers. Militello keeps an extra .38-caliber pistol strapped to her ankle. "It isn't as much as an Uzi or a MAC-10, but every little bit helps," she said, adding that the second guns are legal and conform to department policy.

Guns are not the only weapons used against the police. Blue patrol uniforms in the Potrero district frequently attract thrown bottles, rocks, and bricks, officers say. At l0 p.m. March 22, Officer Tom Buckley and his partner Tom Kracke stopped a car full of teens on a dead-end street near Oakdale and Keith streets. The night was peaceful, quiet and dark except for the twin white beams from the patrol car's headlights.

"Out of nowhere, a barrage of rocks started raining down on us," Buckley said. "Three of them hit the car. If they had hit us, they could have killed us." That kind of incident, the officers said, increases the jitter level among the cops. "Sometimes, you just want to empty your gun into the bushes," Kracke said, adding quickly, "Of course, no one ever does that."

Workload

"It's not unusual to get in your car at the beginning of your shift and see five calls [waiting] on your computer screen," said Militello, whose caseload has soared in her five and a half years at Potrero. "It often stays that way all through the shift." The officers can do little more than "gun and run" each call, meaning they "gun" their patrol cars to each incident, finish as quickly as possible, and "run" off to the next one. Still, they never seem to be able to catch up with their work.

Time is not the only thing in short supply at Potrero Station. Officers say they sometimes are forced to go out into the streets without walkie-talkies, an officer's lifeline in an emergency. Even when they do have radios, there are not enough relay antennas in the district to transmit the calls, officers said. "There are places where you can't transmit out from, like some spots at the Geneva Towers [housing project]," said Officer Danker. "You don't want to be caught there with a dead radio that can't call for help. That could kill you."

Building Camaraderie

The pressures of working in one of the city's scariest districts has galvanized friendships inside the station. "There are cliques in other stations—white against black, gay against straight, men against women," said Officer Ken Cantamount, a five-year veteran of the San Francisco force who sports a huge handlebar mustache. "We don't have any of that here."   ☞

☞ **One Shift's Log:**

One Saturday in May was typical in the number and variety of incidents that the Potrero station cops were called upon to answer in one eight-hour shift.

PM

4:21 Prowler	7:44 Vehicular accident	9:58 Fight with weapons
4:28 Recovered stolen vehicle	7:52 Fight	——
4:36 Fight	7:55 Traffic Congestion	10:06 Citizen standby
——	7:56 Wanted person	10:09 Burglary
5:31 Fight	7:58 Vehicular accident	10:16 Fight
5:41 Check on well-being	7:58 Assault	10:19 Vehicular
5:43 Suspicious person	——	10:22 Fight
5:44 Fight	8:04 Vandalism	10:37 Assault
5:50 Fight	8:07 Vehicular accident	10:45 Shooting
5:56 Assault	8:08 Suspicious person in vehicle	10:51 Fight
5:58 Juvenile disturbance	8:08 Person breaking in complaint	10:58 Noise complaint
5:59 Suspicious person	8:14 Shots fired	——
——	8:14 Vehicular accident	11:00 Alarm
6:27 Alarm	8:35 Noise complaint	11:04 Noise complaint
6:31 Alarm	8:40 Fight	11:08 Noise complaint
6:33 Assault	——	11:11 Burglary
6:35 Person breaking in	9:17 Parking violation	11:12 Prisoner transport
6:36 Juvenile disturbance	9:26 Vehicular accident	11:36 Vandalism
6:50 Person ringing doorbells	9:30 Assault	11:43 Noise complaint
6:53 Burglary	9:46 Vandalism	11:46 Prisoner transport
——	9:48 Assault	
7:22 Traffic congestion	9:54 Sexual assault/rape	
7:44 Vandalism	9:54 Fight	

Source: Adapted from D. Farrell. 1989. "S.F. Cops' Toughest Duty." *San Francisco Chronicle*, May 22: pp. 1A, 7A. Reprinted by permission.

recover within a few weeks, others may experience permanent trauma, which could adversely affect both the department and their personal lives. This disorder has been found to exist in many Vietnam veterans who had been exposed to the stresses and violence of the war experience.

C. A. Martin, H. E. McKean, and L. J. Veltkamp (1986) conducted a study of a group of 53 officers and discovered that 26 percent suffered from posttraumatic stress. Stressors leading to PTSD included shooting someone; being shot; working with child abuse, spouse abuse, and rape cases; being threatened or having family threatened; and observing death through homicide (including colleagues being killed), suicide, or natural disaster. Another study of 100 suburban officers found a correlation between duty-related stress and symptoms of PTSD (Robinson, Sigman, and Wilson 1997). Thirteen percent of the sample met the criteria for PTSD; the best predictors for the diagnosis were associated with a critical event related to the job and exposure to a death-and-life-threat. It was important to note that 63 percent of the respondents stated that a **critical-incident debriefing** (i.e., counseling) would be beneficial following an extremely stressful crisis event.

R. Loo (1986) found that officers experienced the most stress reactions within three days after a critical incident. The majority reported a preoccupation with the traumatic incident (39 percent) and anger (25 percent). Other reported symptoms of PTSD were sleep disturbances, flashbacks, feelings of guilt, wishing it had not happened, and depression (see Table 13.4). Many of the officers continued to report increased anger and lowered work interest one month after the incident. The course of recovery varied, but the average time for a return to "feeling normal" was 20 weeks after the critical incident.

Table 13.4 Common Reaction to Critical Incident Stress

Physical reactions	Emotional reactions	Cognitive reactions
• Headaches • Muscle aches • Sleep disturbances • Changed appetite • Decreased interest in sexual activity • Impotence	• Anxiety • Fear • Guilt • Sadness • Anger • Irritability • Feeling lost and unappreciated • Withdrawal	• Debilitating flashbacks • Repeated visions of the incident • Nightmares • Slowed thinking • Difficulty making decisions and solving problems • Disorientation • Lack of concentration • Memory lapses

Source: A. W. Kureczka, 1996. "Critical Incident Stress in Law Enforcement." *FBI Law Enforcement Bulletin,* Feb./March: p. 15.

Martin and his colleagues concluded from their study that **sensitization training** regarding officers' work with victims, as well as their own victimization, should be conducted early in their careers. Such training may help to increase their empathy for crime victims and cope with their own reactions to the stress caused by dealing with such situations. A. W. Kureczka (1996) believes that officers will not pursue assistance for fear of being stigmatized. In other words, in an effort to preserve their "macho" image, officers remain cautious when discussing their emotional responses to critical incidents.

In terms of cost, PTSD can also have an important impact on the department. It has been estimated (Vaughn 1991), for example, that 70 percent of police officers involved in deadly force incidents leave the department within five years. According to Kureczka, to replace a five-year veteran costs about $100,000, including retraining, benefits, testing for replacements, and overtime. By contrast, prompt treatment costs approximately $8,300; whereas, delayed treatment costs about $46,000. Consequently, quick treatment for officers is not only professional but also cost-effective.

As a routine practice, department policy should mandate that officers visit a mental-health professional for evaluation and further treatment as needed subsequent to any critical incident. Stress-management programs should be provided to all recruits, as well as ongoing stress-education programs for all officers. As an added precaution, Kureczka advocates the use of officers who are specially trained to recognize problems and make referrals as deemed necessary. Such a **peer-counseling program** has been established in the Fort Worth (Texas) Police Department, under the supervision of the Psychological Services Unit (Greenstone, Dunn, and Leviton 1995). Peer counselors are available 24 hours a day, seven days a week and serve voluntarily and without compensation in addition to their regular police duties.

The counselors receive basic training in crisis intervention and critical-incident debriefing.

Finally, counseling services or some type of stress-management program should also be made available to family members. In turn, family members might be able to understand and provide further nurturing and support (see social supports discussion below) to the officer involved. More important, intervention and treatment may serve to circumvent suicide, the worst possible outcome of work-related stress.

Although little is actually known about the amount or effect of PTSD on police officers, it has been suggested that such a disorder might lead to increased brutality by the police. T. Kellogg and M. Harrison (1991), for instance, contend that much police brutality can be attributed to PTSD. Although they present no empirical evidence to support their claims, it seems likely that some officers suffering from posttraumatic stress could vent their anger and frustration on citizens through violence. Consequently, this is an important area for future study. It is important that scholars attempt to determine how widespread PTSD may be among the nation's police, as well as its potential impact on police behavior.

Social Supports and Police Stress

Almost all research on police stress has been based on a **stressor-outcome model**, meaning that a stressful circumstance, or "stressor" leads directly to a negative outcome, such as psychological stress or a physical ailment. Another perspective to the study of stress, however, the **social-supports model**, suggests that an individual may be more or less insulated against the effects of stressors depending on whether he or she has a social-support network—friends, coworkers, and family members—in place. In other words, social supports may help people cope with stressful circumstances and thus lessen the potential negative effects. From this perspective, F. T. Cullen, T. Lemming, B. G. Link, and J. F. Wozniak (1985) studied police stress in five suburban police departments in a large Midwestern city.

The researchers classified police stress along two different dimensions: that involving work and that affecting the officer's personal life. Work-related stressors were chosen that were not infrequent situations but ongoing parts of the police officer's job, such as role problems, court problems, potential danger, and shift changes. Social support measures included two work-related sources, peer support and supervisory support; and two nonwork sources, family support and community support. It was discovered that work stress was most significantly influenced by perceived danger, which could be counteracted by supervisory support. Life stress was influenced not only by perceived danger but also by court problems and shift changes. It was further found that family support counteracted stress in personal life.

It is interesting to note that danger was the only stressor that was significantly related to both dimensions of stress. Although the respondents worked in communities with relatively low rates of serious crime, and 86 percent disagreed with the statement "A lot of people I work with get physically injured in the line of duty," the vast majority of the sample also felt that they had a "chance of getting hurt in my job." In other words, the *potential* of being physically injured was ever present and inherent in their work. Thus, even though policing may not be very dangerous in low-crime communities, the threat of injury is constant and may lead to stressful consequences. Another interesting finding was that both court problems and shift changes were significantly related to stress in personal life but not to work stress. This finding is important in that it "sensitizes us to the possibility that officers may adjust to the more strenuous features of their occupation while at work but nevertheless suffer deleterious effects on their general psychological health" (Cullen, Lemming, Link, and Wozniak 1985, p. 514).

It was clear that supervisory support could mitigate work stress, while family support was helpful in lessening personal-life stress. These findings suggest that departments must establish programs and provide training adequate to deal with stress in both work and personal life, while taking into account various social supports.

Shift Work

Shift work not only adversely affects an officers' performance but also puts an added burden on family and friends. While the rest of society orchestrates their leisure activities around a "day" schedule, officers reserve their activities for days off because on work days many find it difficult to do anything other than eat, sleep, and go to work. According to J. L. O'Neill and M. A. Cushing (1991), relationships with wives, children, and friends are disrupted, and may officers many experience some or all of the following problems (i.e., intolerance to shift work):

- *Sleep alterations*, consisting of subjective self-ratings of poor sleep quality, difficulty in falling asleep, frequent awakenings, and insomnia.

- *Persistent fatigue*, which does not disappear after sleep, weekends, or vacations, thus differing from physiological fatigue caused by physical and/or mental effort.

- *Behavior changes*, including unusual irritability, tantrums, malaise, and inadequate performance.

- *Digestive troubles*, ranging from dyspepsia to epigastric pain and peptic ulcers.

Some evidence indicates that many of the problems associated with shift changes, including sleep problems and fatigue, use of alcohol and sleeping pills, increased sick time, and accidents, can be substantially reduced if schedules are designed to accommodate the body's natural circadian rhythm, which controls sleep-wake cycles. For example, in Philadelphia, three major changes were made in officers' schedules in an attempt to reduce such problems: (1) Shifts were changed every 18 days rather than every eight days, allowing more time to adjust to the change. (2) The rotation shifted forward, from day, to evening, to graveyard, rather than backward as had been the previous practice. Because the typical circadian clock runs on about a 25-hour day, the natural tendency is to shift to a later (rather than an earlier) hour. (3) Consecutive work days were reduced from six to four, allowing officers to catch up on lost sleep and avoiding the cumulative sleep deprivation that night-shift workers often experience (Bain 1988). After 11 months on the new schedule, officers reported significant declines in sleep problems and fatigue on the job. Automobile accidents while at work declined by 40 percent, sleeping pill and alcohol usage dropped by 50 percent, and sick time declined by 23 percent (Bain 1988). There is little doubt that many departments could improve officers' job performance by redesigning traditional shift schedules to coincide more accurately with natural sleep patterns.

Other innovations in shift work might include allowing officers to determine the frequency of their shift rotation with an option to modify it at least annually or semiannually according to seniority. Further, permanent or semipermanent shifts as opposed to rotating shifts might be more desirable. The Michigan State Police, for instance, have instituted such modifications and have allowed individual work sites to make their own choices through majority vote (Finn and Tomz 1997). O'Neill and Cushing (1991) recommend that a minimum number of officers should work the early morning shifts (i.e., shifts that fall between 2:00 A.M. and 6:00 A.M), with callbacks assigned to the day shift so that nonessential tasks are completed during the day. Additionally, they suggest that officers be allowed to bid for another shift at least twice a year and that midnight shifts be limited to four-day weeks. Although shift work cannot be eliminated, different innovative approaches such as the above may mitigate its damaging impact on officers and their families.

Stress and Emotional Problems

There has been a limited amount of research on the relation between stress and emotional problems experienced by police officers; this research has been primarily concerned with alcohol and drug abuse, suicide, and marital and family-related problems, including divorce.

Alcohol Abuse

J. J. Hurrell and W. H. Kroes (1975) have suggested that police work may be especially conducive to alcoholism because officers frequently work in an environment in which social drinking is commonplace. "The nature of their work and the environment in which it is performed provides the stress stimulus" (p. 241). Hurrell and Kroes further contend that some police administrators have reported informally that as many as 25 percent of the officers in their departments have serious alcohol-abuse problems. It should also be noted, however, that other police administrators believe that alcohol-related problems are substantially lower. Although research has established a relationship between high job stress and excessive drinking, there is no direct evidence for high rates of alcoholism among police (Goolkasian, Geddes, and DeJong 1985). J. Brown and E. A. Campbell (1994) found that alcohol consumption and substance abuse are common reactions to PTSD because they serve to mask the underlying stress disorder; however, there is no greater incidence of alcohol-related problems when compared with society in general.

Police departments have traditionally used the "character flaw" theory to deal with alcohol abuse (Hurrell and Kroes 1975). This theory calls for the denunciation and dismissal of officers with an alcohol problem because they will reflect badly on the department's reputation. What is not recognized is that "alcoholism may result from the extraordinary stresses of the job and that eliminating the officer does not do away with the sources of stress" (p.

241). Today, however, many departments are attempting to deal with the alcoholic employee through in-house educational programs and through admittance to outpatient programs designed to deal with such problems.

The following benefits are expected to accrue to those departments that develop procedures to help problem drinkers or alcoholics to recover from their illness:

1. Retention of the majority of officers who had suffered from alcoholism.

2. Solution of a set of complex and difficult personnel problems.

3. Realistic and practical extension of the department's program into the entire city government structure.

4. Improved public and community attitudes by this degree of concern for the officer and the family and by eliminating the dangerous antisocial behavior of the officer.

5. Full cooperation with rehabilitation efforts from the police associations and unions that may represent officers.

6. The preventive influence on moderate drinkers against the development of dangerous drinking habits that may lead to alcoholism. In addition, an in-house program will motivate some officers to undertake remedial action on their own, outside the scope of the department program (Dishlacoff 1976, p. 39).

Drug Abuse

Although there is little direct evidence on the amount of drug abuse among police officers, there is little doubt that along with the general population, the problem is rising.

Narcotics. The principal category of illegal drugs is narcotics. Inside Policing 13.1 chronicles the growing concern with the use of these illegal drugs in policing. In an attempt to reduce this problem, departments utilize drug testing to screen out police applicants who may have a drug-abuse problem (see later discussion). In addition, police administrators are increasingly testing officers on the job for illegal drug use. Because drug use is illegal, and officers are required to enforce laws against it, the usual result of a positive testing is dismissal from the force. In *Guiney v. Roache*, (1989), the courts upheld the Boston Police Department's right to require its officers to undergo urinalysis at any time without any suspicion of drug use.

Anabolic steroids. Another area of growing concern is the abuse of anabolic steroids, which can lead to severe physical and psychological problems. Some of the potential adverse effects of these drugs include increased aggression (known as "roid rage"), increased risk of heart disease, acne, liver damage, and psychological dependence (due to improved strength, athletic ability, and physique). In men, sterility, impotence, and an enlarged prostate gland are also likely to develop from steroid abuse, and in women abuse may lead to menstrual and other irregularities, including increased body and facial hair, baldness, and a deepening voice.

❖ ❖ ❖ ❖

Inside Policing 13.1
Drug Use by Cops Seen as Growing Problem

Top police executives say the use of illegal drugs by law enforcement officers is the biggest problem facing the profession today, and they see a growing trend toward the frequent use of urinalysis to detect drug use among recruits and officers.

"We didn't have this problem in law enforcement years ago," said Neil Behan, of the Baltimore County Department. "Our people, the young people were not using it to the degree that they are using it now," "Society continues to change in regard to narcotic drugs and it's been on the increase these many years." The people recruited 10 years ago, Behan said, were not likely to be drug users. However, he added, the young people that apply for police jobs now are very likely to have used them. "Ten years ago the number one problem in law enforcement was corruption; now the number one problem is the use of illegal drugs."

Richard Koehler of the New York City Police Department's personnel division sees the increased use of drug-detection tests on recruits as a mandate for police officials. "We have a responsibility under state law and the city's administrative code to maintain the fitness of the force. Illegal drug use requires someone to break the law and the use of drugs impairs somebody's ability to function." The department has been giving urinalysis tests to recruits for the past several years. Koehler said that three urinalysis tests are given to recruits: one as an applicant just prior to testing, another while the recruit is still in the training academy, and the last before the end of probation. "We set a tone, particularly up front. We think of it as a socialization process. People are coming from society in general to be police officers with 30 to 35 percent of the population using narcotics, particularly marijuana. So we make it clear in the department that you don't use drugs. If you do, you'll get fired."

The Chicago Police Department also gives urinalysis tests to recruits, as well as to selected in-service officers. As an officer moves up in rank or applies for assignment in a special unit, he or she must submit to a urine test. Over the past 20 months, 1,922 officers from different divisions have submitted to the drug tests. Of these, 81, or 4.2 percent, showed signs of illegal narcotics use. Chicago Police Department policy orders the reassignment to less sensitive positions for any officer who fails a drug test. Charges are then filed with the Police Board to have the officer dismissed from the force.

In New York, as in Chicago, termination is recommended for officers with a chemical dependency. If an officer is suspected of using illegal drugs, the supervisor observes the officer and then calls the department advocate's office to explain the suspicions. The supervisor then has the right to order that officer to take a drug test. If the officer refuses or the test proves positive, he is fired.

"Drug use is a crime," Kohler said. "In order to put the drugs in your body you must commit a crime. It's different from alcohol, which is protected under federal law." Because drug use is a crime, Koehler said, the department has no drug treatment program and no intention of starting one.

The 4.2 percent of the 1,922 Chicago officers who were found to be using drugs is a much lower proportion than the level found among the general population. Still, according to a representative of the Chicago Fraternal Order of Police, there is a problem. "The biggest problem is that many corporations that will identify alcoholism as a sickness have now identified chemical dependency as a sickness and have programs to treat and retain those people in the workplace," he said. "I know of no police department in this country that will retain an officer who has been identified as having a chemical dependency."

Behan said that within the Baltimore County ranks, any use of narcotics is unacceptable. "It's illegal and those who use it should be separated from this kind of work. Other professions should take the same attitude but they do not. They do not expel from their ranks those whom they find to be users." In most departments, Behan said, on-the-job testing has not become a universal practice, ☞

❖ ❖ ❖ ❖ ☞

"there is a trend toward it," he said. "If the abusing continues, you'll probably see an expansion of the idea of checking people. In this department, we give a urine test to every officer going into a narcotics squad. That's the way the trend is going, and you'll probably see more of that, not less."

Although none of the police officials questioned see a problem with substance abuse in their own departments, Behan said there is widespread concern within the law enforcement community. "We're concerned that drug abuse is out of control, especially cocaine, and we want to make sure that as we recruit and put people on special assignment that they are not drug users and do not become drug users after coming to us." At the NYPD, Koehler said, 3 percent of the applicants to the force are turned away because of narcotics use. Koehler said that while other departments using different approaches turn up positive results on 25 to 30 percent of the tests done on applicants, NYPD hopefuls are told that if there is any detection of drug use

they will not be hired. "We tell them that when they take their written test," Koehler said. "From the very beginning of the investigative process all the way through the 18 months they're in the academy and on probation and in the field training program, we indicate that any sign of drug use is going to result in their termination. There has never been an exception where an officer has taken a test and we've gotten a hit. That person's fired."

Koehler believes that the socialization process at the very beginning has led to the 3 percent hits. "Our objective is not to catch people who have ever used marijuana. Our objective is to make sure that they don't use marijuana as police officers. When you look at 3 percent hits, the message is out."

Source: Adapted from *Law Enforcement News*. 1985 "Drug Use by Cops Seen as Growing Problem," September 23, pp. 1, 12. Reprinted by permission.

Although little information is currently available on anabolic steroid abuse in policing, instances of unusual or violent police behavior associated with steroid use have been reported. For example, "60 Minutes" in a 1989 edition, reported several episodes of police violence and abuse of citizens attributed to the use of steroids. There have been other instances of the illegal use or sale of steroids by police (Swanson, Gaines, and Gore 1991). Personal interviews of administrators in 30 police departments across the country indicated that steroid use has been overlooked in policing and that the abuse of these drugs is beginning to become problematic (Swanson, Gaines, and Gore 1991). It should be noted that anabolic steroids are not detected in routine drug testing and therefore must be tested separately.

Besides the potential for violent and unusual police behavior, additional problems relating to steroid abuse include increased officer-to-officer conflicts and officer complaints about the department, its policies and procedures, or working conditions (Swanson, Gaines, and Gore 1991). Because of the potential harm that may accrue from abnormal behavior associated with steroid abuse, police departments must not only educate their officers about the use of steroids but also develop effective policies and programs to eliminate the illegal use of steroids before it becomes a problem.

Suicide

Suicide has become the most dreaded result of a police officer under stress. Although it is difficult to obtain accurate data regarding whether police suicides are higher than those of the general population, it appears to be true, at least in some departments. Most of the early research suggests that it is higher than in the general population. In a comparison of police with 130 other occupations, L. Guralnick (1963) estimated the suicide rate to be 1.8 times that of the general population. Guralnick also found that police were more likely to commit suicide than be killed in a homicide. Richard and Fell (1975) ranked police as the third highest in suicide among 130 occupations, and Violanti, J. E. Vena, and J. R. Marshall (1986) reported that police were three times as likely to commit suicide compared to other municipal workers.

In a more extensive study, J. Dash and M. Reiser (1978), who analyzed officer suicides in the Los Angeles Police Department from 1970 through 1976, found an average rate of 8.1 per 100,000 population for the seven-year period, which was considerably lower than the county, state, and national suicide rates. M. Wagner and R. J. Brzeczek (1983) examined officer suicides of the Chicago Police Department from 1977 through 1979; they found 20 officer suicides during the period, including three retirees. They noted that if one looked only at the numbers, a Chicago police officer was five times as likely to take his life as a citizen of the city; the average suicide rate for Chicago police officers during this three-year period was 43.8 per 100,000. A follow-up study of the Los Angeles Police Department study by R. L. Josephson and M. Reiser (1990) from 1977 through 1988 found an average rate of 12.0 suicides per 100,000, which was up from the 8.1 rate found in the 1978 study. Once again the rate for LAPD officers remained lower than those of the county, state and nation (e.g., California's suicide rate was 14.8 per l00,000 in 1986, and since 1977 the national suicide rate has remained at approximately 12.0 per 100,000 population).

Preliminary data from a 40-year (1950-1990) study of 2,611 Buffalo police officers suggest that the frequency of suicides has increased in the last decade from an average of one suicide every 1.75 years to one every 1.42 years (Violanti and Vena 1995, "What's Killing America's Cops?" 1996)).This same study found that police were eight times more likely to commit suicide than to be killed in a homicide and three times more likely to commit suicide than to die in job-related accidents. The researchers looked at 138 deaths, all white males, including 39 police officers and 99 other municipal workers. Of the 39 police officer deaths, 29 were suicides (74 percent), three were homicides, six were accidental, and one was undetermined. Of the 99 municipal worker deaths, 14 were suicides (14 percent), four were homicides, 77 were accidents, and four were undetermined. According to these numbers, police officers were approximately five times more likely to commit suicide than city workers (74 percent of all deaths compared to 14 percent), a staggering difference and one that needs an explanation.

Data such as these in Buffalo and those found in New York, (Ivanhoff 1994) where there have been 66 suicides over the past decade, 12 of them in 1994, suggest that police suicides are on the rise and may be a significant problem. The New York number is approximately four times that of the general population and compares with those found in Chicago in the late 1970s (Ivanhoff 1994). Part of the problem with making sense of disparate police suicide data is that they vary significantly across departments and may change significantly from year to year or over several years. Because most studies on police suicides focus on one department and are conducted in large cities, little is known about suicides in small or rural departments. Although most data indicate that police officers have a higher risk for suicide than the general population, such results may not hold for the entire country

(Violanti 1995). Nevertheless, it appears that suicide may be a developing problem in policing, at least in larger jurisdictions.

The preliminary results of the Buffalo study indicated that police are at a higher risk for committing suicide for a variety of reasons, including access to firearms (95 percent of the suicides were by firearm), continuous exposure to human misery, shift work, social strain and marital difficulties, drinking problems, physical illness, impending retirement (i.e., separation from police peers and subculture), and lack of control over their jobs and personal lives ("What's Killing America's Cops?" 1996). Other research supports the general tenor of these findings. For example, A. Ivanoff (1994) found that 94 percent of police suicides in New York involved a firearm and that 57 percent were believed to be precipitated by relationship difficulties; T. J. Cronin (1982) and Wagner and Brzeczek found that the majority of police officers committing suicide abused alcohol; Loo (1986) found that 15 percent of police suicides in the Royal Canadian Mounted Police had been exposed to a traumatic work incident; and C. W. Gaska (1982) found a 10-fold risk of suicide among police retirees.

Still others attribute police suicide to the consequences of uncovering corruption in departments. P. Friedman (1968), for example, suggested that many of the suicides in the New York Police Department in the 1930s were possibly related to the Tammany Hall corruption scandal. The increase in suicides in New York in the late 1990s could also possibly be related to a drug ring investigation by the Mollen Commission. Several of the 12 officers who committed suicide in 1994 were part of that investigation.

Interestingly, other findings Ivanoff (1994) also found in New York that officers tend to kill themselves because of personal problems, substance abuse, and depression, not job-related stress. These are continuing life problems that people do not know how to solve. Ivanhoff's study, issued by the New York City Police Foundation, based its findings on surveys of 18,000 patrol officers between 1990 and 1993 and on studies of 57 suicides of officers from 1985 to 1994. These findings are noteworthy because they suggest that police suicides may not result from job stress, which, in turn, may suggest that different types of intervention strategies are necessary. It is clear that more research is needed in order to provide a better understanding of the causes and effects of police suicides and prevention programs.

One of the primary problems of attempting to prevent police suicide is that, traditionally, officers refrain from asking for help. Often they do not want to appear weak in front of their peers, and they see themselves as problem solvers, not persons with problems. In addition, officers fear the possible negative effects on their career if they come forward with a problem. In order to make it easier for officers to seek help, Ivanoff suggests that departments should increase accessibility to confidential psychological services. Officers will be more likely to use such services if they do not have to go through a formal process.

Officers should receive training to help them recognize and avoid psychological factors leading to suicide. It is important to understand that suicide generally results not from a single crisis but from the accumulation of apparently minor life events. Training should begin at the academy before new officers are exposed to the police socialization process. Ivanhoff suggests that **suicide prevention training** should include the recognition of psycho-

logical depression, communication skills, conflict resolution, and maintenance of intimate relationships. It is further important that departments
train supervisors and managers, to recognize the warning signs of suicide
and suggest confidential referrals to those who are in need. As noted earlier in
the chapter, supervisory support can be extremely helpful in mitigating work
stress. In addition, as Violanti (1997) has pointed out, an organizational restructuring of the importance of the police role may be helpful. Recruits
should be made aware that while the role of the police officer is important, it
is not the only role in their lives. Sensitivity training could also be used to encourage officers to actively participate in family activities and establish
friendships outside of policing; the narrow view of "we versus they" should be
strongly discouraged.

Finally, based on the findings that over 90 percent of officers use a firearm to commit suicide, some suicides may be prevented by limiting access to
firearms. Although many departments require their officers to carry their
guns off duty, such a policy should be seriously reviewed. One way to reduce
the availability of firearms, and thus impulsive suicide tendencies, is to eliminate the 24-hour off-duty carry regulation. Another would be to allow officers
voluntarily to store their firearms at the station house or precinct upon completion of their shift (Violanti 1996).

Marital and Family Problems

In the Kroes, Margolis, and Hurrell study on police stressors, officers (all
men) were asked if being a police officer affected their personal lives. If the officer was married, he was asked about his home life; if he was single, he was
asked about his social life. Of the 100 respondents, 81 were married, and 19
were single. Seventy-nine of the married officers felt police work affected
their home life, and 16 of the single officers felt it affected their social life. Of
the married officers, by far the most frequently cited complaint (48) was the
difficulty of maintaining nonpolice friendships. Second was the problem of
spending enough time with their children (25), and third was the problem of
missing weekends and holidays with the family (19). For the single officers,
the most cited problems were the fact that the unusual work hours made it
difficult to date or to attend important social events and, as with married officers, the lack of nonpolice friends. A more recent study of over 400 spouses of
police officers (Alexander and Walker 1996) found that police work also had
an adverse impact on their lives, especially their social lives. The major problems were identified as long hours, shift work, and canceled leave. Surprisingly, dangerous duties and working with the opposite sex did not usually adversely affect officer spouses.

In view of these types of family problems, it has been assumed, as with alcoholism and suicide rates, that divorce rates for police officers are far higher
than normal for the rest of the population. Some research has supported this
view, but other research has indicated that divorce rates for police are no
higher than for many other occupations (the divorce rate for the general population is approximately 50 percent). M. J. Davidson and A. Veno (1978), in
their review of the literature, cite several weaknesses in the studies that support high divorce rates for police, including the failure to consider a number
of factors that strongly influence divorce rates, such as age at marriage and

number of children. J. A. Schwartz and C. B. Schwartz (1975) suggest that young marriages, combined with a lack of understanding of police work, can often lead to divorce.

Police departments that provide any orientation or counseling for the spouses of recruits are still the exception rather than the rule, and until recently there were no such programs

Whether or not police divorce rates are higher than those of the rest of the population is not too critical because police stressors undoubtedly lead to family problems, which, in turn, affect on-the-job performance. It is important, to keep in mind that marital discord appears to be the most significant problem for the suicidal officer. Factors that contribute to marital discord include the following (Territo and Vetter 1981 pp. 218–222):

1. *Overprotection of family members.* Due to the suspicious nature of the work and the trauma and degradation they observe daily, officers often become overly protective of their families, which can lead to resentment by the family members.

2. *Problems with children.* Children may encounter negative reactions from both peers and schoolteachers because of their father's occupation.

3. *Hardening of emotions.* To function adequately on the job, officers often find it necessary to suppress their feelings, which can lead to conflicts with spouses due to communication problems.

4. *Sexual problems.* The pressures and working hours of police work may lead to sexual problems, which, in turn, lead to frustration and anxiety and possibly to the search for release outside the marriage.

Because marital and family problems can have such a devastating impact on job performance, many police departments are developing programs aimed at helping family members to understand and cope with the stressors inherent in police work. The Los Angeles County Sheriff's Department (Stratton 1976), for example, offers an eight-week spouses' training program, which includes an overview of departmental operations and the duties of law enforcement personnel. In Minnesota, the Couple Communications program (Maynard and Maynard 1980) helps officers and their spouses identify issues in their marriage that might produce additional on-the-job stress. The Kansas City (Missouri) Police Department implemented the Marriage Partner program (Saper 1980) to help involve spouses in an effort to reduce stress. In Indiana, the state police initiated an employee-assistance program (Lambuth 1984) designed to help employees and their families deal with emotional problems by referral to proper treatment agencies. Such programs should, in the long run, lead to improved job performance.

Policies and Programs

Based on the literature reviewed, there are a number of policies and programs that could be implemented by police management to help control the stressors encountered by police personnel. Of course, not every department can, or should, attempt to implement all of the recommendations. Each de-

partment has different needs and budgetary constraints and therefore must
decide what type of policies and programs best fit its particular needs. The
following recommendations, however, provide a proper foundation for controlling police stress in both working and nonworking environments:

1. Establish quality-of-worklife activities designed to improve
   communication and increase participation in decision making
   throughout the department.

2. Address workplace environmental issues, including quality of
   equipment, work space, compensation packages, and related aspects.

3. Develop training programs in stress awareness. Police should
   consider stress management as simply another skill to be
   learned, like criminal law or police procedure.

4. Establish specific stress programs. These can be part of a larger
   departmental psychological services, a health program, or a general employee-assistance program.

5. Establish operational policies that reduce stress. Consider the
   effects of shift assignments and scheduling, report writing, and
   so forth.

6. Improve management skills overall, especially in people-ori-
   ented aspects of supervision and management; include stress
   management skills in supervisory practice.

7. Utilize peer-counseling programs. Because peers may have already experienced many of the same problems, they can be of in-
   valuable help to fellow officers.

8. Develop support groups by taking advantage of the natural
   groups that already exist informally and formally within the department.

9. Establish physical-fitness programs that can strengthen the individual to withstand occupational stress. Such programs
   should also address stress-related dietary issues.

10. Encourage family activities as an important source of assistance
    to the officer. In particular, as spouses know more about police
    work and its stresses, they are in a better position to provide sup-
    port (adapted from Farmer 1990, pp. 214–215).

Officer Safety

Between 1987 and 1996, 696 police officers were feloniously killed on
duty and another 639 killed in duty-related accidents, for a total of 1,335. In
addition, 565,400 officers were assaulted over the same 10-year period (FBI,
1997a). In 1996 the 55 officers feloniously killed and 45 accidentally killed
were the lowest in over 20 years (Federal Bureau of Investigation 1997a). In
1997, however, the numbers rose to 64 felonious police deaths and 60 accidental deaths (FBI 1998). The data in Figure 13.1 cover two decades of felonious police killings and show that a significant drop occurred between the first

decade (1978–1987), when 854 officers were killed, and the second decade (1988–1997), when 686 officers were killed.

Figure 13.2 depicts the various circumstances at the scene of the incident at which police officers were feloniously killed or assaulted. For officers killed, the primary circumstance was an arrest situation (e.g., during robberies or burglaries or pursuing suspects, drug-related matters, and other arrests); the second leading circumstance involved investigating suspicious persons or circumstances; the third circumstance was answering disturbance calls (e.g., bar fights, man with gun, family quarrels). The fourth circumstance involved traffic pursuits and stops.

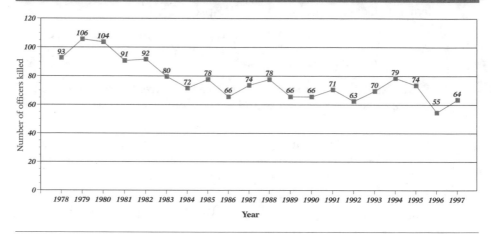

Source: Federal Bureau of Investigation. 1998. "Law Enforcement Line-of-Duty Deaths and Assaults." *Law Enforcement Bulletin*, September: 5; Federal Bureau of Investigation. 1997. *Law Enforcement Officers Killed and Assaulted, 1996*. Washington, D.C.: U.S. Department of Justice, p. 17; Federal Bureau of Investigation. 1988. *Law Enforcement Officers Killed and Assaulted, 1987*. Washington, D.C.: U.S. Department of Justice, p. 29.

For officers assaulted, the leading circumstance was responding to disturbance calls; followed by attempting arrests; the handling, transporting, or maintaining custody of prisoners; investigating suspicious persons or circumstances; and traffic pursuits or stops. The remainder of the assaults took place while various other duties were being performed.

With respect to assault, in 1996 the rate of 12.5 per 100 law enforcement officers dropped 7 percent below the 1995 rate of 13.5, and was 26 percent lower than the 1987 rate of 16.8 (FBI 1997a). The number of assaults that resulted in personal injury was four per 100 officers, which was lower than any other year since 1987. Geographically, the southern states had the highest assault rate at 14 per 100 officers, followed by midwestern and western states with 12 per 100, and the northeastern states with 11 per 100. By population grouping, assault rates ranged from 19 per 100 officers in cities of 100,000 to 249,000 inhabitants to 6 assaults per 100 officers in rural counties. Clearly, there is a significant difference in assault rates depending on what part of the country and on what size city or county department the officer works.

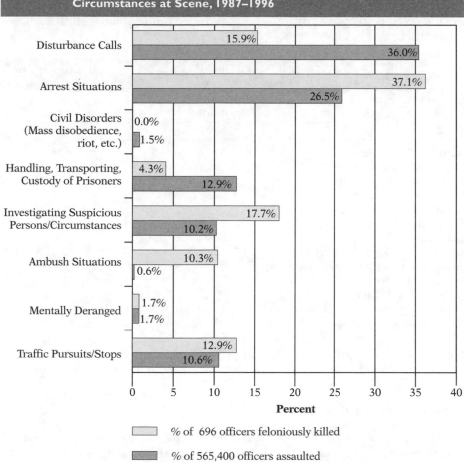

Figure 13.2 Law Enforcement Officers Killed and Assaulted, Percentage of Circumstances at Scene, 1987–1996

❖ ❖ ❖ ❖

Source: Federal Bureau of Investigation, 1997. *Law Enforcement Officers Killed and Assaulted, 1996*. Washington, D.C.: U.S. Department of Justice. Government Printing Office, p. 28.

The final set of data reviewed involves police officers who are accidentally killed and the circumstances at the scene of the incident. As Table 13.5 indicates, from 1987 through 1996, 639 officers were accidentally killed while on duty. This number represents almost half the total number of officers killed over the ten-year period; that is, 639 of 1,335. In addition, the leading circumstance of the accidental death was automobile accidents, which accounted for slightly over half of all accidental police deaths (329 of 639). The second leading circumstance, accounting for nearly one-fifth of the total (116 of 639) was being struck by vehicles (i.e., the combination of directing traffic, assisting motorists, traffic stops, and roadblocks), followed by aircraft accidents, motorcycle accidents, and accidental shootings (e.g., crossfires, mistaken identities, and firearm mishaps). It is interesting to note that in almost every category the number of accidental deaths declined between 1987 and 1996, sometimes substantially (e.g., automobile accidents from 36 to 28 and being struck by vehicles from 18 to 6). Training or policy changes in these areas probably had an impact. As we will discover in the following section, increased training and improved policies can significantly reduce officer fatalities.

Table 13.5 **Law Enforcement Officers Accidentally Killed, Circumstances at Scene, 1987–1996**			
Circumstances at scene of incident	Total	1987	1996
Total	639	74	45
Automobile accidents	329	36	28
Motorcycle accidents	53	5	4
Aircraft accidents	68	5	0
Struck by vehicles (traffic stops, roadblocks, etc.)	48	7	4
Struck by vehicles (directing traffic, assisting motorists, etc.)	58	11	4
Accidental shootings (crossfires, mistaken identities, firearm mishaps)	29	4	1
Accidental shootings (training sessions)	6	1	1
Accidental shootings (self-inflicted)	1 (1988)	0	0
Other (falls, drownings, etc.)	47	5	5

Source: Adapted from Federal Bureau of Investigation. 1997. *Law Enforcement Officers Killed and Assaulted, 1996*. Washington, D.C.: U.S. Department of Justice.

Danger and Police Work

How dangerous is police work? Danger can be considered from three perspectives: perceived, potential, and actual. **Perceived danger** relates to the individual's or public's belief about danger in police work. It is influenced by a variety of factors, including media coverage, television, movies, books, and the actual and reported experiences of officers. In general, many people, including police officers, believe that police work is a very dangerous job. **Potential danger** relates to those situations that could become dangerous for an officer, for example, a felony car stop or investigating a suspicious circumstance. Potentially dangerous encounters are often characterized by a suspect's behavior that adds to the officer's concern (e.g., threats, shouting, challenges to police authority, name calling, and so on). **Actual danger** involves the actual number and rates of injuries and deaths that result from accidents and attacks from citizens.

Another useful way to analyze danger in police work is to categorize it in terms of how it is precipitated; that is, is it initiated by a person or is it a function of the situation? Few occupations include both the possibility and reality of **person-initiated danger**, that is, an attack by another person. **Situational danger** is a function of a particular problem, for example, a high-speed chase in policing, a taxi driver's risk of a traffic accident, the use of certain equipment, or the height at which a person has to work.

One of the more telling aspects of danger to police is that officers initiate a substantial number of the encounters in which they are injured or killed, and they often know that these situations are potentially dangerous. In one study on officer fatalities, D. N. Konstantin (1984) discovered that, contrary to popular belief, most police are not killed in citizen-initiated contacts. He found that approximately 75 percent of incidents resulting in officer deaths were initiated by the officers themselves. In addition, most officers are killed in the types of situations that they know are the most dangerous; the top three incidents were attempting arrests, situations involving robbery, and general car stops. Other situations, in order of occurrence, were assaults on officers, investigating suspicious persons, car stops of known offenders, responding to domestic disturbances, handling mentally deranged persons, and handling prisoners. Even with this knowledge, officers may fail to follow the training and procedures that would reduce the likelihood of injury or death.

A study of 31 officers feloniously killed in California between 1990 and 1994 discovered that an estimated 80 percent of the deaths were *preventable* and primarily the result of "poor tactics, poor judgment, overconfidence, complacency, and rushing in without a plan." Poor positions, such as not having adequate cover or leaving cover too soon, were a significant factor in 84 percent of the deaths (California Commission on Peace Officers Standards and Training 1996, p. xii).

The general conclusions that can be reached from these studies are important if officer fatalities are to be reduced. First is the simple fact that most fatalities occur in situations that the police *know* are dangerous; second, most of the incidents (approximately three-quarters) that lead to killings are *initiated* by the officers themselves. Such conclusions clearly suggest that the police arc often not prepared to handle these potentially dangerous situations. It appears obvious that more thorough preparation and training in these areas could help officers to make better decisions about whether or not to intervene and, once the decision is made, how to handle the situation from the safest perspective. As Konstantin points out:

Officer making a general car stop, which is one of the top dangerous situations leading to officer fatalities. (Photo: corbisimages.com)

Police training emphasis on the great majority of routine encounters that are citizen-initiated is well-meaning but insufficient. Such emphasis should not come at the expense of training officers to approach carefully situations where they themselves make decisions to intervene. (1984, p. 42)

Despite the studies on California presented above, one does not know whether or not these figures are high or low for the occupation as a whole. In other words, how dangerous is policing compared with other occupations? A study by the California Department of Health Services (McLeod 1990) may provide some perspective. The data looked at the mortality rate of 56 occupations for males between the ages of 16 and 64 and compared it with the normal death rate for all working men. The California Occupational Mortality database considers the causes of death regardless of whether the deaths occurred on or off the job; thus, people in the high-mortality occupations tend to die not only more often on the job but from physical or mental ailments (e.g., hypertension, stroke, cirrhosis, or suicide) that may cause death off the job.

Of the 56 occupations listed, deckhands and tankermen (on ships) had the highest mortality rating of 3.93 (i.e., a deckhand's death rate is 3.93 times the normal rate for all working men). The next highest mortality rates, in rank order, were as follows: (2) structural metal workers (3.17), (3) roofers (2.29), (4) industrial helpers (2.22), (5) foresters (2.19), (6) miners and drillers (2.17), (7) operating engineers (2.17), and (8) construction workers (2.13). Police officers and firefighters were ranked 31st with a 1.07 mortality rating. In a separate study of police mortality (Hill and Clawson 1988), it was found that police officers' average age at death appears to be only slightly lower (by seven months) than that of members of 194 other occupations. Thus, it would appear that police work is only moderately dangerous compared to other occupations.

Improving Safety and Reducing Fatalities

From the research presented, it is clear that more training and new or clearer policies are needed in several key areas of police officer safety. There appears to be a need for continual retraining in safety procedures as well. For instance, arrest situations, traffic stops, investigation of suspicious persons or situations, and disturbance calls all need more attention. Since approximately half of all police killings are accidental, departments should review the circumstances in which they occur and review the level of training and policies they provide in these areas. One study of police killings in drug situations (Sherman, DeRiso, Gaines, Rogan, and Cohn 1989), for instance, advised that rehearsing each drug raid could substantially reduce the danger to police.

The FBI in its in-depth studies of officers killed in the line of duty (1992) and of officers who survived a serious assault (1997b) has also made a number of training and policy recommendations. The researchers found that in a significant number of incidents, officers made tactical errors, such as improperly approaching a vehicle or suspect, or failed to conduct a thorough search of a suspect. Increased training was recommended in those areas as well as in the handling of traffic stops, weapons retention, handcuff use, and waiting for backup. With respect to traffic stops, department regulations should include sections on officer safety, including the proper selection of a safe stop location, dispatcher notification, and wearing of soft body armor. Body armor, or bulletproof vests, has been credited with saving more than 2,000 officer lives since 1980; FBI statistics indicate that about 42 percent of police officers killed with guns since 1980 could have been saved if they had been wearing vests ("Congress Ok's ... Body-Armor Fund" 1998).

Weapons retention is another serious problem, where some 16 percent of officers are murdered with service weapons wrested from them or a fellow officer (Witkin 1998). Part of the solution to this problem may lie in technology; the Colt company is developing a personalized gun that uses radio signals that allow the weapon to recognize and respond to a transponder worn by the officer so that it can be fired only by that officer (Witkin 1998).

In addition, the FBI recommends that citizens should be advised of the proper response when stopped by a marked police unit (i.e., they should remain in the vehicle, keep hands in plain view, and wait for further directions from the officer). Finally, since a large number of officers are killed while off duty (approximately one out of every seven), departments should provide a well-defined policy for off-duty performance (e.g., carrying or not carrying of firearms, how to act when observing an offense, and so on).

Police managers, especially first-line supervisors and mid-level managers (i.e., sergeants and lieutenants), can also contribute to the reduction of the number of injuries and deaths (Roberg and Kuykendall 1997). They must be ever vigilant to make sure that officers follow departmental safety and response guidelines. In addition, all incidents involving the use of force and citizen resistance should be reported and used by a department not only to assess the officer's style and discretion but also as a basis for improving future police responses. Any time a police officer or citizen is injured or killed, the department should undertake an immediate and comprehensive reassessment of all related programs, policies, and personnel. This type of response is necessary because police managers need to reduce the fear level of officers if they hope to modify some of the behavior resulting from irrational fear, including verbal abuse of citizens, over-reliance on the use of force, unnecessary and excessive force, and brutality. Police managers must convince officers that officer safety, next to integrity, is

Research has indicated that officer fatalities can be reduced through increased preparation and training, especially in officer-initiated situations. (Photo: corbisimages.com)

❖ ❖ ❖ ❖ the most important priority in the department (p. 332).

Roberg and Kuykendall further suggest that departments undertake an extensive community-education program to instruct citizens how to behave when interacting with officers; this goes beyond the FBI's recommendation about citizens' behavior in traffic stops. Essentially, citizens need to understand that they must cooperate with the police and follow police orders, and that citizen grievances should not and cannot be resolved "in the streets" but rather, if necessary, "in the courts" or through some other formal mechanism. Unfortunately, some people believe that it is their right to challenge police authority at the very moment that authority is being exercised. The police will have problems with such individuals until there is a change in citizen attitudes. Just as the police must modify their behavior in some situations in order to secure public respect and cooperation, citizens must also modify their behavior in order to reduce officers' fear.

Summary

Stress and danger confront the police, but there are methods to reduce both. There are two major categories of police stressors: departmental practices and the inherent nature of police work. The first may include authoritarian structure, lack of administrative support, or minimal participation in decision making; the second may include rotating shift work, boredom, danger, public apathy, and exposure to human misery, including death or injury to fellow officers. In addition, some new forms of stress include efforts toward community policing, especially role conflict and role ambiguity, increased levels of violence with which the police must deal, perceived negative news media coverage, fear of airborne and blood-borne diseases, and for some white officers, cultural diversity and political correctness. In addition, the psychological stress caused by frequent or prolonged exposure to crises or trauma can lead to posttraumatic stress disorder, which can have serious adverse affects, including increased levels of brutality.

Police stress can also lead to alcohol and drug abuse, suicide, and various family problems. Social-support systems (e.g., supervisory and family support) can mitigate against work stress and general life stress. There are numerous policies and programs designed to reduce police stress. Finally, although police fatalities have lessened over the past two decades, policing is a potentially dangerous occupation. Most officer fatalities occur in situations that the police know to be dangerous, and they are typically initiated by the officer; one study estimated that about 80 percent of police fatalities could have been prevented. Clearly, more and better training is needed in how to manage dangerous situations. Policy review, management's insistence on adhering to departmental safety and response guidelines, and community education can all play a role in reducing danger to the police.

Discussion Questions

1. Briefly define the concept of stress; differentiate between the two forms of stress that may affect police behavior.

2. Describe the two major categories of police occupational stressors and provide several examples of each.

3. Discuss at least three types of new sources of stress for today's police.

4. What is posttraumatic stress disorder, and how does it apply to the police?

5. Describe the social supports for the study of stress and their implications for policing.

6. How is alcohol abuse by employees being handled in progressive police departments? Compare this approach with how drug abuse by employees is handled. Why is there such a difference?

7. Briefly describe police suicide rates and what is being done about them.

8. Discuss at least three aspects of police stress that influence the quality of family life. What are some programs that attempt to deal with such problems?

9. List at least five major policies or programs that management could use to help control police stress.

10. What appear to be the major concerns with respect to police danger and fatalities? Discuss several ways in which police safety may be improved and fatalities reduced.

References

Ayers, R. M. and Flanagan, G. S. 1992. *Preventing Law Enforcement Stress: The Organization's Role.* Washington, D.C.: Bureau of Justice Assistance.

Alexander, D. A. and Walker, L. G. 1996. "The Perceived Impact of Police Work on Police Officers' Spouses and Families." *Stress Medicine.* 12: 239–246.

Bain, L. J. 1988. "Night Beat." *Psychology Today* June: 10–11.

Brown, J. and Campbell, E. A. 1994. *Stress and Policing.* West Sussex: Wiley and Sons, Ltd.

California Commission on Peace Officers Standards and Training (POST). 1996.*California Law Enforcement Officers Killed and Assaulted in the Line of Duty, 1990–1994* Report. Sacramento, CA.: California Commission on Peace Officers' Standards and Training.

"Congress OK's $75M Body-Armor Fund." 1998. *Law Enforcement Journal*, May 15: 1.

Crank, J. P. and Caldero, M. 1991. "The Production of Occupational Stress in Medium-Sized Police Agencies: A Survey of Line Officers in Eight Municipal Departments." *Journal of Criminal Justice* 19: 339–349.

Cronin, T. J. 1982. *Police Suicides: A Comprehensive Study of the Chicago Police Department."* Master's Thesis, Lewis University.

Cullen, F. T., Lemming, T., Link, B. G., and Wozniak, J. F. 1985. "The Impact of Social Supports on Police Stress." *Criminology* 23: 503–522.

Dash, J. and Reiser, M. "Suicide Among Police in Urban Law Enforcement Agencies." *Journal of Police Science and Administration* 6: 18–21.

Davidson, M. J. and Veno, A. 1978. "Police Stress: A Multicultural, Interdisciplinary Review and Perspective, Part I." *Abstracts on Police Science*, July/August: 190–191.

Dishlacoff, L. 1976. "The Drinking Cop." *Police Chief* 43: 34–36, 39.

"Drug Use by Cops Seen as Growing Problem." 1985. *Law Enforcement News*, September 1, 12.

Eisenberg, T. 1975. "Job Stress and the Police Officer: Identifying Stress Reduction Techniques," In W. H. Kroes and J. J. Hurrell, Jr. (eds.), *Job Stress and the Police Officer: Identifying Stress Reduction Techniques*, pp. 26–34. Washington, D.C.: Department of Health, Education, and Welfare.

Farmer, R. E. 1990. "Clinical and Managerial Implications of Stress Research on the Police." *Journal of Police Science and Administration* 17: 205–218.

Farrell, D. 1989. "S. F. Cops' Toughest Duty." *San Francisco Chronicle*, May 5: 1A, 7A.

Federal Bureau of Investigation. 1988. *Law Enforcement Officers Killed and Assaulted, 1987*. Washington, D.C.: Department of Justice.

——. 1992. *Killed in the Line of Duty: A Study of Selected Felonious Killings of Law Enforcement Officers*. Washington, D.C.: Department of Justice.

——. 1997a. *In the Line of Fire: A Study of Selected Felonious Assaults on Law Enforcement Officers*. Washington, D.C.: Department of Justice.

——. 1997b. *Law Enforcement Officers Killed and Assaulted, 1996*. Washington, D.C.: Department of Justice.

——. 1998. "Law Enforcement Line-of-Duty Deaths and Assaults." *Law Enforcement Bulletin*, September: 5.

Finn, P. and Tomz, J. E. 1997. *Developing a Law Enforcement Stress Program for Officers and Their Families*. Washington, D.C.: National Institute of Justice.

French, J. R. P. 1975. "A Comparative Look at Stress and Strain in Policemen." In W. H. Kroes and J. J. Hurrell (eds.), *Job Stress and the Police Officer*, pp. 60–72. Washington, D.C.: Department of Health, Education, and Welfare.

Friedell, L. A. and Pate, A. M. 1997. "Death on Patrol: Killings of American Law Enforcement Officers." In G. G. Dunham and G. P. Alpert (eds.), *Critical Issues in Policing: Contemporary Readings*. 3d. ed., pp. 580–608. Prospect Heights, IL: Waveland Press.

Friedman, P. 1968. "Suicide Among Police: A Study of 93 Suicides Among New York City Policemen 1934–40." In E. S. Shneidman (ed.), *Essays of Self Destruction*. New York: Science House.

Gaska, C. W. 1982. "The Rate of Suicide, Potential for Suicide, and Recommendations for Prevention Among Retired Police Officers." Ph.D. dissertation, Wayne State University.

Goolkasian, G. A., Geddes, R. W., and DeJong, W. 1985. *Coping With Police Stress*. Washington, D.C.: National Institute of Justice.

Greenstone, J. L,.Dunn, J. M., and Leviton, S. C. 1995. "Police Peer Counseling and Crisis Intervention Services Into the 21st Century." *Crisis Intervention and Time-Limited Treatment* 2: 167–187.

Grencik, J. M. 1975. "Toward an Understanding of Stress." In W. H. Kroes and J. J. Hurrell, Jr. (eds.), *Job Stress and the Police Officer: Identifying Stress Reduction Techniques*, pp. 163–181. Washington, D.C.: Department of Health, Education, and Welfare.

Guiney v. Roache 873 F. 2d l557 (lst Cir., 1989).

Guralnick, L. 1963. "Mortality by Occupation and Cause of Death Among Men 20-64 Years of Age." *Vital Statistics Special Reports* 53. Bethesda, MD.: Department of Health, Education, and Welfare.

Harr, R. N. and Morash, M. 1999. "Gender, Race, and Strategies of Coping with Occupational Stress in Policing." *Justice Quarterly* 16: 303–336.

Hart, P. M., Wearing, A. J., and Headey, B. 1995. "Police Stress and Well-being: Integrating Personality, Coping and Daily Work Experience." *Journal of Occupational and Organizational Psychology* 68: 133–156.

Hill. K. Q. and Clawson, M. 1988. "The Health Hazards of 'Street Level' Bureaucracy: Morality Among the Police." *Journal of Police Science and Administration* 16: 243–248.

Hurrell, J. J., Jr. and Kroes W. H. 1975. "Stress Awareness," In W. H. Kroes and J. J. Hurrell, Jr. (eds.), *Job Stress and the Police Officer: Identifying Stress Reduction*

Techniques, pp. 234–246. Washington, D.C.: Department of Health, Education, and Welfare.

Ivanoff, A. 1994. *The New York City Police Suicide Training Project*. New York: Police Foundation.

Josephson, R. L. and Reiser, M. 1990. "Officer Suicide in the Los Angeles Police Department: A Twelve-Year Follow-Up." *Journal of Police Science and Administration* 17: 227–229.

Kellogg, T. and Harrison, M. 1991. "Post-traumatic Stress Plays a Part in Police Brutality." *Law Enforcement News*, April 30: 12, 16.

Kroes, W. H., Margolis, B. L., and Hurell, J. L, Jr. 1974. "Job Stress in Policemen." *Journal of Police Science and Administration* 2: 145–155.

Konstantin, D. N. 1984. "Homicides of American Law Enforcement Officers," 1978–1980. *Justice Quarterly* 1: 29–45.

Kureczka, A. W. 1996. "Critical Incident Stress in Law Enforcement." *FBI Law Enforcement Bulletin* 65: 10–16.

Lambuth, L. 1984. "An Employee Assistance Program That Works." *Police Chief* 51: 36–38.

Lardner, G. Jr. 1998. "Crime at Work Often Unreported." *San Jose Mercury News*, July 7: A3.

Loo, R. 1986. "Suicide Among Police in a Federal Force." *Suicide and Life-Threatening Behavior* 16: 379–388.

Lord, V. B. 1996. "An Impact of Community Policing: Reported Stressors, Social Support, and Strain Among Police Officers in a Changing Police Department." *Journal of Criminal Justice* 24: 503–522.

Martin, C. A., McKean, H. E., and Veltkamp, L. J. 1986. "Post-Traumatic Stress Disorder in Police and Working with Victims: A Pilot Study." *Journal of Police Science and Administration* 14: 98–101.

Malloy, T. E. and Mays, G. L. 1984. "The Police Stress Hypothesis: A Critical Evaluation." *Criminal Justice and Behavior* 11: 197–224.

Maynard, P. E. and Maynard, N. W. 1980. "Preventing Police Stress Through Couples Communication Training." *Police Chief* 47: 30, 31, 66.

McLeod, R. G. 1990. "Who Has California's Deadliest Jobs?" *San Francisco Chronicle*, January 22.

Morash, M. and Harr, R. 1995. "Gender, Workplace Problems, and Stress in Policing." *Justice Quarterly* 12: 113–140.

O'Neill, J. L. and Cushing, M. A. 1991. *The Impact of Shift Work on Police Officers*. Washington, D.C.: Police Executive Research Forum.

Pendleton, M., Stotland, E., Spiers, P., and Kirsch, E. 1989. "Stress and Strain Among Police, Firefighters, and Government Workers: A Comparative Analysis." *Criminal Justice and Behavior* 16: 196–210.

Richard, W. and Fell, R. 1975. "Health Factors in Police Job Stress." In W. W. Kroes and J. J. Hurrell, (eds.), *Job Stress and The Police Officer*, pp. 73–84. Washington, D.C.: U.S. Government Printing Office.

Robinson, H. M., Sigman, M. R., and Wilson, J. R. 1997. "Duty-Related Stressors and PTSD Symptoms in Suburban Police Officers." *Psychological Reports* 81: 835–845.

Roberg, R. R. and Kuykendall, J. 1997. *Police Management*, 2d ed. Los Angeles: Roxbury Publishing Co.

Roberg, R. R., Hayhurst, D. L, and Allen, H. E. 1988. "Job Burnout in Law Enforcement Dispatchers: A Comparative Analysis." *Journal of Criminal Justice* 16: 385–393.

Roberts, M. D. 1975. "Job Stress in Law Enforcement: A Treatment and Prevention Program." In W. H. Kroes and J. J. Hurrell, Jr. (eds.), *Job Stress and the Police Officer: Identifying Stress Reduction Techniques*, pp. 226–233. Washington, D.C.: Department of Health, Education, and Welfare.

Saper, M. 1980. "Police Wives: The Hidden Pressure." *Police Chief* 47: 28–29.

❖ ❖ ❖ ❖   Selye, H. 1974. *Stress Without Distress.* Philadelphia: Lippincott.

Schwartz, J. A. and Schwartz, C. B. 1975. "The Personal Problems of the Police Officer: A Plea for Action." In W. H. Kroes and J. J. Hurrell., Jr. (eds.), *Job Stress and the Police Officer: Identifying Stress Reduction Techniques,* pp. 130–141. Washington, D. C.: Department of Health, Education, and Welfare.

Sherman, L. W., DeRiso, D., Gaines, D., Rogan, D., and Cohn, E. 1989. *Police Murdered in Drug-Related Situations,* 1972–1988. Washington, D.C.: Crime Control Institute.

Storch, J. E. and Panzarella, R. 1996. "Police Stress: State-Trait Anxiety in Relation to Occupational and Personal Stressors." *Journal of Criminal Justice* 24: 99–107.

Stratton, J. G. 1976. "The Law Enforcement Family: Programs for Spouses." *Law Enforcement Bulletin,* March: 16–22.

———. 1978. "Police Stress: An Overview." *Police Chief* 45: 58–62.

Swanson, C., Gaines, L., and Gore, B. 1991. "Abuse of Anabolic Steroids." *FBI Law Enforcement Bulletin,* August: 19–23.

Territo, L. and Vetter, H. J. (eds.) 1981. *Stress and Police Personnel.* Boston: Allyn and Bacon.

Terry, W. C. 1981. "Police Stress: The Empirical Evidence." *Police Science and Administration* 9: 61–75.

———. 1985. "Police Stress as a Professional Self-Image." *Journal of Criminal Justice* 13: 501–512.

Vaughn, J. 1991. "Critical Incidents for Law Enforcement Officers." In J. Reese, J. Horn, and C. Dunning. *Critical Incidents in Policing,* pp. 143–148. Washington, D.C.: U.S. Government Printing Office.

Violanti, J. M. 1995. "The Mystery Within: Understanding Police Suicide." *FBI Law Enforcement Bulletin* 64: 19–23.

———. 1996. "Police Suicide: An Overview." *Police Studies* 19: 77–89.

———. 1997. "Suicide and the Police Role: A Psychosocial Model." *Policing: An International Journal of Police Strategies & Management* 20: 698–715.

Violanti, J. M. and Aron, F. 1995. "Police Stressors: Variations in Perception Among Police Personnel." *Journal of Criminal Justice* 23: 287–294.

Violanti, J. M. and Vena, J. E. 1995. "Epidemiology of Police Suicide." *Research in Progress,* NIMH Grant MH47091–02.

Violanti, J. M., Vena, J. E., and Marshall, J. R. 1986. "Disease Risk and Mortality Among Police Officers." *Journal of Police Science and Administration* 14: 17–23.

Wallace, P. A., Roberg, R. R., and Allen, H. E. 1985. "Job Burnout Among Narcotics Investigators: An Exploratory Study." *Journal of Criminal Justice* 13: 549–559.

Wagner, M. and Brzeczek, R. J. 1983. "Alcoholism and Suicide: A Fatal Connection." *FBI Law Enforcement Bulletin* 52: 8–15.

Wexler, J. G. and Logan, D. D. 1983. "Sources of Stress Among Western Police Officers." *Journal of Police Science and Administration* 11: 436–53.

"What's Killing America's Cops? Mostly Themselves, According to New Study." 1996. *Law Enforcement News,* November 15: 1.

Witkin, G. 1998. "Childproofing Guns." *U.S. News and World Report,* June: 25–26.

For a listing of websites appropriate to the content of this chapter, see "Suggested Websites for Further Study" (p. xv). ✦

The Future of Policing

❖ ❖ ❖ ❖

The Future of Policing

Key Terms	
anti-stalking laws	institutionalized organizations
baby-boomers	iron fist
baby bust	less-than-lethal weaponry
coactive policing	mass private property
cyber-terrorism	melting pot
demography	police militarization
ex-urbs	police paramilitary units (PPU)
geographic positioning system (GPS)	retrenchment
	velvet glove
institutional diffusion	

Prediction of the future is always a perilous task. The soothsayer is inevitably wrong on key points and may be embarrassed if the future gyrates wildly away from the divinations. There is a tremendous amount of variety in the nation's police forces with respect to size, structure, and overall quality; which one will be the trendsetter for the future remains to be seen. Further, the importance played by often uncontrollable environmental influences cannot be overestimated. Something unexpected always occurs to undermine even the most reasonable predictions, reminding us that the future will be reasonable in the same way the past is—in retrospect.

Thoughtful observers have noted that police in the United States are in the midst of profound change. Within police departments, shifts in role, function, technology, and philosophy are important trends. Outside departments, changes in character of those being policed, along with changes in government, the academic world, the criminal world, and technology, may lead to changes even more fundamental and far-reaching than those embodied in the community-policing movement and the movement toward militarization. There are so many things going on affecting the American police that trying to make sense of its "present" is already difficult; delineating its "future" is virtually impossible. Nevertheless, this chapter will try to identify trends in present-day policing that indicate directions the police might take in the future.

Environments That Affect the Police

The central argument of this chapter is that to understand the police, one must look at the environments in which they work and the way those environments affect them. These environments, which themselves are changing, can lead to many different possibilities for the police. What the future holds for policing will say as much about Americans as a people as about the police.

Police departments are **institutionalized organizations**—that is, they are responsible for acting on behalf of the values a society holds dear. Unlike economic organizations (businesses), which prosper through their own technical efficiency, police organizations prosper by successfully enforcing society's sense of right and wrong. To do so, they must look beyond themselves to the groups that make up society. Because they serve society, they must respond to pressures from those groups.

Who are these groups? Police departments have to deal with criminals and provide assistance to citizens. They also must address the concerns of mayors, city councils, organizations like Mothers Against Drunk Driving (MADD), business groups, and police unions. They have to deal with prosecutors and the courts, and they must always be sensitive to changes in the law. They have to deal with hostile relations between different ethnic groups. They have to contend with rebellious youth and youth gangs. They always have to keep an eye on the media, which can support or embarrass the police with printed or televised news. Increasingly, they are linking with the military to conduct drug wars. In short, the police have to deal with human relations of far greater complexity than those affecting businesses. The police have the ethical responsibility to enable all these groups to get along, to help solve their problems, and to use coercion when citizens hurt other citizens.

In addition, the police have to respond to technological changes. Consider the ways technology has changed the police over the past century. Installing a two-way radio in a police car in the first third of the twentieth century profoundly changed the delivery of police service. The linkage of these two technologies (car and radio) with the telephone made it possible for citizens to call the station house and for the station house to dispatch a car. This style of patrol, random preventive patrol, is the dominant style today. It was an unlikely prediction 100 years ago.

These groups of people—whether a national president or a local gang—and the whole inanimate realm of technology may be considered environments that influence the police in various ways. This chapter will consider each of these environments and its effects on the police, nationally and locally.

The first and most inclusive is the demographic environment, that is, the character of the American people. The second is the area of federal legislation and programs. The third is the academic world. Also important are the criminal world and the world of technology. Finally, there are two movements within policing—community policing and militarization.

Demographic Challenges

Demographic changes are the most important dynamic affecting police behavior. **Demography** is the study of vital statistics of groups of people, particularly birth, death, and population changes. This section will look at demographic changes in aging, population diversification, rural areas, and incomes.

Age Changes

Two patterns of age-related changes in the population of the United States are important to the future of policing. The first and most politically powerful is the aging of the baby-boomer population. The second is the increase in the numbers of youth.

A world full of oldsters. The United States is a graying population. Nearly 13 percent of the world's population aged 80 and over lives in the

Figure 14.1 The Elderly Population Boom

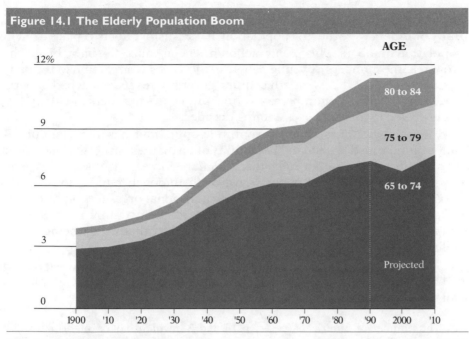

Source: S. Roberts. 1994. *Who We Are: A Portrait of America Based on the Latest U.S. Census.* New York: Random House/Times Books.

United States. Whites live longer than Latinos and African Americans, but much of this difference comes from birth factors: African Americans are three times more likely than whites to die before they are one year old. Once African Americans reach the age of 85, they tend to live longer.

The past century has seen the average life span nearly double, from 41 in 1900 to 75 today. In 1900 those over 65, considered elderly, constituted 4 percent of the population. A century later, they are 10 percent. During the 1980s the over-65 group grew to 20.5 million. By 2030, the over-65 group will mushroom by another 30 million, a tremendous increase (Roberts 1994).

The new elderly pose unique dilemmas for criminal justice. First, among those over 85, three-fourths of the men are still married, but fewer than four of 10 women are. Why? Men die younger than women. This does not mean that the quality of life for surviving women is high. On the contrary, they are one of the populations highly vulnerable to victimization. One in five of those over 85 are institutionalized. As this institutionalized population dramatically increases over the coming decades, there are likely to be sharp increases in white-collar crime in the health-care industry against the elderly.

Second, the elderly, usually dependent on fixed budgets, tend to mobilize in order to vote against tax increases to support social infrastructure. They particularly tend to oppose property tax increases needed to support school budgets. To the extent that education reduces the risk of criminality among the young, one can anticipate increases in juvenile crime to accompany the growing elderly population. It is also likely that the growing numbers of seniors—the most highly mobilized voting population—will resist services that require taxing, including municipal and law enforcement budgets.

The stable youth. The post-World War II period has been characterized as the baby boom, for the large numbers of children born to returning veterans. Yet this population growth has not continued but has instead reversed. **Baby boomers** were the first population in U.S. history not to replace itself in population numbers. This phenomenon has been called the **baby bust**. The growth in the numbers of young people in the 1990s is a reaction to the baby bust; at the end of the twentieth century, growth rates have reached only replacement levels. The numbers of young, unlike the numbers of elderly, are not expected to increase over coming decades.

The demographic stability of youthful populations has important implications for the justice system. The stability of birth rates suggests that (1) over the short term, up to about 2005, there might be increased pressures on juvenile facilities to respond to population growth among juveniles. However, (2) over the longer term there will emerge no additional pressures on resources to keep pace with population growth. This fact, if current trends hold true, will indeed be well received by communities that, other things being equal, will not have to expand services to young people.

The most crime-prone population is widely regarded by criminologists to be between the ages of 18 and 24. By population forecasts, this population will not grow at high rates for many years. Consider:

> The number of Americans between 18 and 24, which has been shrinking since 1980, would continue to decrease until about 1995. But even under the most optimistic projections, it would not exceed the 1980 level for fifty years. (Roberts 1994, p. 254)

Population Diversification

The United States is in the midst of dramatic population transformation. Migration from abroad, large-scale internal migration, and the way in which these migration patterns are distributed across the landscape will profoundly change the face of the U.S. population.

Consider the changing pattern of foreign migration into the country. In the 1980s half as many people emigrated from Europe to the United States as in the 1960s; more than five times as many came from Asia, twice as many from Mexico, the Caribbean and Central America, and nearly four times as many from Africa. Even these groupings mask important regional and local differences. The current census counts 179 ancestry groupings for the Latino category alone (Roberts 1994, p. 73). In the early 1990s, the number of Asians has more than doubled. The long-term implications are clear. By the middle of the twenty-first century, no racial or ethnic group will constitute a majority in the United States (Roberts 1994, p. 246).

Growth and change involve the relocation of many kinds of people. People tend to think of migration in terms of foreign in-migration. Yet this is a proportionally small aspect of overall migration. Blue-collar workers in search of jobs tend to migrate at a much higher rate than their white-collar counterparts. City dwellers in search of a better lifestyle move to the rural hinterland or to the **ex-urbs**, the semirural areas just beyond a city's suburbs. This region is increasingly popular to well-off members of the middle and working classes, who commute to the city to work. Religious groups seek divine meaning though rural settlement. All these are groups on the move. All of them carry the potential for conflicts that the police will have to deal with.

Ethnic diversity and the melting-pot myth. Dynamic changes in ethnic-   ❖ ❖ ❖ ❖
ity will confront Americans in the twenty-first century. Diversity is already remarkable in some areas. In Los Angeles, for example, more than 80 distinct
languages are spoken (Kaplan 1998). These changes may profoundly affect
police services. Consider Asians. In Minnesota alone, for example, a state
seemingly distant from the impact of migration, Asians have tripled their
number from the last census, currently numbering 77,000. Their in-migration creates unique police problems. The prone-out position many officers
use to effect an arrest, for example, is the same position Vietnamese police require when they execute citizens. Vietnamese are sometimes terrified when
"proned-out" and thus are more likely to run from the police (Taft 1991). How
can police deal with public-order problems if they do not share even a common language with the citizens they serve? Language is, after all, the most
fundamental element of culture, from which common ideas of order arise.

As the United States becomes a truly international society, there is a great
demand on police to help us work together, to mediate ethnic frictions and
find common ground. History books sometimes portray U.S. society as a
melting pot, where different kinds of people blend together in harmony. Yet
there is little evidence that Americans "melt together" or that we ever have,
for that matter. On the contrary, some scholars warn that increased contact
among different kinds of peoples contributes to increases in group identity,
particularly group religious identity (Huntington 1996, pp. 67–68).

Religious diversity. Religious changes may be the most far-reaching in
American demographic transformations. The United States is currently
home to 4 million Muslims, five times as many as in 1970. Islam may surpass
Judaism in total population by 2000. Buddhists have experienced a tenfold
increase since 1970. Among Christian faiths, the fastest growing have been
Pentecostal groups, Mormons, and Jehovah's Witnesses. The largest denomi-
nation in the United States is Roman Catholicism with 60 million adherents,
but its expansion is dependent on immigration, especially of Latinos, who
make up 30 percent of this population (Rourke 1998). Indeed most of the
population growth in the next 50 years will come from recent immigrants,
particularly Latinos.

Religious differences are an aspect of cultural differences. Demographic
changes consequently are closely tied to religion. Religion has the capacity to
become the basis of cultural friction across the United States, and cleavages
will increase in number and depth through the twenty-first century. In the
world of tomorrow, police will increasingly take on the responsibility of managing conflicts among religious groups, finding common order among them,
and facilitating their coexistence.

The Transformation of Rural America

One of the more dramatic demographic changes is in the rural environment. In the twentieth century, population was heavily concentrated in metropolitan regions as farm people moved to the cities to find work. This trend
has changed in the last 20 years, as in-migration into cities is balanced and
sometimes overshadowed by out-migration. Growth has dispersed from the
cities to outlying regions. Decentralization has given rise to edge cities, strip
cities, ex-urbs, and rural sprawl. This centrifugal trend is characteristic of

growth at the turn of the twenty-first century. The states recording the fastest growth in rural areas are Nevada, Alaska, and Idaho. As new people arrive, the rural areas tend to lose many of their traditional elements.

The idea of rural communities conjures two related ideas for most people. First, we imagine small towns with a main street, a town square, and farmland or woodland on the outskirts. Second, we think of old-fashioned farm folk, sharing common customs and a common identity, rooted in American traditions. Today, both these images are rapidly disappearing from America's rural landscapes, as they are transformed into ex-urbs inhabited by working commuters, retired people, and others seeking to escape big-city pressures.

R. Weisheit and S. Kernes (1997) identify several changes in rural areas. One is a substantial growth in service industries. Another is that satellite communications has opened rural areas to many occupations that in the past were only practical in the cities. A third is that companies will be drawn to rural areas by the lower crime, lower taxes, lower wages, and more peaceful lifestyle. There are also the "modern cowboys," who include industrial engineers, shopping-center planners, software designers, and others. They can live and work anyplace and are linked by fiber-optic cables and modems (Margolis 1993).

These changes herald new directions in the way rural police do their work. Increasingly, they are developing ways to deal with their new, not-so-rural residents. Drug couriers are using rural areas as principal routs (Weisheit, Falcone, and Wells 1996). Rural police increasingly use citizen surveys to assess the opinions of their constituencies (McGarrell, Benitez, and Gutierrez 1997). Departments are confronting increasing problems with extremist groups (Corcoran 1990). Order problems are expanding, requiring a new breed of rural officer, one trained in problem-solving techniques and skilled in modern technologies. Weisheit and Kernes envision several changes in rural policing to cope with these changes in rural areas:

- The most remote areas will see the rise of live, interactive "video justice" to overcome distance problems. Alaska is already experimenting with live video to conduct court business where the judge and the accused do not have to be in the same site.

- Technology will play an important role in rural crime prevention.

- Improvements in automobiles and highways will be particularly important for rural police.

- There will be dramatic improvements in police communications.

- Technology will play an important role in training rural police.

The following two case studies discuss two dimensions of rural change: the use of community-policing strategies and the expansion of SWAT units. A common thread may be observed in the two offsets: both use multi-jurisdictional efforts to implement their ideas. Multi-jurisdictional efforts and shared intelligence may increasingly characterize the modernization of the rural police.

❖ ❖ ❖ ❖

Case Study 14.1

SWAT in Small-Town America

Rainbow City is a small community of less than 20,000 people, policed by a force of 19 officers. Only two or three cars are fielded per shift. Unlike many small towns, the department had a small tactical team, but the team was equipped only with handguns and shotguns. A Rainbow City detective, Gary Endrekin, was working an overtime patrol shift when Chris McCurley, the head of the Etowah County Drug Task Force, asked Endrekin to be part of a warrants service the following day. McCurley had personally worked up the case on Ezra George Peterson, the suspect and a 50-year-old probationer, and didn't expect any problems.

Officers went to Peterson's house; Detective Endrekin and another officer approached the back while McCurley and others knocked on the front door. They were initially met with silence. When they tried to force entry, they encountered every officer's worst nightmare—a well-armed suspect opening up with an AK-47 assault rifle.

Multi-agency SWAT team members. (Photo: corbisimages.com)

"I was around back with another officer and I heard the door crash in," Endrekin said. "I heard the sound of a high-powered rifle and it sounded like it was fully auto. I ran around to the front and was hit in the legs. Endrekin crawled behind a van on the property, but the suspect seemed specifically to target the wounded detective. He just kept shooting, ricocheting the shots off the ground," said Endrekin.

Without warning, the suspect came out of the house, moving directly toward Endrekin. "He was yelling, 'I'm going to finish you, you son-of-a-bitch'." The experienced detective thought his life was over until his partner, Sergeant Tommy Watts, shot the suspect several times with a shotgun. The suspect went down, but he was not seriously injured because he was wearing body armor.

When the smoke cleared, the suspect had fired more than 200 rounds. Chris McCurley was dead. Gary Entrekin's legs were so badly torn up by the AK-47 rounds that he spent more than two months in the hospital and ultimately had to have one leg amputated. After this tragic incident, Rainbow City purchased H&K MP-5s and Colt AR-15s. The department also provided training with the weapons and upgraded the capabilities of its tactical team.

Should small towns have a SWAT team? Or is a SWAT team an unnecessary move toward militarization, as some critics claim? In Handcock County, Mississippi, Major Matt Karl is the commander of the Special Operations division, a joint-department, special-weapons team. About three years ago, he became concerned that the law enforcement departments in his area did not have the ability to respond properly to a tactical incident. Karl took the initiative to contact managers in two small, adjacent departments, Waveland and Bay St. Louis, and developed a plan for a multi-department tactical team. Three years later, the team consisted of 26 officers, who handled any situation beyond the capabilities of patrol officers. The unit even assisted an adjacent county that did not have a tactical team after a barricaded suspect held the local police at bay for hours.

Source: Adapted from D. Stockton. 1998. "SWAT's Small-Town Question: How Prepared Are You?" *The Law Enforcement Magazine* 22 (4): 20–24.

Delaware State Police Rural Community Policing Unit

The Delaware State Police Rural Community Policing Unit (RCPU) has been in existence since July 1994. By the end of 1995, the unit had completed its first full year of service.

Sussex County, the most rural county in Delaware, has rural communities with high crime rates and few resources to combat them. The purpose of the RCPU, composed of four full-time troopers, is to reduce crime and provide resources to eight targeted communities in the county.

During the first year, the RCPU provided programs in conflict resolution, peer leadership, drug awareness, crime prevention, and neighborhood watch. One hundred and two youths from the targeted communities were sent to Camp Barnes through a grant awarded by the Criminal Justice Council. The unit also found five youths jobs in local businesses and tutored over 50 youths.

In the area of crime, calls for service were down approximately 10 percent. Other notable accomplishments were as follows:

- A drug house was demolished.

- Over 75 wanted persons were apprehended.

- Over 150 criminal arrests were made.

- A local tavern was closed until it met the needs of the community.

- The unit worked with outside agencies to improve homes, streets, and water systems.

- The unit obtained a computerized information system to locate available health resources and employment information.

- Over 100 bicycle helmets were given to youth.

- Fifty infant/child car seats were given to parents.

- The unit conducted operations with local fire departments to discourage drug dealing on weekends.

- The unit joined with local physicians to provide free physicals for youths selected to attend Camp Barnes.

Source: Adapted from D. J. Citro. 1996. "Delaware State Police Rural Community Policing Unit." Internet Site: State Police Home Page Address www.state.de.us/govern/agencies/pubsafe.rural.htm.

Income Inequality and Police Privatization

Another aspect of demographic change is the increasing disparity between the rich and the poor at the dawn of the twenty-first century. The accumulation of wealth is a cultural goal for most Americans. It seems to be bred in the bone of American entrepreneurship, a core value of our culture. However, the growth of the truly rich is occurring against a backdrop of widening poverty. Simply put, the rich are getting richer and the poor poorer, a potentially explosive situation. As a nation, this uneven pattern of income distribution may shift us into two kinds of policing, one public, underfunded and aimed at the control of the poor and so-called dangerous classes, the other private, well funded, and at the beck and call of the rich.

Americans are accustomed to thinking about the police as a public agency. Their public responsibilities, to represent the government and enforce the law, are central to the way most citizens believe the police should behave in a democratic setting. The public role played by the police today, however, may be shrinking. Such is the reasoning of an insightful paper by D. H. Bayley and C. D. Shearing (1998), who argue that we may be entering an age of privatization of police services.

Bayley and Shearing argue that we and other Western democracies are at a watershed in policing. Two changes will mark the future: privatization trends and the search by public police for an appropriate role. Over the past 30 years, the traditional monopoly of the state over police services has diminished. Today in the United States there are three times more private security agents than public police officers.

The trend toward private security is likely to continue, for several reasons. First, the police by themselves can do little about crime. Their behavior is constrained by due process in a democracy, as well as by social and economic variables outside their control. Yet the public fear of crime is not likely to decline and may increase.

> Individualistic democracies are caught between a rock and a hard place with respect to crime control. On the one hand, they are limited by their political values from authoritarian controls, and on other, they are limited by their cultural values from the discipline of less informal social control. (Bayley and Shearing 1998, p. 163)

In other words, the ability of a public police to satisfy public concerns over fear of crime is profoundly limited and unlikely to improve. Private security will begin to fill the gap between public capacity to control crime and public police performance.

Second is a change in the way in which we use physical space. The latter half of the twentieth century witnessed what Bayley and Shearing call the rise of **mass private property**—facilities that are privately owned but used by the public. These include shopping malls, college and school campuses, residential communities, high-rise condominiums, banks, commercial facilities, and recreational complexes. To that list could be added the increasing popularity of gated communities separated from their surrounding areas by tall walls and gates staffed by security guards. Private security specialists are the most likely form of policing for these kinds of facilities. Market-based private security will follow a market-based private economy. The outcome will be policing stratified by class and race.

> Western democratic societies are moving inexorably, we fear, into a Clockwork Orange world where both the market and the government protect the affluent from the poor—the one by barricading and excluding, the other by repressing and imprisoning—and where civil society for the poor disappears in the face of criminal victimization and governmental repression. (Bayley and Shearing 1998, p. 164)

This vision of the future raises important questions. Can we avoid a system where public crime control is acted out primarily against the poor? Bayley and Shearing contend that we can, but only if we make two conscious policy choices. First, poor people need to participate in the market for security. Society should provide poorer communities with the ability to fund their own security. Such funding can only happen with the financial assistance of the federal government, interceding to prevent the continued split of American society into two camps, one well off and mostly Anglo, the other poor and mostly everyone else.

Second, community policing has to become the organizing principle of public policing.

> Since safety is fundamental to the quality of life, co-production between the police and the public legitimates government, lessening the corrosive alienation that disorganizes communities and triggers collective violence. (Bayley and Shearing 1998, p. 165)

Community policing is the only police strategy that incorporates the problems encountered by the poor into decision making by the police. If society does not make a conscious effort to implement community policing and reinforce federal investment in local communities, it is possible that the character of policing could shift to private enterprise for the rich and public, social control for the poor.

Federal Influences

A second major environment influencing the police is the federal government. Washington has played a large role in the development of municipal policing initiatives. Community policing, dedicated to local neighborhoods, exists at least to some extent because of federal support. For example, the National Institute of Justice provides grants to local departments that undertake community policing programs. In short, community policing may not continue without federal support.

Federal Grant Initiatives

The expansion of local policing initiatives has been in response to federal as well as local efforts. The Department of Justice has spent approximately $3 billion annually in the late 1990s to "assist state and local law enforcement and communities in preventing crime" (Sherman et al. 1997). This large federal investment reflects the extent to which street crime has become a national issue. Its influence has both substantive and symbolic implications. Substantively, the impact is limited, frequently amounting to small though sometimes important contributions to individual departments. Symbolically, the impact is large, displaying the federal government's willingness to contribute to local policing, if local police conform to federal expectations.

One area of federal investment at the local level is the COPS program. Under the 1994 Federal Crime Control bill, the President authorized the hiring of 100,000 street cops. Funds for them are being released in successive grant solicitations aimed at the reduction of crime through community policing. They are a financial windfall for local departments.

An example of a solicitation is a specially targeted program aimed at high-crime neighborhoods in 18 cities selected on the basis of high rates of crime and of poverty. In 1998 President Clinton provided funding for 700 officers in these cities. The police can use the funds to attack special problems, such as drugs or gangs, within a particular neighborhood.

The future of federal involvement in local street crime is promising because local communities increasingly lack the will and economic infrastructure to deal with their problems of crime and public order. The form federal investment will take, however, is difficult to forecast. In the 1990s the federal investment focused on fear of crime, problem-oriented policing, community policing, place-based crimes, and drugs and youth gangs. A different political regime in Washington could dramatically change the programs available for grants. Will Americans continue to believe in the strength of our working poor and invest in local areas or will we abandon them, focusing our resources on arrest and prosecution? Might we invest in a dramatically enhanced capacity to keep watch on local areas? Or could we provide tax dollars to local areas to assist in self-help policing efforts, such as the use of vigilante groups and private police? What is known is that whatever legislature and president we elect will affect on local police.

Departmental Diversity and Affirmative Action

Chapter 12 noted the gains made by women and minorities from the late 1980s. Some observers fear that police departments will retreat from affirmative action and equal employment opportunities. Consider the following observation:

> The movement of women into management and command positions in police organizations seems to be diminishing. Consider Pittsburgh PA. There are 1,100 police officers in the department, and 28% are women, the highest percentage in the United States. Six women hold command positions. However, many in the department fear a "backslide." A court order mandating balanced presentation of women and minorities in the department expired in 1991, and women and minority hiring has subsequently slowed. And, in a lawsuit recently settled, eight white men sued the department for reverse discrimination and won their cases. (Janofski 1998)

Hiring women to work as police officers has been an important personnel consideration for the past 30 years, as D. Hale and S. M. Wyland (1999) observed. Yet, women continue to meet "astonishing" resistance from their male counterparts in the department. Many researchers have observed that continued resistance to women in policing, and particularly in patrol work, is strong (Jones 1986; Martin 1989). Hale and Wyland noted:

> The major problem for police departments is not recruiting women—the problem is retention, because many police departments are locked in a "time warp" that perpetuates the myth that only men can do patrol.... Men still perceive police work is a man's domain where women will only get in the way, cannot be depended on for backup, or may get hurt. (Hale and Wyland 1999, p. 454)

A countervailing force to these trends is the dramatic ethnic diversification of the American population and the demands it will place on local policing. The ethnic complexity of many regions can be handled by officers with sophisticated cultural understandings and linguistic skills. In cities with large minority populations, the hegemony of the white male police officer appears to be ending. Thus, although the law may be retreating from equal opportunity, social forces push departments in the direction of diversity.

Academic Influences

A third environment influencing the police is the academic world. One of the surprising developments of the late twentieth century was the dramatic increase in linkages between universities and the police. Historically, universities and police departments held each other at arm's length out of a sense of mutual distrust. By the end of the century, this pattern had begun to reverse itself. Increasingly, universities are contributing to local departments in three vital ways: in education, in research collaboration, and in socializing students to justice perspectives.

Education

The growth of criminal justice education over the past 30 years can only be described as phenomenal. In 1966 there were 39 college and university programs offering bachelor's degrees in criminal justice and law enforcement; 14 offered master's degrees (Sherman 1986). Today, there are more than 1,000 programs offering bachelor's degrees. By recent estimates, 114 programs offer master's degrees and 24 offer doctoral programs. There are estimated to be 1,200 graduate faculty (Academy of Criminal Justice Sciences 1998).

These programs are popular among students and administrators alike, and they are excellent revenue producers for universities. It is likely that programs in criminal justice will continue to grow. Growth will be primarily at the postgraduate level simply because they are approaching the limits of attainable growth at the undergraduate level.

Research Collaboration

The last 30 years have witnessed an accelerated collaboration between the police and the universities, to the benefit of both. The police use the expertise and the research capabilities that universities have to offer, while universities increase their understanding of the police and further enhance their research and policy making. Increasingly, universities are providing training for police and community leaders, offering research and consultation and encouraging collaboration between faculty and local police departments. As federal and state grants over the past decade have increased, the link between universities and local police will probably continue to grow. Police work of the future may be carried on by "Doctor" cops, police with Ph.D.s, committed to community wellness.

Socialization

Many observers of the police have overlooked the extent to which universities have become agents of socialization of the police. University-based criminal justice programs increasingly prepare students for jobs in police departments. J. P. Crank observed that

> Criminal justice programs link students to the culture of policing in a variety of ways.... Guest lecturers expose students to various aspects of local agency life. Internship programs place students in local agencies for a certain number of hours each week for at least one semester, giving students a more practical look at work they will likely be doing when they graduate. After graduation, many students are able to convert their internships to full-time positions.

Part-time faculty are drawn from local agencies and provide in their discussions practical knowledge of the craft of their work.... Department chairs hire these individuals to cultivate and maintain preferred relationships to local agencies. (1998, p. 194–195)

There are several long-term implications of the dramatic growth in the relationships between higher education and local police:

1. The police force of the United States will increasingly be an educated one. Educated officers have employability advantages over their less-educated brethren. They are more comfortable in the increasingly high-tech world of policing. They are more comfortable with the complex accountability requirements in police departments. And, as noted in Chapter 11, they are more effective in dealing with the complex social interactions required in day-to-day work. Moreover, chiefs like to hire educated officers. The day is rapidly approaching when all police in major departments, and most in smaller ones, will have four-year degrees.

2. Criminal justice programs are becoming more politically neutral. Historically, they have tended to be either liberal, housed in sociology or similar types of departments, or conservative, having grown out of two-year programs staffed primarily by former police officers. But in their quest to achieve legitimacy in both the academic and criminal justice environments, department leadership has moved toward the ideological center. This pattern is likely to continue.

3. Criminal justice programs are increasingly accepted as members of their local and regional criminal justice communities. Police departments no longer distrust faculty, and faculty no longer focus on academic criteria of success to the exclusion of contact with local police. Academic research is increasingly concerned with practical problems confronting police departments. University administrators seek local legitimacy for their programs by fostering connections between faculty and local police. In sum, criminal justice programs are for the first time beginning to influence the way justice is carried out in their local communities, a trend likely to continue.

Crime Trends

The future of policing is also influenced by a fourth environment, the criminal world. Indeed, it is tied to the future of crime. If all the crime were to disappear tomorrow, it is unlikely that policing would retain its current form. So scholars must consider trends in order to see how future policing may be done. This section will survey four kinds of crime: gangs, terrorism, cyber-terrorism, and domestic violence.

Gangs

K. Peak (1996) observed a sharp growth in public fears of youth gangs, fears fed by people's apprehensions of outsiders.

> Today there are many youth gangs, usually organized along ethnic lines and including Asian, Black, Hispanic, and White groups. Members usually join the gang either by committing a crime or undergoing an initiation procedure. Gang members use automatic weapons and sawed-off shotguns in drive-by shootings, while becoming more sophisticated in their criminal activities and more wealthy. Crack cocaine and other illegal enterprises have provided a level of wealth and a lifestyle they would probably otherwise not have attained. The availability of guns, a violence-prone film and entertainment industry, and the inherent violence in today's youth only serve to exacerbate the problem. Fear of the criminal justice system is largely absent in these young people. (Peak 1996, p. 8)

The criminal justice system is at a crossroads in its approach to gangs. Research clearly shows that aggressive arrest and sentencing policies, beyond an initial impact, have little effect on gang participation (Sherman 1990). This finding is not surprising. The gang problem is rooted in the conditions of lower-class life, particularly poverty. It tends to be particularly intense in certain areas where social pathologies—delinquency, mental illness, public assistance, and poverty—are concentrated. These conditions are all getting worse, despite programs aimed at improving them.

Some researchers advocate programs narrowly focused on gang members and youth at risk, particularly focusing on education and employment (Miller 1990). Although there is no consensus on what constitutes effective treatment, there is growing agreement that repressive law enforcement is ineffective. Nevertheless, it appears, at least for the short term, that the criminal justice system will continue to use aggressive enforcement, prosecution, and incarceration as the primary way to deal with gangs. There is little political support for an expansion of programs to promote general public welfare, attack root causes, or provide training and education. These factors, considered in the context of long-term demographic trends, make it highly likely that gangs will continue to increase, and policing measures will continue to be ineffective.

International Terrorism

Anyone who has entered an American airport in the past decade cannot help but take note of the elaborate security measures affecting travelers. A bodiless voice constantly reminds you to watch your luggage. You and your carry-on baggage are searched for the presence of metals and drugs prior to entry into the gated areas. Welcome to a high-security zone. This security stems from concerns over terrorist attacks on airplanes, and it is likely to increase.

Concerns over international terrorism were on the rise at the end of the twentieth century. Congress initiated antiterrorist activities with the passage of the Comprehensive Crime Control Act in 1984 and the Omnibus Diplomatic Security Act of 1986. These two acts established federal jurisdiction over terrorist crimes involving Americans when they occurred outside of U.S. territories, and the FBI has taken the lead in antiterrorist activities. It coordinates its activities with international organizations and also works closely with various other state and federal agencies. It provides local police with specialized antiterrorist training (Flynn 1996).

E. E. Flynn has discussed the future of terrorism in the United States and argues that we can expect to see it continue and perhaps increase in frequency and intensity. Should this happen, she believes that the web of civil liberties that characterize U.S. democracy will weaken.

> Looking at the experiences of democratic nations dealing with systematic terrorist assault, one finds not only an expected reduction in the quality of life, but also a disturbing tendency to encroach on the civil liberties of their citizens. Great Britain, for example, is one of the oldest and most stable democracies in the world. Yet, in its struggle with sectarianism and periodic armed insurrection in Northern Ireland, it has instituted at various times such basically undemocratic procedures as internment [and] interrogation-in-depth, as well as search-and-seizure without warrants, censorship, trials without juries, and the admission of hearsay evidence. (Flynn 1996, p. 31)

Internal Terrorism

Terrorism has arrived in the United States with a vengeance. A series of high-profile cases, including the Ruby Ridge incident, the Freemen in Montana, and the bombing of the FBI building in Oklahoma City have revealed the growth of a violent right-wing militancy. Paramilitary groups are not concentrated in any particular region but are widespread across the United States and appear to be expanding.

Terrorism may be directly aimed at police. The best-known case is the Oklahoma City bombing in April 19, 1995, which resulted in the deaths of 168. It was an act of revenge in the retaliation for a highly controversial assault by FBI agents on a religious cult led by David Koresh in Waco, Texas, the year before.

Smaller but more troubling are two cases separated by large distances but similar in implications for antiterrorist efforts. In the first, a security guard was killed and a nurse was severely injured in a bombing of a Birmingham, Alabama, family counseling and abortion clinic on January 29, 1998. The security guard was an off-duty police officer. This was the first recorded death of a police officer from a bombing of an abortion clinic. Both the FBI and the ATF have established a task force to investigate the crime and have issued a warrant for Eric Rudolph. He is associated with a terrorist organization called the Army of God. The search has grown cold, even though there is a $1 million reward on his head (Serrano 1998).

The second case was an incident in 1998 in which a Cortez, Colorado, police officer was shot through the windshield of his truck after stopping what he thought was a stolen truck. Two additional officers were wounded in a subsequent chase. A fourth officer was seriously wounded the following day. Police found three pipe bombs in one of the suspect's camper trailer and two in another suspect's truck. A massive manhunt, involving more than 200 police officers, was carried out. One of the suspects was found shot, with pipe bombs tied to his body. The three suspects were described by the police as trained survivalists.

Troubling about all three cases is that they were carried out against police officers. What is particularly disturbing about the latter two are indications that there may be a terrorist underground in the United States that provides its agents with safe houses. Such a prospect is chilling because it suggests

The threat of biological terrorist attack is of increasing concern. (Photo: United States Department of Defense, April, 1999)

that a growing number of terrorist groups may be interlinked in carrying out deadly antipolice activities.

Other, less-known cases further reveal the potential problem of terrorist antipolice activity. Timothy Thomas Coombs is a member of a right-wing paramilitary group who allegedly shot a state highway patrol officer with a high-powered rifle. The officer had been eating ice cream in his kitchen. No trace of Coombs has been found.

There is wide concern that the United States is inadequately prepared for terrorist activities. By some estimates, the underground network protecting domestic terrorists is growing "exponentially" (Serrano 1998). FBI director Louis Freed observed that the lack of preparedness in U.S. cities and towns is "the greatest vulnerability we have right now" (Quaid 1998). The terrorist events described may be randomly connected. Yet, their importance lies in their symbolic effects which of course is the purpose of terrorist activity. Yet, international research suggests that terrorist efforts inevitably result in an expansion of the state security apparatus (Homer-Dixon 1994).

It is likely that, in the near future, Congress will put forth a counter-terrorism plan. Currently, 43 separate federal agencies share responsibility for anti-terrorist activities, though the FBI carries most of the effort. Further expansion of terrorist activities is likely to result in increased specialized training of local police as well as specialization within the FBI. Another likely response at the local level is an increased emphasis on SWAT teams or **police paramilitary units (PPUs)**.

Cyber-terrorism

Computers are increasingly involved in making command decisions in the American business, military, and social infrastructure. Indeed, they have become so pervasive that it is difficult to think of an area of modern American life that is not computerized. And, as their influence grows, so does their vulnerability to **cyber-terrorism**, or sabotage by hackers. How widespread is such sabotage? It is difficult to measure the extent of it. When malevolent hacking is successful, no one knows that a crime has occurred. However, a recent survey by the Computer Security Institute (a San Francisco-based trade organization) found that more than 64 percent of the companies it polled reported security breaches in the previous year (Mullins 1998a).

Cyber-terrorism is difficult to combat because the level of skill needed to penetrate computer networks is not great. The available software is so sophisticated that it can provide most of the necessary work to enter a network system. It is not much more, comments one FBI agent, than selecting a target, pointing, and clicking.

In February 1998, Attorney General Janet Reno created the National Infrastructure Protection Center (NIPC), an anticyber-terrorism unit inside the FBI. The nation's first top cyber-cop, Michael Vadis, was appointed director of the unit. His goal has been to bring together leaders from both the public and the private sector in efforts to assess and respond to terrorist attacks. The task, he recently observed, is difficult. Large businesses do not want to publicize attempted break-ins to their computers. The day the unit opened, two teenagers were charged with hacking into computers in the Pentagon and 11 military installations. "If we are vulnerable to attacks committed by 15-year-olds, imagine the vulnerability to more concerted efforts by foreign militaries, by foreign intelligence services, and from organized crime" (Mullins 1998b).

Some critics object to the NIPC because they think it represents government's effort to control access to the Internet. To date, no known significant terrorist act has been committed against the Internet. Yet the Internet, designed to withstand nuclear attack, may be technologically uncontrollable. The future of cyber-terrorism is a complete unknown.

Domestic Violence

Domestic violence has historically been a low-priority concern for the police. As discussed in Chapter 7, however, since the Minneapolis domestic violence experiment (Sherman and Berk 1984), this situation has changed. Police officers are increasingly undergoing training for intervention, and police increasingly use arrest as the preferred response (even though research findings on preventive effectiveness of arrest are mixed). All indications are that state and federal legislatures are advancing the cause of arrest and punishment in incidents of domestic violence. The federal government and many states have passed **anti-stalking laws** to protect spouses from abusive partners. In California, the infliction of injury on a spouse is a felony punishable by up to four years in prison.

Technological advances are also in effect in domestic-violence cases. In some places, women who are potential victims have had silent alarms installed in their homes. Some of these alarms are triggered by pushing a button on a necklace (Meadows 1996).

Technology

A fifth chief environment affecting the police is technology. Technological changes have had a far-reaching impact on police. This section examines some state-of-the-art technologies and describes their implications for police work.

Automobile Technologies and Police Effectiveness

Automobiles are increasingly becoming computerized and therefore functionally independent of command and dispatch orders from headquarters. A recently designed computer program called COPLINK uses Windows-type software to enter data, search for more information, obtain a mug shot, and find out if a person is suspected of criminal or gang activity. It is capable of using the **geographic positioning system (GPS)** to reconstruct crime scenes to within a few millimeters of their true location, and it can transmit information at 20 to 40 times the speed of a high-powered home computer unit. It is a wearable crime lab as well: It is designed to be strapped onto an officer's back. It uses a digital camera, laser rangefinder, and voice recorder (Martinez 1998).

The potential of COPLINK is astonishing. When one realizes that the FBI has made available to local police about 60 million or more records by 1995 estimates, one begins to recognize the capacity for routine information checking and surveillance. In the not-distant-future, police will have at their virtual fingertips fingerprint, retinal scan, mug, social security number (SSN), and DNA information on most citizens in the United States, including active files on criminals and suspects. And, it all can be carried in a single automobile. Crime scenes will be scanned by imaging techniques to test for DNA residue, and findings will be compared to SSN records to identify suspects. Police work on ordinary crimes might become effective in a way never imagined—robberies and burglaries could be routinely solved. The automobile, tied into urban camera systems and satellite tracking systems, will be a complete office, information-gathering systems, and surveillance unit. Central headquarters, for purposes other than tradition and social activities, may become obsolete.

Less-Than-Lethal Weapons

The development of a broad technology of **less-than-lethal weaponry** increases the ability of the police to resolve violent encounters without the use of deadly force. Bean bags and pepper sprays have been introduced as potentially nonlethal solutions to encounters that traditionally called for deadly force.

This weaponry also has a dark side: the potential for use as an instrument of torture in encounters that do not require deadly force. TASER weapons were reportedly used in the Rodney King incident to inflict pain on an incapacitated suspect. Police officers dabbed capstan coated Q-tips into the eyes of chained and immobilized nonviolent environmental protesters in California.

A variety of new less-than-lethal technologies are being tested and implemented. Auto-Arrestor™ systems are emerging in high-speed pursuit incidents. The Auto-Arrestor™ system uses electronic pulses to disrupt a fleeing automobile's electronic system and safely stop it. The Sticky Shocker™, a nonlethal compliance weapon, works by shooting a blunt projectile that sticks to the clothing with glue and imparts a short burst of high-voltage pulses (Jaycor 1998).

Such less-than-lethal technologies have demonstrably reduced the incidence of deadly force. In the future, the use of deadly force might drop precipitously as such technologies are further developed. The reason is that in encounters with dangerous suspects, handguns and shotguns are inefficient. They often do not stop suspects, and they carry the potential for striking innocent bystanders. Most suspects survive shooting incidents, which is good from a humanitarian point of view. But many survive and shoot officers, which is bad from any point of view. New less-than-lethal technologies may have the capacity to provide for greater officer safety than current lethal weapons.

Information-Retrieval Systems

Information-retrieval systems are among the fastest-growing technologies used by the police. Automated fingerprint identification systems are transforming the art of fingerprint identification into a science. Even 20 years ago, fingerprint analysis was a frustratingly slow technique; FBI records had millions of fingerprints, but there was no way to sort and compare them except by hand. With high-speed computer cataloguing techniques, fingerprint identification has emerged as a useful technique for suspect identification. Consider these advances in the technology:

> The NCIC-2000 system will enable law enforcement officers to rapidly identify missing persons and fugitives by placing a subject's finger on the fingerprint reader which will be located in patrol cars of the future. The fingerprint reader will then instantly transmit the image to the NCIC 2000 computer at FBI headquarters and, within a few minutes, the computer will relay a reply to the police officer. Futuristic printers installed in patrol cars will permit officers to quickly obtain copies of a suspect's photograph, signature or tattoos, as well as composite drawings of unknown suspects. (Muraskin and Roberts 1997, p. 4)

Online access to criminal history and juvenile records is speeding up suspect identification and background checks. It is possible to acquire the criminal histories of almost everyone for police and citizens alike. Counties will increasingly link to one another to create integrated regional information systems. These systems will be cost-effective because information retrieval can occur through an authorized computer operator (Muraskin and Roberts 1997).

Public Video Cameras and Passive Surveillance

Video cameras unobtrusively mounted to observe public settings are increasingly used to monitor the population. These systems, already widely used in Great Britain, are called (*technologically assisted physical surveillance*). The cameras are intended to aid in the detection, investigation, and prevention of crime. There are concerns about the potential for abuse as well.

❖ ❖ ❖ ❖

Less-than-lethal include pepper spray; here a recruit is sprayed in order that he will understand the effects caused by the spray. (Photo: Mark C. Ide)

For example, how would a citizen feel about having a video camera in front of a bar where fights break out regularly? How would a citizen feel about having a video camera pointed at his or her house? Who should decide?

This technology is current and operational. Baltimore had mounted cameras in 16 downtown locations by the late 1990s. If crimes are not reported, the tapes are disposed of every four days. The cameras are mounted on poles, with signs identifying their purpose. Local officials credit the system for a sharp drop in downtown crime (Carelli 1998).

To what extent are these systems an invasion of personal privacy? One answer is clear. In the twenty-first century, the idea of privacy may be fondly remembered as a part of the lost past, savored like memories of a favorite song.

GPS and Traffic Ticket via Satellite

One of the far-reaching surveillance technologies is embodied in the global positioning system. Through a system of 24 tracking satellites belonging to the Department of Justice, GPS can currently locate individuals within millimeters of their true location. GPS is used today to establish longitude and latitude by surveyors, hikers, the U.S. Coast Guard, and a host of other organizations. It can be used to locate company vehicles and to find one's way through busy urban streets.

GPS holds a great deal of potential for the police as well. The day may be coming when traffic patrol is outdated. Individuals may be caught speeding on routine satellite surveillance and receive their tickets in the mail. Citizens might not even have a police officer on whom to vent their frustration at being caught! GPS also may be used to watch suspects without physically assigning an officer to the task. For both detectives and for patrol, GPS holds the potential to increase workload dramatically without increasing person-hours (Colombo 1997).

Wiretaps

Wiretaps are a preferred tool of the police for surveillance in drug situations. In 1997, 1,186 wiretaps were granted by federal and state judges, permitting agents to listen to more than 2 million conversations, a 3 percent increase over the previous year. Most of the requests, about 73 percent, were for narcotics investigations. Wiretaps were evenly split between federal and local authorities, with federal judges authorizing 569 wiretaps and state judges granting 617 ("Record Total of Wiretaps ... " 1998). This area of surveillance technology thus continues to expand. Because the Internet operates through the telephone lines, expansion of the Internet will be matched by growth in wiretap technology. Further, because of increasing concerns over internal and international terrorism, the use of wiretaps will probably continue to grow.

Trends in Community Policing

A sixth environment affecting the police is inside the police world, namely the community-policing movement. The community policing movement emcompasses a bold set of changes that will continue to have a far-reaching effect on most major police departments in the United States. Yet, it is changing. Not all observers are convinced that the future of policing is community based. Crank (1995), for example, describes a future in which community policing has lost its popularity and a neoprofessionalism movement is underway. In this section we will look at some trends that might affect the community policing movement. Some social forces are favorable to it, and some are not.

Favorable Forces

First among the social forces favorable to the expansion of community policing is its popularity with citizens. Departments with police-community problems will increasingly look to community policing to resolve those problems. Many researchers have cited the popularity of having police officers

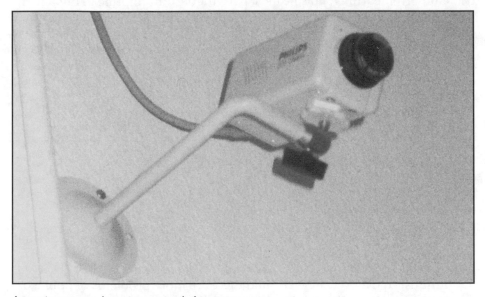

A passive sensor detecting concealed weapons.

walk their beats, a central element of community policing. Community policing mobilizes neighborhoods and consequently is highly regarded by neighborhood groups. It empowers minority groups, who often feel out of touch with municipal police. It provides ordinary citizens with a voice in their local government.

Second, processes of **institutional diffusion** will ensure that aspects of community policing are around for many decades, regardless of other changes in policing. "Institutional diffusion" means that many large departments have programs in place and other departments will tend to copy those programs. Neighborhood watches, for example, will be around regardless of other changes affecting the police. At the state level, an increasing number of states are incorporating community policing elements into their police codes. Community police training has emerged as an important element of peace officer standards and training in many states. In sum, the power of institutional diffusion is not to be underestimated as a force determining the future of policing.

The third force is substantial federal support for, and investment in, community policing. If inner-city areas continue to deteriorate, investment in community policing satisfies both liberal concerns over aid to local communities and conservative concerns over the maintenance of public order. Community policing, in a word, has a capacity to be all things to all people (Mastrofski and Uchida 1997).

The fourth force is the "explosion" of research on the police since the mid-1970s, which has challenged the effectiveness of traditional practices. This openness to research wasn't just a random event but was caused by progressive police administrators. By allowing outsiders into policing, especially critical-minded academics, departments became much less insulated and much more open to constructive criticism.

The fifth force is the emergence of a new breed of police chiefs. These administrators are willing to learn from research and to make changes based on empirical evidence rather than on traditional practice, common sense, or trial-and-error learning. For the most part, they are attempting to implement community policing within their departments. Hubert Williams, a former chief and director of the Police Foundation, suggests that past or current trends in policing did not just occur but "were the cumulative result of conscious, often difficult, decisions made by police executives facing potentially catastrophic consequences if they were wrong" (1990, p. 140).

> Today's law enforcement executives have demonstrated a greater commitment to empirical, often experimental, research than have those in any other part of the criminal justice system. They have sustained this commitment despite sometimes strenuous opposition from their own officers, their mayors, or their ultimate constituents, the public. (1990, p. 140)

Unfavorable Forces

One challenge to community policing, as described by S. Mastrofski and C. Uchida (1997), is that local governments will be pushed toward a more legalistic model of policing. The capacity of local governments, they observed, has diminished over recent years, and there are more problems of public order. At the same time, the public is increasingly unwilling to pay more taxes to address fundamental social problems (Glazer 1988). As N. Glazer observed, the American public seems content to permit the expansion of disorder as a condition of its sense of freedom.

W. Skogan has made similar observations in his studies of disorder in six American cities. The following observation describes the link between policy formation and resource availability:

> The final context for policy formation is that of limits. This is partly a question of resources, which are scarce. It will be difficult to mobilize support for policies aimed at disorder reduction if they cost very much. There are many pressing problems on the American agenda, and when resources can be freed, disorder may not be an obvious target. (Skogan 1990, p. 161)

Skogan further observed the problem in dealing with root causes when public policy requires that police departments focus on proximate causes, particularly criminal conduct. Proximate causes are more likely to be addressed through aggressive strategies than through community policing. Inside Policing 14.1 describes a shift in one department from a community-based model to a legalistic model.

Inside Policing 14.1
COP Lives on in Baltimore Co.

The Baltimore Police Department is reconsidering its recent conversion to community policing, which it pioneered in the early 1980s. Police indicated that they were not abandoning the philosophy but were taking a "hard look" at community policing approaches to some crime problems. The spokesman for the department said they were confronting crime problems that required a more aggressive approach. He noted that "some things, like the widespread armed-robbery problem we had earlier, . . . are best handled through traditional enforcement using informants, conducting aggressive patrol and enforcement strategies and that's what we did."

A patrol commander in a high-crime district with similar sentiments stated that the department has

> redefined our goals and objectives related to community policing. . . . What we've been asked to do by this administration is to take a hard look at our community policing involvement. If it does not reduce crime, if it does not prevent crime, then perhaps we should address whether or not we should be involved in it.

His words showed that community contact was still an important consideration for the police department. However, crime had created demands for enforcement, and officers were needed to carry out hard-nosed, aggressive police work. The department spokesman said,

> We exercise zero tolerance down here and I've got all of my resources devoted to enforcement at this point. That's not to say that I don't go to the community, not to say that I don't listen to the community, their needs, desires, concerns. But whether you want to call it community policing or hard-nosed enforcement, if it reduces crime, we're going to keep doing it.

One of the issues concerning many police officers was the collection of community policing statistics that appeared to have little to do with crime. This upset a number of department personnel. For example, officers were keeping track of the number of community meetings or schools they went to each month. A commander noted that the contribution of this data to crime control was not clear and that the department needed to adopt a more aggressive approach. According to him, ☞

Before[,] they called down and asked us how many community meetings we attended last month. They never asked why, they just wanted to know how many. They wanted to know how many times you went to the schools. They didn't ask why you were there or what you did there, just how many times. I think we just became so involved in that issue that enforcement became just part of what we did, not the main focus. This new guy is bringing us back to that mission and goal at this point in time. Morale in my station has drastically improved.

The refocusing of the department on enforcement resulted in reductions in crimes across the precinct. The rate, the chief noted, was down 6.6 percent, and violent crime was down 12 percent for the first half of 1996. Moreover, the community seemed to like the more aggressive approach. The chief concluded that the more aggressive approach was the way he would probably direct the department in the future.

Source: Adapted from *Law Enforcement News*. 1996. "COP Lives On." December 15.

Police Militarization

A seventh influential environment, also within the world of policing, is the militarization of municipal police. According to a small number of thoughtful researchers, militarization has been going on underneath the peaceful veneer of the community policing movement. It seems likely that two trends within the militarization movement will affect the future of policing: increasing linkages between the police and the military and the increased use of police paramilitary units.

A Police-Military Complex

Historically, Americans have viewed the separation of the police and the military as an essential characteristic of their democratic heritage. This view may be changing. P. Kraska has observed a heightened level of activity linking the military to the police in the United States. He argues that the traditional separation of the police and the military is eroding today.

> Changes in the post-cold war world and in the influence of contemporary militarism—the reliance on military style force to solve problems—are eroding the separation between police and military activity, resulting in a military involved in law enforcement, and the police at times operating "militarily," all under the guise of ameliorating "social problems." (Kraska 1994, p. 1)

He notes recent trends in military involvement in domestic affairs:

- The Washington, D.C., National Guard has used soldiers to assist federal and local police in air and ground transportation, lending military equipment, demolishing crack houses, and flying aerial surveillance missions.

- Portland, Oregon, in 1991 became the first municipality to deploy armed National Guard soldiers to assist local police in drug-related operations.

- Under the auspices of training, the U.S. military in southern Florida and Louisiana is conducting Andean-type exercises using military helicopters. Once the military locates a suspected operation and secures the area, the local police actually search and arrest suspects.

What are the long-range implications of this involvement? Once the federal government advances its policing authority, it seldom retracts it. It is possible that its military role will continue to grow in supplying hardware and manpower and in taking an active role in both municipal and federal policing problems.

The Iron Fist

Some observers of the police refer to the community-policing movement as the **velvet glove**, meaning that community policing is less aggressive than traditional law enforcement, that it focuses on "soft" community relations more than on hard-edged law enforcement. P. Kraska and V. Kappeler (1997) contend that another fundamental change is occurring in policing—a shift toward an **iron fist** approach, namely the spread of PPUs. In recent years, PPUs have been used as an aggressive, militaristic response to solve crime-related problems.

Kraska and Kappeler are concerned that the growth of this kind of policing represents an ominous trend toward the militarization of normal policing activity. Indeed, as they observed, PPUs are frequently financed under federal community policing grants. It seems that while community policing struggles for identity, the growth of PPUs is becoming a core activity of many police departments.

What Kind of a Future?

What does the future hold for U.S. police departments? In light of the environments described that influence the police, it is clear that the future depends not only on the police but also on the American people. The police will be what citizens want them to be. If we want a future of promise and hope, the police can help us get there. If we choose a future that divides us by race, age, and religion, the police will be the instrument of our divisiveness. Whatever the police become, they become so because we ask it of them. This chapter concludes with a discussion of the kinds of departments that may emerge. The authors see the possibility of three major types of departments developing, each reflecting the way police managers adapt to the social, political, and economic milieu of the twenty-first century.

Community-Policing Departments

Departments that have established community-policing programs as their primary mission will be intensely decentralized. Patrol vehicles may provide total offices for line and detective personnel and act as mobile centers for patrol communication in geographical areas. Traditional patrol will have been largely abandoned in favor of proactive patrol and problem-solving assignments. Crime-fighting tactics will be integrated with intensive surveillance in hot-spot areas. All officers will serve in community-policing assignments. Recruitment will focus intensely on officers who can bring the critical linguistic skills needed to police the expanding diversity of urban areas. Pre-service and in-service training will be expanded.

Community-policing departments will have restructured their promotion and reward systems. Rank will be expanded across the street level to encourage competent people to remain line officers. Education will increasingly be used as a criterion for promotion and salary. Peer evaluations will be commonplace, though conducted with an eye toward facilitating effectiveness in preventing and fighting crime.

Neo-Legalistic Departments

Some departments will decide to move away from community policing in favor of achieving or maintaining a legalistic model. Although it focuses on traditional ideas of law enforcement, such a neo-legalistic department makes use of more aggressive elements of community policing and surveillance technologies to advance those ideas.

Traditional administrators will see little reason to adopt community policing when faced with the possibility of increased levels of crime, violence, gang activity, and drug abuse. They may maintain elements of community policing, particularly as it facilitates positive police-community relations, but their focus will be law enforcement. Their departments will use random preventive patrol aided by expanded hot-spot and directed patrols. They will make intense use of crime identification and surveillance technologies.

A number of factors, many beyond the control of the police, will increase pressure on the police to solve problems legalistically. They include intensifying inner-city problems as jobs move to cheaper areas or other countries, less money for municipal services, decreased police budgets, civil liability costs, an over-focus on technology, friction between ethnic groups, and the continued growth of AIDS.

Retrenched Departments

Some police departments will be overwhelmed by crime-related pressures and will have steadily diminishing resources to combat them. Without capable leadership, these departments will retrench, just as the cities they serve are retrenching.

Such **retrenchment** means cutting back to the minimal level of activity needed to carry on highly aggressive police work. These departments, for example, might move from a paramilitary to a full-military style of policing, defining their role as a response to the need for internal security. They will respond aggressively to community problems, straining community relations. They will have a "siege" mentality, trusting no outsiders. They will use new technology to expand surveillance. They will seek out criminal activity, particularly drug and hostage activity that is highly visible, so that solutions will please their political constituents. These departments will be internally focused, abandoning community-policing elements as unnecessary frills.

Conclusion: Forward Into What Future?   ❖ ❖ ❖ ❖

The authors' concerns over the future echo the words of E. Currie. His vision encompasses all elements in the criminal justice system, including the police.

> To sum up, I believe that a new intellectual and political space has been forced open by the widespread and often frightening failures of the strategies that came before. In this space, a new criminological vision and a new public policy toward crime may take root, even flower.
>
> One troubling possibility is that we might go backward. We might adopt the view that the failure of our recent strategies toward crime and toward the more general population of those "at risk" tells us that the problems are much more intractable than we had supposed—so intractable that it isn't worth the effort to do anything but contain them.... We might use that explanation to justify what would amount to urban triage: an even greater withdrawal of resources from the most problematic communities and a de facto policy of allowing them to spiral downward still further. I don't think that will happen; I think the potential social costs are too great and too widely understood. But I don't think it's inappropriately alarmist to suggest it as a possibility. (Currie 1997, p. 414)

And you, the reader, where will you guide the future? The whole conclusion of this book is that the future of policing depends on citizens, that is, on you. Where the police go depends on where you take them. If you have the spirit for it, the energy and the heart, there is hope for policing's future. The task is great. If you become cynical or conclude that the task is too great, then we all may all pay the price of your cynicism.

The twenty-first century offers promise and danger. We are on the brink of an age of unprecedented technological and educational advance. Yet we also face unprecedented socioeconomic problems. The ability of police to ameliorate such problems will depend on the quality of its leadership. And that, of course, will be you. The future of policing is in your hands. Guide it truly.

Discussion Questions

1. Why is the purpose of looking at environments affecting the police?

2. What are institutional organizations?

3. Why is the melting pot a "myth?" Can you think of examples where it is a myth? Where it is not?

4. What is meant by "privatization" of the police? Would you prefer to work for a private police force or for a public one? How would you hold private police accountable for protection of due-process rights of suspects?

5. Identify the ways in which police and academics influence each other. Give examples drawn from your personal experience in school.

6. Of the seven environments that affect the future of the police, which do you think is the most important? Which is the least? Can you identify any other environments that affect the police?

7. Briefly describe each of the three kinds of police departments predicted for the future. Which do you think is the most likely to occur? Why?

8. Identify and discuss the forces favorable and unfavorable to community policing.

9. Do you think that the federal government should play a role in the development of policing in your community? What should that role be?

10. What are current trends in terrorism? Do you think that terrorism over the Internet is a significant problem?

References

Academy of Criminal Justice Sciences. 1998. *ACJS 1997–1998 Guide to Graduate Programs in Criminal Justice and Criminology.* Highland Heights, KY: Academy of Criminal Justice Sciences.

Bayley, D. H. and Shearing, C. D. 1998. "The Future of Policing." In G. Cole and M. Gertz (eds.), *The Criminal Justice System: Politics and Policies.* 7th ed., pp. 150–167. Belmont, CA: West/Wadsworth Publishing.

Carelli, R. 1998. "Law Enforcement Using Technology." *Associated Press: U.S. News.* Internet. May 29.

Citro, D. J. 1996. "Delaware State Police Rural Community Policing Unit." Internet site: State Police Home Page. www.state.de.us/govern/agencies/pubsafe/rural.htm

Colombo, A. 1997. "Police Use of GPS Technology." *Safety and Security* [electronic] *Magazine* 3 (4): 16–18.

"COP Lives On in Baltimore County: Police Brass say They're Not Abandoning the Concept." 1996. *Law Enforcement News* December: 1.

Corcoran, J. 1990. *Bitter Harvest: Gordon Kahl and the Posse Comitatus.* New York: Penguin Books.

Crank, J. P. 1995. "The Community Policing Movement of the 21st Century: What We Learned." In J. Klofas and S. Stojkovic (eds.) *Crime and Justice in the Year 2010,* pp. 107–126. Albany: Wadsworth Publishing

——. 1998. *Understanding Police Culture.* Cincinnati: Anderson Publishing Company.

Currie, E. 1997. "Confronting Crime: Looking Toward the Twenty-First Century." In B. Hancock and P. Sharp, (eds.), *Public Policy: Crime and Criminal Justice,* pp. 411–426. Upper Saddle River, NJ: Prentice Hall.

Flynn, E. E. 1996. "International Terrorism and the United States." In R. Muraskin and A. Roberts (eds.), *Visions for Change: Crime and Justice in the 21st Century,* pp. 19–36. Upper Saddle River, NJ: Prentice Hall.

Glazer, N. 1988. *The Limits of Social Policy.* Cambridge, MA: Harvard University Press.

Hale, D. and Wyland, S. M. 1999. "Dragons and Dinosaurs: The Plight of Patrol Women." In L. K. Gaines and G. W. Cordner (eds.), *Policing Perspectives An Anthology,* pp. 450–458. Los Angeles: Roxbury.

Homer-Dixon, T. 1994. "Environmental Scarcities and Violent Conflict." *International Security* 19–1: 5–40.

Huntington, S. 1996. *The Clash of Civilizations and the Remaking of World Order.* New York: Simon and Schuster.

Janofski, M. 1998. "Pittsburgh is a Showcase for Women in Policing." *New York Times*, June 21: A12.

Jaycor. 1998. *Less Than Lethal Technologies Division*. Internet: www.jaycor.com/eme/ltlt.htm

Jones, S. 1986. "Women Police: Caught in the Act." *Policing* 2(2): 129–140.

Kaplan, R. 1998. "Travels Into America's Future." *Atlantic Monthly* August: 37–72.

Kraska, P. 1994. "The Police and the Military in the Cold-Cold War Era: Streamlining the State's Use of Force Entities in the Drug War." *Police Forum* 4(1): 1–7.

Kraska, P. and Kappeler, V. 1997. "Militarizing American Police: The Rise and Normalization of Paramilitary Units." *Social Problems* 44-1: 101–115.

Margolis, J. 1993. "The Computer Cowboys." *Chicago Tribune*, November 18: Sec. 2, p. 1.

Martin, S. 1989. "Women on the Move? A Report on the Status of Women in Policing." *Women and Criminal Justice* 1(1): 21–40.

Martinez, M. J. 1998. "The Computer on the Beat." *ABCNews.com*. 6/15.

Mastrofski, S. and Uchida, C. 1997. "Transforming the Police." In B. W. Hancock and P. M. Sharp (eds.), *Public Policy: Crime and Criminal Justice*, pp. 196–219. Upper Saddle River, NJ: Prentice Hall.

McGarrell, E., Benitez, S., and Gutierrez, R. 1997. "Getting to Know Your Community Through Citizen Surveys and Focus Group Interviews." In Q. C. Thurman and E. F. McGarrell (eds.), *Community Policing in a Rural Setting*, pp. 97–106. Cincinnati: Anderson Publishing Co.

Meadows, R. 1996. "Legal Issues in Policing." In R. Muraskin and A. Roberts (eds.), *Visions for Change: Crime and Justice in the Twenty-First Century*, pp. 96–115. Upper Saddle River, NJ: Prentice Hall.

Miller, W. 1990. "Why Has the U.S. Failed to Solve Its Youth Gang Problem? In C. R. Huff (ed.), *Gangs in America. Newbury Park*, pp. 263–287. Newbury, CA: Sage Publications.

Mullins, R. 1998. "FBI Eyes Net Crime." *San Francisco Examiner*, April 26: B5, B7.

——. 1998b. "Top Cybercop." *San Francisco Examiner*, April 26: B5, B7.

Muraskin, R. and Roberts, A. 1997. "Looking to the Future of Criminal Justice." In R. Muraskin and A. Roberts (eds.), *Visions for Change: Crime and Justice in the 21st Century*, pp. 1–4. Upper Saddle River, NJ: Prentice Hall.

Peak, K. 1996. "Gangs: Origin, Outlook and Policy Implications." In R. Muraskin and A. Roberts (eds.), *Visions for Change: Crime and Justice in the 21st Century*, pp. 7–18. Upper Saddle River, NJ: Prentice Hall.

Quaid, L. 1998. "Representatives Want Anti-Terrorist Plan." *Wire-News From the AP*. Internet, April 23.

"Record Total of Wiretaps Was Approved by Courts." 1998. *New York Times* May 10: 1:20.

Roberts, S. 1994. *Who We Are: A Portrait of America Based on the Latest U.S. Census*. New York: Random House/Times Books.

Rourke, M. 1998. "More Americans are Going Where the Spirit Takes Them." *Sunday Oregonian*, June 28: E1, E4.

Serrano, R. A. 1998. "Fugitives Give Law Run for Money." *Idaho Statesman*, January 13: D-1.

Sherman, L. 1986. "Higher Education and Police Reform." In M. Pogrebin and R. Regoli (eds.), *Police Administrative Issues: Techniques and Functions*, pp. 233–242. Millwood, NY: Associated Faculty Press.

Sherman, L. 1990. "Police Crackdowns: Initial and Residual Deterrence." In M. Tonry and N. Morris (eds.), *Crime and Justice: A Review of Research*, Vol. 12, pp. 1–48. Chicago, IL: University of Chicago Press.

Sherman, L. and Berk, R. 1984. "The Specific Deterrent Effect of Arrest for Domestic Assault." *American Sociological Review* 49(2): 261–272.

Sherman, L., Gottfredson, D., MacKensie, D., Eck, J., Reuter, P. and Bushway, S. 1997. *Preventing Crime; What Works, What Doesn't, What's Promising.* Washington, D.C.: Office of Justice Programs—U.S. Department of Justice.

Skogan, W. 1990. *Disorder and Decline: Crime and the Spiral of Decay in American Neighborhoods.* New York: Free Press.

Stockton, D. 1998. "SWAT's Small-Town Question: How Prepared Are You?" Police: *Law Enforcement Magazine* 22(4): 20–24.

Taft, P. 1991. "Policing the New Immigrant Ghettos." In C. Klockars and S. Mastrofski (eds.), *Thinking About Police: Contemporary Readings,* pp. 307–315. New York: McGraw-Hill.

Weisheit, R., Falcone, D. and Wells, L. E. 1996. *Crime and Policing in Small-Town and Rural America.* Prospect Heights, IL: Waveland Press.

Weisheit, R. and Kernes, S. 1997. "Future Challenges: The Urbanization of Rural America." In Q. Thurman and E. McGarrell (eds.), *Community Policing in a Rural Setting,* pp. 124–134. Cincinnati: Anderson Publishing Co.

Williams, H. 1990. "Trends in American Policing: Implications for Executives." *American Journal of Police* 9: 139–149.

For a listing of websites appropriate to the content of this chapter, see "Suggested Websites for Further Study" (p. xv). ✦

Glossary

Abuse of Authority   Misuse of power by police that tends to injure a member of the police constituency. It can take the form of excessive physical force; psychological abuse; or violation of civil rights.

Accreditation   A process by which police departments are assessed in terms of standards of competency and professionalism. Accreditation typically involved a rigorous process of self-study followed by external review by an accreditation team made up of an official body of organizations. See CALEA.

Actual Damages   Estimated actual cost of the injury caused, which is paid in compensation.

Actual Danger   Strong likelihood of harm in a situation based on the actual number and rates of deaths and injuries that resulted from similar situations.

Acute Stress   A form of high-level distress caused by sudden emergencies such as shootings of high-speed chases.

Administrative Search   Government inspection associated with regulating certain types of businesses. It does not require a warrant, and if illegal items are discovered during the inspection, they can be legally seized and used as evidence in a criminal prosecution.

Affirmative Action Plan   The attempt by a police department to redress past discriminatory practices by assuring equal employment opportunity, either voluntarily or by court order following legal action.

Aggressive Law Enforcement   Strict police practices in a given area where as many arrests as possible are made, numerous citations are given, and many field investigations are conducted.

Andragogy   An instructural method promoting the involvement of students and instructors in the learning process, stressing analytical and conceptual skills. See also *pedagogy*.

Announcement Effect   Initial modification of people's behavior when publicity surrounds a crackdown; behavior returns to normal when publicity subsides.

Anticipating Danger   Expecting trouble before it comes.

Anti-stalking Laws   Laws against the repeated following, spying on, or otherwise harassing someone such that the victims experiences a "credible threat" of bodily harm. California passed the first anti-stalking law in 1990.

Apprehension   An arrest.

Arrest Rates   The number of persons arrested in relation to all crimes known to the police.

Assailant Geographies   Places that show signs of being dangerous, such as areas that are known for drug exchange.

Assessment Center   A process that attempts to measure a candidate's potential for a particular position using multiple strategies, including job-related simulations and possibly interviews and psychological tests.

Avoiders   Officers who tend to sidestep or ignore problems.

Baby Boomers   Originally children born to returning veterans of World War II, now those born between 1947 and 1964. Baby boomers were the first population in U.S. history not to replace themselves.

Baby Bust   The failure of the baby boomers to replace themselves, reversing the usual trend in populations.

Beat A geographic division used by a department to distribute the workload.

Bertillon System A method to identify suspects, including physical measurements, a detailed description, a photograph, and fingerprints.

BFOQ Abbreviation for **bona fide occupational qualification**, a job-related standard that is permissible under Title VII of the Civil Rights Act. If a particular characteristic (such as the ability to lift heavy weights or run a computer) can be shown to be needed for successful job performance or a "business necessity," it may be allowed as a requirement even though it may discriminate against some protected groups of people.

Bias Crime A crime that is racially or sexually motivated, a hate crime.

Broken-windows Theory A theory of crime that emphasizes the influence of the quality of community life. It suggests that once a neighborhood is allowed to run down, it can be a short time before it becomes inhospitable and infested with crime.

Bureaucracy A term coined by Max Weber at the end of the nineteenth century to identify characteristics that an organization needed to operate on a rational basis.

CALEA Acronym for **Commission on Accreditation of Law Enforcement Agencies**, developed as a result of the combined efforts of the International Association of Chiefs of Police, National Organization of Black Law Enforcement Executives, National Sheriffs' Association, and Police Executive Research Forum. The commission established specific standard that a police department meet before it can become accredited.

Career Path The direction one's chosen profession takes, including broadening of one's position, new assignments, and promotions.

Case Law Written rulings of state and federal appellate courts that define when and how a procedure is to be used.

Centralization Retention of authority and decision making by the top levels of a police department.

Certification A document (license or certificate) that states that a department of individual has met professional standards. It is typically given by a state-level organization.

Chain of Command Levels in an organizational (departmental) hierarchy; the higher the level, the greater the power, authority, and influence.

Change Strategies Management methods used by a department to facilitate change.

Chronic Stress A form of low-level, cumulative distress that includes the day-to-day routine of the job.

Civil Laws Laws concerned with relationships between individuals (contracts, business transactions, family relations) as distinct from **criminal laws**.

Civil Liability Suit A legal action against a police officer, supervisor, chief, or police (or at least the city) for recovery of monetary damages for the negligent behavior of one or more of the above.

Civil Service Commissions Government units that have civil service authority over police organizations, often including discipline and dismissals.

Civil Service Regulations Government policies, which are often state directives, regulating police personnel matters, including selection and promotion.

Civil Service, or Merit, System A selection method for filling government jobs determined by rank order based on the highest combined score on a written exam; oral interview; and physical, medical., and personal requirements; these requirements have often been not job related and therefore discriminatory.

Civilian Review Board Group of citizens charged with investigating allegations of police misconduct.

Class-Control Theory One of four theories to explain the development of police departments: to dominate the working class for the benefit of the industrial elite.

Classical Principles of Organization Rules governing a bureaucracy including specialization of work, assigning of authority and responsibility, discipline, unity of command, scalar chain of authority, centralization of decision making, and small spans of control.

Clean-Beat Crime Fighters Officers who are *Proactive* and *legalistic* but not selective.

Closed System System (organization or department) that does not interact with or adapt to its environment, as distinct from *open system*.

Coactive Policing Strategies in which the police form a partnership with the community. Examples are neighborhood watches and citizen patrols.

Code of Silence The secrecy that line officers maintain about their work-related activities, both from the public and from police administrators. A part of line-officer culture, it is particularly associated with covering up wrongdoing committed by colleagues.

Coercion See *force*.

Coercive Approach Using authority to obtain an appropriate outcome.

Cognitive Employment Tests Tests of a person's ability to synthesize and analyze material.

Command Voice Firmly spoken order.

Commission Approach Use of commissions (groups) of appointed citizens and experts to effect the police reform.

Community The legally incorporated area of a city or county; also people who live in the same area, work for the same organization, or share a common concerns.

Community-accountability Conferences A developing program used as an alternative to prosecuting juveniles, in which the offender admits guilt and the victim is willing to attend a conference. The conference is led by a trained police officer, who insures that everyone has a say. An agreement for repaying the cost of crime to the victim is reached, or else prosecution results.

Community-building Strategy Effort by the police to strengthen the informal social controls among people in an area.

Community Crime Prevention An approach to crime based on the assumption that by changing a community, both through appearance and preventive activities, the behavior of residents can also be changed.

Community-oriented Policing (COP) The initial approach to community policing which had its primary emphasis on establishing a working partnership with the community.

Community Policing See *community policing model.*

Community Policing Model An approach to the relationship between the police and the community that attempts to be responsive to individuals, groups, and the neighborhood without engaging in preference or discrimination. In includes both a working partnership with the community and a capacity to identify and to help solve community problems.

Community-service Officer (CSO) A nonsworn position that is assigned support duties that generally do not require a weapon.

Compstat A process that utilized current crime data to analyze crime patterns on which to base appropriate responses, also known as an anti-crime program.

Computerized Crime Mapping A computer generated map of crime information matched to a geographic area to help officers know where to concentrate their patrol activities.

Consolidation The integration of two or more police departments (also called regional police departments).

Constable Official in medieval England appointed to assist the *sheriff;* later a British police officer.

Constable-nightwatch System A system of law enforcement that began in England and prevailed in cities in the northeastern United States from the 1600s to the early 1800s; the constable provided limited daytime police services while the night watch patrolled after dark.

Consulting-modeling Method of acquiring expertise by analyzing a police department and comparing it to a model of desirable characteristics.

Contact Stage Tactical choices made when an officer approaches a citizen.

Contingency Management Management based on the recognition that many internal and external factors influence police behavior and there is no one best way to run a department.

Continuum of Force A range of possible responses police officers use; from mere presence to deadly force; according to the intensity of resistance of suspects. The continuum provides officers with a standard for training in the use of force.

Contract Law Enforcement A kind of policing that involves an agreement (contract) between two units of government in which one provides law enforcement services for the other.

Controlling The process by which managers determine how the quality or quantity of departmental systems and services can be improved if goals and objectives are to be accomplished.

Co-production of Public Safety A process in which the police and the public become partners in determining the police role and identifying solutions to problems such as crime and disorder.

COPS Acronym for **community-oriented** policing services; a program created by the Crime Control Act of 1994 to hire 100,000 new officers to be used by local departments to help further their community policing efforts. It is administered by the Justice Department's Office of Community Oriented Policing Services.

Covert patrol Patrol officers or detectives working under cover in order to blend into the community.

CPTED Abbreviation for **crime prevention through environmental design**, a strategy by which police and the community work together to control neighborhoods and buildings in order to reduce opportunities for crime. It includes target hardening and territorial reinforcement.

Crackdown An intensive, short-term increase in officer presence and arrests for the specific types of offenses or for all offenses in specific areas.

Crime Clearance Rates The number of Part I Crimes reported to the police divided by the number of crimes for which the police have arrested a suspect.

Crime Control Act See *Violent Crime Control And Law Enforcement Act*.

Crime-control Theory One of four theories to explain the development of police departments: to prevent or suppress criminal activity.

Crime Fighters Groups of officers who view the police role as primarily preventing crime and apprehending suspects by emphasizing police presence and investigation.

Crime Index See *Uniform Crime Reports (Part I Crimes)*.

Crime Repression The control of crime through the omnipresence of patrol activities, traditionally regarded ad the most important patrol function.

Criminal Laws Laws concerned with the relationship between the individual and the government, especially in the areas of public safety and order (driving licenses, theft, rape, and murder), as distinct from *civil laws*.

Critical-incident Debriefing Counseling services provided to officers after and extremely stressful event.

Cultural Diversity A wide variation in racial, ethnic, and gender makeup of a police department, also of a community of society.

Cultural Themes The building blocks of culture. They are areas of activity and ways of common-sense thinking about them widely shared by police officers. Several cultural themes affect how police officers use force. See Inside Policing 9.3.

Culture See *police culture*.

Cyber-terrorism A form of terrorism through sabotaging mainframe computers or computer networks by hackers. Cyber-terrorism is particularly insidious because computers are integral to modern life.

Danger Signifiers Warnings of trouble that include a person's behavior, language, dress, area, age, sex, and ethnicity.

Deadly Force Coercion used with the intent to cause bodily injury or death.

Decentralization Delegation of authority and decision making to lower organizational levels.

Decertification Suspending a police officer or putting the officer on probation.

Deep-pocket Theory In civil suits the idea that officers may have limited financial resources but that higher ranks may have access to funds, usually belonging to taxpayers, to pay damages.

Defeminization Referring to "tough" women police as bitches or lesbians in an effort to neutralize their threat to make dominance.

Definitional Approach Securing information needed to define (categorize) a problem and the role of those involved.

Democracy-police Conflict The discord that arises when the police exercise their authority in a free society based on democratic principles.

Democratic Model An approach to police organization that is not hierarchal and has no formal ranks or supervisors.

Demography The study of vital statistics of groups of people, particularly focusing on birth, death, and population changes.

Detective A specialist who responds to crimes serious enough to warrant a follow-up investigation.

Deterrence The ability to halt an adversary by force rather than threats or reason.

Deterrence Decay A lessening of the discouraging effect of some measure.

Discretion The decision-making latitude of the police on whether to invoke legal sanctions when circumstances are favorable for them.

Discretionary-act Defense An officer's explanation that he or she was acting within lead authority regarding the time, nature, and extent hear she was involved in a required act.

Disorder-control Theory One of four theories to explain the development of police departments: to prevent or suppress mob violence.

Disparate Impact A selection method can be considered to have a legally disparate impact when the selection rate of a group is less than 80 percent of the most successful group, also knows as the four-fifths rule.

Distress Negative stress.

Domestic Violence An assault on or battery of a domestic partner; traditionally handled by the police through arrest.

Double Marginality The situation in which minority police officers are not fully accepted by either the police or members of their own racial or ethnic group.

Due-process Revolution Important changes in procedural laws that had occurred by the 1960s.

Economic Corruption The breaking of the law by officers in order to seek personal financial gain, for example, keeping drug money confiscated from dealers.

Edge Control An officer's having more firepower, skills, and backup than the bad guys and bringing a little more force to bear than is actually needed.

Education Instruction in a general body of knowledge on which decisions can be based as to *why* something should be done on the job; concerned with theories, concepts, issues, and alternatives. See also *training*.

Education Strategy Police plan that provides information and skills to both victims and criminals in hopes of changing the behavior of both.

Educational-incentive Policies Departmental policies that encourage officers to pursue a college degree; such incentives may include tuition assistance or reimbursement, more pay, shift or day-off adjustments, and permission to attend class during work hours.

Empirical Evidence   Proof based on systematic study of data.

Enforcers   Officers who use coercion when the chance arises.

Enticement   A police activity that purposely encourages someone to commit a crime.

Entrapment   Police activity that purposely provides a person with the opportunity and intent to commit a crime.

Environment   Trends and problems in society in general and in communities; these can affect the police.

Environmental Expectations   Concerns of society in general and of particular communities.

Environmental Influences   Legal framework in which police function and the community's input into departmental priorities.

Ethical Formalism   Idea of the absolute importance of doing one's duty. An officer who believes that police should "go by book" is an ethical formalist.

Ethical Relativism   Idea that what is considered good varies with the particular values of groups and individuals.

Ethical Utilitarianism   Idea that it is good results of one's actions that determines whether the action itself is good. For example, telling a lie (generally an unethical act) might save a life (a good result).

Eustress   Positive stress.

Exceptional Clearance   Situation when the police claim to know who committed a crime but cannot make an arrest; the crime is considered to be solved.

Excessive Force   More violence that is needed to carry out a legitimate police task.

Exclusionary Rule   A legal means for controlling officer behavior. All evidence obtained unconstitutionally is not admitted in a state court.

Exigent Circumstances   Unusual situations, for example, when an officer or someone else might be harmed or when the police are chasing a suspect (in "hot pursuit").

Exit Stage   Strategies used to end a police encounter with a citizen.

Exoneration   Clearing an officer of blame when an investigation finds a complaint is essentially true, but the officer's behavior is considered to be justified, legal, and within departmental policy.

Expectation-integration Model   An approach to police work that illustrates how compatible and conflicting concerns of the law, the community, and the police department determine the police role.

External (Citizen) Review   Efforts by individuals and groups outside the department to control the police.

Ex-urbs   Semi-rural areas just beyond a city's suburbs. These regions are popular with well-off business and working-class people, who commute to the city to work.

False Complaints   Unfounded allegations of misconduct.

Field-training Officer   An experienced, well-qualified officer selected and taught to act as a mentor to a new recruit by providing on-the-job training.

Firm Grips   Physical grasps of the body to direct a suspect when and where to move.

Flat Structure Organization design that has few levels with many employees per supervisor, as distinct from *tall structure*.

Fleeing-felon Rule Guideline for use of deadly force in pursuit of someone hastening from the scene of a suspected grave crime.

Follow-up Investigation An official inquiry generally conducted by a detective to develop a case; includes identifying and locating a suspect, possibly obtaining a confession, and disposing of the case.

Force, or Coercion A means of controlling the conduct of others through threats of harm or actual harm. It may be physical or nonphysical. Police force is legitimized by the government, which provides police with the authority to compel observance of the law.

Fourth amendment Amendment to the Constitution with the "right of the people to be secure in their persons, houses, papers, and effects, against unreasonable searches and seizures.

Four-fifths Rule See *disparate impact*.

Frankpledge System A system for keeping order in medieval England based on tithings (10 families) and hundreds (10 tithings).

Fraternal Organization An association that seeks chiefly recognition and benefits for its members, generally organized along ethnic lines.

Garrity Interview Compelled testimony for internal investigations; routing practice but not protected by the fifth amendment and cannot normally be used in a criminal proceeding.

Generalist A police officer who performs a variety of activities, some of which could be assigned to a specialist.

Goals Purposes, objectives, or aims, general statements of big-term purpose.

Good-faith Defense An officer's explanation that he or she did not know that a particular action was against the law.

Good-faith Exemption In reference to the *exclusionary rule*, an officer's defense that he or she honestly thought he or she was acting legally.

GPS Abbreviation for **geographic positioning system**, a system of 24 tracking satellites belonging to the Department of Justice. GPS scan can locate persons within millimeters of their true position. It is used to establish longitude and latitude by surveyors, hikers, the U.S. Coast Guard, and a host of other organizations.

Grass Eaters Police officers who accept graft when it comes their way but do not actively solicit opportunities for graft, as distinct from *meat eaters*.

Gratuity Something of value, such as free or reduced-cost beverages or meals, discount buying privileges, free admission to athletic events or movies, gifts, and small rewards. Most commonly it is beverages or meals. Some officers accept such gratuities from the public.

Group Norms Expected behavior from group members, which can be a powerful factor in resistance to organizational change.

Highway Patrol A state police force whose duties are generally limited to enforcing traffic laws and dealing with accidents on state roads and highways. See also *state police*.

Hostile Work-Environment Harassment A situation in which unwelcome conduct by other workers is so severe or pervasive that it interferes with a person's work performance.

Hot Spots Locations that have a greater amount of crime or disorder than other areas.

Hot Times Periods in which a greater amount of crime or disorder occurs than in other periods.

ICAM Acronym for **information collection for automated mapping,** a program of the Washington, D.C., police department.

Impact Techniques Physical contact between the suspect's body and the officer's body or nonlethal weapons, such as chemical spray or stunning weapons.

Imperative Approach A tactic used by officers wherein they give orders upon initial contact with citizens.

Individual Influences Benefits to members such as job security or pay.

Inertia A condition of doing things as they have always been done before; it is a strong influence in resisting change in police departments.

In-group Solidarity A closeness and loyalty among officers brought about by the perceived danger of police work, the close-knit working relations among officers, concerns that outsiders cannot be trusted, and a common basis of patrol activity.

Innovation The development and use of new ideas and methods.

In-service Training A program to update all department members regularly on a wide variety of subjects.

Institutional Diffusion The process by which organizational forms spread across an institutional sector. The process usually occurs in the following way: a few large police departments adopt a program or design element that is then copied by other departments that have to deal with the same problem. For example, random preventive patrol diffused across police departments as a way to deal with crime after police started using automobiles. The program developed California and rapidly spread across the country.

Institutionalized Organization An organization whose goals, purposes, and policies focus on important societal values. It differs from an economic organization, whose goal is profit through economic efficiency. Institutional organizations face outward to deal with the values of their constituents, whereas economic organizations face inwards to achieve efficient technical production.

Intentional Tort A tort (wrong) that an officer plans to cause some physical or mental harm. See also *tort*.

Internal-affairs Unit Section in a police department to respond to complaints.

Internal (Departmental) Review Efforts by police to control their own behavior.

Investigators Specialists in crimes serious enough to warrant inquiry.

Iron Fist The use of aggressive police strategies, particularly those carried out by police paramilitary units.

Job Analysis Validating selection and testing methods by identifying the behaviors that are necessary for adequate job performance.

Job Redesign An effort to enrich police work by broadening the role in order that the job will its own reward.

Job Related Affecting on-the-job performance, the standard by which job requirements are measured so that they are not discriminatory.

Jurisdiction The geographic area or type of crime for which a police force is responsible.

Kin Policing In early or nonindustrial societies, enforcement of customary rules of conduct by family, clan, or tribe.

Lateral Entry The ability of a police officer, at the patrol or supervisory level, to transfer from one unit to another, usually without losing seniority.

Law Enforcement Assistant Act (1965) A modest grant program that expressed a national concern about the adequacy of local police departments; the act in turn spawned the President's Commission report, which focused attention on police behavior and departmental practices.

Law Enforcement Strategy A police plan that involves stopping suspicious persons, giving citations, and making arrests in hopes of reducing crime.

LEAA Acronym for **Law Enforcement Assistance Administration**, an agency through which the federal government poured literally billions of dollars into the criminal justice system—focusing on the police—in an attempt to improve effectiveness and reduce crime; LEEP, the Law Enforcement Education Program, was established under LEAA.

Leading Motivating others to perform various tasks that will contribute to the accomplishment of goals and objectives.

Learning organization An organization that benefits from, and adapts to, its own and others' experiences.

LEEP Acronym for **Law Enforcement Education Program**, established under *LEAA* to provide financial assistance to police personnel, as well as to others who wished to enter police service, to pursue a college education; it significantly increased police programs in higher education in the mid-1970s.

Legal Expectations Substantive and procedural laws that identify what the police should do and how they should do.

Legalistic Model An approach to police work that makes the standards of law and departmental policy, not politics or personal considerations, the basis for decision making. It emphasizes crime control.

Legalistic Style Policing that insists on enforcing the law in maintaining order.

Less-than-lethal Weaponry Weapons that increase the ability of the police to resolve violent encounters where use of deadly force has traditionally been standard. They include bean bags and capstan (pepper) sprays.

Management Directing individuals to achieve departmental goals efficiently and effectively.

Management-of-demand System The categorizing of requests for police service and matching those requests with different responses.

Management Training Instruction of officers promoted to managerial or executive-level positions; usually involves increased knowledge of management's role, long-range planning, policy development, and allocation of resources.

Manager's Culture Emphasis on both the ends and means of policing; concerned with departmental priorities, policies, and procedures.

Marshal A federally appointed official to keep order in federal territories (U.S. marshal); also a federally appointed local police officer (deputy marshal) and a locally appointed official (town marshal).

Mass-private Property Facilities that are privately owned but used by the public, for example, high-rise condominiums, banks, commercial facilities, and recreational complexes.

Meat Eaters Police officers who actively solicit opportunities for financial gain and are involved in more widespread and serious corruption than *grass eaters*.

Melting pot Metaphor for the idea that immigrants from different countries are assimilated into mainstream U.S. culture, that ethnic differences disappear when different groups live together and share common problems.

Mere Presence An officer's being in view in a situation, the mildest level of force.

Merit System See *Civil Service, or merit, system*.

National Advisory Commission on Higher Education for Police Officers A commission to study the problems of college and graduate education for police in the 1970s; a report in 1978 called for significant changes in virtually all phases of police higher education, including institution, curriculum, and faculty.

Negligent Tort A tort (wrong) resulting from a breach of lawful duty to act reasonably toward an individual whom a police officer might harm.

Negotiated Job Conditions Personnel assignments, allocation of resources, and other aspects of a job that are influenced by police unions instead of decided by management.

Nightwatch In olden times, group of citizens who patrolled at night looking for fires and other problems.

Noble-cause Corruption The abandonment of ethical and legal means in order to achieve good ends. Police may use both violence and subjugation of rights if they are more concerned about the noble-cause—getting bad guys off the streets, protecting victims and children—than about the morality of technically legal behavior.

Occupational Deviance Illegal behavior by an officer in the course of work or under the clock of police authority.

Old-style Crime Fighters Officers who are aggressive and selective, concentrating on felonies.

Omnibus Crime Control and Safe Streets Act (1968) A major piece of legislation to deal with the national concern over crime; it created the Law Enforcement Assistance Administration.

Open System System (organization or department) that interacts with or adapts to its environment, distinct from *closed structure*.

Organization Chart Diagram that depicts the functions, relationships, and flow of communication among designated groups with a police department.

Organization Design The formal patterns of arrangements and in relationships developed by police management to accomplish departmental goals.

Organizational Change A department's adoption of new ideas or behavior; a term often associated with community policing.

Organizational Culture The values, beliefs, and norms that evolve both formally and informally within a police department.

Organizational Expectations The formal and informal concerns of the department about how officers should behave and what they should do.

Organizational Influences Effect of top-level managers and others on department, primarily for its efficiency and perpetuation but also to satisfy its members.

Organizing The process of arranging personnel and physical resources to carry out plans and accomplish goals and objectives.

Pain Compliance Use of pain, without lasting injury, to force a suspect to obey police.

Paramilitary Model Formal pattern where the police are organized along military lines, with emphasis on a legalistic approach.

Particularistic Perspectives Views of the police that emphasize difference among police officers, as distinct from *universalists perspectives*.

Patronage System Unofficial practice in which public jobs are given as rewards for supporting the political party in power.

Pedagogy An instructional method involving a one-way transfer of knowledge, usually facts and procedures, from the instructor to the student, distinguished from *andragogy*.

Peer-counseling Program A program in which police officers who are specially trained to recognize problems associated with stress from critical incidents provide support to colleagues and make referrals as deemed necessary.

Peer Group Officers of the same rank in the department

Perceived Danger Harm that an officer of the public believes to be potential in a situation.

PERF Acronym for **Police Executive Research Forum**, an association made up of college-educated police chief executives; it passed a resolution calling for all police applicants to possess 30 semester units of college, increasing to a minimum requirement of a bachelor's degree for employment in policing.

Person-initiated Danger An attack against a police officer by another person.

Physiological Stress A state resulting from physical, chemical, or emotional factors that can cause biological disease such as high blood pressure and ulcers.

Plain-view Doctrine The principle that what police discover during the performance of their normal duties can be seized. For example, if a police officer stops a person who committed a traffic violation, and the officer sees illegal items in the back seat of the car, then that contraband is in plain view and can be legally taken.

Planning The process of preparing for the future by setting goals and objectives and developing courses of action for accomplishing them.

Police Nonmilitary persons or organizations that are given the general right by government to use coercion to enforce the law and respond to conflict involving illegal behavior.

Police Brutality Excessive force, including violence, that does not support a legitimate police function.

Police Corps A program established under the Crime Control Act of 1994 in which full-time college students will be eligible for up to $10,000 in annual tuition reimbursements; they must agree to work in a state or local police force for at least four years after graduation.

Police Corruption Any forbidden act that involves misuse of an officer's position for gain.

Police Culture The informal, but important relations among police officers and the values they share. Police work is characterized by its own occupational beliefs and values, which traditionally include a perception of the police as sexist and macho.

Police Deviance Activities of officers that inconsistent with their legal authority, the department's authority, and standards of ethical conduct.

Police Field Operations Patrol and investigative functions, which makeup a substantial majority of all work in a police department.

Police Image The favorable representation of the department and the police role, especially to aid recruitment.

Police Legitimacy Public confidence in the police as fair and equitable; it may help to prevent crime through citizens's increased willingness to obey the law.

Police Militarization Departmental changes associated with military strategy and behavior. It includes the language of war, expansion of sophisticated weaponry, application of military technologies in civilian sectors, joint military and civilian-police patrols, and the proliferation of police paramilitary units. See also *PPU*.

Police Misconduct Actions that violate departmental guidelines (policies, procedures, rules, and regulations) that define both appropriate and inappropriate conduct for officers.

Police Power The authority given to government to regulate health, welfare, safety, and morality.

Police Presence See *presence strategy*.

Police Pursuit Chasing a suspect who is trying to avoid arrest.

Police Stressors Sources of stress for police, including departmental practices (e.g. authoritarian structure) and the inherent nature of police work (e.g., shift work, boredom, exposure to human misery).

Police Union Association of police officers to represent the police in collective bargaining with the employer to gain recognition, improved wages and benefits, clear disciplinary procedures, and better job conditions.

Police Violence Use of force to obtain confessions.

Policewoman Female officer who tends to emphasize the traditional police culture, especially its law enforcement aspects.

Police*woman Female officer who attempts to maintain a "feminine manner" while performing police duties.

Political Model An approach to the relationship between the police and the community that sees the police primarily as serving the interests of politically powerful groups. It leads to preferential treatment for some citizens and discrimination against others, that is, corruption.

Posse Comitatus Group in medieval England called out to pursue fleeing felons.

POST Acronym for **peace officers' standards and training**.

Potential Danger Harm that could exist in a situation.

PPU Abbreviation for **police paramilitary unit**, group of police that functions as a military special-operations team, primarily to threaten or use collective force.

Predispositional Theory The idea that the behavior of a police officer is primarily explained by the characteristics, values, and attitudes of that person before he or she was employed.

Preliminary Investigation An initial inquiry conducted by patrol officers of the purpose of establishing that a crime has been committed and to protect the scene of the crime from those not involved in the inquiry.

Presence strategy A police plan that emphasizes the visible activity of the police; also a quality of poise and effectiveness, external calm and internal alertness, that a police officer should acquire for interacting with people.

Prevention Acting to keep a crime from occurring; also working with juveniles to deter them from crime; also using a educational and community-building strategies to deter people from crime.

Private Police Police employed and paid by an individual or nongovernmental organization.

Private World of Policing Police work characterized as politically conservative, close, or secretive and emphasizing loyalty and solidarity.

Proactive Approach Initiated by the police; it applies to the activities of both the officer, such as proactive arrest, and the department.

Probable-cause Defense An officer's explanation that he or she reasonably believed that an action was legal.

Problem-oriented Policing (POP) An approach to police work that is concerned primarily with identifying and solving community problems, with or without input from the community.

Procedural Laws Criminal laws that govern how the police enforce *substantive laws*.

Process-criterion Approach View that prolonged processor effort occurs in which an occupation adopts standards characteristic of professions.

Processing Stage Decisions made between contact and exit from police encounter with a citizen.

Professional-style Officers Police who are somewhat proactive but not selective, believing their work is to serve people. They use coercion if necessary but seek other means first.

Professionalization Movement to help the police be more objective and effective in their decisions by forming a code of ethics, developing a scientifically derived body of knowledge and skill, and providing extensive education and training. These are all means to turn police work from an occupation into a profession.

Psychological Stress A state resulting from physical, chemical, or emotional factors that can cause deterioration of mental health.

PTSD Abbreviation for **posttraumatic stress disorder**, a psychological state caused by frequent or prolonged exposure to crises or trauma.

Public Police Police who are employed, trained, and paid by a government agency.

Public Safety The partial or complete integration of police and fire services.

Public World of Policing Police work presented to the public that tries to avoid controversy and sometimes may involve cover-up of illegal or inappropriate behavior.

Punitive Damages Sums designed to punish the person committing the crime and to make an example.

Quality Circle A management technique by which a group of employees from the same work area volunteer to meet on a regular basis to identify an solve common work problems.

Quality Management See *TQM*.

Quid Pro Quo Harassment A situation requiring the employee to choose between the job and meeting a supervisor's sexual demands.

Race Norming Using different cutoff scores on employment-related tests on the basis of race, color, religion, sex, or national origin.

Random Patrol Police officers patrolling their beats at random (by chance) when not otherwise on assignment.

Reactive Approach Responsive to the request of the citizen for police action, such as an arrest made in response to citizen complaints, generally for a minor offense.

Reasonable Certainty A standard of verifiable evidence whereby a citizen complaint against an officer is considered valid.

Reciprocators Officers who use persuasion if possible.

Recruitment Strategies The various methods used to attract applicants, particularly women and minorities, to become police officers.

Reliability The consistency of a measure in yielding results over time. If other observers conducted the same research in the same setting, they would probably come to similar conclusion.

Resident-officer Program A plan whereby a department provides officers with rent-free or low-rent housing or low-interest loans to purchase rehabilitated homes in low-income or high-crime areas.

Residual Deterrence Continued reduction of crime even after a crackdown is ended.

Retrenchment Cutting back to the minimal level of activity needed for highly aggressive police work.

Reverse Discrimination The charge made by a group—usually white men—who feel that an affirmative-action plan in the selection and promotion process shows bias in favor of minorities and women.

ROP Acronym for **repeat offenders project** of the Washington, D.C., police department.

Rotten-apple Theory of Corruption The idea that corruption is limited to a small number of officers who were probably dishonest prior to their employment. The term stems from the metaphor that a few rotten apples will spoil the barrel; in other words, a few bad officers can spoil a department.

Rule of Law A principle of constitutional democracy whereby the exercise of power is based on laws, not on an individual or organization.

SARA Acronym for **scanning, analysis, response, and assessment**, a four-stage problem-solving process.

Scholarship and Recruitment Program A program established under the Crime Control Act of 1994 that provides scholarships for higher education to in-service police personnel and students (juniors or seniors in high school or college students) who do not currently work in law enforcement and are interested in pursuing it as a career.

Scientific Research Study that is based on observations that are valid (many observers will see the same thing) and reliable (research repeated in the same setting at a different time will yield similar conclusions). See also *validity* and *reliability*.

Screening In Process of identifying police applicants who are the best-qualified candidate for the applicant pool.

Screening Out Process identifying police applicants who are unqualified and removing them from consideration.

Sensitization Training Instructing an officer to be aware of the problems of victims as well as their own victimization; it should be conducted early in their careers.

Service Style Approach to policing that intervenes frequently but often informally in maintaining order.

Service-style Officers Officers who do the minimum to get by, who are not aggressive but are selective.

Sexual Harassment Unwelcome sexual advances that unreasonably interfere with a person's work or create a hostile working environment.

Sheriff Originally an English official appointed to levy fines and keep order in a county; later in the United States an official, usually elected, who enforces the law in rural areas. In addition to patrol and investigations, a sheriff's duties often include managing a jail and providing services for courts.

Shift A working period.

Situational Danger A particular problem on the job, for example, a high-speed chase, that threatens an officer's safety.

Slippery Slope Theory The idea that corruption at a lower level can easily lead to corruption at a higher level.

Social-service Providers Police who believe that all police tasks are important and there are a variety of strategies, rather than police presence and law enforcement, to respond to crime and related problems.

Social-supports Model An approach to police stress based on the premise that individuals are insulated against stressors when they have a support network of friends, family, and co-workers.

Socialization Process by which recruits learn values and behavior from experienced officers.

Socialization Theory Idea that individuals are made part of a group as a result of their occupational experiences.

Special-jurisdiction Police Police who function within a particular type of organization (e.g., college police) that is not part of the basic structure of the police department.

Specialist A police officer who performs a particular kind of activity such as investigation, as distinguished from a *generalist*.

Specialization The division of labor of personnel; the fewer kinds of tasks a person performs, the greater the level of specialization.

Specialized Training Instruction to prepare officers for particular categories of tasks or jobs.

State Police A state force that has bored law enforcement power, conducts criminal investigations, patrols roads and highways, and frequently has forensic science laboratories.

Sting Operation An undercover activity in which police set up fencing outlets and encourage thieves to sell them stolen merchandise.

Stopping Power The symbolic and real importance of hand guns to police culture.

Strategic Management An approach to police work that involves identifying departmental goals and the most effective and efficient way to achieve them; this approach suggests that departments should experiment with alternative police methods.

Strategies Broadly conceptualized plans or activities that affect the attitudes and behavior of individual officers.

Street Cop's Culture Emphasis primarily on achieving results, concern with "street wisdom" and survival.

Stressor-Outcome Model An approach to police stress based on the premise that circumstances of strain or tension lead to psychological or physiological stress.

Structural Characteristics The features that police departments emphasize or do not emphasize, which may be discriminatory, especially against women.

Subculture Police culture as part of a broader societal culture.

Subjugation of Defendant's Rights Overriding a citizen's civil rights in order to obtain a confession.

Substantive Laws Criminal Laws that identify behavior and punishment, distinct from *procedural laws*.

Sudden-emergency Defense Officer's explanation that he or she sometimes has to act from instinct rather than reason.

Suicide Prevention Training Instruction aimed at reducing police suicides by recognizing depression, developing communication skills, resolving conflicts, and maintaining close relationships.

Supervision The management function that focuses primarily on leading and controlling.

Supervisory Training Instruction for officers promoted to first-line administrative positions; it usually includes leadership, specific job requirements, and policies and procedures.

Sustained Complaints Allegations of misdeeds by police that an investigation finds to be justified.

Symbolic Assailant Type of person the police officer thinks is potentially dangerous or troublesome, usually because of the way the person walks, talks, and dresses.

Systematic Theory of Corruption The idea that police corruption arise from the nature of police work and if anti-corruption protocols are inadequate, corruption will spread throughout the department.

Systems Theory The idea that all parts of a system (organization) are interrelated and interdependent.

Tall Structure Organization design that has many levels with few employees per supervisor, as distinct from flat structure.

Task-Force Approach Using a team of officers from two or more police agencies to work together to solve a particular problem that transcends jurisdictional limits (e.g., a drug task force).

Team Policing A group of officers, working as a unit, who are stationed in a neighborhood and are responsible for all police services there.

Testimonial Evidence Proof based on the opinions of others.

Thief Catcher In olden times, a person hired to secure return of stolen property.

Third Degree Coercive police methods including both physical and psychological force.

Tort A civil wrong (not concerned with a contract) in which one person, in violation of a legal duty required by law, causes an injury to another person or damage to that person's property.

TQM Abbreviation for **total quality management**, a customer-oriented approach that emphasizes human resources and quantitative methods in an attempt at continuous improvement.

Training Instruction of an individual in how to do a job; concerned with specific facts and procedures. See also *education*.

Tribal Police Law enforcement bodies on Native American (Indian) reservations.

Unfounded Complaints Allegations of police misdeeds that an investigation finds did not occur as stated.

Uniform Crime Reports (Part I Crimes) An index of the crime rate per 100,000 population of eight major crimes: murder and nonnegligent manslaughter, forcible rape, robbery, aggravated assault, burglary, larceny, motor vehicle theft, and arson.

Universalistic Perspectives Views of police behavior that look for the ways officers are similar, as distinct from *particularistic perspectives*.

Unsubstantiated Complaints Allegations that in the opinion of those making the decision cannot be sustained as either true or false.

Urban-Dispersion Theory One of four theories that explain the development of the police department: to provide an important part of government.

Use Corruption Illegal use of drugs by officers.

Validity Justifiability of a measure as an accurate assessment of the attribute it is designed to assess. Other people are likely to see the same thing the observers sees.

Values Fundamental assumptions that guide a police department and individual members in the exercise of discretion.

Velvet Glove A metaphor for community policing, based on the idea that a less aggressive approach to crime is more effective than hard-edged methods.

Verbalization Persuasive use of words to control a situation.

Victim Survey A study in which scientifically selected samples of the population are asked about being victims of crime.

Vigilante Member of a voluntary band (usually men) who organize to respond to real or imagined threats to their safety; to protect their lives, property, or power; or seek revenge. Characteristic of the old West, they are also active today.

Violent Crime Control and Law Enforcement (Crime Control Act) (1994) The most comprehensive federal crime legislation since the Omnibus Crime Control and Safe Streets Act of 1968; it included the *COPS* program to hire 100,000 police officers.

Virtual Reality Training Instruction by programming data into computers to generate three-dimensional images to create lifelike environments.

Watchman Style Policing that allows great latitude in maintaining order.

Working Notions of Normal Force Standards of acceptable coercion learned on the street, different from what police learn in training.

Zero-Tolerance Policy Many arrests for minor violations and misdemeanors regardless of public sentiment. See also *broken-windows theory*. ✦

Author Index

Subject Index

Civil service system, 437, 458, 533
Civil suits, 23, 371–372, 373
Class-control theory, 38, 534
Classical organizational design, 113, 116, 134
Classical principles of organization, 106–107, 107, 534
Clean-beat crime fighters, 273, 534
Cleveland Police Department, 15, 359
Clinton, Bill, 510
Closed system, 109, 534
Coactive policing, 534
Cobarruviaz, Lou, 449–450
Cochise County, Arizona, 40
Code of ethics (California), 383–384
Code of silence, 293–294, 296, 329, 354, 534
Coercion. *See* force
Coercive approach, 534
Coercive territorial control, 274, 534
Cognitive employment tests, 186, 534
College cops, 400, 421
Colleges with criminal justice programs, 400
Colorado Springs Police Department, 239
Colorado state police, 53
Color-of-law threshold, 374
Colquhoun, Patrick, 34
Columbus Police Department, 15
Combative corruption, 288
Command voice, 315, 534
Commission approach, 47, 534
Commission on Accreditation of Law Enforcement (CALEA), 380, 382, 388, 533
Community, 21, 69–70, 534
Community-accountability conferences, 92, 534
Community-building strategy, 28, 88, 534
Community crime prevention, 92, 534
Community expectations, 24, 29, 70
Community officer (CO), 82, 84–85, 86–87, 88

Community-oriented policing services (COPS), 73, 90, 403, 510, 535
Community-oriented values, 27
Community policing model, 61, 65–96
  accreditation and, 382
  benefits of, 80–81
  Chicago Police Department and, 153–159
  Crime-Control Act and, 402
  crime prevention and, 91–95
  defined, 25, 534–535
  detective-patrol relationships and, 252
  discretion and, 421
  emergence of, 50
  federal support and, 510
  implementation, 150–152
  in-service training and, 203
  job redesign and, 127–129
  in Knoxville, 83
  liability and, 374–375
  middle management and, 143–144
  NYPD resistance to, 144–145
  open system and, 110
  organization design and, 113, 114
  overcoming obstacles, 149–152
  partnerships and, 122
  Portland Police Department and, 116–117
  PPUS and, 119
  and professionalization, 378
  San Francisco and, 148–149
  TQM and, 112
  trends in, 521–524, 525–526
  in Tucson, 84
Community Sector Team Policing Experiment (COMSEC), 72
Community-service officers (CSO), 175, 177, 535–536
Comparative approach, 224

Compensatory damages. *See* actual damages
Comprehensive Crime Control Act, 514
Compstat, 120–123, 164, 237–238, 535
Computerized crime mapping, 227–230, 535
Computer systems, 59, 80
Consolidation, 16, 535
Constable, 34, 36, 37, 535
Constable-nightwatch system, 34, 37, 38, 61, 535
Consulting-modeling method, 379, 535
Contact stage, 312, 313, 535
Contemporary police theory, 109–112, 134
Contingency management, 110–111, 535
Continuous improvement process, 111
Continuum of force, 315–317, 535
Contract law enforcement, 17, 535
Controlling process, 103, 104–105, 134, 535
Cook Co. Sheriffs Department, 15
Coombs, Timothy Thomas, 516
COPLINK, 518
Co-production of public safety, 69–70, 535
COPS. *See* community-oriented policing services
Corporate strategy, 68
Corruption. *See* police corruption
Counterespionage, 58
Counterfeiting, 57
County government law enforcement, 11, 12
County of Sacramento v. Lewis, 370
County police, 12, 18, 193
County sheriffs, 12, 40
Courtesy, professionalism and respect (CPR) policy, 120, 121
Covert patrol, 239, 242, 536
CPTED. *See* crime prevention through environmental design
Crackdown, 66, 234–235, 355, 536